ISBN 978-1-5279-8712-8
PIBN 10925826

1 MONTH OF
FREE
READING

at

www.ForgottenBooks.com

By purchasing this book you are eligible for one month membership to ForgottenBooks.com, giving you unlimited access to our entire collection of over 1,000,000 titles via our web site and mobile apps.

To claim your free month visit: www.forgottenbooks.com/free925826

REPORTS OF CASES

DECIDED IN THE

COURT OF APPEAL

FOR ONTARIO,

DURING PARTS OF THE YEARS 1887 AND 1888.

REPORTED UNDER THE AUTHORITY OF
THE LAW SOCIETY OF UPPER CANADA.

VOLUME XIV.

TORONTO:
ROWSELL & HUTCHISON,
KING-STREET.

1888.

ROWSELL AND HUTCHISON, LAW PRINTERS, TORONTO.

A TABLE

OF THE

CASES REPORTED IN THIS VOLUM

A TABLE

C.

D.

H.

C—VOL. XIV. A.R.

M.

Mc.

ERRATA.

Page 482, line 1 of headnote, for "mortgagee" read "mortgage."
Page 738, footnote, for "PATTERSON, J.," read "FERGUSON, J."

Until recent years the municipalities might in the exercise of their powers over the highways have cut away the street in the front of a man's premises so as to cut off all access to it, without being liable to an action or to make compensation in any form, but under a statute not differing in substance from the language employed in the Railway Act, it was held by this Court in *Yeomans* v. *Wellington,* 5 A. R. 303, that where a highway was raised in such a manner as to cut off ingress or egress to and from his property abutting thereon, the owner of such property was entitled to compensation.

A good deal was said during the argument about the leave of the municipality, but the leave of that body has nothing to do with the case. The railway company is empowered to construct this branch road over any lands between its termini, and in doing so to cross lands used as highways, and to raise or lower the lands so used in order to construct their line on as perfect a grade as they think proper, the only restriction upon their power in this respect being that the highway shall be restored to its former state, or to such a state as not to impair its usefulness. I assume this has been done, but it is clear that the municipal council could not relieve them from this obligation. They have, in the exercise of their powers in doing this, so lowered the street in front of these lots on which it abuts, as to interfere with the owner's ingress and egress from them; if this be so I cannot see why the owner is not entitled to compensation under the words of this enactment.

In *Eagle* v. *The Charing Cross R. W. Co.*, L. R. 2 C. P. at p. 647, a passage is cited from Ricket's case which seems peculiarly applicable to the present case : " Both principle and authority seem to me to shew that no case comes within the purview of the statute unless where some damage has been occasioned to the land itself, in respect of which, but for the statute, the complaining party might have maintained an action. The injury must be an actual injury to the land itself, as, by loosening the foundations of buildings upon it, obstructing its light or its drains, *making it inaccessible by lowering or raising the ground immediately in front of it,* or by some such physical deterioration." More recent cases seem to shew that the language I have cited is too restricted, but we are not concerned with that at present. This case at all events is precisely within the decisions.

If this had been done by the railway company, without the authority of the statute, the claimant could have maintained an action; having done it under the authority of law no action is maintainable, but the damage has been suffered from this exercise of the power of the company in the construction of its railway ; a disagreement has arisen as to the compensation to be paid, or whether any compensation is to be paid, and that being so the statute gives a remedy by arbitration.

I do not at all doubt that the company might at the same time when they gave the notice as to lot 3, a portion of which was taken, and the compensation to be paid in respect of it, have given notice also which would have embraced the compensation to be paid in respect of these lots ; the short answer is that they did not do so. The notice to treat referred to lot 3 only, and when accepted and acted upon by the claimant it constituted a contract between them as to land taken and the damages by reason of its being taken and nothing more, and the execution of the deed for the portion so taken cannot carry the case any further. It is no evidence of a satisfaction or release of the damages now complained of. If I am wrong in my view of the proper construction of the Act, the case is still clearer under the General Railway Act of the Province.

The judgment should I think be affirmed. I know of no authority for compelling a reference to an officer of the Court ; all we can do is to compel an arbitration to which the claimant is entitled under the Act, and the mandamus should go in that form.

OSLER, J. A.—The proceedings out of which the case before us arises are not fully disclosed upon the appeal book. We may infer that the trial before my brother Galt was the trial of an issue raised upon the traverse to a return to a mandamus nisi, by which the defendants were commanded to serve a notice, under which the usual proceedings might be initiated to ascertain the sum the plaintiff was entitled to as compensation or damages in consequence of the defendants having, in the exercise of their powers, injuriously affected certain lands of his by depressing the street in front of them.

The lands in question were lots 3, 4 and 6 fronting on Clifton Avenue, in the town of Niagara Falls. Lot No. 5, which was not the plaintiff's property, was between lots 4 and 6. The defendants had actually taken for the purposes of their railway, a small part of lot 3 only, and the damages claimed were for the injury caused to that lot and lots 4 and 6 by lowering the street in front thereof, to enable the railway to be carried over the highway.

The defendants denied their liability on two grounds:

(1) Because the sum which had been agreed upon and paid for the part of lot 3 actually taken by and conveyed to them, included all damages for depressing the highway in front of that lot and the other two lots; and (2) as to the latter, no part of which had been actually taken, that the alleged injury was not the subject of compensation under the compensation clauses of the Consolidated Railway Act of 1879.

The learned Judge at the trial found, that the plaintiff had been paid in full for the land taken, and the damage done to lot 3, but that he had not received compensation for the injury sustained by lots 4 and 6, and as to this that he was entitled to have his claim investigated by arbitration under the statute. A peremptory mandamus was accordingly directed to issue.

On the question of fact, or mixed question of law and fact, on which the defendants' first objection depends, I entirely agree with the decision below. The terms of the notice to treat, and the deed from the plaintiff to the defendants quite exclude the notion that the parties were

dealing with anything else than the land taken from and
the damage done to lot No. 3. The defendants' notice to
treat, which is the foundation of their contract, is expressly
confined to that lot, and it was carried into effect by the deed.
There is nothing in the evidence to warrant any interference with the contract thus executed.

The case is therefore limited to the damage done to lots
4 and 6, and the sole question is whether they have suffered
any damage for which the Legislature has given a right to
compensation.

It is not contended that the damage suffered by these
lots was caused by the taking of a part of lot No. 3
for the purposes of the railway, and therefore the case
of *The Queen* v. *Essex,* 17 Q. B. D., 447 has no application.
The act which caused the damage complained of is of an
entirely different nature, not connected with or caused by
the actual taking or severance of the land. What the
company have done, in the exercise of their statutory
powers, is to cut away and lower the street in front of the
lots, in such a manner as to obstruct or interfere with the
plaintiff's access thereto.

Now, that damage caused by an act of this nature is
damage to land and properly the subject of compensation
in cases arising under the Railway Act, C. S. C. ch. 6ô or
other Acts containing clauses similar to secs. 5 and 11 sub-
sec. 5, no longer admits of doubt. These clauses are substantially similar to those in the Railway and Lands
Clauses Consolidation Act (Imp.), and in the recent case of
the *Caledonian R. W. Co.* v. *Walker's Trustees* 7 App. Cas.
239, Lord Selborne says, that one of the propositions
established by the numerous decisions of the House of
Lords, which were examined, explained or reconciled in
that case, is that the obstruction by the execution of the
works, of a man's direct access to his house or land, whether
such access be by a public road or by a private way, is a
proper subject for compensation.

The leading cases for that proposition are *The Metropolitan Board of Works* v. *McCarthy,* L. R. 7 H. L. 243 and

Beckett v. *Midland R. W. Co.*, L. R. 3 C. P. 82, and it will
be seen from these and the other case I have referred to,
that the interference with or obstruction of the right of
access which may give rise to a title for compensation
is not necessarily one which occurs immediately in front
of or adjoining the premises affected, Lord Cranworth's
dictum in *Ricket's* Case, L. R. 2 H. L. 175, being to that
extent disapproved of or not followed.

Mr. Cattanach, however, argued that in the case of railways which come under the Consolidated Railway Act
1879 (D.) no liability is imposed to make compensation for
lands damaged or injuriously affected, where no land is
taken, because that Act contains no section corresponding
to section 5 of The Railway Act, C. S. C. ch. 66, which
enacts that the company shall make compensation for the
value of lands taken, and for damages to all *lands injuriously affected* by the construction of the railway, in the
exercise of the powers vested in the company.

This is the only section in which the expression "lands
injuriously affected" occurs. It is also the only section
which in terms expressly enacts that the company shall
make compensation for lands taken as well as for damages
for lands injuriously affected.

Section 11 sub-sec. 5 provides that the company may
agree with the owners of the lands intended to be taken,
or which may suffer damage (that is to say the damage
mentioned in section 5) from the exercise of the powers
granted for the railway touching the said lands, or for the
compensation to be paid for the same, or for the damages.

The mode of ascertaining in a compulsory manner the
amount of the compensation or damages in case the parties
fail to agree is then provided for. Section 9 sub-secs. 10
and 12 of the Consolidated Railway Act, 1879 (D.), are
almost verbally identical with sec. 11, sub-sec 5, and following sections of the Railway Act, C. S. C. ch. 66, and describe the subject of compensation in precisely the same way.

The argument, therefore, from the omission of a section
corresponding to section 5 of the latter Act appears to

prove too much.   It strikes equally at the right to compensation for land taken and damages to land where land is not taken, a right which under the Dominion Act depends altogether upon sec. 9 sub-sec. 10, and must exist in both cases or in neither.

I think it clear that both cases were intended to be provided for by that sub-section, which standing alone and without the aid of an enactment like that contained in sec. 5, is quite wide enough to embrace the damages in question, as they are manifestly damages suffered by land in the exercise of the powers granted by the railway.

I cannot see anything to exonerate the defendants in the fact that they had the leave of the municipality for doing as they did.

The result is that the appeal should be dismissed.   It does not seem necessary to determine whether the compensation clauses of Part I of The Consolidated Railway Act, 1879, or those of The Railway Act, C. S. C. ch. 66 incorporated in the defendants' special Acts, apply.   In either case the company's liability and the procedure for ascertaining it are substantially the same.   The mandamus nisi, and the proceedings which led up to it, are not before us and there may be nothing in them to require amendment or to shew under what Act they were in fact taken. The case was argued by both parties on the assumption that the Act which applied was that of 1879.   I think a similar question has been glanced at, if not decided in more than one case ; Darling v. Midland R. W. Co., coram Boyd, C., not reported ; Clegg v. Grand Trunk R. W. Co., 10 O. R. 767 ; and I am therefore unwilling to pronounce a final opinion upon it here until it becomes necessary to do so.   I will say that I am not convinced that the defendants are subject to Part I. of the Act.   As to their main line and Welland and other branches they were incorporated by Ontario Acts, and although they are now subject to Dominion legislation alone, having been declared to be a work for the general advantage of Canada, I do not concede that the provisions of their special Acts are thereby necessarily superseded. The Act of 1879 recognises three classes of railways, and Part I in which the compensation clauses are found, is not of universal application, being limited to the Intercolonial Railway and to "every railway constructed or to be constructed under the authority of any Act passed by the Parliament of Canada." Whether these defendants are within that class probably depends upon the construction of sec. 5 sub-sec. 1, and sec. 6 of the Act of 1879, and of the special Act of the Dominion, 37 Vict. ch. 68, incorporating them as a Dominion Railway " for the purposes mentioned in and with all the franchises, rights, powers, privileges and authorities conferred upon them by " the Ontario Acts therein recited.

HAGARTY, C.J.O., and PATTERSON, J.A., concurred with OSLER, J.A.

Appeal dismissed, with costs.

STEINHOFF V. CORPORATION OF KENT.

Negligence—Accident—Drawbridge—Liability of municipality.

The defendants constructed a bridge across a navigable stream having in
  it a draw or swing to enable vessels to ply on the river. There
  was not any gate or other protection to guard the approaches to the
  bridge when swung. A horse belonging to the plaintiff, broke away
  from the person in charge of him, escaped out upon the public road
  and ran a distance of about two miles to the bridge, reaching
  it while the draw was open to allow a vessel to pass, and rushing into
  the gap was drowned.
Toms v. *Whitby,* 37 U. C. R. 104; *Sherwood* v. *Hamilton,* 38 U. C. R.
  410; *Price Cataraqui Bridge Co.,* 35 U. C. R. 314 considered.
Held, affirming the judgment of the Court below that the defendant
  municipality could not be made answerable for the loss of the horse.

THIS was an appeal by the plaintiff from the County
Court of Kent.

The action was instituted in that Court to recover damages sustained by the plaintiff through the death of his
horse caused, as he alleged, by the negligence of the defendants.

From the evidence it appeared that the river Sydenham,
a navigable stream, flowing through the village of Wallaceburg, and within the village limits, is crossed by a draw
or swing bridge, so that vessels may pass up and down the
river. That the plaintiff's horse broke away from the
person having charge of him, while on the premises of a
person whom the plaintiff was visiting and ran at a furious
rate for about two miles towards the bridge and reached
it just as the bridge was opened and a vessel passing
through, and dashed along the bridge approach into the
gap and was drowned.

The case came on for trial before Bell, J., of the County
Court on the 17th of December, 1885, when the plaintiff
was examined as a witness, and in the course of his evidence stated that in June, 1884, he had, in company with
a lad named Busha, driven out of town to deliver some
grain some two miles off, and on reaching the place had
driven into the yard and left the horse and buggy in charge
of Busha whilst he (plaintiff) went across the yard some
sixty or seventy feet to look at some turkeys. He further
stated:

"I had just arrived there when I observed the horse getting restless and starting to run. His head was turned toward the road as I had turned him around before I got out. The horse was going to the road, the boy, Busha, holding on to the bridle. It was about one hundred yards to the road. Busha held on until the horse had gone about fifty yards on the main road toward Wallaceburg. The horse then broke loose and ran away toward Wallaceburg."

The defendants did not call any witnesses, but moved for a nonsuit on the grounds that no negligence on their part had been established.

After taking time to look into the cases cited, the learned Judge directed judgment to be entered for the defendants.

The appeal came on to be heard on the 24th of November, 1886.*

J. S. Fraser, for the appellant.
Pegley, for the respondents.

February 7, 1887. HAGARTY, C. J. O.—The nature of the case may be best understood by the following short judgment of the learned Judge

"This is an action to recover damages sustained by the plaintiff through the death of his horse, caused, as he alleges, by the negligence of the defendants.

"From the evidence it appears that the River Sydenham, a navigable stream, flows through the village of Wallaceburg ; that it is crossed within the village limits by a bridge having in it a draw, or swing, to allow vessels to pass up and down the river ; that about 8 or 9 o'clock on the morning of the 19th June, the plaintiff's horse broke away from the person in charge of him and ran at a gallop from some two miles distance in the country towards the bridge and reached it just as the bridge was opened and a vessel passing through, and rushed along the bridge approach into the gap and was drowned.

"I am of the opinion that the plaintiff cannot recover for two reasons : 1. Because he was guilty of contributory negligence in allowing his horse to run away : that the proximate cause of the accident was the runaway, and 2. That the defendants were not guilty of negligence, as in my opinion they were only bound to provide against the ordinary contingencies of travel, and not against such circumstances as existed here.

"The case of *Price* v. *The Cataraqui Bridge Co.*, 35 U.C.R. 314, is almost precisely in point, and if that case was properly decided I do not see how plaintiff can recover here. I therefore direct judgment to be entered for the defendants, with costs."

* *Present.*—HAGARTY, C. J. O., BURTON, PATTERSON, and OSLER. JJ. A.

In addition it may be stated from the evidence that the accident occurred at 9 or 10 a.m., on a fine day : that the plaintiff had turned his horse and vehicle into a place about 100 yards from the high road, leaving him in charge of a lad of 17 years old : that the horse was started and ran towards the road, the boy holding still to his head, and about fifty yards down the road he broke from the boy and ran some two miles (as is stated) towards the bridge.

The plaintiff's claim states it to be the duty of the defendants " to properly guard the approaches of the bridge whenever it shall be swung to avoid accidents and loss of life :" that they negligently omitted to place any guard gate, protection, or signal to avert danger; that plaintiff's horse was lawfully on the road, and the bridge being swung ; and by reason of defendants' negligence and default as aforesaid, the horse unavoidably went over the approach and was drowned.

A steamboat was actually in the " draw' as the horse approached.

If the plaintiff had been driving along the road on this day, he would in all human probability have seen the vessel in the draw, and therefore avoided all danger.

I will assume in his favor that the horse escaped from control without any neglect or default on his part.

I feel very great difficulty in holding that on the facts before us, the municipality is bound to pay for the loss of the horse under such unusual circumstances.

I fully recognise the decisions that hold that a person injured by a defect in a highway or bridge, is not debarred from recovering by the mere fact that his horse shied, balked, or became unmanageable at the critical moment so as (without default on his part) not to be under his control.

If he prove a want of reasonable care in the state of repair of the road or bridge, his accidental loss of control at the time of the accident must not defeat his remedy ; although the accident would not have happened had such control been effectually exercised.

All this is fully discussed in such cases as *Toms* v. *Corporation of Whitby*, 35 U. C. R. 195 ; and in appeal, 37 U. C. R. 104 ; *Sherwood* v. *City of Hamilton*, 37 U. C.R. 410 ; and the large number of cases there cited and discussed.

The general rule governing all these cases is plainly stated by this Court in *Walton* v. *Corporation of York*, 6 A. R. 181.

It is always a question of fact for the jury whether, having regard to all the circumstances, the road or bridge was in a state reasonably fit for ordinary travel.

The subject is fully discussed in the judgments of my learned brothers Burton and Patterson in that case. See also *Lucas* v. *Township of Moore*, in this Court, 3 A. R. 602.

Draper, C. J., in the *Tom's Case*, says, at p. 105 : " I am not giving any support to the doctrine which my brother Morrison [in the Court below] desires to guard himself from encouraging."

On referring to this, we find on p. 227 the doctrine in question is : " I wish to guard myself from deciding that if a horse becoming restive or unmanageable and runs or backs into a ditch, or down a declivity or embankment, on a highway, the municipality is therefore accountable for the consequences, or that they are bound to fence or guard all such places against the possibility of a vicious, balky, or runaway horse running or backing over the highway at such points."

Price v. *Cataraqui Bridge Co.*, 35 U. C. R. 314, cited by the learned Judge, is the nearest in its facts to this, but as I think a much stronger case for a recovery than the present. Plaintiff's horses going down a hill became frightened and ran away ; the driver was thrown out and injured ; they ran on about a quarter of a mile to the east end of the bridge, then along the bridge till they came to the draw which was open to let a vessel pass—they ran in and were drowned. There had been gates which were broken and new ones made, but not yet put up.

The jury found that if there had been reasonable gates the accident would have been avoided, and that gates strong enough to prevent the accident would not have seriously injured the horses, and that there was no negligence on the driver's part.

Wilson, J., after reviewing the authorities, held (apart from a legal objection, as to the company having leased the tolls, &c.,) that defendants were liable.

Richards, C. J., and Morrison, J., held the opposite. The Chief Justice said : "I think they would well discharge their duty to the public if they had persons stationed on the bridge to give notice by signals or otherwise when the draw was open. I do not think they were bound to have gates there to stop passengers, and certainly not to stop horses that had run away and were without any control when they came upon this bridge. * * I think I should hold the facts proved at the trial failed to establish a case against them."

I agree with the learned Chief Justice's view, and also that the case before us is far stronger against the plaintiff. As to signals on a bridge, in a case like this they would of course be useless. We cannot lay down as law that gates should necessarily be there.

It is a question of fact depending on the evidence whether the municipality have been guilty of negligence or failed in their reasonable duty.

In the management of this bridge, we can only expect them to guard against the ordinary requirements of travel and use of the bridge. I hardly think it reasonable to expect them to contemplate the possibility of a frightened horse leaving its driver a mile or two up the road and dashing at their bridge. The horse's presence on the high road was merely as a runaway horse having escaped from control, whether from his owner's stable or from leaping a fence, &c. The mere fact of his having had a driver at one time, a long distance off, and then rushing wholly of his own accord to the bridge, not guided thereto, is, to my mind very distinguishable from the cases that have been before the courts of horses becoming temporarily unmanageable, backing or balking at a critical moment.

I think this case must be decided wholly as to liability for this particular accident, and not as to the defendants' general management as to proper precautions at night, or as to the possibility of a blind traveller seeking to pass, &c.

I repeat that the failure to provide for the contingency of runaway horses rushing to the bridge wholly without control, ought not reasonably to create of itself a cause of action against the county.

For myself I must say that if I had been on a jury to try this case, with a proper charge given to me in accordance with the settled law as to reasonable care and precaution on the defendants' part, I should unhesitatingly find against the plaintiff.

I hardly take the same view as the learned Judge as to the proximate cause of the injury, but I think on the second ground on which he decided against plaintiff he took the right view of the evidence.

I decide nothing as to the liability of bridge managers beyond what is necessary for the decision of this particular case.

I think we should dismiss the appeal.

BURTON and PATTERSON, JJ.A., concurred.

OSLER, J. A.—I also agree that the appeal must be dismissed.

The bridge in question being the defendants' bridge and under their management, if the plaintiff's horse, while being driven along the highway, had become restive or unmanageable and had escaped from his control while upon or approaching the bridge, and the draw being open and unprotected, had fallen into the river without fault on the driver's part I should have thought the case not distinguishable from *Toms* v. *Whitby*, 35 U. C. R. 195, 37 U. C. R. 100 ; *Sherwood* v. *Hamilton*, 37 U. C. R. 410 ; *Grand Trunk R. W. Co.* v. *Boulanger*, Sup. Ct. Can. 1886 ; *Cassels's* Dig. 441.

It would have been for the jury or the judge as the case might be to say whether the defendants had taken proper precautions to prevent the occurrence of accidents at the particular place, and I am not prepared to hold that *Price* v. *Cataraqui Bridge Co.*, 35 U. C. R. 314, gives the rule as to what precautions would have been sufficient. That would be for the tribunal trying the case to decide in view of all the facts; nor ought evidence to be rejected, as it was here, of what precautions were considered usual and proper in the case of similar bridges in the same or in other counties.

It has often been said that every case of this kind must be decided upon its own peculiar circumstances, and the learned Judge holds that under the peculiar circumstances of this case the defendants were not guilty of negligence, as the accident did not result from their default in the performance of any duty they were then owing to the plaintiff. I do not understand him to hold as a matter of law that they were not under any circumstances bound to guard the opening in the bridge by a gate or bar or other sufficient protection, and he could not in my opinion so have held consistently with the decisions in *Toms* v. *Whitby*, and *Sherwood* v. *Hamilton*, with which, as it appears to me, some of the dicta (for there was no decision on that point) of the majority of the Court in *Price* v. *The Cataraqui Bridge Co.*, are not easy to reconcile. What I think he does hold is, that the plaintiff cannot complain of the absence of a guard, because at the time of the accident he was not making use of the road in the the ordinary way, and that the defendants were only bound " to provide against the ordinary contingencies of travel," within which the running away of the horse, under the particular circumstances proved, did not come.

In the *Town of Portland* v. *Griffith*, 11 S. C. R. 333, the plaintiff was held not entitled to recover damages for an accident she had met with, while on the street, because, as Ritchie, C. J., says, she was not at the time using the street " in the way for which streets are provided to be kept in repair, namely, for the passing to and fro of citizens and subjects."

Richards v. *Enfield*, 13 Gray 344, is not unlike this case, and I refer to it because the Massachusetts statute under which it was decided has been said to be not substantially different from ours. See *Toms* v. *Whitby*, 37 U. C. R. 100, 114. The case was that the plaintiff after travelling over a portion of the highway had stopped at the house of one Morton for the purpose of obtaining some corn, leaving his horse tied to a post on Morton's premises. The animal broke loose from the post, regained the highway, and ran homeward, but after going a short distance went down an embankment on the side of the highway, and was injured. One ground on which the Court held the plaintiff was not entitled to recover is thus stated :

"The duty imposed on towns in respect to the repair of highways is, that they shall keep them safe and convenient for travellers, their horses, teams, and carriages: Rev. Stat. ch. 25, sec. 1. The liability of towns for defects or want of repair in highways is intended to be commensurate with this duty. It is only those who are using the highway for legitimate purposes in the usual and ordinary mode who can claim indemnity of a town for injuries caused solely by defects in the highway, or by the combined effect of such defects and pure accidents. In the present case the plaintiff was not travelling at the time of the accident. He had driven his horse out of the highway, and there left him. His use of the road for the time being had ceased as entirely as if he had taken his horse out of the vehicle and placed him in a stable, or turned him into a pasture."

Our decision does not affect a case where animals are allowed to run at large upon the highway, but then they are never allowed to do so attached to a buggy or other vehicle.

Upon the whole I think the judgment should be affirmed. See *Sherman & Redfield*, on Highways, 3rd ed., sec. 250 ; *Jewson* v. *Gatti*, 1 T. L. R. 635 ; 2 T. L. R. 441.

Appeal dismissed, with costs.

In re Macklem and the Commissioners of the Niagara Falls Park.

Construction of will—Forfeiture—Vis major—Expropriation.

T. C. S. devised his estate of Clark Hill, with the islands, lands, and grounds appertaining, to his nephew M. M.'s grandmother, by her will, directed her executors to pay him $2,000 a year so long as he should remain the owner and actual occupant of Clark Hill, " to enable him the better to keep up, decorate, and beautify the property known as Clark Hill and the islands connected therewith."

Held, that the expropriation, under an Act of the Legislature, of part of the Clark Hill estate, did not in any way affect M.'s right to this annuity ; and therefore in awarding compensation to M. for the lands expropriated the arbitrators properly excluded the consideration of any contemplated loss by M. of this annuity. .

A failure by M. to reside and occupy would be in the nature of a forfeiture for breach of a condition subsequent, and his right to the annuity would continue absolute until something occurred to divest the estate which must be by his own act or default : the vis major of a binding statute could not work a forfeiture.

Upon the evidence the Court refused to interfere with the amount of compensation awarded.

THIS was an appeal and cross-appeal from the award of the official arbitrators appointed to value certain lands required to be expropriated for the purpose of forming The Niagara Falls Park, and came on to be heard before this court on the 6th and 7th December, 1886.*

Robinson, Q. C., and *Street*, Q. C., for Macklem.
Irving, Q. C., for the Commissioners.
The facts are clearly stated in the judgment.

February 1, 1887. HAGARTY, C. J. O.—There are cross-appeals in this matter against the award.

It may be most convenient to consider first that of Mr. Macklem, (hereafter called the appellant.)

An award was made of $100,000 in his favor for certain portions of his property to be expropriated.

An Act of last session, 49 Vict. ch. 9 sec. 1, (O.) directs that an appeal be allowed " upon any question of law or fact

Present—HAGARTY, C.J.O., BURTON, PATTERSON, and OSLER, JJ. A.

to the Court of Appeal, and said Court shall have the same jurisdiction therein as a Judge has on an appeal from a report or certificate, under section 192 of the Common Law Procedure Act. Any reference back shall be to the official arbitrators."

Sec. 9, " The judgment of the Court of Appeal shall be final." This section 192 of the Common Law Procedure Act directs that the practice shall be the practice now observed in appeals from a report of a Master in Chancery, and the Judge may upon argument either amend the said report or certificate in any way, and to any extent that he may deem proper, or refer the same back to the Master, County Judge or other referee, for amendment in whole or in part, with such directions as to law or fact as he may deem proper or he may confirm the same.

The result seems to be that we can set aside, confirm, or send back to the official arbitrators, or in effect make such an award as we think the case warrants.

Mr. Macklem appeals on the following grounds :—

1. That the award is contrary to the evidence and the weight of evidence, in that the sum of $100,000 awarded to be paid for the purchase of the land in question is too small, and the evidence shews that the appellant is entitled to a much larger sum.

2. That the arbitrators were not authorized or empowered to value the said lands in two parcels, as they have done ; the respondents' proceedings having been directed to expropriate and acquire the whole of the lands claimed, and not a part or parts thereof, and the appellant's evidence was necessarily chiefly directed to the value of the whole. Nor can the appellant be compelled to part with either of the said parcels for which the said sums of $85,000 and $15,000 respectively have been awarded, without the other of the said parcels.

3. That the annuity of $2,000 bequeathed to the appellant and referred to in the said award, is or will be affected or lost by the taking of the said lands, and the appellant should be allowed compensation therefor, and in this respect the award is contrary to law.

This last objection may be first considered.

The late Mr. Street devised his estate of Clark Hill with the islands, lands, and grounds appertaining, and some farms in the neighbourhood to his mother for life, remainder in fee to his nephew the present appellant. His mother, who outlived him only a few days, by will devised as follows :

" 26th.—I will and direct that so soon as Sutherland Macklem, the son of my daughter Caroline, can and does take actual possession of the real estate and property which under certain conditions expressed in the will of my late son, Thomas Clark Street, he will and may take and enjoy, that thereupon my executors hereinafter named shall during the lifetime of the said Sutherland Macklem, and so long as he remains the owner and actual occupant of the said real estate, pay over to him annually in each and every year the sum of two thousand dollars to enable him the better to keep up, decorate, and beautify the property known as " Clark Hill," and the islands connected therewith."

It was held by the arbitrators that the expropriating of part of the Clark Hill estate did not in any way affect the appellant's right to this annuity.

It was again pressed before us that he might be in danger of losing it by the taking of these portions—that in effect after this expropriation he no longer remained "the owner and actual occupant of the real estate of which he was entitled under Mr. Street's will."

I am strongly of opinion that his right to the annuity is in no way affected by the proposed expropriation. He did enter into possession of the devised estate, and has always since been the owner and has occupied the property known as Clark Hill, the decoration and beautifying of which and the islands connected therewith, appears to be the object in the testatrix's mind in granting the annuity. It is " to enable him the better to keep up, decorate and beautify " that property that it is expressly given.

The appellant has done nothing whatever on his part to work a forfeiture.

The failure to reside and occupy would be in the nature of a forfeiture for breach of a condition subsequent, or if

real estate were involved it might possibly be described
as a contingent limitation, as suggested by Lord St.
Leonard's in the great case of *Brownlow* v. *Egerton*, 4 H.
L. page 207. His right to the annuity continues absolute
until something occurs to divest his estate.

It is proposed to take from him for a public park,
under an Act of Parliament, some 60 or 70 acres of the
whole estate, leaving the Mansion House, and some 30 or
40 acres, still known as " Clark Hill." The estate is thus
curtailed not by his act or default, but by the vis major of
a binding statute.

Many cases were cited on the argument, but the counsel
admitted that they could produce no authority to the effect
that the forcible taking of a part of an estate by statute
was ever held to work a forfeiture.

What has taken place here seems to me to be equivalent,
in legal operation, to the case of these islands crumbling
away by the action of the current or becoming submerged,
and disappearing from view, or of a large section of the
bank of the Niagara falling into the stream and thus
reducing the extent of the estate.

In such a contingency I have no doubt that the owner
and occupant of the Mansion House and residue of the
estate would continue entitled to the annuity under the
wording of this will.

The appellant would be equally free from all charge of
working a forfeiture, as far as his acts were concerned in one
case as in the other. The intention of the testatrix seems
clear that the appellant's ownership and actual occupancy
was the measure of his right to the annuity ; and that it
would be something arising from his act or volition that
would determine such right.

Is it possible for us to suppose that the testatrix contemplated a cesser of the annuity ; on any event such as here
has occurred ? Was she not guarding solely against the
acts of her grandson, contrary to her desire and direction,
as to his ownership and occupancy of the estate ?

We must not apply the terms and incidents peculiarly applicable to the limitations governing the disposition of real estate, to the subject matter of this inquiry, viz., the payment of an annuity contingent in its duration on the continuance of a specified state of things.

But in determining whether an occasion has arisen for its cesser, we may regard it as we find it viewed in the case of a condition subsequent, on the happening of which the vested interest is divested either by devise over, or by reverting to the donor or his heirs.

We are safe, at all events, in assuming that we cannot treat the alleged cause of forfeiture here more favorably than a condition subsequent with a limitation or devise over would be treated.

Lord St. Leonard's in *Brownlow* v. *Egerton* thus speaks: "I know by the authorities that conditions intended to defeat an estate have defeated an estate in contingency just as much as a vested estate,—that they are odious, as it is said in law, and as it is also said by equally high authorities, the Institutes and Shepherd's Touchstone, that they must be submitted to a strict construction; that is, you are not to give a favourable construction to a proviso the object of which is to defeat an estate already created, but that if that estate is to be defeated it must be by clear and express terms, within the limits of the instrument creating it."

Clavering v. *Ellison*, 4 H. L. is a very instructive case as to the manner in which such matters should be construed. Lord Campbell, C., says: at p. 721, citing the *Bridgewater Case*, "Even as conditions subsequent they must be construed strictly and to work a forfeiture there must be shewn a breach of a defined line of conduct which the parties concerned must reasonably have known would work a forfeiture."

He also notices the effect of vis major which prevented the father from returning sooner from abroad to England, the alleged breach being the education of his children abroad.

Lord Cranworth says: "I consider that from the earliest times the cardinal rule on this subject has been this, that where a vested estate is to be defeated by a condition on a

see my way to naming any sum on my own opinion of the
evidence, which would be a more just and reasonable compensation than that awarded. If I ventured to do so I would
have the very unpleasant idea in my mind that I was interfering, to the prejudice of justice, with the opinion of those
who had far better opportunities of ascertaining the truth
than I enjoy.

I am unable to see my way to interfere. I do not deem
it necessary to discuss in detail the objections urged in the
cross-appeal. They relate chiefly to the denial of the
appellant's right to have his expenditure on the bridges
considered, as they were liable to removal as obstructions
to the navigation, and to his uses of the highways, and
reservations by the Crown. I think the arbitrators have
rightly viewed these objections, and I need only refer to
their reasons therefor, which I think are right.

It is not necessary to consider the objection as to their
not specifying the value attached to each of the parcels.
It would have been a most useless proceeding on their part,
and Mr. Irving for the Commissioners consented to abandoning the objection if our decision depended wholly
thereon.

It was suggested on argument that the Crown might
elect to take one or other of the properties to which a
specific valuation is affixed. Our decision rests on the taking
of both of the properties, according to the notice given,

We think under all the circumstances of this case and
the importance of the legal question raised, that the dismissal of the appeals should be without costs.

BURTON J. A.—I agree in the result, but desire to confine my opinion as to the construction of Mrs. Street's will
granting this annuity strictly to what is before us for
adjudication.

I express no opinion as to the effect of a voluntary
alienation by the devisee of any portion of the land
devised by the late Thomas C. Street, nor of the compul-
sary expropriation of the whole property known as the

Clark Hill Estate, but I entertain a very clear opinion that the taking by " vis major," of what has been taken under this award has not the effect of destroying or interfering with the annuity granted by Mrs. Street's will.

It has not been shewn that the arbitrators proceeded upon any erroneous principle in awarding the compensation nor that is not warranted by the evidence.   I agree therefore that we cannot interfere with the amount awarded, and that the appeal and cross-appeal should be dismissed.

PATTERSON, J. A., concurred.

OSLER, J. A.—I concur. I have looked, I think, at all the cases which were cited, and none of them seem to me to support the contention, or more properly speaking the suggestion of the appellant, that the taking, in invitum, of part of the Clark Hill estate works a forfeiture of the legacy bequeathed to him by Mrs. Street's will. He remains the owner and occupant of the mansion house, and the substantial part of the lands and grounds thereto belonging, mentioned in the will of T. C. Street, to enable him the better to keep up, decorate and beautify which, the legacy was given. The fact that an Act of the Legislature has deprived him of the islands and part of the river shore can, I think, no more defeat the legacy than if some convulsion of nature or the ordinary wash and wear of the river had carried them away.

As to the second reason of appeal I agree that the award must be treated as a whole, and adhered to or rejected as such by the commissioners. They cannot take one or more of the parcels, and reject the. others nor can we assume that they have any intention of attempting to do so. On the actual valuation, failing to see that the arbitrators have gone upon a wrong principle, in arriving at it, the evidence is of such a character as to make it impossible for me to say that they have awarded too small a sum. I am equally unable to suggest a satisfactory reason for holding it to be too large.

On the cross-appeal I add nothing to what has been already said, except to observe that some of the objections strike me as unreasonable, particularly those based upon the supposed obstruction of the river by the bridges from the mainland to the islands, and the want of title to the property comprised in the Swayze license. The islands must have been granted to Mr. Street upon the assumption that the bridges would be erected and maintained by him, and no one asks us to believe that it is now intended to take them down in order to preserve the navigable character of the river, or that the public may use or view the islands as part of the park to greater advantage.

As to the Swayze license, I think Mr. Street had a right to regard the property as substantially his own, and to believe that he would never be disturbed in the enjoyment of it, except in the possible event of its being required for military purposes. The Crown through the commissioners has treated it as belonging to Mr. Macklem, and proposes to acquire it as such, and I think the arbitrators have dealt with the legal objections which were taken to the title in the proper way.

Both appeals should be dismissed, without costs.

Appeal and cross appeal dismissed, without costs.

BICKFORD V. CHATHAM.

Railway—Municipal corporation—By-law—Certificate of Engineer—Agreement—44 Vict. ch. 24, sec. 28—Railway station.

A by-law of the defendant municipality provided that upon the construction and completion for running of the E. & H. Railway from Chatham to the C. S. railway crossing by a named day, and the construction and completion within two years from the date of such by-law taking effect of the whole track and road, with stations, freight sheds, sidings, &c., at such crossing, and upon the completion of a bridge across the Thames, &c., and the complete construction of the road in other respects to the satisfaction of the Commissioner of Public Works or an engineer appointed by him; and upon the company running the said road with all necessary accommodations for the public for one week the defendants should forthwith, after the completion of the road and the running thereof for one week, within two years from the day the by-law took effect (which was on the 30th December, 1882), deliver to the E. & H. R. W. Co. debentures to the amount of $30,000. By an agreement made prior to the passing of the by-law the company covenanted with the defendants, amongst other things, to run the road when completed and to construct a station at or near the corner of Colborne and William streets in the said municipality, and in consideration thereof (and other stipulations) the defendants agreed to submit the by-law.

This action was instituted by B. as the assignee of the E. & H. R. W. Co. to compel the delivery of the debentures; and the defendants counter-claimed for damages for breach of the agreement or for a specific performance thereof.

The Commissioner of PublicWorks on the 1st November, 1883, appointed an engineer for the purpose of certifying as required by the by-law.

On the same day the engineer granted a certificate as to the completion of the work.

The defendants claimed the right to have the continuous user and maintenance of the station "at or near the corner of Colborne and William streets" enforced by the Court, the plaintiffs insisting that having constructed the station and used it, though only for a few days, they were not bound to continue the use thereof:

Held, [affirming the judgment of CAMERON, C.J., at the trial (OSLER, J. A., *dubitante*)] that the certificate by the engineer of the substantial completion of the works specified in the by-law established a sufficient performance to satisfy the requirements of the by-law coupled with the fact that the road had been actually run for a week; that the covenants in the agreement were independent, and any non-compliance with the agreement would not constitute a defence to the demand for the delivery of the debentures: But, that under the agreement and by-law the station formed part of the general undertaking, just as much as the main line of road; and that the obligation could not be limited to the construction merely as separable from the user: the defendants were therefore entitled to the specific performance of the contract in respect of such station, and [in this reversing CAMERON, C.J.,] there should be a reference to ascertain the damages of the defendants on their counter-claim.

Held, also, that any objections to the by-law were cured by its registration under 44 Vict. ch. 24, sec. 28, no action or suit to set it aside having been made or instituted within three months, and that the statute applied although the debentures had not been issued.

Per BURTON, J.A.   Apart from the effect of registering under the Act the by-law was valid (*a.*)

THIS was an appeal by the defendants from the judgment of the C. P. D., reported 10 O. R. 257, where, and in the present judgments, the facts are clearly stated; and came on to be heard before this court on the 16th and 17th of September, 1886.*

Robinson, Q. C., and *M. Wilson* for the appellants.
W. Cassels, Q. C., for the respondent.

November 9th, 1886.   HAGARTY, C. J. O.—The agreement between the parties before the submission of the by-law, recites that the company required a bonus of $30,000 in debentures, " payable on obtaining the certificate of the Government Engineer of the completion of the said road, according to the terms of a by-law to be submitted to the electors, and the running thereof for one week,"— thus the company, in consideration of the agreement of the town, covenant to complete the road from Dresden and Wallaceburg to Rondeau Harbour, with steel rails, stations, freight houses, and other necessary accommodation, including certain named stations, &c., at the crossing of the Canada Southern line, &c., and to construct a bridge, &c., and adjoining the bridge a way for foot passengers, and to complete the road in all other respects, &c., to the satisfaction of the Commissioner of Public Works, and to run the road when completed, and to construct a station at or near the corner of Colborne and William streets, &c., and the town, in consideration of the premises, and of the agreement on the part of the company, covenants with them to submit the by-law.

The by-law provides, that upon construction and completion for running of the road from Chatham to the

[(*a*) See, however, *Canada Atlantic v. Ottawa,* 12 S. C. R. decided 17 May, 1886. Affirming S. C. 12 A. R. 234, and holding that a by-law for this purpose is subject to the general provisions of the Municipal Act relating to by-laws for incurring debts.—REP.]

Present :—HAGARTY, C. J. O., BURTON, PATTERSON, and OSLER, JJ.A.

Canada Southern line by a named day, and upon construction and completion within two years from the date of the
by-law taking effect, of the whole track and road from
Dresden, &c., to Rondeau, with steel rails, and stations,
freight houses, &c., and other necessary accommodations,
&c., and with stations, freight houses, switches, and sidings
at crossing of track of the Canada Southern Railway, so that
trains can run off, &c., with platforms of named
length; and upon the completion of a bridge over the
Thames, &c., and upon the complete construction of
said road in other respects, with rolling stock, &c., so as
to connect the town with Rondeau, Blenheim, and Canada
Southern Railway, Dresden and Wallaceburg, to the satisfaction of the Commissioner of Public Works, or an engineer
appointed by him, and upon the company running the
road with all necessary accommodation for the public, &c.,
for one week, the Mayor, &c., shall forthwith after the
said road shall have been completed, and run for one week,
within two years from the day the by-law shall take effect,
issue debentures, &c., payable within eighteen years from
date thereof, and within twenty years from the day on
which the by-law shall take effect, so that the principal of
the debt shall be payable by annual instalments during the
eighteen years—such instalments to be of such amounts
that the aggregate amount for principal and interest in
any year shall be equal, as nearly as may be, what is payable for principal and interest during each of the other
years of such period, one debenture to be payable at the
end of each year from and after the time of issue—when so
issued to be forthwith delivered to the company.

The by-law was to take effect on 30th December, 1882.

The Commissioner of Public Works did, on November
1st, 1883, appoint Robert McCallum as engineer under
the by-law of the town, for the purpose of certifying as
thereby required. On the same date this engineer gave an
imperfect certificate, and again another certifying to a
further examination.

· It may be noticed that the station to be erected at or
near the corner of Colborne and William streets, mentioned

in the agreement, is not specially mentioned in the by-law. A large portion of the defendants' objections referred to this station, both as to its location and accommodation.

On the best consideration I can give to the point, I think the certificate of the engineer of the substantial completion of the works set out in the by-law sufficiently shewed a performance by the company to satisfy its re-quirements, coupled with the actual running of the road for the week. This latter requirement, the learned Chief Justice finds to have been complied with.

The covenants in the agreement appear to me to be independent and not dependent covenants. The company agree to certain stipulations as to the road, and in con-sideration of such stipulations the town agrees to submit the by-law. The company remains liable to the town for any substantial non-compliance with the agreement.

I do not think that the defendants have succeeded in im-peaching the certificate of the engineer, and that the defence as to that ground fails.

I do not see any ground for our interference with any of the Chief Justice's findings of fact either as to the claim or counter-claim. I think that he has taken the right view as to the bridge and the four feet way, and that the company was not bound to connect the bridge on each side with the high ground at some distance from the river.

Objections were urged against the validity of the by-law, the chief ground being that though it was declared to come into force within the year of passing, viz., 1882, yet in effect the levying of any rate to pay off the debenture debt was postponed for two years, or till completion of the work, &c.

This difficulty arose from the peculiar form of the bargain, the liability not to commence till the work was done and certified, &c., instead of issuing the debentures either at once to be held by trustees, or delivered over on proof of sufficient work being done from time to time.

Much might be urged against the lawfulness of the course here taken as being opposed to the spirit if not to the letter of the statute. The ratepayers are asked to vote on a pro-ject which may postpone the imposition of any burden for

several years so long as the statutable period of twenty
years was not on the whole exceeded, and, if the recitals
in the by-law required by the statute (see Municipal Act,
1883, sec. 342, repeating former Acts) were observed, questions might arise as to the statement of the existing debenture debt, literally true when the by-law was to take
nominal effect, but which might be wholly untrue at the
end of two or three years when the assessment would be
first made. Other objections were also taken. But it is
answered that all objections are cured by the 44 Vict. ch.
24 (O.), which was in force when the by-law was passed.

Section 28 declares that every by-law for contracting a
debt by the issue of debentures for a longer term than one
year, shall be registered in the County Registry Office
within two weeks after the final passing, "and every such
by-law so registered and the debentures issued thereunder
shall be absolutely valid and binding upon such municipality according to the terms thereof, and shall not be
quashed or set aside on any ground whatever, unless an
application or suit to quash or set aside the same be made
to some court of competent jurisdiction, within three
months from the registry thereof, and a certificate of the
clerk of said court stating that such suit has been brought,
&c., shall have been registered in said registry office within
such period of three months," &c.

This provision is also in the Consolidated Act of 1883,
also in force when this by-law passed. Section 353, *et
seq.*

It is difficult to see how this stringent provision as to
validating by-laws, can be prevented from operating in
this case. The language is unmistakably clear and precise.

It is conceded that this by-law was registered as directed
and no application made within the three months.

The defendants urge that the clause does not apply
when, as here, the debentures have not been issued.

I think such an interpretation would defeat the plain
object of the Act.

Here work was undertaken and performed in consider-ation of the passing of a by-law, authorising the issue of debentures on completion of the work. It was, we must assume, to give binding force to bargains between muni-cipalities and railway and other companies that the enact-ment was made. If it only applied where debentures had not been issued, the result would apparently be that the wrongful refusal to fulfil the bargain by giving them as agreed, would take the case out of the statute and create a defence for the municipality that would not otherwise have existed.

I think we must hold the objection to the by-law to be cured.

It was strongly objected before us that the learned Judge, while finding that the defendants had succeeded in establishing some of their counterclaim, dismissed the counterclaim, leaving the defendants to their action. His course, we may presume, was adopted to prevent confusion as to the claim for debentures and damages that the defendants might prove to be entitled to.

We can either leave the judgment as framed by the learned Chief Justice, or direct a reference of the counter-claim to ascertain the defendants' amount of damage. I do not see that much will be saved. But on the whole, I think my learned brother should have decided by refer-ence or otherwise, the causes of action in the counterclaim which he held established. I do not care generally to interfere with the exercise of a Judge's discretion in such matters, (*Huggins* v. *Tweed*, 10 Ch. D. 359), but there are reasons, I think in the case before us, requiring the disposal of the claims of the defendants in the pending suit.

The learned Chief Justice decided that the company had reasonably complied with this contract in placing the Colborne street station where it now stands.

He also held that it had been actually used for a week or two, within the time specified, but that the accommoda-tion provided was insufficient, and left the defendants to their remedy therefor by future proceedings.

We have held that such claim should be considered and settled in this suit.

But it appears in evidence that after this short user the company have practically abandoned or discontinued the use of this station, and the Chatham people have in effect to trust wholly to the King street station on the town limit to reach or leave their town, a distance from the Colborne station of nearly half of a mile. The Colborne station being in the centre of business and population, the other in the eastern limit of the municipality.

The defendants claim the right to have the continuous use and maintenance of the Colborne station enforced by decree.

The plaintiffs insist that having constructed the station and used it for a few days they are not bound longer to continue its use.

The agreement made by the plaintiffs was in consideration of the defendants' submitting the by-law for the $30,000 of debentures.

After reciting the agreement to submit the by-law, the company contracted to complete the road with steel rails, stations, and other necessary accommodations, &c.

" And to complete said road in all other respects and to supply the same with all necessary rolling stock and materials so as to connect the town with Rondeau, Blenheim, The Canada Southern Railway, Dresden, and Wallaceburg, to the satisfaction of the Commissioner of Public Works for the time being, or any engineer appointed by him on or before the 30th September, 1883, and immediately upon such completion and continuously thereafter to run the said road with such connection at the crossings of said lines of railways independent of the Grand Trunk Railway Company, unless to give the Grand Trunk Railway Company the right to run over or connect with track and road of said company hereto in such a way as not to stop or interfere with the free traffic on the road of the company hereto, between all of said points, for at least ten years from the completion thereof, and not make arrangements with the Grand Trunk Railway Company without the consent of the council of the corporation of the said town of Chatham, and to erect all necessary work shops and repairing houses or sheds for the said company and the whole road thereof, and establish the same within the town of Chatham.

"And to construct at or near the corner of Colborne and William streets, in the said town, a freight and passenger station with all necessary accommodation, connected by switches, sidings, or otherwise, with said road of the company, upon the council of said town, within three months from the final passing of said by-law, passing another by-law empowering the said company to make its roads and lay its rails along a highway or highways in the said town to said corner, from where the said road would be if the construction thereof were completed in a direct line through the said town, or upon the council procuring for and giving to the said company a right of way along the northerly side of McGregor's Creek (one-half in the water) for the road of said company to or near said corner, and to load from gravel piles, pits, or beds purchased by said corporation adjacent to or adjoining the track of said company, and carry gravel over said road to any place required by the said town for the construction, maintenance and repair of public roads in said town, and for other purposes of the town, for a sum and at a rate for loading and carriage not to exceed three cents per cubic yard of gravel per mile for all distances less than ten miles, and two cents per mile for all distances of ten miles and over but under twenty-five miles, and one and a half cents per mile for all distances of and over twenty-five miles."

It is impossible to read this without being certain that the contracting parties, however they have expressed themselves, contemplated not merely the building of the road and the track from the main line to the named point and station in the town but also the continuous user thereof.

Our duty now is to put ourselves in the position of the parties and endeavour to ascertain what they meant by the words they used.

The first section of the agreement, given above, provides that after the completion and approval of the road it is "to be run continuously for at least ten years from the completion thereof."

Then comes the clause as to Colborne street station.

The town has to authorise the company to lay its rails along the streets up to the corner, and the company agree,

whenever the town desires to draw gravel from its gravel
pits for the repair of its roads in the town, that the company will do so at certain named rates to any place
required by the town.

I read this to be to any point on the contemplated Colborne street track as well as on the main track.

The required permission to lay the rails was given, and
they were laid on Colborne street to the very serious detri-
ment, as is stated, of some of the residents on said street.

I presume the company may equally claim the right
wholly to discontinue the use of this track as to abandon
the use of the station.

The station is to be a freight and passenger station with
all the necessary accommodation, and to be connected by
switches, etc., with the main line at the town limits. The
Colborne street track must, I think, be held to be a passenger as well as a freight track, and it is difficult to understand, under any fair interpretation of the contract, how it
could be used as such if the station at its commencement
be abolished or discontinued.

When we say "a freight and passenger station with all
necessary accommodation," must it not be read as to import
"all necessary accommodation for freight and passengers?"

Who are meant by "passengers?" If the company
construct the station fully equipped for use, but never
allow it to be used, are they providing for passengers?

Primarily the words used seem to import that the station
will be constructed in a proper manner to accommodate
the freight and passenger business, with the ordinary attendance, to receive payment for fares, and to receive and
convey goods offered for carriage.

When a company contracts to construct a freight and
passenger station at a point on their line, with proper
accommodation, I find it impossible to limit the obligation
to the construction merely, as separable from the user.
The very purpose of their incorporation—the reason of
their existence—is as carriers of freight and passengers;
and it seems to me that no amount of literalness in the

way of construction can reduce this agreement to the
barren uselessness contended for by the company. All the
provisions required by the town as to this station and track
to the main line, seem to me to be made and understood
between the parties as with a "going concern"—a railroad
to be run by the contracting parties for at least ten years,
under certain conditions.

We are not informed as to the exact locality of the gravel
pits owned by the town, but I deem it clear that, wherever
they may be, the bargain was to use both the main line
and the side track whenever the corporation wanted to
repair streets from time to time—pointing thus to a continuous user of the track wherever it ran.

Then we have to consider the nature of the bargain.
A large town has this road skirting its limits. It gives
$30,000 to the company in consideration of these agree-
ments. A track from the main line is to be made
into the heart of the business part of the town, and a
station placed at the termination of this track, for freight
and passengers. We must feel ourselves bound by the
absolute and unquestionable rigor of the words used, before
acceding to the company's contention, that they can
abandon the use of the station if not also of this track,
after a few days' formal user.

In my opinion, a fair and reasonable construction of the
agreement and the words used prevent any such absurd
result. I think the whole sense of the words used point
to a continuous user, and that we are not forced to allow
this attempted injustice.

Taking this view of the legal effect of the language used,
it is less necessary to discuss at any length the cases bearing on the subject. Every contract of this character must
depend on its language and object. Our own case of *Jessup*
v. *Grand Trunk R. W. Co.*, 7 A. R. 128, is of a wholly
different character. I was a party to the judgment, and
think it correct.

No case that I have seen or heard of goes the length of
holding that a company can accept the full consideration

6—VOL. XIV A.R.

for their agreement as to stations and special tracks, and
then contend that it is sufficient to do the work, but wholly
decline making any use of it.

I have examined the case of *Wilson* v. *Northampton
R. W. Co.,* L. R. 9 Ch. 279, where many authorities were
cited. The words were simply, "A station to be made on
Nos. 24, 25, and 26, Parish of Wappenham, or some part or
parts thereof." These lots were the plaintiff's property
This was in 1863. There were no words beyond those
cited to enlarge or modify their effect. After seven or
eight years, and before any station was erected, the company proceeded to build their station two miles off, and
refused to put one on the plaintiff's land. It was held
both below and on appeal, that under the circumstances an
inquiry as to damages would be the appropriate remedy.

Lord Selborne's language is instructive. He points to
the extraordinary vagueness of the words used : " If it had
been the intention of the parties to exclude any contract as
to the use of the station when erected, they could hardly
have adopted better words for that purpose, for every word
expressing what they are to do is applicable to the making
of the station and not to the using of it." He says: "The
only word used not vague is 'a station.' I apprehend that
that expression is definite to this extent—it means a stop-
ping-place on the line of railway—that is a place at which
traffic of some description may in a reasonable manner be
taken up and set down by and from the carriages moving
upon the line."

After the long lapse of time, and no station having ever
been built, the Court decided to confine the claim to one of
damage.

The Lord Chancellor says, that "in estimating the
damage the jury might take into account the reasonable
probability that if the company had made the station they
would in their own interest have thought it worth while
to make a reasonable use of it."

BURTON, J. A.—Some objections were taken to the by-
law upon the argument which, if sustainable, render any
consideration of the other points which were argued un-

necessary, and I shall proceed therefore to consider these objections.

No specific defect is pointed at in the pleadings, the defendants contenting themselves with alleging their intention to set up and avail themselves of the various provisions in the Municipal Act relating to municipal corporations, and the rights, powers, and liabilities thereof, and of the Act of incorporation of the railway company.

In the reasons of appeal the objections are stated in this way:

13. "The alleged by-law, under which the plaintiffs claim the debentures, is invalid and is not binding upon the corporation because it does not contain the recitals provided by law; because it does not take effect and create a charge or provide for levying a rate at any certain time or times in or during the financial year in which it was passed, or for two years thereafter, but suspends or postpones the burden to be borne from the then existing ratepayers to future ratepayers; because it does not provide for the issue of debentures or the appointment of trustees to receive the same or make other provisions complying with ch. 70 of 36 Vict. (Ont.); and because the defendants had no power under the Acts relating to Municipal Corporations and the Acts relating to the Erie and Huron Railway Company to grant aid to the plaintiffs in the manner alleged by the plaintiffs to have been done."

It does not appear whether the objections were taken in this form before the learned Judge below—it would almost seem from the way in which the case is disposed of there that the argument had been confined to the question of whether by the Act of incorporation the general provision of the municipal law was restricted and modified.

That point was again urged, but it was further contended that even if the municipality were not so restricted the by-law was void, inasmuch as it did not contain the recitals required by law, and did not provide for the levying an equal rate in each year from the time for it to come into effect, for the payment of the debt and interest.

To this it was answered that no such provision was necessary, and that the by-law having been registered

under the provisions of the Municipal Amendment Act of
1881, sec. 28, had become absolutely valid and binding
upon the municipality.

I do not think that it was intended by the company's
charter to interfere with or restrict the right of any
municipality interested in securing the construction of the
railway in the exercise of its powers under the general
law.

The 19th section extends this power by enabling a portion of a municipality to grant a bonus, but making it
clear, that in such a case, the bonds shall be the bonds of
the municipality.

Section 20, since repealed, as I understand it, made it
compulsory upon the council in certain events to pass a
by-law, and as if the powers of the municipality were
called into existence under this Act of Parliament, which
provides for the immediate conversion into money of the
debentures to be issued, and the transfer of the control of
the fund to others, some protection was required; section
31 declares the trusts on which the moneys shall be held
and paid out.

I do not see that these provisions in any way conflict
with, and ought not therefore to be held to restrict the
general power of a municipality to grant a bonus, and to
retain the debentures until the full construction of the
work according to the terms agreed on; in which case the
directions as to the manner of paying out the proceeds of
the debentures become inapplicable and unnecessary.

Is there then anything in the objection that this by-law
does not comply with the requirements of the municipal
law in respect of by-laws for the creation of debts?

Although as a matter of precaution it has been the
practice in by-laws for aiding railways by a bonus, to
insert the recitals called for by sub-secs. 248 and 250, (I am
speaking now of the Act of 1873,) I have always been of
opinion that there was no legal obligation to do so unless
we are to import into the statute something which is not
to be found there.

It may be well to refer to the history of the sub-sec. No. 4 of the present section 471, formerly section 349 of the previous Municipal Act, under which the by-law was passed.

The provisions of this section and sub-sections 1, 2, 3, and 5, were originally to be found both in the General Railway Act and in the Municipal Act.

It always appeared to me to be something "sui generis" outside of the general power relating to by-laws for the creating of debts.

It differs entirely from the general scheme of the municipal law in allowing debentures to be issued for sums not less than twenty dollars, although by the general law all debentures for less than $100 are declared to be void.

The by-laws could not, in any of the cases mentioned in sub-sections 1, 2, 3 and 5, provide for the immediate levy of a rate, inasmuch as the contingency on which alone a rate would become necessary might never arise.

The liability thus created might extend over any number of years, and is not confined as under the general law to twenty or thirty years.

And the power to assess whenever the contingency did arise, was not to be based on the assessment roll in existence at the time of the passing of the by-law and to be sufficient according to the rate struck upon that roll to pay off the debt as it became payable, (which by the increase in the amount of ratable property might become far in excess of the sum required) but was merely to raise from time to time a sufficient sum to discharge the debt or engagement so contracted.

I think, therefore, as the law stood before the amendment to which I shall presently refer, it is manifest that the class of cases mentioned in it did not come within either the letter or the spirit of those general sections which relate to by-laws for the contracting of debts by borrowing money for any purpose.

By the Municipal Amendment Act of 1871, this section 349, was amended in this way.

The following sub-section is added to section 349 : "For granting bonuses to any railway *   *   and for issuing debentures, payable at such time or times, and bearing or not bearing interest, as the municipality may think meet for the purpose of raising money to meet such bonuses."

It followed what is now sub-section 5.

Shortly after the passing of this amendment, I contended ineffectually before the then Court of Common Pleas, in the case of *Clement* v. *Wentworth*, 22 C. P. 300, that by-laws granting such bonuses and issuing debentures therefor, were subject to all the provisions of the Municipal Act relating to the contracting of debts so as to render it necessary to comply with the requirements of the section corresponding to the present section 248, and except in the case of County Councils, where the debt or loan did not exceed $20,000, requiring the assent of the ratepayers.

That Court held, however, that even in the case of County Councils, the assent of the ratepayers was required. In other words, although the County Councils could, without the assent of the ratepayers, to the extent of $20,000, grant money to aid an ordinary road or bridge company, or in the acquisition of wet lands or the drainage of such lands, and many other purposes; in the case of railway aid, they could not, in the opinion of the Court, grant even $500 without the assent of the ratepayers. I always thought that decision savored more of legislation than interpretation, but it was subsequently followed and adopted by the Legislature in the Act of 1873, although, in my opinion, whether intentionally or not, a very material alteration was made in that Act, by the change in the language used, and the reference to the other sub-sections.

It will be seen, that in the Act based upon this decision, the provision for issuing debentures is to be the same as is provided for other cases under this section : that is to say, they are to be repayable at such times, and for sums not less in amount than $20, as the Council thinks fit ; and whilst the legislature expressly provides that the assent of the ratepayers shall be necessary in conformity with

section 231, nothing is said about the other provisions in reference to a special rate and the other matters referred to
in section 248. It is placed in other words on the same
footing as sub-sections 1, 2 and 3.

Can it be said, unless we are to import into this section
something not to be found there, that a debenture payable
in 25 years, under this sub-section is void, when a debenture
issued under sub-section 2 might clearly be made payable
at any time, or that it would be a violation of this section
to issue debentures in sums of $20, in aid of this railway—
and is it beyond question that the Council, having no
power to contract a debt for this purpose, except under
this section, could burden the ratepayers with a rate which,
under section 248, might be in excess of the sum required
to meet the debt at maturity ?

All that was requisite, if it was the intention of the
Legislature to bring this case within the operation of section 248, regulating the formalities required in by-laws for
the contracting of debts, would have been to say as I think
they did say in the Act of 1871, " it shall be within the
jurisdiction of the councils to contract a debt for the
purpose of granting bonuses to railways," in which case
all the provisions of section 248 as well as of section 231,
would have applied.

All these considerations lead me to the conclusion that
section 471 provides in itself the machinery for contracting
a debt or incurring a liability under its provisions, and that
the legislature did not contemplate that the provisions of
section 248 should apply to such debts or engagements.

The corporation does not propose in this case to borrow
money—it proposes to issue debentures to aid this railway
Whether it may be as material in such a case as in the case
of borrowing to hedge in the power with the restrictions
contained in those sections, it is not for us to say : for some
reason satisfactory to the legislature they have not thought
fit to impose them, but have, on the contrary, left the
council at liberty to make the debentures payable without
restriction at such times as they think proper. The only

condition imposed being that they shall not incur the debt
or liability unless the by-law first receives the assent of
the ratepayers after the notice prescribed in section 231.

I am of opinion, therefore; that apart from the effect of
registering under the Act of 1881, this by-law is valid.

Some of the members of this Court, I am aware, in a
recent case, placed a construction upon these sections of
the statute, different from that which I am expressing,
but the case did not turn upon it, and I am bound to
decide according to my own conviction, and after giving
these reasons full consideration, I am unable to see how
we can place such interpretation upon them without
assuming the functions of the legislature.

No sufficient reason, in my opinion, has been shewn for
interfering with the learned Judge's decision that those
matters, which by the terms of the by-law, were made
conditions precedent to the delivery of the debentures,
had been complied with; for I cannot accede to the defendants' contention that it was obligatory upon the contractor to continue the foot-way on the bridge, along what
may be termed the approaches to the bridge; if that was
what the defendants intended to require, they should have
specified it in the contract.

I have more difficulty in coming to a conclusion as to
the counterclaim.

As to one of the matters mentioned in that counter-
claim, the location of the station on Colborne street, it was
a question of fact whether it was placed at or near the
corner of Colborne and Adelaide streets in compliance
with the terms of the agreement. I do not think we
ought to interfere with the learned Judge's finding in that
respect.

The learned Judge has, however, found that there
were breaches of the agreement established, but in place of
assessing the damages or ordering a reference, has dismissed the counterclaim without prejudice to the right of
the defendants to bring any future action respecting the
continuation of a double track on Colborne street, or to

keep the station on Colborne street open and equipped in all respects suitable for passenger traffic at that station, or the erection of work or repair shops, and the running of passenger trains to the Colborne street station.

Although I incline to agree with the learned Judge below, that it may have been in the interest of all parties concerned, that there should be no adjudication at present upon these matters, the defendants do not appear to acquiesce in that view, and it may be that any assessment of damages might prove futile if they had not the power to deduct them from the debentures which we direct to be delivered over. However that may be, the defendants insist that, as the learned Judge has found these breaches, the damages upon such of them, as damages can be assessed upon, should at once be ascertained, and we think it would be more in accordance with the spirit of the Judicature Act, to direct a reference as to these. According to the finding of the learned Judge, there has not, at present, been any breach as to the workshops, as the business of the company does not, in his opinion, at present require them. This construction of the contract may possibly be open to question, but he has reserved the right of the defendants to take such action as they may be advised as to them at some future time, and it is not absolutely necessary for us to pass upon it.

As to the wrongful continuance of the track upon the street, a claim for damages does not seem to be the appropriate remedy.

A reference will therefore be directed in respect of not keeping the station open and equipped for passenger traffic, and in respect of the running of passenger trains to the Colborne street station, and the order for the mandamus is not to be enforced until after the master's report shall have been confirmed. As to all matters beyond those as to which this reference is directed, the counterclaim is dismissed without prejudice to any future action by the defendants.

7—VOL XIV A.R.

With this variation, the appeal is dismissed ; but as each party has succeeded in part we leave them to bear their own costs of the appeal.

The plaintiffs to be entitled to the costs of the action upon the claim—the defendants to their costs on the counter-claim.

PATTERSON, J. A.—I am satisfied that the defendants are entitled to specific performance of the agreement respecting the station at or near the corner of Colborne and William streets in the sense in which they have asked for it in their counter-claim.

The agreement is between the Railway Company seeking aid by way of a bonus of $30,000, and the town on whose part certain terms are propounded on which the by-law was to be submitted to the voters and passed by the council.

As I read the agreement and the by-law, the station forms part of the general undertaking just as much as what is termed the main line.

The " binding agreement ", in consideration of which the by-law is to be passed, is first to complete the road from terminus to terminus, laid with steel rails, with stations, freight houses, and other necessary accommodations attached and connected therewith, including a station, freight house, and switches or sidings at the crossing of the track of the Canada Southern Railway, so that the trains can run off the track of the company upon it parallel with or adjacent to the track of the Canada Southern Railway Company, with certain platforms. Then come the stipulations concerning the bridge ; and the company is to complete the road in all respects on or before the 30th of September, 1883, and to run the road continuously for at least ten years, independent of the Grand Trunk Railway Company, and to erect workshops, etc., at Chatham ; and then we have the clause immediately in discussion :—

" And to construct at or near the corner of Colborne and William streets in the said town, a freight and passenger station with all necessary accommodation, connected by switches, sidings or otherwise, with said road of the company, upon the council of said town, within three months from the final passing of said by-law, passing another by-law empowering the said company to make its roads and lay its rails along a highway or highways in the said town to said corner, from where the said road would be if the construction thereof were completed in a direct line through the said town, or upon the said council procuring for and giving to said company a right of way along the northerly side of McGregor's Creek(one-half in the water) for the road of said company to or near said corner."

As far as the form of the agreement is concerned, this stipulation is undistinguishable from those relating to the completion of the road with steel rails, and with stations, &c., including the station and platforms at the crossing of the Canada Southern Railway, except in the one particular that the duty of the company was not to arise unless the by-law giving the use of the highways was passed within three months from the final passing of the bonus by-law. The permission to use the highways was given on the 24th of March, 1833, and thereupon the Colborne street station became as much a part of the equipment of the road as the station at the Canada Southern Railway crossing. The absence from the bonus by-law of any specific mention of this station may be explained by the fact that that by-law was passed while the council had yet three months to decide upon requiring the station at that place. We may, I think, fairly assume that both the town and the company contemplated a station being, as a matter of course, provided for Chatham, and there is no reason to suppose that more than one station for Chatham was thought of. The town was to have the option of having it at or near the corner of Colborne and William streets. It is described in essentially the same terms as the stations which by the agreement were to form part of the equipment of the road. "A freight and passenger station with all necessary accommodation," is one of the class included in the phrase, "stations, freight houses, and other necessary accommodation," as used in the agreement and repeated in the by-law.

It was the road so equipped that was to be run continuously for ten years independent of the Grand Trunk Railway Company, and was to be bonâ fide run for one week before the debentures were demandable. Thus the terms of the agreement support the defendants' contention.

The principal, if not the only case which looks like a decision to the contrary is *Wilson* v. *Northampton and Banbury Junction R. W. Co.*, L. R. 9 Ch. 279, in which it was held that under the agreement there in question substantial justice would be better done by awarding damages than by giving specific performance; but that was principally by reason of the indefiniteness of the agreement and of the absence of any express provision for using the station if it should be erected. This agreement, as I understand it, though scarcely as clearly expressed in all respects as it might have been, is not fairly open to the same objections, and is plainly distinguishable from the agreement in *Wilson's Case*.

I understand the "necessary accommodation" to be provided at this freight and passenger station to include all facilities and conveniences usually provided at such stations, in the way of buildings, appliances, officers, and attendants.

In the view we have taken of the effect of the Government engineer's certificate, the ground of complaint on the subject of the station will not enable the town to withhold the debentures, but the station must be maintained and used in the regular and continuous running of the road, as the station for the town of Chatham.

There is nothing to be said against the continuance of the King street station if the company choose to continue it. It is, in my understanding of the matter, outside of the contract which, read in connection with the by-law of 24th March, 1883, requires the Chatham station to be at or near the corner of Colborne and William streets, and the right of the town to the latter station is not weakened by the circumstance that the company has chosen to erect another at a different place.

OSLER, J.A.—As regards the appeal from the judgment in the action I do not, upon the whole, feel justified in dissenting from the conclusion arrived at by the other members of the Court, but I concur in the result reluctantly, and with a good deal of doubt on some points.

The manner in which the engineer's certificate was obtained seems to me open to very strong observation, and it is not easy to think that his appointment and the examination made by him were so made in anything like a fair compliance with the spirit of the by-law.

The finding also as to the station, which was to be erected "at or near" the corner of Colborne and William streets, would, to my mind, have been more satisfactory had it been the other way. I should have thought that when the parties stipulated for that, they meant it; and the evidence shows they meant it, and it is rather a strong thing to say—even treating the question as one of pure fact—that "at or near the corner of Colborne and William streets" may mean at or near the corner of Colborne and Adelaide or some other street in another block, and with other streets intervening. There is the point described. Was it not intended that the station should be relatively nearer to it than to some other street corner? There being no engineering difficulties in the way, and the contractor having deliberately. as it seems to me, determined to take his chances of getting the town—divided against itself—to assent to what he had done, I see little room for a liberal construction either of the by-law or of the evidence on this point.

It is not necessary in this case to determine whether sec. 248 of the Municipal Act applies to by-laws of this nature, even if the point is now open in this Court, as I see no escape from the conclusion that 44 Vict. cap. 24, sec. 28, (O.) validates the one before us. I rather lean to Mr. Justice Patterson's view on this point, and think I so expressed myself when sitting in the Divisional Court in *The Canada Atlantic* v. *Ottawa*, 8 O. R. 201.

As to the appeal from the judgment on the counter-claim, I agree with what has been said.

Appeal dismissed.

ORDER.—That the said judgment be varied by striking out the third, paragraph thereof and by substituting therefor the following paragraph:

"3. And this Court doth further declare that the defendants are entitled to a specific performance of the agreement in the pleadings mentioned as to a station on Colborne street in the said town of Chatham as claimed by the defendants in their counter-claim, and doth further order and adjudge that it be referred to a Master to be hereafter named to ascertain and state the damages, if any, sustained by the defendants up to the date of this judgment in respect of the breach of the said agreement in not keeping open and equipped with all necessary accommodation a freight and passenger station on Colborne street aforesaid, and that as to all other matters referred to in the defendants counter-claim the said counter-claim be and the same is hereby dismissed, without prejudice to any future action or proceedings on the part of the defendants, and that the plaintiffs do pay to the defendants their costs of the said counter-claim forthwith after taxation thereof."

And it was further ordered and adjudged by the said Court that the order for the writ of mandamus should not be enforced until after the report of the said Master shall have been confirmed and the damages, if any, paid to the defendants or allowed to be retained out of the debentures in the said judgment mentioned unless in the meantime the plaintiff give security to the satisfaction of the Master in Ordinary, that they will pay any damages which may hereafter be found payable by them under the said reference. And it was further ordered and adjudged that there should be no costs to either party of this appeal.

[Since carried to the Supreme Court.]

MITCHELL V. GORMLEY.

Partnership in real estate—Dealing with individual share.

The plaintiff and defendant purchased land on joint account for the purpose of reselling, the plaintiff having an undivided one-third share, and
the defendant the remaining two-thirds. A conveyance of the lands
was ultimately made to defendant, he executing a declaration of trust
as to plaintiff's one-third. The defendant with seven others subsequently formed a syndicate to which he turned over his two-thirds
interest at a profit.

Held, [affirming the judgment of POYD, C., 9 O. R. 139,] that this dealing
of defendant with his interest in the land had not the effect of alienating or taking away any part of the partnership estate from the purposes
of that partnership, and therefore the plaintiff had no right to participate in the profit made by the defendant on the sale of his individual
share.

THIS was an appeal by the plaintiff from the judgment
of Boyd, C., reported, 9 O. R. 139, and came on to be heard
before this Court on the 8th of September, 1886.*

McCarthy, Q. C., and *Ritchie,* Q. C., for the appellant.
S. H. Blake, Q. C., for respondent.

The facts clearly appear in the report of the case in the
Court below.

November 4, 1886.   HAGARTY, C. J. O.—I do not think
there can be much difference of opinion as to the legal
effect of the indenture of the 23rd of March, 1882.

Defendant states he owns the land in fee, and that he is
trustee by declaration of trust for plaintiff, as to one undivided part thereof, and he then, for the consideration set
forth, declares that he stands seized of said two-thirds in trust
for seven named persons and himself, and their heirs and
assigns, as tenants in common, in eight equal shares, and
that he will sell and convey as the majority shall in writing
appoint, and he will pay into a bank to the credit of the
parties in his own name and that of another of the eight,
William Anderson, all proceeds of sales of the land.

* *Present :—*HAGARTY, C.J.O., BURTON, PATTERSON, and OSLER, JJ.A.

Then there is a document signed by the eight, declaring that they form a syndicate for the purpose of purchasing two-thirds of this land for $40,000.

The declaration of trust states that the lands had been conveyed to plaintiff and defendant jointly ; and that plaintiff had granted and quit-claimed all his interest to defendant to enable him to sell and convey the land to purchasers of the lots, into which the land had been sub-divided ; and that they desired this instrument to be executed to declare their respective interests therein.

The defendant then declared that plaintiff was entitled to one-third undivided interest therein, and defendant covenanted that he would not sell the lands for less than $60,000 without plaintiff's written consent.

It appears that frequent letters and telegrams were passing between the parties before, and each was apparently anxious that the other should endeavour to sell the whole property, and I judge from the correspondence that both were wlling to sell, either in whole or in undivided moieties.

For instance: Defendant on the 16th of the month telegraphs to plaintiff, " Wills and Wilson willing to go with you in syndicating ⅓. We will arrange ⅔."

Answer from plaintiff: "Don't care to be connected with syndicate, as not knowing the parties to it—rather close out. Will do my best to syndicate ⅓ here."

Then plaintiff writes : " I would much rather sell my whole interest than be bothered with syndicates. Have been trying as hard as I could to syndicate the other ⅓ interest, but so far I have been unable to do so."

The case cannot be put more favourably for the plaintiff, than to assume his position that the parties were, to all intents and purposes, co-partners as dealers in real estate bought on speculation, to be sold again at a profit.

Conceding this, we have then to inquire what has defendant sold, and in what way plaintiff can claim any interest in the proceeds of such sale ? The defendant has certainly only professed to sell his undivided ⅔, and the plaintiff's interest in the remaining ⅓ remains just where it was.

In that sense, it is not easy to see that any part of the partnership property or assets has been alienated or taken away from the purposes of the partnership, viz.: a sale at a profit. Especially in a case of a partnership of unlimited duration, it seems to be clear that either partner may transfer or sell his share or interest. His right so to do seems unquestioned. If contrary to any of the conditions of partnership he do so, he may be liable therefor to his co-partner. The effect of such an act is chiefly discussed as to its effect in working a dissolution.

In Lindley, ed., 1878, p. 228, the matter is discussed : " The question whether an assignment by a member of an ordinary firm of his share of it, dissolves it or gives the other members a right to have it dissolved, has not been much considered in this country. * * Where the partnership is at will, an assignment and notice thereof, must it is conceived, operate as a dissolution. * * Whether an agreement by an ordinary partner, to hold his share in the partnership in trust for other persons entitles his co-partners to dissolve, has never been determined. Considering, however, the effect of notice to them of the existence of the trust, they would probably be held entitled to have the partnership dissolved in order to be relieved from their embarrassment. The cestui que trust clearly does not become a partner with the partners of his trustee."

The same subject is discussed at length in *Story* on Partnership (ed. 1881), sec. 307, and especially in the copious notes ; *Collyer* on Partnership, Am. ed., (1868) 151, in notes.

There seems, therefore, to be no question of the co-partner's right to sell or transfer his share at all events in the absence of provision to the contrary.

In the present case, I think I should find on the evidence that plaintiff up in Winnipeg was just as ready to sell his one-third interest on his own account as defendant his two-thirds here in Toronto, and I see nothing to warrant our holding on what is laid before us that either party was debarred from so doing, or compellable to account to the other for any profit made on the transaction.

On this short point this appeal must turn. The plaintiff's one-third interest remains to him untouched. Except on his own terms he is not called upon to join in any sale of the whole interest in any part of the property. He may be entitled to treat the creation of the e new interests as a cause for dissolution, and to pray a partition of the property, if he have the right to treat this as a case of actual partnership.

We are not called on to decide this question one way or the other. I refer to such cases as *Dale* v. *Hamilton*, 5 Hare 269 ; and in appeal, per Lord Cottenham, 2 Phill. 266 ; *Darby* v. *Darby*, 3 Drew. 495, in which is a very elaborate judgment of Kindersley, V. C.

Counsel had argued strongly that there could not be a partnership in the purchase of land to be sold on joint account at a profit.

The decision was, that it would be considered in the same light as land bought with funds of an existing partnership for partnership purposes, and was converted out and out into ordinary partnership assets, and that the share of a deceased partner in part of the unmortgaged real estate passed to his personal representatives.

I also refer to *French* v. *Styring*, 2 C. B. N. S. 357 ; *Nakers* v. *Barton*, 20 W. R. 388 ; *Cowell* v. *Watts*, 2 H. & Tw. 224. And among American cases, *Brubacker* v. *Robinson*, 3 Penn. 297 ; *Galbraith* v. *Moore*, 2 Watts 86. These two last are cited in notes to American ed., 2 C. B. N. S., in *Styring* v. *French* ; *Story* on Partnership, secs. 82-3, and these cases there cited ; *Fall River Company* v. *Borden*, 10 Cush. 458 ; *Kraner* v. *Arthurs*, 7 Penn State, 165 ; *Ludlow* v. *Cooper*, 4 Ohio State, 1.

I think the appeal must be dismissed.

BURTON, J. A.—It is not necessary, I think, in this case to consider how far the co-owners of property purchased with a view to a sub-division and sale, for the purpose of profit, become partners to any, and if any, to what extent, as I think the conclusion arrived at by the Chancellor, that there was no dealing by the defendant with the joint property out of which he has made a profit in which the plaintiff is entitled to participate, is the correct one.

The case may be much simplified by putting the syndicate operations entirely out of view, and supposing that the defendant had sold out his interest altogether to a stranger; it would have been impossible to say that, in the absence of agreement, he could not do so, or that his co-owner could claim to participate in the profit made upon the sale. The parties might have stipulated, as is frequently done in similar cases, that one co-owner should not part with his interest without first offering it to his co-owner, but in the absence of stipulation, I do not see what the plaintiff has a right to complain of.

The defendant may possibly have placed himself in somewhat of a dilemma in giving two declarations of trust, in one of which he covenants that he will not sell for a less sum than $60,000, whereas in the other he covenants to sell and convey the lands and tenements as the members of the syndicate, or a majority of them may appoint, but that is a question with which we are not at present concerned.

Upon the short ground that the defendant has not disposed of any portion of the joint property but merely of his own interest, I think the action was properly dismissed.

PATTERSON and OSLER, JJ.A., concurred.

Appeal dismissed, with costs.

KLŒPFER v. GARDNER.

Assignment for benefit of creditors—Disputing assignment—Right to dividend.

The mere fact that a creditor disputes the validity of an assignment made by his debtor for the general benefit of creditors, is no ground for the assignee refusing to pay such creditor his dividend out of the money realised from the estate ; the assignment having been sustained in the action brought by the creditor to impeach it.

The law on this question under assignments for the benefit of creditors prior 22 Vict. ch. 96, and the cases thereunder, considered.

Decision of the Queen's Bench Division, 10 O. R. 415, reversed.

THIS was an appeal by the plaintiff from a judgment of the Queen's Bench Division refusing an order to set aside the judgment entered for the defendant and for a new trial, and came on for hearing before this Court on the 16th November, 1886.*

Osler, Q.C., and *W. Nesbitt*, for appellant.
Creasor, Q.C., for respondent.

The facts are fully stated in the report of the case in the Court below, 10 O. R. 415, and in the present judgment.

December 23, 1886. OSLER, J.A.—This is an appeal from the judgment of the Queen's Bench Division, affirming the judgment at the trial in favor of the defendant, Mr. Justice O'Connor dissenting.

The facts may be very shortly stated.

The defendant is assignee for the benefit of the creditors generally of the firm of McKenzie & McKinnon, against whom the plaintiff, subsequent to the assignment, recovered judgment and issued an execution, under which the property assigned was seized as being the property of the execution debtors. The defendant claimed it, and an interpleader order was made directing the trial of an issue in the usual form. At the trial the issue was decided in favor of the assignee, on the ground that the plaintiff before the recovery of his judgment had assented to and acquiesced in the assignment, and was estopped from disputing its validity. The defendant subsequently proceeded to carry out the trusts of the deed, and collocated the plaintiff as a creditor for a dividend of $962. The other creditors contended that the plaintiff, by attempting to destroy the assignment, had forfeited the right to take any benefit under it, and the assignee having refused, at their instance, to pay the dividend, this action was brought.

At the trial, and afterwards in the Divisional Court, it was held that the plaintiff was not entitled to recover because he had elected to disclaim and repudiate the assignment, and the sole question now presented for decision is, whether in the case of an unconditional assignment, for the benefit of creditors generally without preference or priority, a creditor is precluded from taking any benefit under the deed merely because he has unsuccessfully attempted to defeat it.

I am of opinion that this question must be answered in the negative. The cases which have been relied upon in support of the judgment below are inapplicable to an assignment of this nature. They will all be found to have arisen upon composition deeds, or deeds by which a debtor assigned property or part of it for the benefit of a class of creditors, or of all his creditors, upon certain conditions, which in a former state of the law he could legally impose upon them, as for example that they should assent to the deed within a limited time and should release the assignor from all further demands.

Such was the case of *Field* v. *Lord Donoughmore* 1 Dr. & War. 227, the leading case on the subject. There, the plaintiff at first refused to assent to a composition deed and brought an action against the debtor, but afterwards filed a bill to be admitted to the benefit of the trust.

Lord St. Leonard's said:

"This Court in letting in one of a class of creditors to the benefit under such a deed as this, is bound to see that he has performed all its fixed conditions. This a necessary preliminary to the right of such a creditor to participate in the fund. The object of all such deeds is to protect the estate from being torn to pieces, and this Court when called upon to effectuate them is bound in the first instance to inquire, whether the arrangements to protect the estate which were entered into by the debtor and his creditors have or have not been faithfully performed; and in every case where it finds any creditor to have deviated from and disturbed that arrangement it is bound to deprive him of all benefit under the deed."

So, in *Watson* v. *Knight*, 19 Beav. 369, the deed was for the benefit of those creditors who should execute it by a certain day, and provided that all who should *not* execute it should be excluded. The plaintiff not only delayed beyond the time, but set up a claim adverse to the deed. The Master of the Rolls said that if she intended to come in she must have released her judgment, and it was her duty to inform the trustees without delay that she intended to do so, and to claim under the deed.

The question has arisen in some cases in our own Courts. In *McKay* v. *Farish*, 1 Gr. 333, the debtor had made an assignment of his assets for the benefit of all his creditors, who should execute the deed and release their demands. The plaintiff refused to execute it, sued the debtor, and seized the goods assigned. The trustee as here, interpleaded, and the plaintiff having failed to defeat the deed filed a bill to compel him to administer the trust and to admit him to participate in its benefit A motion was made to compel the trustee to pay the balance of the trust estate into Court. The rights of the parties were not finally decided, but the Court considered the plaintiff's equity too doubtful to warrant them in making the order. The Chancellor said :

"The object of all parties in entering into arrangements of this kind is to prevent the estate being squandered * * the debtor stipulates for an absolute release from liability to those who participate in the proposed benefit; while the creditors consent to release preexistent rights, preferring the composition secured by such a deed, coupled with the immunity thereby furnished to the debtor, to the uncertain fruit of litigation.

Such an appropriation on the part of the debtor is purely voluntary; he may annex any condition not inconsistent with the rules of law. It was open to the creditors * * to have either accepted or rejected his proposal. They might either have come in under the deed or stood upon their original rights, but it is obvious that they could not have been permitted to claim under both. The provision made by deeds like the present * * is substitutional not cumulative, and creditors must elect whether they will stand upon their original rights or accept the composition offered in lieu thereof."

Joseph v. *Bostwick*, 7 Gr. 332 was a similar case, and the creditor who had contested the validity of the assignment was held to have forfeited all right to share in its benefit.

The recent case of *In re Meredith, Meredith* v. *Facey*, 29 Ch. Div. 745, cited on the argument, and referred to in the judgment below, merely follows *Field* v. *Lord Donoughmore* and *Watson* v. *Knight*. All these cases proceeded upon the ground that the assignor was at liberty to make terms with his creditors and to insist that those who intended to participate in the benefit of the trust created by him should do so on the terms he proposed, in other words should become parties to an agreement whereby in consideration of the composition offered or of the giving up by the debtor of his property, they should release him from further demands.

In such a transaction, therefore, creditors were put to their election either to accept the terms offered or to stand upon their original rights. If they took the former course they became preferred creditors, creditors of the class for whose benefit the deed was intended; if the latter, they were outside of the deed altogether, and their election against the deed might be manifested not only by setting up an adverse claim, but by merely bringing an action against the debtor or by delaying to assent to it within a reasonable time.

Now, however, that a debtor is no longer at liberty to exact terms from his creditors or to require their assent to the assignment, or to prefer one class of creditors to another, there is nothing to put a creditor to his election. His remedies against the debtor are not interfered with. If the assignment is valid within the Act, he must submit to it, but even if he has failed in an attempt to avoid it he remains a creditor within its very terms, his position as it seems to me, not being different from that of a creditor in bankruptcy or insolvency, who is entitled to prove his debt notwithstanding that he has attempted to set aside the proceedings. See also *Janet* v. *Woodward*, 1 Edwards, Ch. N. Y. 195.

Had it been thought that the old rule was applicable to assignments under the present law, it is singular that no trace is to be found of an attempt to enforce it, as numerous instances must have occurred since 22 Vict., ch. 96, of creditors proving under an assignment which they have first endeavoured to defeat. *Bank of Upper Canada* v. *Thomas* 2 E. & A. 502.

In *Schreiber* v. *Fraser*, 2 Ch. Ch. R. 271, an unreported case of *Jacques* v. *Foster* is cited in which it was held that a creditor may sue the assignor, and still take the benefit of the trust deed, where the deed contains no release.

I am therefore respectfully of opinion that the appeal should be allowed. I think the plaintiff would also be entitled to succeed on the ground, indicated by Mr. Justice O'Connor, that if he was defeated on the interpleader because he had assented to, or in effect become a party to the assignment he could not be defeated in this action on the ground, that by interpleading he had elected against it. If he *was* put to his election, he had elected in favor of the deed just as much as if he had executed it, and his subsequent attempt to defeat it might have been restrained: *McKay* v. *Farish*, 1 Gr. 333; *Bank of Yarmouth* v. *Blethen*, 10 App. Cas. 293.

HAGARTY, C.J.O., BURTON and PATTERSON, JJ.A., concurred.

Appeal allowed, with costs.

RE NIAGARA FALLS PARK.

FULLER'S CASE.

Niagara Falls Park—Road·Company—Expropriation of franchise—
48 Vict. ch. 21, (O.)

The Statute 48 Vict. ch. 21, (O.,) does not empower the commissioners
appointed thereunder to expropriate the rights of a road company or
to close up any part of the road for the purposes of the Niagara Falls
Park.

THIS was an appeal by Henry H. Fuller, Cynthia Fuller,
Valancey E. Fuller, John B. Smyth and Eliza Smith his
wife, the present proprietors of part of a road formerly
owned by the St. Catharines, Thorold, and Suspension
Bridge Road Company, under the circumstances stated in
the judgment, and came on for hearing before this Court
on the 7th and 8th of December, 1886.*

Robinson, Q. C., and *J. W. Nesbitt*, for the appellants.
Irving, Q. C., for the commissioners.

February 1, 1887. PATTERSON, J. A.—The St. Catharines, Thorold, and Suspension Bridge Road Company
owned a road thirteen miles long, extending from St.
Catharines to the town of Clifton, and thence following
the bank of the Niagara river to Table Rock The "road,
roadway, franchises, and rents " of the company were, by a
vesting order of the Court of Chancery dated the 9th of
June, 1862, vested in one Brown, and were afterwards
acquired from him by the appellants.

On the 27th of October, 1882, the appellants executed
a deed for the purpose of conveying the central portion of
the road to the Township of Stamford, retaining about
five miles at each extremity of the road, on which portions they continued to collect tolls.

The portion now directly in question is that which
extended from Table Rock northerly along the river.

* *Present.*—HAGARTY, C.J.O., BURTON, PATTERSON, and OSLER, JJ.A.

The commissioners for Niagara Falls Park, appointed under 48 Vict. ch. 21 (O.,) included about seven-eighths of a mile of the road, extending from Table Rock to the " Clifton House," in the boundaries laid out for the park. They gave notice in January, 1886, to the appellants that they required to purchase or take, subject to the provisions of the Act, and for the objects and uses therein mentioned, the lands of which the particulars were contained in a schedule annexed to the notice. The schedule read as follows :

" The rights, whatever they are, vested in the persons in the notice described in the roadway lying upon that part of the reservation known as the Military or Government Reservation in front of Lots 129, 144, 145, 159 of the original survey of the Township of Stamford, now within the Town of Niagara Falls, and lying within the lands by the said map described of the Niagara Falls Park, together with the toll, house, gates and lands connected therewith.

" By the term roadway above mentioned is understood the stone and gravel road over the within limits, including the right to collect legal tolls in respect thereof."

By another notice, dated the 1st of May, 1886, the commissioners expressed their intention to issue their warrant to the official arbitrators " to determine the price to be paid for the purchase, free from incumbrances, of the lands or pieces or parcels of land mentioned in the said notice in manner provided for by the said Act, and by the Revised Statutes respecting the Public Works of Ontario ;" adding the following offer :

" And further take notice, that we the said commissioners are willing to fix as the price to be paid for the pieces or parcels of land mentioned in the said notice as follows : The sum of two thousand and five hundred dollars, which said sum as a whole is in respect of the separate parcels hereunder set forth :

For the Toll House, Toll Gate and appurtenances................$ 500

For the Roadway from the Table Rock to the northern extremity of Lot 144, near the Brunswick House—say at the southern boundary of P. S. Clark's Lot No. 43 1,050

For the Roadway from the northern extremity of Lot No. 144, and southern boundary of P. S. Clark's Lot No. 43, to the north ern boundary of the Park where it crosses the Roadway.... 950

$2,500

The arbitration took place, and resulted in the award which is the subject of this appeal, the arbitrators fixing $2,900 as the amount to be paid "for the absolute purchase, free from incumbrances, of all those pieces or parcels of land particularly mentioned and described in the said schedule hereunder written;" the description in the schedule being the same in effect, and almost the same in terms, as in the schedule to the notice of January, 1886.

There are five reasons of appeal set out in the formal notice, but substantially they impeach the award on two general grounds, viz., inadequacy of the amount awarded, and want of power in the commissioners to expropriate the rights of the appellants in the road.

The former of these objections raises a question which we may not be able to pronounce upon for the reason that the second objection appears to be well founded.

The statute, by the fifth section, empowers the commissioners " to select such lands in the vicinity of the Falls of Niagara, within Ontario, as in their opinion proper to be set apart for the purposes set out in the preamble of this Act." Those purposes are " to restore to some extent the scenery around the Falls of Niagara to its natural condition, and to preserve the same from further deterioration, as well as to afford to travellers and others facilities for observing the points of interest in the vicinity." The sixth section shews that the lands are to be " arranged in in order to secure the enjoyment of the same as a public park."

After the approval of their selection of lands by the Lieutenant-Governor in Council, the commissioners are, by section 9, to " proceed to ascertain the value of the lands selected and approved as aforesaid, with a view to the same being purchased under the authority of this Act for the objects and uses hereinbefore mentioned." And so on through various other sections we find that the object of selection and purchase and payment of what is usually styled " value," but sometimes " price," is *land*. In the second section it is declared that " land " or 'lands ' shall include any parcel of land, stream, park, water-course, fence, and wall, and any easement in any land."

The right to collect toll is not covered by this definition,. and that right, coupled with correlative duties, or enjoyed on condition of performing certain services in respect of the road, is what belongs to the appellants. The road itself is a public highway. It has been usual, following an expression used by Heath, J., in *Dovaston* v. *Payne*, 2 H. Bl. 527, to speak of the right of the public to use a public highway as an easement; but as pointed out in very distinct terms by Lord Cairns, L. J., in *Rangeley* v. *The Midland Railway Co.*, L. R. 3 Ch. 306, 311, that expression is not accurate. " An easement," he remarked, " must be connected with a dominant tenement. In truth a public highway is not an easement; it is a dedication to the public of the occupation of the surface of the land for the purpose of passing and repassing, the public generally taking upon themselves (through the parochial authorities or otherwise) the obligation of repairing it. It is quite clear that that is a very different thing from an ordinary easement, where the occupation remains in the owner of the servient tenement subject to the easement." See also *Goddard* on Easements, ch. 1, sec. 1, where the distinction between an easement, a license, and a *profit a prendre* is shewn.

The term " easement," therefore, in the definition before us will not cover the rights of a road company under our provincial statute; and even in the inaccurate application of the term to this highway the so-called easement would be in the public, and not in the appellants.

The tenth section of the statute connects with the word " lands " the word " rights." It enacts that for the purpose of ascertaining and determining the *price* to be paid for the *lands*, the commissioners may agree with the respective *owners* as to the price and terms of payment, subject to the provisions of the Act; and if they are unable to agree, the *prices to be paid* shall be determined by the provincial arbitrators in the manner provided for by the revised statutes respecting the public works of Ontario; and all the provisions of the said Act, in regard to the mode of determining the compensation to be paid for lands or other property or rights to be acquired by the

Commissioner of Public Works, shall apply as nearly as
may be in determining the *compensation* to be paid for
lands or other property or rights to be acquired for the
purposes of this Act; but in lieu of making any tender,
the commissioners may name *a price* which they are willing to fix as the price to be paid, and notice thereof shall
stand in lieu of a tender And it further declares that "the
compensation agreed to or awarded shall be the *price to
be paid* for the *lands or rights* described in the agreement
or award in case the same are taken under this Act, or by
the authority of the Legislature of this Province, within
two years after the passing of this Act."

This section 10 deals with procedure only, and although
the person who drafted it has, probably from having open
before him the Act respecting public works, adopted from
that Act the expressions "property" and "rights," instead
of adhering to the word "lands," which is uniformly
employed elsewhere throughout the statute, this use of
those words cannot be held to extend the powers expressly
given to the commissioners by the sections under which
those powers are directly bestowed. We find the word
"compensation" used in some sections, but it is used inter-
changeably with "price" or "value," etc. "Compensation money for lands taken" in section 17—and we find
the word "property" again used in section 16—"the person conveying lands or property selected under this Act"—
but this reference to the power of selection, which extends
only to lands, makes it clear that lands only are meant.

Again, the agreement or arbitration under section 10 is
to be with the *owners*, and the definition of that term, by
section 2, points only to estates or interests different in
their nature from the rights of the road company.
"Owner" or "owners" in this Act, besides including any
person in whom the legal and equitable estates are vested,
shall also include a mortgagor, guardian, trustee, and committee, and every guardian, trustee and committee shall
have authority to agree as to compensation under this
Act, and to bind the person of whom he is guardian, trustee, or committee."

The commissioners evidently felt the difficulty insepar-
able from the attempt to bring these rights, or this franchise, under the terms of the statute, as appears from the
offer of the three sums of money as price to be paid for the
toll house and gate, and the two portions of the roadway,
specified in the notice of the first of May. They correctly
read the statute as empowering them only to take land as
defined in section 2, and their offer is accordingly to pay
for land, though, as it appears the land was a public highway, and was not land which the appellants could have
sold and conveyed.

Under the circumstances, no rights having been acquired,
and no interference with the existing state of things having
yet taken place, there is no reason for in any way strain-
ing the ordinary force of the language of the statute.

If rights like those in question are intended to be the
subject of expropriation, the Legislature can remove all
doubts, and at the same time provide for valuing and making compensation for them without the necessity of any
attempt being made to bring under provisions respecting
land a class of interests which should be valued in view of
considerations different from those usually applicable when
the soil itself is to be taken and paid for.

The extinguishment of such rights as those of the appellants in respect of the roads would seem to come fairly
enough within the objects set out in that part of the preamble which speaks of affording facilities for observing the
points of interest in the vicinity of the Falls, though probably not essential to the purpose of the statute. The road
is intended to be continued as a highway, as the statute
makes clear by the provision in section 14 (4) for removing
it in a certain event, somewhat farther from the bank of
the river, which provision applies to a part of the road
outside of the park as laid out by the commissioners as
well as to that within its limits, thus apparently authorising a further interference with the road company's rights
than that contemplated by the award.

The Legislature can easily meet the case by an appropriate declaration if the existence of a right to collect tolls
within the park is inconsistent with the scheme. Possibly
it may be considered, having regard to the declared object
of affording facilities to travellers for seeing objects of
interest in the vicinity, some of which, like the Whirlpool
and the Whirlpool Rapids, cannot be seen from the park as
laid out, that the extinguishment of the tolls should not be
confined to the part of the road that happens to fall within
the park; and if there is legislation on the subject it will
probably be considered that inasmuch as it will necessarily
touch only this one road, it ought to deal with the circumstance on which some discussion before us turned of the
appellants having in this locality only five miles of road
which will be reduced by whatever portion is expropriated.

It may not be out of place to refer to the case of *Attorney General* v. *Mercer*, 8 App. Cas. 767, as bearing on the
construction of the word "land" in the Act before us, as not
including rights of all kinds, even though in some way
connected with land. In that case it was argued that
"escheat" was a species of reversion, and passed under the
term "lands" in the British North America Act; but that
argument was not acceded to, though the effect contended
for was given to the combined force of the words "lands,
mines, minerals and royalties" (p. 777).

The appeal should be allowed, with costs; and the award
set aside, with costs.

OSLER, J. A.—I think it is clear, upon the proper construction of the Act 48 Vict. ch. 21 (O.), that the commissioners
were not authorized to expropriate the rights of the appellants in the St. Catharines, Thorold, and Suspension Bridge
Road Co., or to take or close up any part of that road for
the purposes of the park. These rights were acquired
under statutory authority, and the lands over or on which
they are exercised cannot, in my opinion, be taken or
expropriated for another and inconsistent purpose, unless
the power to do so is expressly, or by necessary implica-

tion, conferred by the Act.   Such a power is not conferred by the terms of the Act in question any more, for instance, than to acquire a line or franchise of a railway company, had its line extended through the area of the intended park. The appeal should therefore be allowed.

I may refer to the case of *Bronson* v. *Ottawa*, **1 O. R.**, 415, where I had occasion to consider a somewhat similar question to that involved in this branch of the appeal, and noticed several of the authorities bearing upon it.

HAGARTY, C. J. O., and BURTON, J. A., concurred.

Appeal allowed, with costs.

RE BUSH AND THE COMMISSIONERS OF THE NIAGARA FALLS
PARK.

Niagara Falls Park—Expropriation of land—48 Vict. ch. 21, (O.)—Compensation for land taken—Effect upon part left—Easement.

The statute 48 Vict. ch. 21, (O.,) authorized the taking of land for the purpose of a public park, and defined land, as including "any parcel of land, stream, * * and any easement in any land." There was no express provision for compensation for lands injuriously affected, the compensation, price, or value mentioned in the Act, being only for the land taken. Fourteen acres of an estate of 33 acres owned by B. were taken for the park. The 33 acres were separated by a road from another property owned by B. and leased by him for the purposes of an hotel for a term of twenty years from February, 1881. The water supply for the hotel was, and had been for thirty years derived from springs on the fourteen acres.

The Court refused to interfere with the amount of compensation awarded, and the appeal was therefore dismissed, except as to the question of the supply of water for the hotel property. As to that, it being an easement which passed to the tenant under the lease, and being "land" within the meaning of the Act, the fourteen acres might be expropriated, leaving the easement to be enjoyed by B. as appurtenant to the hotel property ; or it might be extinguished, in which case it would be a proper subject for compensation, and it not appearing upon the material before the Court whether or not this had been considered, the award was referred back to the arbitrators, but under the circumstances without costs to either party.

Per PATTERSON, J. A., although the statute made no express provision for compensating the owner for the part of his land not taken, it was fair and reasonable to add proportionately to the price of the part taken for any diminution in value of the part left when dissociated from the other ; and therefore the arbitrators were right in acting upon that view in determining the amount of compensation.

THIS was an appeal by the owner of lands sought to be expropriated for the purpose of forming the Niagara Falls Park, and came on for hearing before this Court on the 7th and 8th of December, 1886.*

Cattanach and *Symons,* for the appellant.
Irving, Q. C., for the commissioners.

February 1, 1887.   HAGARTY, C. J. O.—In the judgment of this Court in the Macklem case, (*ante* p. 20) we have made certain remarks of general application to the course taken by the official arbitrators in the performance of their duties

Present.—HAGARTY, C. J. O., BURTON, PATTERSON, and OSLER, JJ.A.

under the statute, and respecting the powers thereby vested
in this Court of examination and review. We approved of
the principles adopted by the arbitrators as set forth in their
reasons.

I do not propose to repeat those remarks. Up to a
certain point of difference they are equally applicable to
the present case.

The appellant has a property close to the Falls, divided
by the ferry road from the "Clifton House." His property
is about 33 acres in extent. He has a handsome residence
on the high ground, which appears to divide his property.
From this a very splendid view is enjoyed. The upper
part is about 18 acres. The front portion of this property,
lying below the ridge and consisting of about 14 acres, is
the part proposed to be taken for the public park. It extends for about 1,000 feet in frontage along the road on
the Niagara River. It has been laid out as an ornamental
ground.

The sum of $34,000 has been awarded as compensation.
The owner considers this as below the proper compensation and appeals to this Court. A number of witnesses
called by him estimate the value of this piece of ground
in various sums, ranging from $75,000 to $100,000. One
witness went as high as $15,000 per acre.

On the other hand, witnesses called for the Government
made their estimates at about $25,000. Some of them
spoke of $2,000 per acre.

I feel bound to say that a close perusal of the evidence
leaves on my mind the strong impression that the witnesses for the lower valuation appear to have viewed the
matter in a far more sober and intelligible aspect than
those called by the appellant. We cannot be surprised to
find the referees hesitating to accept as fairly proved that
the appellant had been offered in good faith such a sum as
$75,000 for this portion. I do not propose to analyze the
evidence on this head, and I have no desire unnecessarily
to impugn the honesty of witnesses. But I cannot avoid
the avowal that I am unable to accept as a ground of de-

cision the idea of value by the principal witnesses for the appellant.

The main, if not the whole groundwork of the high valuations, appears to be the cutting up of the property into lots either for restaurants, curiosity shops, &c., &c., or for villa residences, &c.

The impression left on my mind is, that the prospects of a remunerative demand for lots for such purposes are of a very shadowy character, and both the evidence adduced and the personal knowledge of the referees, derived from their careful examination of the ground, must, I think, have produced the belief that no such demand existed or was likely to exist. An examination of the large map prepared by the commissioners, shewing the entire range of properties to be expropriated, would not induce the belief that any active demand for high-priced lots for business or other purposes, had failed to be satisfied in consequence of land not being in the market. We do not overlook the argument that the appellant—the wealthy owner of an estate like this—would not be likely so long as he continued to own this residence, to sell the front to be cut up into shops, &c., with their back premises towards his mansion house, as we cannot but feel the force of the evidence as to the great deterioration that would thus be caused to the rest of his estate. But if he chose to sell his river frontage for such a purpose, he has the right to insist that it is worth what it would bring in the market. In this view I have fully considered the weight to be attached to the evidence and the suggested offers made to him. The result of the decision is that something like $2,300 per acre has been awarded to the appellant.

The attractions of the great cataract are indisputable. But amongst the millions who have come to gaze and wonder, there does not appear to have existed any strong desire to reside permanently or even for any considerable portions of the year within sound or sight of its marvels. The demand for land either for business or pleasure purposes does not seem to be ever in excess of the supply.

I am wholly unable to say that the referees have made an estimate of compensation not warranted by the evidence before them.

I am quite satisfied, as in the Macklem case, with the manner in which the referees have treated the questions raised as to the highways and alleged reservations along the river bank.

There remains to be considered a question raised as to the supply of water from this land to the " Clifton House," also the appellant's property. It is water containing sulphur in small quantities, and the lessee of the " Clifton " speaks very favourably of its value and its user in the hotel, and states that though it is hard to place a value on it he would rather pay $4,000 or $5,000 than lose it. His term is for twenty years from February, 1881. The lease conveys the premises " with all the privileges and appurtenances thereto belonging." This privilege had existed, it is stated, under the former lease, and had been in existence as far back as in Mr. Zimmerman's time. The case was apparently presented to the arbitrators in the shape of a damage done to the " Clifton House," another property of Mr. Bush. In the reasons no direct reference is made to the water supply, but they say " The arbitrators are of opinion that the." Clifton House," which is separated from the land taken by a public road, cannot be considered as a part of the same property so as to justify the arbitrators in awarding compensation for injury done to it by the expropriation of the land taken, if such injury was done." The remarks point to the question of the use of the expropriated land by the guests of the hotel. It was argued before us chiefly on the ground of injury to the " Clifton." It strikes us as rather suggesting a different aspect of the case. The land to be taken has for about thirty years supplied the hotel with this water by gravitation through pipes, and the user of this water is valued at a considerable sum by the hotel people. It may be looked upon in two views. As a valuable commodity existing on the land taken; as a quarry or oil well, &c., &c. It seems to us that at all events so long as the relation of landlord and tenant exists between

Mr. Bush and the "Clifton House" it would not be in the power of the landlord to cut off this supply. It passed by the lease as an easement or as a "privilege or appurtenance" therein mentioned. It is a continuous, if not also a necessary easement, and the land to be taken would in that sense be the servient tenement. A sale by Bush thereof would not destroy that servitude. Here the land is to be taken from him not by his own act or will.

I do not see how the Province thus acquiring it would obtain a larger title to it, as to any patent existing servitude like this. At the expiration Mr. Bush, if still the owner of both properties, could, it may be assumed, put an end to this servitude.

The law on this subject may be fully explained by such cases as *Watts* v. *Kelson*, L. R. 6 Ch. Ap. 166, *Wheeldon* v. *Burrows*, 12 Ch. D. 31.

The point was not discussed before us as to the land continuing liable to this servitude in the hands of the Province, or whether its existence would interfere with its use as a public park. The fact of the two properties being severed by a public road under which we must suppose the pipes to pass, cannot affect the legal obligation as between Mr. Bush and his tenant. If this supply of water was, as it were, a commodity for which, apart from the unity of ownership, the hotel tenant paid an annual or other sum from time to time to the appellant, I think the arbitrators might properly have considered it in their estimate of compensation; not on the principle of damage to another property by its possible deprivation, but as a source of value in the actual property to be taken.

All these suggested aspects of the case should properly be viewed and considered by the arbitrators.

PATTERSON, J. A.—Mr. Cattanach contended that the lands expropriated ought to be valued on the scale suggested in the report of the Committee of the House of Lords in 1845, by adding fifty per cent. to the marketable value in consideration of the compulsory taking of the property.

The report is given in full, with copious extracts from
the evidence taken by the committee, in the 3rd edition of
Hodges on Railways, published in 1863. A perusal of the
report and the evidence will show that no hard and fast
rule can be deduced from them that would be practically
applicable in the very different circumstances of this
country, even as to the mode of ascertaining the market
value, and the suggestion as to the fifty per cent. does not
appear to have received the sanction of any judicial decision, or to have been acted upon in legislation.

Mr. Cattanach referred to *Regina* v. *Essex*, 17 Q. B. D.
447, and particularly to the language of Lord Esher, M. R.,
at p. 451, as an instance of the affirmance of the principle
of the committee's report. I do not so understand it, but
I nevertheless regard it as having a useful bearing upon
the operation of the statute under which this matter arises,
48 Vic. ch. 21, (O.)

The statute authorizes the taking of land for the purposes of the park, and defines land as including any parcel
of land, stream, pond, watercourse, fence, and walk, and
any easement in any land. It provides for the commissioners dealing with the owners as to prices to be paid
for lands taken, and for settling the price by arbitration in
case it is not agreed upon; but, as 1 have had occasion to
point out in another case, the price, or value, or compensation—those three words being used as meaning the same
thing—is always for the land taken. There is no express
provision for compensation for lands injuriously affected.

The probability of lands in the neighborhood of the park
being injuriously affected by anything contemplated by
this statute may be so remote as to preclude any comparison with the exercise of the statutory powers of a railway
company, and therefore no provision for compensation as
in cases of that kind should be looked for in the statute.
When the whole of a property is taken, and its value paid,
that is the end of the matter, and an adjoining owner may
be, and apparently is, treated by the statute as having no
more interest in the use to which the land may be put by

the Crown than by the former owner. But when a part only of a property is taken, the taking of that part may depreciate the remainder, and in that way injuriously affect it. Now, although the statute, providing as it does only for payment of the value of the land taken, makes no express provision for compensating the owner for the depreciation of what is left; it is easy to shew, by a fair and reasonable construction of its enactments, that the case is really covered.

The commissioners treat with the owner, who puts his price on what they propose to take. What they are to pay is the price which it is reasonable for him to ask. Given the value of the whole property, it by no means follows that half that amount is the reasonable selling value of half the property. A fair test is what will be the value of the half retained when dissociated from the other, and if that is less than half of the original value, it is fair and reasonable to add proportionately to the price asked for what is taken. The price to be fixed by the arbitrators I take to be the price which would have been fairly and reasonably asked by the owner. In this way compensation is given for injuriously affecting the part not taken.

I think the language of the Master of the Rolls in *Regina* v. *Essex*, supports this construction. The passage cited by Mr. Cattanach, although occuring in a discussion of the Lands Clauses Act, which does in terms provide for lands injuriously affected, are yet so general as to be not inapposite to the point I am making:

"The compensation given under the Lands Clauses Act is based on this theory, that the claimant is selling his land to the persons who are to pay compensation, but he is to have more than he would have as a mere vendor, because he is compelled to sell. If he is treated as a vendor, I quite understand that an ordinary vendor in an ordinary dealing would require a larger price for some portions of his land than he would for other portions; as for instance, a man would not sell a part of a lawn or part of a garden close to his house for the same price as he would sell the

same quantity of land on the other side of an intervening
wood and situate a mile from his house. It is not a
reasonable view that he would sell on the same terms ; he
would require a larger price. He would not sell the land
and get compensation in respect of the injury done to his
house separately, he would get more for the piece of land
he was selling; and I suppose that any tribunal would give
him on a compulsory sale more for that land."

This is not at all equivalent to the committee's suggestion of the 50 per cent. addition to the market value. It
simply affirms that when one is compelled to sell a part of
his property, the price of that part may properly include
compensation for the injury done by taking it to the part
which remains ; and it illustrates the fallacy of attempting
to lay down a rule like that suggested. Market value
means what a purchaser will give as the worth of the
thing he buys, and the term is used in that sense in the
evidence, and in the report of the committee. An acre of
land a mile from the house, and with an intervening wood,
may have a market value as high as an acre in the park,
or garden, which is worth, to the owner, three or four times
as much. .

When the arbitrators made their award, in August, 1886,
they may not have seen a report of the judgment in
appeal in *Regina* v. *Essex*, which, though delivered in April,
is contained in the September number of the Law Reports ;
but they applied to the statute, as we learn from their
memorandum of reasons for their decisions, the same rule
of construction on which, in my opinion, the direction to
value the land taken is obeyed by awarding the price
which the owner, in view of the effect of the taking of a
part upon the part that is left, might reasonably have demanded for the part taken, and which construction is, I
think, borne out by the observations of Lord Esher in *Regina*
v. *Essex*. They say, "when only a part of the land is
taken the compensation to be given should be assessed, not
only with reference to the market value of the land taken,
but also with reference to the injurious effects upon the
part not taken, and the deterioration in the value of the
whole lot, and that the real inquiry is, what was the fair

market value of the land *before* the taking, and what is its
fair market value *since* the taking, in view of the uses to
which the land is, or might be devoted, and the uses to
which it is to be put under the taking, and the probable
effect of such use upon the value of land remaining, and
that the difference is the proper measure of compensation;
but merely conjectural or speculative damages are not to
be included."

If my reading of the statute is correct, the arbitrators
have also read it correctly. If I am wrong, and the statute
ought to be more strictly and literally construed, then certainly the appellant has no reason to complain of the view
on which the arbitrators profess to have acted.

On the question of the amount awarded there is very
little to say. An appeal lies, it is true, on questions of fact
as well as on questions of law. But when the fact for decision is a matter so peculiarly depending upon estimates
and opinions of value as it is in this case ; and when the
award represents the conclusion of the persons who have
had means of forming an estimate of the reliance that
ought to be placed on the testimony adduced which we do
not possess, as well as of exercising their own judgment,
which they have a perfect right to do, bringing to the task
whatever knowledge they may have of the locality and
the properties, and their general acquaintance with the
subject, as to which we are not expected to deal as experts,
and are not likely to be better informed than they or more
capable of forming a correct judgment; it is obvious that
we cannot interfere unless we find that some wrong principle has been acted on, or something overlooked which
ought to have been considered.

I speak, of course, only of the question of reviewing
the award, not of interference on the ground of misconduct or any like ground which does not arise in the case
before us.

Some observations were made in this case by Mr.
Symons. and also by counsel for the appellant in another
case, respecting the constitution of the tribunal of official
arbitrators under the provisions of the Public Works Act,

the three arbitrators being appointed by the Government, which is not inappropriately spoken of as one of the litigant parties, and the Act permitting the appointment even in view of a particular contest.

The remarks of counsel were not addressed to the composition of the present board, but to the principle of the statute.

It is easy to see that the power is one capable of abuse, and one is pleased to find that the case which gives occasion to criticise the law under which the tribunal exists involves no reflection on the tribunal itself.

This being so, we have to deal with the award as we should do with an award of arbitrators appointed in the ordinary way; and, as I have said, it is impossible under the circumstances for us to attempt to set our judgment on the mere question of value against that of the arbitrators.

The appeal ought therefore to be dismissed, were it not for the question respecting the supply of water to the "Clifton House."

The arbitrators refused to entertain the question of injury to the "Clifton House," and in that form of the question I think they were perfectly right. The subject of dispute was the land separated from the "Clifton House" by the travelled highway.

But when we learn that the "Clifton House" derives a valuable part of its supply of water from the spring on the land proposed to be taken, the water being conducted to it by an underground pipe, we perceive that the water is a profitable product of the land, and we are uncertain whether or not it entered into the arbitrators' estimate of the price to be awarded for the land.

We understand that the appellant has leased the "Clifton House" for a term of which fifteen years or thereabouts are unexpired The easement in respect of this supply of water would seem to have passed to the tenant by the lease, under the law acted on in *Watts* v. *Kelson*, L. R. 6 Ch. 166. At all events it would be proper for the arbitrators to assume that it did so pass.

It is "land" within the definition in the statute, and the commissioners cannot deprive the tenant of it without dealing directly with him.

After the expiration of the term, if both the tenements, dominant and servient, remained vested in Mr. Bush, his enjoyment of the water brought from one tenement to the other would lose the technical character of an easement. It would be a beneficial use of the one tenement by conducting the water from it to his other tenement, but would not be an easement which is something enjoyed in or over the land of another. If he conveyed away the servient tenement, he would not reserve by implication the easement. According to *Wheeldon* v. *Burrows*, 12 Ch. D. 31, an express reservation would be necessary. His conveyance of the servient tenement, pending the term in his tenant of the " Clifton House " which is the dominant tenement, and without reservation of the easement, could not affect the tenant's right, but the grantee would take the land subject to the easement during the residue of the term, and free from it thereafter.

The expropriation of the land is equivalent to a conveyance in fee. As Mr. Bush might make a conveyance reserving the easement, so may the commissioners expropriate the land leaving the easement to be enjoyed by him as appurtenant to the " Clifton House."

If they should take that course, or if they have already dealt with the matter in that view, it should be made clear that they do so, and that the compensation awarded is on the basis of the reservation of the easement.

If on the other hand the easement is intended to be extinguished, which is the import of the action taken by the commissioners, it is a proper subject for compensation —for the residue of the term to the tenant, and thence forward to the appellant. In his case it will take the form of compensation for the spring as a profit producing part of his land. Should it happen that that has already been taken into consideration—which is not indicated by the materials before us, as we understand them —there will be no more to do in that matter, but to make the fact clear on the award; but if not, the matter should be considered and disposed of. The amount of the compensation is a matter on which we do not attempt to form any opinion.

The appeal must be allowed, and the award referred back to the arbitrators; but inasmuch as the main object of the appeal fails, and we are not able to say whether or not the matter on which we refer the award back is one of much substance, I think it should be allowed, without costs.

BURTON and OSLER, JJ.A., concurred.

Appeal allowed, without costs.

PRESTON V. CORPORATION OF CAMDEN.

Municipal Corporation—By-law—Drainage—Injury to land—Negligence— Findings of jury—Compensation—Secs. 91, 576. *Municipal Act,* 1883.

The defendants enlarged a drain running through the plaintiff's land ; the earth taken from which they deposited on either side and left it there. The plaintiff sued for damages to his land, &c., by reason of such depositing of the earth. It was admitted that the work was done under a by-law, passed under sec. 576 of the Municipal Act, (1883,) and it was not suggested that the by-law was defective in any way. The jury found that the defendants were not guilty of any negligence, but that the plaintiff had suffered damage in consequence of the execution of the work.

Held, [reversing the decision of ROSE, J.,] that upon these findings judgment should have been entered for the defendants ; that a cause of action could not accrue from the doing of a lawful act, unless in a negligent manner ; and that the plaintiff's remedy, if any, was by arbitration to obtain compensation under the Municipal Act of 1883, sec. 91.

THIS was an appeal by the defendants from a judgment of Rose, J., and came on for hearing before this Court on the 17th of November, 1886.*

M. Wilson, for the appellants.

Pegley, for the respondent.

The facts appear in the judgment of this Court.

February 1, 1887.   HAGARTY, C. J. O.—Appeal from Rose, J., entering judgment on findings of a jury.

The plaintiff owns land within the incorporated town of Dresden, which is, or was, part of Camden township. An old drain, called the Hensin drain, ran through his lot, finding its outlet into the River Sydenham, which was within a few chains of the north part of plaintiff's lot of five acres.

On 7th September, 1885, the defendants passed a by-law, adopting the report of their engineer, Mr. Coad, "to provide for draining parts of the Gore of Camden," and direct the doing of the work in accordance therewith. The report, &c., is set out in the by-law.

Present.—HAGARTY, C. J. O., BURTON, PATTERSON, and OSLER, JJ.A.

The report describes the proposed drain. It is to be brought from a named point " to an old drain known as the Hensin drain," then along that drain northward to the river—total length of the work, 155 rods. An annexed profile shewed the depth, &c. Certain named lots were assessed, but none inside Dresden.

This old drain appears to have been a mere farm drain.

The usual advertisement was made in a Dresden newspaper, and notice given to the Mayor of Dresden.

The work was done ; the old drain across plaintiff's land much deepened and widened ; the earth was thrown up on either side and left there. He complains much of the damage done to him and his land and crops and fence, and a valuable tree cut down.

There was much discussion at the trial, plaintiff insisting that the work was negligently executed, and specially urging the leaving of a very large quantity of earth of bad quality on his land, &c.

The defendants denied all negligence, and urged that the plaintiff's remedy (if any) should be compensation by arbitration.

The case was thus left to the jury :

1. Was there any negligence in constructing the drain ? If so, state what it was. Jury—No.

2. What injury or damage was caused to the plaintiff's land by leaving the earth on the side of the drain, that is, to what amount in value ? Jury—$50.

3. And what by digging the larger drain excluding the injury arising from the sides of the drain caving in ? In answering above questions 2 and 3 consider the character of the soil, its condition, whether wet or dry, and generally whether any benefit resulted to the plaintiff's land from the increased drainage. Jury—$50.

4. What injury was caused by the drain caving in ? Jury—None.

5. What do you allow for the value of the fence removed ? Jury—$6.

6. And what for injury to the crops ? Jury—$5.

7. And what for the tree ? Jury—None.

8. On the whole, do you consider the enlarging of the drain a benefit or an injury ? Jury—An injury.

These questions and answers may be better understood by the discussions in presence of the jury when they brought in their verdict.

His Lordship—" I think I quite understand your answers. You say there was no negligence in constructing the drain, that the injury caused to the plaintiff's land by leaving the earth on the side of the drain amounted to $50, and by digging the larger drain $50. You further say there was no injury caused by the drain caving in; you say you allow $6 for the fence removed, $5 for the injury to the crops, and nothing for the tree. On the whole you think the enlarging was an injury and not a benefit.

His Lordship (To Counsel)—What do you conceive to be the result of these findings ? They find no negligence in the construction of the ditch.

Mr. Pegley—They do not say whether there was negligence in leaving the dirt on the side.

His Lordship—I left the two questions to them, negligence in constructing and leaving the earth on the side, so they find neither was negligent. There was no negligence in the mode of construction which caused the caving in, and they say the caving in was no damage anyway, and then they say it was not negligent to leave the earth in that way, but that it caused you an injury of $50, and that the increase in the size of the drain caused you an injury of $50, the injury to you from the fence and the other $5 each, that is $10, you suffered as injury for which you would be entitled as compensation.

It is clear, therefore, that the defendants are declared not guilty of any negligence in executing the work authorised by the by-law or in leaving the earth thrown up from the drain. But they find a damage to the plaintiff by the execution of the works.

If, therefore, the work was properly and carefully done, and the doing of it was lawful under a lawful exercise of municipal authority, the case, as is strongly urged by defendants, would appear to be one in which redress could only be obtained in the mode provided by the Statute.

It never could have been intended by the Legislature that a person claiming damages for acts lawfully done with due care should have the option of either bringing an action or seeking compensation by arbitration. What would the action be for ? It would have to be for some illegal act or some proved negligence or wrongdoing in the execution of a legal act. But if the act be wholly lawful, and be lawfully and carefully done, I am satisfied the only remedy must be that provided by the Act.

There would seem to be no reasonable doubt of the right of the township of Camden in executing a drainage work to enter an adjoining municipality to obtain an effective outfall. In doing this they have to observe certain statutable directions. This case is not embarrassed by any consideration of imposing any burden of assessment on the municipality of Dresden. The drain is carried a very short distance, a few chains, across the plaintiff's and another man's land into the river.

No objection is taken to the form or regularity of the by-law, and it is proved that it and the plans, report, &c., were duly served on the Mayor of Dresden and duly published in the Dresden *Times*, newspaper. No action whatever appears to have been taken thereon by the Dresden council.

Sec. 591 declares : " If any dispute arises between individuals, or between individuals and a municipality or company, or between a company and municipality, or between municipalities as to damages alleged to have been done to the property of any municipality, individual or company in the construction of drainage works, or consequent thereon, then the municipality, company or individual complaining may refer the matter to arbitration, as provided in this Act, and the award so made shall be binding on all parties."

It appears to me to be clear that this section governs the case before us, and that the plaintiff here was in a position to require a reference as between him and the defendants.

Sec. 486 specially directs as to claims of the owner of lands " entered upon, taken or used " by the corporation in the exercise of any of its powers, or injuriously affected thereby, and compensation is to be settled by arbitration. The procedure for arbitration is set out in sec. 387 *et seq.*

I am unable to agree with the views of my learned brother as to the effect of these findings. All negligence is negatived, including the incumbering of the land with the earth. I cannot lay down that they are legally bound to remove it as á question of law, and I do not think that the case is like that of *Rowe* v. *Rochester*, 22 C. P. 319, where trees cut in clearing or making a road were felled on plaintiff's land and left there. The throwing of trees on plaintiff's land was not an act done in the exercise of any lawful work on his land or connected therewith.

Nor am I able to agree that there can be any recovery by action for matters involving damage only allowed to be sought by arbitration. We must be careful in not thus defeating the intention of the Legislature that such claims should only be dealt with in the manner they prescribe. My learned brother would not have so held except on the assumption that a part of the claim, such as the non-removal of the earth, could be recoverable on these findings.

I fear we have no alternative but to set aside this judgment, and direct judgment to be entered for the defendants in the usual manner.

I do not think it necessary to review the authorities. The general questions on the Drainage Acts have been before this Court before now.

OSLER, J. A.—In this case I think that on the findings of the jury the proper judgment to be entered was a judgment for the defendants. At the trial it was admitted that the work was done under a by-law, and it was not suggested that the by-law was defective in form or substance or for want of authority to pass it. So far as it authorizes work to be done in the town of Dresden it was passed under section 576 of the Municipal Act of 1883, it being necessary to continue the drain into a municipality other than that in which it was commenced in order to find fall enough to carry away the water.

If the work was done under the authority of the by-law and it was done as the jury have found, without negligence, how can the plaintiff recover in an action? If he has any remedy at all, and I am far from saying he has not, it is by arbitration to obtain compensation under the Municipal Act. *VanEgmond* v. *Seaforth*, 6 O. R. 599, is, with great submission, not an authority for the plaintiff. When the corporation in cleaning out or deepening the stream there in question cast earth and soil, &c., upon the plaintiff's lands, they did it absolutely without any authority, and were mere trespassers. Here, for aught that appears, the leaving the earth on the banks on the plaintiff's land beside the ditch was the best and most feasible way of disposing of it, and if the plaintiff thereby suffers injury he must proceed for compensation in the way I have pointed out.

Appeal allowed with costs.

McGIBBON v. NORTHERN RAILWAY COMPANY.

Railway—Negligence—Fire caused by cinders from engine—Evidence—
Withdrawing case from jury—Practice.

In an action for negligence by reason of which it was alleged that fire
had escaped from a locomotive of the defendants, and the plaintiff's
property was destroyed ; there was evidence that the engine had
passed only a short time before fire was discovered in a manure heap,
and which communicated to the destroyed property ; that a strong
wind blew across the track towards the manure heap ; that there was
no other known source from which the fire was at all likely to have
come ; that the wind was not in a direction to have caused sparks from
a steam saw-mill close by to reach the premises, and that cinders were
found in the straw lying on the manure heap by those who went to extinguish the fire.
Held, that from these facts, there was evidence for the jury that the
mischief was caused by the locomotive.
The evidence further shewed that the engine had run ninety miles without the ash-pan having been emptied ; that ignited substances were
found upon the manure heap, which were too large to pass through the
net of the smoke stack, and it was alleged must therefore have come
from the ash-pan ; that the ash-pan was perfectly good and so constructed that it was difficult for ashes to escape from it ; and that the
possibility of any escape would be prevented by emptying or partly
emptying the pan.
Held. [reversing the judgment of the Court below. 11 O. R. 307,] that the
jury might have found as legitimate inferences of fact that the fire escaped
because the pan was full, and that that result might with reasonable care
have been avoided ; that there was therefore sufficient evidence of negligence to go to the jury, and that a nonsuit was improper.

THIS was an appeal by the plaintiff from a judgment
of the Common Pleas Division refusing an order to set
aside the nonsuit entered at the trial and for a new trial ;
and came on for hearing before this Court on the 16th of
November, 1886.*

Lash, Q. C., for the appellant.
Robinson, Q. C., and *G. D. Boulton*, Q. C., for the
respondents.

The facts giving rise to the action are clearly set forth
in the report of the case in the Court below, (11 O. R.
307) and in the present judgments.

Present.—HAGARTY, C. J. O., BURTON, PATTERSON, and OSLER, JJ. A.

February 1, 1887.   HAGARTY, C. J. O.—I have hesitated longer over this appeal than any other which I have had before me for a long period.

There is no subject on which there seems to have been a wider divergence of opinion among judges of late years than that of the boundary between evidence sufficient to be submitted to a jury, and evidence which the trial judge has the right to rule to be insufficient.

It seems idle to attempt to reconcile all the decisions or expressions of opinion on the subject. It remains, and perhaps from its nature, must remain a debatable land, with an ideal instead of a fixed or agreed on line of boundary. It is idle to attempt a logical definition.

The well known canon as to the distinction between evidence on which twelve reasonable men *could* not reasonably find for the plaintiff, and evidence on which such men *ought* not so to find, helps but little in many cases. I could very shortly dispose of the case if I could stop it on the latter state of facts, or if I had to decide it on my view of the evidence. But I cannot do so here unless I am prepared to hold the case within the first state.

The only branch of the evidence which would warrant submitting the case to the jury seems to be as to the ash pan being allowed to be too full.

I see nothing in the point chiefly pressed at the trial as to any negligence in putting on steam at the particular place where the shunt was being made. The engine seems to have been in perfect order, and well constructed and protected as to emission of sparks, and if the fire had been clearly shewn to have been caused by sparks from the smoke stack, I think the case would have failed. I think there was evidence sufficient to be submitted to the jury that the fire came from the engine.

One of the plaintiff's witnesses says that cinders fall from the engine underneath from the ash pan: that when steam is put on they sometimes fall, and "when you have got a long run and the ashes are shaken down till the ash pan is full, if another blast is put on the consequence is some of the ashes fall out."

He says, that a cinder, such as the witnesses describe, could not get through the bonnet. He also says, he has known occasions when he had to clean out the ash pan for purposes of draught in a run of 88 miles when burning wood, and he has seen ashes escape from the ash pan on the route.

The defendants' witnesses proved the good construction of the engine. One of them says as to the distance run :

Q. Could they run that far without the ash pan being full ? A. Yes.

Q. It would depend on the number of times they shook it down, and so on ? A. Yes.

Q. Now, if the ash pan is full, the coals must necessarily fall out ? A. The ash pan is so constructed, with the mouth turned up, that it is very difficult for ashes to escape from it.

Q. If the ash pan is full, the ashes will be liable to get shaken out ? A. Yes.

Q. And I suppose if the ash pan is full, and the engine starts quickly, there is a tendency in the ashes to shake out of the ash pan ? A. Yes."

This evidence helps the plaintiff's contention. It is forcibly put by my brother Patterson, that the defendants' clear evidence of the proper construction of the ash pan, and the difficulty of ashes escaping from it, points to the presumption that it must have been full or else there would have been no such escape of cinders.

I have, therefore, after very long consideration and some wavering of opinion, arrived at the conclusion that in the present state of the authorities, we are bound to hold that the case should not have been withdrawn from the jury.

I say this with regret, as I am painfully aware of the very slight evidence which often satisfies a jury where the liability of a railway company is concerned.

As to costs, I do not think the defendants should be called on to pay for the trial. I cannot find that the point on which our judgment turns was presented to the learned Judge or his ruling sought thereon, nor that attention was called to it in such a manner that the question bearing directly on the point as to the state of the ash pan could have been put to the witnesses called for the defence. The

claim at the trial seems to me to have been rested on other
grounds, and the importance of the point on which we
interfere, was apparently passed over.

BURTON J. A., concurred.

PATTERSON, J. A.—In my opinion this case ought to have
gone to the jury. The reasoning of Mr. Justice Rose upon
the evidence agrees with my own view formed from perusing the reporter's notes.

There was abundant evidence from which the jury might
have found that the plaintiff's barn was burned by fire
communicated from the barn of Mr. Columbus, and that
that barn had been set on fire by the burning straw of the
manure heap.

Two witnesses at least supposed they had effectually put
out the fire in the manure heap, but they seem to have
been mistaken. The fire may have run along to where
the straw lay beside or under the barn without their having noticed it, or it may have been an independent fire
caused by whatever set fire to the manure heap. It would
amount to precisely the same thing, if the fire came from
sparks carried by the wind, whether the straw took fire
and the fire from it ran to the barn, or whether some
sparks settled at once on the barn and set it on fire. The
fact that the fire in the barn and the fire in the straw came
from the same source might well have been found by the
jury. It is not easy to see on what treatment of the
evidence any other conclusion could be reached.

Then where did the fire come from ? Here the evidence
leading to the inference that it came from the locomotive
could not have been withdrawn from the jury.

There is evidence that the locomotive had passed just
before the fire in the straw was perceived; that a strong
wind blew across the track towards the straw; that there
was no other known source from which the fire was at all
likely to have come; that the wind was in the wrong
direction to have carried sparks from the mill; and that

burning cinders were found on the manure heap by those who went to put out the fire.

From these facts the jury would have been clearly justified in finding that the mischief was done by the locomotive. What then is the evidence on the issue of negligence?

The plaintiff does not prove any faulty construction in the locomotive, and on that point the defendants make assurance doubly sure by giving evidence, which seems to be treated as incontrovertible, that everything was the best of its kind and in perfect order. They make it clear that the meshes of the net over the smoke stack were as small as could be used without disabling the engine, and they go farther and prove that, while some sparks will inevitably escape notwithstanding the use of the smallest meshes and the most perfect spark arresters, those sparks would be nothing like the pieces of cinder that were found on the manure heap. They demonstrate, in short, that those pieces of cinder did not escape from the smoke stack.

As to the ash pan we have the evidence of several skilled witnesses that it was perfectly good, and one of them said it was so constructed, with the mouth turned up, that it would be very difficult for ashes to escape from it. But they all agree that if the ash pan is allowed to become full the ashes are liable to be shaken out; and one witness, being asked, " Do they ever fall out when steam is put on ?" Answered: " Oh yes, they sometimes fall; and when you have got a long run and the ashes are shaken down until the pan is full, if another blast is put on the consequence is some of the ashes will fall out "

There is no direct evidence that I notice of the condition of the ash pan on this occasion, but from the evidence we have I think the jury might well have inferred that it was full.

It is not pretended that it was cleaned out after leaving Toronto that morning. It ought perhaps to be assumed that it was empty at starting, though that is not actually said by any one. A witness for the plaintiff, who had been an engine driver, was asked " How far will an engine run

without her having her ash pan cleaned out ?" and he answered, " that depends a great deal on the work to be done
along the road.   I have known occasions on which I had
to clean out the pan between here [Toronto] and Cobokonk,
88 miles, when burning wood.   I had to clean it out for
the purpose of draught."

One of the defendants' witnesses speaks of the Canadian Pacific Company's engines running from Owen Sound
to Toronto, 120 miles, without having the ash pan emptied.
But no one tells us that the pan may not be so full that
the security against fire afforded by its careful construction will be lost before the ashes are piled so high as to
obstruct the draught.

Penetanguishene is said to be ninety miles from Toronto.

If the engine had run all that distance without the ash
pan being emptied, and if the fire was caused by ignited
substances from the engine which, being too large to pass
through the net of the bonnet, must have come from the
ash pan ; and if their escape might have been prevented by
emptying or partly emptying the pan, of all of which facts
there clearly was evidence, it seems to follow of necessity
that it was competent for the jury to find further as legitimate inferences of fact that the fire escaped because the pan
was full, and that that result might, with reasonable care,
have been avoided ; in other words, that there was negligence in the working of the engine.

I think we ought to allow the appeal, with costs, and
make the rule for a new trial absolute.

OSLER, J.A.—I do not dissent from the conclusion at
which the other members of the Court have arrived, but I
concur reluctantly.

The evidence which we think should have been submitted to the jury does not really seem to have been
relied upon at the trial or pressed upon the attention of
the learned judge.   Had its importance then been noticed
it is more than probable that it would have been capable
of explanation, and that the learned Judge would not have

withdrawn the case from the jury. It seems only too
probable that the result will shew that the parties are
incurring a needless expense and prolonging litigation to
no purpose.

Appeal allowed, with costs.

SEABROOK V. YOUNG.

*Jurisdiction—Pleading—O. J. A. Rules 128, 146, 147, 148, 189, 240—
Trespass—Mesne profits—Title to land—R. S. O. ch. 44, sec. 28—
Judgment in ejectment—Estoppel.*

Under the system of pleading in the High Court of Justice and in County
Courts under the Judicature Act, Rules 128, 146, 147, 148 240, where
a material fact is alleged in a pleading, and the pleading of the opposite party is silent with respect thereto, the fact must be considered as
in issue. *Waterloo Mutual Fire Ins. Co.* v. *Robinson*, 4 O. R. 295, approved of.

And where in an action of trespass for pulling down fences and for
mesne profits the plaintiff alleged his title at the time from which
he claimed to recover mesne profits; and the defendant, in his statement of defence, denied that he committed any of the wrongs in the
plaintiff's statement of claim mentioned, and denied that he was liable
in damages or otherwise on the alleged causes of action.

Held, that on these pleadings the title to land was expressly brought in
question, and the jurisdiction of the County Court ousted.

Held also that the defendant was not estopped from raising the question of
jurisdiction at the trial, because of his omission to file an affidavit under
R. S. O. ch. 43, sec. 28, that his pleading was not vexatious, or for the
mere purpose of excluding jurisdiction; such an omission being a mere
irregularity for which the plea might have been set aside, but not
operating to confer jurisdiction where the defence in fact raised the
question of title.   *Campbell* v. *Davidson*, 19 U. C. R. 222, followed.

The statement of claim presented a cause of action within the jurisdiction, and the defendant could not have demurred; it depended upon
his pleading whether the jurisdiction would be ousted, and therefore
Rule 189 did not apply to prevent the raising of the question of jurisdiction at the trial.

It was contended that the defendant was estopped from disputing the
plaintiff's title by his admissions and by reason of the plaintiff having
recovered a judgment in ejectment against the defendant's tenants;
but the plaintiff's claim was for damages for pulling down fences and
for mesne profits for a period of five or six months prior to the date of
the ejectment, and the admissions of title did not go further back than
the ejectment.

Held, that the judgment against his tenants was evidence against the
defendant, at the date of the writ of ejectment, but that title was really
in question, and necessary to be proved in respect of the period for
which mesne profits were claimed prior to the ejectment.

THIS was an appeal by defendant Young from the County Court of Carleton, and came on for hearing on the 23rd November, 1886.*

Alan Cassels, for the appellant.
Read, Q.C., and *Sparks*, for the respondent.

The facts are stated in the judgment of the Court, which was delivered

March 1, 1887, by OSLER, J. A.—This is an appeal by the defendant Young from the judgment of the Judge of the County Court of the county of Carleton discharging an order nisi for a new trial.

The principal question to be considered is the jurisdiction of the Court to try the action. In the reasons of appeal several objections are made to the Judge's charge for misdirection, but as they were not taken at the trial (nor indeed by the order nisi,) they are not now open to the defendant. The objection as to want of jurisdiction, we cannot avoid entertaining and giving effect to if well founded, though we do so with regret at this stage of the cause, very heavy costs having been incurred and the merits appearing to be wholly with the plaintiff.

The action is an action of trespass for breaking down the plaintiff's fence, and for mesne profits from the 27th January, 1881, the day when the plaintiff's title accrued, until the 16th March, 1882, when possession of the premises in question was delivered to him in an action of ejectment.

The statement of claim alleges that the plaintiff became the owner of the land, being part of the north east ¼ of 18 in the 9th concession Goulbourne, on the 27th January, 1881, the defendant Young being then the owner and in possession by his tenants, the other defendants, of the south east quarter of the same lot : that he caused the division line to be run between their lands by a provincial

land surveyor, and put up a fence thereon, which the
defendant tore down, and prevented the plaintiff from
occupying twelve acres of his land, which twelve acres the
defendants cropped and pastured for the season of 1881,
and until the spring of 1882 : That on the 20th June, 1881
the plaintiff brought an action of ejectment against the
defendants, the Kitts, to recover the land, of which action
the defendant Young had notice, and might have defended,
and that judgment was entered in the action in March,
1882, and possession then delivered to the plaintiff.

By the statement of defence, the defendant Young
"denies that he committed any of the wrongs in the plaintiff's statement of claim mentioned, and he also denies that
he is liable in damages or otherwise on the alleged causes of
action, or any of them."

It was strenuously urged that an action of this nature
could not be brought in the County Court under any circumstances, a contention in which I do not agree. It
depends upon whether the title is brought in question by
the pleadings or upon the evidence, and it need not necessarily be brought in question, or denied in such an action as
this more than in an action for use and occupation : *Harold*
v. *Stewart*, 2 C. L. J. N. S. 245 ; *Neale* v. *Winter*,
9 C. P. 394. Under the former system of pleading the
plaintiff might, by pleas raising the proper issues, be
compelled to prove : 1, His title : 2. His re-entry : 3.
The defendant's liability by reason of his possession, and,
4th. The amount of damages. *Rosc. Nisi Prius* 14 ed.,
875 ; *Cole* on Ejectment, page 639.

In some cases the issue raised by the pleadings was
equivocal, and it could not be seen until the trial whether
the title was brought in question or not.

The first question then is, whether upon the pleadings
as now framed and as presented in this case, the title is to
be considered as brought in question.

A new system of pleading as regards the Common Law
Divisions of the High Court, and the County Courts, was
introduced by the Judicature Act, and instead of raising

distinct issues for trial, each party is now required to set forth a concise statement of the material facts on which he relies constituting his cause of action or defence : Rules 128, 147. Admissions are to be made, either in pleading or by notice, of such material allegations in the statement or defence as are true: Rules 146, 240; and save as provided in certain special cases, the silence of a pleading as to any allegation contained in the previous pleading of the opposite party is not to be construed into an implied admission of the truth of such allegation : Rule 148.

My own view of the construction of these rules coincides with that expressed by Armour, J., in *Waterloo Mutual Ins. Co.* v. *Robinson,* 4 O. R. 295, viz., that where a material fact is alleged in a pleading, and the pleading of the opposite party is silent with respect thereto, the fact must be considered as in-issue. A pleading may, of course, be so framed, as in *Richardson* v. *Jenkins,* 10 P. R. 292, as to be insensible unless it is read as admitting some or all of the facts alleged on the pleading of the opposite party ; or the parties may so conduct themselves at the trial as to waive or dispense with proof of such facts, and may treat them as proved or admitted ; but where they are not thus admitted or expressly admitted by pleading or notice they are in issue, and must be proved.

Here the plaintiff alleges, as he was obliged to do, his title at the time from which he claims to recover the mesne profits. The statement of defence not only contains no admission in terms, but expressly denies all liability in damages or otherwise on the causes of action stated.

It seems to me that we cannot do otherwise than hold that the title is expressly brought in question on these pleadings.

It was urged that the defendant had omitted to comply with the requirement of sec. 28 of the County Court Act, R. S. O. ch. 43, to file an affidavit that his pleading was not pleaded vexatiously, nor for the mere purpose of excluding jurisdiction, &c. ; and we infer from what is stated in the judgment of the learned Judge that he thought the title would be brought in question by the pleadings; but he held that the defendant was estopped from raising the question of jurisdiction at the trialbecause of his omission to file the affidavit.

In this I am unable to agree. Assuming that it was necessary to file the affidavit, the omission was a mere irregularity for which the plea might have been set aside, but it could not operate to confer jurisdiction where the plea raised the question of title. This point was so decided in *Campbell* v. *Davidson*, 19 U. C. R. 222 (a).

It seems also to have been considered in the Court below that it would be a violation of Rule 189 of the Judicature Act to permit the defendant at the trial to raise the question of jurisdiction. I hardly see the force of this suggestion. Rule 189 relates to demurrers, and the statement of claim presents a cause of action quite within the jurisdiction. The defendant could not have demurred. It depended upon his pleading whether the jurisdiction would be ousted.

Taking this view of the case, it becomes less material to consider the other questions raised at the trial, and argued here as to the defendant, Young, being estopped by his admissions and by the judgment in ejectment, from disputing the plaintiff's title.

The case of *Neale* v. *Winter*, 9 C. P. 394, clearly shews that the judgment in ejectment against the tenants was evidence against their landlord, (who had notice of, and might have defended the action), of the plaintiff's title at the date of the issue of the writ of ejectment; and *Barnett* v. *Guildford*, 11 Ex. 19, is an authority that the entry under the writ, or otherwise, will relate back to the accrual of the actual title so as to enable the plaintiff to recover for trespasses committed prior to the entry.

There appears, however, to be some difficulty on the evidence, in supporting the plaintiff's claim to the full extent. It seems clear that the verdict was based on a claim for damages for pulling down the plaintiff's fences,

[(a) See now 50 Vict. ch. 8 sched. R. S. O.. 1887, ch. 46, sec. 26.—REP.]

and for mesne profits for a period five or six months prior to the date of the ejectment. The defendant, through his tenants, was in actual possession, cultivating up to an existing fence. Upon that possession the plaintiff entered, removed the existing fence, and placed it some distance back upon the land so occupied.

Therefore there was an entry upon an actual possession, and the plaintiff could only justify his right to make it by proving his title.

The title he alleged and relied on accrued in January, 1881. The fence was pulled down in May, while the writ of ejectment was not issued until the 20th June, 1881. The judgment, therefore, did not carry his title back far enough, even if on the pleadings it was open to the plaintiff to rely on it as an estoppel to the date of the writ. The defendant's admission of the plaintiff's title and assent to his taking possession which were also relied on as an estoppel went no further, so that the title was really in question, and necessary to be proved in respect of the period between the 27th January, 1881, and the date of the writ of ejectment: *Green* v. *Kain*, 18 U. C. R. 626; *Neal* v. *Winter*, *supra: Adams* on Ejectment, 4th ed. (by Waterman), 454.

The case is precisely the same as if the defendant being in possession had sued the plaintiff for breaking down and removing the existing fence; the plaintiff must have proved his title to justify the entry on defendant's possession.

The plaintiff's real difficulty, however, arises on the pleadings, as they shew that there was nothing before the learned Judge which he had jurisdiction to try.

The appeal must, therefore, be allowed, but we do not think it right to give costs here or below.

We must assume, from the course the defendant took at the trial, that he from the first intended to treat the title as being in issue, and he might have applied for a prohibition at a very early stage of the cause, or for a writ of certiorari, at a comparatively trifling expense. Instead of taking one of these courses, a petty case involving no more than $60 or $80, has been made the subject of a most

costly litigation.   There have been two trials, besides
chamber motions and motions in term, culminating in an
appeal book of ninety-eight pages which contains much unnecessary matter, and the printing of which alone, as we are
informed, has probably cost upwards of $100.

Appeal allowed, without costs.

─────

HOUSTON V. McLAREN.

Lease, lessee, and lessor—Covenant to build fences.

The lease from the defendant to the plaintiff contained the usual covenant
 by the lessee to repair fences, &c., but the lessor agreed "*to build the
 line fence between the premises hereby demised and the farm of D. M.,
 should the same be required during the currency of the lease.*"
The evidence shewed that there was no line fence between the farms, but
 that there was a fence upon D. M.'s land about twenty-four yards south
 of the boundary line. The plaintiff alleged that this fence was out of
 order; and that the defendant would not repair it, and that in consequence damage had been done to his crops by cattle, and he contended
 that the stipulation as to the line fence being "required during the
 currency of the lease," was fulfilled by the fence on D. M.'s land being
 out of repair.
Held, [affirming the judgment of the Court below] that no liability could
 accrue under the defendant's covenant until something occurred to disturb the state of things existing at the time the lease was made, and
 that the covenant was designed to meet such a contingency as D. M.
 refusing to allow entry on his land to repair the fence, or his requiring
 the line fence to be built.
Per OSLER, J.A., the language of the covenant being indefinite, evidence
 was properly admitted to explain it.

THIS was an appeal [by the plaintiff from the County
Court of the county of Carleton, and came on to be heard
before this Court on the 23rd and 24th of November, 1886.*

The facts are clearly set forth in the judgment of
Hagarty, C.J.O.

* *Present* :—HAGARTY, C.J.O., BURTON, PATTERSON, and OSLER, JJ.A.

Alan Cassels, for the appellant.
Lash, Q.C., for the respondent.

March 1st, 1887.   HAGARTY, C. J. O.—This is an appeal
by the plaintiff from the decision of the Judge of the
County Court of Carleton, dismissing the action.

By lease for five years, from 20th March, 1832, defendant demised a lot with certain named exceptions to
plaintiff. The lease was under the statutable form, and
contained, among other covenants, terms and condition s,
not in question in this litigation, the following covenants :

" And the said lessee covenants with the said lessor * *
And to repair : and *to keep up fences* * * And the said
lessor hereby undertakes and agrees to build *the line fence
between the premises hereby demised and the farm of Donald McLaren, should the same be required during the
currency of this lease.*"

South of the demised farm was the farm of Donald
McLaren, The whole dispute was as to the fence bound-
ing an eight acre field which ran for about two hundred
yards east and west. Plaintiff alleges that this fence
became out of repair, that the landlord would not repair
it, though requested, and he claims large damages for
injuries to his crops during two seasons by cattle.

It is conceded that this fence to the eight acre field is
in some distance on Donald McLaren's farm, and a line
fence on the true line between the two farms would run
to the north of the existing fence. This latter fence was
the only protection to the eight acre field on the south,
although clearly on Donald McLaren's land. The plaintiff admits that it is only the bad state of that fence that
he complains of.

He says that when he entered the defendant shewed
him where the true line really was, and he only cultivated
up to that, and that McLaren every year comes over it
and cuts the meadow up to the true line. It was a small
bit of meadow, about twenty-four yards, between the
existing fence and the true line.

It seems that it was the only fence between the farms, and the respective occupants let their cattle run in common over the rest, consisting of pasture and scattered bush.

Donald McLaren never, up to the bringing of the action, required the line fence to be erected, but was content to leave things as they were.

He says: ."It was not a very good fence until last year, and there was so much trouble and grumbling about it that I took and mended it myself after 15th June, on account of saving that strip of hay, and another thing, to keep people quiet.'

He also says: "It was just the fence of that eight acre field—there was no other fence—that was the fence that was to protect this field."

Again, he says that fence had been on the south side of the field about twenty years.

The defendant insists that the tenant agreed to keep up all existing fences, and that whether this fence was or was not actually on the demised premises, it was the existing fence, and the only fence for the protection of this field, and was to be repaired as such, and that the landlord's covenant to build the line fences was in effect to provide for the contingency of the adoption of the true line if required by Donald McLaren.

After taking a great mass of evidence on both sides the learned Judge found: " I construe the covenants in the lease 1st: that of the tenant to the landlord 'to repair' and 'to keep up fences' to be intended that the plaintiff was to protect the property leased him by so keeping up the fences, and I find so accordingly: 2ndly, I further construe the covenant of the lessor to mean under 'the Line Fences Act,' that if the owner of the occupied adjoining lands, Donald McLaren, should require the line fence between his premises and the property demised to the plaintiff Houston by the defendant, then the defendant John McLaren should build it, and not the tenant; and I find that he did not so require it during the tenancy, and before action brought: I therefore enter a verdict for the defendant."

The parties here made two special and separate contracts on the subject of fences. First, as to the general fences of the farm which the tenant must uphold.

Secondly, as to a line fence between the farm and Donald McLaren, if required during the term.

It would seem reasonably clear that if no necessity should arise, not then existing, for a line fence, the parties contemplated things remaining as they then were.

The plaintiff seems to construe " if required " to mean if this existing fence became insufficient to protect the land from cattle, &c. He also urges that he could not be expected to keep up or repair a fence admitted to be not on the demised land, but on Donald McLaren's land. This would be a strong argument if the latter had forbidden or prevented the tenant going on his land to make repairs.

I do not think that under a general covenant to keep fences in repair it would be a defence for the tenant to urge, that because it appeared one of the fences used for the protection of the land was actually ten, twenty, or sixty feet on to the land of another person so long, at all events, as such person was raising no objection, and acquiescing in the existence of that fence as the fence used for years for the protection of the farm. So far from there being any difficulty as to repairing this fence, as being off the premises, the plaintiff states that the landlord actually did some repairs to it, and McLaren, on whose land it was, also did some repairs to it.

Then, what was the object in this covenant on the landlord's part ?

The tenant might be willing to take the ordinary burden of repairing fences, as he could judge by observation of the measure, and extent of his liability. But if the ordinary line fence between this farm and Donald McLaren's would have to be wholly built along a different line, he would naturally provide that in just such a case the landlord should bear the cost.

The extended form of the statute of the words, "And to keep up fences," reads thus : " And also will, from time to time, during the said term, keep up the fences and walls of or belonging to the said premises, and make anew any parts thereof that may require to be new-made in a good and husband-like manner," &c.

It is not necessary to decide the question, but I incline to the opinion that the general clause in the lease applies to all then existing fences used for the protection of the farm, and would be properly applicable to this fence so long as it remained as it then was.

The adjoining proprietor, Donald McLaren, might at any time assert his rights, and refuse to allow any entry on his land for repair, &c. Such a contingency appears to me to be designed to be met by the wording of the landlord's covenant; and that until something would be done to disturb the existing state of things, the landlord's liability would not arise. I therefore consider that the learned judge was right in dismissing the action.

I have seldom, if ever, seen a case more deplorable as to the amount of costs to which these unfortunate litigants have been put than is disclosed in this appeal. There have been three trials. To say nothing of the two first, we find at the last trial 155 foolscap pages of reporters' notes, which include over 40 pages of the arguments of counsel. We have an appeal book of 106 pages, in which these arguments are printed.

The whole subject matter arose from the non-repair of a piece of fence which one man says he would rebuild for $20 or $22, and the highest estimate was about $40, the truth probably lying between the two.

There are parties who, instead of making the repairs when the party liable refuses to do it, and suing for the outlay, prefer to inflame the damages by leaving the place open for two seasons, and then demanding payment for all injuries to successive crops.

I think the appeal should be dismissed.

BURTON, J. A.—I have a very clear conviction that the tenant's covenant to repair and keep up fences would only extend to fences on the demised premises, and would not include the fence of the eight-acre field, which was entirely upon Donald McLaren's land. The mere circumstance that it was used for years as the fence for the protection of the crops upon the farm could not extend the language of the covenant to a fence not upon the demised premises, but that consideration alone does not give us much assistance in the determination of the question which is now before us, which is the proper construction to be given to the lessor's covenant, which is in these words: " And the said lessor hereby undertakes and agrees *to build the line fence between the premises hereby demised and the farm of Donald McLaren, should the same be required during the currency of this lease.*"

It is in evidence that at the time of the execution of the lease the tenant was under the impression that the fence in question was on the line of the demised premises. Had he known the fact, subsequently disclosed, to him, that it was some distance from the line, there would be much force in the argument that the plaintiff's covenant was intended for the protection of the tenant in the event of Donald McLaren allowing his fence to fall into disrepair.

The covenant, moreover, is not confined to the small portion of the line fence which might be required between the eight-acre field and the adjoining farm, but is general in its terms, so that if the plaintiff's contention be well founded, he had a right at any time to call upon the defendant to build the whole of the line fence between the farm demised and that owned by Donald McLaren. The learned Judge below has construed the words as meaning that if Donald McLaren, at any time during the term, insisted on his legal right of having the line fence put up between them, in such a contingency, the burden of erecting that fence should not be thrown upon the tenant, although subsequent to its erection the burden of keeping it in repair might be thrown partially upon him.

Looking at all the surrounding circumstances, I incline to that view, although it is sufficient for the purpose of this appeal to say, that I am not satisfied that the conclusion of the learned Judge is wrong.

I agree, therefore, in dismissing the appeal.

PATTERSON, J. A.—I agree that this appeal must be dismissed. My judgment does not turn on the force of the tenant's covenant to keep up fences. I am not prepared to hold that the fence of the eight-acre field formed a subject of special consideration when the lease was made, and I see no good reason for supposing that the landlord had it in his mind to bind his tenant to repair that fence which was wholly on the land of Donald McLaren; nor do I think that the circumstance that that fence was the only protection from cattle which might, but for it, pass from the south across the intervening strip of land which belonged to McLaren, and so reach the part of the field covered by the lease, would enable the landlord to enforce against the tenant the duty of keeping that fence in repair under the covenant which in its extended form is in terms limited to fences " of, or belonging to, the said premises." In the landlord's covenant the premises are more particularly described as " the premises hereby demised," but I take " the said premises," in the other covenant, to mean precisely the same thing.

I proceed entirely on the construction of the landlord's covenant, in which I agree with the learned Judge in the Court below. It is " to build the line fence between the premises hereby demised and the farm of Donald McLaren, should the same be required during the currency of this lease." Now, having regard to the surrounding circumstances, as explained in the evidence, particularly to the facts that there was no line fence between the farms, and no separation further than what depended on the fence across the eight acres; and that the farms had been up to that time occupied in that way; and that it was the intention that the plaintiff should occupy the defendant's farm

in the same way as it had before been occupied, or to the
absence of any indication to the contrary ; while there
always was the right in the owner of the adjoining farm
to require the line fence to be built under the provisions
of the law in that behalf, I think the covenant is intended
to provide, in the interest of the tenant, that if that event
happens the burden shall be undertaken by the landlord.

The construction contended for on the part of the plaintiff would bind the defendant to fence in any part of the
line, hitherto unfenced, where the plaintiff might take a
fancy to enclose a field. If any such thing were contemplated, or if this eight-acre field had been thought of as
particularly affected by the covenant, or if the plaintiff,
who was taking the farm, and covenanting to keep the
existing fences, meant to bind the defendant to fence in
any part not before under fence, we should have doubtless
found something to point more specifically to that intention. We have nothing of the kind, not even such words
as " or any part thereof," but only the general reference to
the line fence between the farms, which at once suggests
the statutory requirement as what was contemplated.

That the eight-acre field was not, in fact, in contempla -
tion, is proved by the plaintiff when he speaks in his evidence of learning from the defendant, two weeks after he
had entered under the lease, that the fence was on Donald
McLaren's land. When the lease was made, that was
obviously treated as a fenced field, and as the matter was
then understood, though not, as I think, in legal effect, the
plaintiff's covenant to keep up fences would have included
that fence. If, then, it was intended to bind the defendant to fence any part of the line which the plaintiff might
ask him to fence, the enclosure of a new field must have
been intended, and one does not see why the defendant
should not have undertaken to fence the other sides of the
field, or to enclose a new field that did not happen to come
to the line. These considerations go to satisfy me that in
construing the word " required " in this covenant as meaning "demanded by the owner of the adjoining farm," and the

building of the line fence as the performance of the statutory obligation, and not the erecting of a fence on any part
of the line which the tenant might designate, we are not
doing any violence to the understanding of the parties to
the lease, while we impose no limitation on the language
used, which is not shewn to be proper by the reading of
the whole instrument together.

OSLER, J. A.—The fence which the lessor covenanted to
build was the *line* fence between the demised premises
and the adjoining farm of one Donald McLaren, and it
was only to be built " should the same *be required* during
the currency of the lease." The language of the covenant
is vague, and evidence was properly admitted to explain it,
as it does not necessarily mean that the lessee was the
person who might require it. See *Harris* v. *Moore*, 10 A.
R. p. 10. I think the learned Judge properly held, in view
of the surrounding circumstances and the situation of the
parties, that the contingency they meant to provide for was
that of its being required by McLaren, the owner of the
adjoining farm.

I concur in dismissing the appeal.

Appeal dismissed, with costs.

Re Knight v. Medora and Wood.

Division Courts—Prohibition—Jurisdiction.

The judgment of the Queen's Bench Division, (11 O. R. 138) refusing to order prohibition to a Division Court, was affirmed on appeal on the ground the defendants were liable to repair the road in question, which was not a public road " vested as a Provincial work in Her Majesty or in any public department or board," and that the title to land was not brought in question ; but

Held, (disagreeing with the Court below, and affirming *Mead* v. *Creary*, 8 P. R. 374, 32 C. P. 1), that the notice under 48 Vict. ch. 14, sec. 1, amending 43 Vict. ch. 8, sec. 14, disputing the jurisdiction, is only required when a suit otherwise of the proper competence of the Division Court has been brought in the wrong Division, and the want of such notice cannot give the Division Court jurisdiction if the title to land is brought in question. (HAGARTY, C.J.O., expressing no opinion on this point.)

THIS was an appeal by the defendants from the judgment of the Queen's Bench Division, (reported 11 O. R. 138) and came on to be heard before this Court on the 10th and 11th of March, 1887.*

McCarthy, Q. C., and *Pepler*, for the appellants.
Arnoldi, for the respondent.

The facts are fully stated in the report of the case in the Court below.

March 22, 1887. PATTERSON, J. A.—This is an appeal from the judgment of a Divisional Court of the Queen's Bench Division, refusing a writ of prohibition asked for by the defendant municipality to restrain the Fourth Division Court of the district of Muskoka from proceeding with the trial of the action, on the ground that title to land comes in question.

The action is brought to recover damages for an injury sustained by the plaintiff's horse by reason of the defective state of a bridge on a highway in the township of Medora.

The highway is a public road, but the defendants contend that it is not one which they are bound to repair

Present.—HAGARTY, C. J. O., BURTON, PATTERSON and OSLER, JJ.A.

because it was constructed by the Government as a colonization road, and, as they assert, comes within the class of roads with which they are forbidden, by section 542 of the Consolidated Municipal Act, 1883, to interfere.

This position they advanced in the Division Court, and at the same time contended that that Court had not jurisdiction to investigate it because it involved an inquiry into title to land.

The learned Judge was of a different opinion, holding that the duty of the municipality to repair the public roads was not dependent on the ownership of any estate in the soil of the highway. That opinion was sustained by the judgment now appealed from, and I cannot say that the appellants have created in my mind any doubt of its correctness.

It was considered in the Divisional Court that the application for prohibition could not be entertained by reason of the objection not having been taken in the Division Court by a notice given in the mode and within the time prescribed by the 14th section of the Division Courts Act, 1880. If that section applies, it is made clear by the addition made to the section in 1885 by 48 Vict., ch. 14, sec. 1, that prohibition will not lie. I am satisfied, however, that section 14 deals only with the question of jurisdiction as between one Division Court and another, and that it was in this respect correctly interpreted in *Re Mead* v. *Creary*, 8 P. R. 374, 32 C. P. 1, where the language of the section is examined and reasons for the conclusion are given, to which I have nothing to add.

Some opinions were expressed in the Divisional Court, the learned Judges not all taking the same view, as to whether or not the road in question came within section 542, so as to be excepted from the general class of public roads which the municipality is bound to repair.

I do not enter upon that discussion. If it involved the question of title, the prohibition ought to go. But if not, as I agree in thinking, it is a question for the Division

Court, and does not properly arise for discussion on this notice.

The Consolidated Municipal Act, 1883, provides, in section 526, that subject to exceptions and provisions thereinafter contained, every municipal council shall have jurisdiction over the original allowances for roads, and highways, and bridges, within the municipality.

Section 527 declares that every public road, &c., in a city, &c., shall be vested in the municipality, subject to any rights in the soil which the individuals who laid out such road, &c., reserved, and except any concession or other road taken and held possession of by an individual in lieu of a street, &c., laid out by him without compensation therefor.

Section 525 had declared that unless otherwise provided for, the soil and freehold of every highway or road altered, amended, or laid out according to law, shall be vested in Her Majesty, her heirs and successors.

I do not know that the precise effect of these two sections in their present form has ever been the subject of decision. In *Sarnia* v. *Great Western R.W. Co.*, 21 U.C.R. 59, Mr. Justice Burns suggested a reading which would reconcile their apparent conflict, and his suggestion was approved by Draper, C. J., in *Mutton* v. *Duck*, 26 U.C.R. 61. But section 527 differs from the corresponding section in the C. S. U. C. ch. 54, with which Mr. Justice Burns dealt, by containing what seems to be a recognition of original allowance for roads as coming within its scope, by the express exception of certain concession lines.

We have not now to consider the effect of these sections on the title to the soil. It is sufficient to note that the duty of the municipality to repair the roads is not made to depend on the title to the soil, nor is it co-extensive with that title.

The duty is cast by section 531 on *the corporation*, which evidently means the corporation which has jurisdiction over the particular road. The language of section 530 distinctly bears out this understanding of section 531.

Certain roads and bridges being wholly within townships are under the jurisdiction of the county council, and over others there is joint jurisdiction in two municipalities. These are examples of jurisdiction, and consequent liability to repair, in one municipality while the soil is in another or in the Crown.

We have then the general liability of the township to repair all roads within its jurisdiction, and we have the declaration that all the public roads within its limits are within its jurisdiction, save as excepted. Section 542 excepts roads of a certain class, and the whole question is whether or not this road comes within that class.

In describing the class, the word " vested " happens to be used : " No council shall interfere with any public road or bridge vested as a Provincial work in Her Majesty, or in any public department or board." The word is not used in the sense of vested in estate, as appears from its being applied to public departments or boards. It apparently means " under the control of." But however this may be, the inquiry is whether the road is one of the class which the council is forbidden to interfere with, and that is not a question of title.

That is all we have now to decide, and the appeal must for the reasons I have given be dismissed.

OSLER, J. A.—I agree in dismissing the appeal for the reasons stated in the judgment of my brother Patterson. The only question is, whether the liability to repair the road is cast upon the defendants by the Municipal Act, as it undoubtedly is by the terms of section 531, unless the road is one of the class mentioned in section 542, viz., a road vested as a Provincial work in Her Majesty, or in any public department or board. Such an inquiry might be entered upon for the purpose of shewing where lay the jurisdiction to manage and control, and the consequent liability to repair the road, without involving any question of title.

In the Court below it appears to have been held that even if the title had been brought in question, prohibition would not lie, because the defendants had omitted to leave with the clerk of the Court the written notice disputing the jurisdiction mentioned in sec. 14 of the Division Courts. Act of 1880, as amended by 48 Vict., ch. 14, sec. 1 (O). But in the case of *Mead* v. *Creary*, 8 P. R. 374, 32 C. P. 1, it was expressly held that this notice was only required when a suit otherwise of the proper competence of the Division Court had been brought in the wrong division, and that the section did not operate to give jurisdiction in default of notice in cases in which the Division Courts Act declares that those Courts shall not have any jurisdiction among which is an action in which the title to any corporeal or incorporeal hereditament shall be brought in question.

The amendment to section 14 subsequently introduced by 48 Vict., ch. 14 (O.), merely requires that the notice shall be in writing (which, perhaps, already sufficiently appeared) and expressly takes away the right to prohibition " in any such suit," that is suits of the character which section 14 relates to, but is not of general application. *Mead* v. *Creary* was not cited in the Court below, and I retain the opinion there expressed as to the proper construction of section 14, founded on the reasons given by Cameron, C. J., in the same case in 8 P. R. 380. It may be, as my brother Armour says, that the case of *Clarke* v. *McDonald*, 4 O. R. 310, must now be taken to be overruled by the subsequent case of *Chadwick* v. *Ball*, 14 Q. B. D. 855, which overruled *Oram* v. *Brearar*, 2 C. P. D. 346, on the authority of which *Clarke* v. *McDonald* was decided ; but none of these cases have any application to the present. In all of them it was a mere question of local jurisdiction, whether the action had been brought in the proper Court or Division, and whether jurisdiction so far had not been conceded by the omission to plead to it or give the notice disputing it. As Lindley, L. J., observes in *Chadwick* v. *Ball*, the enactment does not touch the question of the jurisdiction of the superior Court to prohibit where there is no jurisdiction, because the words extend the jurisdiction of the inferior Court; that is, they give the particular Court under the English Act and the particular Division under ours, in default of plea in one case and of notice in the other, jurisdiction over a suit which ought, primâ facie, to have been brought in another Court or Division, but not over one which no Court or Division had authority to entertain at all.

HAGARTY, C. J. O.—I agree with the judgments just delivered. I wish to express no opinion as to the effect of section 14 of the Division Courts Act of 1880, ch. 8, as to the effect of not objecting to the jurisdiction, until a case arises calling directly for a decision.

BURTON, J.A., agreed with PATTERSON and OSLER, JJ.A.

Appeal dismissed, with costs.

SHIELDS v. MacDONALD.

Jurisdiction of Judge—O. J. A. sec 48—Agreement—Counter-claim.

A Judge has jurisdiction under sec. 48 O. J. A. to make a compulsory order referring not only questions of account, but also all the issues of fact in any action to an official referee.

Ward v. *Pilley*, 5 Q. B. D. 427, followed.

The plaintiff's claim was upon a verbal agreement entitling him to one half of certain commission received by the defendant ; and his case depended on his being able to prove the agreement, and to shew that he performed the services which were to form the consideration for it ; if the plaintiff succeeded in establishing the agreement and the performance, the taking of an account would necessarily follow. The defendant filed a counter-claim, as to which there was no question that it would be proper to direct a reference either to arbitration or to an official referee. Two days after the action was commenced, the defendant's solicitor wrote suggesting that all accounts between the parties should be settled by arbitration. The plaintiff subsequently made a motion to refer to an official referee under sec. 48, and the defendant moved to refer to a named arbitrator, or to some other arbitrator to be named by the Court. The affidavit filed in support of the defendant's motion, stated the belief of the deponent that the whole matter could be settled by a reference to an arbitrator to be appointed by the Court, who would have authority to decide as to the validity of the alleged agreement : the Court being of opinion that the real contest was as to the person to whom the reference should be made, refused to interfere with the discretion exercised by WILSON, C. J., in referring the action to the referee, though made without the consent of the defendant.

THIS was an appeal from the judgment of Wilson, C. J., directing a reference of all matters in question to an official referee, and came on for hearing on the 10th of September, 1886.*

Hector Cameron, Q. C., for the appellant.
Tilt, Q. C., for the respondent.

November 4, 1886. OSLER, J.A.—This is an appeal from an order made by the Chief Justice of the Queen's Bench Division referring all the questions and issues of fact and questions of account raised by the pleadings to an official referee, to be tried by him pursuant to sec. 48, Ontario Judicature Act.

*PRESENT—HAGARTY, C.J.O., BURTON, PATTERSON, and OSLER, JJ.A.

The plaintiff had given a notice of motion for an order to refer to an official referee under the 48th section of the Act, and the defendant a notice of motion for an order to refer all questions in dispute between the parties to a person named in the notice or to some other person to be approved of by the Court, "as arbitrator, with all the powers of a Judge at the trial."

The learned Chief Justice being of opinion that there was "no substantial difference between the parties but who should be referee," determined, upon the whole, to make the plaintiff's motion absolute.

The defendant now contends that this order should not have been made until the determination by the Court of the question of law and fact raised by the pleadings as to the existence of the agreement sued upon, this question being entirely independent of the question of accounts, and not so mixed up with it that it could not be severed from the reference of the account. It is also contended that it is not shewn that the plaintiff's claim involves a prolonged examination of documents and accounts, but only that the defendant's counter-claim may involve it, and, therefore that the plaintiff's claim ought first to be determined.

I do not think that there are any satisfactory reasons for interfering with the order of the learned Chief Justice.

The first question is, whether he had jurisdiction to make it. It is made under sec. 48 of the Ontario Judicature Act, which corresponds with sec. 57 of the English Act, and provides that in any cause or matter requiring any prolonged investigation of documents or accounts which cannot conveniently be made before a Judge or conducted by the Court or Judge directly, the Court may order any question or issue of fact, or any question of account arising therein, to be tried before an official referee.

The plaintiff's case depends in the outset upon his ability to prove the agreement (a verbal one) set up in the statement of claim, under which, as he alleges, the defendant was to pay him one-half of all the commission received by him for settling the accounts and collecting moneys due to a firm in which they were both interested, under a large railway construction contract, and also for managing and attending to an arbitration with the Government in respect of such contract. But if this agreement is proved, and the plaintiff can shew that he has performed the services on his part which were to form the consideration for it, an examination more or less prolonged will necessarily follow, of accounts of moneys received by the defendant in respect of commission and in connection with the expenses of collecting and realising the assets, and of the arbitration with the Government.

As regards the defendant's counter-claim, there seems to be no question that it is wholly a matter proper to be referred either to arbitration, or to an official referee under sec. 48, O. J. A.

The affidavit of the plaintiff in support of his motion states that the matter is one requiring a prolonged examination of documents and accounts, and that he verily believes that it cannot conveniently be tried before the Court or Judge directly. The only answer made to this is the affidavit of the defendant's solicitor, who says, in effect, that the defendant has been advised not to give the particulars of his expenditure until the plaintiff proves the agreement alleged in the statement of claim.

The defendant does not deny that in that event a prolonged examination of accounts will become necessary, and therefore it cannot be said that the learned Chief Justice was not justified in acting upon the plaintiff's affidavit and holding that the action was one involving a prolonged investigation of accounts, and therefore within the 48th section of the Judicature Act. But it is said that as there is a substantial question of liability to be determined, namely, the existence of the alleged agreement, upon which the taking of the accounts will depend, that question ought to be determined in the ordinary way and not sent to a referee. In support of this objection the case of *Clow* v. *Harper*, 3 Ex. D. 198, was cited. In that case the order of reference was made under the Common

Law Procedure Act, and the decision has been observed upon and distinguished again and again, as having proceeded, either upon the ground that under the circumstances of the particular case it was a wrong exercise of discretion to refer the action, or upon the ground that the reference was not under the Judicature Act but under the Common Law Procedure Act. See *Goodwin* v. *Budden*, 42 L. T. 536 ; *Hoch* v. *Burr*, 43 L. T. 425 ; *Martin* v. *Fyfe*, 49 L. T. 107 ; S. C. 50 L. T. 72.

In *Ward* v. *Pilley*, 5 Q. B. Div. 427, which was followed in the last case cited, Bramwell, L. J., speaking of the power of the Court under sec. 57, says: " I think that wherever the Court has jurisdiction to refer any question of account to an official referee it also has jurisdiction to refer to him any other question arising in the action. I believe that not long since a notion got abroad that under sec. 3 of the C. L. P. Act we had power to refer questions of account, and not other matters, but that mistake we set right in a case which we decided in this Court at the last sittings. There is this strong objection to referring some only of the issues and leaving others to be tried by a jury, that you have two trials instead of one, and so involve double expense." Brett, L. J., says : " In cases within sec. 57 what is it that the Court is empowered to refer ? I am of opinion that if a case is once brought within that section the Court may send to the official referee not only the issues of account but all the issues in the cause."

I am not sure that this is entirely consistent with all that was said by the Court in *Longman* v. *East*, 3 C. P. D. 158, but the practice appears from the other cases referred to, to be uniformly settled in accordance with the opinions I have just quoted.

The learned Chief Justice, therefore, had jurisdiction to make the order referring all the issues of fact and questions of account in the action to the referee, and the only other question is whether his discretion in making it was improperly exercised. That is a ground on which this Court should be slow to interfere. If the defendant had from the outset taken the stand that he desired the question of agreement or no agreement to be tried in the ordinary way as a distinct issue from the question of the accounts, it might well be that the learned Chief Justice would not have thought it proper to send that issue for trial before a referee, particularly if it had appeared that there was no certainty of any matter of account being tried at all.   So, also, if there had been any distinct severable issue or charge of fraud unmixed with the accounts, which, however, is not suggested.

Here it is manifest that the defendant has always contemplated a reference as the proper way of settling the accounts.   Two days after the issue of the writ his solicitor, apparently repeating a proposition which had been previously made, writes suggesting that all accounts between the parties should be settled by arbitration. The affidavit filed in support of the defendant's motion to refer also states the belief of the deponent that the whole matter can be settled without a reference back to the Court, by a reference to an arbitrator appointed under the C. L. P. Act or otherwise, who would have authority to decide, in the first instance, as to the validity of the alleged agreement.   And lastly, the defendant's notice of motion asks for a reference to the arbitrator named in the notice, or to some other arbitrator to be named by the Court.   Under these circumstances I think it was properly held that the real contest between the parties was as to the person to whom the reference should be made, for the difference under our practice between a compulsory reference of the whole action to arbitration and a reference of all the issues of fact in the action to a referee, is in this case, if not merely formal, at least not important.   Under a reference in the latter form the parties must move for judgment on the findings of the referee, but as regards an appeal from the award or a motion to set aside the findings of the referee, their rights are substantially the same.

I am therefore of opinion that all the objections to the order fail, and that the appeal should be dismissed.

BURTON, J. A.—The question here is one of some importance as affecting the right of parties to have their cases, if they desire it, adjudicated upon by the ordinary tribunals and in the ordinary way, although the matter assumes rather a technical shape in consequence of the acts of the parties themselves, and resolves itself, in my opinion, into a question of whether the learned Judge had jurisdiction to refer the whole of the issues under sec. 48 of the Judicature Act against the consent of the defendant. I do not doubt that if he had granted the defendant's application, and referred the action to the same party, he would have been warranted in doing so. If, therefore, he had jurisdiction I agree with the other members of the Court that we could not under the peculiar facts of this case interfere with the learned Judge's discretion in referring the matter to him.

But the question of jurisdiction to refer under this section is one of grave importance, and but for the one decision of *Ward* v. *Pilley*, 5 Q. B. D. 427, I should have thought it clear that the learned Judge had no jurisdiction to make the order he has made, if that order, as drawn up, correctly embodies his judgment, which on a perusal of his reasons I should have thought very doubtful.

Now, as I have always understood sec. 48, the Court can only send such questions to the referee as are brought within the terms of the section. That is, any issue requiring any prolonged examination of documents or accounts or any scientific or local investigation.

But then it is not every issue requiring a prolonged examination of documents or accounts which can be referred—it must be such as cannot, in the opinion of the Court, conveniently be tried before a jury or conducted by the Court or judge directly.

If any part of a cause or matter is brought within these terms the Court might according to my reading of the section, borne out by the authorities I shall presently refer to, by compulsion at any time order that part of the cause, or rather the issues and questions of fact coming within that definition, to be tried by an official referee.

We have the high authority of Lord Bramwell for holding that even where the parties consent the power of the Judge under this section is still confined; that is, he has no jurisdiction to order the action to be referred, but merely to send, for the decision of the referee, any question or issue of fact or any question of account, but that questions of law cannot be sent to him even by consent of the parties: *Longman* v. *East*, 3 C. P. D. 158.

Lord Justice Brett in the same case says " I do not think because one issue in the cause is brought within the terms of sec. 57 the Court or Judge have power to order all the issues in the case to be sent to the official referee, unless those other issues are so mixed up with that issue that although they are different issues in form, yet in substance there is really only one issue."

I do not think the case of *Goodwin* v. *Budden*, 42 L. T. N. S. 536, which was the decision of a Divisional Court, whilst the judgment from which I have been quoting was that of the Court of Appeal, conflicts with it, although the remarks of some of the Judges, referring in a great measure to a decision of *Clow* v. *Harper*, 3 Ex. D. 198 under another statute, may appear to do so. The case falls rather within the class of cases referred to by Brett, L. J., in the extract I have just given, for the issues were so interwoven that it may have been necessary to go into the question of accounts in order to determine the other issue, the question of partnership, and although as I have said *Clow* v. *Harper* was decided under a different statute in which the right to refer compulsorily was less restricted, the counsel who argued in support of the order in *Goodwin* v. *Budden* admits the distinction between it and *Clow* v. *Harper*, where he says there was " a question of liability which went to the root of the matter, and before that was decided no question of account arose, but that was not the present case at all"; and again to refer to the judgment of the Court of Appeal in 3 C.P.D., Lord Justice Cotton says at p. 160: "There may be certain issues so connected with the matters of account, or with the matters requiring local inquiry or scientific examination, that it would be hardly possible fairly to deal

with the issues not of that special character, without sending them to the same person who is to deal with those
requiring scientific examination or local investigation, or
matters of account. But, in my opinion, it would be wrong
even if there is any jurisdiction, which I do not say there
is, to refer all the issues in a cause to a referee simply
because there is a matter of account which can only be
properly dealt with by him."

The opinions of these learned Judges seem very clearly
to bear out the view I have expressed, that the learned
Judge had no jurisdiction, without consent, to deal with the
issue which is contested in this case, viz., the existence of
any binding agreement between the parties, failing which
no investigation of accounts would be necessary at all.

The utterances of Bramwell and Brett, L.JJ., in the case
in 5 Q. B. D. seem certainly to be in conflict with their earlier
decisions in the case from which I have quoted, and go the
full length of holding that "if once a case is brought within
the section, the Court may send to the official referee, not
only the issues of account, but all the issues in the
cause."

It does not strike me as being a case in which, according
to the old adage, second thoughts can be said to be best,
nor do I think the reason given by L. J. Bramwell, that by
referring some matters and not others "you have two trials
instead of one, and so double expense," a very satisfactory
one, inasmuch as if the main issue is disposed of by the
judge or jury adversely to the party claiming the account,
that second trial becomes unnecessary.

I gather, however, that in such a case as the present
where we are told that the question of liability involves a
question of law as well as fact, and could more conveniently be disposed of by a jury under the direction of a
Judge or by the Judge himself, none of the Judges I have
named would if the matter had come before them in the
first instance have made the reference.

As, however, this later decision, which though not
absolutely binding upon us is one we ought to follow, seems
to settle the question of jurisdiction, I am not prepared to

say that under the circumstances we should interfere with the discretion which has been exercised, and therefore I agree in dismissing the appeal.

HAGARTY, C. J. O., and PATTERSON, J.A., concurred.

Appeal dismissed, with costs.

NEVITT V. McMURRAY.

Estoppel by deed—Vendor's lien—Registration of plan—Offer to sell—Acceptance of offer—Conditional offer.

McM., in building a house, by mistake built part of it on the land of the adjoining owner B. On discovering this he applied to B. with a view of purchasing a portion of B.'s lot, and B. on 29th July, 1880, wrote : "I hereby offer to sell you twenty-five feet frontage for the sum of $250, to be paid six months from this date, otherwise this offer to be null " * * and B. accepted such offer at the foot in the words, "I hereby accept the above offer." McM. seven days after registered a plan as No 327, alleged to be of his own property, but which included the 25 feet as part of lot M., and the next day executed a mortgage on lot M. with a description, which included the 25 feet, and which was assigned to the defendants the Q. S. Co. B.'s offer to sell to McM. was not acted on within the six months limited, and B. afterwards, in January, 1883, sold and conveyed the 25 feet (which was called lot 40 on his [B.'s] plan No. 396, registered 26th January, 1883,) to McM. for $400, payable $100 cash and mortgage for $300, and which mortgage was at the instance of B. taken to his daughter N., the plaintiff. The O. S. Co. subsequently sold under the power of sale in their mortgage to the defendant W.

In an action by N. to realise her mortgage, it was

Held, [reversing the judgment of PROUDFOOT, J.,] that the original dealing between B. and McM. created no binding contract on the latter, it being merely an option given him ; and he not having completed the purchase within six months the subsequent sale and conveyance by B. to McM. was upon a new and distinct contract. No interest in the 25 feet [lot 40] passed to the O. S. Co. under McM.'s mortgage, and the subsequent conveyance to him "fed the estoppel" created by his prior mortgage to the extent only of McM.'s interest which was that of owner of the equity of redemption, or owner of the 25 feet (lot 40) charged with $300, and it made no difference that the $300 mortgage was taken to the plaintiff instead of to B., the effect of the whole transaction being that W. was the owner of lot 40 subject to a first mortgage of $300 in favor of the plaintiff and to a second mortgage of the O. S. Co.

B. having by his dealing with McM. created in him the status of owner, and in the plaintiff that of mortgagee, was not, nor was the plaintiff in a position to complain of the registration of plan 327.

Doe Irvine v. *Webster*, 2 U. C. R. 234 ; *Doe Hennessey* v. *Meyers*, 2 O. S. 424, observed upon.

THIS was an action commenced in the Chancery Division by the plaintiff Elizabeth Ellen Nevitt, against J. Saurin McMurray, Valancey E. Fuller, The Omnium Securities Company (limited), and Margaret Wiseman, claiming (1) possession of certain land in the city of Toronto from the defendants the Omnium Securities Company and Wiseman, (2) an order declaring that a certain plan (No. 327) registered by the defendants McMurray and Fuller so far as the same affected such land was a cloud upon the plaintiff's title thereto, and ordering its removal from the registry so far as it affected such land ; and (3) damages against McMurray and Fuller for having so wrongly registered such plan.

The several defendants having put in defences the case came on for trial before Proudfoot, J., at the Sittings in Toronto on the 24th October, 1885, who on the 30th of that month gave judgment dismissing the action as against all the defendants, with costs.

Against that judgment the plaintiff appealed, and the case came on for hearing before this Court on the 14th September, 1886.*

Robinson, Q.C., and *A. Cassels*, for the appellant.

Moss, Q.C., for the respondents the Omnium Securities Co.

Meek, for the respondent McMurray.

F. W. Hill, for the respondent Wiseman.

Bicknell, for the respondent Fuller.

The other facts clearly appear in the judgments.

December 23, 1886. HAGARTY, C.J.O.—It appears to me that if we have to decide this case in favor of defendants, it must be only by the application of the doctrine of estoppel, and as far as the apparent merits are before us, by a most unjust application of a doctrine unknown to all the

Present—HAGARTY, C. J. O., BURTON, PATTERSON, and OSLER, JJ:A.

acting parties, and in no way influencing their dealings with each other.

Before considering whether we are forced to do this injustice it may be well to notice points in the case which have influenced the decision below. The learned Judge considered that the defendant McMurray had an equitable interest under the contract with Beaty which was never terminated, and that the settlement under which Beaty made the conveyance to McMurray was a continuation, or rather completion, of the original bargain.

I am unable to concur in this view.

I think the expiration of six months from the date of Beaty's letter of 29th July, 1880, without any action on McMurray's part, put an end to any interest in the latter.

Beaty writes: " I hereby offer to sell to you, &c., &c., for the sum of $250, to be paid six months after this date, otherwise this offer to be null. I agree to pay off encumbrances on this when paying off whole."

McMurray writes at foot : " I hereby accept the above offer."

This is a unilateral contract. It binds Beaty if acted on; it does not in any way bind McMurray, who need not take it unless he pleases. It is merely an option given to him. For six months the land continues bound, awaiting as it were, the signification of McMurray's acceptance.

This not being signified, I think the land is free.

The absence of anything binding on McMurray is to my mind the material fact.

I regard it as a mere option or right of pre-emption for a named time. Fry on Specific Performance, 2nd ed., 475 : " Where the contract is in any wise unilateral, as for instance in the case of an option to purchase, a right of renewal, or of any other condition in favor of one party and not of the other, then any delay in the party in whose favor the contract is binding is looked at with especial strictness." Several cases are in the books where a right of pre-emption of an estate was devised, election to take having to be signified in a named time: *Austin*, v. *Tawney*, L. R. 2 Ch. 143; *Brooke* v. *Garrod*, 3 K. &

J 612. In this last case, Wood, V. C., says : " The right of
pre-emption was a privilege given to Mallows, and being so
the conditions were conditions with which he was obliged to
comply strictly. The case is somewhat analogous to a case
between vendor and purchaser where time is made of the
essence of the contract, and the parties have not by their
dealings waived their rights as to time being of the essence
of the contract."

This decision was upheld by Lord Cranworth, C., on
appeal, 2 DeG. & J. 62. He uses words of general
application : " I have more than once had occasion to say
that I think this Court has gone to too great an extent in
departing from the precise terms of the contracts into
which the parties have entered, and so in effect making
other contracts for them. If a contract can by fair construction be divided into two contracts, $i. e.$, one contract
to do an act, and another to do it at a certain time, the Court
may say that these are independent stipulations. But if
the contract be that on payment of a sum of £1,000 at or
before a specified day a certain act shall be done on my
part, I am at a loss to see why I can properly be called on
to do the act if the money be not paid at the day, or why
I should be compelled to perform not my contract but
another contract into which I have not entered. If cases
are found in the books which go to that extent, I can only
say that I cannot see the principle on which they are
founded."

Barclay v. *Messenger*, 22 W. R. 522; *Weston* v. *Collins*,
13 W. R. 510 ; 34 L. J., Ch. 353. In the last of these an option
was given to a tenant to purchase the property at the end of
the term if he gave six months notice to lessor and paid
£2,000 as and for the purchase thereof. He gave the
notice in time, but did not pay or tender the purchase
money, alleging that owing to the lessor's delay in
furnishing an abstract he was unable to complete the
conveyance. The Lord Chancellor said that if the
lessee chose to comply with the conditions the lessor
is bound, but previously there is no mutuality of contract. " It is in fact a conditional offer by the lessor,
and the conditions must be observed before the offer
becomes binding. It is a mistake to apply to stipulations
of this kind the rules applicable in this Court to ordinary

contracts for sale of real estate." He goes on to explain
that it is a unilateral contract; that delivery of the notice
and payment of the purchase money were both conditions to
be fulfilled by the lessee before the lessor became bound ;
that it was true that the lessee would thus have to pay
the whole purchase money before he could ascertain that
the lessor could make a good title, but he could recover
back the money if title could not be made. *Barclay* v.
Messenger, before Jessel, M. R., is much to same effect.
The judgment is valuable from its references.

I do not concur in the view that Beaty was called upon
to do anything in reference to any incumbrances on the
property. The whole burden of moving in the matter
within the specified time was on the defendant McMurray.

Even if he were not bound, as Lord Westbury states, to
pay or tender the money, I do not see that Beaty was
bound to take any step. He had agreed to remove the
incumbrances when he paid off the charges on the whole
property of which this was a part, and we know not when
they became due.

I am also unable to agree that the final settlement
between them was anything but a new bargain and contract.

As to the filing of the plans, I think any claim in
respect of this fails.

No filing of a plan by McMurray could operate to
deprive Beaty of his property, and damages could not, I
think, under the circumstances be claimed for such filing.
When the plan was filed, McMurray had a claim upon the
land which he had the right to turn into an absolute
interest. Had he done so the plan would be right.

I do not see how his sending his cheque for $100, after
some fourteen, instead of six, months, to Beaty, and which
was never used by the latter, can affect the right. If any
money was to be sent, why not the $250 ?

We have now to consider the argument that the effect
of the passing of the estate to McMurray by the deed
from Beaty, was to " feed the estoppel " created by

McMurray's conveyance to the Society now represented by the defendants, the Omnium Securities Company.

The deed to the latter was a statutable short form of mortgage in fee—no recitals, but a covenant that McMurray was seized in fee simple.

. Under the law laid down half a century ago in our Courts, in *Doe. Hennessy* v. *Meyers*, 2 O. S. 424, and *Doe Irvine* v. *Webster*, 2 U. C. R. 224, and *McLean* v. *Laidlaw*, *ib.* 222, such a deed will create an estoppel. The deed in the first case having neither recital nor covenant—the latter having no recital but covenants for seizin in fee and the " common clause of warranty of title."

It is too late to question the soundness of the law so long laid down and acted upon in the dealings with real estate in this province; and in the Supreme Court in *Trust and Loan Co.* v. *Ruttan and Covert*, 1 S. C. R. 564, Mr. Justice Strong points out the necessity of adhering thereto. I do not think anything can be made of the suggestion that some interest passed by McMurray's mortgage, as he had then the option of obtaining title within the six months. The interest must be a legal existing interest or estate.

But when we are asked, as here, to apply the doctrine of estoppel in its most odious form, to deprive an innocent owner of his estate, it is a very unpleasant consideration that if it were not for our being bound to follow these old authorities there is every reason to believe that the law there laid down is opposed to modern decisions and would not now be upheld in England.

I refer to the judgment of Lord Cairns, C., and James and Mellish, L.JJ., in *Heath* v. *Crealock*, L. R. 10 Ch. 22, and the full discussion and judgment of Sir Geo. Jessel in *General Finance Co.* v. *Liberator Building Society*, 10, Ch. D. 15.

The remarks of that eminent Judge as to estoppel generally are worthy of attention. He asks the counsel can they produce any authority for the proposition that an estoppel can be created by covenant? They answer

they have found none.   He considers that a covenant only
imports that if he have not the power to convey the legal
estate he will pay damages.

We certainly should not extend this doctrine further to
help to work, to my mind, startling injustice.

We must now see what was the effect of Beaty's deed.
The bargain undoubtedly was that McMurray was to pay
$100, and $300 secured on the land, in all $400.   What
then passed by the deed ?   If the defendants' argument be
sound, then on the instant of its execution and delivery
the fee simple passed to " feed the estoppel" created by the
former mortgage by McMurray, making good what was
worthless when given to the company—in effect applying
Beaty's land to secure McMurray's mortgagees.   When
Beaty conveyed he was as to three-quarters of the purchase
money an unpaid vendor.   We must see what actually
passed by the deed.

In *Sugden's* Vendors and Purchasers, 671, 4th ed., it is
stated that in the case of a vendor who has actually conveyed,
the lien remains though he has no longer the estate ; the
principle is that the lien for the purchase money represented
the estate which in equity no longer was his—this right the
conveyance did not defeat—here the purchaser upon the
execution of the contract becomes in equity owner of the
estate, and the money belongs to the vendor—if all the
money is paid, he obtains the estate itself—the money is in
exchange for the estate, a deposit is part payment, therefore
part payment *to that extent* constitutes the purchaser
actually owner of the estate ; consequently, if the contract
do not proceed without the fault of the purchaser, the seller
to recover the equitable ownership must pay the deposit
which, representing a portion of the interest in the property, is a lien upon it.

In another view the lien of the vendor for all the money
may, upon receipt of a portion of the money from the
purchaser, be considered as transferred to that extent to
the purchaser.

2 Story Eq. 561, 13th ed. The lien of the vendor of real estate for the purchase money is wholly independent of any possession on his part, and it attaches to the estate as a trust equally whether it be actually conveyed or only be contracted to be conveyed. * * The principle upon which Courts of Equity have proceeded in establishing the lien in the nature of a trust, is that the person who has gotten the estate of another, ought not in conscience as between them to be allowed to keep it, and ought to pay the full consideration money.

The subject is very fully treated at p. 561 and following pages and in the copious notes. " To the extent of the lien the vendee becomes a trustee for the vendor."

Page 578 : " When vendee has sold the estate to a bonâ fide purchaser without notice, if the purchase money has not been paid, the original vendor may proceed against the estate for his lien, or against the purchase money in the hands of such purchaser for satisfaction, for the latter not having paid his money takes the estate cum onere, at least to the extent of the unpaid purchase money."

That the vendor's lien is assignable, even by parol, is discussed and admitted in this Court in *Armstrong* v. *Farr*, 11 A. R. 186, citing *Dryden* v. *Frost*, 3 M. & Cr. 670 ; 2 W. & Tud. L. C. 321 ; *Sugden* on Vendors and Purchasers, 653.

In *Rice* v. *Rice*, 2 Drew. 80, V. C. Kindersley says that the vendor's lien and equitable mortgage by deposit are equities of equal worth. The lien is a right created by a rule of equity without any special contract, the other is created by contract.

Kettlewell v. *Watson*, 26 Ch. D. 507, in appeal. Lindley, L. J., gives the judgment of the Court.

" The primâ facie right of an unpaid vendor of land to an equitable lien upon it to the amount of his unpaid purchase money is too well established to be disputed. The right arises whenever there is a valid contract of sale and the time for completing that contract has arrived and the purchase money is not duly paid ; there is no necessity for the vendor to stipulate for the lien, and although the lien arises from and may, in one sense, be said to be created by the contract of sale, still no contract to confer the lien is necessary, and in that sense the lien may be said to arise independently of contract."

I think it reasonably clear that when he delivered the deed, Beaty had his lien or equitable charge on the premises for all his unpaid purchase money, and that the estate or interest conveyed to McMurray was burdened and charged with the unpaid amount, and that whatever passed to feed the estoppel (if anything passed) was confined to the interest acquired by McMurray and subject to the charge, and the defendant company and those claiming through them have nothing except subject to that charge. They can take nothing but what McMurray got.

We are not embarrassed by any question as to Beaty waiving his vendor's lien, which constantly arises. In my view it is immaterial whether a mortgage was taken back to himself or to the plaintiff at his request.

If taking this mortgage to a third person would force us to finding that this was an abandonment or waiver of lien, which I am not prepared to admit, still up to the giving of that mortgage what was McMurray's estate, and where was it? If it went at once to feed the estoppel, it went charged with the vendor's lien. If it remained in McMurray until he executed the agreed on mortgage, I consider he had an interest passing by such mortgage.

It is immaterial to plaintiff and to the justice of the case whether the unpaid purchase money remains as a charge or lien on the estate, or was secured to her by the mortgage on the estate.

The defendants must, I consider, stand or fall by the argument that the whole interest passed by the deed to enure to the benefit of the old mortgage. They cannot desire to argue that McMurray's interest did pass to them encumbered and charged with the unpaid $300.

And yet, so it appears to me that we must hold, as laid down in the "Vendors and Purchasers," McMurray became owner of the estate to the extent of what he had paid. The plaintiff cannot object to such a limited interest.

vesting in him. But he became, as it were, trustee for the vendor as to the unpaid portion ; and if neither mortgage, nor bond nor note had been given therefor, still such would be his position.

We have no difficulty here as to the claim of any purchaser without notice. All we have to decide is, whether, with the law as to unpaid vendors in the state in which we find it, it can be possible wholly to destroy their rights by the application desired by defendants of the alleged law of estoppel.

It may be necessary to direct some amendment in the pleadings to meet the view of the law here adopted.

PATTERSON, J. A.—The plaintiff's case as set out in her statement of claim may be shortly stated thus :

Robert Beaty being owner of a lot designated as lot 40, on plan 396, which was prepared and filed by him, sold lot 40 to the defendant McMurray for $400, of which $100 was to be paid in cash, and $300 secured by mortgage on the lot. On the 1st of January, 1883, Beaty made a deed conveying the lot to McMurray in fee, and McMurray, as part of the same transaction, made the mortgage for $300, making it at Beaty's request, to the plaintiff: that McMurray made default and the plaintiff foreclosed him : that after this the plaintiff discovered that the defendants McMurray and Fuller had, on the 5th of August, 1880, while the lot belonged to Beaty, filed a plan numbered 327, in which they included the lot in question as part of their lot M: that on the 6th of August, 1880, McMurray made a mortgage of lot M to the Anglo Canadian Mortgage Company, which devolved upon the defendants the Omnium Securities Company, who sold under the power of sale, in December, 1883, to the defendant Wiseman, taking back a mortgage from her for $1,200 : and the plaintiff claims (1) against the Omnium Company and Wiseman possession of lot 40 ; (2) the removal from the registry of plan 327 so far as it affects lot 40; and (3) damages against McMurray and Fuller for registering the plan 327.

Plan 327 was filed on the 5th August, 1880, with a certificate signed by the defendants McMurray and Fuller stating that the plan shewed correctly the manner in which they had subdivided the lands embraced in it.

I understand that those defendants, or at all events the defendant McMurray, had a survey made on the 23rd of July, and that the surveyors had completed and certified a plan on the 27th July, including in lot M all the land as far south as a fence. This, in fact, embraced about five feet six inches frontage on Northcote avenue which belonged to Mr. Beaty, and on which the defendant Mc-Murray, being misled by the fence, had inadvertently encroached with his building. On the same day on which the plan was filed, the 5th of August, and before it was filed, it was altered by removing the southern line of lot M 19½ feet further south, and thus including in it the whole of the 25 foot lot which was afterwards known as lot 40 on Mr. Beaty's plan number 396.

The only connection of McMurray with the title at this time arose from the offer he obtained from Mr. Beaty on the 29th of July to sell him the lot. This offer, and Mr. McMurray's acceptance, have been fully discussed by his lordship the Chief Justice. It was obtained after the survey had led to the discovery of the encroachment on the lot.

I entirely agree with the view that that offer was conditional on payment of the money within six months; that the acceptance of it by McMurray was an acceptance of the condition that the offer was to be void if he did not pay the money at the day ; and that when he made default in that payment he ceased to have any further interest in the land. I do not attempt to add anything to what has been said on that topic.

The reliance which has been placed on this offer and acceptance as authorizing the filing of the plan has no support from the Registry Act.

The statute (R. S. O. ch. 111, sec. 82) while it does not in so many words say that the person to file a plan is the

owner of the sub-divided land plainly contemplates the
owner as the person. It does not assume to authorize the
sub-division. That is an act of ownership. But it requires
that, when a sub-division is made, the person who makes
it shall file his plan ; and thenceforward the registrar is to
adopt an index founded on the plan, and is not to register
any instrument affecting the land or any part . thereof,
executed after the plan is filed, unless it conforms to the
plan.

It is clear that the existence on the files of the registry
office of an unauthorized plan may inconvenience the owner
of the land it affects to deal with, and lead to confusion in
the investigation of titles.

If actual damage is suffered from it, an action for
damages will, I do not doubt, lie against the wrongdoer ;
but the rule that governs the analogous action for slander
of title will prevent a recovery when there has been no
actual damage, which is the present case : *Malachy* v.
Soper, 3 Bing. N. C. 371.   On that branch of the case the
plaintiff therefore fails.

But to proceed for an order to take the unauthorized
plan off the files is a different thing ; and McMurray not
being the owner at law or in equity, but having only a
right to become owner on payment of $250, there is no
reason why immediately after the fifth of August, 1880,
an order should not have been made, if it had then been
asked for, compelling him to remove or amend the plan.

Nor do I see clearly why, at that time, Mr. Fuller could
have successfully objected to being made a party to such a
proceeding. The plan was, as it appears, filed by McMurray for his own purposes, and when filed it embraced more
of Beaty's lot than when it was signed by Fuller on the
27th July. But on the latter date it covered five feet six
inches of Beaty's land, and Fuller, although he may have
joined for some purpose of McMurray's, nevertheless did
join in certifying the plan with a view to its being filed,
and could scarcely have complained if ordered to join with
McMurray in undoing what was on the face of it, and also

18—VOL XIV A.R.

in reality, their joint act. Whatever were their relations between themselves, or their respective interests in the other lands touched by the plan, they were equally strangers to the title of Beaty's lot, and wrongdoers as to him.

We find, moreover, that Fuller took a mortgage from McMurray of lot M with other lots, bearing date the 28th July, 1880, a date earlier than the filing of the plan, and even a day before the date of Mr. Beaty's offer. I speak now only of the date the mortgage bears, for this document, like several others before us, is obviously misdated, as is shewn by its referring to the plan by its registry number of 327, and by its reciting other mortgages which were not made earlier than the 6th of August.

But although the plan was unauthorized and might have been ordered off the files in August, 1880, we must consider whether, like the plan which was the subject of the decision in *Chisholm* v. *Oakville,*12 A. R. 225, it may not have come to enure to the benefit of McMurray or his assigns by reason of the subsequent dealings which I am about to notice

On the sixth of August, 1880, the defendant McMurray made a mortgage of lot M to the Anglo-Canadian Mortgage Company, having at that time no estate in that part of it which consisted of Mr. Beaty's lot 40. It is asserted on the part of the defence that the company took, as against McMurray, an estate in fee by estoppel, and that that estoppel would be fed by any estate or interest in the land afterwards acquired by McMurray. This is advanced on the authority of the class of cases which includes *Doe Hennessy* v. *Meyers,* 2 O. S 424; *Doe Irvine* v. *Webster,* 2 U. C. R. 224; *Featherstone* v. *McDonell,* 15 C. P. 162, and other cases in our courts. That the mortgage deed was such as to create an estoppel cannot be denied without impugning the authority of those cases, and as remarked by Strong, J., in *Trust and Loan Co.* v. *Ruttan,* 1 S. C. R. 564, 584, it is now too late to question them in this province. I have certainly no desire to do so, or to narrow the effect of the doctrine which, applied in circumstances

like those of any of our reported cases, tends to give purchasers what they bargain for and what their vendors
profess to sell ; deprives the estopped party of nothing
that in honesty and fair dealing he ought to retain ; and
does not operate unjustly upon the rights of third parties.
As remarked by Nelson, J., in *Van Rensellaer* v. *Kearney*,
11 How. 297, 326 : " It is a doctrine, therefore, when
properly understood and applied, that concludes the truth
in order to prevent fraud and falsehood, and imposes silence
on a party only when in conscience and honesty he ought
not to be allowed to speak."

In this case we are asked to apply the doctrine in a
mode and for a purpose which would, it is to be feared,
make it the instrument of injustice.

Properly applied, as it is by holding that whatever
beneficial interest was acquired by McMurray in the lot
enured to the advantage of his mortgagees, the doctrine
will have its legitimate and salutary effect, and all the
effect it ought to receive.

I do not feel called upon to inquire whether there ever
was a time when a person claiming by estoppel could have
made good, even in a court of common law, his title to any
further interest in the land than that which had accrued
to his grantor to his own use, because at the present day,
when equitable rights are recognised by the courts as
fully as legal rights, the inquiry what was the real extent
of the interest acquired creates no embarrassment, and the
concession of that interest to the claimant by estoppel
gives its full operation to the principle.

What estate did McMurray at any time acquire ?

In 1882 he agreed to buy from Mr. Beaty lot number 40,
as laid down on Beaty's registered plan number 396, for
$400, $100 to be paid in cash, and $300 secured by mort-
gage of the lot. Beaty accordingly made him a deed, dated
the 1st of January, 1883, and McMurray paid $100 and exe-
cuted a mortage bearing the same date for $300, but made it
to the plaintiff instead of Beaty, at the request of Beaty
who had money belonging to the plaintiff in his hands as

her agent, $300 of which he invested on her behalf by appropriating it to his own use and holding the mortgage for her.

This is another of the instances of misdating. The deeds cannot have been completed before the 26th of January, as appears from their referring to plan 396, that being the number affixed to the plan when it was filed on the 26th.

The transaction left McMurray the owner of the equity of redemption, or of the lot charged with $300. Whether we regard the making of the mortgage as the important and operative act, or look upon McMurray simply as purchaser of land on which his vendor retained a lien for $300 of unpaid purchase money, the practical effect is probably the same, though it may be of some technical consequence to the plaintiff to be able to maintain that she had the legal estate.

The deed and the mortgage were part of one transaction. The land never vested in McMurray free from the charge, whether we call it a vendor's lien or a trust to execute the mortgage. I do not know that there was any written memorandum of the bargain; but the Statute of Frauds would not prevent the recognition of such a trust, because, as it is expressed in *Story's* Equity Jurisprudence, sec. 759 : "Where one party has executed his part of the agreement in the confidence that the other party would do the same, it is obvious that if the latter should refuse, it would be a fraud upon the former to suffer this refusal to work to his prejudice."

The argument for the defence appeals to the doctrine of instantaneous seizin which was given effect to in common law actions of dower, such as *Potts* v. *Meyers*, 14 U. C. R. 499, and *Smith* v. *Norton*, 20 U. C. R. 213; 7 U. C. L. J. 263, and also at common law with respect to a registered judgment in *Ruttan* v. *Levisconte*, 16 U. C. R. 495, and rests on the contention, which, with reference to the subject of title by estoppel, is, I think, now raised for the first time, that when the legal estate passed from Beaty to McMurray by his deed, it eo instanti fed the estoppel, and vested in the loan company in priority to the mortgage for the purchase money.

If this were the result, it is one which could not have been avoided by any expedient such as executing the mortgage before the deed ; because the mortgage executed by a man who had not yet acquired the title, would have operated only by estoppel, and the earlier estoppel of the loan company would have prevailed.

What was chiefly attempted before us was to shew that the vendor's lien had been lost by the introduction of the plaintiff into the transaction, as if she had lent $300 to McMurray with which he paid off the vendor, and as if it became a purchase for $400 cash, in place of the real bargain for $100 cash and a $300 mortgage.

Ingenious as this way of dealing with the evidence is, it would not, even if it could be adopted, really alter the position. Before the money could be procured the mortgage had to be given, and given in accordance with the form which, on the suggested theory, the bargain would assume. It would be as if Beaty said : " I will sell you the lot for $400 if you pay me the $100 you have, and get some one to lend you $300 on mortgage of the lot to make up the $400." At no instant of time would the lot be free from the charge, or held by McMurray to his own use except to the value of the $100 he paid.

In whatever way the matter is put, the contention really is that the form of the transaction should so far override the reality as to enable the company to take the land at the expense of the plaintiff whose money paid for it ; and in whichever way it is argued the defence, in my opinion, fails.

The plaintiff has, if I am right in the view I have taken, the legal estate, the defendants Wiseman and the company having the equity of redemption.

The case of *Chin* v. *Barnet*, 11 Sergt. & R. 389, to which my brother Osler has called my attention, seems very like the present case in its facts. There a person made a conveyance in fee of lands to which he had only an equitable title, and afterwards acquiring the legal estate he executed a mortgàge in pursuance of the terms of his purchase to secure part of the purchase money. The Supreme Court of Pennsylvania held that the legal estate passed to the mortgagee to whom a court of equity would have compelled the purchaser to execute a mortgage. The doctrine of estoppel is not discussed in the judgment, further than by the remark that it did not operate in favor of the grantee.

But whether the plaintiff has the legal estate or only a charge representing the vendor's lien, there is still the same right of redemption in Mrs. Wiseman and the company.

The action seems to have been brought and possession claimed against the defendants Wiseman and the company as if they were mere wrongdoers holding possession without any title. In this particular the plaintiff misunderstood her position, as has been shewn. She would nevertheless, in my view respecting the legal estate being in her, be entitled in strictness to eject the defendant Wiseman, who is in possession, and the action, as originally framed, might have been dismissed as against the Omnium Securities Co. I should say it might properly have been dismissed with costs if the company had been content to treat the action as one for the recovery of possession, and had simply disclaimed possession; or had merely asserted a right to redeem the plaintiff. They have, however, disputed the plaintiff's title and claimed priority over her, and they have failed in that contest, for which reason I should not have considered them entitled to costs.

But the plaintiff now amends by asking relief against the company and Mrs. Wiseman as in a foreclosure action. She has successfully met their attacks upon her title and established her right to the relief she asks; and should therefore, as I think, have judgment with costs against those defendants, the appeal being allowed as to them, also with costs.

Then returning to the question of the plan 327, and of the proper judgment as to the defendants McMurray and Fuller:

I am not prepared to hold that a mortgagor of land deprives himself, as of necessity, by the mere fact of making a mortgage, of the right to sub-divide the land and file a plan, though one can imagine circumstances that might give the mortgagee a right to object to his doing so.

Now when Mr. Beaty, by his bargain with Mr. Mc-Murray and the conveyances in pursuance of it, created in McMurray the status of owner and in the plaintiff that of mortgagee, he was no longer, nor was the plaintiff, in a position to complain of the plan. It was as if he sold the lot to McMurray as lot 40, and McMurray had then made it a part of lot M on his plan. If any objection were at that time open it must have been by reason of something not now brought before us.

For this reason I think that the prayer for removal or change of the plan is one which cannot in the present state of things be entertained. If the plaintiff is redeemed she of course will be no longer interested about the plan. If on the other hand she obtains a final judgment for foreclosure or sale, she may be entitled to a declaration that the southern portion of lot M is identical with lot 40 on plan 396, and perhaps to an order under section 84 of the Registry Act to amend plan 327; but in the meantime no such order can be made, and the judgment so far as it dismisses the action against the defendants Fuller and Mc-Murray should be affirmed. They were made parties only by reason of the filing of the plan. Mr. Fuller's share in that business, although as I have already remarked, it might once have prevented his maintaining that he was not a proper party to an action to remove or alter the plan, was wrongful only from inadvertence, and he cannot justly be charged with having caused the litigation. The appeal ought, therefore, to be dismissed as against him with costs.

Mr. McMurray's position is materially different, because all the difficulty and expense are directly traceable to his acts and defaults. He succeeds in the action, and on this appeal, by the effect of circumstances which, in relation to

the merits of the contest, may not inappropriately be
called accidental circumstances; he gets his costs in the
court below, which possibly he might not have done if
the judgment in his favor had proceeded on the views on
which we have acted; but while we dismiss the appeal as
against him I am satisfied that we ought to dismiss it
without costs.

No case has been made by Mrs. Wiseman for relief over
against the company; but, as their transactions are not
closed, she ought not to be prejudiced in regard to any
claim she may have, and may properly have it so noted in
the judgment if she wishes.

OSLER, J. A.—The real contest in this case is between the
plaintiff and the defendants the Omnium Securities Company and Margaret Wiseman. The claim against the
defendants McMurray and Fuller may be laid out of view
for the present.

The facts upon which the case turns are simple enough

On the 5th August, 1880, the defendant McMurray was
the owner of a strip of ground 100 feet in front on Northcote Avenue, by about 114 feet in depth.

On that day he caused to be registered a plan dividing
it into four lots, the most southerly of which was described
as lot letter. M. The whole frontage of the lots as described on the plan was, however, 125 feet, made up by
an encroachment upon the land of the adjoining owner on
the south (Mr. Robert Beaty), thus giving to lot M as described a frontage of 44 ft. 7 ins., instead of 19 ft. 7 in.,
the residue of the 100 feet after taking off the three lots to
the north of it.

To the additional twenty-five feet thus included in lot
M, McMurray had absolutely no title whatever beyond a
conditional option or privilege of purchasing it on payment
to the owner of the sum of $250 within six months from
the 29th July, 1880.

A plan of the 100 feet parcel had been already prepared
for McMurray, and it appears to have been amended and

then registered by him on the strength of having this option. (Reg. Plan 327.)

By a mortgage dated the 6th August, 1880, McMurray then conveyed in fee lot M. as described in the plan, to the company now represented by the defendants, the Omnium Company, to secure the sum of $1,000. This mortgage contained the usual mortgagors' absolute covenants for title, &c., &c. Other mortgages for similar amounts were at the same time taken by the company on the other lots, as described on the plan, and they were all given and received in substitution of a mortgage then held by the company from McMurray's immediate grantor, one Culbert, upon the 100 feet parcel.

McMurray not having availed himself of the option of purchase, Beaty brought an action of ejectment against him, and on the 26th January, 1883, registered a plan of his own land, in which the twenty-five feet in question were described as lot No. 40. (Reg. plan 396.)

After this, by a deed dated the 1st January, and registered on the 4th April, 1883, Beaty conveyed lot 40, as described in the last mentioned plan, to McMurray in fee for the expressed consideration of $400, of which $100 was paid down, and a mortgage was given by McMurray to Mrs. Nevitt the plaintiff, Beaty's daughter, for the balance, on the lot in question.

In the month of December following, the Omnium Company sold lot M, plan 327, to the defendant Wiseman under the power of sale in their mortgage, taking back a mortgage for the balance of the purchase money.

The question is whether the right of the Omnium Company and their grantee is superior to that of the plaintiff, or Beaty, in respect of the latter's unpaid purchase money?

This question can be answered in the affirmative only by an application of the doctrine of estoppel which would not merely exclude the truth but would also perpetrate injustice. It is a doctrine of which the late Master of the Rolls said, that it appears no longer necessary in law and no longer useful, and should be carried no further than a Judge is bound to carry it.

So far as the fact is material there is no reason to doubt that the Anglo-Canadian Mortgage Company (with whom the Omnium Company is identified) had notice from the registry office that McMurray had no title to the south 25 feet of M, and their grantee, Mrs. Wiseman, is in the same position.   As to it no estate, *i. e,.* no legal estate or interest, passed by McMurray's mortgage to them, which, so far as it was operative at all, was so by estoppel only.   According to the decisions in our own courts in *Doe Irvine* v. *Webster,* 2 U. C. R. 224, and a line of subsequent cases by which we are bound, the terms of that mortgage were sufficient to create an estate by estoppel in the company's favor against McMurray which would be fed or become an estate in interest on his subsequent acquisition of the title from Beaty to the extent of the title so acquired.

I agree that at the expiration of six months from the date of Beaty's conditional offer, the right of McMurray and of the company to take advantage of it was absolutely gone.   It was not an ordinary contract of purchase by which both parties were bound.   Beaty was bound, but McMurray was not, and it was necessary for him to shew a strict compliance with the conditions on which alone he was entitled to exercise the option.   In addition to the authorities already referred to on this point, I may notice that of *Ball* v. *The Canada Company,* 24 Gr. 281, where the leading cases are reviewed and the distinction acted on between an ordinary agreement for sale and purchase (time being of the essence of the agreement), and a conditional offer.   The result of the cases is thus stated by the Vice-Chancellor :

"I understand the rule to be well settled that where there is a right or option to purchase given, which is to arise on certain specified conditions, then in order to obtain a specific performance a literal compliance with such conditions must be shewn, unless, owing to no default on the part of the person having the option they could not be performed."

I also agree in holding that the proper, indeed the necessary, inference from the evidence is, that the final sale to McMurray was the result of an entirely new agreement and not an implementing or completion of the original offer. The only practical importance of this, however, in the view I take of the case, is that Beaty can insist as against all parties that the purchase money was $400 instead of $250.

Beaty then being the owner of the land in January, 1883, and entitled to deal with it as he pleased, conveyed it to McMurray and received $100 on account of the purchase money. On what principle is he to be deprived of his right to be paid the residue ?

The defendants make two answers. First, they say that the conveyance to McMurray at once operated to feed the estoppel created by his mortgage to them so that it immediately became an estate in interest to the exclusion of and in priority to every one else ; and secondly, that the result of the transaction between McMurray and Beaty was that the former borrowed $300 from Mrs. Nevitt, the plaintiff, and therewith paid Beaty, so that the purchase money was in fact discharged, Mrs. Nevitt taking as security for her loan a third mortgage on the property, and being postponed, not only to the mortgage to the Omnium Company, but also to another which had been subsequently given to the defendant Fuller.

With regard to the last contention, I feel compelled to differ from the view of the evidence taken by my brother Proudfoot.

I look upon the deed and mortgage as parts of the same transaction, the latter having been made to the plaintiff at Beaty's request and as a matter of convenience, but nevertheless as representing the unpaid purchase money. I think Beaty placed Mrs. Nevitt in his position, transferring his unpaid purchase money to her, and that she stands in his shoes and has all the rights he had in respect of it. That was the real substance of the transaction, and I think we should adopt this view, which the evidence, to my mind, fairly bears out, rather than that which seems to have found favor at the trial, and which of course was fatal to the plaintiff's claim.

What then were Beaty's rights ? How far did his conveyance to McMurray enure to feed the estoppel under the mortgage to the defendants ? Their contention as I have said, is that the whole estate passed to them, so that Beaty's right to his unpaid purchase money is cut out. I am glad to think that the doctrine of estoppel cannot be made to work so monstrous an injustice as that.

At the moment of the execution of his conveyance, Beaty retained his vendor's lien for the unpaid purchase money. To that extent McMurray did not acquire the entire legal and equitable estate in the land, and to that extent, therefore, did not acquire it in the same right as that in which he had professed to make the former conveyance. The vendor's lien was not lost, as the authorities shew, by merely taking a mortgage on the land sold for the balance of the purchase money, and I think the defendants have not pointed out any other circumstances from which an intention to waive it is necessarily to be inferred.

The subject of estoppel by deed is discussed in *Rawle* on Covenants, ed. 1873, from which at page 399 I make the following extract:

" To create this estoppel, it is also considered necessary that the after-acquired estate should be held by the grantor in the same right as that in which the former conveyance was made. Thus where one conveys land in his own right with covenants for title, and subsequently acquires title thereto as trustee, the doctrine of estoppel is held not to apply, and it is deemed immaterial whether in the conveyance to the former grantee the trust is express or implied."

Among the cases cited by the author is *Kelly* v. *Jenness,* 50 Me. 44. There defendant had mortgaged to the plaintiff with covenants for title. There was a prior mortgage by the defendant's grantor Clark to one Blake, outstanding, which was subsequently assigned to the defendant. It was proved that though absolute on its face, the assign-

ment had been paid for, with the exception of a small sum,
with the money of one Hill, to whom it was again assigned
by the defendant. It was held that the first assignment
did not enure to the benefit of the plaintiff as Jenness'
grantee by force of the estoppel created by the covenants,
except as to the sum paid by Jenness with his own money.

The Court say :

"If Jenness took the assignment of the mortgage
charged with a trust, it was not of the same character
and of the same estate as in his deed (mortgage)
to Kelly. He was here a mere trustee. There can be no
division or separation of the effects of the assignment. He
did not take a conveyance and afterwards have engrafted
thereon a trust : allowing the legal estate to vest absolutely and for a time before any trust arose. The assignment was charged with a trust as soon as executed. If
he had acquired for himself the legal and equitable title
he would have been estopped by reason of the covenant.
All the cases rest on the general principle that the estate
must be subsequently acquired by the grantor in his own
right, in fact and substance as his own property without
intervening rights in third parties. While the law is
careful to see that an after acquired title purchased and
paid for by the grantor shall enure, it is equally careful to
guard against any inequitable result by enforcing the rule
where the substance is wanting, and the rights of others
are impaired."

I agree, therefore, in thinking that the deed enured in
favor of the Omnium Company only to the extent of the
interest which McMurray really acquired under it, and
that the equitable interest which remained in Beaty still
exists unaffected by the estoppel, and may be enforced by
the plaintiff against the land.

I see no reason why this should not be done by foreclosure of the mortgage, or by sale in the present action,
amending the pleadings to meet the case.

It will be necessary to prevent confusion arising hereafter from the same piece of land having been described
on two different plans, and, therefore, whether the defendants redeem or are foreclosed, or the vendor's lien is
enforced by a sale of the land, the judgment should con-

tain a declaration which, as it seems to me, would be quite
sufficient for the purpose, that lot No. 40 as described on
plan 396 is identical with the south 25 feet of lot M as
described on plan 327, since in any event the title must
hereafter be made through two instruments in which the
same parcel is differently described.

The case against the defendants McMurray and Fuller
remains to be considered. As the action was framed, and
as it was tried, the only relief sought against them was
in the shape of damages for having wrongfully registered
plan 327 against the piece of land which Beaty subsequently described as lot 40, on plan 396. Against the
other defendants possession of the lot was demanded and
rectification of the plan 327 so far as it affected lot 40.
As to the defendant Fuller, I think the judgment in his
favor was put upon the right ground, namely, that he was
not a party to the registration of the plan. The plan he
signed was altered and amended, no doubt, in good faith,
but still without his authority, and was registered as
altered, but without being again signed or ratified by him.
As to McMurray I concede that when he caused the plan
to be registered it was a futile and unauthorised act on
his part. The offer of the 29th July, 1880, gave him no
right to register a plan upon Beaty's land and Beaty
might have compelled its removal or correction. But
when the same land was afterwards conveyed to McMurray,
though by a different description, surely Beaty's right to
complain of the registration as an act causing damage
was substantially gone.

McMurray or his assigns might then at all events have
registered a new plan, or adopted the former one ; and the
right of Beaty or his assigns would simply be, to have such
plan rectified or cancelled on non-payment of the mortgage.

The only parties interested in a claim of that nature,
(damages against the original filer of the plan being out
of the question,) are the owners of the equity of redemption, and the relief might properly be granted as incidental
to the foreclosure action or other action in which the
mortgage or vendor's lien is enforced.

For that purpose, McMurray and Fuller are not necessary parties, as they have been already foreclosed, and
have no longer any interest in the property, and no case
can be made against them by amendment. Therefore the
judgment at the trial in their favor must stand.

We are not at liberty to vary it as regards the costs,
merely because (as to the defendant McMurray at least)
we support it for other reasons than those assigned by the
learned Judge. It does not appear that costs were given
for any other reason than that the defendants had succeeded
in the action. No question of principle is involved; and if
we interfered with the judgment in that respect, we
should be entertaining an appeal for costs strictly in the
discretion of the Judge, which we are prohibited from
doing.

I do not differ as to the disposition of the costs of the
other parties and of the appeal.

BURTON, J.A., concurred in the conclusion arrived at on
the grounds stated in the judgment of Patterson, J.A.

Appeal allowed.

SCOTT v. CRERAR.

Libel—Evidence—Expert evidence.

On the trial of an action for a libel contained in an anonymous letter circulated among members of the legal profession, charging the plaintiff with unprofessional conduct, no direct evidence was given to shew that the defendant was the author of the letter, but the plaintiff relied upon several circumstances pointing to that conclusion. The Judge at the trial refused to admit some of the evidence tendered.

Held, [reversing the judgment of the C. P. D., (11 O. R. 541,)] that evidence of the defendant being in the habit of using certain uncommon expressions, and which occurred in the letter, was improperly rejected ; but

Semble, a witness could not be asked his opinion as to the authorship of a letter ; and

Per BURTON, and OSLER, JJ.A.—Evidence of literary style on which to found a comparison, if admissible at all, is not so otherwise than as expert evidence.

THIS was an appeal by the plaintiff from a judgment of the C. P. D. refusing a motion to set aside a nonsuit entered at the trial, and for a new trial, which is reported 11 O. R. 541, where the libel complained of, and the material evidence in the case sufficiently appear. The appeal came on to be heard before this Court on the 25th of November, 1886.*

McCarthy, Q.C., and *W. Nesbitt*, for the appellant.
Robertson, Q.C., for the respondent.

March 1, 1887. HAGARTY, C. J.—The circumstances under which this action for libel is brought are most peculiar and unusual, and we trust they may retain their peculiar character so long as the reputation of the Ontario bar is precious in the regard of its members.

I do not propose to repeat them, they are so very fully detailed in the judgment in the Common Pleas Division.

The grounds of appeal may be shortly stated.

That the learned trial Judge erred in withdrawing the case from the jury for insufficiency of evidence of publication.

Present.—HAGARTY, C. J. O., BURTON, PATTERSON, and OSLER, JJ.A.

2. For rejection of evidence tendered to shew the style of defendant's composition and diction, with a view to comparison of the libellous documents in composition and diction with his customary and usual style.

3. Error in refusing to admit evidence to shew the working of the caligraph machine alleged to have been used in preparing the libellous documents complained of, and of caligraph machines in general.

The alleged rejection of evidence may be first considered.

The first witness, Mr. Parkes, was asked, after stating that he was not acquainted with defendant's style : " Are there expressions in this letter peculiar, would you say, to any person ?

Defendant objects to this question.

After a discussion as to a manner of speaking, and his peculiar way of expressing himself, and plaintiff's urging that a man may have acquired a style of speaking or writing such that a person who knows that style can speak of it, the learned Judge said, " I decline to receive evidence of defendant's style of composition." The result was, that the question was not answered as to expression. The witness had already said he was not acquainted with defendant's *style*.

Mr. Martin stated that after receiving the circular he wrote to defendant acknowledging its receipt, assuming him to be the writer. He said, " Upon reading it I had not the slightest doubt."

The Court.—" Stop. That will not do at all. Why did you do it ? Because you thought Mr. Crerar was the author I suppose ? "

Ans.—" Yes."

" Why did you believe it ? "

Ans.—" Because from reading it I thought from the style it was Mr. Crerar wrote it."

Mr. Robertson, for defendant, objects, and witness retires.

Just before this last evidence, given by Mr. Martin on his recall, Mr. McCarthy renews his contention of yesterday that he should be allowed to examine witnesses as to the habit of the *defendant in conversation in the way of using certain expressions so as to establish the style of the defendant,* and cites *Jones* v. *Richards,* 15 Q. B. 439 ; *Wills* on Circumstantial Evidence, 139, 149, and 176 ;. *Brooks* v. *Tichbourn,* 5 Ex. 929.

His lordship holds that in all these cases reference was had to a comparison of written documents, and expresses the opinion that the evidence is not admissible.

We thus see that the Court held that habits of expression in conversation could not be given.

Wadell, an expert as to caligraphy, was examined. He was asked : " If you were allowed to print with this machine (then in Court), is it your opinion you could identify this work with this machine ?"

Objected to.

" Or would you be able to say it was not the work of the machine ?"

Objected to.

Objections sustained.

As we understood in argument, the machine was there, and it was desired by plaintiff that he should be allowed to work it, and that this was not allowed,

Mr. Walker stated he had conversation with defendant about the plaintiff prior to the letters. He is asked, "From the expressions used in your conversation did you recognize the authorship of these letters ? "

Objected to.

Objection sustained.

Mr. Cameron had stated that in the work of the machine in question the " e's " were sometimes blotted in the top.

He is then shewn a brief in a case which I assume to have been the work of this machine, and he is asked whether the " e" in that is blotted. He answers that the tops and the bottoms also are blotted.

The Court.—" I decline to receive that; Mr. Cameron says he is not an expert."

This answer is unimportant. I only refer to it to illustrate what, with deference, strikes me was an error in this case throughout in requiring a witness to be an "expert" who is testifying to matters within his own knowledge.

I think the [result of the] rulings in this case had the direct effect of preventing evidence being given which should have been admitted.

There seems to be a clear and intelligible difference between what is called expert evidence and some of the rejected evidence here.

An expert in literary style knows nothing personally of the controversy, but he is asked (assuming for the argument that such evidence can be given) whether a contested writing is or is not in the style of an acknowledged writing.

This is one thing. But it is wholly another thing to ask a witness whether a certain most peculiar expression, say an oath, a whimsical phrase, etc., has ever been heard by the witness before, and if so, from whose mouth or conversation.

In the evidence here we have some most singular forms of expression, certainly not of general use, nor in general knowledge, except of experts in wonderfully constructed colloquialisms.

Many of them are noticed in the judgments, and they are of startling originality, at least to minds imperfectly educated in the vocabulary of what is called "slang."

It appears to me that a witness may be asked as to such expressions where and how he has heard them before.

We are not discussing the force or weight of such evidence, but simply its admissibility.

On the argument my brother Patterson suggested that the rule of evidence would be the same here as if it was a prosecution for sending a threatening letter. In such a proceeding I have at present no doubt that a person receiving the contested documents might well be asked as to specially peculiar expressions or colloquialisms in it, and from whom he had heard them. This has nothing to do with what is called expert evidence. *Brooks* v. *Tichbourn*, 5 Ex. 932, 14 Jur. 1122, is illustrative of the general principle.

In *Brooks* v. *Tichbourn*, 5 Ex. 932, 14 Jur. 1122, the Court held that it was proper to shew that the alleged writer of a letter in which the name was wrongly spelled had on other occasions in his genuine letters so spelled it.

"The object," said Parke, B., "is not to shew similarity of the form of the letters and words of writing of a particular word or words, but to prove a peculiar mode of spelling a word which might be evidenced by the plaintiff having orally spelt it in a different way, or written it in that way once or oftener, in any sort of characters, the more frequently the greater the value of the evidence, for that purpose one or more specimens written by him with that peculiar orthography would be admissible."

I presume by "orally spelt it" is meant if he was heard to say, or told some other person that it should be so spelt. The words are the same in the Jurist report.

If a word were spelled in some unusual way, giving it a different sound from the correct pronunciation, I think it would be admissible to shew that the person or prisoner charged as the writer so always pronounced it.

A multitude of instances can be found in the great Tichborne case in which peculiar spellings and expressions and grammatical eccentricities are given in evidence. Letters proved to have been written by the genuine Roger are placed side by side with those of the impostor, and the marked difference of language and expression pointed out and discussed, not as the result of expert criticism, but as plain matters of fact and direct ordinary testimony.

Taylor on Ev., ed. of 1885, p. 1586 : "When a writing is proved to be genuine the witnesses, the jury, and the Court may all examine it with the disputed writing, and exercise their judgment on the resemblance or difference, hand-writing, form of letters, the use of capitals, stops, paragraphs * * * the adoption of peculiar expressions, orthography of words, grammatical construction of sentences, and the style of the composition. Of course all this must be always open to the argument that it was most easy to counterfeit a style or words of expression.

If a man be indicted for sending a threatening letter, and it is found graced by certain eccentric expressions which owe their parentage and place in English literature to the late Thomas Carlyle ; if the letter spoke of " Dead Sea Apes," " Mud Angels," "Owl-eyed Pedantries," "Opaque Flunkeyisms," &c., is it possible that it could not be given in evidence that the prisoner—perhaps the only person in the locality—was in the habit of adorning his conversation and correspondence with these and similar well-known Carlylisms ?

We may take another instance. A stranger stops at a tavern at night ; he hears two men talking in the bar-room, both well known to him. They leave before he resumes his journey. After a while he hears cries of murder and for help, and hears a voice using some very peculiar oath and objurgation. A man is found slain. Cannot this traveller, a witness called at the trial, be first asked what words he heard, and then had he ever heard the expression before, and then be allowed to tell that he had heard it in the bar-room from a person there, the person charged being proved by other evidence to have been in the bar, though the traveller could or could not identify him ? I think it impossible to reject it. It falls under the head of circumstantial evidence—a link, possibly a very weak one—in the chain.

One learned Judge objected to this expression, considering that instead of a chain of links, it would he more correct to call the evidence as strands in a cord, one of which might be too weak, but the whole not being absolutely dependent upon it.

Of course the force of such evidence as I have been discussing is open to obvious objections. We are only dealing with its admissibilty.

Starkie on Evidence (1863), p. 901, says : "An artful person may not only deceive by speaking or writing, but may also create false and deceptive appearances, calculated to induce others to draw false conclusions from them. He may act as well as speak a lie, and may deceive by false facts as well as false impressions." Commenting on the arguments against the receipt of such evidence, he says : " The answer seems to be that although a possibility exists that such appearances may have resulted from contrivance and design, yet that much less danger is to be apprehended from the reception of such evidence of actual facts than would result from receiving evidence of mere statements of facts."

It must be remembered, however, that these remarks are made on the general principle of receiving evidence of all circumstances to which witnesses depose as to what they saw or noticed as connected with the *corpus delicti*.

We may refer to *Best* on Evidence (ed. 1883), ch. 1, p. 281, on direct and circumstantial evidence: " As regards admissibility, direct and circumstantial evidence stand, generally speaking, on the same footing * * circumstantial evidence, whether conclusive or presumptive, is as original in its nature as direct evidence."

He cites a very instructive case, *Regina* v. *Exall*, 4 F. & F. 922, where, in an elaborate charge, Chief Baron Pollock, as to a combination of circumstances taken together being sufficient to raise a reasonable conviction, although no one of them would be sufficient to raise more than a reasonable suspicion. This case has elaborate notes appended.

Lord Cairns, C., says in the *Belhaven Peerage Case*, 1 App. Cas. 279 : " In dealing with circumstantial evidence, we have to consider the weight which is to be given to the united force of all the circumstances put together. You may have a ray of light so feeble that by itself it will do little to elucidate a dark corner. But on the other hand you may have a number of rays, each of them insufficient, but all converging, and brought to bear upon the same point, and when united producing a body of illumination which will clear away the darkness which you are endeavoring to dispel."

Lord Coleridge, in *Regina* v. *Francis*, L. R. 2, C. C. R. 132, points out that the law of evidence is the same in criminal and civil suits in speaking of the admission of other acts being allowed to be given in evidence to shew a guilty knowledge in a prisoner as to the act charged, apart from any statutable provision on the subject.

See also such cases as *Regina* v. *Garner*, 3 F.& F. 681 ; *Regina* v. *Geering*, 18 L. J. M. C. 215 ; *Best* on Evidence— *passim.*

On the whole, I have come to the conclusion that the course taken at the trial and the rulings of the Court have prevented the admittance of evidence, which I think should have been allowed. Of its weight, I express no opinion. To prevent misunderstanding, I may state that of course, a witness cannot be asked his opinion as to the authorship of the letters, that is the function of the jury.   The learned Chief Justice below, says, as to one part of the evidence : " But the plaintiff has made, as part of his case, the declaration on oath of the defendant that he did not use the envelope received in Messrs. Cameron and Witherspoon's office for the purpose of enclosing the circular to Mr. Mc-Kelcan, which must, it seems to me, entirely deprive the plaintiff of the right to take the opinion of the jury, for there is nothing upon which the jury could reasonably find that the defendant did write and publish the libel, the burden to prove which rests entirely on the plaintiff.

I cannot accept this as a general principle. In many cases in which fraud was charged, the plaintiff called the defendant and examined him closely in all parts of the case. The defendant peremptorily denied all fraud on his part, but the plaintiff successfully proved such frauds by the other circumstances of the case to the full satisfaction of the Court or jury.

A late instance of this, was in *Baillie* v. *Walsh* in this Court (not reported.)

As I think there must be a new trial, I abstain from discussing the weight of the evidence.

BURTON, J.A.—After the doubts expressed by the learned Chief Justice of the C. P. D., as to there being reasonable evidence for the jury on the trial of this case, I cannot say that I am entirely free from doubt, but I do not feel justified on that account in dissenting from the conclusions of my learned brothers that there were facts in evidence sufficient to call upon the defendant for an answer, and that the nonsuit therefore should be set aside, but I wish not to be understood as agreeing in the view apparently taken by the plaintiff at the trial, that it was proper to ask a witness whether from his knowledge of the style of the defendant, he was of opinion that the letter in question was written by him, and I dissent from the view that evidence of style if admissible at all, is so, otherwise than as expert evidence.

A witness of ordinary capacity and experience may be able to state whether a particular letter of the alphabet resembles one made by a caligraph produced and worked before him, from having seen the documents printed by the same machine, at least with as much certainty as a witness who is called upon to say whether a particular paper was written by a person with whose handwriting he is familiar, from habits of correspondence, or from having seen him write. There are few questions of fact so perplexing as the identity of handwriting, as every Judge upon the bench must have seen in his experience. For many years a comparison of handwriting, that is, the collation of one paper with another, for the purpose of proving that both were in the same handwriting, was regarded as a test so fallacious that it was rejected, and it was not until 1854 that it was by statute made admissible as evidence in England.

But a person offering an opinion on the question of a writer's style should be competent not only to form a judgment as to the resemblance to that of the defendant, but also whether it is genuine or a mere imitation.

It is quite possible that although, as in the case of the celebrated rejected addresses, a great majority of casual readers might be deceived, an experienced critic might be able at once to point out passages which would prove conclusively that they could not be genuine, and it appears to me that if such evidence is receivable at all it could only be from witnesses who had first satisfied the Court of their skill and competency in the particular matter of inquiry. The fact that no case has been found in which such evidence has ever been received is, to my mind, almost conclusive against its being receivable.

But if receivable it must be from a skilled witness.

Lord Denman, commenting upon the practice of calling a witness to give an opinion as to the genuineness of hand-writing, says : " But to call a witness who could barely read or write to. speak of his own knowledge and judgment in handwriting, would rather tend to throw ridicule than any degree of light on the cause, and to ask a man whose ordi-nary avocations have not specially qualified him to form a judgment of another's style, for his opinion upon it, would be open to the same criticism."

Mr. Massey, in his History of England, in stating his rea-sons for differing from the conclusions of many eminent men as to the authorship of Junius, refers to this fact, and says : " The best evidence of this description is loose and unsat-isfactory. Nothing is so easy to imitate as style. The history of literature abundantly proves that fact. Pope, Johnson, Scott, Byron, and many other great authors have had numerous imitators more or less successful. Junius had many copyists both in Parliament and in the press. There is a letter in the *Gentleman's Magazine* of 1770, which might be read for one by Junius." |*The Vindica-tion of Natural Society*, by a late noble lord, was by many good judges believed to have been the production of Bolingbroke, until the ingenious deception was avowed by Burke, and the writer there avows his inability to discover any remarkable similarity, adding, " Some superficial re-semblance there is indeed in the style and sentiments such as any writer might acquire with a little trouble."

Reference has been made to threatening letters or letters . in which the writer has intimated an intention to commit a particular crime. Those letters are receivable, if shewn to contain statements of facts which could have been known only by the accused and the prosecution, but I should be surprised to find that they had been received, simply because the style resembled that of the accused.

In my opinion it would be most unsafe to receive such evidence, it would be acting upon bare suspicion and not evidence at all, and is altogether different from circum-stantial evidence, consisting of a variety of minute facts,

all when placed together forming a chain of circumstances
tending to bring home guilt to the accused.

In the case suggested by the learned Chief Justice of the
unusual words used by parties shortly before and at the
time of a murder, I should say there could be no question
of the relevancy of that evidence, it is simply evidence of
two facts having a most material tendency to identify the
parties using them with the murderer, not different in principle from shewing the men first seen, and those seen in
the immediate vicinity of the murder wore a peculiar cap
or head dress.

The *Tichbourn Case* referred to on the argument was
very different. The Claimant there had written a number
of letters, and letters from the real Sir Roger were produced
for the purpose of shewing that those written by the
Claimant could not have been written by the same person,
and that the Claimant was consequently not the person he
represented himself to be, inasmuch as the orthography
and style, if you will, of the one, was altogether different
from that of the other ; but that is no authority for holding
that evidence of style is, receivable to prove a man guilty
of writing a particular letter.

The witnesses might probably (and the inclination of my
mind is that they could) be asked whether the defendant
was in the habit of using peculiar or unusual expressions,
and if similar expressions were found in the letter it would
be a legitimate argument to the jury, that they might
from that, coupled with other circumstances, draw the con--
clusion that the defendant was the writer, but I should
think that any judge trying the case would warn the
jury of the extreme weakness of that kind of
evidence, inasmuch as the writer of such a letter,
with the view of diverting suspicion from himself,
would naturally use expressions which would have that
tendency, especially if the peculiar character of those
expressions would be likely to fix the authorship upon
some one else.

I merely desire to say that so far as the learned Judge excluded evidence of the nature I have indicated, he was justified in doing so, even if the evidence of experts be admissible for the purpose of proving style, which, as at present advised, I much doubt.

PATTERSON, J. A., concurred.

OSLER, J.A.—I do not wish to decide anything more than seems to be called for by the course taken at the trial, and I cannot help thinking that the discussion both here and in the Court below has taken a wider range than was warranted by a consideration of the evidence actually tendered, and the rulings of the learned presiding Judge. I fully agree, however, that there was evidence which ought not to have been withdrawn from the jury of the publication of the alleged libels by the defendant.

It would be improper to express, and I do not express any opinion as to the weight of the evidence, or how a jury should regard it. The argument addressed to us by Mr. Robertson might prove of convincing force if addressed to a tribunal whose duty it is to judge of facts, but as addressed to us it served only to shew how many circumstances there were for the consideration of such a tribunal. The fact to be proved was that the defendant published the alleged libels, and as they were not in manuscript this could only be done by evidence of circumstances from which the jury might draw the conclusion or inference that he had done so. For this purpose the evidence offered and admitted was, as it seems to me, with one exception, relevant, and I shall not further discuss it. The exception I allude to is the evidence of H. D. Cameron, as to his having written to his brother, advising him not to produce at the trial the type-writer on which the alleged libels are supposed to have been printed. His evidence, so far as it was pressed, does not go far enough to implicate the defendant with his action in writing that letter.

A great deal has been said as to the propriety of admitting evidence of the defendant's style, as it has been called,
and it is in reference to this that I said that the discussion
appeared to have taken a broader range than the occasion
called for. What the plaintiff proposed to do is shewn by
what took place on the morning of the second day of the
trial.

"Mr. McCarthy renews his contention of yesterday that
he should be allowed to examine witnesses as to the habit
of the defendant in conversation using certain expressions
so as to establish the style of the defendant, and cites *Jones*
v. *Richards*, 15 Q. B. 439 ; *Wills* on Circumstantial Evidence, 139, 149 and 176 ; *Brooks* v. *Tichtourn*, 5 Ex. 929."

Strictly thus limited, and for the purpose of shewing
that the defendant had used, or was in the habit of using,
expressions similar to those found in the alleged libels, the
evidence tendered, apart from all consideration of its value,
was, in my opinion, relevant, and was indeed admitted
without objection at a later stage of the case. It was, however, evidence of facts, not opinion or expert evidence. It
would be for the jury to say what, if any, inference ought
to be drawn from such facts, not for the witness who
proved them to express an opinion of his own as to the
authorship of the libels, and the learned Judge, with perfect propriety, rejected such statements as that the witness
" thought from the style " it was the defendant who wrote
them.

If, however, by evidence of " style " is meant the comparison of the alleged libels with some letter or other
admitted composition of the defendant, as for instance one
of those filed at the trial for the purpose of shewing a
general similarity in habit of thought, construction of
language or turn of expression, no evidence of that
kind was tendered at the trial, and such evidence must
be that of experts or skilled witnesses giving their
opinion,—not that either of the documents was written
by the defendant, but—that both were written by the
the same person, and the document to be proved must be

treated much in the same way as one written in a dis-
guised handwriting, but in which experts discover, or profess to discover, the structural peculiarities which are seen
in the natural and admitted handwriting of the alleged
writer. Every objection which has been urged against
professional evidence of this kind applies with ten-fold
force when used for the purpose of proving " style " in the
sense in which I am now referring to it. The physical
test afforded by the actual visible handwriting is wanting,
and the ease with which a practised writer imitates or
adopts the style of another is too well known to need
illustration.

The question is to some extent discussed in the notes to
Campbell v. *Spottiswoode*, 3 F. & F. 421, 422, 457.

I agree that the appeal must be allowed.

Appeal allowed, with costs.

DICKEY v. McCAUL.

Conversion—Sale of goods—Title—Receiver—Possession of goods.

Held, [reversing the judgment of the C.P.D.] that the defendant could not
be held liable for a conversion of the goods in question, by reason of
his having joined in a bill of sale of them, and having accepted and
assigned a mortgage for the balance of purchase money thereof ; no
other act of interference with the property on his part being shewn,
they never having been in his possession or control, and he never having
had the power to deliver up or retain them so as to make a demand
upon and refusal by him, evidence of a conversion ; he having acted
in such sale of the goods as the agent, and by the authority of another
only.
The plaintiff J. I. D. could not maintain an action for the conversion of
the property in question ; for assuming that it was the property of those
under whom he claimed, which was one of the matters in controversy,
it did not become vested in him until after the alleged conversion ;
neither could J. D. maintain the action, he never having had the actual
possession of the property but a mere right as receiver appointed by
the Court to obtain the custody if it belonged to those whom he
represented, which would not support the action, though it might form
the ground of a special application to the Court for a mandamus or
attachment or other appropriate relief.

THIS was an appeal from the Common Pleas Division,
discharging the defendant's motion to set aside the judgment at the trial.

The action was for the conversion of a screwing machine
and tools connected therewith, and was tried before
Hagarty, C. J., at the Toronto Spring Assizes, 1884.
The plaintiffs had judgment, which was afterwards
affirmed by a Divisional Court of the Common Pleas
Division, from whose judgment this appeal was brought,
and came on to be heard before this Court on the 9th and
10th of December, 1886.*

Moss, Q. C., and *Falconbridge*, Q.C., for the appellants.
W. Cassels, Q. C., for the respondents.

The present judgments set forth the facts fully.

March 1, 1887. BURTON, J. A.—Two questions
arise on this appeal. First, whether the receiver, Joseph

*Present.—BURTON, PATTERSON, OSLER, JJ.A. and ROSE, J.

Dickey, has shewn any title sufficient to maintain this action; and if so, whether the acts complained of constitute a conversion.

The action was instituted, originally, in the name of James Isaac Dickey, on the 16th June, 1883, but in what way his title was shewn does not appear, but I assume that it was under the vesting order made on the 8th April, 1882, an order made several months after the alleged conversion, and about which I shall have something to say presently.

It was deemed necessary to amend the statement of claim, and that amendment appears to have been made very shortly before the assizes at which the case was tried.

The present claim, as amended, is based entirely on the right of Joseph Dickey, as the receiver appointed by the Court of Chancery of the estate of Dickey, Neill & Co., a firm consisting of the plaintiff, James Isaac Dickey, John Neill, senior, and one Nathaniel Dickey, who dissolved partnership in October, 1876.

The machines and other things in question unquestionably formed part, originally, of the assets of that firm, and the proceeds, if they ever got into the hands of the receiver, assuming that the machines were, when sold, still the assets of that firm, would be distributable among them, and James's name appears to have been retained simply for the purpose of shewing that he had acquired the interests of the other members of the firm and was the person entitled to call the receiver to account. It is a case in which the Judicature Act is made responsible for a system of pleading which can scarcely be regarded, in this instance, as an improvement on the simple pleading which would have been used before its passage.

The defence appears to have been framed in answer to James Isaac Dickey's claim, the 2nd, 4th, and 6th paragraphs of which would probably have afforded a complete answer to his claim, inasmuch as Mrs. Neill, as the representative of her husband, was part owner of the property, and equally entitled with James to deal with it.

It is necessary, in order to understand the case, to give a brief history of the proceedings consequent on the dissolution of the partnership of Dickey, Neill & Co., and I shall do so as concisely as I can, as I gather them from the evidence.

A bill was filed by John Neill to take an account of the partnership dealings, which was brought to a hearing on the 12th June, 1878, when a decree was made and the plaintiff Joseph appointed receiver of the estate and effects of the partnership, and a reference to the master to take the accounts directed.

The suit and all other matters in difference between the parties were afterwards, on the 12th March, 1879, referred to arbitration, the arbitrator being empowered to give instructions to the receiver, who was required to observe them in the same manner as if they were given by all the partners.

An award was made in pursuance of this submission on the 22nd March, 1880 ; John Neill having, in the meantime, died, and his widow, Elizabeth Neill, been appointed his executrix.

Among other things, the arbitrator found that among the undisposed of assets of the partnership were. "a quantity of patterns, tools. &c., in the possession of John Neill's estate, which he valued at $600, and which he stated were thereinafter more particularly referred to in the award ; also a quantity of other tools, &c., in the possession of the receiver.

He refers here to two classes of goods, one in the possession of John Neill and one in the possession of the receiver. Those in the possession of John Neill he values at $600, and says he shall refer to them again in the award.

In paragraph three of the award, in taking the accounts, he charges John Neill, as I read it, with certain tools and patterns received from the partnership, and valued by Messrs. Hickey & Fenson ; and also, as I understand it, with a quantity of other patterns, core boxes, belting, master taps, and other small tools, &c., left on the premises of John Neill's estate, which he values at $600 ; and these

same tools, &c., so valued at $600, he directs that she shall
have the option of transferring to James at that figure in
part payment of her indebtedness to him upon the taking
of the accounts.

It is not at all clear upon the evidence whether the
machine and taps in question were or were not included
in these things valued at $600 ; but it is not, in my view,
material, as it is, I think, abundantly clear that the
machine itself was attached to the building, and all the
articles were in the possession of Mrs. Neill, and never
were in the possession of the receiver.

The building in which the business of Dickey, Neill & Co.,
had been carried on, was the property of Mrs. Neill, and
since the dissolution of that firm, had been occupied by
other firms, and latterly by the firm of John Neill & Sons,
consisting at the time of the alleged conversion, of her
sons, who used all the tools, &c., in question, together with
goods belonging to themselves, which they assigned to
the defendant when they made their assignment to him
for the benefit of creditors on the 24th September 1881.

The defendant in pursuance of the trusts of the assignment, proposed to sell the property and effects assigned to
him ; but inasmuch as it was thought that the premises
belonging to Mrs. Neill and the property she owned, would
sell with the property assigned much more advantageously
together as a going concern, it was suggested that the
whole should be sold together, and accordingly on the 7th
November, 1881, an auction sale took place at which
Messrs. Morrison were adjudged the purchasers.

At the sale, however, James Dickey appeared and for-
bade the sale of the articles in question, and they were
accordingly withdrawn, although Messrs. Morrison subsequently declined to carry out their purchase unless these
things were included, and negotiations ensued in consequence, resulting in Mrs. Neill's withdrawing her objection to their being included and joining in a bill of sale
with the defendant, the effect of which was to transfer

22—VOL XIV A.R.

the interest which each had in the goods they respectively claimed.

Before proceeding to discuss the receiver's right to bring this action, it is as well to consider James Isaac Dickey's position.

These goods are part of the goods awarded to Mrs. Neill, or they are not; if they were, the vesting order made by the Master on the application of James, and with the consent of the receiver, to which she was no party, and made without notice to her, could not have the effect of divesting her title or rather that of her mortgagee, for at that time she had mortgaged the property to Mr. Kingstone·

I sent for the original papers, and in the affidavit of Joseph Dickey, the only one used on the occasion, after the description of the machinery, &c., the following significant words are interlined, " Now in my custody and possession as such receiver aforesaid." The affidavit being made long after the possession had passed to Morrison.

These words have not been inserted as they should have been in the order, but instead of them the following words are used, " being stored thereon for or on account of the said receiver." This was an ambiguity which might have been cleared up by evidence, and I think, with deference, that the learned Judge erred in refusing to allow evidence to be given at the trial to shew that they never were in the receiver's possession; but assuming that the goods in question were not those awarded to Mrs. Neill, then they still remained, it is true, part of the assets of Dickey, Neill & Co., but were not in the possession of the receiver, nor stored for the receiver, and for the same reason would not pass under the vesting order; but how does this vesting order assist the receiver ? It was not made until months after the alleged conversion. It purported to be made for the purpose of carrying out a sale made by the receiver, who from that time, at all events, ceased to have a title, and yet he now seeks to recover for a conversion of the same goods in his own name. Then what right had the receiver to bring the action, if the property was vested in

Mrs. Neill by the award ? He had neither possession, property, nor right of possession ; but even were it otherwise, we were referred to no authority for such an action by a receiver in our own Courts In some of the United States the receiver occupies the position of a statutory assignee, and is expressly empowered to sue in his own name, but with us he is merely an officer or representative of the Court, and when once in possession, any interference with that possession is punishable as a contempt; and when a party to the suit is in possession and wrongfully refuses to give up possession, a like remedy is open, but the Court would be assuming the functions of the Legislature if it attempted to vest power in a receiver not recognised by law.

This action is brought for a conversion which, if it occurred at all, was either on the 7th November, 1881, or the 25th February, 1882. As I understand the cases, in order to constitute a conversion there must be a wrongful taking or using or destroying of the goods, or an exercise of dominion over them inconsistent with the title of the owner.

A mere wrongful sale not in market overt without delivery, as for instance a sale by the sheriff in execution of goods let for hire to the defendant, is no conversion, for it does not affect the property in the goods : *Fitzhugh* v. *The Lancashire Waggon Co.*, 6 H. & N. 502.

In the case of *Johnson* v. *Stear*, 15 C. B. N. S. 334, the same rule is recognised. Erle, C. J., in delivering judgment, says : The defendant wrongfully assumed to be the owner in selling, and although the sale alone might not be a conversion, yet by delivering over the dock-warrant to the vendees in pursuance of such sale he interfered with the right which Cumming had of taking possession if he repaid the loan.

So in *England* v. *Cowley*, L. R. 9 Ex. 126, Bramwell, J., refers to an action of this kind in this way : " The substance of the action is the same as before the Common Law Procedure Act, and although in the form of declaration there given the words used are, "converted to his own use or wrongfully deprived the plaintiff of the use and possession of the plaintiff's goods," the gist of the action is the conversion, as, for example, by consuming the goods or by refusing the true owner possession, the wrongdoer having himself at the time a physical control over the goods. Now here the defendant did not 'convert' the goods to his own use either by sale or in any other way, nor did he deprive the plaintiff of them."

And Kelly, C. B., in the same case, says: "Apart from mere dicta, no case so far as I am aware, can be found where a man not in possession of the property has been held liable in trover unless he has absolutely denied the plaintiff's right, although if in possession of the property any dealing with it inconsistent with the true owner's right would be a conversion."

But in the present case there was no intention on the part of this defendant to sell or transfer any goods but those which had been assigned to him as trustee. It is clear that the property was withdrawn from sale at the auction. It never was in the defendant's possession or claimed by him in any way; he, on the contrary, declined to let the purchaser at the sale take it when he demanded it after the sale, and it was only when Mrs. Neill consented to withdraw her objections that he agreed to join her in a bill of sale for the purpose of transferring their several and respective interests in the property to Morrison, she as executrix of her deceased husband in the property in question; he as the trustee of the Neills' in the property assigned to him; each intended to convey only the property in which they claimed an interest.

It would be contrary to every principle of justice if such a transaction could be held to amount in law to a conversion, and the acceptance of a mortgage, which was at once transferred to the holders of the previous incumbrance upon it cannot, I imagine, carry the case any further. There was no interference with the possession by the defendant, and the true owner could not be affected either by the bill of sale or by the mortgage. He is as free as ever to pursue any remedy which was at any time open to him, and the defendant has obtained no advantage, directly or indirectly, from the transaction.

As to the admission made in the 2nd, 4th, and 6th paragraphs of the answer, if they stand alone they might afford no defence to the plaintiffs' claim; but the defendant denies the allegations in the statement of claim, which threw upon the plaintiff the necessity of proving that they are the proper parties to sue, and that there was a conversion. I think they have failed on both points, and that the appeal ought, therefore, to be allowed and the action dismissed with costs.

OSLER, J. A.—I think the only question we shall find it necessary to decide is, whether there was evidence of a conversion by the defendant, though the plaintiffs' title is also denied, and a further question has been made as to the damages.

There are two plaintiffs, and their cause of action as set forth in the statement of claim, is that the plaintiff Joseph Dickey was the owner of the property in question, holding it as receiver appointed by the Court of Chancery. That the defendant knowing this, wrongfully converted it, and that, subsequent to the alleged conversion, the plaintiff James Isaac Dickey became solely entitled to receive it from the other plaintiff, if in his possession, or the proceeds realised from a sale thereof, and any damages which that plaintiff might recover from the defendant.

The nature of the claim and the facts of the case are peculiar. One of the plaintiffs seeks to recover damages, not on his own account, but for the benefit of his co-plaintiff for an alleged conversion of property which he sold to the latter after the conversion.

The machine in question was formerly the property of Dickey, Neill & Co., a firm composed of Nathaniel Dickey, the plaintiff James Isaac Dickey, and John Neill, who carried on business as iron founders in the premises known as the Soho Foundry.

Their partnership was dissolved in October, 1876, and Neill, to whom or to whose wife the premises belonged, continued the business under the name of John Neill & Sons from that time until his death in October, 1879. His widow, Elizabeth Neill, became his executrix and devisee, and his two sons carried on the business in partnership until the 24th September, 1881, when they made an assignment to the defendant for the benefit of their creditors "all their assets and estate, property, goods, chattels and effects, including among other things all the plant, material, tools, and machinery belonging to them in and about the premises known as the Soho Foundry."

During all this time the machine remained in the foundry, and was used in the business as carried on by Neill and afterwards by his sons.

The defendant proceeded to carry out the trusts of the assignment, and in order to dispose of the estate to the best advantage, it was thought advisable to sell the business as a going concern. For this purpose Mrs. Neill by the following letter dated the 12th October, authorized the defendant to sell the leasehold of the foundry premises :

" Sir,—I hereby authorize and instruct you to offer for sale on the 24th inst., the leasehold premises on Esplanade and Front streets, in which the business of J. Neill & Sons has heretofore been carried on, along with the assets of the said firm, so as to enable the whole with the building on the said leasehold premises to be sold in one block as a going concern, and I agree in the event of a sale being made to execute all deeds or instruments, and do all acts necessary to enable the said leasehold premises to be vested in the purchaser thereof."

On the 7th November, 1881, defendant caused the assets of the estate and the unexpired term of the lease to be offered for sale by auction, and two persons named Morrison became the purchasers at the sum of $15,800. The machine, which was a fixture on the premises, was put up for sale with the rest of the property, but according to the evidence of the plaintiff James Isaac Dickey and of the defendant, it was not sold because the plaintiff claimed it and forbid the sale.

The Morrisons subsequently refused to carry out their purchase unless they got the machine, which with four or five other articles which had been actually sold, appears to have been claimed by Mrs. Neill as hers, or as belonging to the estate of her late husband, and, as to this machine at all events, were not the property of R. & J. Neill. On the 15th November, a valuation of these articles was made by the defendant with the view of ascertaining the value of Mrs. Neill's interest in the purchase money, at the foot of which she signed the following :

" With reference to the above plant, tools, and machinery, I hereby consent and agree that such shall be included and form part of the property sold by auction on 7th November, 1881, to Morrison Brothers for the sum of fifteen thousand eight hundred dollars. Said property being known as the Soho Foundry property.
ELIZABETH NEILL."

The sale was afterwards carried out by a bill of sale dated the 25th February, 1882, made between Elizabeth Neill, widow and executrix of John Neill, of the first part, the defendant of the second part, and the Morrisons of the third part. This instrument recites that R. & J. Neill used in their business a quantity of plant, machinery, &c., which had been in the possession of their father, John Neill, at the time of his death, but which then belonged to his widow and executrix, besides other machinery, tools, &c., belonging to themselves. It recites the assignment by the sons to McCaul of their own property, and that all parties interested in the leasehold, plant, machinery, &c., had authorised and permitted McCaul to sell the same and to apply the proceeds among the parties entitled thereto, in accordance with their respective legal rights. Then it recites that McCaul, on the 7th November, 1881, had caused the leasehold premises and chattels afterwards described, including the machine in question, to be offered for sale, and that the Morrisons had become the purchasers at $15,800, of which $5,000 had, at the request of Mrs. Neill, been paid to defendant ; and a mortgage, dated 12th January, 1882, had been given to him upon the said machinery and chattels as additional security for the balance.

Then it is witnessed that McCaul and Mrs. Neill, respectively, bargain, sell, assign, &c., to the Morrisons, inter alia, the screwing machine and tools, &c., " all which goods and chattels are now situate upon or in the foundry and premises lately occupied by the firm of T. Neill & Sons, commonly called the Soho Foundry; and all the right, title, &c., of her, the said Elizabeth Neill, as executrix as aforesaid and otherwise, and of the said J. H. McCaul as trustee as aforesaid and otherwise in and to the same, &c."

Mrs. Neil and the defendant respectively covenant that they have done no act to incumber, &c.

The defendant, by the direction of Mrs. Neill, took a mortgage (as recited in the bill of sale) for the balance of the purchase money, which he afterwards assigned to F. W. Kingstone in substitution of another mortgage on the same property which had been made to him by Mrs. Neill in the month of June, 1881.

Soon after the sale, James Isaac Dickey went to Morrison with the view of getting the machine. Morrison was using it. Dickey wanted him to buy it, but he claimed it under the bill of sale. The plaintiff did not otherwise attempt to obtain the machine from the Morrisons, who subsequently failed, and the machine was sold by their creditors' trustee.

The defendant was not shewn to have been in occupation of the foundry or in possession of the machine at any time, and, so far as the evidence goes, did not in any other way than has been described meddle with or assume title to, or dominion over it.

It was in fact, a fixture but no point was made of this.

It was objected at the trial that the defendant had not taken possession of, or delivered the machine. Neither party offered any evidence on this point, but it was held there, and afterwards in the Divisional Court, that the giving of the bill of sale and taking back a mortgage was a conversion and that the defendant could not be permitted to say he had not exercised such a control or dominion over it as would amount to a conversion.

The contention was renewed before us, and it was strongly argued that the defendant was not shewn to have had the actual possession of, or physical control over the machine, and would not be guilty of a conversion by merely selling it, or joining in a bill of sale and taking back a mortgage upon it, at the request of the person as whose agent he sold it.

The difficulty of determining in many cases what acts do and what acts do not amount to a conversion, has often been observed upon. In *Hiort* v. *Bott*, L. R. 9 Ex. 86, Bramwell, B., said that a good description of what constitutes a conversion is, "Where a man does an unauthorized act which deprives another of his property permanently or for an indefinite time." Such an act, as distinguished from a mere trespass (looking at the nature of the action for conversion), implies that the wrongdoer is in possession of, or has exercised some direct control over the property converted, or has some ostensible title to it by means of which he detains it from the rightful owner, or by transferring which he has enabled another to obtain and dispose of it. A mere assumption of title to or dominion over property, as by selling it, &c., not followed by some physical interference with it by the seller, or directly caused by him, inconsistent with the right of the true owner, is not a conversion. It is this to which Lord Ellenborough refers in *McCombie* v. *Davis*, 6 East 538, and not the mere case of assuming to sell or assuming to buy, when he says a man is guilty of a conversion "who takes my property by assignment from another who has no power to dispose of it, for what is that but assisting that other to carry his wrongful sale into effect"; and the same observation applies to *Baldwin* v. *Cole*, 6 Mod. 212 : cited in that case. See also *Cooper* v. *Chitty*, 1 Burr. 20 ; *Fine Art Society* v. *Union Bank*, 17 Q. B. D. 705.

The following authorities support this view:

The Lancashire Waggon Co. v. *Fitzhugh*, 6 H. & N. 502, was an action for an injury to the plaintiff's reversionary interest in certain waggons which had been let by them to one Pell, under an execution against whom the defendant had seized and sold them. Pollock, C. B., said : " We think if there was no conversion, except in selling, that .that is no conversion in law, and therefore no cause of action. But the plaintiffs new assign that the conversion did not consist in the mere sale, but in the delivery also, and in causing the purchasers to use and damage the waggons. The new assignment shews a cause of action."

Hilbury v. *Hatton*, 2 H. & C. 822. A person who had no title wrongfully took possession of, and sold a vessel to one T., who bought her professedly, but without their authority, on behalf of. the defendants, and then took possession of and let her for hire. The defendants afterwards ratified what he had done. It was held that T., by buying *and taking possession*, was guilty of a conversion of the vessel, and that the defendants were liable because they had ratified his act.

In *England* v. *Cowley*, L. R. 8 Ex. 126, the plaintiff, the holder of a bill of sale, was in possession of, and proceeding to remove the goods comprised in his security, and was told by the landlord, who intended to distrain on the following day, that he would not allow them to be removed. This was held not to be a conversion, as the plaintiff should at least have attempted to insist upon their removal.

Bramwell, B., said : " The gist of the action is, the conversion, as, for example, by consuming the goods or by refusing the true owner possession, the wrongdoer having himself at the time a physical control over the goods."

Pollock, B. : " The defendant never was in possession. No doubt cases might be put where a wrongdoer, though not in actual possession, uses such force or contrivance as to interfere entirely with the dominion of the true owner ; but here there was a mere assertion of right. The plaintiff should have insisted upon the. removal of the goods if he intended to challenge the defendant's assertion in an action of trover."

Kelly. C. B. : " The plaintiff was in actual possession. Apart from mere dicta no case can be found where a man not in possession of the property has been held liable in trover unless he has absolutely denied the plaintiff's right, although, if in possession, any dealing with the property inconsistent with the true owner's right would be a conversion."

I have not succeeded in finding any case where " an absolute denial of the owner's right " by one not in a position to enforce such denial has been held to be a conversion.

The general question was much discussed in *Fowler* v. *Hollins*, L. R. 7 Q. B. 616, and L. R. 7 H. L. 757. There the defendants, who were brokers, purchased from one Bayley certain cotton which he had fraudulently obtained from the plaintiff, the real owner. They were ignorant of Bayley's fraud, and took delivery of the cotton and forwarded it to one of their ordinary clients, who accepted it as if they had bought it for him.

The only point decided was, that any one who, however innocently, obtains possession of the goods of a person who has been fraudulently deprived of them, and disposes of them whether for his own benefit or that of any other person is guilty of a conversion.

Brett, J., discusses the difficulties which sometimes arise in determining what is such an exercise of dominion in contravention of the real owner's rights as to amount to a conversion, and speaking of the case where one has dealt with goods as if they were his own without having had the possession of them, says that in no case can a man be guilty of a conversion who has not by himself or his agent had possession of the goods in dispute. He adds: " So if one enters into a contract to sell as if they were his own the goods of another, whether the form of the contract be such as would assume to pass the property at once or such as could only pass the property on a subsequent delivery, I apprehend that the mere fact of making such a contract is not a conversion."

In Dom. Proc., in advising the House, Blackburn, J., said: " The case against the defendants does not rest merely on their having entered into a contract with Bayley, or merely having assisted in changing the custody of the goods, but in their having done both. They knowingly and intentionally assisted in transferring the property in the goods to Micholls, that Micholls might dispose of them as their own, and the plaintiffs never got them back."

Baron Cleasby : " If this was the ordinary case of a. broker merely acting as middle-man and making the contract between two principals, and having himself no interest in either contract, then the mere making of the contract would not, I conceive, involve any responsibility to third parties. And how far the intermeddling with the goods themselves by delivering them would do so, admits. of question, and might depend upon the extent to which the broker could be regarded, as having an independent. possession of the goods and delivering them for the purpose of passing the property. For example, an auctioneer delivers possession for the purpose of passing the property,. and it would not be disputed that he would be liable as upon a conversion to the true owner."

Lord Cairns said that the defendants had acted in relation to the sellers in a character beyond that of mere agents : " They exercised a volition in favour of Micholls & Co., the result of which was that they transferred the dominion over and property in the goods to Micholls in order that Micholls might dispose of them as their own, and this, I think within all the authorities, amounted to a. conversion."

The " exercise of volition," which Lord Cairns speaks of, was the actual taking possession of the goods by the defendants and forwarding them to their vendee.

Cochrane v. *Rymill*, 40 L. T. 744, illustrates the case of the auctioneer, put by Baron Cleasby, supra, as also does the case of *The National Mercantile Bank* v. *Rymill*, 44 L. T. R. 767, where conversely the auctioneer was held not. liable, not having delivered the goods on a sale made by him.

Hiort v. *Bott*, L. R. 9 Ex. 86, already cited, was an action of trover for barley which, by the fraud of one Grimmett, who professed to act as broker between the plaintiff as buyer and defendant as seller, the plaintiff had forwarded to the defendant at the railway station at Birmingham, at the same time sending him the invoice and a delivery order, which made the barley deliverable to the order of the consignor or consignee. The defendant believing, as Grimmett told him, that it was a mistake, and with the view of returning the barley to the plaintiff, thoughtlessly indorsed the delivery order to Grimmett who, by means of it, then obtained delivery of the barley and disposed of it. It was held that the defendant was guilty of a conversion. He had the ostensible title to the possession of the goods, and by his unauthorised act in indorsing the delivery order assumed a control over their disposition and caused them to be delivered to a person who deprived the plaintiff of them.

In the case before us the title to the machine was not vested in the defendant. It was not in his possession or under his control, and at no time does it appear to have been in his power to deliver up or retain it so as to make a demand upon and refusal by him evidence of a conversion.

It is plain that so far as he can be said to have sold at all he did so only as the agent and by the authority of Mrs. Neill. I say so far as he can be said to have sold at all because I think it clear, as a matter of fact, (which the recital in the bill of sale does not estop him from proving) that he did not sell the machine at the auction sale, and it was only by the subsequent assent of Mrs. Neill that it was treated as being included in and forming part of the property then sold. And if the transaction is looked upon as having been carried into effect and completed by the bill of sale, I can see no reason why the defendant is to be considered as conveying by it anything but the property which he held as trustee of R. and J. Neill, Mrs. Neill being made a party for the express purpose of conveying that which she claimed as her own.

We are not in a position to draw any inference of fact as to the actual delivery of possession of the machine. We have not the advantage of any finding on the subject, and the plaintiff offered no evidence of it though the objection that the defendant had not delivered it was pointedly raised at the outset of the case.

Upon the whole, I am of opinion, with great respect, that the authorities I have referred to well warrant us in holding that the defendant was not guilty of a conversion of this property either by joining in a bill of sale or by accepting and assigning a mortgage for the balance of the purchase money, no other act of interference by him being shewn.

As I think the appeal should be allowed on this ground, it is unnecessary to decide whether the plaintiffs have proved their title. It was argued for the defendant that the machine became the property of Mrs. Neill, under the award made in the partnership action of *Neill* v. *Dickey,* but I have not been able to convince myself that this is made out. It is not identified as being part of the property with which John Neill's estate was charged by the arbitrators, or as being included in the lot of tools, &c., valued at $600.

On the other hand, there are difficulties in the plaintiffs' way more or less formidable.

James Isaac Dickey, in whose name the action was originally brought, clearly cannot maintain it upon any title acquired under the vesting order or sale by the receiver, which is what he relied upon at the first trial, as that was made in April, 1882, many months after the date of the alleged conversion. As the case is now framed, he does not assert any title in himself at that date, and as between him and Mrs. Neill, the executrix of his deceased partner, the sale to the Morrisons, though a sale out and out and not professing to be made for the benefit of the estate, could hardly be treated as a conversion, as it did not place it out of the power of the surviving partners or of the receiver to take the machine or to pursue their remedies for its recovery, or their right in respect of it against the Morrisons, in whose hands it remained, and on the same premises where it had always been : *Patterson* v. *Thompson*, 9 A. R. 346-7 ; *Buckley* v. *Barber*, 6 Ex. 164 ; *Rothwell* v. *Rothwell*, 26 U. C. R. 179 ; *Brady* v. *Arnold,* 19 C. P. 42.

As regards Joseph Dickey, who was added as plaintiff after the first trial, it is more than doubtful whether he can maintain an action in his own name as receiver for the

conversion of property, the legal title to which was never
vested in him, and of which he never had the actual possession. A mere right to obtain the custody of a chattel will not
support an action of trover, though it may form the ground
of a special application to the court for a mandamus or
other appropriate relief. *Addison* v. *Round*, 4 Ad. & E.
799.

If in November, 1881, the receiver's appointment had been
completed by giving the security required by the decree
(*Edwards* v. *Edwards*, 2 Ch. D. 291 ; *Defries* v. *Crew*, 11
Jur. N. S. 360) he might have been in a position to move
to attach Mrs. Neill or the defendant for contempt, or to
apply to the court to restrain them from interfering with
the property or to compel its delivery up to him if in their
possession; but that is a very different thing from bringing
an unauthorised action of trover in his own name months
after he had sold or professed to sell the property in the
cause in which he was receiver.

I refer to *Campbell* v. *Lepan*, 19 C. P. 31 ; *Re Hopkins*,
30 W. R. 601 ; *Yeager* v. *Wallace*, 44 Pa. 294.

PATTERSON, J.A., and ROSE, J. concurred with OSLER,
J.A.

Appeal allowed, with costs.

REGINA V. HOWLAND.

Contempt of Court—Solicitor—Locus standi of applicant.

The decision of PROUDFOOT, J., 11 O. R. 633, finding that the solicitor
for the respondent in a quo warranto proceeding had committed a contempt of Court by reason of having written a letter which he published in
a newspaper commenting upon a decision of the Master in Chambers,
and directing the solicitor to pay costs to the applicant, the relator
in the proceeding, was affirmed.—[BURTON, J. A., dissenting.]
Per BURTON, J. A.—As it appeared that the ground on which the application was based, viz., prejudice to the applicant's case, had ceased to
exist at the time the application was heard, the proper course would
have been to dismiss it so far as the applicant was concerned. The
Court, might on its own motion have punished the contempt shewn to
its officer, even though the quo warranto proceedings were not still pending, but that course was not adopted : the learned Judge proceeded solely
on the ground that the applicant had a locus standi, and gave him the
costs of the application ; and the appeal should therefore be allowed.

THIS was an appeal by Henry O'Brien, solicitor for the
defendant, from the judgment of Proudfoot, J., reported
11 O. R. 633, where the facts giving rise to the proceeding against him and the grounds of the present appeal
are clearly set forth. The appeal came on for hearing on
the 12th January, 1887.*

S. H. Blake, Q. C., and *Lefroy,* for the appellant.
Bain, Q. C., and *Kapelle,* for the respondent.

March 1, 1887. PATTERSON, J. A.—I am satisfied, after
a careful consideration of this case and of the authorities
to which we have been referred, that no reason has been
shewn for differing from the learned Judge in his views of
the letter which is the subject of complaint, or of the duty
of the Court in the matter.

The grounds on which the judgment is objected to are
thus stated in the appellant's reasons of appeal.

1. The letter in question was nothing more than a legitimate comment upon the judgment which had already been
delivered by the Master in Chambers, and its matter is not

Present.—HAGARTY, C.J.O., BURTON and PATTERSON, JJ.A., and
FERGUSON, J.

such as can, in accordance with precedent, rightly be adjudged to constitute a contempt of Court.

2. No appeal from the judgment commented on was in fact pending at the time that the said letter was written; therefore, the said letter cannot rightly be adjudged to have been written with any view to influence any Judge of any Court.

3. Judgment having been delivered in the case with regard to which the letter in question was written, there is no ground in law or in reason for saying that the solicitor for one of the parties had not a right to publish such a letter.

4. The relator had no locus standi on this motion, inasmuch as his rights were not in any way affected by the publication of the letter in question.

5. The letter was written in respect of an official of the Court, who, as was objected at the time of the argument before him, had no jurisdiction to entertain the matters in question between the parties, and therefore cannot be considered as having held a judicial position.

6. To hold such a letter as that in question, written under the circumstances under which it was written, to be a contempt of Court, would be an unprecedented infringement on the liberty of the subject and not in accordance with British law or British liberty.

We have not to exercise any judgment on what may be called the merits of the contest before the learned Master in Chambers, either touching the jurisdiction of the Master or the qualification of the Mayor. The former question, though raised and debated before the Master, and at a later date before a Judge in Chambers in *Wilson* v. *Duncan*, 11 P. R. 379, and now formally stated as the 5th reason of appeal, was very properly not pressed before us. It was a question between the relator and the defendant in the quo warranto, and the decision upon it, as well as that upon the qualification, would have been reviewable on the appeal from the Master, if that had been gone on with.

The question of the qualification was made the occasion of the remarks which are complained of as a contempt of Court, and though we have nothing to decide respecting the qualification, it will be proper to advert a little more particularly to those remarks inasmuch as the appellant,

besides questioning the right of the Court below to entertain the charge of contempt on the information of this
relator, contends that no contempt was committed.

The part of the letter to the newspaper on which the
charge is founded is thus expressed:

" You say Mr. Howland made a bad blunder in running
without a proper qualification. It was perhaps natural to
assume this, on the supposition that the law was correctly
expounded last Tuesday. We contend it was not so, but
will speak of that hereafter. Mr. Howland's advisers,
however, had to take the law as they found it. How then
did it stand before the election ?

" 1. Ever since we have had municipal institutions it has
been assumed that a husband properly rated, and whose
wife has the necessary property, had the right to vote and
qualify in respect of that property. The generally received
and acted upon opinion was that the property had under
such circumstances the right to representation, and that this
right was in the husband. The whole country has acted
on this view, and the right has never been questioned until
now   It might have been brought up at any time since
the Married Woman's Act of 1859, but was not.

" Chief Justice Richards, probably the best authority on
such matters in Canada, had held in 1871 that under such
circumstances the husband had the right we contend for in
the Howland case. This decision has never been overruled, is consistent with common sense, and with the universally accepted opinion on the subject.

" Under these circumstances the counsel who advised
Mr. Howland that his qualification was sufficient were
amply justified in so doing. They did so advise Mr.
Howland plainly and distinctly when asked by him. If
they were wrong surely the blame should rest on them, and
not on the person who had been unhesitatingly advised that
he had the qualification required by law.

" You may naturally ask, Why then was the decision the
other way ? This question I am unable to answer. The
delivered judgment affords no answer. The arguments addressed were simply ignored, and the authority relied on
by us, so far from being explained or distinguished, was
not even referred to. This is eminently unsatisfactory to
both the profession and the public—an officer of the Court
over-ruling the judgment of a Chief Justice, who, above all
others in our land, was skilled in matters of municipal law.

But the Legislature on both sides of the House, on the matter being presented, at once admitted that the interpretation of Chief Justice Richards was correct and according to the original intention of the Legislature; and thereupon declared that to be the case, and removed the apparent difficulty."

We have here a criticism, not of the decision only, but also of the conduct, of the learned Master in his discharge of the functions of a Judge of the High Court under a statute, which, (as for the purpose of this appeal is not questioned,) conferred that jurisdiction upon him.

He is charged with having simply ignored the arguments addressed to him in support of the opinion of counsel on which Mr. Howland is said to have acted; and so far from explaining or distinguishing a decision of Chief Justice Richards, to "have not even referred to" it in the judgment he delivered; "an officer of the Court overruling the judgment of a Chief Justice who, above all others in our land, was skilled in matters of municipal law;" thus doing what was eminently unsatisfactory to both the profession and the public, and giving a decision inconsistent with common sense and with the universally accepted opinion on the subject of the right of a husband to qualify upon the property of his wife.

It has been contended that this must be treated on the footing of something written and published without reference to pending litigation. It is perfectly clear from the appellant's own affidavit that his contention cannot be acceded to. He shews that he had an appeal in contemplation as one of two courses open to his client, and that he gave notice of appeal on the same day that he wrote the letter, and only abandoned the appeal three days later when the other course was definitely decided on—and, more than this, the letter itself expressly refers to the contemplated appeal in the following passage with with it concludes:

"This being the case, Mr. Howland has decided not to keep matters in abeyance by asking for a stay of proceedings pending appeal, and instead of relying upon a reversal of the late judgment by a higher authority, has deter-

mined to go at once to the people, encouraged thereto
partly by your own manly utterance on the subject, and
by the universal expressions of sympathy and support
which he has received.

" It may be necessary as a question of costs to appeal
from the recent judgment, but that does not now affect the
question before the electors."

For the purpose of the inquiry whether by the writing
and publication of the letter a contempt of Court was committed, those acts must be taken to have been done while
the matter of the quo warranto was pending. The right
of the relator to set the Court in motion when he applied
three days after the letter was written is a different matter
and must be considered by itself.

In *Metzler* v. *Gounod*, 30 L. T. N. S. 264, there was a
verdict for the plaintiff, with leave to defendant to move
for a nonsuit or new trial, and, before the time for moving,
the defendant circulated amongst the people at a concert a
printed document giving an account of the dispute, which
the plaintiff complained of, and moved to commit the defendant. It was held that nothing was pending before the
Court when the document was circulated.

To make that case applicable as a precedent, it should
appear that in this case nothing was said or done to shew
that an appeal was in contemplation, whereas the facts are
the other way ; but the motion in *Metzler* v. *Gounod* was
not refused on the one ground only, but also on grounds
touching the character of the paper and the distribution of
it being to a limited number of a particular class of people.

I have not seen any case that comes nearer the point on
this branch of the appeal.

In addition to the publication pending the litigation,
there is the more serious consideration of the character of
the letter itself, which removes the case from those of the
class of the *Plating Co.* v. *Farquharson*, 44 L. T. N. S.
389 ; *Daw* v. *Eley*, L. R. 1 Eq. 49, and some of those which
arose in connection with the Tichborne litigation, where

the matter touches only the interests of the parties and no attack upon the Court is involved.

The imputations of disregard of his duty as a Judge, or of unfitness for the position, which would be naturally understood to be conveyed, and are indeed very plainly expressed in the remarks of the appellant, are calculated to weaken confidence in the administration of justice in the very important department where the learned Master presides; and, emanating from a barrister so well known and of the standing of the appellant, and with so much show of authority by references to opinions of counsel, universal understanding of the profession, judicial decision, and legislative action, of which the general reader cannot test the correctness, but must, and almost of course will, take upon trust, the aspersions may have an influence which might not attend similar utterances by a disappointed litigant smarting under the application of some rule of law that he does not understand.

We have not, it is true, to pronounce upon the legal question on which the learned Master is so confidently charged with having gone wrong, but it is not possible to read the appellant's letter without feeling that his interest in the subject must have betrayed him into making assertions of matters both of law and of fact which in cooler judgment he would have acknowledged to be open to much discussion ; and as to which he would have seen the propriety of merely asking the editor to whom he wrote to suspend judgment until the Master's decision had been reviewed in appeal. For example, he would not have treated it as unquestionable that the ruling of Chief Justice Richards in the *Prescott* Election case (*H. E. C.* 3) which we are told is the decision referred to, respecting the effect of the Elections Act of 1868 in giving a husband, who lived with his wife on his wife's freehold land, a vote as owner in the right of his wife, as a decision upon the construction of the Municipal Institutions Act ; and if he contended that in principle it governed the construction of the latter Act, notwithstanding a slight difference in the wording of the

Acts, he would doubtless have put it as a matter of opinion only.   Further, he would have taken account of the not unimportant change in the law respecting the property of married women by the Act of 1872, a year later than the trial of the *Prescott Case*, by which some rights which remained in the husband under the Act of 1859 were done away with, and which was much discussed in this Court in *Furness* v. *Mitchell*, 3 A. R. 510, as well as in other cases there cited; and of the further enactment in 1877 when the law took the form now found in R. S. O.   He would probably also have considered that the difference between freehold estates, which were the subject of some decisions, and the leasehold upon which the question now arose, might enter into the discussion.   He would scarcely have ventured to say that the delivered judgment of the Master afforded no answer to the question why his decision differed from the opinion given by counsel to Mr. Howland, when the reasons which were put in writing by the Master, as we find them in the report in 11 P. R. at p. 271, and a copy of which the appellant had before him when he wrote, state distinctly that it was because Mr. Howland had in law no interest whatever in his wife's leasehold property, and because the municipal law required as a qualification an estate to his own use and benefit in his own right or in right of his wife.   Nor would he have asserted that the arguments of counsel were ignored and the authority relied on not even referred to, because in addition to stating the reason for his decision, the Master did not also commit to writing the reasons why he did not apply to the municipal law, and to the leasehold qualification of the Mayor of a city, a decision which, if the *Prescott Case* is that referred to, was not under the municipal law, though the letter seems to say it was, but was under a provision relating altogether to freehold estates, and to the qualification of voters, besides being open to other suggestions already made.   The real position of the matter, if reflected on by the writer, could scarcely have been thought to warrant so severe a stricture as that the officer of the Court presumed to overrule the judgment of a Chief Justice.

The surprising inaccuracies involved in this last statement point decidedly to the absence of that reflection
which might reasonably be looked for when a gentleman
in the position of the appellant animadverts upon the
exercise of his judicial functions by an officer of the Court;
but the same thing is, to my mind, more plainly apparent
from the assertion that "the Legislature on both sides of
the House, on the matter being presented, at once admitted
that the interpretation of Chief Justice Richards was correct and according to the original intention of the Legislature and thereupon declared that to be the case, and removed the apparent difficulty."

This statement imports something ex post facto as further proof of the Master's alleged delinquency. If it has
any foundation on which a lawyer can assert its accuracy
it has escaped my attention.

The Legislature passed no declaratory law. What was
done was, by 48 Vict. ch. 37, (O.) to repeal the qualification
clause, 46 Vict., ch. 18, sec. 73, (O.) with an amendment made
by 48 Vict., ch. 39, sec. 4, (O.) and substitute another clause, in
which in place of declaring that the persons to be elected
Mayors, &c., must "have in their own right or in the right
of their wives, as proprietors or tenants," &c., &c. : declared
that no person shall be qualified to be elected Mayor, &c.,
unless, inter alia, one who "has or whose wife has, as proprietor or tenant," &c., &c.

There is much sounder reason for arguing that by this
change of the law the Legislature recognised the existing
law as being what the Master declared it to be, than for
the assertion contained in the appellant's letter. The Act
not being declaratory, it is needless to say that it did not
declare anything on the subject of the decision of Chief
Justice Richards, nor need it be said that it did not in any
way deal with the law concerning elections to the legislature on which his decision was given—but it may be noted
that while it altered the law respecting the qualification of
Mayors, &c., it left untouched the clauses regulating the
qualification of voters which are those to which the decision might be supposed more directly to apply.

It is not necessary to refer at any length to the affidavit
of the appellant filed in explanation of the circumstances
under which the letter was written. It has been considered
in the Court below, and given effect to as leading, in connection with other considerations, to no other order being
made than the order to pay the costs. It shews the absence of any intention on the part of the appellant to
evince disrespect for the learned Master or to impute par-
tiality in his decisions ; and while in stating that the letter
was written as a citizen in the interest of a candidate supported by the writer at the late election, but unseated by
the judgment of the Master whose apprehension of the
law differed from that of the advisers of the candidate, it
accounts for the state of feeling under which the letter was
written, it does not concede that after cooler consideration
the writer thought the letter too strong in its language or
too reckless in its assertions.

The honesty of the appellant's belief in the propriety of
what he did cannot relieve the Court of its duty to deal
with the matter in view of its effect, actual or potential,
upon the administration of justice.

A striking illustration of this is found in the case of *The
Sheriff of Surrey*, 2 F. & F. 236. The High Sheriff honestly believing that a direction given by the Judge holding
the assizes, to clear part of the Court-room was illegal and
an infringement of the rights of the people, directed his
officers not to obey another order of the kind. The Lord
Chief Justice, Cockburn, having heard his explanation,
pointed out the error under which he had acted, and concluded by saying, " You have stated, and the Court is perfectly assured that you, as an honorable English gentleman,
neither have intended nor are capable of offering any personal indignity to Her Majesty's Judges ; but the course
you have pursued is clearly a contumacious contempt of
the Court, and a most serious reflection on the authority
of the Judges' commission, which emanated from the
Crown, and demands, especially from the High Sheriff, as
one of Her Majesty's most important officers of justice,
obedience and respect. I consider it my duty, Mr. High
Sheriff, to fine you £500."

There is no question involved respecting the right, which is a salutary one, and which no one now-a-days would desire to abridge, to discuss, in the public press or otherwise, the proceedings and decisions of the Courts, or even the conduct of a Judge or his fitness for the office he holds, all of which are matters of importance to the public at large, though the right may not be put on the ground taken in some American State Courts where the Judges are elective, and where, for that reason the right seems to be asserted for the people to scan their doings and sayings like those of their elected representatives or local officers.

The idea of this letter being intended as a fair and temperate comment on the decision or the conduct of the Master cannot be seriously entertained.

To say nothing of the character of its contents at which I have already glanced, it is enough to bear in mind not merely that the Master's decision was reviewable by an appeal to a Judge, but that an appeal was spoken of in the letter itself as a step about to be taken, to see how far removed such an appeal to the public is from legitimate comment or discussion.

There is a case reported in L. R. 8 Q. B. 134, *Regina* v. *Lefroy,* in which a Judge of the County Court on the hearing of a judgment summons had made some strong obsevations on the conduct of the attorney for the party, imputing to him misconduct towards his client. The matter was referred to the registrar to ascertain what means, if any, the party had, and pending that inquiry, the attorney wrote a letter which was published in a local newspaper, commenting on the conduct of the Judge and saying, as to one statement made by the Judge, "The statement was a monstrosity, and as I can now say without fear of an arbitrary or tyrannical abuse of power, an untruth." The County Court Judge cited the attorney to appear at the next Court to answer for his contempt, and the attorney obtained from the Court of Queen's Bench a prohibition on the ground of want of jurisdiction in the Judge of the inferior Court to punish summarily any contempt but con-

tempt committed in the face of the Court. The decision
is not upon any point that arises now; but I refer to
the case because the act complained of was not very unlike
that which is the subject of the present proceeding, and
the law is discussed by Cockburn, C. J., and by Mellor and
Quain, JJ., without any intimation of doubt, as to such an
act being punishable as a contempt by a Superior Court.

The offence in *Ex parte Turner*, 3 Mont. D. & D. 523,
was also very similar to that now charged.

We have been referred to *Shortt* on Literature and *Morgan's* Law of Literature, where the general subject is dealt
with and the leading cases cited. I may also refer to *Paterson's* Treatise on the Liberty of the Press, Speech and Public Worship, in the seventh chapter of which the result of
the decisions is succinctly and accurately given. At p. 121
of the work, where the author states the principles on
which the jurisdiction in question is exercised, there are
these observations : " As in the case of proceedings in Parliament, the business transacted in Courts of justice comes
home to every one, and there is no reason why all that is
done there should not be open to every kind of observation
both in speech and in the press. * *. Courts, as may be
supposed, are sometimes well spoken of and sometimes the
reverse. And as the administration of justice is of equal
importance to the making and reforming of the law, and
is entitled to be surrounded with a dignity appropriate to
its place in the constitution, the same occasions for collision
arise where free comments are made on the exercise of so
high a function. Courts of law must therefore, as in the
case of Parliament, be credited with sufficient power to
vindicate and protect their procedure against attacks, for
as Courts are the appointed means of adjudicating on all
disputes, and for discovering all sufficient materials to that
end, their labors would be often- futile, if irresponsible
volunteers intruded crude opinions and speculations, founded
as they must usually be, on defective data. The first
requisite of a court of justice is that its machinery be left
undisturbed ; and this cannot be effected unless comments
be all but excluded until the Court has discharged its functions."

Our attention was also called to a paper by a correspon-
dent of the Albany Law Journal (33 Alb. L. J. 145). The.

writer discusses the question of constructive contempt with ability, but without an adequate grasp of the English course of practice, and the editor adds a reference to a number of American cases in which the subject had been considered. One of these, *Story* v. *The People*, 79 Ill. 45, was cited to us on the argument.

Little is to be gained in this discussion from the American decisions for the reason, pointed out in a note at p. 333 of the first volume of *Kent's* Commentaries, that the Courts have to a great extent, particularly the United States Courts, been deprived by legislation of the power to deal summarily with contempts except when committed in the face of the Court, and also by reason of the introduction of the element of the popular election of the Judges into the discussion in the State Courts.

Nor is it necessary to look beyond the English books, if indeed we need go any farther than our own reports, to find clear authority for the jurisdiction and for its exercise in the present case.

In *Hawkins's* Pleas of the Crown, it is said (vol. 2, p. 220) that the most remarkable instances of contempt seem reducible to six heads which are set out, No. 3 being "contemptuous words or writings concerning the Court," and of this particular it is said (p. 221): "It seems needless to put any instances of this kind which are generally so obvious to common understanding." But the definitions of contempt most usually cited are those by Lord Hardwicke, which are thus quoted from 2 Atk. 271 by Harrison, C. J., in *Regina* v. *Wilkinson*, 41 U C. R. 47, at p. 98: "1. Scandalizing the Court itself: 2. Abusing parties who are concerned in causes: 3. Prejudicing mankind against persons before their cause is heard."

The rule for an attachment in *Regina* v. *Wilkinson* was argued before the Chief Justice and Mr. Justice Morrison. The charge was for contempts coming under the first definition and also for constructive contempt by the publication of an article calculated to prejudice a party to the litigation. The Chief Justice held that contempt of both

classes had been committed, and I do not understand his-
learned colleague to have held a different opinion upon that
point, though he considered that under the circumstances
the complainant had lost any right to ask the Court to interfere for his individual protection, and that he could not
compel the Court to notice the direct contempt which the
Court itself had not thought fit to do during the four
months that had passed since the publication.

That case recognised the right of the Court to punish
both kinds of contempt, which is a different thing from its
being bound to proceed for contempt 'of the Court itself
upon the information of a private suitor.

"The power which Courts have of vindicating their own
authority by punishing contempt committed in or out of
Court, is coeval with the common law and stands upon im-
memorial usage, for which I would refer to the *King* v.
Almon, Wilmot's Opinions, 254." Per Parke, B., in
Miller v. *Knox*, in H. L. 4 Bing. N. C. at p. 613.

Skipworth's Case, L. R. 9 Q. B. 230, contains, in the judgment of Blackburn, J., a valuable exposition of the law
concerning contempt of Court by conduct and words constituting a personal attack upon a Judge, as well as calculated to affect pending proceedings, but I need not now do
more than refer to it. It also affords an instance in point
on the other branch of this appeal which I have yet to
deal with. It is that which is set out in the fourth reason
of appeal, viz., the locus standi of the applicant.

The argument is that inasmuch as the motion was not
made until after, though on the same morning as the service on the part of Mr. Howland of notice that his appeal
was not to be proceeded with, the relator had ceased to be
in danger of prejudice from the appellant's letter, and that
though the writing and publication of the letter was a contempt of Court, the right of the relator to complain of it
had ceased.

The Plating Co. v. *Farquharson*, 44 L. T. N. S. 389, was
relied on, and it supports the proposition, which has been
acted on also in other cases, that when a discussion in print

of the merits of a contest can no longer affect the proceedings the Court will be slow to interfere; and it contains a
pithy remark of James, L. J., which is not meant to be
taken very literally, that applications the object of which
is to mulct a party in costs are themselves a contempt by
wasting the time of the Court.

We do not find in the materials before us any such precise statement of dates as there would most likely have
been if the particular form in which this objection was
argued had been thought of when the answer was made in
the Court below.   Indeed it is only by a liberal reading of
the 4th reason of appeal that any place for the objection
is found.   We were orally told by counsel how the two
things, the motion to commit and the notice of abandoning
the appeal stood in point of time.   I think one trod on the
heels of the other, and perhaps the notice was the fore-
most; but in my opinion the matter cannot turn on any
such inquiry.

The fallacy is in treating this order on the principle of
an injunction granted at the instance of a suitor, to whom
an injunction ought not to have been granted to stay an
act from which he could not possibly suffer, and which had
ceased to be, if it ever was, a wrong against him.

The objection is answered as soon as it is shewn that the
appellant was properly held to have committed a contempt
against the Court itself, unless it can be maintained that
the Court could not properly proceed upon the information
of this relator.

No authority has been produced which goes that length.
Cases like *The Plating Co.* v. *Farquharson* are distinguished
by the circumstance that the judgments deal with matters
which concerned only the litigant parties.

But in none of those cases, nor in the opinion of Morrison,
J., in *Regina* v. *Wilkinson,* is the power of the Court
denied.

In *Skipworth's Case* the motion was for a rule upon
Skipworth only, but the Court, upon the materials laid
before it upon that motion, directed the Tichborne claimant
also to be called upon.

The right of the Court to proceed for the punishment of
contempt cannot, as I apprehend, be challenged on the
ground that its information came from one who might not
have been able to insist on such action being taken at his
instance or on his behalf alone.

A question of another kind naturally suggests itself. If
the contempt is held to be established and at the same time
it is held that the relator was too late in complaining, is it
logical to give him his costs ?

No such question has been presented by counsel, but one
cannot help feeling that it is one that deserves an answer,
and that the answer is not far to seek.

In the first place it is not held that the application, made
when it was, and looking at it only from the relator's point
of view, must, by reason of any disabling rule of law or of
practice, necessarily have been rejected.

In the next place there would be some difficulty, and
probably an insuperable difficulty, in making out that this
was not an appeal for costs only, unless on the ground that
the application ought to have been dismissed.

Further, the imposition of costs is really in the nature
of a penalty for the contempt. The form of the order is
unimportant and can be changed when necessary. Strictly
speaking it should have been either a formal adjudication
of contempt, in which case a fine might have been in form
imposed, or a forbearance to make any order on condition
of the costs being paid. That was what was done in *Littler*
v. *Thompson*, 2 Beav. 129, and what has been done here is
the same in substance.

As to the title of the relator to his costs, it may be said,
as was said by Whiteside, C. J., in *Corkery* v. *Hickson*, 10
Ir. C. L. 174 : " It was proper that the question should be
raised, and the person who did it should get his costs irrespective of what other proceedings he may have been
advised to take." These last words refer to an action for
libel brought upon the same writing which was complained
of as a contempt, the bringing of which, it was urged, disabled the applicant from invoking the summary jurisdiction of the Court.

In *Bowden* v. *Russell*, 36 L. T. N. S. 177, the application for commitment was given up and an injunction asked for, but Malins, V. C., said that the conduct of the plaintiff, who had published or circulated copies of his statement of claim in a pending action, was so improper that he must pay the costs of the motion.

In *Brook* v. *Evans*, 6 Jur., N. S. 1025, Stuart, V. C., held that the published article was not such as to call for interference, but as he did not approve of the publication of it, he would not dismiss the application with costs, but made them costs in the cause, so that the party who succeeded before him might in the event have to pay them.

The appeal should therefore be dismissed, with costs.

HAGARTY, C.J.O., and FERGUSON, J., concurred.

BURTON, J. A.   The application to commit Mr. O'Brien was made to my brother Proudfoot, by a party to the proceedings in the case of *Regina* v. *Howland*, (a proceeding to unseat the defendant as Mayor on the ground of disqualification), and was based on the right of the applicant to seek the interference of the Court on the ground that the case was still pending, and the tendency of such a publication as that which was complained of to interfere with a fair trial and equal justice to all parties.

There can be no difference of opinion among us as to the importance of the Court having the power to punish as a contempt any attempt to prejudice the minds of the Court the witnesses, or the public whilst a case is still pending. It is in the interest of the community not less than of the litigants that such a power should be freely exercised in such cases so as to secure the pure and fearless administration of justice; but I entertain a very strong opinion that this extraordinary power of punishing summarily as for a contempt, an act not committed in the face of the Court, ought not to be exercised where the proceedings have terminated and where something has been published which only so far trangresses the rules of law as to be a technical contempt, but is wholly unattended with mischievous consequences. Where the act complained of is of that character, the complainant may, as was remarked by the late Chief Justice of this Court, be safely left to the ordinary remedies which the law has provided.

Whenever, therefore, it appeared that the grounds on which the application was based had ceased to exist before the application was made, the proper course would, in my opinion, have been to dismiss it so far as the relator was concerned.

I do not at all question the right of the Court itself when a publication is brought to its notice, which reflects injuriously upon the Court or its officials by imputing to them false, corrupt, or dishonest motives, or in any other way so that the natural or necessary consequence would be to bring odium upon the administration of the law, and thereby to weaken the confidence of the public in it, to punish the party guilty of that contempt in a summary way, even though the suit or matter to which the publication relates is not still pending; and if it appeared in the present case that the Court had taken upon itself to punish this as a contempt of that nature, I am free to admit that a very different question would have presented itself for adjudication, as whatever might be my own opinion upon the subject of this letter being a publication of that character, I should naturally hesitate before coming to a conclusion different from that of the learned Judge of first instance; but no such question, in my view of the matter, arises here, and I express no opinion therefore as to whether the letter was or was not of that description.

Neither the learned Master whose decision was reflected upon, nor the Court have thought proper to institute any proceedings ; on the contrary, the learned Judge proceeds solely on the ground that the applicant had a locus standi, inasmuch as the writing of the letter before the proceedings were ended was a contempt punishable summarily and his judgment proceeds entirely upon that ground, and gives to the applicant the costs of the application, and the formal order recognises the fact that no prejudice can now result to the relator from the publication, and therefore does not make any order except that the writer shall pay to the relator his costs of the application.

I do not find a single expression in the judgment to shew that if this matter had been brought under the notice of the Court even by the learned Master himself after the termination of the proceedings, he would have thought it a proper subject for a summary application.

Mr. Bain relied upon the case of ex parte *Turner*, 3 Mont. D. & M. 523, as shewing that the fact that proceedings, had terminated made no difference.

The remarks of the learned Judge in that case upon the point were not material to the decision, not only because the proceedings were still pending, the minutes of the decree having yet to be settled, but also because the acts complained of would be equally a contempt, whether the proceedings were pending or had terminated.

The libel there complained of, charged that the Chief Judge in Bankruptcy had in co-operation, if not in conspiracy with the opposite solicitors, with the taxing officer, and with the registrar of the Court, committed a series of frauds, robbed the public, and prevented improvements in the Court of Bankruptcy, and the learned Judge expressly deals with the matter as falling within the class of cases to which I have referred as being designed or calculated to destroy confidence in the Court, and to degrade it in the opinion of the public. " If," he says, " I am right in saying that this is the conclusion to be drawn from the charges, can we for a moment hesitate at arriving at the conclusion that it was a gross and scandalous contumacy of the learned Judge, that it was a gross libel upon him which ought to be visited as a contempt ? "

I do not think it sufficient, in a case of this nature, to say that the Judge had the power so to deal with it if he had thought proper, because I cannot be sure that if the learned Judge had been called upon, after the termination of the proceedings, to deal with this letter as a constructive contempt solely in consequence of its reflections upon the learned Master, he would have felt called upon to do so. I must confess that I share the opinion expressed on more than one occasion by the late Sir George Jessel, that on all motions of this kind we should be careful to see that a cause cannot be fairly prosecuted to a hearing without injury to the parties to it, unless this extreme step be adopted, and "that he had always thought, that necessary though it be, it was necessary only in the sense in which extreme measures are sometimes necessary to preserve men's rights, that is, if no other pertinent remedy could be found."

If an appeal lies against an order to commit for contempt, which seemed to be admitted upon the argument, it equally lies against this order to pay the costs, which is substantially the same thing. The Court has made an adjudication, and as a consequence of that, has ordered Mr. O'Brien to pay the costs.

I regret that in this case there should be any difference of opinion, but I feel compelled to deal with it in the same way as if Mr. O'Brien were suffering imprisonment for the contempt, and I cannot avoid seeing that the judgment was arrived at on the same grounds as those which were referred to in the notice of motion and on no other.

I am of opinion, therefore, that the appeal should be allowed.

Appeal dismissed, with costs.

[This case has since been carried to the Supreme Court.]

GAULT v. SHEPARD.

*Landlord and tenant—Verbal lease—Change of tenants—Surrender in law
—Estoppel.*

The plaintiffs by their agent, in June, 1881, verbally leased to S. & W. for
three years certain premises in which the latter carried on business in
partnership for about a year when W. sold out his interest to one D.
who in partnership with S. carried on the same business for about ten
months when S. withdrew from the partnership and sold out his
interest to D. who agreed with S. to pay all rent then due or to become
due in respect of the premises which he continued to occupy and pay
rent for. The plaintiff without authority drew for a quarter's rent on S.
& D. who refused to accept it ; and a fire having occurred on the premises
the piaintiff expended the insurance money in repairs with D.'s consent.
Default having been made of six months' rent due on 15th December,
1883, the plaintiffs instituted proceedings against S. & W. for the
recovery thereof :

Held, [reversing the judgment of the Court below] that although the
plaintiffs were cognizant of the several changes in the partnership and
the occupation by D. of the premises, these acts were not evidence of a
surrender in law, and that they were not estopped from enforcing payment of the overdue rent against S. & W.

PATTERSON, J.A., *dubitante.*

The doctrine of surrender by act and operation of law applies as well to a
term created by deed as to one created by parol.

Lawrence v. *Faux,* 2 F. & F. 435, distinguished.

THIS was an action in the County Court of Middlesex
by Gault Bros. & Co. of Montreal, against F. E. Shepard
and J. McF. Wilson, to recover the sum of $250, being for
a half year's rent of a certain store and premises in St.
Thomas, which plaintiffs had verbally leased for a term of
three years from 15th June, 1881, to the defendants.

It appeared that the defendants had carried on business
in these premises from that date until the 4th of July,
1882, when the partnership was dissolved, the defendant
Wilson withdrawing therefrom, who sold out his interest
in the partnership to one W. W. Disher, and the business
was then carried on in the name of Shepard & Disher who
assumed all the liabilities of Shepard & Wilson, amongst
others, the tenancy between the plaintiffs and the said
firm. That in May, 1883, the firm of Shepard & Disher
was dissolved by Shepard withdrawing therefrom, who
sold all his interest in the business to Disher, who continued to carry on the business in the said premises, and

who stipulated and agreed with Shepard to pay the rent due, and to become due, in respect of the leasehold.

The statement of defence further set up that Disher entered into possession of the said premises as tenant to the plaintiffs, who accepted him as such, and received rent from him as such tenant, in the room and stead of the defendants Shepard and Wilson; and that thereby the plaintiffs fully released and discharged the defendants from the payment of said rent, and which formed the plaintiffs' only claim in the action.

On the examination of the defendants, it was elicited that the several changes in the firm were all effected without any consultation or arrangement with the plaintiffs, or with one Morton who acted as agent of the plaintiffs in letting the house, &c.

The action came on for trial before His Honor Judge Davis and a jury, on the 2nd of June, 1885, when the two defendants, together with one Lindop a contractor, were examined as witnesses, and the facts proved were substantially those above stated. At the conclusion of the arguments of counsel, His Honor in charging the jury, remarked as follows:

"There has been a good deal of argument but the matter is really within a very narrow compass. These defendants, Shepard & Wilson, in the first place were tenants of these premises in St. Thomas, and agreed to take a lease for some three years. It appears Wilson went out and Disher went in with Shepard, and then Shepard went out and Disher only remained. The landlord, who lives in Montreal, was paid his rent until the last six months, and when he came to claim his last six months' rent from the original parties, Shepard & Wilson, they repudiated all liability, and said Disher was the man he should look to. He did not take that view of it, but said he had made a bargain with Shepard & Wilson and would hold them to it. They might do what they liked with Disher but he would not release them.

It has been said here that although there was no intention to give up the original lease, the law would imply a giving up. That is a legal proposition as to what the inference is from these letters. If there was verbal testimony it would be a proper thing to submit to a jury for them to find out what the intention was; but the law is clear that where the inferences are to be drawn from written correspondence, and where the meaning of the parties is to be drawn from that written correspondence,

it is the duty of the Court to interpret that. I t· · upon myself the
duty of doing so, but I leave the matter to you of saying what is due the
plaintiff. There is some $250 and interest, which is easily calculated.
That is the amount they are entitled to, and there is nothing to reduce it.
The only question is, whether it is due from Disher, or the original parties
Shepard & Wilson. Mr. Morton was called, and put his views beyond a
doubt. He says there was no intention to release these parties, and his
veidence you heard. Other parts of his testimony would appear to conflict, and you are urged to determine that the lease was really given up.
You must, however, take the man's whole evidence. Then we are driven
back to the correspondence. If there is any mistake with regard to this
matter, the defendant will have an opportunity of moving, in the proper
place and time, to have the verdict set aside. * * Verdict for the
plaintiffs for $261.25."

In July term following, the defendants moved to set
aside the verdict as entered for the plaintiffs, and for a new
trial.

After hearing counsel for all parties, His Honor directed
a new trial, remarking that, " After carefully considering
the facts and hearing the arguments of counsel, and upon
referring to the cases cited, I think there was some evidence
to go to the jury, and that the same should have been submitted to them at the trial. On that ground, therefore, I
grant a new trial without costs."

Thereupon the plaintiffs appealed to this Court and the
appeal came on to be heard on the 9th of September,
1886.*

Gibbons, for the appellants.
G. T. Blackstock, for the respondents.

The other facts of the case and the authorities cited
appear in the judgment.

November 4, 1886. OSLER, J. A.—This was an action
to recover half a year's rent upon a lease of certain premises in the town of St. Thomas. The defence relied upon
was a surrender of the lease by the act and operation of
law before any of the rent claimed had become due.

Present.—HAGARTY, C.J.O., BURTON, PATTERSON, and OSLER, JJ. A.

The plaintiffs had a verdict at the trial, which was afterwards set aside, and a new trial granted as to the defendant Wilson, the learned Judge of the County Court being
of opinion that there was evidence of a surrender, which
he ought to have submitted to the jury. The present
appeal is from that decision.

This case appears to me to involve a question of some
importance as regards the position of the landlord of a partnership firm, in the constitution of which changes which
he cannot prevent, occur during the term of the lease, and it
is necessary to examine the facts somewhat closely.

The tenancy was for a term of three years from the 15th
of June, 1881, at a rental of $500, payable quarterly.

A lease under seal was produced executed by the plaintiffs, but, according to the evidence of the defendants it had
not been delivered to or accepted by them, and it was
stated without contradiction that the only lease between
the parties was a verbal one. I do not, however, attach
any importance to that fact in the present case, as
the doctrine of surrender by act and operation of law
applies as well to a term created by deed as to one created
by parol: *Davison* v. *Gent*, 1 H. & N. 744.

The present action is not an action for use and occupation,
or upon any covenant on the tenants' part, (for, as I have
said, there was none), but is simply the ordinary action
upon a lease for the rent reserved, depending upon the continued existence of the term granted. The sole question,
therefore, is whether there was evidence for the jury of a
surrender of the term by the act and operation of law.

The general rule is stated in *Phené* v. *Popplewell*, 12 C.
B. N. S. 334. "Anything which amounts to an agreement
on the part of the tenant to abandon and on the part of
the landlord to remain in the possession of the premises
amounts to a surrender by operation of law." And in the
same case, per Byles, J.: "It is extremely difficult to reconcile all the cases on the subject. It seems, however, to be
plain from them all that when there is an agreement between landlord and tenant that the latter shall relinquish
and the former resume possession of the premises, and that

agreement is acted upon by change of possession that amounts to a surrender by act and operation of law within the 3rd section of the Statute of Frauds."

The rule is easily applied in the simple case of the tenant giving up and the landlord resuming possession of the premises, particularly if the tenancy be a yearly one, or where, as in *Nickells* v. *Atherstone*, 10 Q. B. 944, and *Davison* v. *Gent*, 1 H. & N. 744, the landlord, with the consent of the tenant, actively intervenes and re-lets them to a new tenant, and the former goes out of possession; but there is more difficulty where the tenancy is of a term of years and the tenant seeks to convert into or treat as an implied surrender, what was in its origin a transfer of his own interest, invalid for not being under seal, by raising against the landlord an estoppel out of his subsequent dealings with the person to whom he has thus transferred the possession. And the difficulty is not diminished where the original lease was to two or more, and one only transfers his interest and possession. To such cases I think the language of the late Chief Justice of this Court in *Nixon* v. *Maltby*, 7 A. R. 371, is peculiarly applicable. The tenant has placed his landlord.

" In what may be called a dilemma, and the acts of the landlord ought to receive the most favourable construction, and unless they are absolutely incompatible with the continued existence of the lease they should not be held to be so."

And in *Oastler* v. *Henderson*, 2 Q. B. D. 575, Brett, L. J., said:

" There can be no estoppel by mere verbal agreement. There must be in addition to such agreement some act done which is inconsistent with the continuance of the lease. If after the agreement, the landlord actually takes possession or does what virtually amounts to it, if he not only attempts to let, but actually does let, then there is a palpable act done with regard to the premises raising an estoppel within the rule laid down in *Nickells* v. *Atherstone*, 10 Q. B. 944, following *Lyon* v *Reed*, 13 M. & W. 285."

See also per Bayley and Holroyd, JJ., in *Johnston* v. *Huddleston*, 4 B. & C. 934, 939.

In *Hamerton* v. *Stead*, 3 B. & C. 478, a tenant from year to year entered into an agreement during a current year for a lease to be granted to himself and another person, who from that time entered and occupied jointly with him. It was held that by this agreement and the joint occupation under it the former tenancy was determined. And in *Sheppard's* Touchstone, p. 302, cited in *Davison* v. *Gent,* supra, it is said that it is a surrender if the new lease be to the lessee and a stranger. In cases of this sort the act of the landlord is unequivocal. *Graham* v. *Whichelo,* 1 Cr. & M. 188, comes nearest to the present case. That was an action for rent upon a lease made in March, 1827, to Whichelo and Hull of premises occupied by them as partners, for a term of three years, with the option of extending it to seven years upon giving notice to that effect. The partnership was dissolved in 1828, Whichelo retiring from business, and the landlord was informed of it soon afterwards. In January, 1829, Hull entered into partnership with one Smart, and they carried on business in the name of Hull & Smart until September, 1831. Notice requiring the extension of the term was given in January, 1829, in the name of and signed by Whichelo & Hull. In February, 1829, the landlord gave Hull a letter to his attorney, stating that the lease for the extended term might be made to Hull & Smart, but no lease was ever prepared or executed. Receipts for rent were proved as received from Hull after the dissolution of Whichelo to Hull, and as from Hull & Smart after the commencement of that partnership. It was held that Whichelo remained liable for the rent accruing in 1831.

Bayley, B., distinguished the case from *Thomas* v. *Cooke,* 2 B. & Ald. 119, on the ground that in that case there had been an assent of all three parties to the arrangement by which the underlessee became the immediate tenant to the original landlord. He then says :

" If it could have been made out that the plaintiff agreed to give up Whichelo, and that Whichelo assented, and that Smart agreed to become tenant, the principle of *Thomas* v. *Cooke* would apply, but this case is different because there was no agreement on the part of Graham (the landlord) to give up Whichelo, or on the part of Smart to be bound as tenant."

And see *McDonell* v. *Pope,* 9 Hare 705.

To apply these authorities to the present case. Is there
evidence of an agreement or conduct manifesting an assent
or agreement on the part of the plaintiffs to the creation of
a new tenancy, and of such a nature as to estop them from
asserting their right under the former tenancy ?

The facts relied upon by the defendants are those relating (1) to the payment of the rent and (2) to the execution
of certain repairs upon the demised premises.   The defendants were in partnership from the 15th June, 1881, the
date of the lease, until the 4th July, 1882.   Wilson then
sold out his interest in the firm to one Disher, who became
partner with Shepard in his stead.   There was no written
agreement.   Wilson said that Disher agreed with him to
assume the lease and the half year's rent due on 15th June,
1882, in connection with other liabilities and contracts of
the firm, and to see the plaintiffs about it.   He made no
arrangements with them to relieve himself from the rent,
nor did they or their agent take any part in the arrangement with Disher or agree to it.   " I supposed," he says,
" that I was released from liability, as Shepard and Disher
were to pay the future rent."   Mr. Morton, a bank agent
in St. Thomas, who had acted for the plaintiffs in letting
the premises to the defendants, said that he knew of the
change in the firm, and that Disher had bought out Wilson
and gone in with Shepard, and that being in Montreal
shortly afterwards he mentioned the fact to the plaintiffs,
who " made no objection to it."   No receipts for rent were
produced, but Shepard said that after Disher came in the
rent was paid by Shepard and Disher.

Shepard and Disher's partnership continued until 1st
May, 1883, when Shepard also retired, selling out his interest to Disher, and paying the latter $200 on account of the
half year's rent which would be due on the 15th June following.   It did not appear when this rent was in fact paid
to the plaintiffs, but it was no doubt paid as the
rent now sued for is the half year's rent from the 15th
June to the 15th December, 1883.   Wilson said that the
first notice he had that the plaintiffs claimed anything

27—VOL XIV A.R.

from him was on the 22nd June, 1883, that is to say about
a week after the rent sued for became due.

The plaintiffs appear to have been informed of Shepard's transfer to Disher about the 20th or 21st May, 1883.
On this part of the case the only other fact necessary to be
noticed is that spoken of by Morton, the bank agent, who said
that a draft (not produced) made by the plaintiffs, presumably on Shepard & Disher, was refused acceptance by them,
and was returned dishonored in May, 1883. The amount
of the draft was not mentioned. It may, perhaps, be inferred, though nothing is said about it, that it was for a
quarter's rent due in the previous month of March.

A little before the middle of May, 1883, the premises
were injured by fire, and the insurance company paid the
amount expended by the plaintiffs in putting them in repair. The repairs were done by the order of the plaintiffs
and with the consent of Disher, who had then left the
premises and who gave the carpenter the key.

On this state of facts I consider that a jury could not
properly infer a surrender by operation of law of the lease
to Shepard & Wilson. Whatever may have been the rights
of Shepard, Wilson and Disher as between themselves,
their arrangements were made between themselves alone,
independently of the plaintiffs.

As regards the rent, nothing can be made of the draft
upon Shepard & Disher as they had not authorized it and
refused to accept it even if its acceptance would have
made any difference. All that is proved is that the rent
was paid, but that alone cannot justify the inference that
the persons remitting it were accepted and treated by the
plaintiffs as their tenants.

Lawrence v. *Faux*, 2 F. & F., 435 cited by Mr. Blackstock,
is distinguishable. There, a receipt for rent was in fact,
proved, and was held to be evidence of the surrender by
operation of law of a former tenancy. But it was on its
face expressed to be for money paid as rent due by the
person paying it as a tenant of the premises: and the
case was thus brought within the rule of *Thomas* v. *Cooke*,
2 B. & Ad. 119.

Then as to the repairs. I fail to see how they can be treated as inconsistent with the continuance of the defendants' tenancy. They were not done with the view of resuming possession of the property, but of protecting it. It was a gratuitous act for the benefit of the tenants, and not an exercise of ownership. Upon this point I quote another passage from the judgment in *Nixon* v. *Maltby,* 7 A. R. 371, where the Chief Justice speaking of the effect to be attributed to acts done by the landlord upon the demised premises (in that case a farm), says:

"If the lease had been of a dwelling house and a fire had occurred by which the roof had been burned off, and the tenant had gone away as the defendant did without a word to his landlord, and the landlord had thereupon put a new roof on the house, and had or had not (it matters not which) placed a caretaker in charge, his doing this could not be an eviction. It would be properly referable to his right to preserve his property, and it would not alter the case, if under his lease the tenant were bound to repair, without excepting accidents by fire."

Upon the whole it appears to me that the appeal should be allowed.

HAGARTY, C. J. O., and BURTON, J.A., concurred.

PATTERSON, J. A.—I do not dissent from the judgment proposed by my learned brothers, though I cannot free myself from a strong impression that the learned Judge was right when he held that there was evidence on which the respondents had a right to have the opinion of the jury.

The plaintiffs let the house to the mercantile firm of Shepard & Wilson, knowing that it was for the purposes of their business that they took it.

Then Wilson retires, and the firm becomes Shepard & Disher, from whom the plaintiffs regularly receive the rent.

Then Shepard retires, and Disher alone remains.

The plaintiffs knew of these changes.

They once drew on Shepard & Disher for rent, but the draft was dishonored.

An alteration was made in the premises at the request of Disher.

When a fire occurred and repairs had to be done it was from Disher that the key was obtained, and to him it was returned.

During all this time no reference is made by or on behalf of the plaintiffs to Wilson, and there is no direct evidence that the plaintiffs, who were informed that Wilson had sold out to Disher, supposed Disher to be sub-tenant of Wilson or of Shepard & Wilson.

I should have thought these facts sufficient to submit to the jury on the question whether the plaintiffs had not accepted Disher, or Shepard & Disher, as their tenants in lieu of Shepard & Wilson.

The evidence might not be of the strongest, and it is encountered by some other evidence, so that on the whole one may feel that the verdict ought to be for the plaintiffs, though on a full discussion a jury might not come to that conclusion. It is with much hesitation that I concur in the judgment allowing the appeal.

Appeal allowed, with costs,

RACE v. ANDERSON ET AL.

Arbitration—Evidence secretly communicated to arbitrator.

In the conduct of arbitrations the rule is inflexible that the arbitrators must be scrupulously guarded against any possible charge of unfair dealing towards either party ; therefore where one of the parties·to a reference, who had been examined as a witness, after the evidence had been closed and the matter argued, sent by mail his affidavit explaining some portion of his evidence, to the arbitrator, but which was not received by him until after he had written out the view in accordance with which he subsequently made his award ; the Court affirmed the judgment of the Court below setting aside the award.

THIS was an action commenced in the County Court of Perth by Thomas H. Race against John Anderson and George Hudson, the statement of claim in which set forth that the defendants had made a promissory note for $250 in favor of Adam Ballentine, which was by him assigned to plaintiff and which remained unpaid.

The defendant filed a statement of defence denying all the allegations in the statement of claim ; alleging that the plaintiff was not the lawful holder ; that there was not any consideration for making said note, and the same was assigned to plaintiff without consideration ; that such note was an accommodation note, and that the payee Adam Ballentine was the beneficial plaintiff.

The action was tried at the County Court Sittings on the 12th June, 1885, before Judge Lizars, and a jury, when Adam Ballentine was added as a party plaintiff, and a verdict was given for the plaintiff subject to the award of A. M. McKinnon, Esq., Master at Guelph, who on the 30th September, 1885, made his award in favor of the plaintiff, increasing the verdict entered for him to $134.10, and ordering the defendants to pay the costs of the reference.

On the 6th November following Anderson gave notice of appeal from said award, on several grounds, amongst others that (the 4th) set forth in the present judgment.

After hearing counsel for all parties, the learned Judge
on the 6th of April, 1886, set aside the award, observing
in the course of his judgment as follows :

"The 4th objection seems to me under the authority of *Waters* v. *Daly*,
2 P. R. 202 ; *McEdwards* v. *Gordon*, 12 Gr. 333, and the cases of *Walker*
v. *Frobisher* ; *Dobson* v. *Groves, &c.*, to be fatal, and that the award cannot be upheld. The receipt by the referee of Hudson's letter and affidavit are exactly in point with the facts which governed the decision in
McEdwards v. *Gordon.* The award of the referee will therefore be set
aside, as in *Herring and Napanee, Tamworth, and Quebec R. W. Co.*, 5
O. R. 359, with costs."

The plaintiff thereupon appealed to this Court, alleging
the following, amongst other grounds therefor :

(1) That the arbitrator had prepared his written judgment before he received the affidavit of the defendant
Hudson, and the award was prepared in accordance with
such judgment.

(2) That the said affidavit was sent to the arbitrator by
the defendant Hudson, through the post office, and it was
impossible for the arbitrator to know the contents of the
letter until he had opened it.

(3) That the receiving of the affidavit by the arbitrator
was not, under the circumstances, a receiving it in evidence
within the meaning of the cases ; and

(4) That the affidavit of the defendant Hudson, sent to
the arbitrator, should not under the circumstances and
manner in which it was received by the arbitrator, be permitted to defeat the plaintiff's claim ; and under the
circumstances could not invalidate the award.

The appeal came on to be heard before this Court on the
13th of September, 1886.*

Lash, Q. C., for the appellant.
Moss, Q. C., for the respondents.

In addition to the cases referred to in the judgment, *Re
Plews and Middleton*, 6 Q. B. 845, was cited.

November 4, 1886. The judgment of the court was
delivered by

Present.--HAGARTY, C.J.O., BURTON, PATTERSON, and OSLER, JJ.A.

HAGARTY, C. J. O.—This is an appeal from the decision of the learned Judge of the county of Perth, setting aside an award.

A reference by consent was made at the trial to Mr. McKinnon, Master of the High Court of Justice at Guelph.

He made his award, after much discussion of various accounts and dealings, against the defendants.

This award was moved against on several grounds. The 4th ground alone requires notice : "That the arbitrator received in evidence against defendant Anderson, the affidavit of defendant Hudson after the evidence had been taken on said reference, and the same argued."

On this objection the award was set aside.

The defendant Hudson was examined at some length at the reference, and there is no doubt but that his evidence was very material to the case.

Mr. McKinnon makes an affidavit in which he states that after taking all the evidence, he considered the case and prepared a written judgment of his findings ; after having done this (but before signing it) he received a letter from defendant Hudson :

"ARTHUR, ONT., SEPT. 9, 1885.
"A. M. McKINNON, ESQ.,
          "Master in H. C. J., Guelph.
                    "RACE vs. ANDERSON.
"DEAR SIR,—
    "On my examination before you on this matter my evidence seemed to be of an unsatisfactory nature, but I am now convinced that the evidence of A. Ballentine regarding the $200 and $100 cheques is right, and so take the liberty of sending down herewith my written affidavit to that effect.
                    "Yours truly,
                              "GEO. HUDSON."

He says he had no intimation of any intention to send this.

It came by post, and had he known its contents he would not have opened it, but having opened it could not help but discover the contents. That the affidavit enclosed in no way affected his award, he having previously come to a final determination on the matters, and his award would have been the same had the letter never been received, and he did not accept it as evidence or mark it filed. He says he would have returned it to Hudson had he not thought his motives might be misconstrued, and he thought it preferable to return it with the papers, so that he could not be blamed for concealing the fact of its being sent to him.

Neither party cast any reflection whatever on the good faith or honesty of purpose of the referee, and there is certainly nothing before us to warrant any such imputation. But we cannot but regard it as unfortunate that the referee did not, before executing his award, communicate to the parties interested, the fact of Hudson's communication, bearing as it did on a vital portion of the inquiry.

No principle is more important to be preserved intact than that which declares that every referee must scrupulously hold the balance evenly between litigant parties, and to hear nothing and know nothing (so far as is possible) urged or presented to him for or against one of the parties in the absence of the other, or without that other having the opportunity of knowing or answering it.

The language in *Russell* on Awards, ed., 1878, is worth quoting: "An arbitrator can hardly be too scrupulous in guarding against the possibility of being charged with not dealing equally with both parties. Neither side can be allowed to use any means of influencing his mind which are not known to and capable of being met and resisted by the other. As much as possible the arbitrator should decline to receive private communications from either litigant respecting the subject matter of the reference. It is a prudent course to make a rule of handing over to the opponent all written statements sent to him by a party, and to take care that no kind of communications concerning the points under discussion be made to him without giving information of it to the other side."

We may fully believe the referee's statement that he was not influenced by this communication. Lord Eldon's words in *Walker* v. *Frobisher*, 7 Ves. 70, cited by my brother Osler in *Cruickshank* v. *Corby*, 30 C. P. 480, are very much in point. "The arbitrator swears it had no effect upon his award. I believe him. He is a most respectable man. But I cannot from respect for any man do that which I cannot reconcile to general principles. A Judge may not take upon himself to say whether evidence improperly admitted had or had not an effect upon his mind. The award may have done perfect justice, but upon general principles it cannot be supported."

In the case before us it is known to the parties that sworn testimony bearing most materially upon the merits was submitted to the referee, and an award was made without the other parties having any knowledge of such fact or opportunity of objecting to it.

I think we must dismiss the appeal. In this particular case it may be somewhat of a hardship, but the leading principles that govern references to arbitration must be preserved inviolate.

I may refer to the Lord Chancellor's remarks in *Drew* v. *Drew and Leburn,* 2 Macq. at pp. 8 and 9, *Harvey* v. *Shelton,* 7. Beav. 455 ; *Cruickshank* v. *Corby,* 30 C. P. 466, and 5 A. R. 415.

Appeal dismissed, with costs.

MILLER v. CONFEDERATION LIFE INSURANCE COMPANY.

*Life insurance—Misstatement in application for—Suppression of facts—
  " Best of knowledge and belief"—Fresh corroborative evidence.*

M. applied to the defendants to effect an endowment policy on his life,
and received a printed form of application containing a number of
questions. Subjoined to the questions was a declaration which he
signed, to the effect that the foregoing answers were true to "the best of
his knowledge and belief," and that he agreed that this proposal and
declaration should be the basis of the contract, and that if any misstatements or suppression of facts were made in the said answers or in those
to the medical examiner the policy was to be absolutely void and all
moneys received as premiums forfeited. The policy recited the above
declaration as the basis of the contract. The medical examiner's report
did not propound any questions to be answered by the assured.
Among the questions and answers in the application were: " Have
either of your * * brothers * * ever had * * pulmonary * *
or any other constitutional disease ?" to which the answer was in the
negative. It appeared that one brother who had died at 17 was an
overgrown lad, and had spat blood several times, and that medical
men whom he had consulted had apparently thought lightly of the matter.
There was no evidence that he had died of pulmonary disease.
Another brother had also spat blood, but on consulting physicians they
  seemed to have thought there was nothing seriously wrong.
The assured was also asked whether he had " had any serious illness,
  local disease, or personal injury, and if so of what nature ?" The
  answer was, "broken leg in childhood ; confined to bed three days with
  a cold." It appeared the applicant was rendered permanently lame
  from the effects of the accident. About three years previous to his
  application the assured was thrown from a load of hay and sustained
  personal injuries for which he brought an action against the Township
  of S. Although bruised and shaken and incapacitated from work he
  fully recovered. All mention of this was omitted. He was also asked
  as to the medical men whom he had at any time consulted, and in his
  answer omitted the names of those attending him during the last mentioned accident.
Held, [affirming the judgment of the Q. B. D. 11 O. R. 120,] that it was
  not a misdirection to leave it to the jury to say whether the answers of
  the assured were reasonably fair and truthful to the best of his knowledge and belief. That the applicant's declaration was in all its parts
  governed by the qualification "to the best of my knowledge and
  belief ; " that the answers were not warranted to be absolutely accurate,
  and that there were no such misstatements or suppression of facts as
  would vitiate the policy.
Held, also, that the discovery of new evidence which was merely corroborative of evidence given at the former trial was no ground for a new
  trial. (HAGARTY, C. J. O., *hesitante.*)

THIS was an appeal by defendants from a judgment of
the Queen's Bench Division, reported 11 O. R. 120, where
and in the judgments herein the facts giving rise to the
action and the points decided are so clearly stated as to
render any further statement of them here unnecessary.

The appeal came on to be heard before this Court on the 11th November, 1886.*

S. H. Blake, Q.C., and *Alan Cassels* for the appellants. *McCarthy*, Q. C., and *McMichael*, Q.C., for respondents.

December 23, 1886.   HAGARTY, C. J. O.—We have first to determine the important legal question submitted to us by the defendants. It may be briefly stated to be this. Did the assured warrant the absolute truthfulness of his statements and answers, or, as plaintiffs contend was it only that his answers and statements were warranted to be made in good faith and in the honest belief of the assured in their truthfulness and accuracy ?

To the questions answered in the application the insured made this declaration.

I, the said George Miller, (the person whose life is to be insured) do hereby warrant and guarantee that the answers given to the above questions (all which questions I hereby declare that I have read or heard read) are true, to the best of my knowledge and belief; and I do hereby agree that this proposal shall be the basis of the contract between me and the said association, and I further agree that any misstatements or suppression of facts made in the answers to the questions aforesaid, or in my answers to be given to the medical examiner, shall render null and void the policy of insurance herein applied for, and forfeit all payments made thereon. It is also further agreed that should a policy be executed under this application, the same shall not be delivered or binding on the association until the first premium thereon shall be paid to a duly authorized agent of the association, during my lifetime and good health, I, (the party in whose favor the assurance is granted), do also hereby agree that this proposal and declaration shall be the basis of the contract between me and the said association. Dated at Markham this 5th day of December, 1883.

He was examined by the medical officer who sends in his report containing answers to seventeen questions which he gives after his examination of applicant.

Present—HAGARTY, C.J.O., BURTON, PATTERSON, and OSLER, JJ. A.

At the foot of the report is written ; " I hereby certify that I have made true, full, and complete answers to the questions propounded to me by the examining physician and I agree to accept the policy when issued on the terms mentioned in within application and to pay the association the premium thereon.

GEORGE MILLER,
Applicant.

Witness, J. R. TABOR, Examining Physician."

Dr. Tabor died before the trial, so we are wholly uninformed as to the form or nature of the statements made by the applicant to him or of the manner in which the information was elicited. The answers are the doctor's answers. The applicant then certifies in effect that he has truly answered whatever questions the doctor put to him.

I think it impossible to hold that there is any absolute warranty as to what is contained in this report. It would be making the assured, in effect, guaranteeing the correctness of the doctor's course of examination and the sufficiency of his questions and personal manipulations to ascertain the true state of the applicant and his freedom from disease or tendency thereto.

Then as to the applicant's own alleged absolute warranty of the truth of his answers, I am of opinion that the declaration is in all its parts governed by the qualification " to the best of my knowledge and belief."

Mr. Blake argued strongly that the subsequent part in which he agrees that any misstatement &c., made in the answers shall avoid the policy. I cannot agree in this. When he speaks of the answers he must be held to mean the answers that he has given in good faith so far as his knowledge or belief or information extended. I do not think any ordinary man making such a declaration would not so understand it.

It is clear that parties may if they please contract for the absolute truth of answers given and statements made on an application for insurance, and the recent case of *Thomson* v. *Weems*, 9 App. Cas. 671 in the Lords, clearly and fully points this out. But the language must be intelligibly clear in such a case. The late Chief Justice Cockburn, in 1863, in *Fowkes* v. *Manchester Assurance Association*, 3 B. & S. 923, laid down principles of construction which have never I think been questioned, and govern this case. It is a judgment frequently cited both here and in England.

In *Thomson* v. *Weems*, Lord Blackburn quotes Lord St. Leonards's words in *Anderson* v. *Fitzgerald*, 4 H. L. C. at p. 507, and says that " before a contract is held to have the effect of a warranty it is necessary to see that the language is such as to shew that the assured as well as the insurers meant it, and that the language in the policy being that of the insurers if there is any ambiguity it must be construed most strongly against them."

This question has been dealt with in the judgments of the learned Judges of the Queen's Bench Division and I need not further discuss it.

This view of the law disposes of most of the objections taken in the rule for new trial bearing on the directions given to the jury.

It was further complained that the learned Judge did not direct that the written statement or affidavit of the insured in his action against the Township of Scarborough should be taken as conclusive proof of the truthfulness of the facts therein stated : this objection is untenable. The jury had not here to consider whether the deceased did or did not in bad faith try to impose on the township as to the extent of his injuries. The evidence of the doctor who then attended him strongly led to the conclusion that he had exaggerated his alleged injuries. It was proper evidence to submit to the jury as an admission made by assured. As to the materiality of the alleged misstatements, the direction on this point was as follows :

HIS LORDSHIP—" What I tell you, gentlemen of the jury, is this : If you think there is anything in these answers which was calculated to mislead the defendants and induce them to enter into the contract, when they otherwise would not have done it, then your verdict should be for the defendants. But, if on the other hand, you think the answers reasonably fair and truthful, to the best of the knowledge and belief of the man, I think your verdict should be for the plaintiffs."

I do not think this can be complained of.

On the remaining branch of the case we have to consider the application for a new trial on the weight of evidence and the alleged discovery of fresh evidence. If the Court of Queen's Bench had in its discretion granted a new trial on payment of costs, I think, on the whole, I should have been better satisfied. I think the evidence obtained from Manitoba after the trial should, under the circumstances, be received if another trial were ordered, and might be important.

Only two Judges heard the case. The learned Chief Justice considered that a new trial should be granted. Mr. Justice Armour held otherwise. The evidence has been fully discussed in the judgments delivered below. To grant a new trial to defendants would in all probability be of little service to them, as the nature of the case and its circumstances would probably place them in a disadvantageous position before the jury.

My learned brothers, as I understand, think that there should not be a new trial. I do not positively dissent from that view, but, as already expressed, I would feel better satisfied with a different result.

BURTON, J. A.—The defendants place their appeal upon three grounds. 1st. That there was misdirection on the part of the learned Judge in holding that the statement in the declaration " that any misstatements or suppression of facts in the answers to the questions in the application, or in the answers to be given to the medical examiner, shall render the policy null and void," was not an absolute warranty on the part of the assured, but was qualified by the words in the earlier portion of the declaration in which he warranted that his answers to the questions contained in the application were true " to the best of his knowledge and belief." 2nd. On the ground that, even assuming it not to be an absolute warranty, the answers given were so manifestly untrue that no other conclusion can be fairly drawn than that they were wilfully untruthful representations or suppressions, and that the verdict should on that account be set aside and a new trial granted.   3rd. On the ground of the discovery of new evidence.

I propose to deal with these in their order.

I think that one of the cases relied on by the defendants counsel is, when properly considered, a most conclusive authority against the contention that these statements must be regarded as unqualified and absolute warranties. I refer to the case of *Fowkes* v. *The Manchester, &c., Ins. Co.*, 3. B. & S. 917.

There the language of the policy was that if any state-ment in the declaration was "untrue" the policy shall be void.   This was the language of the completed contract, the policy itself, not of the preliminary negotiations leading up to the contract, but of the contract itself; and it was there contended that the policy was the true statement of the contract between the parties, and, therefore, that a statement which the company had shewn its intention to make material by inquiring about it, being untrue, neces-sarily avoided the contract.   But, it was answered, the declaration is declared to be as much part of the policy as if it had been set forth therein; and therefore to ascertain the meaning of the words, if any "statement in the declara-tion is untrue," you had to refer to the declaration itself, and reading those words with the light thrown upon them by the declaration the true construction of the language of the company was, that in order to avoid the policy the statement must be designedly untrue, that is, untrue to the knowledge of the assured.

There also, as here, there were passages in the declara-tion itself which were apparently inconsistent; first, that if any statement was untrue it should avoid the policy and create a forfeiture of all premiums paid; untrue meaning primâ facie inaccurate, not wilfully false.   The question was whether, looking at the whole instrument, it was to be taken in that sense.

The Court, there, in applying the rules of construction
refer to a very well known rule that in all deeds and
instruments the language used by one party is to be
construed in the sense in which it would be reasonably
understood by the other. The declaration thus far meant,
primâ facie, that any statement which was untrue in the
sense of being inaccurate was intended, and when the
assured agreed that that should be the basis of the contract, that made it a warranty. But following it were these
words : " And if it shall hereafter appear that any fraudulent concealment or designedly untrue statement be contained therein the policy shall be void."

It will be seen that the declaration there varies from the
declaration in the case before us in this, that in this one
the declaration commences with a reference to a statement
which if untrue to the knowledge and belief of the party,
shall vitiate the policy, followed by others not in terms so
restricted.

In the case from which I am quoting the warranty
seems to be in terms unrestricted, but is followed by the
words relating to fraudulent concealment. And how is it
dealt with ? " I think a common person," says Lord
Blackburn, " reading this declaration would read ' and,'
at the beginning of the last clause, as pointing out the consequence of an untrue statement just as if it had begun
' so that if it shall hereafter appear, &c., the policy shall be
void,' so that the declaration when read as a whole meant
only that if there was a designedly untrue statement the
policy should be void, and not otherwise."

Cazenove v. *The British Equitable*, 6 C. B. N. S. 437,
was very different. There the condition was, that the
policy should be void in case any fraudulent or untrue
statement was contained in any of the documents. The
statement being untrue was held to vitiate the policy. But
I see that at least one of the Judges also held it to be
fraudulently untrue.

Of course if parties enter into contracts of that nature
they must be bound by them, but I think that most insurance companies have in recent times adopted the advice ten-

dered to them by Lord St. Leonards, in *Anderson* v. *Fitz-gerald*, 4 H. L. at p. 514. where he pointed out the unfairness of issuing policies such as it is now contended this policy is, but which we hold it is not: " I think," he says, " it is very important to impress upon companies that they ought not to issue policies in this shape, and I think they would do well if they were to place the word ' wilful ' before the word false statement in that last branch of the clause. So, if it is their intention to exclude materiality, I think it would be but honest and fair so to state upon the face of their policies, so that persons who are really not competent to form a judgment upon such question may at once upon the face of the policy see what risks they run, for remember that the proviso inflicts upon the family the loss not only of the sum assured but of all the sums, possibly a great portion of the savings of a man's life, which have been paid for the policy itself."

I think these remarks apply equally to the answers given to the medical examiner, the words, " to your knowledge and belief," applying equally to them, but there is the further difficulty that there is no evidence before the Court of what these answers were. The medical officer has noted what he takes to be the result of the information he elicited by inquiry from the assured, and the assured has certified that he gave him true answers to the questions propounded to him, but what those questions and answers were we can only gather inferentially.

I agree, therefore, that the learned Judge was correct in holding that in point of law the answers were not warranted to be absolutely accurate. Whether they were wilfully or intentionally false, false to the knowledge of the assured, and intended to misrepresent matters to the company, is another question ; and upon that the onus probandi is upon the company, who are, of course, entitled to be protected not only against intentional frauds but against any wilful misstatements in reply to questions which they deem material to be considered in deciding upon the risk ; but then the jury are the proper parties to decide these questions under a proper direction.

It was urged with great force, and the argument is entitled, no doubt, to very great weight, that it is almost impossible to believe that the assured intended to defraud the company by palming off upon them a bad life, from the circumstance that he, so far from urging the company to take the risk, did everything in his power to be relieved from the contract, and from the further fact that he was not insuring in the expectation that the money would in the course of a short time be payable to his family, but on the endowment plan under which the insurance money would on his attaining a certain age be payable to himself, for which he paid a much higher rate of premium.

The first answer complained of is that in reply to 13 B.: " Have either of your grandparents, uncles, aunts, brothers, or sisters ever been insane or had pulmonary, scrofulous, or any other constitutional disease ? " He replied in the negative.

Considering the class of persons of whom such inquiries are frequently made, I think the question might have been framed in terms to be more easily understood. Every one knows of what in common parlance is styled " consumption," which a great many medical men would even in the witness box speak of as phthisis, but it would be farcical so to describe it in a question of this kind to be answered by an ordinary applicant for assurance the describing it however under the general head of pulmonary disease is scarcely less open to objection.

But it is urged that this answer is untrue because one of the brothers did, it is alleged die, from pulmonary disease, and another had been under medical treatment for it. This of course would be no answer unless there was evidence that the assured knew it.

The evidence seems to shew that the brother who died did feel some uneasiness about his health some years before and that he spat blood three times and consulted Dr. Aikins about it, but Dr. Aikins treated the matter lightly, and told him it was a slight inflamation of his right lung, and that he could get rid of it without much trouble.

There is no evidence that William did die from pulmonary disease, nor that the answer made by the assured " that he did not know but he thought it was from growing too fast" was not strictly true; it was ample to put the company upon inquiry ; no objection can be taken to the way in which that question was left to the jury or with the jury's finding [upon it, no other finding could have been correct.

As to the other brother the evidence is if anything weaker; he, too, had been spitting blood on two or three occasions about twelve years previously, and went into town to consult Dr. Aikins who was absent from the country, and he was examined by a gentleman who had charge of his practice in his absence who told him that as far as he could see there was nothing the matter with him he awaited the return of Dr. Aikins and then consulted him who does not appear to have thought that there was anything seriously the matter with him, and Dr. Aikins is not called.

It is difficult to see how the jury could truthfully have said there was any misstatement in that answer.

Then as to the answers as to his own health.

He was asked : "Whether he had had any serious illness, local disease, or personal injury, and if so of what nature ?" It is to be noted that the question differs from that contained in the application in *Moore* v. *Connecticut,* 41 U.C.R. 497 ; 3 A. R. 250; 6 S. C. R. 624; 6 App. Cas. 644; where the word " serious " was omitted, and where the warranty was more absolute in its character than the present.

In the case of *Insurance Co.* v. *Wilkinson,* 13 Wallace 222, the question of the meaning " serious personal injury" was much discussed, it being contended that if the applicant had at any time received a serious personal injury, although he had entirely recovered from its effects, the omission to disclose it was a breach of the warranty.

The Court below refused to place such a construction upon it, saying, the idea is that such a construction is to be put by the courts upon the language as an ordinary person

of common understanding would put upon it when addressed
to him for answer. The strict construction which would
make the word " any " an indefinite term so as to include
all injuries, even the most trifling, would bring a just
reproach upon the courts, the law, the company itself, and
its business.

The Supreme Court in affirming the decision, whilst
deciding that the mere fact that an injury was deemed
serious at the time was not in itself sufficient to render its
mention necessary, held, on the other hand, that when a
question arises on a trial the jury, and not the insurer,
must decide whether the injury was serious or not. In
deciding this were they to reject the evidence of the ultimate effect of the injury on the party's health, and other
similar considerations ?   That would be to leave out of
view the essential purpose of the inquiry, and the very
matters which would throw most light on the nature of
the injury with reference to its influence on the insurable
character of the life proposed.

Looking then at the purpose for which the information
was sought, and the difficulty of answering whether an
injury was serious in any other manner than by reference to its permanent or temporary influence on the
health, strength or longevity of the party, the Court held
that the Judge properly directed the jury that the language
was to have a reasonable construction in view of the purpose for which the question was asked, and must have
reference to such an accidental injury as probably would
or might possibly have influenced the subsequent health or
longevity of the assured.

The answer of the assured in the present case was :
" Broken leg in childhood ; confined to bed three days with
a cold ; " and it was shewn that the applicant was rendered
permanently lame from the effects of the broken leg.

It is contended that he had about three years before met
with a serious accident, for which he had brought an action
against the township of Scarborough, and that the omission
to mention this could not have been otherwise than
intentional.

It does not, however, appear that he was at the time of the application suffering from the effects of the accident, and although it was strongly urged to the jury that in his own sworn statement on his examination in the suit he instituted against the township of Scarborough he had spoken of it as a serious accident, the medical man who attended him does not appear to have so regarded it, and it was a question for the jury to say whether it was or was not a serious accident.

Questions 17 and 18 may be considered together. In the first of these he is asked for the name and residence of his usual medical attendant, and on what occasions and for what diseases have his attendance and advice been required.

In reply he gave the name of Dr. Tabor, adding " for a cold." I do not understand the paragraph in brackets following the word "required," as part of the inquiry, but an intimation to the assured that a non-compliance with what is there referred to might cause delay.

In the question immediately following he is asked whether he had consulted any other medical man. If so, for what and when, to which he answered: "Dr. Aikins, of Toronto, examined me when I was sick from cold." I do not see how these answers can be fairly objected to. Dr. Tabor was his usual medical attendant, and it is true, as we have seen, that he, whilst attended by him, went to consult Dr. Aikins. He is not asked whether he had at any time been attended by any other medical man, but whether he had consulted any medical man.

Even if I did not fully agree with the jury in the conclusion at which they have arrived that would be no reason for interfering with the verdict, so to do would be in fact to substitute the Court for the jury.

I agree also with the Court below that the evidence said to have been discovered since the trial is not new evidence, as that term is understood in this connection; the same facts were before the jury, and all that can be said is that the facts referred to in the affidavit of the assured now relied on would be corroborative of those sworn to by Dr. Knill and other witnesses.

I agree therefore that no sufficient ground has been shewn for depriving the plaintiffs of their verdict and granting a new trial.

The appeal should in my judgment be dismissed.

PATTERSON, J. A.—The plaintiffs are the executors, the widow and the children of George Miller.

They seek to recover the amount of an endowment policy for $10,000 effected by George Miller with the defendants on the 5th of January, 1884.

George Miller died on the 14th of August, 1884, in Manitoba. He had lived in this Province in the township of Markham until after the date of the policy.

The defendants resist the action on the ground of incorrect and untrue answers by the insured to questions contained in the application papers. In their statement of defence they make many charges of falsehood and bad faith, which it would serve no purpose to refer to in much detail, because the greater part of them are not at all borne out by the evidence. We may confine our attention to those brought specifically before us in the reasons of appeal, where they are thus set out :

(a). That none of his brothers or sisters ever had pulmonary or any other constitutional disease. (Application 13 B, medical report 8 and 10 A).

(b). That he had had no serious illness, local disease or personal injury, except a broken leg in childhood and an illness of three days from cold. (Application 14 A, medical report 11).

(c). That his usual medical attendant was one Dr. Tabor, and that he had been attended by him for a cold, and that he had not required the services of a physician, except as aforesaid, for the past seven years or for any serious illness during that period. (Application 17).

(d). That he had not consulted any other medical man except one Dr. Aikins, who examined him while suffering from the cold. (Application 18).

(e). That no material fact bearing upon his physical condition or family history had been omitted in the foregoing questions and the answers thereto. (Application 20).

It is contended for the defendants that the applicant under their contract warrants absolutely the truth of his answers to the questions which he is himself required to answer, and also the truth of answers to questions framed for the medical examiner and contained in a document called the Medical Examiner's Report. But that document does not propound any questions to be answered by the applicant. It has nearly three dozen questions for the physician to answer, as to many of which he must necessarily form his opinion and frame his answers from information obtained from the applicant during his examination of him; and it is undoubtedly important and necessary to secure truthful answers to all questions which the physician may ask. The applicant is therefore required to certify that he has made true, full, and complete answers to the questions propounded to him by the examining physician. He did so certify in this case, but we have no information concerning the questions put by the physician, and consequently no evidence that the applicant gave any untrue, evasive or incomplete answer to that officer.

We may therefore lay aside this paper and look only at the other which contains the questions required to be answered in writing by the applicant himself.

It is dated at Markham, the 5th day of December, 1883.

It contains an undertaking by the applicant in these words:

"I, the said George Miller, (the person whose life is to be insured) do hereby warrant and guarantee that the answers given to the above questions (all which questions I hereby declare that I have read or heard read) are true, to the best of my knowledge and belief; and I do hereby agree that this proposal shall be the basis of the contract between me and the said association; and I further agree that any misstatements or suppression of facts made in the answers to the questions aforesaid, or in my answers to be given to the medical examiner, shall render null and void the policy of insurance herein applied for, and forfeit all payments made thereon."

The defendants argue that this contains a warranty of the absolute truth of every statement contained in the answers, but that argument cannot for a moment be acceded to. It is not pushed to the length of denying all force to the phrase " to the best of my knowledge and belief ;" but it is urged that the terms " misstatements or suppression of facts " must be read without qualification.

But to do so would be to separate those words from the context, for which there is neither reason nor necessity. The language is that of the party seeking to enforce the contract, and we must be satisfied that the sense in which we are asked to enforce it is that in which the other party understood it when the contract was made.

The undertaking is one undertaking, and not two. In the first part of it the applicant defines the extent to which he warrants and guarantees the truth of his answers. They are to be true to the best of his knowledge and belief. In the latter part he discloses what shall be the consequence of a breach of that engagement, namely, the avoidance of the policy and forfeiture of his payments, whether he has stated what he knew to be false or sup- pressed what he knew to be true.

It may be scarcely necessary to say that this undertaking, understood as I agree with my learned brothers in this court and in the court below in interpreting it, is sufficient to demand from the applicant the uberrima fides which is insisted on in one of the reasons of appeal. That the defendants, in framing the undertaking in this form, went as far as was required for their protection is shewn by the case of *Roe* v. *Bradshaw*, L. R. 1 Ex. 106, where it was held that when one swears to the best of his knowledge and belief, his statement imports that he is entitled to entertain the belief he expresses.

The answers alleged to be untrue and dishonest, though enunciated in the reasons of appeal as five separate answers, and though they are in fact answers to five ques- tions, really cover only two subjects, one touching the family history of the applicant, and the other his own history.

He was asked (question 12) about his brothers, and, after four answers which are not impeached, answered that one was dead ; and then to the question " at what age and of what disease did he die ? " he replied " 17 years of age : can't say : he was over-grown." This was followed by question 13 B : " Have either of your grand-parents, uncles, aunts, brothers, or sisters ever been insane, or had pulmonary, scrofulous, or any other constitutional disease ? " to which he answered " No."

It appears that the brother William, who died at 17, and who was an overgrown lad, had at some time or other been spitting blood. From this it is contended that he had a pulmonary disease which ought to have been stated in answer to question 13 B.

It is impossible to say as a proposition of law that spitting blood imports pulmonary disease. I believe the only evidence touching the matter, as a question of fact, is that of Dr. Knill, who said that bleeding of the lungs was, or indicated, pulmonary disease.

The defendants did not go so far as to expressly prove that the blood spat by the brother came from his lungs. It seems probable that it did, and there are some things in the evidence that suggest the belief that the insured was of that opinion. The idea conveyed by what is said is that William may have burst a blood vessel. There is no medical evidence, nor indeed any direct evidence at all, of the cause of his death or of the nature of his constitution. He is said to have grown too fast. The plaintiff John Miller speaks of that. But that was disclosed in the application, and was there stated in reply to the question about his death, which would seem to have been sufficient to put the defendants upon inquiry.

The objection taken is not that the cause of the brother's death was not disclosed, but that it was untruly stated that he had never had a pulmonary disease. This objection does not give sufficient weight to the terms in which the question 13 B is framed, and which make it clear that it relates only to constitutional diseases, and moreover to such constitutional diseases as may be hereditary.

The term "pulmonary" is etymologically extensive enough to include every disease of the lungs however slight and however temporary, just as the term "personal injury" is appropriate to a black eye as well as to a broken skull; but when the defendants contend for that wide interpretation in this place, and particularly when they at the same time insist that the answers are warranties—on which principle your policy might be forfeited by the discovery that your grandfather, who lived to be a hale octogenarian, had in his schoolboy days been laid up for a week with inflammation of the lungs—the extravagance of the result makes it proper to observe closely the true purport of the question.

You are asked respecting "pulmonary, scrofulous or other constitutional disease," in other words constitutional disease whether pulmonary, scrofulous or of any other type; and the reference to ancestors and collateral relatives proves that the diseases pointed at are also hereditary diseases, a characteristic which would itself shew that only constitutional diseases are meant.

I can find nothing in the report before us, either in the shape of a statement of fact or a scientific opinion upon facts in evidence, proper in my judgment to support a finding that the young man suffered from consumption or from any other constitutional disease. So to hold from the bare fact that at some time he bled from the lungs would be to act on conjecture and not upon evidence.

When I say the bare fact that he bled from the lungs, I do not forget that his death is attributed on the part of the plaintiffs, or was attributed by the insured, to his growing too fast. If we assume, as common knowledge, that a lad of seventeen, or under, who grows too tall, will probably be of a weaker constitution, and more liable to such misadventures as the bursting of a blood vessel, than a boy of a different physique, that would not be enough to entitle us to pronounce him a sufferer from constitutional disease; but whatever overgrowth may imply, it implied for the information of the defendants when they read the answer to question 12.

John Miller, the plaintiff, who is a brother of the insured, is said also to have had attacks of pulmonary disease in the form of colds, for which he took medical advice, and some twelve years ago he spat blood. I need not go into the details of the evidence on this point, because it falls short of shewing constitutional disease; the doctor whom he consulted was not called; his ailments whatever they were, are not brought home to the knowledge of the insured; and when the idea of the asserted warranty is laid aside, the evidence ceases to be material.

The fact that three brothers had hæmorrhage from the lungs is certainly suggestive of a family tendency to pulmonary weakness; but the evidence, when applied to the issue on this record, not only falls short of what the defendants require, but is in one respect singularly strong against them. I find this in the letter from the manager to the medical examiner of 12th December, 1883, and the answer to it of 1st January, 1884, respecting the cold — or as the defendants would now express it, the pulmonary disease— which the applicant then had or recently had had; proving that attention was specially given to this particular subject before the application was accepted; and in the evidence given by John Miller that after he himself had had hæmorrhage more than once, Dr. Aikins examined him and said that as far as he could tell there was nothing the matter with him, and that Dr. Aikins had also examined the insured and, as John expresses it, "sounded him all over and said there was nothing wrong with him." Dr. Aikins was not called.

The incident in the history of the insured himself which it is charged he ought to have disclosed is an accident in 1880, when he was thrown from a load of hay, and sustained personal injuries for which he brought an action against the township of Scarborough. He appears to have been a good deal shaken and bruised, but fortunately

broke no bones, and although incapacitated for some time
for work by reason, amongst other things, of a pain in his
back caused by the fall, he fully recovered. He set forth
his injuries in a deposition in the action against the township, and if, as seems to be conceded, he rather exaggerated
them, I see no sound reason for allowing it now to be
asserted in favor of his representatives that what he said
was not substantially true. Still it is only evidence to be
dealt with along with whatever other evidence there is
upon the issue on the personal injury question. It indicates
that he thought he was seriously if not permanently injured;
but Dr. Lapsley, who attended him for a few days after
the accident, did not think that he was so much hurt as
he supposed; and the event justified the doctor's opinion,
and demonstrated also that the injuries did not permanently affect the health of the insured. Dr. Armstrong,
who also attended him, died before this action.

The question is: " 14. A. Have you had any serious illness, local disease or personal injury, and if so, of what
nature?" and the answer: " Broken leg in childhood. Confined to bed three days from a cold."

We may not be able to fully understand why all mention of the accident is omitted. It is not possible, to me at
all events, to suppose it was forgotten. Yet the case is by
no means one for assuming mala fides or even for feeling
very strongly that a jury ought to find that the question
was not answered to the best of the knowledge and belief
of the party interrogated. I am not prepared to lay it
down that the accident ought to have been mentioned,
though I think it would have been better to do so, and
should have expected to find it done.

The question, it will be noticed, is not the same as in
applications like that discussed in *Moore* v. *Connecticut
M. L. I. Co.*, 41 U. C. R. 497; 3 A. R. 230; 6 S. C. R. 634;
6 App. Cas. 644, where the applicant after answering to a
long list of specific diseases, is asked: " Have you had any
other illness, local disease or personal injury? And if so,
of what nature? How long since, and what effect on
general health?"

Here the inquiry is only respecting *serious* illness, local disease, or personal injury. The word "serious" qualifies all the three subjects, as is, I think, plain enough from reading the question, and is confirmed by looking at the report of the medical examiner, who is asked, "Has the person ever had any serious injury or illness ?"

Now, as the result of the evidence is that whatever George Miller may have thought or said of himself when he was examined in his action against the township over three years before he effected this policy, he was not seriously injured by his fall, it is difficult to perceive any difference in principle, or any important difference in degree, between this fall from the load of hay, all bad effects of which were gone before the insurance, and any one of the accidents by which boys may be lamed for a day or two, such as the upset of a coasting sleigh. In neither case is the injury serious or severe.

It is worth while to observe that, no reason appearing for surmising that the fall had left any injurious effect, there can have been no indirect motive in omitting to state it, to which may be added an observation made in the court below that the accident and the lawsuit must have been well known to the local agent of the defendants who was present when the application was filled up. The local agent was not called as a witness, and Dr. Tabor the medical examiner is dead. The doctor probably also knew of the accident ; but if he did, and if he knew that whatever harm it had done was only temporary, and was never serious, it would be unreasonable to expect him to put it into his report as a severe injury. He would have done just what he did, that is, mention the broken leg which had lamed Miller for life, and say nothing of the upset.

The objection that when interrogated respecting the medical men whom he had at any time "consulted," the applicant made no mention of Dr. Lapsley or Dr. Armstrong who attended him on the occasion of the fall from the load of hay can scarcely be considered on this motion, except in connection with the charge for omitting to mention the accident itself.

The question ought to have been answered fully, notwithstanding that it may not have been necessary to class
the accident as a serious or severe personal injury.

But the practical point at present is whether the issue
upon the charge of not fully answering to the best of the
applicant's knowledge and belief has been properly disposed
of, or should be sent back to another jury.

The doctors, Lapsley and Armstrong, were no doubt
" consulted " within the meaning of the question : " Have
you consulted any other medical man ? If so, for what
and when ? "—and the boy upset while coasting down hill
would literally " consult " the doctor if he asked him to
feel if his leg was broken ; but it would be hopeless to
expect a jury to find bad faith in omitting to name the
doctor, if the occasion of the attendance or consultation was
excusably omitted from the answer to the question respecting serious or severe injuries.

The rule nisi in the Court below was for a new trial for
misdirection, and on the law and evidence, and also by
reason of the discovery of new evidence. It also asked
for a nonsuit or judgment for the defendants, but those
alternatives must have got there per incuriam.

At the trial several objections to the charge of the
learned Judge were taken ; one contention, if not the main
contention, being the same which has been insisted on
before us, based on the assumed warranty of the absolute
truth of the answers in the application paper.   That
objection was, as I have shewn, untenable.

The defendants seem to have charged that the answers
were not only untrue but were fraudulently untrue. I am
not sure that this is in direct terms charged in the pleadings.
It is so in one of the reasons of appeal, and I therefore
suppose it must have been so urged before the jury. If
that supposition is correct it will probably account for the
stress which the learned Judge seems, from the reporter's
note of his charge, to have once or twice laid on the question whether the applicant wilfully misrepresented or
suppressed the facts. According to my reading of the

contract, the question for the jury was, whether the impeached answers were true to the best of the party's knowledge and belief. It may be difficult to distinguish that question from the question of fraudulent misrepresentation or concealment; and having regard to the actual contest upon the question of the warranty, which was the burden of the objections taken at the trial and renewed in the rule, I should be at a loss to lay my finger on any material passage in the charge which the defendants can reasonably complain of as misdirection, and still more at a loss to find a reason for supposing that any substantial wrong or miscarriage has been occasioned by the charge.

This is a fortiori the case if I am right in considering that the defendants made no case for the jury except upon the rather collateral and unimportant issue of the omission to insert the names of Drs. Lapsley and Armstrong in one of the answers.

I do not see this last point noted as an objection taken specifically to the charge, though it is perhaps included in the general contention as to warranty, which is the ground on which it finds a place in the rule nisi.

For the reasons I have given, and without entering upon a discussion of the authorities which have been noticed in the Court below and by his lordship the Chief Justice and my brother Burton, I am of opinion that the verdict and judgment ought not to be disturbed.

The judgment of the Judicial Committee of the Privy Council in *Moore* v. *Connecticut M. L. Ins. Co.*, which will be found in 6 S. C. R. 695, as well as in 6 App. Cas. 644, will be found to afford ample authority for this disposition of the case.

Then as to the so-called newly discovered evidence.

It would probably have been objected to, and very likely with success, if it had come a day or two sooner and had been tendered at the trial.

The application papers bear the dates 5th and 6th of December, 1883. The applicant answered the questions about his health as of the first of those dates. The new

evidence consists of his declarations made more than four
months later, *i. e.*, on the 15th of April, 1884, concerning
his inability to travel with safety by reason of a cold
caught some time in March, apparently after the middle of
the month.   Dr. Knill gives the 19th as the day of his first
visit to him, and Miller's affidavit mentions the 20th as the
day on which he had proposed to start for Manitoba.

There is also a letter written on the 25th of April, 1884,
by Miller, in which, referring to an application for a permit about the 1st of July, 1883, he said: " I have been
sick nearly all the time since, and had to stay, after having my car loaded on March 19th, 1884."

The defendants wish to use these papers as evidence
that Miller must have been in bad health on the 5th of
December, 1883.   But they had investigated that very matter before they accepted the application.   The illness of the
preceding summer had been mentioned by Miller, and
nothing could well be stronger evidence of his recovery
from it than Dr. Tabor's letter of 1st January, 1884,
on the subject:

" His constitution is better than our average of to-day's
young men and I think a good risk.   With regard to the
cold, I have taken special notice, both before and since
your note, and made thorough enquiry.   He had been
breaking a colt and got pretty warm, so the reaction was
the cold referred to.   I have again examined him, he can
expand fully five inches in forced respiration."

This is in perfect accord with the affidavit when it
describes the illness that made it dangerous to undertake
the journey in cold weather as having been contracted in
March, 1884.

Apart from this, I am not satisfied that this is new
evidence the discovery of which should afford ground for
a new trial.   The defendants had at the trial Dr. Knill's
direct evidence of the very facts stated in the affidavit;
and it is by no means satisfactorily shewn that with
reasonable diligence on the part of the gentlemen who
acted in Manitoba for the defendants, the documents would
not have been found in good time for use at the trial.   But

the nature of the evidence itself would certainly not warrant the granting of a new trial merely to enable the defendants to tender it.

I think the appeal should be dismissed.

OSLER, J. A.—I do not think it necessary to add anything to what has been said, having arrived at the opinion after a careful examination of the case, that the appeal should be dismissed, for the reasons assigned by my brother Armour in the Court below, and in the judgment of my brother Patterson, which I have had an opportunity of reading.

Appeal dismissed, with costs.

[This case has been since carried to the Supreme Court.]

WOODRUFF v. McLENNAN.

Foreign judgment, action upon—Defence—False swearing by plaintiff at original trial—Rejection of evidence of.

In an action upon a foreign judgment the defence was that the same had been recovered by reason of the plaintiff fraudulently misleading the court at the trial by swearing to what he knew to be untrue. The matter in dispute was a claim for extra services in hauling logs for a greater distance than required by a written contract, and the contest was upon the question whether the services were or not within the terms of that contract. On this question the evidence of the plaintiff and of one of the defendants, and of other witnesses, was given at the trial in the foreign court, when the contract and certain letters were put in, and the judge's charge to the jury shewed that the whole evidence had been clearly brought to the attention of the court, and it was now sought to establish the falsehood of the plaintiff's evidence with regard to the claim for extra services.

Held, [affirming the judgment of the Common Pleas Division, BURTON, J. A., dissenting] that evidence under the defence was properly rejected at the trial; for what the defendants proposed to do was to try over again the very question which was in issue in the original action. The charge of fraud was superadded, but that charge involved the assertion that a falsehood was knowingly stated, and before the question of scienter was reached a conclusion of fact adverse to that which had been arrived at by the foreign jury would have to be adopted.

Per BURTON, J. A.—In admitting evidence under the defence the court would not be assuming to re-try the issues disposed of in the foreign court. The finding upon those issues being conclusive, cannot be questioned here; but it can be shewn that the decision arrived at was obtained by fraud practised upon the foreign court, and that right cannot be defeated, because, in order to establish it, it becomes necessary to go into the same evidence as was used on the former trial to sustain or defeat that issue. The issues are not the same, for if the facts now discovered could have been shewn at the former trial they would have secured a different result.

The authority of decisions of the English Court of Appeal, and the case of *Aboulof* v. *Oppenheimer*, 10 Q. B. D. 297, discussed.

THIS was an action commenced in the Common Pleas Division by Henry M. Woodruff against John K. McLennan and Benjamin Killmaster, upon a judgment recovered by the plaintiff against the defendants in the Circuit Court of the United States, for the sixth Circuit and Eastern District of the State of Michigan, on the 4th of December, 1883, for the sum of $3,260.54, with interest from that date, together with costs of suit, &c., from which was to be deducted a judgment recovered by the defendants against one John Prieur, leaving due on the judgment recovered by the plaintiff the sum of $3,168.86.

The defendants by their statement of defence, denied the recovery of the judgment against them as alleged, and contended that they were not in any way subject to the laws of the State of Michigan; and, further, they alleged that the judgment so recovered against the defendants was so recovered by the fraud and false swearing of the plaintiff and others whom the plaintiff suborned to swear falsely, and that the plaintiff ought not to be assisted by the Court here to enforce the same.

Pursuant to an order made by the Master in Chambers on the 22nd of June, 1885, particulars shewing the facts and circumstances of the alleged fraud by which the plaintiff recovered the judgment in question, were delivered by the defendants as follows:

"Joseph Prieur, a witness on behalf of the plaintiff, states in his evidence at the trial when the judgment in question herein was recovered:

"That the defendant McLennan gave him leave to bank above section 20.

"That the south-east of the south-east of twenty was a splendid banking ground and would hold forty million feet.

"That before the letter of the 23rd December, 1880, was received by him from defendants he was told that everything was satisfactory.

"That after the receipt of this letter, he had a conversation with the defendant McLennan, and told him he had commenced to haul the logs as directed in that letter, and that he expected to be paid for the difference in expense, that the defendant did not object but said there would be no difference: that driving would cost more than hauling.

"That if he had not received this letter he would have banked on the south-east of section 20: that he built his dam and cleared the creek for this purpose in view, and that he banked below only because he was told to do so.

"That the additional expense of banking at the lower ground was two dollars a thousand feet, much smaller loads being hauled to the lower ground than to the upper and the distance being greater.

"That he made the road to the lower banking ground after he received the direction from the defendant McLennan.

"That the defendant McLennan told him that no damage was done by his not cutting the timber off the "Forty," that it could be cut next winter; that it was not cut because the defendant told him to leave it uncut.

"That the defendant McLennan took some 150,000 feet of culled logs, and allowed nothing for them.

"That the defendant McLennan agreed to pay half the cost of repairing the dam, and has paid no part of it.

"That the expense of driving logs from the upper to the lower ground would be from fifteen to twenty cents a thousand feet.

" That he was not told by the defendant McLennan that only some Nor- way pine should be banked on the south-east of section 20.

" That he commenced the construction of the road from the one dam to the other about the time he commenced to haul, and constructed only a short piece about eighty rods at that time : that this portion was constructed merely to extend the first banking ground, and give additional space,

" That before he was directed not to bank on the upper ground, not a log had been banked on the lower ground.

" These statements were false and were so made by the said Prieur for the fraudulent purpose of assisting the plaintiff in recovering judgment."

Thomas Ballentine, a witness on behalf of the plaintiff, states :

" That the account settled by himself and the defendant McLennan, included an item of $146.50 for one half the expenses of repairing the dam ; an item of $79.56 for discounts on moneys that had been paid by Gustin and Merrill, and that these items were not objected to."

These statements are false.

Peter White, a witness on behalf of the plaintiff, states :

" That the defendant McLennan told him that the logs could be banked on the south-east of the south-east of section 20.

" That the roads were constructed with reference to this ground, and all pre- parations made to bank there.

" That when the defendant McLennan told him not to haul any more logs to. the upper ground, he said he could not bank anywhere else, as there were no roads ; that Mr. Prieur then instructed him to continue the small branch road, which had been made to give a little additional space, down to the lower ground.

" That loads of 1,500 feet were hauled to the upper ground and loads of only 1,000 feet to the lower and that the additional expense was a dollar per thousand a mile.

" That the defendant McLennan told Prieur not to be in a hurry about cutting the " Forty" on section Twenty-two, but to go on hauling and stop cutting.

" That the defendant McLennan marked about 150,000 feet of culled logs.

" That the logging road to the lower ground was not made till after the receipt of the letter from McLennan to Prieur.

" These statements were false and made with the fraudulent purpose of enab- ling the plaintiff to recover judgment."

The action came on for trial before Mr. Justice Galt, at Toronto, on the 23rd October, 1885, who after hearing the evidence, gave judgment in favor of the plaintiff for the amount claimed; against which the defendants moved at the November Sittings of the Divisional Court, and to enter a verdict for the defendants, " on the ground that upon the whole case as made out at the trial the defendants are entitled to a verdict or judgment in their favor, and that the verdict or judgment entered at the trial is con- trary to law and evidence and the weight of the evidence and because the defence raised by the third paragraph of the statement of defence was established, and because it.

was not proved that the Court in which the alleged judgment sued on was recovered, had jurisdiction in that behalf and because the recovery of the said judgment was not duly proven.

" Or for an order setting aside the verdict or judgment and granting a new trial on the ground that the learned judge improperly rejected evidence tendered on behalf of the defendants, as appears by the notes of the said trial, and refused to allow the defendants' witnesses to speak of conversations with Prieur's foreman and other witnesses who gave evidence for the plaintiff on the trial in Michigan, which conversations would have established that the evidence given by them on said trial was false on other grounds." Which application was, on the 6th of March, 1886, by the unanimous judgment of the Court dismissed with costs.

The defendants thereupon appealed to this Court on the ground, amongst others, that if the case made by them be well proved, the foreign judgment was not in any way binding upon this Court, as there is no rule of law which makes such foreign judgment binding. It is a mere matter of comity, and if such judgment was obtained by the fraud and perjury of the plaintiff and his witnesses in that action, then they submitted that such judgment could not stand.

They further submitted that, in any event, the learned Judge's finding at the trial was contrary to the whole weight of evidence. That the evidence in the case was almost conclusive against the case put forward on the part of the plaintiff, and was such as to have entitled the defendants to a verdict, and in any event they submitted that if a new trial should be ordered judgment should be entered for them.

The appeal came on to be heard on the 14th of March, 1887.*

*Present—HAGARTY, C.J.O., BURTON, PATTERSON, and OSLER, JJ. A.

S. H. Blake, Q. C., and *Lash*, Q. C., for the appellants,. referred to : *Abouloff* v. *Oppenheimer*, 10 Q. B. D. 295, and cases therein cited ; *Magurn* v. *Magurn*, 11 A. R. 178 ; *Commercial Bank* v. *Wilson*, 3 E. & A. 277.

Bain, Q. C., and *Rapelle*, for the respondent, referred to *Godard* v. *Gray*, L. R. 6 Q. B. 139 ; *Ellis* v. *McHenry*, L. R. 6 C. P. 228 ; *Bank of Australasia* v. *Nias*, 16 Q. B. 717 ; *Flower* v. *Lloyd*, 10 Ch. Div. 327 ; *Smith's* Leading Cases, 8th Eng. ed., vol. 2, pp. 830-2-4 ; *Story's* Conflict of Laws, 8th ed., p. 827.

The other facts of the case clearly appear in the present judgments.

May 10, 1887.   PATTERSON, J. A.—This action is upon a judgment recovered in Michigan by the plaintiff against the defendants.

The defence is, that the plaintiff fraudulently misled the United States Court by swearing to what was untrue to his knowledge at the trial of the original action.   The case of *Abouloff* v. *Oppenheimer*, 10 Q. B. D. 295, is relied on as warranting that defence, and this appeal is from the decision of the Divisional Court of the Common Pleas Division holding the defence invalid, and sustaining the judgment pronounced at the trial by Mr. Justice Galt.

The original action was brought by the plaintiff as the assignee of one Prieur upon a contract made by Prieur in September, 1880, with the defendants who are lumberers, to cut into saw logs, haul, bank, run, and deliver into certain boom limits all the merchantable White Pine and Norway Timber standing and down on certain designated lands in Michigan, for the price of four dollars per thousand feet.   The work was to be done during the season of 1880-1881.   The price was to be paid thus: $1.75 per 1,000 feet when the logs were skidded in quantities of not less than 500,000 feet ; $1.75 when banked in quantities of not less than 500,000 feet ; 25c. when delivered below the dam on Denton Creek in quantities not less than one million feet ; and the balance when delivered in quantities of not less than one million feet. The defendants agreed to furnish the plaintiff with banking ground for banking the logs upon sections 19 and 20, and the right of way to and from the banking grounds on those sections for the purpose of hauling logs; and it was agreed that the logs should be banked upon Denton Creek on section 19, unless a dam should be constructed above section 20, on the creek, before banking commenced, in which case the logs might be banked on section 19 or section 20.

The contract contains other provisions which need not now be referred to.

Denton Creek is shewn by the plans in evidence to run in a north-westerly direction, entering section 20 near the south-east angle of that section, crossing the section obliquely, entering section 19 from the north-west quarter of section 20, and then running westerly across the northern half of 19. The sections are each a square mile, and are surveyed into quarter sections, which again are divided each into four square parcels of forty acres each. The logs were all to be cut at a distance from the sections 19 and 20, except such as grew on the south-east forty acres of 20, which was the part of the section highest up the creek.

This explanation may serve to make more intelligible what I have to say respecting the only part of the contest in the Court in Michigan with which we are concerned. There were several items of claim and counter-claim litigated there; but the only one which concerns us was a claim for hauling logs for a greater distance than required by the contract. It was a claim for extra services; and the contest was upon the question whether the services were within the contract or were extra.

The plaintiff had begun to "bank" logs on the south-east forty acres of 20, having first constructed a dam on the creek above section 20. The defendants wrote to him on the 23rd of December, 1880, in effect forbidding him to bank more than 500,000 feet at that place, and requiring him to bank the remainder lower down the creek on lot 19, which required hauling upwards of a mile further.

The claim was for $1.50 and he recovered $1 a thousand for some three millions of feet so hauled.

Upon the question whether or not this was extra work, the evidence of the plaintiff and of the defendants or one of them was given at the trial, and it is said there were one or two other witnesses examined : and the contract and the letter I have spoken of, as well as another letter written by or for the plaintiff, and on which the defendants relied as involving an admission against the plaintiff's claim, were in evidence.

We have been furnished with a report of the charge to the jury, from which it appears that the whole evidence was fully before the attention of the Court. After commenting on the considerations bearing on the dispute, the learned Judge is reported to have thus stated the general question :

"The substance of all this is, that if you find that defendants designated section 20 as the banking ground, and upon the faith of such designation Prieur went on and built a dam and put himself to expense, the defendants were bound to furnish him with a proper banking ground upon that section, and if they failed to do so or directed him afterwards to go on and bank upon another section, that is upon section 19, the plaintiff would be entitled to recover the extra expense of banking there. It is claimed on the part of the plaintiff that he was put to the extra expense of $1.50 per M. On the other hand it is denied by defendants that there was any such expense, and that it would cost very nearly or quite as much to have banked upon section 20 and floated them down to section 19 as it cost to haul them to section 19 and bank them there."

The fraud charged against the plaintiff is in his swearing that if he had not received the letter of the 23rd of December he would have banked on the south east of the south east of section 20 ; and that he built his dam and cleared the creek with this purpose in view ; and that he banked below only because he was told to do so ; with some other statements less directly bearing on the issue, such as that the banking ground on 20 would hold four millions of feet, and that he had not begun to make the

log road to the lower ground on 19 until after receiving
the letter; and it is now sought to establish the falsehood
of the statements imputed to the plaintiff by evidence of
teamsters and others who worked in the winter of 1880 in
the Michigan woods.

It seems to me impossible to deny that what the defendants propose to do is to try over again the very question
which was in issue in the original action. The charge of
fraud is superadded; but that charge involves the assertion that a falsehood was knowingly stated, and before the
question of scienter is reached a conclusion of fact adverse
to that arrived at by the Michigan jury must be adopted.
The attempt is not to prove some extrinsic fraud or imposition upon the Court, but to induce the Court here to deduce
from evidence which either conflicts with other evidence
or is at most indirect evidence, a state of facts different
from that found by the tribunal before which both parties
were heard, and which had all the means of testing their
credibility that their appearance and demeanour and the
other testimony given at the trial may have afforded. The
banking of the logs at the lower ground was nothing that
the plaintiff might not have done under the terms of his
contract, though he does not appear to have been bound to
do so after constructing the dam above section 20; and
the defendants seem to have been bound to find him banking ground on 20, in case he decided to bank on that section; and the United States Court had to try whether, by
banking on the lower section he was put to more expense
in the carrying out of the contract, which did not end with
the banking but extended to the driving and delivery of
the logs, than he would have been at if the defendants had
not interfered by their letter of the 23rd of December.
Amongst the considerations which properly entered into
that inquiry, whatever their weight may have been, was
the time at which the log road to the lower ground was
made, and perhaps also, though I think of less importance,
the capacity of the banking ground on the south-east forty
acres of 20. I say this seems the less important considera-

tion, partly because the contract apparently bound the
defendants, having regard to the construction of the dam,
to find sufficient ground on 20 if required, and partly
because the letter assumes the beaver meadow on the south-
east corner of 20 to be of sufficient extent, while it objects
to the logs being banked there. These were, however, matters collateral to the issue. It is impossible to say what force
they may have had in the minds of the jury; and if we
should concede a right so capable of being put to a fraudulent use as the right to re-open here and now the matter
litigated in Michigan five years ago there would be difficulties, probably insuperable, in the way of our holding
that the statements alleged to have been dishonestly made
by the plaintiff misled the Court or jury so as to occasion
a wrong decision upon the question of fact.

It is not contended that any decided case affords authority for the position taken by the defendants except the
case of *Aboulof* v. *Oppenheimer.*

The point actually decided in that case, cannot be said
to resemble that for which the defendants now contend.
The foreign judgment there was for the return of certain
goods of the plaintiff, or in default for the payment of
their value. The defence pleaded was, that the judgment
was obtained by the gross fraud of the plaintiff and her
husband acting in collusion with her, in representing to
the foreign Court that the goods were not in the possession
of the plaintiff and her husband at the time of the suit,
while the goods were all the time in their possession and
concealed by them. This defence was demurred to, the
allegations of the defence being of course admitted by the
demurrer. The position taken was, therefore, that the
judgment of the foreign Court must be held to be binding
in the English Court in favor of the plaintiff, who admitted that the facts were the opposite of those on which the
judgment was founded; that she had had all along the
goods which the defendants were enjoined to deliver, and
the value of which she was now seeking to enforce against
them; and that it was by her own fraud that the foreign

Court was induced to give the judgment in her favor. The argument there used that these allegations of fraud must have been brought before the foreign Court, could not aid the plaintiff who admitted that she had committed the fraud. The rule that the foreign judgment is conclusive as to the matters litigated in the foreign Court, whether that rule is founded on the comity of nations, or on the same principle of contract that makes an award binding on the parties who agree to a reference, is in effect a rule of evidence. The judgment is evidence of the facts found by it, and in ordinary circumstances, conclusive evidence. The exceptional position in *Abouloff* v. *Oppenheimer* was, in the admission that the facts were not as found by the judgment, which admission by itself would possibly have been a sufficient reason for refusing to enforce the judgment, and in the further admission that the plaintiff had misled the Court and procured the untrue finding in her favor by her gross fraud. The contention as put by Lord Coleridge was, " that, although the Russian Courts at Tiflis were led to decide against the defendants through believing a false state of facts to exist, owing to the fraud of the plaintiff, nevertheless the defendants are not now at liberty to say that the judgments against them were procured by that fraud;" and he added the obvious truth that " certainly this contention seems unreasonable."

It is true that the opinions expressed by the Lord Chief Justice and the Lords Justices in delivering their judgments, seem to go so far as to assert the right of the court in an action upon a judgment—I do not say a foreign judgment, because the doctrine applies equally to all judgments domestic as well as foreign—when the defendant alleges that the Court was led to a wrong conclusion by false evidence fraudulently adduced by the plaintiff, to try, as an issue of fact dependent on the weight of evidence, the correctness of the conclusion on which the judgment is founded. The case of perjury alleged to have been committed by the plaintiff is instanced. I suppose the same rule must apply whatever shape the fraud assumes,

whether perjury, subornation of perjury, or the fraudulent
use of honest testimony—as *e. g.*, in a case of mistaken
identity—as proof of what the plaintiff knows to be
untrue. But, in any form of the charge, the investigation of the truth of the allegation which must be established before the question of fraud is necessarily reached,
namely, the falsehood of what was sworn to in the original action, will ordinarily be undistinguishable from a
re-trial of the original [issue. The credibility of the witnesses, whether parties or strangers to the action, will be
a matter for decision in one case to exactly the same
extent as in the other.

It is necessarily with much self-distrust that one ven-
tures to hesitate before adopting the dicta of the eminent
Judges who decided the case of *Aboulof* v. *Oppenheimer* ;
but while, as I apprehend, the decision in that case rests
on principles that are not open to question, I cannot suppose the general remarks that were not necessary for the
decision of the case to have been intended to lay down so
wide a rule as it may be possible to deduce from what is .
reported to have been said.

It is not said that even a charge of fraud will warrant
the Court in trying over again the same issue that was
tried in the original action ; but it is said that the question,
whether the original Court was or was not misled, cannot
have been in issue there. I confess my inability to follow
this distinction without understanding the word " issue "
in what seems to me too narrow and technical a sense.

Take the extreme case of alleged perjury committed by
the plaintiff in giving his evidence upon the material question in controversy between him and his adversary. The
issue, in substance and reality, though perhaps not in
technical form—if, indeed, technical forms can now be said
to exist in our procedure—is the truth or falsehood of what
the plaintiff swears to. If, afterwards, the plaintiff, when
seeking to enforce his judgment, admits, as in *Aboulof* v.
Oppenheimer, that his whole case was a fiction, and all his
evidence perjury, cadit quœstio ; but if what is presented

is a charge of perjury on the one hand met by a traverse on the other we have, to my apprehension, the same issue as in the original action, or one which involves the issue originally tried, and which cannot be found for the defendants without reversing the former finding.

The doctrine in discussion has not yet, so far as I am aware, been brought to the test of practical application in any English case. It is commented upon in *Pigott* on Foreign Judgments, at p. 108, and the remarks of the learned writer concur with the views I have attempted to express in suggesting the danger of violating established principles by adopting it in its widest extent as a general rule. It may be that the test of actual application to the facts of particular cases may lead to a better definition of the limits to which the rule is intended to extend. These limits were indicated by Lord Coleridge when he said (p. 302): "The English Courts are not either trying or even re-discussing any question which was or could have been submitted to the determination of the Russian Courts," an observation which could not, in my judgment, be truly applied to the investigation which the defendants urge the Court to undertake.

Voinet v. *Barrett*, 55 L. J., Q. B. 39 ; 34 W. R. 161, decided last November in the Court of Appeal is an instructive case, and the latest I have seen on the subject of the effect of a foreign judgment, and the principles on which it is held to bind the parties to it.

I agree with the Court below in holding that the judgment of the United States Court must be taken to conclude the question of the liability of the defendants, and I therefore think the appeal should be dismissed.

HAGARTY, C. J. O.—The decision of the Court of Appeal in *Abouloff* v. *Oppenheimer*, 10 Q. B. Div. 295, was in itself the inevitable result of the course of decision on the point presented. Where it is asserted that a judgment of a foreign Court sought to be enforced in England was obtained by the gross fraud of the plaintiffs in fraudulently representing that certain goods the subject of the suit were not in the plaintiffs' possession, and by fraudulently concealing from the Court that they were in their actual possession, and concealed by plaintiffs except as to so much of them as they had fraudulently and secretly disposed of, and the plaintiffs admit the truth of the defence, but demur to it as insufficient in law, no other judgment than one overruling the demurrer seems to have been possible.

It is solely from the remarks of the very learned Judges that a far wider field of discussion than was necessary for the decision of the question in issue, has been opened. From the language of some of the Judges especially of Lord Esher, then Lord Justice Brett, the whole merits may be again discussed on the same or other evidence, and the whole case in effect tried over again, and the same eminent judge considers (p. 305) that the same rule will apply to an English judgment recovered in a Court other than the Court in which it is sought to be enforced.

Assuming that the plaintiff in the former suit swore falsely; that of course would be considered his fraud; and the defendant swore directly the opposite, and the Judges or the jury gave credit to the plaintiff and disbelieved the defendant, it can, of course, be argued on the remarks made that when an action is brought to enforce the judgment the defendant can plead plaintiff's fraud and perjury, and on a new issue try the case again.

The often cited words of De Grey, C. J., in the *Duchess of Kingston's Case*, apply to English as well as to foreign judgments. Throughout all the older cases it strikes me the vitiating fraud spoken of was not the direct contradictory statements on oath of the parties or their witnesses on one side asserting that the other had given untrue against his true statement of disputed fact, but rather that the recovery was collusive, that defendant had never been served with process, that the suit had been undefended without defendant's default, that the defendant had been fraudulently persuaded by plaintiff to let judgment go by default, as suggested in *Ochsenbein* v. *Papelier*, L. R. 8 Chy. 695, or some-fraud to defendant's prejudice committed or allowed in the proceedings of the other Court, and other instances cited by Lord Selborne from Mr. Justice Story, vol. 2. 732.

Abouloff v. *Oppenheimer*, was before the Court of Appeal in 1882. Four years before, in 1878, *Flower* v. *Lloyd*, was decided before Sir Wm. James and Lord Justices Thesiger and Baggallay.

The former very eminent Judge, with Lord Justice Thesiger's concurrence, 10 Chy. D. 333, said : " Where is litigation to end if a judgment obtained in an action fought out adversely between two litigants, sui juris and at arm's length, could be set aside by a fresh action on the ground that perjury had been committed in the first action, or that false answers had been given to interrogatories, or a misleading production of documents, or of a machine, or of a process had been given ? There are hundreds of actions tried every year in which the evidence is irreconcilably conflicting and must be, on one side or the other, wilfully and corruptly perjured. In this case, if the plaintiffs had sustained, on this appeal, the judgment in their favor, the present defendants, in their turn, might bring a fresh action to set that judgment aside on the ground of perjury of the principal witness and subornation of perjury ; and so the parties might go on alternately ad infinitum. * * Perjuries, falsehood, frauds, when detected, must be punished and punished severely ; but, in their desire to prevent parties litigant from obtaining any benefit from such foul means, the Court must not forget the evils which may arise from opening such new sources of litigation, amongst such evils not the least being that it would be certain to multiply indefinitely the mass of those very perjuries, falsehoods, and frauds."

Baggallay, L. J., said, that he desired to reserve to himself the right to deal with the general question, if the case should arise where it would be clearly proved that a judgment had been obtained by the fraud of one of the parties, which judgment but for such fraud would have been in favor of the other party.

If we accept the argument of defendants, in this case, and the defendants should, on a new trial, succeed and get judgment, I do not see why, on the same principle, the

plaintiff could not bring a fresh suit on the original cause
of action and reply to the defence of judgment recovered
that the recovery was had by defendants' fraud and perjury.

Looking at the length to which the observations of the
learned Judges in *Aboulof* v. *Oppenheimer*, may be
legitimately extended, covering the whole field of domestic as well as foreign judgments, I think our proper course
is to wait for a decision in which the question comes
directly for judgment. The consequences are too momen-
tuous if we revolutionise, as it were, the hitherto universal belief in the finality of the judgment of a Court of
competent jurisdiction where both parties have been fairly
heard, and their controversy apparently determined.

All laws, and as far as practicable, all interpretations of
laws, ought to be for the general good government and
guidance of the public, and it is assuredly not for the
general good to decide till we are told directly so to do by
a superior authority that there is no finality in a judgment
of a competent Court not appealed from or set aside.

OSLER, J. A., agreed with PATTERSON, J.A.

BURTON, J. A.—If the dictum attributed to Sir Montague
Smith in the case of *Trimble* v. *Hill*, 5 App. Cas. 342, in the
Privy Council, means only that where in a colony an enactment precisely similar to an Act passed by the Imperial Parliament has received a construction by the Court of Appeal
in England, that construction should be adopted and acted
upon by the Courts of the Colony until a contrary determination has been arrived at by the House of Lords, I do
not think that any exception could be reasonably taken to
it; but if it is intended to express the view that an Appellate Court in a Colony is bound under any circumstances
to follow a decision of the English Court of Appeal, I
must respectfully but decidedly dissent from that view.
The very greatest respect is due and should be paid to the
decisions of that tribunal, but in performing the functions
entrusted to us as an Appellate Court, we are bound, in

my opinion, to exercise the right to act upon our own judgment, governing ourselves by the same rule as the Judicial Committee profess to act upon, viz., "not to depart from the decision arrived at by the Court of Appeal unless entertaining a clear opinion that the decision arrived at is wrong."

Looking at the eminence of the Judges at present constituting the Court of Appeal in England, the occasions in which any Colonial Court would feel justified in disregarding a judgment of that tribunal, must be very rare ; but in cases where a clear opinion of its incorrectness is entertained, the suitor is entitled to the independent judgment of the Colonial Court.

In the case referred to by my learned brothers of *Abouloff* v. *Oppenheimer*, I agree not only in the judgment pronounced, but in the reasoning, if I may be allowed without presumption to say so, of the very able Judges who delivered it ; and that being so, I need scarcely add that I am unable to concur in the judgment just delivered.

It appears to me, with great respect, to be a fallacy to say that the Court is assuming to retry the issues disposed of at the trial, or to be exercising the powers of an Appellate Court from the decision of the foreign tribunal. The finding upon those issues is conclusive, and cannot be questioned here, but it can be shewn that the decision arrived at was obtained by fraud practised upon the Court and that right cannot be defeated, because in order to establish it, it becomes necessary to go into the same evidence as was used on the former trial to sustain or defeat that issue.

Assume, for instance, that the issue on the former trial had been, whether or not the plaintiff had executed a release of the cause of action, which was alleged to be lost, and a number of witnesses had been produced, some of whom proved that they had read the instrument before execution, and had seen it executed, and that it was a release, whilst others proved that they had also been

present, and that the instrument so signed was a conveyance of a lot of land, and the jury came to the conclusion
that the latter was the correct conclusion, and found a
verdict accordingly, which was affirmed by a judgment,
could it possibly be contended that if the plaintiff came
to this country and invoked the assistance of our Courts it
could not be shewn that subsequently to the judgment he
had produced the release from his possession, and admitted
the fact that he had suborned the witnesses to give false
evidence at the former trial? No evidence could be received
to prove simply that the former finding was erroneous, but
evidence that the plaintiff had knowingly misled the Court
by his own false testimony, or that of his accomplices would
clearly be receivable.

Or assume in a collision case the usual amount of inconsistent evidence had been given, each witness truthfully
giving his evidence as the facts appeared to him from his
own standpoint, the finding of the foreign Court either
way would be conclusive in an action here upon the judgment; but if the defendant were in a position to shew that
since the recovery he had discovered and was enabled to
prove that the plaintiff had instructed the helmsman to
run down the other vessel, can it possibly be the law that
that could not be shewn as an answer to the action in this
country.

The issues are not the same, although if the facts now
discovered could have been shewn at the former trial they
would have secured a different result.

In the *Aboulof Case* the plea was demurred to, and
held to be a good plea; the facts therefore there alleged
whether proved by evidence or admitted on demurrer,
would have been fatal to the plaintiff's recovery.

If issue had been taken, the inquiry would, to a certain
extent, have involved the same issue as that disposed of
in the foreign Court, viz., whether the goods in question
were or were not in the possession of the defendants; but
that inquiry would be merely incidental to the real issue,
viz., whether a fraud had been practised on the Court

and proof of the actual possession by the plaintiff and her husband, and the concealment of that fact would conclusively have established that issue in favor of the defendants.

It is not disputed, and could not of course be disputed that the Courts of this country in dealing with a foreign judgment will not inquire whether the foreign Court pronounced a judgment correct in point of law, or accurate in point of fact, but in the words of Chief Justice Grey, although it is not permissible to shew that the foreign Court was mistaken, it may be shewn that it was misled.

I admit that in a case like the present the defendants may find a difficulty in sustaining the issue they have raised upon the pleadings, but with that we are not at present concerned; I entertain no doubt of their right to raise it, and entertaining that view, I am of opinion that the evidence tendered was improperly rejected.

From a careful perusal of the evidence, I think there was a misapprehension on the part of one of the Judges in the Court below that the learned Judge at the trial, although at first declining to receive the evidence, had subsequently agreed to do so. I feel convinced that that was not the intention of the learned Judge, and that the counsel engaged in the case did not so understand it.

The learned Judge had from the first emphatically and consistently declined to receive evidence of the nature first tendered and rejected.

On the occasion when he intimated his willingness to receive evidence, the only question then under discussion was as to the making of the road; it was near the close of the case upon the cross-examination of the plaintiff. The defendants had, during the whole case, been not only in examination of their own witnesses, but in the cross-examination of the plaintiff's witnesses prevented giving evidence of the nature first tendered, and it is, I think, clear that the learned Judge never receded from that position, and that no one at the trial imagined that he did.

It would have placed the defendants in a very unfavourable position at that stage of the case when the defendants might be unable to procure the attendance of the plaintiff's witnesses for the purpose of cross-examination, and I should require very clear evidence not only of the learned Judge's change of view, but of the acquiescence of the defendants' counsel in the altered state of things, before disposing of the case on such a ground.

It is not necessary to express an opinion as to whether a litigant in an English Court would be able to obtain relief against a judgment obtained in due course on the subsequent discovery that it was obtained by means of evidence wilfully false to the knowledge of the plaintiff himself : but when a party invokes the assistance of an English Court for the purpose of enforcing a foreign judgment so obtained, I cannot believe that fraud practised upon a foreign Court by a party to the suit for the purpose of deceiving it and securing a wrong decision is not a good answer to an action in this country to enforce that judgment.

That is what the defendant are endeavouring to shew here. Whether the evidence which has been excluded will be sufficient to make out that defence would be for the Judge or jury trying the case. I am of opinion that it was perfectly competent to the defendants to shew that the plaintiff wilfully misled the Court by evidence, either of himself or his witnesses, which he knew to be false; and when he comes to the Courts of this country to enforce a judgment so obtained he must fail, if the Court or jury trying the case here are satisfied that the judgment has been obtained by such fraudulent means.

I express no opinion upon the merits of this case ; but on the ground that the evidence tendered was improperly rejected, I think the appeal should be allowed and a new trial ordered.

Appeal dismissed with costs.
BURTON, J. A., dissenting.

MATTHEWS V. THE HAMILTON POWDER COMPANY.

Master and servant—Negligence—Liability of master for neglect of fellow servant—Intervention of master.

In an action for damages by the administratrix of M., an employee of the defendant company, who was killed by an explosion of defendants' powder mills, caused by a portion of the machinery being out of repair, it was shewn that W., a director of the company, had sometime before the explosion, when the works were idle, given directions to C., the superintendent and head of the works, to have the defective portions of the machinery repaired before recommencing operations, but C. neglected to attend to it, and the repairs were not made. It was not shewn that W. in any way assumed to direct the practical working of the mills, or that he had any special knowledge or ability to do so, and there was no suggestion that C. was an incompetent or improper person to employ.
Held, reversing the judgment of the Queen's Bench Division, 12 O. R. 58. that the intervention of W. had not taken the case out of the general rule of law, that the defendants were not responsible for an accident due to the negligence of a fellow servant, which C. was.

THIS was an appeal by defendants from the judgment of the Queen's Bench Division reported 12 O. R. 58, and came on to be heard before this Court on the 30th of March, 1887*

Robinson, Q.C., and *E. Martin*, Q.C., for the appellants.
W. Nesbitt, and *J. W. Elliott*, for respondent.

The facts are fully stated in the report of the case in the Court below, and in the present judgment.

June 29, 1887.   HAGARTY, C. J. O.—It seems clear, on the authorities, that Corlett the manager or superintendent of the Mills must be held to be in the position of a fellow servant of the deceased workman.

Cockburn, C. J., says, in *Howell* v. *London Steel Company*, L. R. 10 Q. B. 64:

"Since the case of *Wilson* v. *Merry*, (a) in the House of Lords, it is not open to dispute, that in general the master is not liable to a servant for the negligence of a fellow-servant although he be the manager of the concern."

Present.—HAGARTY, C. J. O., BURTON, PATTERSON, and OSLER, JJ.A.

(a) L. R. 1 H. L., Sc. 326.

Blackburn, J. "There have been several cases in which, whether vice-principal or manager, the person has been held a fellow-servant."

In the late work of Mr. *Pollock* on Torts, p. 84, *et. seq.,* Am. ed., p. 67, the principle is discussed and authorities reviewed. At p. 87 the position of foreman, manager, or superintendent is examined.

The judgment of the Queen's Bench now in appeal admits the general law, but the learned Chief Justice who pronounced the judgment of the Court decides the case in favor of the plaintiff on what he considers an important distinction, viz.; the intervention of Watson, a director of the defendant company. The head office of the Company is in Montreal—a branch office in Hamilton—Corlett had the whole practical management of the Powder Mills, some 15 miles from Hamilton. He hired and dismissed the men and did all the superintendence and management subject to orders from the board, and was hired and paid by the month. Orders for the manufacture of powder were sent to him by the board from time to time. He was to manufacture the powder. Watson sends money to him to pay the men, &c., and he is supposed to look after the repairs. Watson says (in answer to a question as to orders to Corlett respecting the machinery) : "I went out every six months and saw if there was anything wrong, and he (Corlett) was ordered to report if there was anything wrong; we went round the works together and examined if there was anything that required to be done."

In Sept., 1884, the mills were shut down, when the Company had received a large order for powder and were anxious to start again as soon as possible. Dent's evidence is that there were repairs required to be done to the "shakers" which were in the building called the "crackers," and that without such repairs it would be dangerous to run them. He was working at the press wheel. He says : "Mr. Watson came to him with Corlett. Watson asked if he could have the crackers and the wheel done by 10th October, Dent replied that he could. Watson then said 'that will do Mr. Corlett;' that is all Mr. Watson said to me ; what was said after I do not know." In another part of his evidence he says he was told by them as to repairing the shaker part of the crackers, the hangers and the pins; that was what was to be done. New sills, he said, were required and were prepared. After this he proceeds : " But by and bye an order or something came, the crackers were left as they were and started to work without the new sills being put in."

According to Dent's testimony it was wholly Corlett's fault that these repairs were not done, and the mills were started some time before 10th Oct., and the explosion took place on the 9th Oct.

We have now to decide whether the learned Chief Justice is right in holding that Watson's intervention has taken the case out of the general rule of law.

We must see what the alleged intervention was :

It is not shewn that Watson in any way assumed to direct the practical working of the mills, or that he had any special knowledge or ability so to do.

There is no suggestion that Corlett was an incompetent or improper person to employ, and it was his duty to see that the machinery was in a safe state of repair and on. his information the directors would naturally have to depend. Watson came at long intervals to make inquiries and see how matters were going on. He is informed of certain defects and he at once, in effect, directs them to be remedied, and the necessary repairs to be executed, and leaves in the belief and understanding that they will be put to rights before the mill is again started. Corlett neglects to attend to this. Every workman in the mills knows that all matters of this kind are left wholly to Corlett.

I do not think we can place this intervention of Watson on any grounds more favorable to plaintiff than to treat it as I now suggest.

While the mills are shut down Corlett writes to the board of directors that certain specified repairs are required. The board at once directs him to have the repairs executed before work is resumed. He neglects their orders, resumes work, and in consequence the explosion takes place.

They have no reason whatever to suppose that Corlett will neglect his duty.

I am unable to draw any intelligible distinction between what did occur and the case now suggested.

Or, if the whole board had visited the mills and on having the defects stated to them by the manager, and they gave the same directions that Watson gave, the case is not further advanced.

Lord Cairns, in his often quoted words, (*Wilson* v. *Merry*, L. R. l H. L. Sc. 328) says : "What the master is in my opinion bound to his servant to do, in the event of his not personally superintending and directing the work, is to select proper and competent persons to do so, and to furnish them with adequate materials and resources for the work. When he has done this he has, in my opinion, done all that he is bound to do. And if the persons so selected are guilty of negligence, that is not the negligence of the master."

A company or incorporation must be treated in the same way as an individual on this point.   Per Lord Blackburn in *Howells* v. *Landore Steel Company*, L. R. 10 Q. B. 62.

Nor can I see much distinction between our case and that of the trusted manager failing to inform his employers, the Company, of the existence of defects.

If the principal be aware of defects in machinery, and with that knowledge permit or passively allow the work to proceed, I can understand holding him liable.

But that is very different from, at once on acquiring the knowledge, directing the necessary repairs and the cessation of work until that be completed.   If there be no interference whatever and no knowledge of defects, trusting to a competent manager, it would seem from the cases that the principal is not liable for injury to a workman, the result of the negligence of his fellow servant the manager.

It does not seem intelligible that the principal's position should be made worse by the fact that he periodically comes to make inquiry—ascertain that there are defects and promptly directs their reparation and a cessation of work so as to ensure against danger until the defects be cured.

In the case before us it was especially a matter for the manager to attend to properly and in addition to his ordinary duty to attend to such matters. He had the express orders of his employers to do what was required.

I have not found any authority specially defining the measure of permitted interference.

Blackburn, J., says in *Howells* v. *Landore Steel Company*, p. 65, "When the master personally interferes he is liable for his personal negligence just as the individual servant would be."

In *Allen* v. *New Gas Company*, 1 Ex. D. 261. Huddleston, B., delivering the judgment of the Court says : "To establish negligence against the defendants the plaintiff must prove that the defendants undertook personally to superintend and direct the works, or that the persons employed by them were not proper and competent persons, or that the materials were inadequate or the means and resources were unsuitable to accomplish the work. * * Here there was no evidence that the defendants undertook personally to superintend and direct the works, on the contrary from the fact of this being a joint stock company the direct inference would be the other way."

I may also refer to the remarks as to interference in in such cases as *Roberts* v. *Smith*, 2 H. & N. 248 ; *Ormond* v. *Holland*, E. B. & E. 105 ; *Smith* on Negligence p. 68, Am. ed., 45 ; and as to giving directions to have repairs made or precaution taken, see *Smith* v. *Dowell*, 3 F. & F. 238; *Durgan* v. *Munson*, 9 Allen, 396; *Smith* on Negligence 45.

There is a marked difference between English and American laws on the "fellow workman" question. Of course we have to follow the former.

With some regret I arrive at the conclusion that on the authorities by which we are bound, the appeal must be allowed.

BURTON, PATTERSON, and OSLER, JJ.A., concurred.

Appeal allowed, with costs,

CULVERWELL V. BIRNEY.

Principal and agent—Sale of land—Commission to agent—Offer to purchase
—Conditional acceptance—Inability of purchaser to carry out offer—
Sale to another person pending negotiations.

The plaintiff had been employed by the defendants to procure offers for
the purchase or exchange of three blocks of land owned by them and he
accordingly procured from one R. an offer at an estimated price of
$97,000 which he submitted to the defendants, and which they, on the
10th September, 1884, accepted conditionally that R. would agree to
a variation of the terms of his offer. R. being then absent from the
country, the plaintiff, without any instructions, agreed on behalf of R.
to the proposed variation. R. returned shortly afterwards, and on the
18th September, signed a formal ratification of the plaintiff's act, but it
was not shewn that this was ever communicated to the defendants.
Meanwhile the defendants being pressed for money by a mortgagee of
one of the properties had arranged a sale of that property to one S., at
a price $8,000 less than it was valued at in the offer of R., part of the
consideration given by S. being some of the same lands offered by R. in
exchange, of which it appeared that S. and not R. had the control ; and
by a subsequent arrangement the defendants' other two properties were
sold to R. The defendants and S. were brought together during the
negotiations arising out of R.'s offer.
Held, [reversing the judgment of the C. P. D. 11 O. R. 265,] that as between R. and the defendants, the matter had never passed beyond the
stage of negotiation ; R.'s offer was not one that he could carry out,
and therefore the plaintiff was not entitled to commission upon the offer
of R., or alleged contract of sale made with him ; neither was he entitled
to anything either on the footing of his agreement òr *quantum meruit*
by way of commission on the sales that were actually made.

THIS was an appeal by the defendants from the judgment of the Common Pleas Division, reported 11 O. R. 265,
where and in the present judgments the facts giving rise
to the action are fully stated, and came to be heard before
this Court on the 22nd of March, 1887.*

W. Nesbitt, for the appellants.
J. K. Kerr, Q. C., and *J. A. Paterson,* for the respondent.

June 29, 1887.   PATTERSON, J. A.—The plaintiff's statement of claim sets out a retainer of the plaintiff by
the defendants to procure an offer for the purchase
or for the exchange of a large amount of real estate,
situate in the city of Toronto and elsewhere, and their

Present.—HAGARTY, C.J.O., BURTON, PATTERSON, and OSLER, JJ.A.

agreement "to allow and pay to the plaintiff on his effecting a sale or exchange of such property, a commission of one and-a-half per cent upon the purchase money or price which he should obtain therefor, on any such sale or exchange." Then the statement avers that the plaintiff procured an offer for the exchange of the property at the price of $97,000, which offer he submitted to the defendants who accepted it on the 10th of September, 1884.

The claim is for commission on this alleged transaction.

The defendants, by their statement of defence, admit all the plaintiff's allegations of fact, and set out that the offer and acceptance were between one Radford of the one part and the defendants of the other part, and were dated the 6th and 10th days of September, 1884 ; that it was part of their agreement with the plaintiff that the purchaser should be a man of substance sufficiently capable of carrying out the agreement ; and that the plaintiff represented Radford to be such a man : that the plaintiff was aware that it was necessary that the agreement of September should be carried out forthwith, because the defendants' property was subject to mortgages under which proceedings for sale were being taken : that about the middle of September the plaintiff informed the defendants that Radford was unable to complete the contract, and asked them to release him, which at first they refused to do; but that on the following day in the presence of the plaintiff and of Radford, they being persuaded thereto by Radford and the plaintiff, agreed to release Radford, and the contract was then cancelled : and that it was further understood and agreed between the plaintiff and the defendants that the defendants were to be released from all claim for compensation on the part of the plaintiff. They go on to allege as one reason for Radford's inability to perform the contract, that he was not the owner of all the land he offered the defendants ; and they further charge that the plaintiff acted throughout the transactions as agent for and in the interest of Radford.

They conclude with the following summary of their defence :

"9. The defendants say that the said plaintiff is not entitled to be paid the sum he claims by reason of the said Radford not being possessed of sufficient means to complete and carry out the said agreement, and by reason of the said Radford not being the owner of the property referred to in the said agreement as his, and because the plaintiff induced the defendants to abandon the said contract, and because the plaintiff waived, released, and abandoned all claim or right to compensation which he had against the defendants under and by virtue of the matters set forth in the plaintiff's statement of claim."

The evidence bearing on the defendants' allegation of the abandonment by general consent of the bargain with Radford is contradictory. We have no finding of fact upon the issue. The allegation is supported by the testimony of the defendants themselves, principally by that of Joseph Birney, and that evidence seems to me to derive added weight from what we learn of the somewhat complicated history of the transactions. I do not think, however, that it is necessary for us to find the fact one way or the other, because the other allegation that Radford's offer on which the action is based was not one that he could carry out, and therefore not such a sale as would entitle the plaintiff to commission, is, in my understanding of the undisputed facts, fully established.

The defence specifically admits the making of the contract with Radford by Radford's offer of the 6th, and the defendants' acceptance of the 10th of September. Substantially those dates may serve all purposes, but the force of the evidence on the denial of Radford's ability to carry the contract out will be more distinct if we note that the contract was really not concluded before the 18th, even if it became at that date binding on Radford. His offer of the 6th was accepted on the 10th with a variation, substituting $2,800 cash for lands to that amount of those offered in exchange; and, Radford being absent, an assent to the variation was given in his name by the plaintiff. But the plaintiff had no power to bind Radford, and the assent did not become operative until the 18th, when it is said Radford ratified it.

In the mean time difficulties had arisen from proceedings by a mortgagee to sell the defendants' Queen Street property; and, in connection with efforts made to raise money enough to have the impending sale postponed, it appeared that the Moosejaw lands, which formed an important part of those offered by Radford, belonged to or were controlled by Shaw; and the defendants were driven into a separate dealing with Shaw for those lands in exchange for the Queen Street property, and had to submit to a loss of $8,000 on that property, that is to say, Radford was to take it at a valuation of $60,000, and it was valued only at $52,000 in the exchange with Shaw.

Radford and Shaw had a disagreement about this transaction which they arranged by Shaw giving Radford $1,800; but the inability of Radford to carry out his bargain with the defendants, as far as the Moosejaw lands were concerned, cannot be said to admit of a reasonable doubt; nor can it be disputed that when the sale of those lands was made by Shaw, the ratification of the assent to the variation of his offer had not been given by Radford.

It is questionable whether it was ever communicated to the defendants; but apart from that, it was of later date than Shaw's sale.

The plaintiff himself explains that he had the Moosejaw lands in his hands for sale on Shaw's account, and that it was his suggestion, to which Radford assented, that Radford should buy the lands from Shaw and allow the plaintiff to offer them to the defendants.

The plaintiff, speaking of the agreement between Shaw and the defendants for the exchange of the Queen street property for the Moosejaw lands, makes it a point to shew that there was an understanding that what was done was " subject to the Radford sale.' The meaning of this may not be quite apparent, but we may take it to be as paraphrased by the plaintiff's counsel in the question, "Upon that, anything that was done must be conditional upon the Radford contract if Radford chose to wish it to go on ?" To which the plaintiff answered, " Yes."   But Radford did not avail himself of this privilege to insist on accounting to the plaintiff at the rate of $60,000 for the Queen street lands ; but he accepted the $1,800 from Shaw, and let the defendants lose the $8,000 and the Moosejaw lands pass under Shaw's agreement.

This $1,800 arrangement was evidenced by a writing which is produced, dated the 22nd of September, and which shews what appears also from the oral testimony, that a Mr. Cossitt and another person were associated with Shaw in the purchase of the Queen street property.

The circumstance that this document is dated after the so-called ratification of the 18th of September does not affect the position that the defendants had no contract binding upon Radford when their transaction with Shaw took place, nor does it weaken the proof of the other two facts on which the defendants rely—viz., that Radford never had such control of the Moosejaw lands as to be able to sell them as his offer professed to do, and that if the stipulation spoken of by the plaintiff, that the defendant's bargain with Shaw was to be subject to the Radford sale, pointed to any arrangements between Radford and Shaw by which the former could have insisted on the lands going under his offer to the defendants, he did not so insist.

This seems to me to completely answer the case made by the plaintiff in his statement of claim.

The defence may be shortly stated thus : true it is that the plaintiff procured an offer on paper, of lands and money to the amount of the $97,000 for which the defendants authorized their lands to be sold, but the offer was not a real one, because it comprised lands that Radford did not own, and had not power to sell.

It might be truly added that these facts were always within the knowledge of the plaintiff, but that is not, as I apprehend, a very material circumstance.

The transaction between the defendants and Shaw is material only as an episode which throws light on the position of Radford in relation to the Moosejaw property.

A good deal of the evidence was given concerning efforts made by the defendants, sometimes in concert with Radford, to raise money to meet the exigencies of the mortgages on the defendants' properties.

All this I take to be collateral to the issue. It may be that if these mortgages had been less pressing, and there had therefore been more time to work out the transaction, the proposed sale and exchange with Radford might have been carried out after all. But that is a matter of speculation only. The plaintiff knew of the mortgages, in fact the bargain expressly provided that Radford was to buy subject to them, and the pressure they caused is just one of the surrounding circumstances which, by bringing the defendants into contact with Shaw, led to the episode which goes so far in aid of the defence.

The remaining question is, whether the plaintiff is not entitled to something, either on the footing of his agreement for $1\frac{1}{2}$ per cent. or quantum meruit, by way of commission on the sales that were ultimately made.

These were the sale of the Queen street property to Shaw or Cossitt or some one, and of the Bronte and Nelson farms to Radford.

I have pointed out that the plaintiff has not claimed commission on these transactions, and I think he was well advised in not doing so.

They are transactions entirely outside of the scope of his retainer and were not brought about directly or indirectly as the result of anything done by him on behalf of the defendants.

One of the transactions I have perhaps sufficiently noticed. It was a sale which yielded $8,000 less than the sum for which the property was valued at in the sale to Radford. It was made while the plaintiff was insisting on the Radford sale being adhered to, and was brought about by the pressure to which the defendants were subjected by the mortgagees, and not in any way as a service rendered by the plaintiff to the defendants.

The other sales were brought about in much the same way, the defendants being forced into them by Shaw who had got in one of the mortgages which covered all the property, and, the defendants being unable to provide for it, would make no terms that did not include the sale of the Bronte farm to Radford who had some particular reason for wishing to get it.

I am of opinion that we should allow the appeal with costs, and dismiss the action, with costs.

OSLER, J. A.—The plaintiff sues to recover his commission on a sale or exchange of the defendants' lands made to one Radford. Armour, J., found that throughout the whole transaction, in respect of which commission was claimed, he was acting as the paid agent of and on behalf of Radford, and was so acting without the consent or knowledge of the defendants, and that therefore he was not entitled to recover any commission. The Common Pleas Division while not dissenting from the finding of fact, held that he was entitled to recover the difference between the commission he had received from or was to be paid by Radford, and that which the defendants had agreed to pay him—viz., one-half per cent, amounting to $485.

The defendants contend, 1st. That no sale or exchange of their property or contract therefor was obtained by the plaintiff under which he can claim the commission sought to be recovered ; 2nd. That the sales in respect of which the commission was allowed by the Court were not effected by the plaintiff, and are not those in respect of which commission is claimed by the pleading in the action ; 3rd. That as the plaintiff acted throughout the whole of the transactions for which the commission is claimed as the paid agent of Radford without their knowledge or assent, he is not entitled to recover any commission from them, as Armour, J., held at the trial.

The case made by the plaintiff on the pleadings is, that he was employed to procure an offer for the purchase of the defendants' lands, or for the exchange thereof for other property. That he procured an offer for sale and exchange at the price of $97,000, which he submitted to and which was accepted by the defendants on the 10th September, 1884, whereupon he became entitled to the agreed commission, at the rate of one and-a-half per cent on the price.

We may assume, for the present, that under the terms on which he was employed, it would have been sufficient for the plaintiff to procure a binding contract of sale or exchange, or a person ready and willing to enter into such and complete it on terms proposed or assented to by the defendants. The first question, therefore, is, whether he succeeded as he alleges in obtaining such a contract in fact, and in considering this, it will be necessary to examine the evidence with some minuteness.

The defendants' agreement with the plaintiff is contained in a memorandum in the following terms: " August 28, 1884. A sale or exchange being made to your customer of our properties, we will pay a commission one and a-half per cent. on the properties sold." Then follows a note of the properties and the price affixed to each. They consisted of a block of shops on Queen street, valued at $60,000; a farm in Nelson, $; and a farm in Bronté, $; in all $97,000, subject to incumbrances, amounting in all to $54,000, of which one was a mortgage to a Dr. McCausland for $5,000 or $6,000 which included all three properties.

The plaintiff immediately went to see Radford, a person for whom he had already been acting in land transactions, and whom he had a day or two previously informed that he expected to have such properties as these placed in his hands, and obtained from him an offer dated 6th September, 1884, to exchange for them a number of houses and lots and a quantity of farm lands in Manitoba and the North

West Territories, the latter being known as the "Moosejaw lands," of nearly equal nominal value, and to pay $200 to balance the exchange. The defendants were to have the option of selecting certain other properties in lieu of some of those offered.

The Manitoba lands consisted of 3,360 acres to be selected by the defendants out of a list of 26 farms of 240 acres each, at $7 per acre, subject to a mortgage of $2 per acre.

Of these properties the plaintiff already had lists from Radford for the purpose of disposing of them and was entitled to recover a commission from him if he succeeded in doing so.

This written offer was not obtained from Radford until some verbal negotiations had taken place between him and Culverwell, and it was not submitted to the defendants until some further similar communications had passed between them, and the lowest terms they would submit to had been ascertained.

On the 10th September the defendants wrote at the foot of Radford's offer the following :

"We hereby accept the within offer of bargain and sale per exchange, on terms and conditions therein mentioned, excepting that we are to be paid $3,000 in lieu of the $200 mentioned,—viz., $1,000 in cash and $2,000 in three months from completion of our titles, and lands to the amount of $2,800 to be deducted from those to be selected by us from said list of Manitoba farms on same basis of prices and incumbrances or out of city property offered at Radford's choice. And if the Rose avenue house is not similar to house on corner of Rose and Dunn avenue, we to have some other property of equal margin instead."

Radford had gone away to the United States immediately after leaving his offer with the plaintiff, and his address was not known.

The plaintiff swore that he had authorized him to communicate with one Brown as regarded the limit of the cash payment, and that Brown had told him he thought Radford would go as high as $3,000.

The defendants' counter-proposal having been made, a difficulty arose in Radford's absence as to accepting it. The parties went to the office of one Shaw, who was Radford's solicitor, and who was undoubtedly concerned with him in land transactions and interested in, if not actually the owner, of the Moosejaw property included in Radford's offer, to see what could be done. There was no evidence that either Culverwell or Shaw had authority to assent to the defendants' terms, and they appear to have insisted that if the former undertook to do so he should have written instructions to that effect from Shaw. The latter thereupon gave him the following note :

10th Sept., 1884. Dear Sir,—I would, in the absence of Mr. Radford, authorize you to accept the proposal of the Messrs. Birneys by way of acceptance of Radford's offer as far as the condition of payment of $3,000 in lieu of the $200 mentioned in said offer is concerned, I agreeing to furnish the said sum of $3,000 as stipulated for on the benefit thereof accruing to me, Radford arranging for the $6,000 required to placing Birneys' property in satisfactory position, and my receiving a proportionate interest in the same, or a satisfactory arrangement being come to in reference to my property and the above sum of $3,000 between the said Radford and myself.

The $6,000 referred to in this letter, was the McCausland mortgage which Radford was to assume, and which bore interest at the rate of two and-a-half per cent per month ; and the property which the writer alludes to as his, was the Moosejaw property, of which Culverwell swore Shaw was the owner, and that it was then in his, Culverwell's hands, to sell for him. He said that the defendants had desired to withhold the Bronté farm, but that as Radford would not deal for the other properties without it, he had suggested that Shaw should transfer the Moosejaw property to Radford, and allow him, Culverwell, to offer it, in the course of the verbal negotiations which preceded the written offer, and that this Radford had authorized

him to do ; having, it may be supposed, some understanding on the subject with Shaw.

On the strength of Shaw's letter, Culverwell wrote
beneath the defendants' proposal, the following :

"I agree to the above exceptions and conditions on
behalf of the said Radford as his agent. September 10th,
1884, 9 p. m. J. T. CULVERWELL, agent to conditional
acceptance only."

He said that he signed it with this limitation, because
he was agent for the Birneys' property, and that he got
the written instructions from Shaw to accept, "just merely
as a conditional offer for Radford to ratify afterwards."

At this time the mortgagees had advertized the property for sale on Saturday, the 13th September, and it
became necessary at once to get a statement of the amount
due, and to arrange for a postponement of the sale. With
some difficulty they were induced to agree to postpone for
two weeks on payment of $400 before the time fixed for
the sale, but the defendants found themselves unable to
procure it within the time, and Shaw refused to make an
advance on foot of the conditional agreement. He offered,
however, to obtain the amount from a friend, if the defendants would turn over to him the Queen Street property at
$52,000, taking in exchange on account the Moosejaw lands.
Culverwell objected to this, insisting that if such an agreement was made it should be subject to the Radford agreement, and that it should not interfere with his commission.
The defendants assuming apparently that the latter was a
binding agreement assented to this, but as Shaw's friend
insisted on controlling the Queen street property himself,
and the money could not otherwise be obtained, an agreement was made between Shaw, acting for one Cossitt, and
the defendants, on the morning of the 13th September, by
which the Queen Street property was transferred at $52,-
000 (instead of $60,000, the price at which it was to have
been assumed by Radford) and at the last moment the
$400 was advanced and the sale postponed for a fortnight.

On the 18th September Radford unexpectedly returned. Some dispute arose between him and Shaw as to the right of the latter to intervene and acquire the Queen street property, but nothing was then settled between them as to it. It is alleged that in the evening of that day at an interview between the defendants, Culverwell and Radford, the latter signed a memorandum, which now appears annexed to the other papers, as follows :

" I hereby ratify conditional acceptance of offer of Birney Bros. to me of certain property in this city on Queen and Richmond streets and two farms in the vicinity of Burlington and Port Credit, made by J. T. Culverwell, as my agent, which he accepted conditionally for me.

The defendants swore that they knew nothing of this memorandum, and that Radford had always refused to commit himself to anything, though he claimed the benefit of Shaw's agreement in case he should be able to raise the money to pay off the mortgage. If necessary to do so, I should find as a fact that the alleged ratification was not communicated to the defendants.

I think it clear that notwithstanding the stipulation in Shaw's letter, Radford did not mean to bind himself absolutely to assume or provide for the $6,000 mortgage, and if he was insisting upon the benefit of Shaw's agreement as to the Queen street property, it seems highly improbable that he would commit himself to an agreement under which he would have to assume it at a very much higher price.

The mortgagees continued to press for payment, and ultimately the negotiations between the defendants and Radford came to nothing, in consequence of his inability to raise the amount required to pay off the mortgage within the extended time, and he told the defendants they had better try to carry out their agreement with Shaw. In the meantime, however, aware of his own inability, but determined to make some profit out of the transaction, he had, on the 22nd September, assigned to Shaw for an expressed consideration of $1,800, all his supposed interest

in the Queen street property, consenting that Shaw should
be at liberty to carry out his own agreement with the
defendants, which he afterwards did, though not without
some changes to their disadvantage.

Upon this state of facts it appears to me that the plaintiff has entirely failed to prove that he procured any such
contract as he has alleged in his statement of claim. It
is manifest that his conditional acceptance of the defendants' terms did not bind Radford to anything. The
defendants had not agreed that their counter-proposal
should be kept open until his return, nor would the pressing nature of the mortgagees' claim admit of their doing
so. They were of necessity driven to make other arrangements in order to meet it ; and this, so far as the plaintiff
and Radford were concerned, in the absence of any binding acceptance of the terms they had offered, they were at
liberty to do. The agreement made by them, accordingly,
with Cossitt through Shaw for one of their properties, put
an end to the Radford offer, which embraced them all.
Nor could Radford's subsequent ratification of the plaintiff's conditional acceptance, even if communicated to the
defendants, establish the contract which that acceptance
purported to conclude, since it was one entirely inconsistent with the Shaw agreement which Radford was then
asserting his right to, and treating as in force. Radford
might perhaps have obtained, as he in fact attempted to
obtain, the benefit of that contract as against the defendants, and might afterwards have arranged with them to
carry out his original proposal as to their other lands, but
his doing so depended upon his ability to make arrangements in respect of the McCausland mortgage, which he
evidently never considered himself bound to do, notwithstanding the stipulation to that effect in Shaw's instructions to Culverwell. In short, as between Radford and the
defendants, the matter never passed beyond the stage of
negotiation ; whether it was to pass into contract or not
depended, as I have said, upon the former being able to
arrange with the mortgagees.

I have not overlooked the memorandum signed by one of the defendants between the 10th and 13th of September, as to paying commission on the whole sale. The plaintiff was then doing all in his power to prevent the defendants from dealing with Shaw, (a course they were forced into taking) and to prevent the larger proposal, productive of so much advantage to himself, from being broken up, and the defendants may have 'been under the impression that there was something binding between themselves and Radford. But, inasmuch as there was no sale or binding contract of sale in fact, such a memorandum must be valueless.

I am, therefore, of opinion, that the plaintiff is not entitled to commission upon the alleged sale to Radford or contract of sale made with him. The recent case of *McKenzie* v. *Champion*, 12 S. C. R. 649, may be referred to, and see also *Benningfield* v. *Kynaston*, 3 T. L. R. 279.

The next question is, whether commission is recoverable in respect of the contract of sale or exchange which was in fact afterwards made and carried out by the defendants.

In *Green* v. *Bartlett*, 14 C. B. N. S. 681, Erle, C. J. says : " The question whether or not an agent is entitled to commission on a sale of property has been repeatedly litigated, and it has usually been decided that if the relation of buyer and seller is really brought about by the act of the agent he is entitled to commission, although the actual sale has not been effected by him."

Has the plaintiff brought himself within this rule ? I am of opinion that he has not.

As regards the Queen street property it appears to me difficult to suggest any fair ground of argument in his favor. He not only took no part in promoting or bringing about the bargain with Shaw or Cossitt, but, acting in Radford's interest and his own, in order to secure a large commission on a single sale of all the properties together, used all the means in his power to prevent it. I do not think he can now, having failed to effect a binding agreement with Radford, be heard to say that he procured the other agreement.

As to the Bronté and Nelson farms; it appears that
after all negotiations with Radford upon the offer submitted through the plaintiff were at an end, the defendants in
pursuance of two different agreements dated respectively
the 7th October and the 13th November, 188 , conveyed
these farms to Radford. According to their evidence,
which does not seem to be contradicted, they were forced
into selling the Bronté farm which they desired to retain
in their own hands, by the refusal of Shaw to relieve it
from the McCausland mortgage, which covered all three
properties, unless they would sell it to Radford, who had
long been desirous of procuring it; and the agreement to
sell the Nelson farm followed because of their inability
otherwise to carry out the terms of the agreement they
had made respecting the Bronté farm.

Apart from the difficulty of holding that agreements
thus brought about resulted directly or naturally from the
plaintiff's exertions, we have the fact distinguishing this
case from that of *Green* v. *Bartlett*, 14 C. B. N. S., 681,
that it was not by means of the plaintiff's intervention or
introduction that Radford became aware that these properties were in the market. As vendor and purchaser the
parties were not brought together by him: they merely
came together again after his intermediate negotiation had
failed, and the agreements they finally arrived at were
entirely independent of that which he had attempted to
make, were different in their terms, and not entered into
by his intervention or procurement.

If then, the plaintiff has not so performed his special
contract as to entitle him to commission, are there any
circumstances from which a contract may be implied to
pay him, as upon a quantum meruit for his labour and
services in endeavouring to find a purchaser? Here again
I think the answer must be in the negative. The case is
not like that of *Pricket* v. *Badger*, 1 C. B. N. S. 296
where the plaintiff having succeeded in finding a person
ready to purchase on the defendant's terms, the latter has
refused, or has been unable to sell, and has rescinded the

agent's authority. As is said by Crowder, J., in *Simp-son* v. *Lamb*, 17 C. B. 603, 618, if it could be shewn that the agent was, by the wrongful act of the principal prevented from carrying out the work on which he was engaged, he would be entitled to a reasonable remuner-ation for what he had done. There is no evidence of that kind here, or of any contract to pay a reasonable compensation if the authority to sell was revoked before a valid contract of sale, or a person ready to become a pur-chaser, was procured.

The observations of Jervis, C. J., in the last case are much in point.

" The right of the agent to be re-imbursed depends upon the terms of the employment. A general em-ployment may carry with it a power of revocation only on payment of a compensation for what may have been done under it, but there may be a qualified employment under which no payment shall be demandable if counter-manded. In the present case I think the evidence shewed that the employment was of that qualified character—like the case of the house agent or the shipbroker—the plain tiffs taking the business on the understanding that they were to have nothing if they did not sell the advowson : taking the chance of the large remuneration they would have received if they had succeeded in obtaining a pur·chaser."

For the foregoing reasons I am of opinion that the appeal should be allowed ; but I desire to add with reference to the particular ground on which my brother Armour dis-posed of the case at the trial, that taking the facts to be as he found them, I should not as at present advised be dis-posed to differ from his judgment.

It may be less difficult in the case of an exchange of lands to infer knowledge on the part of the vendor or vendee that the broker he employs is the paid agent of the opposite party and receiving a commission for making for that party the best bargain he can, and the assent of the vendor to employ the broker on those conditions ; but ad-hering to the view expressed by the Court of Common Pleas in *Culverwell* v. *Campton*, 31 C.P. 342, I have no doubt that that knowledge and that assent must be proved to entitle the broker to his commission. What I have said has of course no application to the case where the broker merely introduces the parties to each other, or brings them together leaving them to make their own bargain.

HAGARTY, C. J. O., and BURTON, J. A., concurred.

Appeal allowed with costs.

ARSCOTT V. LILLEY.

False imprisonment—Action against justice of the peace —Costs— R. S. O., ch. 73, sec. 19—Objection to appeal—Irregularity.

The provisions of R. S. O.. ch. 73, sec. 4, protect a magistrate from an action for anything done under a conviction so long as the conviction remains in force ; not where the conviction does not justify what has been done under it.

The plaintiff being in custody on a warrant issued by the defendant L. on a conviction had before him under the Vagrant Act, applied to be discharged under the Habeas Corpus Act, the plaintiff electing to remain in custody at London to attending before the judge in Toronto, and on the 4th of February an order was made on that application for her discharge, which order was duly received by the gaoler on the 6th. Meanwhile a fresh warrant had been issued by L. on the 4th and delivered to the gaoler, who, by direction of the County Crown Attorney, detained her for two hours after receipt of the order for her discharge when another warrant was prepared, and she was again arrested. In an action brought for such arrest and imprisonment for two hours, the jury found the plaintiff was entitled to a verdict, but that she had not sustained any damage which the learned judge before whom the case was tried treated as a verdict for the defendants, but refused the justice his costs (11 O. R. 285). On appeal to this Court the dismissal of the action was affirmed, but

Held, reversing the judgment of the Court below, that sec. 19 of R. S.O., ch. 73, has not been repealed by any of the provisions of the Ontario Judicature Act ; and therefore the dismissal of the action should be with costs to the magistrate, as between solicitor and client.

Where a conviction is affirmed on appeal to the sessions the warrant of distress or commitment may be issued by the convicting justice.

Held, also, that the plaintiff could not object to the appeal as irregular, on the ground that, having been begun by both defendants, it was continued by only one.

Per OSLER, J. A.   If there was anything in the objection, it should have been taken by way of substantive motion to strike out the appeal for irregularity.

THIS was an appeal by the defendants Lilley and Hutchinson, and a cross-appeal by the plaintiff from a judgment of the Common Pleas Division reported 11 O. R. 285, where and in the report of the case between the same parties at page 153 of the same volume and in the present judgments the facts and circumstances giving rise to the action are fully and clearly set forth.

The appeal came on to be heard on the 29th and 30th of March, 1887.*

McCarthy, Q.C., and *R. M. Meredith,* for the plaintiff in the Court below.

Aylesworth, for the defendant Lilley.

The defendant *Hutchinson* in person.

Present.--HAGARTY, C.J.O., BURTON, PATTERSON, and OSLER, JJ.A.

MAY 10, 1887.   PATTERSON, J. A.—This action is against
Charles Lilley, the Mayor of London East, and Charles
Hutchinson, the County Crown Attorney for Middlesex,
to recover damages for the arrest and imprisonment of the
plaintiff.

The action was commenced on the 17th of March, 1885.

The statement of claim contains eight complaints or
counts.

1. That on the 24th of September, 1884, the defendants
and each of them caused and procured the plaintiff to be
taken into custody, and to be brought into custody before
the defendant Lilley and detained in custody for a long
time, and thence taken in custody through the streets to
the common gaol, and there imprisoned for two days.

2. That on the 24th of September, 1884, the defendants
and each of them *falsely and maliciously and without
reasonable and probable cause, caused and procured, &c.,*
as in the first count.

3. That on the 25th of September, 1884, the defendant
Lilley falsely and maliciously and without reasonable and
probable cause refused—at the instance of and in conspiracy with the defendant Hutchinson to deprive the
plaintiff of her liberty, and to keep her confined in gaol
contrary to the provisions of the statute relating to summary convictions and appeals therefrom—to admit the
plaintiff to bail after she had been committed under a
warrant purporting to have been made by Lilley.

4. That on the 18th of December, 1884, the defendants
and each of them, caused and procured the plaintiff to be
arrested and kept in close custody until the 6th of February,
1885, when she was discharged by an order of the High
Court of Justice.

5. Charging the same as in the 4th count, but as done
falsely and maliciously and without reasonable and probable cause.

6. That on the 6th of February, 1885, the defendants,
and each of them, caused and procured the plaintiff to be
arrested and taken into custody and detained in the common gaol for six hours, until released by the gaoler under
the said order of the High Court of Justice.

7. That on the 6th of February the defendants, and each
of them, knowing that by an order of the High Court of

Justice the keeper of the common gaol was ordered to release the plaintiff, who was in his custody, conspired together to cause and procure the keeper to detain the plaintiff, and did cause and procure him to detain her two hours.

8. Undistinguishable from the 7th.

It appeared that on the 24th of September, 1884, the plaintiff had been convicted before the defendant Lilley " for that she did on the 24th day of September, 1884, at the town of London East, unlawfully keep a certain bawdy house and house of ill-fame for the resort of prostitutes, and is a vagrant within the meaning of the statute entitled An Act respecting Vagrants," and was sentenced to be imprisoned in the common gaol at hard labour for six months. She was committed to gaol under a warrant issued by Mr. Lilley on the 24th of September, in pursuance of the conviction, and remained there two days, when she was liberated on bail pending her appeal to the General Sessions.

The appeal was heard at the Sessions in December, and the conviction was affirmed.

Thereupon a second warrant was issued by the defendant Lilley on the 18th of December, and the plaintiff was arrested and recommitted to gaol. That warrant recited the conviction of the 24th of September, and the sentence of six months, and directed the keeper of the gaol to imprison the plaintiff at hard labour for the period of six months, taking no notice of the fact that she had already suffered two days imprisonment.

The plaintiff sued out a writ of habeas corpus, to which the gaoler returned the warrant of the 18th of December as the only reason for the detention of the plaintiff; and on the 4th of February, 1885, an order was made by a Judge of the High Court at Toronto, for the discharge of the plaintiff.

The plaintiff was not brought before the Judge upon the return of the writ, having elected not to be taken before him, but remained in gaol at London. She could not, therefore, have complained of the detention from the time of the making of the order in Toronto until it could, in the ordinary course, reach the gaoler at London, nor does she complain of the detention during that interval further than as part of her general complaint that everything done under the second warrant was illegal. Her 6th, 7th, and 8th counts are founded on her detention for a couple of hours after the receipt by the gaoler of the order for her discharge. She was so detained, and there is no doubt that that was at the instance or by the advice of the defendant Hutchinson who wished to have another warrant ready for her re-arrest, and she was re-arrested at the door of the gaol on a new warrant prepared by Mr. Hutchinson and signed by Mr. Lilley on the 6th of February. She remained six hours longer in custody, when the sheriff, becoming apprehensive of liability, directed the gaoler to let her go, and she was for the time set free.

The whole history, only part of which I have noticed, is full of surprises. Unexpected opportunities for doing things the wrong way seem to have started up at every step, and seldom to have been let slip. One matter of surprise is, why the sheriff interfered with a person who was not his prisoner. The effect, however, was to set her free until the 18th of March, when she was arrested again. We have nothing directly to do with this last arrest, because the plaintiff had begun this action during her interval of liberty ; but it cannot be passed without notice, because the plaintiff sued out a new writ of habeas corpus on which, in May, 1885, she was again discharged, giving occasion for the discussion of questions of law to which it will be necessary to allude : *Regina* v. *Arscott*, 9 O. R. 541.

The plaintiff also brought an action against these defendants to recover the penalty of £500 sterling under the Habeas Corpus Act, 29 Charles II. ch. 2, sec. 6, on the ground that, having been set at large upon habeas corpus, she had been recommitted for the same offence ; and in delivering the judgment of the Divisional Court of the Queen's Bench Division in that action, the learned Chief

Justice dealt with most of the questions arising on the facts to which I have been adverting, which may make it unnecessary now to discuss those questions at much length.

We have in this case an appeal and a cross-appeal.

The action was tried before the Chief Justice of the Common Pleas, who entered, as the verdict of the jury, a verdict for the defendants, and gave judgment dismissing the action, but not giving the defendants costs. That judgment was affirmed in the Divisional Court. The defendant Lilley appeals against the disallowance of his costs, and the plaintiff objects by way of cross-appeal to the verdict for the defendants.

The cross-appeal should be considered first.

There seems some uncertainty as to just what took place when the verdict was rendered. The extract given us from the shorthand notes is this: "The jury returned at 3.05 p.m. and handed a paper to his Lordship. His Lordship.—The jury find in favor of the defendants, they find that the plaintiff is not entitled to any damages." The contention now is, that the plaintiff had been illegally arrested, and that she was therefore entitled to a verdict in her favor for at least nominal damages.

It would, I imagine, be hopeless to expect a jury to find differently on the subject of damages. The plaintiff was convicted and sentenced to six months imprisonment at hard labor, and she has got off without serving out her sentence. Still, if any of her legal rights have been violated, she has a case for nominal damages. But how do the facts help her?

She obtained her discharge on her appeal to the Sessions on her undertaking with sureties to return to imprisonment if the conviction was affirmed; and apart from her undertaking her sentence stood, and the judgment of the Sessions was, that it should be enforced. The fact of her recommittal therefore was no wrong to her. The original warrant to the gaoler was not effete. If she had voluntarily returned to gaol or had been surrendered by

her bail, no further warrant was necessary. But she complains of being re-arrested under the warrant of the 18th
of December because reciting, as it did correctly, the sentence for six months, it directed the gaoler to imprison her
for that term, without noticing the two days imprisonment
before the appeal ; and she further contends that the defendant Lilley having already issued one warrant on the conviction was incapacitated from issuing another.

These objections, if well founded, would not, as I at
present think, be met by the provision of R. S. O. ch. 73,
sec. 4, which protects a justice of the peace from an action
for anything done under a conviction until the conviction
has been quashed, because they do not depend on the inval-
idity of the conviction. The point is, that the conviction
did not justify what was done.

I may as well say, at this place, that I think the conviction was good for the reasons given by Wilson, C. J., in
Arscott v. *Lilley*, 11 O.R. pp. 180 to 182, and that I shall
not attempt to add anything to what he has said on that
subject.

I do not see any good reason for holding that the power
of the magistrate did not extend to issuing the second
warrant. By what authority did he issue the first ? Not
by virtue of anything expressly enacted in the statute.
All the provisions of the Act of 1869, 32 & 33 Vict. ch. 31
(D.), necessary to refer to on this subject are identical with
those in C. S. C. ch. 103. The jurisdiction of the justice to
enforce his own conviction is assumed in both statutes, and
the express provisions recognise the jurisdiction, and merely
regulate its exercise in particular classes of cases. Thus
section 52 of each statute provides that in one case " the
defendant shall be served with a copy of the minute of the
order before any warrant of commitment or of distress is
issued in that behalf." Section 63 provides that when
a defendant adjudged to be imprisoned, is already in
imprisonment upon another conviction, the warrant
of commitment shall be forthwith delivered to the
gaoler, "and the justice or justices who issued the

same" may order that the imprisonment for the subsequent offence shall commence at the expiration of the
previous sentence. Section 86 of the Act of 1869, like
sec. 71 of the C. S. C. ch. 103, declare that " After a case
has been heard and determined, one justice may issue all
warrants of distress or commitment thereon," the object
of the section as shewn by the context being to make it
unnecessary that two or more justices should join in enforcing a conviction merely because two or more were
required to make the conviction. The next section in
each statute is supplementary, being that " It shall not be
necessary that the justice who acts before or after the
hearing, be the justice or one of the justices by whom the
case is or was heard or determined." And to make it clear
(as I apprehend the purpose of the clause) that the general power of the justice is not affected by an unsuccessful
appeal, we have section 70 of 1869, (or 66 of ch. 103) to
which so much argument has been addressed, declaring
that " In case an appeal against any conviction or order be
decided in favour of the respondents, the justice or justices
who made the conviction or order, or any other justice of
the peace for the same territorial division, may issue the
warrant of distress or commitment for execution of the
same, as if no appeal had been brought." Other sections,
in fact every section where the issue of a warrant by way
of execution is referred to, concur in bearing out the
same reading of the statute. See *e.g.*, sections 57, 59, 61,
and 62, the same numbers in both statutes, and sec. 75
of 1869, which is 67 of ch. 103.

Then, as we do not look to this statute for the original
power to issue a commitment, we find nothing in it to prevent
the justice issuing more than one on the same conviction.
If he chose to amuse himself by issuing a fresh one every
morning no actionable wrong would be done to the convict; and if the convict happened to escape from custody
or to be at large when under his sentence he ought to be
in gaol, and was arrested under any one of those warrants,
I do not understand on what principle the fact that that

37—VOL XIV A.R.

was not the first warrant issued by the justice on that conviction would give him an action of trespass against the justice.

On the other objection to this warrant I have very little to add to what was said by Wilson, C. J. His opinion inclined very strongly against the objection, though he did not pronounce so decidedly upon it as upon the other. My opinion is at least as decided as that which he expressed, which would be quite far enough to go upon this appeal in which the plaintiff has assumed the burden of convincing us that she ought to have had a verdict.

The order for the plaintiff's discharge upon the habeas corpus is not an adjudication against these defendants that the arrest ordered by the warrant was illegal. The judgment upon that application is not in appeal before us. Looking at the warrant we see that upon its face it is perfectly regular, reciting a valid conviction and ordering the enforcement of it in the terms of the conviction itself, and we know that nothing was done under the warrant that the conviction did not authorize. If a longer term of imprisonment had been actually suffered than the six months, a question might have arisen as to where the blame lay. The plaintiff had it in her power to have all danger, if any existed, of too long an imprisonment removed. She was advised to apply by habeas corpus, and perhaps owing to the omission to return any but one cause of detention, —which is one of the surprises I spoke of—she was discharged. I do not doubt she could have found ample protection by other means, but I need say no more on that topic which has been dealt with by Wilson, C. J., whose views I adopt.

In discussing the arrest made after the discharge of the plaintiff on the 6th of February and the matters connected with it, I wish to confine myself to the aspect of the proceedings which concerns the plaintiff's rights. Looking back on the course actually taken, one can see that the occasion for some observations that have been made would not have arisen if nothing had been done towards the re-arrest of the plaintiff until the order on the habeas corpus application had been actually carried out; and, looking back after the event, it may be thought that the interests of the community would not have suffered, and that possibly the ends of justice would have been substantially served, if the plaintiff had taken the opportunity to do what we are told she has since done, and leave the country before a fresh warrant could overtake her.

It is obvious, however, that as far as her legal rights are concerned, the precise moment at which she was re-committed to serve out the remainder of her sentence is not a material consideration.

The order on the habeas corpus application was made at Toronto on the 4th of February, 1885. The plaintiff had chosen to remain in the gaol at London in place of being brought before the Judge in Toronto. Had she not so elected, but had let her writ be executed according to its tenor, she would have been discharged from custody when the decision was pronounced. The legal effect of the order was to discharge her at once, but by her own consent she had to remain in custody till the order reached the hands of the gaoler, which was not until the 6th.

On the 4th the defendant Lilley had issued a warrant, prepared by his co-defendant, which was unobjectionable in form and substance, and it was on that day delivered to the gaoler.

The defendant Hutchinson, however, seems to have thought it better to have the plaintiff re-arrested after being formally set at liberty under the order. Accordingly we find him writing on the 5th of February to the gaoler, and saying, amongst other things: " I think it possible an order may come to discharge Mrs. Arscott from the original warrant, but unless the order prevents your doing so, you should detain her on the warrant given you yesterday, and I want to see the order so as to decide the question. I will be responsible for all you do under my instructions.''

She was thereupon, as I have already mentioned, detained about two hours after the order came, and then a new warrant having been issued, the last arrest before action took place under it. From what I have already said it follows, in my opinion, that nothing was done by the defendant Lilley of which the plaintiff can complain as a wrong to her.

There was no detention under the warrant of 4th of February, except for the two hours on the 6th. During the intervening day or day and a half from the pronouncing of the judgment in Toronto, I take the legal position to be that she was there by her own arrangement, or, what is probably the same thing in effect, under the commitment of the 18th of September. But the actual detention for the two hours seems to have been at the instance of the defendant Hutchinson, and it is apparent that but for his interference the order would have been obeyed as soon as it came.

There is, therefore, no sufficient reason for holding the plaintiff entitled to a verdict against the defendant Lilley, and as to him the cross-appeal must be dismissed, with costs.

If there is any different right as against the defendant Hutchinson, it is only in respect of the two hours. But after a good deal of consideration, I am not able to say that the present verdict should be disturbed. I do not profess to have a perfectly clear opinion on the legal position created by the order made in Toronto, the voluntary submission to imprisonment till it arrived in London, the warrant of the 4th of February on which, if the plaintiff had been in Toronto, and had been there discharged by the Judge, she might properly have been arrested before or on the morning of the 6th, and the force, whatever it continued to be, of the first warrant of all. It is not impossible that with a fuller knowledge of the facts, including the terms of the plaintiff's arrangement to remain in London in place of being brought on her writ to Toronto, some position might be worked out shewing a clear right of action. We are told simply that she elected not to appear. The object to be gained by changing the verdict into one for nominal damages for the plaintiff is not one calling for astuteness on the part of the Court. If a clear legal right had been in-

vaded the Court would make every fair intendment in aid ·
of the action, even though no actual damage had been
suffered. But when the absence of actual damage is the
one fact that is clear, and the legal right has to be groped
for in doubt and confusion, the case is not one in which the
verdict for the defendant should be interfered with.

The cross-appeal, therefore, fails as to both the defendants, but should be dismissed, without costs, as to the
defendant Hutchinson.

A preliminary objection was taken to the prosecution
by the defendant Lilley of his appeal without the other
defendant joining. Both defendants gave notice of appeal,
and they joined in the appeal bond, but the defendant
Hutchinson decided not to proceed farther, and gave notice
to that effect to the plaintiff, and the defendant Lilley
proceeded alone. There is nothing in the objection, even
if it can properly be raised at this stage after the settling
of the appeal book and the receiving and answering the
separate reasons of appeal given by the one defendant.
See *Watson* v. *Cave*, 17 Ch. D. 23.

The circumstance that a joint appeal bond was given is
not a disadvantage to the plaintiff. On the contrary she
apparently has the security of Lilley for whatever costs or
damages may have been occasioned by Hutchinson's failure
to prosecute his appeal, and she has been able, without
bringing a substantive appeal and without giving security,
to bring forward her cross-appeal against both defendants.

The question upon the appeal is, whether the provision
of R. S. O. ch. 73, sec. 19 entitling a justice of the peace
who succeeds in his defence to an action for anything done
by him in the execution of his office to his full costs, to be
taxed as between attorney and client, is so inconsistent
with the Judicature Act as to be repealed by the force of
section 90, sub-sec. 2 of which includes in the repeal "any
enactment inconsistent with this Act."

The asserted inconsistency is not with anything in the
body of the Act, but with Rule 428, which has force as
part of the statute, and which provides that, "subject

to the provisions of the Act, the costs of and incident to
all proceedings in the High Court shall be in the discretion of the Court," &c.

In the Court below, (11 O. R. 285,) the decision that the
repeal affected this statute and left the costs in the discretion of the Court under Rule 428, was given with much
hesitation in view of the opinions expressed in the House
of Lords in *Garnett* v *Bradley*, 3 App. Cas. 944, to the
effect that the Judicature Act did not do away with the
right to costs given by statute to particular classes of persons.

I think I should myself have yielded to the force of
those opinions and held the defendant Lilley entitled as of
right to his costs; but the doubt has now been authoritatively resolved in the defendant's favor by the re-enact-
ment in the new Revised Statutes of the former provision.
This is a recognition and affirmance of the clause as
unaffected by the repealing section of the Judicature Act,
and is not the revival of an effete or repealed enactment.
Therefore its effect for our present purpose is immediate,
notwithstanding that the Revised Statutes do not become
operative at once.

The appeal must be allowed, with costs.

OSLER, J.A.—As regards the defendant Lilley's appeal
against the judgment of the Common Pleas Division
depriving him of his costs, it appears to me that the
plaintiff has not succeeded in shewing that the judgment
was improperly entered for the defendants at the trial.
I mean that we cannot assume that the finding of the
jury was not in fact a finding for the defendants, but
that it was, as is suggested, a finding for the plaintiff
without damages, on which judgment should have been
entered for the plaintiff for nominal damages.

Taking the finding and judgment as reported, the
defendant recovered judgment in an action in which he
was charged as a justice of the peace for something done
by him in the execution of the office. That being so he

was by force of section 19 of the Justices' Protection Act entitled to his costs, a right of which the Court prior to the Judicature Act had no power to deprive him. It appears to me to be clearly settled by more than one decision that the Judicature Act 'and rules have not altered the law in this respect, and that where a special privilege as to costs is conferred by statute upon certain individual litigants the general jurisdiction of the Court or Judge over costs does not extend to deprive them of such privilege. The effect and intention of the Act and orders is only to regulate the mode in which costs are to be dealt with in cases where the Court antecedently had jurisdiction either acquired or statutory, to award costs: *Hasker* v. *Wood,* 54 L. J. 419 ; *Re Mills's Estate,* 34 Ch. D. 24. Moreover, as my brother Patterson has pointed out, this construction has now been placed upon the Act in question as re-enacted in the new Revised Statutes.

The defendant Lilley's appeal must therefore be allowed as regards his costs of the action ; the appeal of the defendant Hutchinson on that point was abandoned.

As regards the defendant Lilley's right to continue an appeal on his own behalf which was begun as a joint appeal by the now defendants but which one of them discontinued, I do not see how any objection on that point can now be open to the plaintiff, as she has made use of the appeal to bring forward and sustain a cross-appeal upon the merits of the whole case, as against both defendants.

If there was anything in the objection it should have been taken by way of substantive motion to strike out the appeal for irregularity. A respondent cannot use the appeal for the purpose of a cross-appeal, and at the same time argue that it is not regularly before the Court. The positions are inconsistent. I agree substantially with what my brother Patterson has said in disposing of the cross-appeal. It ought to be dismissed, but as regards the defendant Hutchinson, without costs. Speaking for myself I think it impossible to pass over without some

mark of disapproval, the latter's conduct in reference to
the order of Mr. Justice Galt discharging the plaintiff.   It
was not his duty to interfere with the operation of that
order in any way.   As an officer of the Court he should
have known that it was the duty of the gaoler to obey it
at once, and he ought not to have advised any other course.
I am aware that what was done proceeded from an excess
of zeal, which has indeed occasioned all this troublesome
and expensive litigation, and not from an improper motive ;
but officers should know that while the order of a Court
or Judge stands unreversed, it is not to be canvassed. but
obeyed.

HAGARTY, C. J. O., and BURTON, J. A., concurred.

Appeal allowed, with costs.

*Cross-appeal dismissed, with costs to defendant Lilley—
without costs to defendant Hutchinson.*

ARSCOTT V. LILLEY.

Vagrant Act, conviction and commitment under—Discharge under Habeas Corpus Act—Penalty of £500 stg. under sec. 6 of Act.

The plaintiff had been convicted under the Vagrant Act and sentenced and committed to the common gaol for six months, but was discharged on *habeas corpus* for irregularity in the warrant of committment, whereupon a fresh warrant on the same conviction was sued out and the plaintiff was re-committed thereon.

In an action brought to recover the penalty of £500 stg. imposed under sec. 6 of the Habeas Corpus Act (31 Ch. 2 c. 2) as having been "again imprisoned or committed for the same offence" the Queen's Bench Division held the section did not apply and dismissed the action, with costs.

On appeal that judgment was affirmed, with costs.

THIS was an appeal by the plaintiff from the judgments of the Queen's Bench Division (11 O. R. 153) where and in the next preceding judgment the facts are fully stated.

The appeal came on to be heard before this Court on the 3rd of March, 1887.*

McCarthy, Q.C., and *R. M. Meredith*, for the appellant.

Aylesworth, for the respondent Lilley.

The respondent *Hutchinson* in person.

May 10th, 1887. PATTERSON, J. A.--This is an action to recover from the defendant Lilley who was mayor of the town of London East, and from the defendant Hutchinson, the County Crown Attorney for Middlesex, the penalty of £500 stg., under the Habeas Corpus Act, 31 Charles II. ch. 2, sec. 6.

The plaintiff was convicted before the defendant Lilley of an offence under the Vagrant Act, and sentenced to six months imprisonment. She was committed to the common goal under a warrant issued in execution of the conviction, and was discharged on habeas corpus for an irregularity in the warrant.

Present—HAGARTY, C. J. O., BURTON, PATTERSON, and OSLER, JJ.A.

38—VOL XIV A.R.

Thereupon the defendant Hutchinson sued out from the defendant Lilley a fresh warrant on the same conviction, and upon it the plaintiff was re-committed.

She claims the penalty on the ground that her case comes within the meaning of section 6, under which a person discharged by habeas corpus is not to be "again imprisoned or committed for the same offence by any person or persons whatsoever other than by the legal order or process of such Court, wherein he or they shall be bound by recognizance to appear, or other court having jurisdiction of the cause."

In the Divisional Court (11 O. R. 153) it was held that the section did not apply and the action was dismissed.

The learned Chief Justice who delivered the judgment of the Court discussed in an exhaustive manner the whole subject, which included several matters that were more directly in question in the other action between the same parties in which judgment has just been given. It would serve no useful purpose to enter now upon a separate investigation of the construction of the Habeas Corpus Act, and its bearing upon the present litigation, because we should be merely traversing the same ground and repeating the same arguments which led to the conclusion against the plaintiff in the Court below. We content ourselves with expressing our concurrence with the judgment pronounced by Chief Justice Wilson and dismiss the appeal.

HAGARTY, C.J.O., BURTON, and OSLER, JJ.A., concurred.

Appeal dismissed, with costs.

THE CANADA ATLANTIC RAILWAY COMPANY V. THE COR-
PORATION OF THE TOWNSHIP OF CAMBRIDGE.

*Municipal corporation—Bonus to railway—Equality of votes—Casting vote
of clerk—R. S. O. ch. 174, secs. 154, 317—Promulgation.*

In 1880, (before the passing of 46 Vict. ch. 18, (O.) a municipal council.
with the view of granting a bonus to a railway company, caused to be
submitted to the vote of the ratepayers a by-law to raise money for that
purpose. At the voting thereon the votes for and against it were
equal, and the clerk of the municipality, who also acted as returning
officer, verbally gave a casting vote in favor of the by-law.

Held, [reversing the judgment of the C. P. D., 11 O. R. 392] that section
152 of the Municipal Act, R. S. O., ch. 174, is not applicable to the
case of voting on a by-law , and therefore the casting vote of the clerk
was a nullity, and the by-law did not receive the assent of the electors
of the municipality within the meaning of R. S. O., ch. 174, sec. 317 ;
as such a defect could not be cured by promulgation of the by-law.

Held, also, following *Canada Atlantic* v. *Ottawa*, 12 A. R. 234, and *S. C.*
12 S. C. R. 377, that the by-law was bad for non-compliance with sec.
330 of the Municipal Act, R. S. O. ch. 174, the section corresponding
with section 248 of 36 Vict. ch. 48.

Per BURTON, J. A. The provisions of section 248 of the Municipal Act
of 1876, 36 Vict. ch. 48, do not apply to by-laws for granting bonuses to
railways, and the judgment of the Supreme Court of Canada in *Canada
Atlantic R. W. Co.* v. *Ottawa*, 12 S. C. R. 377, does not so decide.

THIS was an appeal by the defendants from a judgment
of the Common Pleas Division, reported 11 O. R. 392, and
came on to be heard before this Court 25th and 28th of
March, 1887.*

J. Maclennan, Q.C., for the appellants.
McCarthy, Q.C., and *Chrysler* for the respondents.

The facts clearly appear in the former reports and in
the present judgments.

May 10, 1887.   OSLER, J. A.—This is an appeal from
the judgment of the C. P. Division, affirming the judgment
of Rose, J., at the trial.

The action is for a mandamus to compel the defendants
to sign, issue, and deliver to the plaintiffs debentures of
the municipality to the amount of $20,000, to which they
allege they are entitled under the terms of a by-law of the
municipality, passed on the 22nd March, 1880, and a declaration is also sought that the plaintiffs have complied with.

* *Present* :—HAGARTY, C.J.O., BURTON, PATTERSON, and OSLER, JJ.A.

all conditions of the by-law necessary to entitle them to the debentures.

The validity of the by-law was contested on several grounds, but I think the only questions which require serious consideration are :

1. Whether the by-law, which was one to raise upon the credit of the municipality money not required for its ordinary expenditure and not payable within the same financial year, in order to grant a bonus to a railway company, received the assent of the electors of the municipality in the manner provided by the Municipal Act.

2. If the by-law was so assented to, whether the defects and errors apparent upon its face, arising from its non-compliance with the requirements of section 330 of the Act, were cured by its promulgation.

It is unnecessary to examine the evidence at length.

The first question depends entirely upon the right of the clerk of the municipality, who was returning officer for the occasion, to give a casting vote on summing up the votes for and against the by-law.

If he had such right the by-law was carried by a majority of one. If he had not, then, inasmuch as the ballot votes for and against it were equal, the by-law was not carried by a majority of the duly qualified electors voting thereon, and therefore did not receive the assent required by the Act.

The 26th February 1880, was the day appointed by the by-law for taking the votes of the electors, and the 1st of March following, for the summing up by the clerk of the votes given for and against it.

There were two polling sub-divisions in the municipality, at one of which the clerk acted as deputy-returning officer.

On the 1st March the votes were summed up by the clerk in his capacity of returning officer, from the statements of the deputy returning officers, 87 votes for and 87 against the by-law. The ballot votes thus being equal the clerk, believing that he had a right to give a casting vote "to decide the election," as he expressed it, verbally gave it in favor of the by-law, and, having done so, certified that the majority of the electors had voted in its favor. On the 22nd March it was finally passed by the council.

The statutory enactments which are to be considered in this case are those found in the R. S. O. ch. 174, as amended by 42 Vic. ch. 31, (O.)

Section 559, sub-section 5, provides that no municipal corporation shall incur a debt for granting a bonus to a railway company unless the by-law for that purpose shall before the final passing thereof, receive the assent of the electors of the municipality in the manner provided by the Act. Section 330 contains a similar provision in the case of a by-law creating a debt not payable in the same financial year.

A group of sections 286 to 318, together with another group—116 to 169, so far as the latter are applicable, prescribe the proceedings which are to be taken for ascertaining the assent of !the electors, the subsequent proceedings in the case of a scrutiny, and the condition on which the power of the council to pass the by-law arises.

The vote is to be taken by ballot, section 298.   Certain classes only of electors can vote, sub-sections 301, 302; and at the close of the poll the deputy-returning officers are to make out and sign a written statement, shewing *inter alia* the number of votes cast for and against the by-law; sub-sections 305 and 147, sub-section 5.   The ballot papers are, then, together with these statements and certain other particulars, to be sent to the clerk, whose duty on receipt thereof is thus prescribed by section 310 :

"The clerk, after he has received the ballot papers and statement before mentioned of the number of votes given in each polling place, shall, at the time and place appointed by the by-law,   *   *   without opening any of the sealed packets of ballot papers, sum up from such statements the number of votes for and against the by-law, and shall then and there declare the result, and forthwith certify to the council, under his hand, whether the majority of the electors voting upon the by-law have approved or disapproved of the by-law."

If a scrutiny is granted, the County Judge is at a time and place appointed, upon inspecting the ballot papers and hearing such evidence as he may deem necessary, and upon hearing the parties, to determine in a summary manner whether the majority of the votes given is for or against the by-law, and certify the result to the council.

Section 317 then enacts that any by-law which is carried by a majority of the duly qualified electors voting thereon, shall, within six weeks thereafter, be passed by the council. This section, read in connection with section 286, sub-section 3, merely prescribes a time within which the by-law is to be taken into consideration by the council and per- fected. It does not cast upon them an imperative duty to pass it at all events. If not passed within the time limited it drops: *Canada Atlantic R. W. Co.* v. *Ottawa*, 12 S. C. R. 377.

If the clauses I have hitherto referred to are, as the defendants contend, the only ones which govern the case, they do not leave it in doubt that the majority in favour of the by-law is to be ascertained by the clerk from the statements of the deputy-returning officers alone, and that it is only a by-law which is carried by the votes of the duly qualified electors voting thereon which the council can pass. If there is not a majority of such votes, the by-law is simply not carried. Presumitur pro negante.

The plaintiffs, however, contend that section 152, which confers upon the clerk the right to give a casting vote at an election for members of the council, where two or more candidates have an equal number of votes, is by force of sec. 299 made applicable to the case of voting on a by-law.

This section which is one of the second group already mentioned, under the heading "Voting on By-laws," enacts that the proceedings at the poll (that is the poll of votes on the by-law).

" And for and incidental to the same and the purposes thereof shall be the same as nearly as may be as at municipal elections, and all the provisions of sections 116 to 169 inclusive, of the Act, so far as the same are applicable, and except so far as is herein otherwise provided, shall apply to the taking of votes at such poll and to all matters incidental thereto."

This is a loose way of applying a large group of sections which have a general bearing on the procedure of voting by ballot, and a very cursory examination will suffice to shew that among those thus compendiously included are several which are entirely excluded by the qualifying words, and others which are repeated verbatim ; an observation which seems to meet the argument that section 152 would not have been included, or would have been specially excluded if it had not been intended that it should have some application.

Before referring to section 152, we must notice the clerk's duty as returning officer at a municipal election. After receipt of the ballot papers and statements of the votes given at each polling place, he is to cast up the number of votes for each candidate from such statements, and at the town hall at noon on the day following their return to him, is to publicly declare to be elected the candidate having the highest number of votes, section 151.

Then follows section 152, on which the plaintiffs rely : " In case it appears upon the casting up of the votes as aforesaid that two or more candidates have an equal number of votes, the clerk of the municipality * * whether otherwise qualified or not, shall, at the time he declares the result of the poll, give a vote for one or more of such candidates, so as to decide the election."

Upon the best consideration I can bring to the question, and after having twice heard it very fully argued (the first time on the motion for mandamus, which was dismissed, 3 O. R. 291, on the authority of *Grand Junction R. W. Co.* v. *Peterborough*, 8 S. C. R. 76, on the ground that the remedy was by action) I incline to the opinion that the force and effect of this section is wholly confined to the proceedings at a municipal election, and that it cannot be held to apply to the case of voting on a by-law consistently with the other provisions on that subject.

A consideration of the essential difference in the nature of the two proceedings will, I think, make this clear. An election for member of a municipal council ought to be effectual. It should result in the return of somebody, that being what it is held for: and not less so, if the polling of every vote on the voters' list happens to result in a tie between the candidates. The business of the municipality must be carried on, and therefore where the votes on each side are equal, the clerk, whether otherwise qualified or not, gives a casting vote pro hac vice, on one side or the other, in order to *decide the election*. Until he has done so, each candidate is in the same position, neither of them has won, neither lost, and the clerk's vote is effectual, on whichever side he casts it. It decides the election.

On the other hand no necessity exists for a by-law to create a debt or to grant a bonus to a railway company. It is voluntary, first with the electors to carry it, and afterwards with the council to pass it. And so where there is an equality of votes, the case is one in which, unless we can clearly see that the Legislature has otherwise enacted, the maxim already mentioned might well apply. Though it is not necessary that such a by-law should be carried, it must be carried before the council can pass it; and it cannot be carried without the assent of certain qualified electors, an assent, which as I read the Act, is withheld, unless a sufficient number of them, that is to say a majority of those voting thereon vote in favor of it. The 317th section is a plain declaration that the only by-law which a council has authority to pass is one which is carried by a majority of the duly qualified electors voting thereon. Suppose, then, the votes of such electors, as ascertained by the clerk from the statements of the deputy-returning officers, are merely equal for and against the by-law; and we may also suppose, without weakening the argument, that the votes of all the qualified electors on the list have been polled; there is no majority either way, it is true. But if there is not a majority in its favor, is not that fatal? The by-law being already lost, what remains to be *decided* by the clerk? If it be held that in such case he has a vote by virtue of section 152, it is not in the nature of a casting vote which may be effectually given for or against the by-law.

The only effectual vote which he can give is one in favor of the by-law, since a vote against it would be merely thrown away. If we accede to the plaintiffs' argument, we must hold that the Legislature intended that where the votes of the qualified electors are equal for and against the by-law, which therefore so far has not been carried by the votes of the qualified electors, it may be carried by the vote of a person who may not be a qualified elector at all. In short, they wish to read the statute as if it provided that where the votes are equal and therefore there is not a majority for the by-law, the clerk may convert the equality into a majority by giving his possibly otherwise unqualified vote. I think that section 317 is a distinct declaration to the contrary of this, and I fail to see that any valid argument can be drawn in support of the contention that there must be a nominal majority one way or the other, from the fact that section 310 directs the clerk to certify whether [the majority of the electors voting upon the by-law have approved or disapproved of it. The same form of expression is found in the Municipal Act of 1873, section 231, sub-section 6, and also in the Act of 1866, in neither of which can it be plausibly argued that there is anything to be found extending the clerk's right to give a casting vote at an election to the case of voting on a by-law. So, also, a scrutiny of the ballot papers before the County Judge may result in a tie, yet his duty, in the language of the section 315, is to determine in a summary manner whether the majority of the votes given is for or against the by-law, and to forthwith certify the result to the council.

Nor can I accede to the argument that because the clerk's name was on the voters' list in fact, that gave him any right to vote as and when he did vote. His right to vote at that time and place, depended entirely upon whether he could do so as clerk and returning officer by virtue of section 152. He could no more vote as an elector on a day subsequent to the polling day than any other elector who had omitted to vote on that day could do so.

Other arguments against the clerk's right to vote as returning officer, under section 152, may be found in sections 301 and 302, by which special classes of persons are selected from the general voters' lists, and who constitute the duly qualified electors who may vote upon a by-law.

Section 315 also indicates that the Judge, upon a scrutiny, is to ascertain the result of the voting from the ballot papers taken from the sealed packets returned by the deputy-returning officers.

I cannot but think it also improbable that the Legislature, in adapting the procedure of voting by ballot to the case of by-laws requiring the assent of the electors, meant to alter the principle which had up to that time been recognised, that the clerk, in such a case, should not have a casting vote.

Section 321 of the Municipal Act of 1883 now expressly enacts that the clerk shall not have a casting vote, and in the judgment of my brother Rose at the trial it is said that this had been pointed to as a declaration by the Legislature that such a clause was necessary. The argument was not renewed before us, and it does not appear that any weight was attached to it in the Court below, but it seems sufficient to say that the question was then under consideration in the Courts in reference to this very by-law and it may well have been thought desirable to make the matter clear for the future.

As I am for the foregoing reasons of the opinion that the by-law did not receive the assent of the electors within in the meaning of section 317, it is unnecessary to say much on the question of promulgation and its effect. I observe that the notice or advertisement of the by-law states that it has been approved by the Lieutenant-Governor in Council. Whether this was really the case we do not know. If it was, it was a perfectly futile proceeding, as such a by-law requires no assent.

The by-law is, on its face, open to at least two other formidable objections arising from non-compliance with the terms of section 330, viz. : (1) that no day is named in the financial year in which it was passed on which it was to take effect; the day named being one anterior to its passage; and (2) that it makes the debt intended to be created payable more than twenty years from the time it was passed.

I take it to be now settled by the recent decision of the Supreme Court, *Canada Atlantic* v. *Ottawa*, 12 S. C. R. 365. affirming the view which has always prevailed in our own Courts, that the section referred to and its predecessor, section 248 of the Municipal Act of 1873, apply to by-laws incurring debts for bonuses to railway companies. That this was the ratio decidendi, or an element of it, in that case seems to me clear from the passages of the judgment at pp. 369, 374, and 375 of the report. How far promulgation can be held, by force of section 321, to cure defects of this nature, where no debentures have been actually issued under the by-law need not now be decided. Nor need we determine whether promulgation is, as was argued for the defendants, an answer merely to an application to quash the by-law, the council being still at liberty to attack its validity in any action to enforce rights alleged to have been acquired under it. For, assuming that where promulgation makes a by-law proof against a motion to quash it after a certain time, it establishes also its validity for all purposes, yet it cannot validate a by-law which ordains something not within the competence of the council to pass: and by section 323, where a by-law which requires the assent of the electors has not received such assent, an application to quash it may be made at any time. A *fortiori*, therefore, such an objection is fatal in an action on the by-law.

I respectfully think that the appeal should be allowed.

HAGARTY, C. J. O. and PATTERSON, J. A. concurred.

BURTON, J.A.—I agree in thinking that the by-law was
not carried by a majority of the qualified electors voting
upon the by-law within the meaning of the Municipal Act.

I do not think that the decision in the same company
against Ottawa at all decides that the provisions of sec.
248 (I speak of the Act of 1873) apply to by-laws for
granting bonuses to railways. It was unnecessary so to
decide in that case, as the judgment of this Court was
upheld on other grounds.

No doubt, as Mr. Justice Gwynne points out, all
the provisions of sec. 231 do apply, are in fact expressly
made applicable by the statute, so as to render the assent
of the ratepayers requisite, but it is a non sequitur that
because that section applies, sec. 248, which is not in terms
made applicable, should also apply, and manifestly it cannot apply to many of the cases of by-laws under sec. 47,
the section under which the by-law was passed, and which
alone authorises its passage.

It is not material to the decision in this case, and I refer
to it only for the purpose of shewing that I do not acquiesce in the view that that is a proper construction of the
statute.

Mr. Justice Gwynne, no doubt, indicates that that is his
opinion, and that opinion is unquestionably entitled to
every respect; but I do not agree with it, and adhere to
the view which I have on more than one occasion expressed.

I agree, however, in the result.

Appeal allowed with costs.

JAMES TEMPLETON MOXLEY v. THE CANADA ATLANTIC
RAILWAY.

AND

RICHARD MOXLEY v. THE SAME COMPANY.

*Railway—Fire from engine—Negligence—Evidence—Withdrawing case
from jury.*

In an action for damages for negligence the complaint was, that owing to
want of repair, negligent construction or management, sparks or ignited
matter had escaped from an engine of the defendants and caused a fire
which had spread and destroyed fences and trees on the farms of the
plaintiffs.
The evidence did not directly shew the cause of the fire, but it shewed
that an engine (No. 4) had passed the place of the fire about an hour
and a half before it or the smoke from it was perceived, and that another
engine (No. 406) had passed about an hour and a quarter later or about
a quarter of an hour before the smoke was perceived. Engine No. 4
was said to be out of order and was a wood-burner, but it was not shewn
that there was any defect in No. 406, which was a coal-burner, and it
was assumed at the trial that it was properly constructed and in good
condition. Evidence was given, in the shape of depositions taken before
the trial, of two employés of the defendants, to the effect that an engine
properly constructed and in good order could not throw dangerous
sparks, or sparks which would not be dead before they reached the
ground; and one of them said that a greater quantity of fire would escape
from a wood than from a coal burner. Two witnesses who were near at
the time of the passing of the engines said that they saw no smoke or fire
till after both trains had passed.
It was contended that the probabilities were very much against the fire
having been caused by No. 4, although the engine was shewn to be in
bad order, and that, as the case depended altogether upon inferences
from circumstantial evidence, there was not a case for the jury. The
case was however submitted to the jury, and a verdict rendered for the
plaintiff.
Held [BURTON, J. A., dissenting,] affirming judgments of the Queen's
Bench and Common Pleas Divisions refusing orders *nisi*, that there was
evidence from which the jury might infer that engine No. 4 was the
cause of the fire ; it was a presumption of fact depending on the circumstances of the case, and it was for the jury to fix the weight which
should be given to it.
Per BURTON, J. A. It was incumbent upon the plaintiffs to furnish evidence not only of negligence but of its connection with the loss ; and
this was not done by shewing that the fire broke out an hour or two
after engine No. 4 passed, another engine which might have caused
it having passed in the meantime, and the judge ought to have withdrawn the case from the jury upon the ground that there was no evidence of the issue which the plaintiff was bound to establish, fit for
them to take into consideration.

THESE were two actions, brought respectively in the
Queen's Bench Division and the Common Pleas Division,

in which, under the circumstances detailed in the judgments, verdicts had been rendered in favor of the respective plaintiffs, which verdict was in each case moved
against at the sittings of the Divisional Courts, and such
motion was in each case refused with costs.

The defendants thereupon appealed to this Court; and
by an order made in Chambers by Hagarty, C. J. O., it
was directed that one case in appeal to this Court and
one appeal book should be printed and filed for the purposes of the said appeals, and that the said appeals should
be heard together; and the appeals were set down simultaneously for that purpose accordingly, and came on to be
heard on the 4th day of March, 1887.*

Lount, Q. C., and *Chrysler*, for the appellants.
Osler, Q. C., for the respondents.

The points relied on by counsel appear in the judgments.

May 10, 1887.   PATTERSON, J. A.—After much consideration I am of opinion that our proper course is to dismiss these appeals.   I cannot say that I have any serious
doubt of the correctness of that conclusion, yet there are
some things which do not appear to have been so fully
investigated at the trial as to make the jury's finding in
all respects satisfactory, or even to make it perfectly
clear what view of the evidence the finding proceeds upon.

There is no difficulty as to the sufficiency of the evidence
to warrant a finding that engine No. 4, which drew the
freight train, was out of order.   There is nothing that can
be urged against that finding which was not equally open
in *McLaren* v. *The Canada Central R. W. Co.*, 8 A. R. 564;
and I shall not now add anything to what was said on the
subject during the argument.   I shall merely note two late
cases on the subject of entries by servants in the course of
their duty, *The Earl of Dumfries*, 10 P. D. 31, and *The
Solway*, 10 P. D. 137.

The trouble has been with respect to the question of the cause of the fire ; and having arrived at the conclusion I have mentioned, I shall now confine myself to some remarks upon the leading features of the evidence as it bears on that branch of the case.

The charge is that the company by negligent construction or negligent management of its engines caused the fire from which the plaintiffs suffered.

Three regular trains a day were run by the company to and from Ottawa, that is three each way. The regular time for passing Eastman's station, eleven miles from Ottawa and near the farms of the plaintiffs, for one freight train going to Ottawa was 11.30 a.m. and for the passenger train 12.01 p.m.

On the 19th of August, 1884, these trains passed the farms at or about the regular time ; and within a few minutes after the passenger train had passed, fire was seen in some combustible matter on the ground within the railway fences and about fifteen feet from the metal track. The fire, or rather smoke, was seen from some distance, and the fire spread rapidly into the lands of one of the plaintiffs, from which it passed to the lands of the other, burning fences and trees, whether living timber or only fallen or dead timber does not seem very clear, and doing other damage.   One witness describes the burnt tract " all a brulé bush any way ;" and others speak of it as dry swamp and slash ; but no one tells us in what state the railway land was, or what was the kind of combustible matter in which the fire began.   The season is described as very warm and dry, and it may be that the grass, weeds, brambles, or whatever else, which grew on the side of the ditch where the fire is said to have started, was easily inflammable, and that the fire ran through the grass and herbage to the adjoining farm, being fanned and carried by the wind which we are told was blowing from the S.W. to the N.E.; but when we understand that the origin of the fire was on the railway property and no great distance from the track where any cinder dropped from the ash pan of an engine would fall, and where sparks from the smoke stack would naturally fall if not carried off the line by the wind, it would have been more satisfactory to have known whether or not the company had taken all reasonable ·precautions against danger from the fire inevitably thrown by an engine of the best construction and in the most perfect order.

This last remark may perhaps assume something contrary to the evidence before us. We have been accustomed to take it to be a fact so well established as to be judicially recognised, that no spark arresting contrivance which can be used without interfering with the working of the engine, will altogether prevent the escape of sparks capable of setting fire to combustible matter. That was the basis of the decision in *Vaughan* v. *Taff Vale R. W. Co.*, 5 H. & N. 629, and it has been noticed and acted on in cases without number both in England and in this province, amongst which I may note *Smith* v. *London and South Western R. W. Co.*, L. R. 5 C. P. 98; *McCallum* v. *Grand Trunk R. W. Co.*, 30 U. C. R. 122 : 31 U. C. R. 527, and *Jaffray* v. *Toronto, Grey, and Bruce R. W. Co.*, 23 C. P. 553, as cases in which the negligence for which the company was liable consisted in allowing dry combustible materials to remain on the track.

The witness Farmer who lives near the railway says that he had several times that season put out fires on the track which he attributed to passing engines. His evidence, if reliable, might have been of importance in connection with the condition of the track, if attention had been directed to that subject. In *Smith* v. *London and South Western R. W. Co.*, the fact of fires occurring here and there, though not on the railway itself, was considered material on the question of the duty of the company to keep the railway property in a reasonably safe condition.

But we have in this case evidence which apparently went to the jury as proof that an engine properly constructed and in good order, whether burning wood or coal, could not throw dangerous sparks, or sparks which would not be dead before they reached the ground.

That evidence is found in depositions of James Ogilvie, the defendants' locomotive foreman, and Morley Donaldson, their master mechanic or locomotive superintendent. I refer to these depositions, which I observe were received as evidence for the plaintiffs against the objection of the defendants' counsel, without expressing any opinion on their admissibility as evidence against the company. The question whether the objection was not a "just exception" under R. S. O. ch. 50 sec. 165 has not been raised before us and I give no opinion upon it. Ogilvie was a witness at the trial and repeated the opinion expressed in his deposition.

This is one of the unsatisfactory incidents of the trial, The jury may, for aught we know, have adopted the opinion of these men who seem to have been looked upon as experts, though there is nothing in the evidence to indicate any special acquaintance with the subject to qualify either of them to assume that character. It is obvious that unless the hitherto universally received idea of the inevitable danger from a steam engine is entirely wrong, evidence like that of these men will expose railway companies to serious risk ; because, once a fire is traced to a locomotive, the inference of negligence must follow as of course.

If the fire was caused by negligence with which the company is properly chargeable, it matters not which of the engines threw or dropped the fire. In the actual contest at the trial, and as far as we can judge in the whole conduct of the action, the attempt was to establish negligence of only one kind, viz., in relation to the condition of the locomotives, and the only locomotive open to attack on that score seems to be No. 4 which drew the freight train.

We have no formal statement in the appeal book of what the finding of the jury was, but the whole argument has proceeded upon the understanding that it condemned No. 4 as the offender.

The argument for the appellants is that there was not a proper case made against that engine for the reasons :

40—VOL XIV. A.R.

first, that an hour and a half having elapsed from the time it passed until the fire was discovered, the inference that the fire was caused by a spark or cinder from that engine is not reasonable; and, *secondly*, that another engine having passed shortly before the discovery of the fire, the probability that that engine occasioned the fire is greater, or at least is equal to the probability that it was caused by No. 4. This is enforced not only upon the facts I have referred to, but the further fact sworn to by Farmer, that an hour or so after the freight train went by, he was on the track looking for sheep and could see a mile each way, and saw no smoke or fire; another witness also saying that there was no fire till after both trains passed, or that he saw none, for he was at a distance. The contention is, that in this state of the probabilities, and the case depending altogether on inferences from circumstantial evidence, there was not a sufficient case to submit to the jury, but that at all events the weight of evidence is so much against the probability of the fire having come from No. 4 that there ought to be a new trial.

The first point raises the question of the respective functions of the court and jury. Whose province is it to determine how the balance of probability inclines?

The question is important and the answer may not be found in any direct decision; but after the best consideration it has been in my power to give, I have not been able to convince myself that the court could undertake the decision without usurping the functions of the jury.

There is a dissertation on circumstantial evidence in *Starkie* on Evidence, 4th ed. pp. 839 et seq. on which the learned writer founds four propositions which he treats as essential to circumstantial proof, illustrating each of them in its turn. They are: First, that the circumstances from which the conclusion is drawn be fully established; Secondly, that all the facts be consistent with the hypothesis; Thirdly, that the circumstances should be of a conclusive nature and tendency; Fourthly, that the circumstances should, to a moral certainty, actually exclude every hypothesis but the one proposition to be proved. In illustrating the third proposition the writer remarks that "such evidence is always insufficient when, assuming all to be proved which the evidence tends to prove, some other hypothesis may still be true; for it is the actual exclusion of every other hypothesis which invests mere circumstances with the force of proof;" and after some further observations directed more particularly to evidence in criminal cases, he says: "Thus in practice, when it is certain that one of two individuals committed the offence charged, but it is uncertain whether the one or the other was the guilty agent, neither of them can be convicted."

The hypothesis in discussion is, that No. 4 caused the fire. The circumstances are sufficient to lead to the conclusion that one engine or the other did the mischief, and there is not any evidence to found a different hypothesis. But how does the proof sustain the hypothesis that No. 4 was the one? Does it leave it uncertain which of the two it was? That is the question, but it is as I understand it a question for the jury and not for the Court. The discussion of circumstantial evidence to which I have adverted, occurs in a chapter devoted to the duty of the jury, the duty of the court being discussed in a separate chapter, and the remarks of the learned writer lay down the principle on which a jury should be directed to deal with the evidence.

The cases which have turned on the duty of the Court, on an issue of negligence, to withhold from the jury evidence which is as consistent with the absence as with the presence of negligence, are merely illustrations of the rule that the person on whom the onus of proof lies must give evidence on which a jury can reasonably find in his favor. A scintilla of evidence was held to be insufficient in such cases, long before the decision of *Ryder* v. *Wombwell*, L. R. 4 Ex. 32. Thus in *Toomey* v, *The London Brighton and South Coast Ry. Co.*, 3 C. B. N. S. 146, we find Williams J. saying, "A scintilla of evidence or a mere surmise that there may have been negligence on the part of the defendants clearly would not justify the Judge in leaving the case to the jury. There must be evidence on which they might reasonably and properly conclude that there was negligence;" and the learned Judge gave a reason for care in this respect which has been adopted in several other cases and which has the same force to-day as when he stated it thirty years ago, viz.: that "every person who has had any experience in courts of justice knows very well that a case of this sort against a railway company could only be submitted to a jury with one result." In *Cotton* v. *Wood*, 8 C. B. N. S. 568, which is usually cited in support of the formula that the evidence is insufficient if equally consistent with the presence or absence of negligence, a woman having partly crossed a crowded street and having safely passed in front of an omnibus, was alarmed by another vehicle and turned back, when she was knocked down by the omnibus, the driver of which had seen her cross, but happened to be looking another way when she turned back. He was on his proper side of the road and was driving at a moderate pace. The question for the Judge did not differ from the ordinary question. Was there evidence that the accident was caused by the negligence of the driver ? and the formula which I imagine took its rise from a remark of Erle C. J. that, as far as the evidence went, there appeared to be just as much reason for saying that the woman came negligently into collision with the defendant's horses and omnibus as for saying that the collision was the result of negligence on the part of the defendant's servant, really expresses no more than the rule enunciated by Williams, J., in Toomey's case. The question now raised is, in my judgment, different, and is more like that which arose in *Peart* v. *Grand Trunk R. W. Co.*, 10 A. R. 191, when it was held that the jury must pronounce upon the evidence.

Since writing the remarks I have now read, I have seen the report of *Wakelin* v. *The London and South Western Ry. Co.* in the House of Lords, 12 App. Cas. 41. I refer to the judgment of Lord Halsbury, C., who treats the rule under which a plaintiff fails, if the circumstances established are equally consistent with the defendant's denial as with the plaintiff's allegation of negligence, as I have done, as in effect the proposition "Ei qui affirmat non ei qui negat incumbit probatio." There are also remarks by Lord Fitzgerald which deserve attention. He discusses opinions expressed in the Court of Appeal by Lord Esher, M. R., and adds : " If the noble and learned Master of the Rolls means that if the evidence is such that the jury might reasonably come to a conclusion in favor of the plaintiff, or might reasonably draw a contrary inference, the case is to be withdrawn from the decision of the jury and a verdict and judgment go for the defendant, I desire to say that I am not to be taken as acquiescing in that proposition."

But if the question were properly one for the Court, I am not prepared to hold that the probabilities were evenly balanced, much less that those throwing the blame on the noon train preponderated. This position embraces both points, the nonsuit and the new trial. To do so I should have to hold in effect that the lapse of time between the passing of No. 4. and the discovery of the fire was an insuperable obstacle in favor of No 4. The discovery of the fire was by persons who saw the smoke from a distance, when the fire had evidently taken firm hold of the combustibles and was breaking into dangerous activity. It is impossible for us to say that it had not smouldered for an hour and a half in the ditch, particularly as we have no information concerning the state of the ditch or the railway lands.

Then if the evidence would have justified the finding that No. 4 caused the fire if no other train had passed, how can we say that it was as likely or more likely that the later engine did the mischief? Those are inferences of fact, and the company could not reasonably complain if the jury drew the inference in accordance with the evidence of the company's servants, who swore that neither engine could have set the place on fire unless it was out of order.

I may have my private opinion of the value of that expert testimony, but that is entirely apart from what we have now to deal with.

We should in my opinion dismiss the appeals.

OSLER, J. A.—It is not necessary to advert to the evidence which was given for the purpose of shewing that engine No. 4 was out of repair and in a dangerous condition. I think it is abundantly sufficient to support the finding of the jury on that point. Was there also evidence from which they might infer not only that this particular engine was out of repair, but also that it was the cause of the fire?

After it passed, and before the fire was noticed, another engine of the defendants attached to a passenger train passed over the line in the same direction, and the fire was discovered a short time, perhaps from 15 to 20 minutes, afterwards.

The first engine passed at about 10.40 a.m. and the other about noon or a few minutes after.

The second engine was, as my brother Rose informs us, assumed at the trial to have been in good repair and not open to objection on the ground of improper construction or otherwise; and though nothing is expressly said about it in the evidence and it is now urged that there is no evidence on the subject, I think we must take it that the parties acted on this assumption, especially as we find it so stated in the appellant's reasons of appeal. No doubt the respondents felt that they could not attack this engine with any hope of success ; and the appellants' argument that it may have been the cause of the fire must rest upon the hypothesis that it was in such good condition that they would not be responsible for any fire accidentally or inevitably caused by it. If it was in bad condition it was immaterial whether the fire came from it or from engine No. 4. I quite agree that a plaintiff cannot recover who merely gives evidence of a state of facts which is equally consistent with the injury of which he complains having been caused by a fire for which the defendants would, as by one for which they would not, be responsible. The principle was very clearly laid down and enforced in the recent case of *Wakelin* v. *The L. & S. W. R. W. Co.* 12 App. Cas., 41. It has, however, no application to the present case. As Channell, B. remarks in *Smith v. The same defendants,* L. R. 5 C. P. Ex. Ch. 42, the two causes of fire suggested are not of equal probability, and there was therefore evidence for the jury that the fire was caused by the more probable of the two causes. That the fire was caused by engine No. 4 rather than by engine No. 406, is a presumption of fact depending on the circumstances of the case, and it was for the jury to fix the weight which should be given to it. *Taylor* on Evidence, secs. 169, 170, 171' 6th ed.

Where there is conflict or doubt as to the proper inference to be drawn from the facts in proof, or if the evidence is such that the jury might reasonably come to a conclusion in favor of the plaintiff, or might reasonably draw a contrary inference, the case is for the jury to decide.—See per Lord Fitzgerald in *Wakelin's Case, supra.*

We have it stated by Mr. Ogilvie, the defendant's, locomotive foreman, that the second engine No. 406 was a coal burner, and that a coal burning engine when in good condition will not throw a dangerous spark.

The other engine, besides being out of repair, was a wood-burner, and from such an engine, as the same witness says, a greater quantity of fire will escape than from a coal burner.

We have, therefore, two possible causes of fire, (conceding so much to the defendants in opposition to Ogilvie's evidence), the coal-burning engine, which being such and in good order was at least not likely to throw a dangerous spark, and the wood-burning engine which being such and also out of order, was liable and likely to do so. Of these two causes, assuming the engines to have passed at the same time, or one immediately following the other, and the fire not to have broken out for an hour and a half or two hours afterwards, it would be for the jury to say, and there would be evidence which could not be withdrawn from them, whether the fire was caused by the

engines, and if so whether it was more likely to have been
caused by the engine which was in a dangerous condition
than by the one which was not so.

It may also be laid down that if only engine No. 4
h ad passed, the case could not, under the circumstances,
h ave been withdrawn from the jury, merely because an
hour and a half elapsed after it passed until the breaking
forth or rather until the discovery of the fire.   If in both
these assumed cases the jury, judging of the probabilities
from the facts, might infer that the fire was caused by the
dangerous engine, I do not think that the passage, just before the fire of another engine unlikely to throw dangerous
sparks, is a fact which so weakens the probabilities of which
the jury are to judge, as to warrant us in saying that there
was no evidence on which they could reasonably come to
a conclusion in favor of the plaintiffs.   This no doubt was
a circumstance and one to be carefully weighed, but if it
would not be unreasonable for them to find that a spark
might smoulder an hour and a half or two hours before
breaking into flame, or smoke, visible at the distance of half
a mile (and certainly no Judge or Court could lay down that
without usurping the province of the jury), I see no reason
why they might not assign the origin of the fire to the
dangerous engine rather than to the other.

The question, therefore, being, what was the cause of the
fire ; unless we can hold that the lapse of time alone is
enough to make it so improbable that engine No. 4 was
the cause, that the Judge ought to have nonsuited, the
appearance on the scene of engine No. 406 is only an element
in the case, of the weight of which as making the probability of the plaintiff's contention the jury were the proper
judges.   We could not set aside this verdict consistently
with our recent decision in McGibbon v. The Northern Ry.
ante 91. I think there was no miscarriage at the trial either
in the reception of the evidence, (so far as any question was
raised on that point) or otherwise, and therefore in my
opinion the appeals should be dismissed.

HAGARTY, C. J. O., concurred.

BURTON, J. A.—I am of opinion that there was no evidence to go to the jury of one of the facts which it was incumbent upon the plaintiff to establish in order to recover.

I do not question that there was evidence of alleged faulty construction of engine No. 4 which could not have been withdrawn from the jury if the origin of the fire had been traced to sparks or burning cinders from that engine, although I am of opinion that the evidence is very weak, and had I been upon the jury I am not at all clear that I could have come to their conclusion. If the abusive epithets poured upon that engine by the plaintiff's counsel could be received as evidence, a very strong case would have been made out; but after a very careful perusal of the evidence I do not find that the character given to the engine was at all warranted by the evidence.

There is not a particle of direct evidence to shew what caused the fire. No doubt if the fire had broken out shortly after the passing of engine No. 4, no other cause for the fire being shewn, the jury might properly enough have been asked to draw the inference that sparks from that engine had caused the fire; but I entertain a very strong opinion that no such inference should or ought to be drawn when it is shewn that no trace of fire was seen until after the passing of the second engine, upwards of an hour subsequently, in an exceptionally dry season, and that it was discovered some 10 or 15 minutes after the passing of that second engine, it being common knowledge that all engines do emit sparks and cinders which might have caused the injury, notwithstanding that they are of the best construction, and are worked without negligence.

· There is positive evidence that the second engine had passed before the discovery of the fire, and there is no evidence to the contrary; whilst there is evidence from witnesses who passed over the road in the interval, who swear that they saw no traces of fire and must have seen it, if it had been there.

41—VOL XIV A.R.

Under these circumstances the duty, in my opinion, devolved upon the Judge to say whether upon these facts it could be reasonably inferred that the fire was caused by engine No. 4.

The rule which is usually referred to in cases of negligence as to the duty of the Court to withdraw a case from the jury, when the evidence is equally consistent with the presence or absence of negligence, is not confined to proofs of the fact of negligence only, but extends to the proof of any fact which it is incumbent upon the plaintiff to establish in order to entitle him to recover.

A mere surmise that the fire may have escaped from that engine and caused the injury would not justify the Judge in leaving the case to the jury; nor would he be entitled to do so because there was evidence which would tend to shew that if the injury were traced to that engine, the jury might properly infer that it was an actionable injury. There must be evidence upon which the jury might reasonably and properly conclude that the fire did escape from it, and cause the loss; if the evidence was consistent with either view, that the fire came from engine No. 4 or from the second engine, it would not be a question for the jury. Here the natural presumption in the absence of any direct evidence would be that the fire came from the second engine.

This is clearly to my mind a question for the Judge; it was incumbent upon the plaintiff to furnish evidence, not only of negligence, but of its connection with the loss, in the relation of cause and effect. This I submit is not done by shewing that the fire broke out an hour or two after it passed, another engine which might have caused it, having passed in the meantime, and it became, in my opinion, the duty of the Judge to have withdrawn the case from the jury, upon the simple ground that there was no evidence in support of the issue which the plaintiff was bound to establish, fit for them to take into consideration.

I confine myself entirely to this question and think we are bound in considering it, to place ourselves in the posi-

tion of the learned Judge, when the motion was made for
a nonsuit, and to give the judgment which he should then
have given. Taking that position I think the evidence
which was objected to, and to be found in the depositions
of Ogilvie and Donaldson, should have been rejected not only
on the grounds referred to by my brother Patterson, but
on the further ground that judges do know as well as juries
what is the usual and normal state of things, and that it
is a matter of common and universal knowledge that no
locomotive worked by steam ever has been, or ever can be
constructed, which can be effectively operated without
throwing fire capable of causing such a loss as the present.

Upon any other theory there must be an entire revo-
lutionising of the law of evidence in cases of this kind;
and the mere fact of an engine throwing fire would be
primâ facie evidence of negligence, of which from the
earliest decisions on railway law, we are aware is not
so.

I think, therefore, that, it was in accordance with a long
line of decisions to some of which I shall refer, the duty
of the Judge to have held that there was no evidence.

So far back as *Jewell* v. *Purr*, 13 C. B. 916, Maule J.,
laid it down that the question was not whether there was
literally no evidence, but whether there is none that ought
reasonably to satisfy a jury that the fact sought to be
proved is established.

Toomey v. *London and Brighton Railway*, 3 C. B. N. S.
150, lays down the law as it is laid down in the most
recent cases, that there must be evidence on which the
jury might reasonably and properly conclude that there
was negligence—the fact in that case sought to be established.

Wheelton v. *Hardisty*, 8 El. & Bl. 232, is to the same
effect. The rule is correctly laid down in *Ryder* v. *Wombwell* 8 E. &. B. 262, approved of by the Privy Council, the
Court of last resort from the decision of this Province, in
Giblin v. *McMullen*, L. R. 2 P. C. 331.

On the argument of that case, the counsel for the appellant admitting that the Bank were gratuitous bailees,
therefore not responsible except for the highest degree of
negligence, insisted that it was a question of fact for the
jury, and that after the defendant's case had been gone
into and the jury had pronounced a verdict upon all the
evidence on both sides, it was not competent to the Court
to direct a nonsuit.

It was held that it was the duty of the Court to do what
the Judge ought to have done at the trial, and the rule
laid down that in every case before the evidence is
left to the jury there is a preliminary question for the
judge, not whether there is literally no evidence, but whether there is any upon which a jury may properly proceed
to find a verdict for the party producing it upon whom
the onus of proof is imposed.

If, therefore, the plaintiff's evidence in that case was
such that the Judge ought to have considered that it fell
short of proving the bank to have been guilty of that species
of negligence which should render them liable to an action,
he ought to have withdrawn the case from the jury.

In *Lovegrove* v. *The London and Brighton Railway*,
1 Ex. D. 255, Mr. Justice Willes laid it down that it is
not enough for the plaintiff to show that he has sustained
an injury under circumstances which may lead to a suspicion, or even a fair inference that there may have been
negligence on the part of the defendants, but he must go on
and give evidence of some specific act of negligence on the
part of the person against whom he seeks compensation ;
and he held that the case should have been withdrawn
from the jury.

I refer, also, to Mr. Justice Gwynne's remarks in *Storey*
v. *Veach*, 22 C. P. 164, and to Lord Tenderden's language,
cited by Cresswell, J., in *Avery* v. *Bowden*, 6 El. & Bl.
953 : "If the evidence was such that the jury could only
conjecture, but not Judge, it ought not to go to the jury ;
that the onus was on the party offering the evidence, and
that he, if he offered any evidence consistent with either
supposition of facts, was not entitled to have it put to the
jury."

I refer also to the language of Lord Bramwell in *Ellis* v. *The Great Western Railway*, L. R. 9 C. P. 557, "when testimony is equally consistent with two things, it proves neither. This may seem a subtlety, but it is not," and to the most recent expression of opinion on the subject in the House of Lords, in *Wakelin* v. *London and South Western Railway*, decided within the last four months. The question there was, negligence being shewn, whether there was any evidence to connect such negligence with the accident.

The man was found dead on the railway track, and the Lord Chancellor remarked, one may surmise and it is but surmise and not evidence, that the unfortunate man was knocked down by a passing train while on the level crossing ; another of the learned Lords, "Mere allegation or proof that the company were guilty of negligence is altogether irrelevant, and therefore the plaintiff must allege and prove not merely that they were negligent, but that their negligence caused the injury. The evidence shews that the injuries were caused by contact with an engine belonging to the respondents, and I am willing to assume that they were in certain respects negligent. The evidence goes no further. It affords ample material for conjecturing that the death may possibly have been occasioned by that negligence, but it furnishes no data from which an inference can reasonably be drawn that as a matter of fact it was so occasioned."

And Lord Fitzgerald uses language very pertinent to the present case. After saying that there was evidence of negligence, he proceeds : "It fell short of proving that the immediate and proximate cause of the calamity was the negligence of the defendants. We are left to mere conjecture as to whether it was the causa causans, and that we cannot resort to. The plaintiff undertakes to establish negligence as a fact and that such negligence was the cause of her husband's death. She failed to do so and the proper course to have adopted at the close of the plaintiff's case was to have directed a verdict for the defendants."

It is, in my judgment, precisely in such a case that a Judge is called upon to intervene. What facts were there

here in evidence from which the inference that the fire came from the first engine could reasonably be drawn ? Surely it was the province of the Judge to decide that. Could any man say otherwise than as a matter of the purest speculation from which engine the fire came. If I had been trying this case without a jury, I should have said the only inference I can draw is, that it came from the last of the two engines; but that is not the way, as we all know by experience, in which a jury would deal with such a case against a railway company ; and I quote the language of the late Lord Cairns as peculiarly applicable to a case of this nature after stating that it would be a serious inroad on the province of a jury if in a case where there are facts from which negligence may reasonably be inferred, the Judge were to withdraw the case from the jury upon the ground that in his opinion it ought not to be inferred, it would on the other hand, place in the hands of jurors a power which might be exercised in the most arbitrary manner if they were at liberty to hold that negligence might be inferred from any state of facts whatever.

In that case negligence was the fact sought to be established ; in this the fact that the fire escaped from an engine alleged to be defective is what it was incumbent on the plaintiffs to prove. It is not a case in which the Judge is called upon to decide the somewhat difficult point whether the facts in evidence are such from which the emission of fire which caused the loss could be legitimately inferred, but whether it was proper to allow a jury to draw an inference which, under any circumstances, would be mere guess work.

With very great deference to those who differ from me in this matter I am compelled to hold that it was a pure question for the Judge, and I do not think any new principle has been established in the recent cases; but that the law is, and always has been, and ought to be, that a jury should not be allowed to find a verdict upon a mere surmise ; and that in the present case there was no evidence upon which a jury could properly find that the fire came from the first engine.

The rule we shall be adopting is, in my humble opinion, not only going back to the old days when a scintilla of evidence was deemed sufficient, but is substituting for a scintilla of evidence mere conjecture, founded upon a basis of the barest possibilities, and thereby allowing the jury to decide the case upon chance and not upon proper and legal evidence.

I desire before concluding, to refer to the illustration taken by my brother Patterson from Mr. Starkie's work in reference to a criminal case, as the case seems to my mind to support the view which I have been endeavoring to explain; the learned author says:

"Where it is certain that one of two individuals committed the offence charged, but it is uncertain whether one or the other was the guilty agent, neither of them *can* be convicted." In other words it would become the duty of the learned Judge to direct a verdict of acquittal, for no one could pretend to guess what might be the result if the jury were allowed to pass upon it.

As to the suggestion that the company might be liable for negligence in allowing weeds to grow on the side of the track, it is sufficient to say that no such case is made in the claim; and it is impossible to say what answer might have been set up had it been raised on the trial, or even on the argument before us.

For these reasons I think the appeal should be allowed, and a nonsuit entered.

BURTON, J. A., dissenting.

Appeal dismissed, with costs.

SMITH v. THE CITY OF LONDON INSURANCE COMPANY.

Fire · Insurance—Misdescription of premises— Waiver—Statutory conditions, variation of.

The plaintiff applied to the agent of the defendant company whose head office was in London, England, to insure a house which was described as a building two stories high and built of *burds*, which was written and intended by the agent for the word "boards." On the back of the application was a diagram of the building on which was marked in black, the colour in which all frame buildings were required to be shewn. The house was destroyed by fire during the currency of the policy issued by the head office, which was for a brick house, the general manager swearing that he had read the application as being in respect of a brick house, the premium charged being that charged on brick while one-half per cent. more would have been charged on a wooden building. The agent, however, swore that he considered a solid board house (that is one with the boards laid flat on each other, in this case being six inches wide) was a safer risk than a brick house, and he fixed the premium rate at one and one-half per cent., and it was admitted that he had authority to do so.

The company having refused payment of the insurance, an action was commenced to recover the amount after a lapse of more than thirty days from completion of the proofs of loss, but less than sixty days thereafter which, by a variation and addition to the statutory conditions, indorsed on the policy, was stipulated for.

After action the company, under the 16th statutory condition, demanded an arbitration as to the value of the premises destroyed, the result of which was an award finding the value to have been $2,500, and the loss payable to the plaintiff $1,700 ; while the jury at the trial of the action found that the plaintiff had truly represented the property as having been worth $3,500, and estimated his loss at that amount.

Held, [affirming the judgment of the Court below, 11 O. R. 38] that there having been no misrepresentation on the plaintiff's part, no mutual mistake, and the defendants not having proved that they granted the policy in consequence of any mistake on their part the parties were *ad idem* and the plaintiff was entitled to judgment for the amount of the award.

Held, also, that the stipulation that no action should be brought until the expiry of sixty days after proof of loss was not a just or reasonable variation of the statutory conditions.

Per BURTON, J. A.—The words of the 17th statutory condition being that the loss should not be payable until 30 days after completion of the proofs of loss created a privilege in favor of the companies, and the statute does not contemplate any further extension, but simply that the company shall be entitled to that delay unless under their charter or by agreement that period is shortened.

THIS was an appeal by the defendants from a judgment of the Q. B. D. reported 11 O. R. 38, where, and in the present judgments the facts are fully stated, and came on for hearing before this Court on the 7th of March, 1887.*

*Present.—HAGARTY, C. J. O., BURTON, PATTERSON, and OSLER, JJ.A

Robinson, Q. C., and *C. Miller*, for the appellants.
Osler, Q. C., and *W. Nesbitt*, for the respondent.

May 10th, 1887.   OSLER, J. A.—This is an appeal from the judgment of the Queen's Bench Division, affirming the judgment in favor of the plaintiff at the trial.

The action is upon a fire insurance policy for $2,500, dated the 3rd July, 1883.

A short statement of the facts will explain the grounds of the defence.

The defendants are a foreign corporation, carrying on business in this country through a general manager and local agents appointed by him.

On the 3rd July, 1883, the plaintiff made an application to defendants, through one Stafford, their local agent at Renfrew, to insure the property which was afterwards burnt, for the term of one year from that date.   The company's usual printed form of application was filled up by the agent from the answers of the plaintiff and his own knowledge of the premises derived from personal inspection.   The property was described as a building, two stories high, &c., built of "burds" covered with shingles, situate and being No.   on the west side of Raglan street, block 2, No. 79 Goad's Plan.   It was a wooden building made of boards six inches wide, laid flat one on top of another.   The word "burds," (which is very distinctly thus written in the application), was written and intended by the agent for the word *boards,* and seems to be a mere mis-spelling of that word.

On the back of the application is a diagram of the building; and the printed direction to the agent at the top of blank space left for the diagram, requires that brick or stone buildings shall be shewn in *red,* and frame buildings in *black.*   The diagram shews the buildings in *black.*   The general manager said that he considered a building made as this one was made a frame building.

The present cash value of the property was stated to be $3,500; and in answer to the question, is any incendiary danger threatened or apprehended? the plaintiff said: "No."

The local agent fixed the rate for the premium at $1\frac{1}{2}$ per cent. His authority to fix a rate was not denied. This was the rate for a brick building. He said that he considered a solid board building a safer risk than a brick building, and would not rate it any higher. The tariff provided no special rate for a board building.

The policy issued by the company insures " the property hereinafter described, and more fully described in the requisition for insurance," that is to say, "on the building only of a two story brick building, situate," &c.

The general manager swore that he read the application asking for an insurance of a brick building, and that the rate upon a wooden building would have been two per cent.

The usual statutory conditions are printed on the face of the policy. The only ones necessary to be noticed are the 16th and 17th. The former provides for a reference to arbitration in case of a difference arising as to the value of the property insured or amount of loss, and the proportion, if any, to be paid by the company; and the latter declares that the loss shall not be payable until thirty days after the completion of the proofs of loss, unless otherwise provided by statute or the agreement of the parties.

After the 22nd condition follows the notice.

" VARIATIONS IN CONDITIONS."

"This policy is issued on the above statutory conditions with the following variations and additions, &c., &c.

* * * * * * * * * * *

The loss shall not be payable until sixty days after completion of the claim."

Some time after the insurance was effected, the tenants of part of the premises quitted possession, and at the time of the fire the main part of the building was, and for several months had been, unoccupied.

There was no evidence that incendiary threats had been made. It was said that the tenants were people of doubtful character, who had been tarred and feathered by the law abiding and respectable inhabitants of the village, and had been compelled in consequence to leave the premises; and there was some evidence from which the jury might have inferred that the plaintiff apprehended incendiary damage during their occupation, and had insured himself for that reason.

The fire occurred on the 15th April, and notice was given to the company on the same day by telegraph to the general manager. On the following day blank forms of claim papers and proofs of loss were forwarded by him to the local agent to be handed to the plaintiff, and instructions were given to a valuator to appraise the loss.

Under the 16th statutory condition, at the company's request an arbitration was held respecting the value of the property insured and the amount of the loss. The arbitrators found that the value was $2,500, and the loss $1,700.

Upon a full examination of the evidence, I am quite satisfied that we cannot interfere with the judgment upon any question of fact on which the jury have found. The defendants very strongly urge that the finding as to the value of the property at the time of the insurance, and of the loss, is against evidence. If the jury had found the other way it might have been more satisfactory, but this is all that can be said. They found that the plaintiff had not misrepresented the value in the application, and that the value and loss had been truly stated as being $3,500. There was evidence which, if they believed it, warranted these findings.

It was argued that the award, under the 16th statutory condition, was conclusive as to the value and loss; but that is not the case. It is no evidence that the plaintiff misrepresented either. The arbitration, under the 16th condition, takes place only when a difference arises as to the value (that is, the value at the time of the fire) of the property insured, of the property saved, or the amount of the loss ; and the only effect of the award is to fix the amount of the loss and of the company's liability. Here, notwithstanding the finding of the jury, the judgment against the company must be limited to $1,700, the amount awarded.

The findings that the vacating of the premises by the Bromleys was not material to the risk in the sense of increasing it, and that there was no incendiary danger threatened or apprehended at the time of the application are supported by the evidence ; and I must add, after a careful examination of the evidence, that I do not take so strong a view of the incorrectness of the finding on the last point as the learned Chief Justice in the court below seems to entertain.

The grounds on which the claim is disputed are substantially two. The first, that there was really no contract between the parties ; and the second, that the action was prematurely brought.

The first objection proceeds entirely upon this, that the company took the word spelt " burds " in the application to mean *brick*, and issued the policy describing the subject matter of insurance as a *brick* building. In the language of the statement of defence they say : " That if the plaintiff intended to insure the building as a wooden one, no contract was made by reason of a want of mutual understanding between the parties as to the subject matter of the agreement ;" in other words the contention is that the parties never were *ad idem*. Now it is not suggested that there was any misrepresentation or fraud on the plaintiffs' part in describing the building he meant to insure. Apart from the mis-spelling of the word "boards" the property was sufficiently described and identified to the defendants by the other words of description, and by its being marked on the plan or diagram where, in accordance with the agent's instructions, it is shewn in black as a wooden or frame building, as it in fact is, and not in red as it should have been in the case of a stone or brick

they building. The defendants do not allege or prove that
would not have insured the building at all if they had
noticed that it was a wooden one. They say, at least they ·
now say, that it would have made a difference of $\frac{1}{2}$ per cent.
in the rate. They intended, however, to insure the building mentioned in the application, although owing to their
own mistake they did not charge as high a rate as they
otherwise would or might have done. It is not proved
that the plaintiff knew or had reason to suppose that he
was being charged a smaller premium than he would have
been charged for a brick building, or that the defendants
would not have insured a wooden building at all : and,
therefore their mistake in describing it as brick in the
policy would be no notice to him that they were contracting with him under a mistake on their part which
induced the contract. I think they shew nothing but a
falso demonstratio, a mere misdescription not affecting
the contract.

There having been no misrepresentation on the plaintiff's
part, no mutual mistake, and the defendants not having
proved that they granted the policy in consequence of any
mistake on their part, this objection fails. It is also to be
observed that the defendants have recognised the policy
as an existing contract of insurance, whatever defence they
might set up to their obligation to perform it, by calling for
further proofs of loss, and the magistrate's certificate mentioned in condition 13, after they had notice of the error in ·
the description, a thing they clearly had no right to do except
upon the footing of an existing contract. I think also
that the plaintiff may invoke the second condition, which
as against the defendants is a part of the policy, and
which provides that the policy sent to the insured is
intended to be in accordance with the terms of the application unless the company point out in writing (which I
take to mean a writing apart from the policy) the particulars wherein the policy differs from the application.

The next question is, whether the action was brought
too soon.

The fire occurred on the 15th April. Proofs of loss were received by the local agent on the 26th or 27th April, and were forwarded by him to the general manager, who received them on the 5th May. The action was commenced on the 4th June.

The defence on this ground arises on the 17th condition and its variation, and is thus pleaded :

"The alleged policy was subject to a condition as follows: 'The loss shall not be payable until 30 days after completion of the proofs of loss unless otherwise provided by statute or the agreement of the parties, and to a certain just and reasonable variation thereto printed in the manner that said Act requires,—namely, 'the loss shall not be payable until 60 days after completion of the claim;' averment that the action was brought before thirty days after completion of the proofs of loss, and before sixty days after completion of the claim, and so at the time the action was commenced no cause of action had accrued under the policy."

By this pleading the defendants treat the time of the completion of the proofs of loss as one thing, and that of the completion of the claim as another ; and the condition and variation as providing a different period of delay in each case. As pleaded, therefore, the latter would seem to be an addition to the statutory condition rather than a variation, if the completion of the proofs of loss and the completion of the claim are two different things. I think, however, that they are convertible expressions, both meaning the same thing. The claim is not complete until the proofs of loss are completed : when the latter are completed the claim is complete. The effect of the variation (if a valid one) simply is to substitute one period of delay for another.

This is the construction the defendants relied on at the trial, where the objection taken at the close of the plaintiff's case was, that the action had been brought within sixty days from the delivery of the claim papers, that is the proofs of loss, to Stafford, the local agent. This being incontrovertible, the answer was, that the variation was unreasonable. In the discussion which arose upon that question, the learned trial Judge observed that thirty days had elapsed before the action was brought; to which it was only answered, that the proofs of loss were not complete until the magistrate's certificate had been procured, and that as this had not been demanded before the 24th June, the action brought on the 4th of June was premature, because brought before completion of proofs of loss a contention which was, of course, quite untenable.

I have noticed the manner in which the case for the defence was presented at the trial, because it was pressed upon us that even if the variation of the 17th condition was held to be unreasonable, the action was nevertheless premature as having been brought within thirty days from the completion of proofs of loss, as that time did not run from the delivery of the claim papers to the local agent on the 26th and 27th April, but from the 5th May, when the general agent received them.   But this was not the objection taken at the trial, nor was it suggested there, or in the court below, that the local agent had no authority to receive the claim papers.   On the contrary, it was assumed at the trial that the sixty days began to run from the time of their delivery to Stafford, and no question as to the extent of his authority was submitted to the jury, for whom there certainly was evidence on the point, the written appointment which the general agent spoke of, not having been produced.

Unless, therefore, the defendants can maintain the variation of the 17th condition as a just and reasonable variation, or as an agreement between the parties, with the justice and reasonableness of which the Court has nothing to do, the statutory condition will govern the case, and it is, in my opinion, not now open to the defendants to say that under that condition the action was not brought in proper time.

First, then, are the defendants at liberty to insist upon this variation as an absolute unqualified agreement by the plaintiff that the loss shall not be payable until sixty days instead of thirty days after the completion of the claim or

proofs of loss, as provided by the statutory condition ?   I
think not. That condition differs from the other statutory
conditions in this, that while providing for a delay of thirty
days as primâ facie just and reasonable in all cases, it
contemplates two ways in which it may be "otherwise
provided," namely, by statute or agreement of the parties.
Unless otherwise provided in one of these two ways, that
is to be the limit of the delay ; and where it is in either of
these ways so otherwise provided, the justice and reasonableness of the provision cannot come into question under
the 6th section of the Act; for a statute provides for it in
one case, and the permitted agreement of the parties in the
other.   Both stand on the same footing : you can no more
inquire into the justice and reasonableness of the agreement than you can into that of the statute.

Now the provision which the defendants rely upon here
is not pleaded as an agreement which excludes the application of the 6th sec. of the Act, and it can only be held to
be one by virtue of the general rule, exemplified by
Watkins v. *Rymill*, 10 Q. B. D. 178, and that class of
cases, that if a document in common form is delivered by
one of two contracting parties to and accepted by the other
without objection, it is binding upon him, whether he
informs himself of its contents or not.   Conceding for a
moment that a policy of fire insurance, the conditions of
which have been so specially provided for by statute, is
such a document, the agreement thus sought to be raised is
qualified by the defendants themselves by the express proviso that it shall be deemed to be in force only so far as by
the Court or Judge it shall be held to be just and reasonable to be exacted by them. Therefore if it be an agreement at all it is a qualified one, and its justice and reasonableness are by the terms of the contract, if not by force
of the statute, a matter for the Court or Judge to determine.

This variation, therefore, whether it be regarded as a
mere qualification of the contract evidenced by the policy
and conditions (and perhaps that is the proper way to look

at *any* additions to or variations of the statutory conditions) or as a variation *exacted* by the company and not
depending upon agreement at all, must be dealt with just
as any other variation of a statutory condition, and is in
force or binding only so far as it may be held to be just and
reasonable to be exacted by the company. My brother
Rose, at the trial, held that it was not just and reasonable.
I see no ground on which I can safely say that he should
have held otherwise. In *Ballagh* v. *The Royal Mutual Insurance Co.*, 5 A. R. 87, it was held by this Court that the
reasonableness of a condition is to be tested with relation
to the circumstances of each case at the time the policy
is issued, differing in this respect from the case of *May* v.
Standard, 30 C. P. p. 51, in which that Court had decided
a few months previously that it should be regarded in the
light of those existing at the time at which the condition
was sought to be applied. And in several cases in this
Court the opinion has been expressed by my brother
Patterson without, so far as I have noticed, any dissent on
the part of the other members of the Court, that

"Conditions dealing with the same subjects as those given
by the statute and being variations of the statutory conditions should be tried by the standard afforded by the
statute and held not to be just and reasonable if they impose
upon the insured, terms more stringent or onerous or complicated, than those attached by the statute to the same
subject or incident." *May* v. *Standard*, 5 A. R. 622; *Ballagh*
v. *Royal*, 5 A. R. 107; *Butler* v. *Standard*, 4 A. R. 395.

For the purposes of the present case it is sufficient to say
that if it be limited to such conditions only as do not affect
the risk, I concur in the view thus expressed by my learned
brother. The only circumstance existing at the date of the
policy, which has been relied on in support of the justice and
reasonableness of this variation of the statutory conditions
is, that the defendants are a foreign corporation having their
head office in London. But the statutory conditions were
framed as well for foreign as for home corporations, and
thirty days was considered a reasonable delay in all cases;
and as the action against the company must be brought

within a year next after the loss or damage occurs it seems
quite as much time as any company ought to demand to
make inquiry into the loss and determine whether to pay
or to contest it.

The variation which they have in this instance exacted
has no relation to the risk, and it appears to me to be purely
arbitrary, and therefore unjust and unreasonable to be
exacted from the insured. For the foregoing reasons I
I think the appeal should be dismissed.

HAGARTY, C. J. O., and PATTERSON, J. A., concurred.

BURTON, J. A.—The only point upon which I desire to
add anything is as to the construction of the 17th statutory condition, and I do so because it strikes me in a
different light from any that I have seen advanced.

If the words of that condition had been that the loss
shall be payable in thirty days after completion of the
proofs of loss unless otherwise provided by statute, or the
agreement of the parties, there would be a good deal of
room for discussion as to whether the mere acceptance of
the contract with the varied condition upon it was a
sufficient agreement of the parties within the meaning of
the statute. But that is not the way in which the condition is expressed. It is that the loss shall not be payable
until thirty days after the completion of the proofs of loss
unless otherwise provided by statute or the agreement of
the parties; it is a privilege given by law to the companies,
and the statute does not seem to contemplate any further
extension, but simply that the company shall have that
delay unless under a statute, by which is meant I fancy,
the statute incorporating them, or by their own agreement
that period is shortened.

I agree, therefore, in dismissing the appeal.

Appeal dismissed, with costs.

[This case has been carried to the Supreme Court.]

McKenna v. McNamee.

Executory contract—Destruction of subject-matter by vis major—
Rescission of contract.

Where an executory contract is entered into respecting property or
goods, if the subject-matter be destroyed by the act of God or *vis major*,
over which neither party has any control, and without either party's
default, the parties are relieved.

The defendants, who had had a contract with the Government of British
Columbia for the performance of a public work, but had forfeited it,
after a part of the work had been done, agreed with the plaintiffs that
the latter should do the remainder of the work under the contract, and
should receive ninety per cent. of the amount of every estimate issued
till the completion of the work. The written instrument embodying
the agreement referred to the contract as an existing one, but the fact
was, as was fully known by all the parties, that at the time of making
the agreement the contract had been forfeited, and the Government had
taken possession of the works. No advantage was taken by the defendants; the plaintiffs had examined the contract with the Government,
and understood as well as the defendants the exact position of affairs;
but all trusted to the possession of certain influence by which they
hoped to get back the contract, and resume work upon it.

Held, affirming the judgment of the Q. B. D., that the failure to obtain a
restoration of the contract destroyed the whole consideration for each
party's agreement or undertaking.

Cunningham v. *Dunn,* 8 C. P. Div. 443, applied, and followed.

THIS was an action instituted originally in the Queen's
Bench Division by John P. McKenna and Robert Peter
Mitchell, against F. B. McNamee & Co., the statement of
claim in which, amongst other things, set forth that on
the 24th day of February, 1880, the defendants contracted with the government of British Columbia to construct and erect certain works in that province, commonly
known as the Esquimault Graving Docks, for which the
defendants were to be paid by the said government the
sum of $350,000: that on the 29th day of July, 1882, the
defendants had performed a portion of such work, but by
far the larger portion remained unperformed; and that on
the last mentioned day, by an indenture under seal made
between the defendants of the first part and the plaintiffs
of the second part, and executed by all the parties thereto,
the defendants, in consideration of the covenants therein
contained on the part of the plaintiffs to execute the works
in connection with the said docks, contracted and agreed
to take the plaintiffs into their service and employment in

the completion of the said works, and to pay them 90% of the price agreed to be paid to the defendants by the government of British Columbia, under the said contract with the government; that at the time of entering into this agreement the defendants were in default with regard to the performance of certain conditions contained in their contract with the said government, and in consequence thereof the government took possession and were then in possession of the said uncompleted works, and were proceeding with the erection and construction thereof at the cost, charges and expenses of the defendants; but that the defendants represented to the plaintiffs that the government had only so taken possession of such works temporarily and until the defendants should be in a position to resume operations thereon, and it was understood between the defendants and the plaintiffs, that upon the plaintiff Robert Peter Mitchell (one of the members of the plaintiffs' firm) proceeding to British Columbia the said uncompleted works would be handed over by the government, so that the plaintiffs could at once proceed to perform the work remaining to be done under the defendants' contract with the government.

It was also stated that the said R. P. Mitchell proceeded to British Columbia and requested the government to hand over to him, as representing the defendants, the said uncompleted works, with a view to the plaintiffs at once proceeding to complete the same, but after considerable negotiation the said government refused so to do, nor did the defendants, as they had agreed to do, take the plaintiffs into their service in connection with the completion of such works, although the plaintiffs were at all times ready and willing to enter upon the said service: and the plaintiffs claimed

(1) $100,000 as damages for the breach by the defendants of their agreement above set forth to take the plaintiffs into their service in connection with the completion of the said docks.

(2.) $25,000 for the work done and the services performed by the plaintiffs for and at the request of the defendants.

The action came on for trial at Ottawa, before Rose, J., without a jury, on the 7th of November, 1885, when, after hearing the evidence, he gave judgment in favor of the plaintiffs, reserving the question of costs until after an account should be taken of what was due the plaintiffs; which, on the 8th of March, 1886, the Divisional Court, on the application of the defendants, ordered to be set aside, and the action dismissed, with costs.

The plaintiffs thereupon appealed to this Court, and the appeal came on for hearing on the 31st of March, 1887.*

McCarthy, Q. C., *W. Nesbitt*, and *Clement*, for the appellants.

Lount, Q. C., for the respondents.

The other facts appear in the judgment.

May 10, 1887.   HAGARTY, C. J. O.—The agreement between the parties of 29th of July, 1882, recites that by a deed of 24th of February, 1880, defendants had agreed to do certain work for the Government of British Columbia, part of which had been done, and the larger part remained to be executed. That the plaintiffs had agreed with defendants to enter upon the work under the contract and to do it, and that defendants had agreed to take plaintiffs into their service and pay them 90 per cent. of the stipulated price, and the plaintiffs agreed to do all the work yet to be done under the contract according to the deed of 24th of February, 1880, and that they would faithfully perform all the conditions therein. Then the defendants covenanted in consideration of the premises that plaintiff should be paid 90 per cent. of the amount of every estimate issued on the works till the completion thereof, &c; the plaintiffs to pay for the building material belonging to defendants at a valuation, and further, that out of the first estimate after the commencement of the work by plaintiffs they shall be paid by defendants 90

per cent. of the value of the work done by them, and so
as to all subsequent estimates.   By an instrument of equal
date the defendants appointed Mitchell, one of the plaintiff's their attorney, to proceed with the works at Esquimault Harbour, and to receive all warrants for payment
therefor, but not to draw the money deposited with
Government as security for performance of the contract
or the 10 per cent. withheld by the Government from
the commencement of the works.

At the time of making these agreements it was fully
known to all the parties that the British Columbia Government had, under the powers given them in their contract
with defendants, entered upon and taken possession of the
works and put an end to the contract, and that defendants
were then in default.   This is admitted in the claim, and
that defendants represented to plaintiffs that the Government had only taken temporary possession until defendants
should be in a position to resume work, and that on Mitchell
(a plaintiff) going to British Columbia the works would be
handed over so that plaintiff could at once proceed.

The claim states that the Government would not consent
to the work being proceeded with, and the plaintiff claims
$100,000 for damages for not taking plaintiffs into their
service for the completion of the work, and $2,500 for
services performed by plaintiffs about the matter.

The defence states that it was well known that the
Government had taken possession: that all parties believed
that defendants would be allowed to resume and complete
the work: that the contract contained provisions against
sub-letting, as was then known, and that it was fully
understood that the agreement should not take effect unless
the Government would allow defendants to go on with the
works, and it was treated as an escrow, contingent on
such allowance: that all exertions were used on all
sides to endeavour to get such consent and allowance, but
in vain, and that all the expenses incurred were on plaintiffs' behalf in endeavouring to obtain such consent, and
defendants did not request same to be incurred, but they
were incurred at plaintiffs' risk.

It was clear from the evidence and was found by the trial Judge and candidly admitted on the argument, that when and before the agreement was executed all parties were fully aware that the Government had entered upon and taken possession under the clauses of their contract. The plaintiffs also had fully examined the various provisions of that contract, The denial of the plaintiff Mitchell of this important knowledge, as remarked by my learned brother Wilson, C. J., tends very much to shake our faith in his general evidence.

I think it very clearly shews that no advantage whatever was taken by defendants in dealing with the plaintiffs; that they equally understood the exact position of affairs, but all trusted in their possession of certain influences by which they hoped to get back the contract, and resume work upon it.

In the instrument the contract is treated as existing. We must put ourselves in the position of the executing parties, and read their contract as they understood it.

All the matters contracted for are based upon there being an existing bargain with the British Columbia Government. The plaintiffs are to finish the work under it, and the defendants are to pay them 90 per cent of the amount of every estimate issued on or under it until completion. There is no absolute obligation on defendants' part to do or to pay anything except arising out of the contract and derivable from it. There is no express agreement that it is an existing contract; it is assumed so to be.

The evidence fails to disclose any untrue representation made by defendants to induce the plaintiffs to enter into the bargain. All seems to have been done at the risk of the actually broken contract being restored by the Government.

Their failure to obtain such restoration destroyed the whole consideration for each party's agreements or undertakings.

If a landlord had entered for condition broken on his lessee for years, and the latter contracts with a third person to dispose of the term to him or to allow him to receive the rents of under-tenants, or divide the same in specified proportions with him, each being fully aware of the forfeiture and the landlord's action, but contracting, in words like those in the present agreement, as if the term still existed, trusting to their being able to induce the landlord to forego his right and waive the forfeiture, I am of opinion that in the absence of fraud or misrepresentation, either party would be relieved from the other's attempt to enforce the bargain.

The law seems reasonably clear that where an executory contract is entered into respecting property or goods, if the subject matter be destroyed by the act of God or vis major, over which neither party has any control, and without either party's default, that the parties are relieved. In *Taylor* v. *Caldwell*, 3 B. & S. 833, Lord Blackburn thus states the law :

"There are authorities which, as we think, establish the principle that where from the nature of the contract it appears that the parties must, from the beginning, have known that it could not be fulfilled, unless when the time for the fulfilment of the contract arrived some particular specified thing continued to exist, so that when entering into the contract they must have contemplated such continuing existence as the foundation of what was to be done, there, in the absence of an express or implied warranty that the thing shall exist, the contract is not to be construed as a positive contract, but as subject to an implied condition that the parties shall be excused in case, before breach, performance becomes impossible from the perishing of the thing without the fault of the contractor ; * * in the course of affairs men, in making such contracts in general would, if it were brought to their mind, say that there should be such a condition."

He then discusses the authorities and adds : " In none of these cases is the promise in words other than positive, nor is there any express stipulation that the destruction of the person or thing shall excuse the performance ; but that excuse is by law implied, because from the nature of the contract it is apparent that the parties contracted on the basis of the continued existence of the particular person or chattel."

Of course in that case there was the unexpected destruction by fire of the Music hall, respecting the use of which the contract had been entered into.

I have a very strong opinion that the general principle stated by Lord Blackburn, must apply even more distinctly in a case like the present, where parties choose to bargain respecting a contract as existing, which they equally know has been put an end to by competent authority, and which neither of them, except as a matter of grace, can possibly recall to existence.

Cunningham v. *Dunn*, 3 C. P. D. 443, seems to support the same view. By charter party defendants' ship, after loading " dead freight " at Malta, proceeded to Valentia and loaded a cargo of fruit for plaintiff. At the time of making the contract the plaintiff knew that the " dead freight " to be shipped at Malta would consist of military stores, and he knew that by the law of Spain a vessel with warlike stores on board must not be allowed to load at a Spanish port. Application was made to the Spanish Government to relax the prohibition, but it was refused.

The ship arrived at Valentia ready to take the cargo for plaintiff. On finding that permission to load would not be granted, she departed.

This was the breach.

Held by Lords Justices Bramwell, Brett, and Cotton, that plaintiff could not recover, for, through the act of a superior power, the parties were unable to perform their respective duties under the contract, the plaintiff being unable to load the cargo, and the defendant to receive it.

I refer to the reasons of the learned Judges : Bramwell, L. J., at p. 447, points out that defendant appears to have believed that the prohibition would not be persisted in.

Ford v. *Cotesworth*, L. R. 4 Q. B. 127, 5 Q. B. 544 *Appleby* v. *Meyers*, L. R. 2 C. P. 651, are referred to on the general question.

It seems to me that *Cunningham* v. *Dunn* is decided on a principle which should apply to this case. The contract was absolute on its face. Both parties knew of the Spanish law which, unless relaxed in their favor, would prevent its performance. They contracted, trusting to its being relaxed, just as here they contract absolutely knowing that the contract was forfeited, but hoping and trusting to the forfeiture not being insisted on.

In the Divisional Court the decision in defendants' favor seems to be rested on an implied conditional execution in the nature of escrow. This may be so, but I prefer placing my decision on what seems to be a broader principle.

I also refer to *Couturier* v. *Hastie*, 5 H. L. Cas. p. 681 and to *Pollock* on Contracts, ed. 1885 p. 370. After noticing the cases of subsequent destruction of subject matter he says : " But sometimes the same kind of impossibility results from the present existence of a state of things not contemplated by parties, and the performance is excused to the same extent and for the same reasons as if that state of things had supervened ; where this impossibility consists in the absolute non-existence of the specific property or interest in property which is the subject matter of the agreement, it is evident that the agreement would not have been made unless the parties had contemplated the subject matter as existing," &c.

I think the appeal should be dismissed.

BURTON, PATTERSON, and OSLER, JJ.A., concurred.

BANK OF MINNESOTA V. PAGE.

District Court—Appeal, right of—R. S. O. c. 90 s. 4—Order under Rule
80—45 Vic. c. 6 s. 4—Motion to High Court—47 Vict. c. 14 s. 4—
Costs security for—Dismissal of action.

There is an appeal to the Court of Appeal from the judgments of
the District Courts of the Provisional Judicial Districts. Section 34 of
R. S. O. c. 90 imports that when by the law in force with regard to
County Courts an appeal lies from those courts to the Court of Appeal,
it lies also from the District Courts.

An order for leave to sign judgment under Rule 80 is in its nature final
and not merely interlocutory, and therefore such an order if made in a
County Court would be appealable by virtue of 45 Vict. c. 6, s. 4 (O.),
and is also appealable when made in a District Court.

47 Vict. c. 14, s. 4 (O.), assumes the existence of the right of appeal from
District Courts ; and the optional right to move against the verdict in
the High Court, provided by sub-sec. 5, is not the appeal referred to in
the first part of the section, in the words "subject to appeal."

On the 5th Nov., 1885, an order was made requiring the plaintiff to give
security for costs within four weeks and in default that the action should
be dismissed with costs, unless the Court or Judge on special application for that purpose should otherwise order. Within the four weeks
the plaintiff obtained a summons, with a stay of proceedings, for "further time to perfect security for costs," and on the 10th Dec., 1885, an
order was made extending the time till the 23rd Dec., 1885, but not providing that the dismissal of the action should be the result of non-compliance with its terms. Security was not furnished within the time so
extended, and it was contended that after that the action was dead,
and there was no jurisdiction to make an order in it.

Held, that the action never became dismissed under either of these orders,
and that a motion to dismiss was regular and necessary.

Whistler v. *Hancock*, 3 Q. B. Div. 83 ; *King* v. *Davenport*, 4 Q. B. Div.
402 distinguished.

Leave to sign judgment under Rule 80 should not be granted save where
the case is clear and free from doubt, and under the circumstances of
this case an order for such leave, made by the Judge of the District Court
of Thunder Bay, was reversed.

THIS was an appeal by the defendant from an order pronounced by the Judge of the District Court of the provisional judicial district of Thunder Bay on the 23rd day of
June, 1886, and came on for hearing before this Court on
the 16th day of May, 1887.*

The facts are clearly stated in the judgment.

G. H. Watson, for the appellant.

Aylesworth, for the respondents.

In addition to the cases mentioned in the judgment,
Fuller et al. v. *Alexander Bros.*, 47 L. T. 443; *Lloyd's Bank-*

* *Present.*—HAGARTY, C. J. O., BURTON, PATTERSON, and OSLER, JJ.A.

ing Co. v. *Ogle*, 1 Ex. D. 310 ; *Standard Discount Co.* v. *La Grange*, 3 C. P. D. 67 ; *Carter* v. *Stubbs*, 16 Q. B. D. 116, were referred to.

June 29, 1887. The judgment of the Court was delivered by

OSLER, J. A.—This is an appeal from an order made by His Honor John M. Hamilton, the Judge of the District Court of the Provisional Judicial District of Thunder Bay setting aside a præcipe order for security for costs, dismissing the defendant's motion to dismiss the action for want of prosecution, and non-compliance with the order for security for costs, and giving the plaintiffs leave to enter final judgment under Rule 80 of the Judicature Act for the amount of the claim as indorsed on the writ.

The plaintiffs moved to quash the appeal on the grounds : 1. That no appeal lies to this Court from any judgment or decision of the Judge of a District Court of a Provisional Judicial District. 2. That if an appeal lies as in cases of the judgment or decision of a County Court, none lies as regards this particular order under 45 Vict., ch. 6, s. 4 (O.), it being merely interlocutory and not in its nature final.

The last objection I consider not open to the respondent. We have already entertained appeals from orders of this kind ; see *Nelson* v. *Thorner*, 11 A. R. 620; *Collins* v. *Hickok*, 11 A. R. 616. I think, moreover, that the language of the section prevents the application of those cases in which under the English Judicature Act orders are, as regards the procedure for appealing from them, held to be interlocutory. Such an order is in its nature if not, in form, final, and not merely interlocutory, even though it has to be carried into effect by entering judgment in pursuance of it.

The other objection is more serious, involving as it does the proposition that there is no right of appeal from the judgments of the District Courts of the Provisional Judicial Districts. I think, however, that it cannot be supported.

The R. S. O. ch. 7, sec. 28, and ch. 90, sec. 29, enact that
the Lieut.-Governor may form Provisional Judicial Districts out of the unorganised tracts of country bordering
upon and adjacent to Lakes Superior and Huron.

Sec. 33, of ch. 90, enacts that a District Judge shall be
appointed in each district who shall have the same powers,
duties, and emoluments as a County Judge. And sec. 34,
provides, inter alia, that the laws now in force or which
may be hereafter passed with respect to county and division courts, or the power, authority or jurisdiction of
the judge of such court, shall, unless it is otherwise
provided, or unless there is something in the context indicating a different intention, apply to each of the said
provisional judicial districts, and to every such district
thereafter established.

It appears to me that, without at all infringing upon the
spirit or letter of the rule that an appeal must be given
by express words and not by inference, or by an equitable
construction of the language of an Act, this section does
by its very terms import that where, by the law in force
with regard to County Courts, an appeal lies from those
Courts to the Court of Appeal, it lies also from the District Court of a provisional judicial district. With respect
to County Courts a law was passed which, as we have
held, gives a right of appeal in the case of such an order
as we have now before us. And, it not being otherwise
provided, and there being nothing that I am aware of in
the context which indicates a different intention, it seems
by the very words of the Act to apply to the provisional
judicial district.

Then the 47th Vict. ch. 14, sec. 4, assumes the existence
of the right of appeal, providing that the court shall, in
addition to the jurisdiction possessed by county courts,
have jurisdiction and hold plea *subject to appeal* in certain
specified cases; and sub-sec. 5 provides that in every case
where the cause of action is beyond the jurisdiction possessed by county courts, and a verdict exceeding $200 is
obtained, the party entitled to move against it may, *instead*

of moving in the district court, move in the High Court
for such rule or order as he thinks himself entitled to.
Whether in that case any appeal will lie from the judgment given by the High Court, is a question not necessary
to decide ; but I wish to point out that there is merely an
option given to move in the High Court instead of in the
District Court; and that the language of the section
appears to import that the motion referred to is one
against the judgment at the trial of the cause, and not
against an order made on a summary proceeding in Chambers.   The fact that it is merely optional to move in the
High Court destroys the argument that the right to move
there is the appeal referred to in the first part of the
section.

Proceeding then to the appeal itself, the defendant first
objects that the learned Judge had no jurisdiction to make
the order complained of, the action being then, as it is
said, dead, or no longer in existence, in consequence of the
plaintiff's omission to comply with the terms of the order
for security for costs.   That was an order issued by the
clerk of the Court on præcipe on the 5th November, 1885,
whereby it was ordered that the plaintiffs should, within
four weeks from service, give the usual security for costs;
and it was also ordered that in default of such security
being given, the action be dismissed, with costs, unless the
Court or Judge, on special application for that purpose,
should otherwise order.   Within the time limited by
this order for giving the security, the plaintiffs obtained
a summons with a stay of proceedings for "further time
to perfect security for costs," and on the 10th December,
1885, an order was made, after hearing counsel for the
parties, that the plaintiffs should have until the 23rd
December, 1885, in which to secure the defendant's costs.
No further proceedings were taken in the action until the
21st April, 1886, when the defendant took out a summons to dismiss the action for non-compliance with the
orders of the 5th November and 23rd December, and this
summons was by consent enlarged from time to time until
the 23rd June, 1886, when it was discharged.

The case on this point seems to me quite distinguishable from *King* v. *Davenport*, 4 Q. B. D. 402; *Whistler* v. *Hancock*, 3 Q. B. D. 83, and similar cases cited by Mr. Aylesworth. There the orders dismissed the action in default of delivery of the statement of claim within a certain time, and no order to extend the time or for a stay of proceedings was made within the time limited. But here the order was made in pursuance of a reservation contained in the original order on a summons taken out within the time limited and containing a stay of proceedings.

The action, therefore, never became dismissed under that order, and as the order of the 10th December did not expressly provide that the dismissal of the action should ipso facto be the result of non-compliance with its terms, the defendant, in my opinion, properly treated it as being still in court, and the motion to dismiss was regular and necessary.

Upon the merits, I am of opinion that summary judgment under Rule 80, should not have been ordered.

On such an application leave may be granted to defend on payment of money into Court, or on other terms which the judge may think fit to impose; or the plaintiff may have leave to sign judgment. If the case is not one for taking one or the other of these courses, the defendant simply defends unconditionally.

Leave to sign judgment ought not to be granted save where the case is clear and free from doubt.

In *Runnacles* v. *Mesquita*, 1 Q. B. D. 416, the Court said :

" This is a new power, and it is a discretion which must be exercised most scrupulously. I think we must not hesitate to establish a precedent that when the defendant goes beyond the mere form of stating that he has a good defence, and states what his defence is, and gives reason for thinking that his defence is substantial and will be sustained in evidence, the defendant ought not to be compelled to pay money into Court as a condition to his being allowed to come in and defend the action."

And in *Ray* v. *Barker*, 4 Ex. D. 279, 284, Cotton, L. J.,
states the rule for both cases thus :

" If the defendant's affidavit sets up a good defence, the
Court has no discretion and cannot order the money
claimed to be paid into Court. But an alternative is
allowed in which leave to defend may be given—namely,
where the defendant discloses such facts as may be deemed
sufficient to entitle him to defend ; and it is this state of
facts to which the discretionary power given by Rule 85
is directed. The affidavit may not make it clear that
there is a defence, but the defendant may be able at the
trial to establish a bonâ fide defence."

Now here the plaintiffs sue as endorsees of a promissory
note for $1,000, made by the defendant in favor of one
M. F. Farrell or order, dated 5th December, 1884, payable
5th October, 1885. This, at least, is the claim as disclosed
on the affidavits, though it is not stated in the special
endorsement on the writ in such a way as to entitle the
plaintiffs to sign judgment for non-appearance.

The ground on which leave is sought to sign judgment is, that there is no defence to the action, because
the defendant has, since the order for security for costs
was granted, admitted to Farrell and to one of the
plaintiff's solicitors, and to a third person that she
owes the debt sued for. These admissions she denies or
explains in her affidavit in answer, and she swears that
she is not defending the action for the purpose of delay,
but because she believes she has a " good legal, substantial,
and just defence thereto,"—namely, that the note in question was made to Farrell for an immoral and illegal consideration, the nature and particulars of which are fully
set forth and disclosed in her affidavit, as also are other
grounds of defence, which she swears she relies upon, but
which may or may not be available to her.

She also swears that she believes that the plaintiffs are
not the bonâ fide holders of the note, and that the suit
is really brought by them for the benefit and on behalf
of Farrell, and that they have no better right to enforce

it against her than he would have if her statement as
to the real consideration is true. She also sets forth the
circumstances in detail on which her belief is founded.

The affidavits filed for the plaintiffs in support of the
motion for leave to sign judgment, (sworn before the depo-
nents were aware of the defence intended to be set up,)
very strongly corroborate her contention on this point,
and support the inference that the plaintiffs merely
received the note from Farrell for collection, and have no
other interest in it than as his agents.

The affidavit of the plaintiffs' assistant cashier in
reply is much too loosely and equivocally phrased to be
of much value in rebutting this inference. As an answer
to or explanation of facts adversely alleged, it should
have entered into particulars which must have been
within the knowledge of the deponent or some other
officer of the bank, and should not have been so drawn
that its verbal accuracy might be satisfied if there had
been an advance of fifty cents, or perhaps only a lien
for collection charges.

No affidavit was filed in the Court below denying the
defendant's statement as to the nature of the consideration.
Such an affidavit coupled with one shewing distinctly how
and when the plaintiffs became bonâ fide holders for value,
might, when read with the affidavits as to the admission
of the debt, and that one of the notes given for the purchase money of the property had been already paid, have
left it open to the learned Judge to make an order for
leave to defend conditionally on reasonable terms; but, as it
is, the affidavits disclose a defence on the merits, which, in
my opinion, ought to be left to be tried in the usual manner.

I refer to *Barber* v. *Russell*, 9 P. R. 433; *Ontario Bank*
v. *Burk*, 10 P. R. 561; *Hughson* v. *Gordon*, ib., 565;
Nelson v. *Thorner*, 11 A. R. 616; *Collins* v. *Hickok*, ib.
620; *Dobie* v. *Lemon*, 12 P. R. 64.

I think that so far as the order complained of permits
plaintiffs to sign final judgment in the action the appeal
should be allowed.

The other branch of the order must be dealt with by the learned Judge. The costs of the motion to quash the appeal for irregularity, it having been set down out of time, must be borne by the defendant, but may be set off against the costs of the appeal.

Appeal allowed, with costs.

CHAPUT v. ROBERT.

Penalty—Qui tam action against two defendants—R. S. O. ch. 123, sec. 11—Action by several plaintiffs—Residence of plaintiffs out of jurisdiction—Demurrer—Misjoinder of defendants.

In an action by several plaintiffs qui tam against two defendants for penalties for not registering their partnership under R. S. O. ch. 123, of which sec. 11 gives the right of action to, " any person " who may sue.
Held, reversing the judgment of the Court below : (1) That under the above section and the Interpretation Act, any objection to the action being brought in the name of more than one person could not prevail : (2) That the circumstance that the plaintiffs resided out of the jurisdiction could not defeat their action : (3) That the joinder of two defendants for several penalties was not a ground of demurrer ; and
Per OSLER, J. A.—There was no inconvenience or impropriety in joining these two defendants in one action.

THIS was a qui tam action, instituted in the County Court of the County of Carleton, by Charles Chaput, Edouard St. Denis, Louis Napoleon St. Arnaud, and Louis Elie Geoffrion, trading under the name of " L. Chaput & Co.," against Olivier Robert and Maria Richardson McDonell, carrying on business at Ottawa under the style or firm of "McDonell, Fitzsimmons & Co.," and who formed such partnership on or about the 10th day of April, 1885. and had since continued to carry on business at Ottawa. The statement of claim charged that the defendants did not, within six months next after the formation of such partnership, cause to be delivered to the registrar of the city of Ottawa, in the county of Carleton, being the registration division in which they carried on, or intended to carry on business, a declaration in writing signed by them as the several members of such co-partnership, as required by the statute in that behalf, namely, chapter 123 of the Revised Statutes of Ontario, and contrary to the said statute, whereby an action had accrued to the plaintiffs to demand and have one hundred dollars from each of the defendants, as well for the Queen as for themselves; and that the plaintiffs, in consequence of such default had been caused and had suffered loss of time and of money, delay, and considerable damages, in the prosecution of their just claims, rights and demands against the said defendants.

The defendants demurred to the plaintiffs' statement of claim, alleging that the same was bad in law, on the ground that there cannot be more than one person plaintiff or informant in an action under the statute referred to, and that no person can be such plaintiff or informant if resident out of the province of Ontario, and that the defendants could not be sued together in one action for several penalties.

Upon argument thereof before the junior Judge of the County Court the learned Judge allowed the demurrer, with costs.

From that judgment the plaintiffs appealed to this Court, and the same came on for hearing on the 12th of May, 1887.*

Belcourt, for the appellants, referred to *Myers* v. *Baker*, 3 H. & N. 802; *Atcheson* v. *Everitt*, Cowp. 389; *Cole* v. *Coulton*, 2 E. & E. 695; *Rex* v. *Clarke*, Cowp. 610.

J. Maclennan, Q. C., for the respondents, cited *Burstall* v. *Beyfus*, 26 Ch. D., at 38-9; *Wharton's* Confl. of Laws, secs. 4-108-833.

June 29, 1887. PATTERSON, J. A.—Several plaintiffs join in suing, qui tam, for penalties for the neglect of the defendants to register their partnership under R. S. O. ch. 123.

* *Present.*—HAGARTY, C.J.O., BURTON, PATTERSON, and OSLER, JJ.A.

The defendants demur to the statement of claim, and they have judgment in their favor in the County Court of the County of Carleton, from which judgment the plaintiffs appeal.

The learned Judge has not certified the reasons for his judgment. We have therefore to deal with the several grounds of demurrer stated in the pleading, and insisted on in argument before us.

The first objection taken is to the joinder of several plaintiffs. The statute, section 11, giving the action to *any person* who may sue, it is contended that only one person can sue, and that even the declaration of the Interpretation Act, that in each of the Revised Statutes words. importing the singular number shall include more persons of the same kind than one, is powerless to give the right of action to more than a solitary plaintiff.

The provision must be, of course, read along with the clause which declares that it is not to apply to any Act with the intent and object of which it is nconsistent, or if the interpretation which the provision would give to the word is inconsistent with the context; but there is no inconsistency between the registration of partnerships, which is the object of the Act, and the joinder of two plaintiffs in a qui tam action for the penalty incurred by disobeying the law, nor does the context contain an inconsistent expression. The exception extends also to any Act in which it is declared that the provision shall not apply. The defendants do not find any such declaration in the Act, but they urge that the penal character of the section requires that the language shall be construed strictly. It is giving a strict construction to the language to understand it to mean what the Interpretation Act declares it means; but, were it not so, the occasion would not be one for the application of the canon appealed to. No greater burden is put upon the offender by being sued by two persons; one penalty only is demanded, and his defence is not prejudiced by the joinder.

No authority has been produced in support of the objection. No principle is violated by recognising the right of several to join as plaintiffs. It has always been a usual form of legislation to give the action to one or more. In *Bradlaugh* v. *Clarke*, 8 App. Cas. 354, several statutes are referred to in which the penalty, in whole or in part, was given "to him or them" who should sue. In *St. Leonard's Shoreditch* v. *Franklin*, 3 C. P. D. 377, one or two others are quoted where the expression happens to be 'the person or persons." How far back that form of enactment may be traceable I do not know, but we find it in use four hundred years ago in 4 Hen. 7 ch. 20, which is directed against collusive actions on penal statutes, and enacts that " If *any person or persons* hereafter sue with good faith any action popular, and the defendant or defendants in the same action plead," &c., &c.

Mr. Belcourt referred us to the case of *Myers et al.* v. *Baker*, 3 H. & N. 802, which was an action by several plaintiffs brought upon a statute which gave the penalty "one-half to His Majesty, his heirs and successors, and the other half to *any person* who shall sue for the same." No fault was found with the joinder of more plaintiffs than one, although that statute was not, like ours, expanded by an interpretation Act.

I do not think there is any foundation for this first objection. The second objection, which is also to the persons of the plaintiffs, is stated to be that they reside in Montreal. In support of it Mr. Maclennan cited authorities for the principle that one country will not execute the penal laws of another. But in this instance we are asked merely to execute the law of our own Legislature.

That law gives the penalty to any person who shall sue for it in our courts. Whether an alien could sue is not the question, for the objection is not that the plaintiffs are not British subjects and residents in Canada, but merely that they do not live in the province. I see no ground in legal principle for the objection, but it wants foundation in fact. The allegation in the pleading is that the plaintiffs carry on business at the city of Montreal under the name, style and firm of L. Chaput & Co. They may live in Ottawa, where they sue, so far as shewn by the pleading,. which is all that, on this demurrer, we have to look to.

The third objection, and the one mainly relied on, is that the claim is for a separate penalty against each defendant, and that the defendants ought not to be joined in one action.

This is a merely formal objection, and is not the subject of demurrer. Mr. Maclennan referred to the case of *Burstall* v. *Beyfus*, 26 Ch. D. 35 ; but whatever the effect of that decision may be on the propriety of joining the defendants in one action, it does not shew that the objection can be taken by special demurrer, but the contrary.

If it were necessary to decide the question of the right to join the defendants in this action, the case of *Rex* v. *Clark*, 2 Cowp. 610, cited by Mr. Belcourt, might be usefully referred to.

The only answer necessary to give to the objection is, that clearly it cannot, under our present system, be raised by demurrer.

I have no doubt that the appeal should be allowed.

OSLER, J. A.—I am of opinion that this appeal should be allowed.

The demurrer is on the ground that the statement of claim discloses no cause of action.

Three plaintiffs (a partnership firm) sue two defendants to recover from each of them a penalty to which it is alleged he has rendered himself liable under the Act relating to the registration of co-partnerships.

The first question is, whether there is any legal rule or principle which says that a qui tam action may not be brought in the name of two or more persons jointly to recover one or more penalties. No case was cited to us which so decides, nor is it so laid down in any of the standard text books which I have looked at.

An infant cannot bring such an action, as we recently
held in *Garrett* v. *Roberts*, 10 A. R, 650, but that is because
he is obliged to sue by his guardian, and the statute
18 Eliz. ch. 5, requires an informer to exhibit his writ in
his proper person, and to pursue the same by himself or
by his attorney in Court. And in the case of *St. Leonard's Shoreditch* v. *Franklin*, 3 C. P. D. 377, it was held
that a corporation could not be common informers under a
statute which made the penalties imposed by it recoverable by the "person or persons who shall sue for the
same." Lord Coleridge said :

"Undoubtedly the corporation may be in one sense
included within the terms 'person or persons.' But the
Act must be construed *secundum subjectam materiem*,
and I must ascertain whether it would be reasonable
that a corporation should be within those words."

Then he goes on to say that the general current of
authority seemed to shew that a corporation could not
be common informers, and to point out the reasons which
still existed for not giving an extended construction to
the words "person or persons," as used in the Act. It
is unnecessary here to consider whether a general interpretation Act such as our R. S. O. ch. 1, sec. 8, sub-
sec. 13, which declares that the word "person" shall
include any body corporate or politic, might have made
a difference in the decision.

None of the reasons, therefore, on which these cases
depend has any application to the present case. The
statute says that the penalty may be recovered by "any
person" suing as well on his own behalf as on behalf of
Her Majesty, and the Interpretation Act, sec. 8, sub-sec.
23, enacts that words importing the singular number
only shall include more persons of the same kind than
one, and the converse. Sub-sec. 38 of the same section
enacts that every Act, shall be deemed remedial, and
shall receive such fair, large, and liberal construction
and interpretation as will best insure the attainment
of its object according to its true intent, meaning,

and spirit. Whatever, therefore, might in former times have been urged in favor of the strict construction of a penal statute on a point of this kind, unless some reason exists in principle which forbids the application of these provisions to the Act now in question, it appears to me that they are properly invoked in support of the construction the plaintiffs contend for.

The case of *Meyers* v. *Baker*, 3 H. & N. 802, is an instance of a qui tam action brought by two plaintiffs suing jointly as common informers, under a statute which imposed a penalty of £50, to be recovered by action, &c., one-half to His Majesty and the other "to any person who shall sue for the same." There were several pleas and a demurrer, and the case was tried before Cockburn, C. J. The defendant had a verdict, which was moved against unsuccessfully on the ground of misdirection. The objection here taken would have been decisive, but it does not seem to have occurred to the bench, or to the bar, that it was tenable; and the fact that it was not taken affords a strong argument against its validity. The suggestion that if several persons may join in suing for a penalty, it may be possible to form an association or partnership for such a purpose, or for two or more persons to combine to bring an action which one might have hesitated to bring alone, seems to me more ingenious than practical.

The Court is possessed of ample power to restrain any abuse of its process, and on principle I can see nothing improper in the bare fact of two persons suing jointly for a penalty, especially where they happen to be a firm or partnership which may have been injured by the act or omission by which the penalty is incurred. Such a case was *Myers* v. *Baker*, and such, for anything we know, may be this case also. Further, in the case of *St. Leonards* v. *Franklin* may be seen instances of statutes passed in times when the language of Acts of Parliament was more verbose and redundant than in modern days, in which penalties are given to the "person or persons," or to "any person or persons" who shall sue for the same as common informers, And I think a very slight examination of the statute book would shew that this was not an uncommon form of expression. So *Blackstone* Com., vol. 2, p. 447, *Kerr's* ed., speaks of "penalties given by particular statutes to be recovered in an action popular; in other words, to be recovered by him *or them* that will sue for the same."

The case, therefore, simply resolves itself into the question whether we are at liberty to read the word "person" as "person or persons," and for the foregoing reasons I think we are. For the same reasons I think we cannot follow the three American cases I have noticed, in which it is held that two persons cannot maintain a joint action as common informers: See *Hill* v. *Davis*, 4 Mass. 137; *Vinton* v. *Walsh*, 9 Pick. 87; *Ferrett* v. *Atwell*, 1 Blatch. C. C. R. 151.

As regards the joinder of the plaintiffs, the case is unaffected by the Judicature Act and rules. There are two joint demands, though against two several defendants; and this brings me to the next question, namely, whether the defendants can be sued together in one action for several penalties, neither being interested in the demand made against the other. Looking at the form in which the objection has been taken, namely, by demurrer, I think this question must be answered adversely to the defendants.

If, as against one of the defendants, no cause of action had been shewn, he might no doubt have objected by demurrer, or possibly by motion: *Scottish Widows' Fund* v. *Craig*, 20 Ch. D. 208; *Burstall* v. *Beyfus*, 26 Ch. D. 35. But a perfectly good cause of action against each of them is here set forth on the statement of claim. I think Rule 91, relating to the joinder of defendants, must have a construction similar to that which has been placed on Rule 89, which deals with the joinder of plaintiffs, and we must hold that the action cannot be defeated merely by the joinder of defendants who have no common interest in the causes of action sued for. Rule 91 provides that all persons may be joined as defendants against whom the right to any relief is alleged to exist whether jointly, severally, or in the alternative; and that, substituting " plaintiffs " for " defendants," is the language of Rule 89.

In *Booth* v. *Briscoe*, 2 Q. B. D. 496, the English rule which corresponds to the latter rule was construed as meaning that where there are different plaintiffs, who are seeking wholly different relief, they may be joined. In that case eight plaintiffs joined in bringing an action of libel, though no joint injury was shewn, and though they would, before the Act, have been compelled to bring eight separate actions, it was held by the Court of Appeal that they might be rightly joined, and the decision was followed by the same Court in the subsequent case of *Gort* v. *Rowney*, 17 Q. B. D. 625. The Court there said, " There is no limit to the power of joinder under the rule; but the power of joinder would be subject to other rules, therefore the defendant, if he finds himself embarrassed, may apply to have one of the plaintiffs struck out; or if the Judge thinks the claims of the different plaintiffs cannot properly be dealt with together, he may make an order to strike out one of the plaintiffs, or may direct that there shall be separate trials."

It appears to me that, conversely, this is the measure of relief to which one of several defendants is entitled. Rule 103 provides that no action shall be defeated by reason of the misjoinder of parties, and rule 115, that the Court or Judge may order separate trials of the several causes of action, or may make such other order as may be necessary for the separate disposal thereof.

These rules appear to give ample power to the court to prevent inconvenience or injustice arising from the joinder of defendants whose interests or liabilities are unconnected, even where the claim against each may be of a similar character. As a rule it is undesirable that independent claims against several defendants should be made the subject of an action, but in the present case I see no inconvenience or impropriety in such a course.

The remaining objection is that the plaintiffs being residents out of the jurisdiction cannot maintain an action, for a penalty given by a penal statute. I confess to a certain difficulty in appreciating the force of this objection, which broadly stated is, that non-residence disqualifies even a subject from bringing a penal action. Admitting that a penalty imposed by our laws cannot be sued for, or a judgment therefor enforced in the Courts of a foreign country, on the principle that the penal laws of one State will not be taken notice of by the Courts of another, how does that affect the right of the resident of a foreign country to resort to our own tribunals ?

It has long been settled that an alien friend may sue in our Courts in personal (and now in any) action, and in *Pisani* v. *Lawson*, 8 Scott 182, it was held that he might maintain an action of libel even though he had never been in this country.

"It may be laid down as a general rule that all persons sui juris, and not otherwise specially disabled by the law of the place where the suit is brought, may there maintain suits to vindicate their rights, and redress their wrongs;" *Story's* Conflict L., sec, 565.

Blackstone speaks of a suit and judgment at law for a penalty as a means not only of recovering but of acquiring property. Penalties that are given at large to any person that will sue for the same

"are placed as it were in a state of nature, accessible by all, but the acquired right of none: open, therefore, to the first occupant who declares his intention to possess them by bringing his action, and who carries that intention into execution by obtaining judgment to recover them." Comm. (*Kerr's* ed.), vol. 2, p. 448.

Such actions are called popular actions because given to the people at large; but I find no authority for saying that no one can make the popular action his own private action unless he is a resident of the country where he sues.

No hint of such a disability is to be found in the books.

On the merits I think there is nothing in the objection, and am of opinion that the appeal should be allowed.

HAGARTY, C. J. O., and BURTON, J. A., concurred.

Appeal allowed, with costs.

NORTHCOTE V. BRUNKER.

Liquor License Act—Sale of liquor after notice—Drinking to excess—Form
of notice—R. S. O. ch. 181, sec. 80—Intoxicating liquor.

In an action by a married woman against an innkeeper, under R. S. O.
ch. 181, sec. 60, for having supplied liquor to her husband, after a
notice, as follows : "I hereby forbid you, or any one in your house,
giving my husband William Northcote any liquor of any kind from this
day,"   *   *   the jury found that the husband was an habitual drunkard, and that intoxicating liquor had been furnished to him after such
notice by the defendant, who knew the husband well, as also the reason
for giving the notice, and rendered a verdict in favor of the plaintiff for
$20.

In the following term the defendant moved to set aside that verdict, and
to enter a nonsuit or grant a new trial.   After argument the learned
Judge ordered the verdict to be set aside and a nonsuit entered. which,
on appeal to this Court, by reason of an equal division of the Judges,
was affirmed.

Per HAGARTY, C. J. O. and OSLER, J. A., the notice was insufficient in
omitting to state that the plaintiff's husband had the habit of drinking
to excess.

Per BURTON and PATTERSON, JJ. A.—The notice as given was sufficient.

Per BURTON, PATTERSON, and OSLER, JJ.A.—It was not necessary to forbid the supplying of "intoxicating liquor," the words used "liquor of
any kind" being sufficient.

THIS action was instituted in the County Court of Vic-
toria by the plaintiff against William Brunker, an inn-
keeper, to recover $200 damages under the statute (R. S.O.
ch. 181, sec. 90), which provides that the husband, wife,
&c., of any person who has the habit of drinking intoxicating liquor to excess may give notice in writing, signed
by him or her, to any person licensed to sell, or who sells,
or is reputed to sell, intoxicating liquor to the person having such habit; and if after such notice the person notified
suffers to be delivered any such liquor to the person having
such habit, the person giving the notice may, in an action
for personal wrong, recover such sum as may be assessed
for damages, &c.

The plaintiff, it was shewn, sent to the defendant a
written notice, which is set out in the judgment of Patterson, J. A.

The action came on for trial at Lindsay, before the Judge, of the County Court and a jury on the 8th of June, 1886, when the case set up by the plaintiff was fully sustained, and the jury returned a verdict for the plaintiff and $20 damages, which, in the following term, the defendant moved to set aside, and to enter a nonsuit or grant a new trial, on the ground of insufficiency of the notice. The County Judge held that the expression in the letter " any liquor of any kind " was sufficient to satisfy the section; but (2) that the notice was insufficient, because it did not contain a statement that the plaintiff's husband was a person who had the habit of drinking intoxicating liquor to excess, and ordered a nonsuit to be entered.

The plaintiff thereupon appealed to this Court, and the appeal came on for hearing on the 6th of April, 1887.*

Hudspeth, Q. C., for the appellant, contended that the verdict in favor of the plaintiff had been properly found, and ought not to have been set aside, as the notice given by the plaintiff was sufficient, the Act describing the persons who may give such notice, as well as the persons to whom such notice may be given, as also the persons in respect of whom such notice may be given—that is, any person having the habit of drinking to excess ; which is a fact capable of being established on the trial, as well as the other facts required to maintain the action ; for instance, that the person giving the notice, as well as the person to whom it is given, come within the descriptions contained in the statute.

D. J. McIntyre for respondent. The notice proved to have been given in this case is clearly not sufficient in this, that it does not forbid the defendant furnishing intoxicating liquor, nor does it say that the person to whom the liquor is not to be delivered has the habit of drinking intoxicating liquor to excess. Besides, the Act provides that the notice to be given shall be " not to deliver intoxicating liquor to a person having such habit."

The intention clearly is, that the person served with a
notice is to be informed that the person to whom he is
not to sell or give such liquor is a person who has the
habit of drinking intoxicating liquor to excess; and the
statute being in its nature penal, its words must be strictly
construed : *Jackson* v. *Kassell*, 26 U. C. R. 341 ; *Harding*
v. *Knowlson*, 17 U. C. R. 564. *Hardcastle's* Stat. Laws,
249, 251 were referred to.

May 10, 1887. HAGARTY, C. J. O.— The substance
of the sections, on which this action is founded, seems
to be that where a person has the habit of drinking
intoxicating liquors to excess, a notice in writing may
be given by certain named relatives to any person
licensed to sell, &c., " not to deliver intoxicating liquor to
the person having such habit." What, therefore, must
such a notice contain ?

Is it sufficient to say, " Do not give my husband any
liquor of any kind from this day ?"

The statute does not prescribe a form of notice as is to
be found in many analogous enactments.

The Ontario Interpretation Act, sec. 34, says : " Where
forms are prescribed, slight deviations therefrom not affecting the substance or calculated to mislead, shall not vitiate
them."

It seems to me that the " forms prescribed " here mean
when forms are given by the statute itself, and that the
enactment is framed to meet the occurrences of clerical
errors or trifling variance in words.

In my view this clause does not aid us much in the
solution of this question.

To warrant the giving of such a notice, the person named
must have the habit of drinking intoxicating liquors to
excess.

The offence of the tavern keeper is the giving such
liquor " to the person having such habit," after receiving
written notice not to give it to the person having such
habit.

If the notice in no way shews the *status* (as it were) of the drunkard, or assigns no reason whatever for the forbidding his having any liquor—if the mere order not to give must be obeyed at the tavern keeper's peril, then this notice is sufficient.

But I must say that it is contrary to all the ideas that I have entertained as to the requirements of a statute of this kind to hold the bare command of the wife, unexplained in any way as to the reason or ground of giving it, to be sufficient.

I am strongly of opinion that any notice under this statute should carry with it the reason of its existence. It is argued that all this is matter of evidence.

I do not think that is any answer. In the present case the evidence shewed that the defendant knew the person well, and the reason of the giving the notice. It may be so in this case—it may not be so in another.

An inn-keeper may receive this notice respecting a person who may be either an absolute stranger to him, or a person of whose habits he is wholly ignorant.

If the notice from the wife contained the information that he was given to excessive drinking, that might be a warrant for the inn-keeper's refusal to give him liquor. But a mere forbidding like this, giving no reason whatever on which it is grounded, seems to me to be defective, not merely in form but in substance.

If a statute created a liability like the present for selling goods in a shop to an insane man, and the notice was to be given exactly as here directed, would it be safe to hold it sufficient to simply forbid the shop-keeper from selling to him?

I think it would be most unreasonable to omit the cause of the proceeding. When a man is peremptorily forbidden to do an ordinary legal act in his business, I think he should be told why he is so forbidden.

In such a case he might be left completely in the dark as to whether it was for insanity or drunkenness, or some other statutable incapacity that the mandate was given to him.

We must not give in to the specious argument that the defendant was perfectly aware of all the facts, and could not possibly have been misled. But, although it be a " liquor case," we must decide it on some principle of general application.

If the statute had omitted the words "in writing " would it be sufficient for the wife simply to say to the defendant, " I forbid you giving liquor of any kind to my husband.'' I think it would not suffice.

The statute says, "not to deliver intoxicating liquor to the person having such habit." I think this is a substantial direction that the notice must state the existence of such habit in the person named. It could be stated either in the earlier part that he was a person in the habit of drinking, &c., or at the end of the notice.

Its total omission is in my judgment a most substantial defect.

Had the notice contained the statement as to the husband's habit to drink intoxicating liquor to excess, I would endeavour, if possible, to hold that any liquor of any kind "was sufficient to satisfy a statute requiring a notice ' not to deliver intoxicating liquor.' "

But without an averment of the habit of drinking to excess, it seems almost too much to hold the words used sufficient. The existence of that habit is the foundation of the right to give to give the notice and create the liability for disobeying its requirements.

Spice v. *Bacon*, before the Court of Appeal, 2 Ex. D. 463 fairly points out how far the Court can go to relieve against a formal error.

That was an action against an inn-keeper for loss of a guest's goods. The Imperial Act 26-7 Vic., ch. 41, sec. 1, limited the inn-keeper's responsibility to £30, except where the goods were lost, stolen, &c., through the wilful act, default, or neglect of the inn-keeper, or his servants.

Sec. 3 required the inn-keeper to have at least one copy of the 1st section of the Act exhibited in a conspicuous place, &c., in order to have the benefit of the Act.

The copy exhibited by defendant in his inn, by a printer's error, omitted the word "act," and the exception read, "through the wilful default or neglect, &c.," instead of "*act*, default or neglect."

The Court of Appeal held the omission fatal.

Lord Cairns, L.C., after expressing his regret, says: he had no doubt but that there was a bona fide intention on defendant's part to give a notice in exact compliance with the statute; and further says that at first sight it rather appeared it was an omission of a word not material to the sense, but after noticing the omission of the word "act," he remarks that there is nothing in the notice—no statement which admits the common law liability for goods lost by the wilful "act" of the inn-keeper or his servants—and if that be so the omission entirely alters the operation of the section of the statute.

Sir A. Cockburn, C. J., adds : "I quite concur in thinking that if this were a mere clerical error we might hold the notice sufficient to meet the requirement of the Act, as still being a copy. But when we find an omission of that which is material, with a view to a clear and distinct statement of the rights and liabilities of the parties respectively, we have an omission which is far beyond a mere clerical error. It is an omission of a substantial part of the notice."

There was nothing in the evidence to lead to the belief that the guest was or could have been in any way misled or influenced by the omission.

So in the case before me, I feel bound to hold, with a view to the rights and liabilities of the parties, that the notice should in some intelligible way shew the right, viz. : that the husband had the habit of drinking to excess, and the liability of the inn-keeper, if he gave liquor to a person with such a habit after notice. The notice is, in my opinion, substantially defective.

I rest my opinion wholly on the words of the section, and I hold that the law requires the notice to be a warning not to give liquor to a person having the habit of drinking to excess.

I am surprised to hear the objection that ordinary people, without legal education, would be misled by requiring such a statement to be made in the notice. For my part, I should think that ninety-nine people out of every hundred would at once take it for granted that such a notice should, in some shape or other, state the person not to be given liquor had the habit of drinking to excess.

BURTON, J. A.—This is an action brought by a married woman under "The Liquor License Act" against a licensed tavern-keeper to recover damages in consequence of his having sold intoxicating liquor to her husband after being notified by the plaintiff not to do so

The case was tried by a jury who assessed the damages at $20. A nonsuit was, however, moved for on the ground that the notice given was insufficient inasmuch as it did not use the words "intoxicating liquors," but forbade the defendant to give her husband "liquor of any kind."

The learned Judge upon this point held, and I think correctly, that the notice was sufficient.

The statute in question is partly remedial and partly penal.

The tendency of modern decision is to narrow materially the difference between what is called a strict and a beneficial construction. All statutes are now construed with a more strict regard to the language, and criminal statutes with a more rational regard to the aim and intention of the Legislature than formerly, and in a remedial statute everything is to be done in advancement of the remedy that can be done consistently with any construction that can be put upon it.

And these decisions have now been made obligatory upon the Courts by a declaration of the Legislature that every Act, and every provision and enactment thereof shall be deemed remedial, whether its immediate purport be to direct the doing of anything which the Legislature deems to be for the public good, or to prevent, or punish the doing of anything which it deems to be contrary to the public good, and that they shall receive such fair, large, and liberal interpretation as will best ensure the attainment of the object of the Act.

And in the same direction is the enactment which declares that where forms are prescribed, slight deviations therefrom, not affecting the substance or calculated to mislead, shall not vitiate them.

Such, then, being the tendency of modern decision, and the spirit of recent legislation, it appears to me we should be giving a very narrow construction to the words of this notice, if we held it to be insufficient.

The evidence shews very clearly that the defendant was not misled, as indeed he could not be misled by a term which is in common use, and the meaning of which is perfectly understood.

I think that the learned Judge was right in refusing to give effect to that objection.

But the learned Judge held that the notice was insufficient because it did not state upon the face of it the grounds upon which she became entitled under the statute to give this notice.

With great respect I think the objection untenable.

The Act provides that in the case of a particular class of persons, viz.: persons who are in the habit of drinking intoxicating liquor to excess—the husband, wife, parent, child of age, brother, sister, master, guardian, or employer of such person may do—what? Give notice in writing, signed by him or her, to a tavern-keeper not to deliver intoxicating liquor to such person. All that the statute requires is that the notice shall be in writing—that it shall be signed by the person giving it, and that it shall indicate the person to whom the liquor is not to be given.

Why should the Courts take upon themselves to say that the notice to be effectual shall go further than the Legislature has thought fit to prescribe; and what possible good would be attained by the notice containing the allegation that the party to whom the interdict extends is given to the habit of drinking to excess, which might be true, or untrue, in fact?

Every person must be presumed to know the law, and
when tavern-keepers receive a notice signed by a person filling the relationship to the person referred to in it, which the
statute recognises—he has all the notice which the statute
requires, and afterwards delivers liquor to that person at
his peril. If the plaintiff fails at the trial to prove that
the person mentioned in the notice was in the habit of
drinking intoxicating liquor to excess, she must fail; if she
does prove it, then the tavern-keeper has received the
requisite notice and should suffer the consequences.

It appears to me, with great deference, to be confounding
what it is incumbent upon the plaintiff to prove, with what
it is necessary to state in the notice.

The Legislature never intended that a notice of this
nature should be submitted to the close scrutiny of a
pleading under a special demurrer, but that it should
simply shew that it is given by one of the parties occupying relationship to the person referred to in it, within the
terms of the Act. I think we may fairly assume that the
Legislature with the knowledge that the class of persons
intended to be benefited by the Act were generally too
poor to spend money in obtaining legal advice, intended to
make the notice as simple as possible and consistent with
the object in view—that of warning the tavern-keeper.

The learned Judge proceeds a good deal on the ground
of this being a penal law; there is a portion of the law
which gives a penalty: but I should not regard that portion
of it which gives a right of action to the injured wife as
falling within that definition.

In a recent case in the Court of Appeal, under a very
similar statute, interrogatories were administered which the
defendant declined to answer on the ground that the action
was for a penalty, and that therefore no interrogatories
were allowed; but the Master of the Rolls said it was
clear that this was not a payment of money which
came within the doctrine which prevented the Court of
Equity from allowing discovery by way of interrogatories
in actions for a penalty. The payment was treated in the

Act of Parliament as a payment by way of damages, and not by way of penalty. It was not a payment imposed upon the defendant by way of punishment, but for the purpose of compensating the plaintiff. It had no characteristic of a penalty.

The Lords Justices concurred. *Adams* v. *Batley*, Times Law Rep. vol. 3, p. 511.

But as I have already pointed out, all statutes, whether penal or not, are now as a matter of fact construed by the same rules. The distinction, as explained by Baron Bramwell, in the case of the Alexandria, now means little more than that the penal provisions, like all others, are to be fairly construed according to the legislative intent as expressed in the enactment—the Courts refusing on the one hand to extend the punishment to cases which are not clearly embraced in them, and on the other equally refusing by any mere verbal nicety, forced construction, or equitable interpretation to exonerate parties clearly within their scope.

The plaintiff in this case has proved that her husband came within the description in the statute, and that she gave notice to the inn-keeper; and she has proved further that the defendant was fully aware of her husband's habits.

I think it would be a matter to be regretted if the action were to be defeated on such an objection. And for the reasons I have given, I think the appeal should be allowed, the nonsuit set aside, and the verdict in favor of the plaintiff restored.

PATTERSON, J. A.—The plaintiff's statement of claim sets out five facts, and the statement of defence is a simple denial of all the allegations contained in the plaintiff's statement of claim.

The alleged facts are (1) that the plaintiff is the wife of William Northcote; (2) that the defendant is an inn-keeper licensed to sell, or reputed to sell intoxicating drinks; (3) that William Northcote has the habit of drinking intoxicating liquor to excess : (4) that the plaintiff on the 20th of May, 1885, gave the defendant notice in writing, signed by her, not to deliver intoxicating liquor to her husband ; (5) that the defendant did within twelve months after such notice, either by himself or his clerk, servant, or agent, otherwise than in terms of a special requisition for medicinal purposes signed by a medical practitioner, deliver or suffer to be delivered from the building or place occupied by the defendant as an inn, intoxicating liquor to the said William.

There was a verdict for the plaintiff, the whole contest before the jury being, as I gather from the charge of the learned Judge which is very fully reported, upon allegation 3, respecting the man's habits.

Leave had been reserved to move for a nonsuit on the ground of the insufficiency of the notice mentioned in allegation 4, and the defendant moved accordingly.

The notice was in these words :

"MR. BRUNKER,—Sir :—I hereby forbid you, or any one in your house giving my husband, William Northcote, any liquor of any kind from this day, the 20 of May, 1885, and oblige me,

"MRS. H. NORTHCOTE."

The action is brought under R. S. O. ch. 181, the short title of which is "The Liquor License Act."

Sec. 90 enacts that "the husband, wife, parent, brother, sister, guardian or employer of any person who has the habit of drinking intoxicating liquor to excess   *   * may give notice in writing, signed by him or her, to any person licensed to sell, or who sells, or is reputed to sell, intoxicating liquor of any kind, not to deliver intoxicating liquor to the person having such habit," &c.

Two objections were taken to the notice, and both have been insisted on before us, viz.: that the notice did not designate the liquor as *intoxicating* liquor, and that it did not inform the defendant that the plaintiff's husband was a person who had the habit of drinking intoxicating liquor to excess.

The learned Judge did not give effect to the first of these objections. His view of it is thus expressed in his judgment:

"It is contended for the defendant that the notice is defective in not using the words 'intoxicating liquor,' to this it is replied that the words 'any liquor of any kind' in the notice must include intoxicating liquor, and that the interpretation clause of the Act, sec. 2, defines the word liquor as comprehending intoxicating liquor. It must be observed that this clause only defines the meaning of the word when used in the Act."

But the word "liquor" popularly means intoxicating liquor. The defendant is a dealer in such liquors and could not be in any way misled by the use of the word, and certainly "any liquor of any kind" includes intoxicating liquors of any kind.

As I read the interpretation clause of the statute, the word "liquor," when used in the Act, not only comprehends intoxicating liquor, but is restricted to that meaning. It is to be "construed to mean and to comprehend all," &c. The clause was the same in the Act of 1874, 37 Vict., ch. 32; but most of the numerous clauses, and all of the forms of the R. S. O. in which the word "liquor" is used without being qualified by the word "intoxicating," come from the Acts of 1876, (39 Vict., ch. 26,) and of 1877, (40 Vict., ch. 18). The word was not employed in the same general way in the Temperance Act of 1864, commonly known as the Dunkin Act, yet when that Act is referred to in the Act of 1876, sec. 27, its prohibition is said to be of the "sale of liquor." The R. S. O., ch. 182, is "The Temperance Act of Ontario." Like the Dunkin Act, it has a definition of "Intoxicating Liquor," but none of "liquor" by itself. Yet we find in sec. 40, of ch. 182, the word "liquor" used to denote liquors which it is made unlawful to sell without license by the Liquor License Act—meaning, of course, intoxicating liquor.

It is common knowledge that, as the learned Judge observes, the word popularly means spirituous liquor. The dictionaries recognise that as its most common application. It is not pretended that the defendant understood it in any other sense. This notice was not the first he had had from the plaintiff. He says he obeyed the first one, which was

in 1882. The next was in 1884. He avows his decision
to disregard the notice now in question, arguing that
Northcote is not a drunkard, and that he could get liquor
at another tavern.

Now when I see how the word "liquor" is used by the
Legislature in these chapters, 181 and 182, and further
note the provision of the Interpretation Act, "when forms
are prescribed, slight deviations therefrom not affecting the
substance or calculated to mislead shall not vitiate them,"
a provision which is perhaps more applicable in principle
than in its literal force, but which brings statutory forms
distinctly within the general rule that every provision is
to receive such fair, large and liberal construction as will
best insure the attainment of the object of the provision,
according to its true intent meaning and spirit, I cannot
see any reasonable ground for differing from the learned
Judge upon this part of the question. The very compre-
hensive term "any liquor of any kind" clearly includes, as
the learned Judge remarks, intoxicating liquor, and I do
not know why too large a warning should be held to be no
warning within the statute. If the plaintiff had undertaken to enumerate the descriptions of liquor, including in
the list soda water as well as whiskey, the notice would
have been inoperative as to soda water, but I apprehend it
would be valid as against whiskey, or the other specified
intoxicating liquors. Utile per inutile non vitiatur. The
construction would be somewhat like that upon which a
bastardy order was supported in *Regina* v. *Goodall*, 2
Dowl. P. C., N. S. 382. The application for that order
should have been made to the justice by the guardians
alone, but the order recited that the application was made
by the guardians and overseers. Patteson, J., held it good,
saying that the application was made by the guardians
who, under the Act of Parliament, were the proper persons, and that if it had been alleged to have been made by
the guardians, overseers, clergyman and all the inhabitants
of the parish, it would be immaterial as long as the right
persons applied.

The case of *Allen,* appellant, and *House,* respondent, 7 M. & G. 157, is of the same class. The question was the sufficiency of a notice of objection to the retention of the respondent's name on a voters' list, the objection being that the words "as householders" had been added to the form given by statute. Tindal, C. J., said, "If the insertion of those words could have misled the party objected to, then the notice, not being in strict compliance with the form given in the Act, would have been bad * * I think, however, that the principle utile per inutile non vitiatur applies, it not being shewn that the party was misled or that he was put to any inconvenience or extra expense. In common parlance the list in question was made out in respect of £10 householders." And Cresswell, J.: "If the departure from the prescribed form had been likely to divert the attention of the party to a wrong list, I think the notice would have been bad. But this notice could not possibly have that effect."

In *Chaney* v. *Payne,* 1 Q. B. 712, one question was, the validity of a conviction of the master of a ship for continuing in charge of the ship after a pilot had offered to take charge. The conviction was drawn up after a general form given by statute. Lord Denman, C. J., said : "This second conviction follows the form given in the Act of Parliament, and the only objection suggested to it is, that although it states the consent of the corporation of Trinity House to have been given to the prosecutor, yet it does not state that the offence was committed within the jurisdiction of the Trinity House ; therefore that the consent of the Lord Warden of the Cinque Ports may have been that which the Act requires. The answer is, that though the Act requires such consent, yet the form of conviction does not contain any allusion to it. It was necessary to prove it, but wholly unnecessary to state it in the conviction. Assuming, therefore, that the statement is defective for the reason suggested, it is of no consequence, for utile per inutile non vitiatur."

The case of *Mountcashel* v. *O'Neill,* 5 H. L. C. 937 ; 2 Jur. N. S. 1030, cited by the Chancellor in *Gemmell* v. *Garland,* 12 O. R. 139, which turned on the sufficiency of an affidavit which had to be filed by way of notice from a tenant to his landlord of the planting of trees, in pursuance of an Act of Parliament, is a strong authority against holding a variance from a statutory form fatal so long as the document really conveys the proper information, and the more recent case of *Ex parte Stanford.* 17 Q. B. D. 259, goes far in the same direction, and has the weight of a decision of five out of the six Lords Justices by whom the argument was heard, the sixth not disputing the principle but differing as to its application.

We were referred by Mr. McIntyre to *Jackson* v. *Kassel*, 26 U. C. R. 341, as an instance in which a literal compliance with a statute was held to be essential. That decision, which, though clearly sound, is perhaps an extreme instance of its class, can scarcely be used as a guide in the present case. It was under a statute which declared that no action should be sustained under its provisions against the putative father of an illegitimate child, for maintenance of the child, unless the mother had within a limited time filed an affidavit declaring that the person sued was " really the father of the child." An affidavit omitting the word "really" was held insufficient.

The Court had there to give effect to prohibitive words. We have to deal with a provision intended to prevent the furnishing to persons addicted to excess, the means of intoxication, by any one who receives written notice of the desire of some one occupying one of the specified relations, that liquor shall not be furnished. Care is taken that the notice shall come from the proper person by requiring it to be signed, and it must convey the intended information; but no form of words is prescribed in which that intimation must be conveyed.

I think the notice before us is quite sufficient to convey the information, and we know that as a matter of fact it did so.

But the learned Judge held the notice bad because it did not state that the husband had the habit of drinking intoxicating liquor to excess.

That he, in fact, had that habit, is found by the jury, and might well have been found upon the defendant's own evidence if there had been none other.   He was therefore a person of the class described in section 90.

It would doubtless be considered unjust to visit a tavern-keeper with penal damages under this statute in case he had not reasonable notice that the person to whom he was notified not to give liquor was one of those described in section 90, but the statute does not require an intimation of that fact to be set out in that writing by the wife or other person giving notice under the section.   Such an intimation, if set out, would have no further effect than to inform the party notified that the proceeding was taken under the statute.   The fact of the habit would always have to be proved, if not admitted.

The mere fact of giving the notice, signed as the statute requires, would probably be as effectual an intimation without as with the express statement that the person named was asserted by the party giving the notice to be one of those with regard to whom the section 90 permits such a notice to be given.

But, however this may be, it seems to me very plain that we have no warrant from the language of the section for reading into it the requirement that the person who gives the written notice shall, in that notice, state that the husband, wife, child, brother sister, ward or servant, who is not to be served with liquor, has the habit of drinking to excess, and that we are not required to do so on any ground of principle or necessity.   The reasons to the contrary seem to me very cogent.

The effect urged as proper to be given to the clause certainly does not lie on the surface.   The persons intended to benefit by it must, to a great extent, be persons whose education and training have not qualified them for extracting by ingenious inference a meaning which the Legislature could have put in plain words, if so minded ; and we cannot but see that the clause is meant to be acted on by these people themselves, as by the plaintiff in this case, without calling in professional assistance.

The respondent's argument rather credits the Legislature with preparing a pitfall than with providing a practical remedy for a serious evil.

No injustice can be done to the liquor seller as long as his liability is restricted to cases where he has notice that the person is addicted to excess, whether the notice comes to him by writing or from his personal knowledge of the man or otherwise; but to recognise his right to avow full knowledge of the man's habits, and to justify his disregard of the notice on the ground that it did not put in writing what he well knew all the time would, in my judgment, require a very clear indication that that was the meaning and intention of the statute.

I think the appeal should be allowed, with costs.

OSLER, J. A.—I regret that there should be any difference of opinion in this case, and the more that the defendant's conduct, as described by the evidence, shews that on what the laity might call the merits of the case, he is not deserving of favorable consideration.

But with the merits of the case we are not now at all concerned. We have only to see whether the notice, which is the foundation of the right of action, complies with the requirements of the statute. If it does not, there was no notice, the defendant's legal right to sell intoxicating liquor to any one he pleased was not abridged, and he cannot be made liable to the penalties of the Act.

The question as presented here, must be decided in precisely the same way as it would be in a case where the notice had been given to a person who, at the time of service, had never heard of the husband of the person giving it or his habits; in other words, the notice must in all cases convey the same minimum of information to the recipient.

Then the question is, what that information must be? The statute prescribes no form, and it must be spelt out of the enactment. The notice in this case is complained of on two grounds. 1. That it forbids defendant to give North-

cote "any liquor of any kind," instead of using the term
"intoxicating liquor," and 2. That it does not state that
he is a person who has the habit of drinking intoxicating
liquor to excess.   As to the first objection, though not free
from doubt, I do not dissent from the judgment below.
The term liquor, when used in connection with selling it
or delivering at a tavern, has probably, in common parlance, if not indeed in the legislative tongue, come to be a
convertible term with intoxicating liquor.   My doubt is
whether, as the notice is intended to limit or restrain a
legal right, it should not describe the thing forbidden as
the statute describes it, and not, by using the comprehen-
sive terms "any liquor of any kind," lead the tavern-
keeper to suppose that he is forbidden to sell harmless as
well as hurtful potations.   The fault is, that the prohibition
is too wide and may be embarrassing unless the defendant
happens to compare it with the statute.   The case on this
point seemed to me, I confess, distinguishable from cases
where notices, convictions, &c., have been upheld where
there was merely over-statement or surplusage of information.

The other objection I consider fatal.   The Act as regards
the tavern keeper is extremely stringent and highly penal
in its terms, and the defendant's liability to the penalty is
not dependent upon his knowledge that the person to
whom after the receipt of the notice he delivers liquor had
the drinking habit, though his ignorance of it may possibly
in the view of a jury or judge trying an action or information, affect the quantum of the penalty.   The fact must be
proved, but his ignorance of it is no defence.

When the Act says that the wife of any person who has
the habit of drinking intoxicating liquors to excess may
give notice, signed by her, to a licensed or reputed seller,
not to deliver such liquor to the person having such habit,
I cannot regard it as requiring less than that the notice
shall state or shew in some way on its face the circumstances which authorise it.   It must appear to be given by
a person standing in a certain legal relationship to the per-

son to be affected by it, the latter being also a person who has the habit of drinking, &c., to excess. A notice not to deliver to the person having such habit, appears to me necessarily to comprise the description of the person regarding whom the right to give it has arisen, and it is only a person " so notified," that is, notified not to deliver, and to such a person so described who incurs the penalty for disobedience. Moreover, if, as I think, the ignorance of the tavern keeper is no defence, (the prohibition, where the circumstances exist, being absolute), it is most reasonable that the notice should contain the information in order that he may know that the habit has been acquired, or is believed by the person who undertakes to give the notice to have been acquired, and so, that the notice has not been given wantonly or without just cause existing, or believed to exist. That, of course, is not a reason for placing a construction on the statute which its words will not bear, but where they do bear, as I respectfully think, the construction I have indicated as the right one, it may serve to shew that it is also a reasonable one.

I am not impressed with the argument so forcibly urged by Mr. Hudspeth, that the construction which has been placed upon the section will destroy its usefulness. I agree that the Act was mainly intended for a class of persons not accustomed to construe statutes, or to extract its meaning from a loosely framed clause; yet, I think most persons drawing their information from the statute itself, and not acting upon a merely confused impression of its requirements, and without looking at the section, would frame the notice so as to give the information which I think it ought to give.

I think the appeal should be dismissed.

The Court being equally divided in opinion, the appeal was dismissed, with costs.

HUGGINS V. LAW ET AL.

Executors—Guardian—Infants—Payment of infants' moneys to guardian.

Moneys bequeathed directly to infant legatees and which had been invested by the defendants, the executors of the testatrix, were demanded of and received from them by one F., a solicitor who had obtained from the Surrogate Court his appointment as guardian of the infants. F. subsequently misapplied the moneys and absconded.

Held, [reversing the judgment of FERGUSON, J., HAGARTY, C. J. O., dissenting,] that the defendants were not liable.

THIS was an appeal from the judgment of Ferguson, J., reported 11 O. R. 565, where the facts giving rise to the action are fully and clearly stated, and came on to be heard before this Court on the 1st day of April, 1887.*

McCarthy, Q. C., and *Bain,* Q. C., for the appellants.

Moss, Q. C., and *Guthrie,* Q. C., for the respondents.

June 29, 1887. BURTON, J.A.—The question of the right of a guardian under our own Statute, R. S. O. ch. 132, to give a valid discharge to the executor of personal property bequeathed to the infants, for whom he has been appointed guardian, comes in this case, I believe, for the first time before the Courts of this Province for adjudication.

By the appointment the guardian is invested with authority to act for and on behalf of the infant, to prosecute actions in his name, and he is to have the charge and management of his or her estate, real and personal, and the care of his or her person and education.

I should suppose it to be beyond question that although the guardian would, under this Statute, be driven to sue in the infants' names to recover from a stranger property to which the infant is entitled, the property when recovered would remain under the charge and management of the guardian; and if that property so recovered consisted of farming stock or perishable property it would

Present.—HAGARTY, C. J. O., BURTON, PATTERSON, and OSLER, JJ.A.

be proper for him to convert it into money, with the view
to performing the duties of his position and providing for
the maintenance and education of his wards.

It is not necessary to consider what would have been
the relative positions of the guardian and the executor in
the case of a legacy vested in the infant at the time of the
testator's death, but not payable until the majority of the
infant.

My own view of such a case would be that as the infants'
right to sue would not accrue until after the office of
guardian had come to an end, the guardian could be in no
different positio n; and besides, in such a case, by the express
terms of the will, the executor, not the guardian, is made
the trustee, to hold it until the time of payment arrives.

That is not the present case. The property is bequeathed
directly to the infants, " to be divided equally amongst
them, share and share alike, after payment of the just
debts and funeral and testamentary expenses of the testatrix." So that if there were funds on hand sufficient to
pay those debts and expenses, the executor would have
held the property to which the infants were entitled in
specie; and it is very difficult indeed to understand why
the trustee specially empowered by law to take charge of
and manage that property, which by the very terms of the
will was to be divided among the infants after payment of
the debts, should not be entitled to give a valid discharge.
It is true that if driven to assert his rights he would have
to sue in the name of the infant. But is there anything
inconsistent in this ? the law having provided in language,
which apart from decisions I should have thought very
clear, that the guardian should have the control and management of the property. If the testatrix, even in the case
of a pecuniary legacy, had directed it to be paid to a guardian appointed by the will, it is quite clear that the executor could not refuse to pay it over to him, and insist on
converting himself into a trustee for the infant until he
attained the age of 21.

I think it will be found that the statutory guardian is
entitled to the possession of all property in which the.

infant is interested, and for which by law, or express contract, or other provision no other custody has been provided.

If, for instance, by the terms of 'this will it had been provided that the division should be made on the children attaining 21, it would have been a clear indication that the executor was the party intended by the testatrix to act as trustee for the infants in the management of their property until they attained that age. But the very reverse is the case here. The law says that the custody of the children and their education shall be vested in the guardian. The will says the infants are to be entitled to this property so soon as the debts are paid, and this was the only property to which they were entitled; how, then, is the guardian to perform that duty if the control and possession of the estate is denied him, and is to remain in the executor?

I apprehend that if there had been funds on hand sufficient to pay the debts and funeral expenses, the executor would have had no power to convert the personal estate into money. What, then, would have been the consequence? Is it to be supposed that the executor was bound to retain in specie the property belonging to the infants, and to have imposed upon him a trust to take care of it until the children attained their majority? I think the answer is, your duties are at an end when you have paid the debts, except that you are by the terms of the will when that is accomplished to divide the property among the children. You can only safely do so after a guardian has been duly appointed by the proper Court, but upon that being done you can safely relieve yourself from further responsibility and obtain from him a legal discharge.

Unless some direct authority can be produced, I am prepared to hold that that this is and ought to be the law governing such a case as the present.

I will proceed now to consider the authorities which have been cited in favour of the view that the payment to the guardian was wrong.

In the first place it may be remarked that no direct authority was referred to for that position, and so far as I have been able to ascertain no such authority can be found.

The case of *McCreight* v. *McCreight*, 13 Ir. Eq. 314, a decision of the Lord Chancellor of Ireland, is an authority the other way.

That was a decision under an Irish Statute analogous to the English Act, 12 Ch., 2nd ch. 24, as to the right of the testamentary guardian, who by the terms of that Act is entitled "to the custody, tuition, and management of the infants' goods, chattels and personal estate," to receive the property belonging to the infants and to give a valid discharge.

The judgment goes much farther than I have thought it necessary to go in support of that view, both on the ground that the legacies were not then payable, and because the powers of a testamentary guardian are of a much more limited character than those of a guardian appointed under our Act, who is bound by law to give security for the property coming into his hands.

Blake v. *Blake*, 2 Sch. & L. 26, is certainly no authority against it. It simply decides that when the executor has paid off the debts of the estate, even though the executor is named as testamentary guardian, the Court will, on the application of some of the beneficiaries direct the fund to be paid into Court.

The case of *Orrok* v. *Binney*, Jacob 523, decided twenty years later, by no means affects the view that this may not have been a valid payment.

There the suit was instituted by an executor twelve years after the testator's death, (and where it was admitted that the fund was not required for the payment of debts) to compel certain persons, in whose names a fund from which some legacies were to be paid had previously stood, to transfer that fund into the name of the executor. The Court being apprised that this fund was one belonging exclusively to infants, directed it to be brought into Court, it not appearing that it was required for immediate use for the maintenance and education of the children.

Neither of these cases establish that a payment over by the executor of a legacy, or the distributive shares of infants, to a guardian duly appointed, would not be a good payment.

It is of course clear enough that independently of the statute, when a legacy is given to an infant, an executor cannot safely pay it to the infant, or to his father as natural guardian, without the sanction of the Court; but I am unable to find any case, although there are dicta, I admit, to be found in text books, that a guardian duly appointed is not entitled to receive it and give a valid discharge, and there are authorities to be found where such payments have been recognised as valid. *Grant* v. *Tallmadge*, 1 John Ch. 3; *Morrell* v. *Dickey*, 1 John Ch. 153.

The case of *Re Cresswell*, 30 W. R. 244, is no authority, in my opinion, for the contention that such a payment would not be good. It merely decides that a testamentary guardian is not a person entitled to funds paid into Court, within the meaning of the Legacy Duty Act, and was not intended, as is mentioned in a recent work (*Eversley* on Domestic Relations) to impugn the accuracy of the Irish decision, from which the learned author draws the deduction that under ordinary circumstances, a testamentary guardian is entitled to give a receipt for funds coming to his infant ward, but not to have funds paid out to him which have been paid into Court under that Act.

The fact that the executors had actually invested the money appears to me to be perfectly immaterial, and with great deference I think the effect of the decision of this Court in *Cameron* v. *Campbell*, 7 A. R. 336, has been misapprehended. All that that case decides, or was intended to decide, was, that so soon as the debts were paid and the executor assented to the legacy, it became a trust fund, so as to render the Statute of Limitations inapplicable.

It is scarcely necessary to refer to authorities for the, I might say almost elementary, proposition that a trustee cannot relieve himself from liability to his cestui qui trust

by transferring the trust fund to another on an agreement
that he should asssume the trust; and I have already
pointed out that if this fund at the time of the death of
the testator, either by the terms of the will or otherwise,
had been in the hands of some one other than the guardian
to be held for the infant till twenty-one, it is clear that the
latter would neither have had the right to demand a transfer, nor could the trustee have relieved himself from responsibility by making such a transfer. That to my mind
is too clear for argument; but I dispute the doctrine that
a person in possession of property of the infant can, by a
voluntary dealing with that property and investing it in
securities, deprive the guardian of the infant of his right
to claim the property into which it had been converted.

A remark of Vice-Chancellor Blake, in *Galbraith* v.
Duncombe, 28 Gr. 27, at the first blush would appear to
give countenance to such a view. As applied to the
facts of that case the language attributed to the learned
Judge is perfectly correct, inasmuch as the testator had
directed by his will that certain legacies should be paid
to the children on coming of age, and the executors
were directed to place the money on deposit in a savings
bank in the meantime. It is quite clear, therefore, that
the executor would have been guilty of a breach of
trust in removing it from the place of deposit selected
by the testator, and handing it to the guardian. If it was
intended, as has been suggested, to decide more than this,
and to lay down in general terms that because the executor
had invested money belonging to infants, and to which
they were presently entitled, he became incapable of handing it over to their guardian, I must respectfully dissent,
and I submit with deference that no authority can be cited
for such a position.

Whenever the debts of the testatrix in the present case
were paid, the executors' duties ceased: they found themselves in possession of property belonging to these infants,
to the possession and control of which their guardian
when appointed was solely and exclusively entitled. The

dealing by the executors with that property by investing it could not deprive the guardian of his right still to demand and insist upon the control of the property itself, or its proceeds; and although the executors by their action had constituted themselves trustees, so that they could not transfer the trust to a stranger, they were still entitled, as they were originally, to transfer the property to the legal guardian of the infant—the person to whom, and to whom alone, the law had entrusted the custody and care of the infant and the charge and management of his estate.

If the executors had adopted the scripture precedent of wrapping the money in a napkin and hiding it in the earth, it seems almost conceded that the guardian would have been entitled to demand it. I should have hardly thought the argument that the executors by adopting the more prudent and proper course of investing it, had changed the relation of the parties, worthy of serious consideration, but for the strenuous manner in which it was pressed upon us at the Bar and the fact that the learned Chief Justice has adopted it. It seems to me to be brought back at last to the question: Was the guardian the party entitled by law to this property at any time? If so, can the executors by investing it deprive him of his right?

Another case cited below was *Flanders* v. *D'Evelyn*, 4 O. R. 704.

That case might have been disposed of on the short ground that a foreign guardian had no locus standi in our Courts.

The learned Judge in the Court below felt bound by these decisions, but for which he appears to have inclined to the view that the payment was good.

I see no reason whatever for construing the words of this Act of Parliament otherwise than in their natural and ordinary sense; so construed they seem to indicate beyond all doubt that the guardian, and he alone, is entitled to the possession of the property which the testatrix bequeathed to these infants; that being so, no act of the executor could deprive him of that right, and the executor did not by the proper and prudent course which he adopted, deprive himself of the right he would have had immediately after the death of the testatrix, to relieve himself of responsibility by handing over the property, if there had then been a hand to receive.

I find no decision other than those I have referred to against this view, and the decision of the Lord Chancellor of Ireland is in favor of it.

I am, therefore, of opinion, that the executor was rightly advised when he paid over these moneys to the guardian, although it is deeply to be regretted that through the neglect of some one, sufficient securities were not taken for the due performance of his duties.

I think therefore the appeal should be allowed.

PATTERSON, J. A.—This action is brought by five legatees of Eliza Jane Lee against her executors James Law and Margaret English.

The pleadings state all the essential facts with substantial correctness.

The statement of claim shews that the testatrix by her will, dated the 26th of August, 1874, devised and bequeathed her real and personal estate to be equally divided, after payment of debts, &c., among her eight half-brothers and sisters, of whom the plaintiffs are five ; that the testatrix died on 26th March, 1875, and the defendants proved the will and possessed themselves of the estate ; and that the plaintiffs have not received their shares, which they state as being $500 each as of the 26th of March, 1875; and they ask for administration of the estate.

The answer of the defendants is that the estate amounted to $3,336 after paying debts, &c. : that upon getting in the estate they invested it in good mortgage security and paid their shares to the three eldest legatees as they came of age : that they desired to do the like by the plaintiffs, but that the parents of the plaintiffs were unwilling that they should retain and manage the estate, and procured the

' appointment, in December, 1883, of a Mr. Fennell as guardian of the plaintiffs: that the guardian demanded payment over of the estate, threatening legal proceedings to compel the defendants to account and pay over; and that the defendants thereupon, on the advice of counsel, paid over the moneys to the guardian, who released them by deed dated the 17th of March, 1882.

The trouble arises from the fact that the guardian embezzled the money and absconded, and that his sureties are, as it is said, worthless.

The decision of the Court below is that under the facts, which are substantially as above stated, the defendants are not discharged.

This result, against which the defendants appeal, is one of decided hardship upon them. They must, of course, submit to the inevitable; but whether this is the inevitable result of the law as it exists is a question that deserves serious consideration.

The appointment of the guardian was under R. S. O. ch. 132, and 44 Vict. ch. 16 (O.).

The revised statute authorized the appointment of a guardian by the Surrogate Court only when the infant had no father living. The Act of 44 Vict. authorized the appointment of the father himself, or, with the consent of the father, of some other suitable person, requiring also, when the infant is of the age of fourteen years or over, the consent of the infant; and it declared that a guardian appointed under that Act should have like authority over the person and property of the infant as a guardian appointed under the revised statute, and should give security in the same manner.

The revised statute requires the Judge to take from the guardian a bond in the name of the infant in such penal sum and with such securities as the Judge directs and approves, having regard to the circumstances of the case, conditioned that the guardian will faithfully perform the trust, and will, when the ward becomes of the full age of 21 years, or whenever the guardianship is determined, or

sooner if thereto required by the Surrogate Court, render
to the ward a true and just account of all goods, moneys,
interest, rents, profits or property of the ward which come
into the hands of the guardian, and will thereupon, without delay, deliver and pay over to the ward the property
or the sum or balance of money which may be in the hands
of the guardian belonging to the ward, deducting therefrom and retaining a reasonable sum for the expenses and
charges of the guardian ; and it declares that the guardian
shall have authority to act for and in behalf of the ward ;
that he may appear in any Court and prosecute or defend
any action in the name of the ward; and that he shall
have the charge and management of the ward's estate, real
and personal, and the care of his or her person and education, with further powers as to apprenticing him.

In the present case all the requirements of the statute
seem to have been carefully complied with.

The appointment was made upon the written consents
of the father and the mother of the plaintiffs and of the
two plaintiffs who were over 14 years of age.

The only estate belonging to the infants was the legacy
of their half-sister. It was stated by the guardian in his
petition and accompanying affidavit as of or about the value
$1,500, which seems to have been an underestimate, as he
received from the defendants $2,500, or a little more, which
included interest from the investment of the money.

In the bond, the guardian was bound in $3000 and two
sureties in separate sums of $3000 each.

The security was taken in contemplation of the principal
money coming into the hands of the guardian, as is clear
from a memorandum of the Judge of the Surrogate Court,
which is in evidence. It was made a week before he
granted his order for the issue of letters of guardianship,
and reads thus :

RE HUGGINS.—Affidavit of execution of bond wanted.
Affidavit of execution of consent of infants must show
that it was explained, and their consent given freely.

These affidavits must be entitled in the Court and matter.

The usual rule is, that the bond should be for double the amount of the estate. Why is it not so here ? Unless there is some good reason I think the bond must be for greater sum. The estate will be many years in the guardian's hands, and if properly managed will increase at least for first four years. The security should be strictly sufficient. 30th November, 1881.

The same thing further appears from an affidavit made by Mr. Fennell, on the 28th of November, that he would " faithfully manage the estate of said infants, and pay over to them as they attain the age of twenty-one years each her and his respective shares of said estate."

The learned Judge's understanding of the functions of the guardian seems to me to be in accord with the plain words of the statute.

If the declaration that the guardian shall have the charge and management of the real and personal estate of the ward, illustrated as it is by the terms of the bond which he is required to give to account, and to deliver and pay over the property, sum or balance which may be in his hands when the ward comes of age, does not empower him to receive on behalf of his ward and to give an acquittance for money belonging in presenti to the ward, but for which the ward, by reason of infancy, cannot give a binding acquittance, the statute has been framed very unhappily, and is calculated, as proved by what has happened in this case, to mislead careful people and not merely the unwary.

There is no a priori reason for attributing to the Legislature the intention that the statute shall be understood in a sense different from that conveyed by its language, or that its operation upon the rights of individuals is to be controlled by importing into it rules which Courts of Equity may have adopted for their guidance when called upon to deal with the property of infants, but to which the statute makes no allusion.

The jurisdiction of the Court in respect of the property of infants and its power to direct guardians or other trustees in their management of that property, or to take it out of their hands and assume the care and management of it, is not open to dispute.   In the exercise of that juris. diction it may be the general rule of the Court to require that money shall not remain in the hands of the guardian, executor, or other trustee, but shall be paid into Court. The limits of the rule may be flexible or rigid; in its application to guardians under our statute there may be a question how far the difference of circumstances, such as the security required from the guardian and the mode in which money in Court is invested in this country, should modify the English rule; but taking the general rule to be, that the Court, when appealed to, will insist on taking charge of the fund, the power and the right of the guardian to get in the estate, of whatever it consists, and to manage it until interfered with by the order of the Court, and as a consequence to acquit the person who pays over money or hands over property of the infant to him, seems to be distinctly and unequivocally conferred by the statute.

The office of guardian under our statute resembles in its nature and incidents, but with some differences, that of testamentary guardian under the statute 12 Car. 2 ch. 24.

The English cases to which our attention has been chiefly directed relate to testamentary guardians. No question like that now in discussion appears to have arisen in any of them, or in any Canadian case; yet I find, as I think, support in them for the view of our statute which I have expressed, and I find nothing opposed to it in any of the authorities as I understand them.

In *Macpherson* on Infants it is said, p. 270 : "If the infant is not a ward of Court the guardian or other person entrusted with his property must act as to the real estate according to his own powers as guardian or trustee; he must also follow any special directions, and he may exercise any powers contained in the instrument under which the infant is entitled; and he must, in the absence of such directions or powers, call in the money due to the infant and invest it in the three per cents. or in the purchase of any existing charge on the infant's real estate ; or he may leave it out if he finds it on good mortgage security; but if he lays it out in mortgages of any other real estate than the infant's, or if he leaves it out, or having got it in invests it, upon personal security, he does so at his own risk, even though he has express authority to lay out the money in such manner as he shall think most for the infant's advantage, and though the borrower is unquestionably solvent at the time."

At p. 272 I read : " Infants as well as adults are bound by the composition or release of a debt by a guardian, executor or trustee if the act appears to have been for the benefit of the trust estate."

In *Eyre* v. *The Countess of Shaftesbury*, 2 W. & T. L. C. 693, the judgment of Lord Commissioner Gilbert is copied from his own report (Gilb. Eq. Rep. 172) where the case appears under the name of *Shaftesbury* v. *Shaftesbury*, and not from the short note in 2 P. Wms. 103. Arguing for the survival of testamentary guardianship, the Lord Commissioner used this illustration : " But in this case the authority must, from the nature of the thing, be joint and several ; for one alone *must receive the money* of the infant, and not meet altogether for that purpose."

In *Mitchell* v. *Richey*, 13 Gr. 445, where the rule of equity requiring the money to be paid into Court was discussed, Mowat, V. C., points out the distinction which seems to me so important in this case. He said (p. 451) : " The learned counsel attached great importance to the enactment that a guardian appointed to an infant by the Surrogate Court shall have the care and management of his or her estate, real and personal. But the English statute 12 Charles II. ch. 24 sec. 9, appears to give testamentary guardians powers quite as large ; and the case I have referred to [*Blake* v. *Blake*, 2 Sch. & L. 26] shews that in securing the property, the Court of Chancery does not proceed on any want of authority in the guardian to manage it," and he proceeded to expound the reason why the Court, for the safety of the infant, took the management of the estate out of the hands of the guardian without imputation of dishonesty or of want of legal right— reasons which I venture to think are susceptible of modifi-

cation when security is given under our statute, but which
are entirely consistent with the validity of the acquittance
from the guardian to the person who pays him the infant's
money.

The 11th chapter of *Macpherson* on Infants is devoted
to the subject of guardianship by appointment of a Court
of Equity, an ancient jurisdiction of the Court representing the king as parens patriæ.

It is explained that the jurisdiction is exercised only
when there is property to act upon, and that in order to
give the Court jurisdiction the expedient of settling a
small sum of money, £100 apparently being sufficient, upon
the infant has been resorted to.

The difference is pointed out between the case where a
suit is pending when the Court takes charge of the property and appoints a guardian of the person only, and one
where there is no suit, when a guardian of the estate as
well as of the person is appointed.

In the latter case the guardian has to give security extending to the whole amount of the capital of the infant's
personal estate and two years' income of his real estate, if
any.

The same subject is dealt with in 2 W. & T. L. C. in the
notes to *Eyre* v. *Shaftesbury.* It is there said : " The
Court, although no suit be pending, will appoint a guar
dian upon the petition either of the infant himself or of
some other person on his behalf without a bill having been
filed, even where a testamentary guardian has been appointed, if he declines to act : and, as was done in the
principal case, if there are conflicting claims for the guardianship they may be settled upon petition. And where
there is no suit relative to the infant's property, a guardian
will be appointed for the person and estate of the infant,
and he does not thereby become a ward of the Court.
When a suit is pending, a guardian *for the person* only will
be appointed, as the Court will manage the estate, and, as
before observed, the infant then becomes a ward of Court."

I make this and other quotations without noticing the
cases cited by the writers, though I have examined many
of them, as to discuss them would occupy much time without advancing the argument.

Further on the annotator says : " Although the guardian *of the estate and person* of an infant may be appointed, a receiver of the rents and profits of his property will not be appointed unless a bill be filed."

The incident of the giving of security, both in respect of the character of the security and of its extent, attaches to guardianship under our statute in the same way as to guardianship by appointment of the Court of Chancery under the English law, and it is in addition to the incidents which belong to testamentary guardianship under the statute of Charles. It seems to me to make it unnecessary, if not illogical, to apply to guardians under our statute the reasoning upon which the rule as to trustees who do not give security, including testamentary guardians and, as in *Orrok* v. *Binney*, Jac. 523, executors, are ordered to pay the trust money into Court.

It may be that in every case in which such an order has been made it was for the benefit of the infant that the Court should take charge of the fund ; but the practice of the Court, as stated in the extracts I have read, to appoint guardians of the estate when no suit is pending, and to take charge of the estate only when there is a suit, is conclusive against the assertion of want of power in the guardian lawfully to receive the money and effectually to discharge the person who pays it.

Another reason appears to be assigned for executors not paying over legacies to testamentary guardians in England, as I gather from *Macpherson* on Infants, where, at p. 273, there is this passage : " The statute 12 Charles II. ch. 24 empowers guardians appointed under its provisions to take ' the custody, tuition, and management of the goods, chattels, and personal estate ' of their wards : but the remedies given by the statute are only co-extensive with those of guardians in socage who seem not to have any legal interest in the personal estate of their wards : and the payment of legacies to the testamentary guardian has not been practised by executors. The safe and simple course is, for the executor to pay such legacies into the bank at the time when he would, but for the infancy, pay them to the legatees ; the legatees, when of age, may peti-

tion for the money, and it will be applicable in the meantime for their maintenance. This is the proper arrangement under the statute 36 Geo. III. ch. 52, which enacts "
&c., going on to give the 32nd section of the Act respecting
legacy duties.

At another place (p. 31) the author explains that there
is no legal authority for attributing to the guardian in
socage any interest in the chattels of the heir.

The force, whatever it may be, of the reason founded on
the alleged incapacity of the testamentary guardian to
bring an action respecting the personal estate of his ward
—or, to apply the observation more directly, an action to
recover the legacy from the executor—does not extend to
our statute, which gives unrestrained authority to the
the guardian to act for his ward and to prosecute any
action in the name of the ward, and an executor with us
cannot avail himself of the easy method of discharging
himself, which the Legacy Duty Act provides for the executor in England.

Our Legislature has indicated its apprehension of the
right of a guardian to deal with the estate of his ward by
including guardians with executors, administrators, and
other trustees in the provision for the allowance of their
remuneration out of the trust estate by R. S. O. ch. 107,
sec. 36, &c.

But though no decision in England or here precisely
meets the form of the present question, it is not so in the
United States or in Ireland.

In *The Children of Genet by him as their Guardian* v.
Tallmadge, Admor., &c., 1 Johns. Chy. 3, decided in 1814
by Chancellor Kent, the New York statute respecting
guardians was in question. It is cited as " Stats. N. Y.
Sess. 36, ch. 75." I have not access to the book referred
to, but I take the provisions to be the same as found at p.
334 of the 2nd vol. of the Rev. Stat. of N. Y. of 1852.
They follow the Statute of 12 Car. 2nd, ch. 24, as to testamentary guardians, using almost the same language, and
sec. 10 provides that every guardian appointed as directed

by the Surrogate Court shall have the same powers as a testamentary guardian. In the Genet case the adminis-- trator had paid the money into Court, and the infant leg- atees petitioned to have it paid out to their father, who had been appointed their guardian. Kent, C., said : " The petitioner in his character of guardian is entitled to the money, though in his character of father, or guardian by nature merely, it seems he would not be." Then, after dis- cussing the cases on the subject of the father's right, he continued: "In all these cases the question seems to have been whether the legacy to a minor could be safely paid to the father as father or natural guardian merely, and it does not appear to be anywhere denied that a guardian duly ap- pointed by the competent authority was authorized to receive legacies or distributive shares belonging to his ward. On this point I do not see that any doubt can arise. The statute of this State, to which I have already referred, contemplates the recovery at law, by the guardian, of legacies and distributive shares, on giving approved security to account to the infant on his coming of age. The guardian is by the general nature of his trust entitled to the possession and care of the personal and of the rents and profits of the real estate of the infant, and I do not feel myself at liberty to deny to the guardian on any terms whatever the possession of this distributive share."

Morrell v. *Dickey*, 1 Johns. Chy. 153, was another case in the same year 1814, before Kent, C., who followed his own decision in *Genet's Case*, ordering money belonging to an infant to be paid to an officer of the Court, and to be paid out to the child's mother when she was appointed guardian in that State and had given the competent security.

I understand that the statute law and the decisions upon it are in general the same through the various States. I have read an interesting case before the Supreme Court of Vermont in 1837, *Sparhawk* v. *Administrators of Buell*, 9 Vt. 41, where it is said (p. 73): " Upon two grounds then, we think that Buell was originally bound to see to the payment of this legacy whenever the legatees should come of age, or should have a guardian properly appointed."

Then there is the important case of *McCreight* v. *Mc-Creight*, 13 Ir. Eq. 314, decided by Lord Chancellor Brady, in 1849, under the Irish Statute 14 & 15 Charles II. ch. 19, which is analogous to the English Act of 12 Charles II. ch. 24. The attempt was to charge the executor with money paid while the plaintiffs were minors to their testamentary guardian, who died' insolvent. The case resembled the present one in that particular, and it happened that there, as here, the payment had been made on the advice of counsel, the opinion of Mr. Pennefather, who a few years afterwards became Lord Chief Justice of Ireland, being printed in a note to the report. The judgment of the Lord Chancellor contains an exhaustive discussion of the law and the authorities. He founds part of his argument on the right of action which he holds to extend to the personal estate, notwithstanding the reference in the statute to such action as a guardian in socage might bring, thus finding by his construction of the Irish Act what is in our statute provided in express terms, and he concludes thus: " Upon the whole of the case it appears to me, and I cannot say that I entertain any serious doubt on it, that this guardian, deriving his authority from the will of the testator, was entitled by the force of the power and authority given by the statute to such a guardian, to give a discharge for the general personal estate of the infants, and I think the fund in question here is not stamped with any character which distinguishes it from general personal estate, or withdraws it from the operation of the same principle."

I understand this last observation to refer to the circumstance that by the terms of the will the fund was only payable to the legatees on attaining 21, or on marriage with the consent of the guardian.

This decision bears out to the full my view of the effect of our statute as applicable to the case in hand, and the facts were by no means so strong as in the present case. The payment was to a testamentary guardian who had given no security, and it was one which the Court, if applied to before hand, would not have sanctioned. Such an application would have been disposed of on the principle established in the same Court by Lord Redesdale's decision in *Blake* v. *Blake,* 2 Sch. & L. 26.

I am not aware of any reference to *McCreight* v. *McCreight* in the English Courts except by Mr. Justice Fry, in *Re Cresswell,* 45 L. T. N. S. 468; 30 W. R. 244, where the decision is spoken of without disapproval. See *Lewin* on Trusts, ed. of 1885, where *Re Cresswell* and *McCreight* v. *McCreight* are referred to. Also see reference to same cases in *Eversley* on Domestic Relations.

Then if I am right in the opinion that the guardian had power to receive the money and give a valid discharge, the defendants ought to succeed unless there has been something done by themselves to make the payment a breach of their duty to the plaintiffs.

It is argued that there is something in their technical position of trustees of the fund, and that the principle that a trustee cannot by his own act divest himself of his trust, comes in some way into operation.

" When a fund is given to a person on certain trusts and he is appointed executor, as soon as he has severed the legacy from the general assets and appropriated it to the specific purpose he dismisses the character of executor and assumes that of trustee. Indeed, the assent of the executor to the legacy, however proved, converts him into a trustee :" *Lewin* on Trusts, 157, citing *Phillipo* v. *Munnings,* 2 M. & Cr. 309 ; *Dix* v. *Burford,* 19 Beav. 409, and other cases.

Assuming the defendants to have changed their character from executors to trustees, whether in an imperceptible manner, of which, as remarked by Lord Romilly in *Lord Brougham* v. *Poulett,* 19 Beav. 119, *Phillipo* v *Munnings* is a familiar example, or by the formal appropriation of the residue to the legatees, the important question is what were the trusts on which they held the money ?

By the will the money belonged in presenti to the infants. The trust was to pay it to them, and all that stood in the way of its being paid over as soon as ascertained was the want of a competent hand to receive it.

Therefore, when the guardian became clothed with authority to act for the infants and to manage their estate, the trustee by paying over the money was fulfilling his trust, not relinquishing it.

The situation was not like that of the executor in *Galbraith* v. *Duncombe*, 28 Gr. 27, who was directed to keep the money in a savings bank till the children were of age, and who had accepted that trust.

If we still had Courts of Common Law as in former days we had, and an action for money had and received had been brought by the guardian in the name of the infants against the defendants, like the action of *Burrows* v. *Gates*, 8 C. P. 121, I see no reason to doubt that the action ought to succeed.

I think the appeal should be allowed, with costs ; and the action dismissed, with costs.

OSLER, J. A.—I have given this case the best consideration in my power, and am of opinion the executors cannot be held liable to replace the moneys of the infants paid by them to their fraudulent guardian Fennell.

The words of the Act are wide enough and plain enough to lead anyone to conclude that the guardian had power to receive and to give a valid discharge for these moneys. It may be that when it is necessary to seek the aid or intervention of the Court in respect of moneys belonging to an infant which have not actually reached the guardian's hands, the Court, acting on the beneficial practice hitherto observed by it, will refuse to order such moneys to be paid over to the guardian, and will require them to be paid into and invested by the Court; but I think the authorities do not compel us by, as it were an expost facto application of the practice, to defeat a payment, which, as it seems to me, the statute justified the executors in making.

Therefore, for the reasons assigned in the judgment of Mr. Justice Patterson, I concur in allowing the appeal. I think under the circumstances it may properly be allowed, without costs.

HAGARTY, C. J. O.—The will of E. J. Lee appointed the defendants executors, and left her estate directly to her mother's children, to be divided equally, share and share alike, after payment of debts, &c. The legatees were eight in number, all then under age.

Testatrix died 26th March, 1875. Some of her moneys were then outstanding on mortgages. The executors state that they got in the estate and paid the shares of three of the legatees as they became of age. They invested the moneys on good mortgage security (as was stated on argument) in their individual names.

On the application of the legatees' mother and step-father one Fennell was appointed guardian by the Surrogate Court, 7th December, 1881. He applied to the executors for the estate, and they called in the estate, accounted with the guardian, and paid over all to him, he allowing $100 to be retained by them for their services.

Fennell appears to have embezzled the money, and has left the country, and it is alleged that the sureties given by him to the Surrogate Court are worthless. The legatees now seek to recover from the executors, and my brother Ferguson has decided in favor of the claim and the executors appeal.

It is a most unfortunate case in every aspect, and one in which I would much more willingly concur than differ from the rest of the Court. The executors appear to have been anxious to perform their duty, and gave up the estate to the guardian under legal advice.

It appears clear from the authorities that the executors in this case have constituted themselves trustees of this fund for the legatees.

The bequest in *Tyson* v. *Jackson*, 30 Beav. 385, was substantially in the same form as here. The executor was not declared a trustee by the will.

The M. R. says : " It is clear when the executor retains
the money for payment of the legacy that he becomes, as
in *Philippo* v. *Munnings*, 2 M. & Cr. 309, a trustee of that
particular fund or sum of money so retained distinct from
his character as executor.   It is as distinct as if the testator had directed his executors to pay the legacy over to
A. B. in trust for a legatee, and it had been actual'y paid
over, A. B. would then be a trustee for the legatee.   So
here the executor who has retained that sum of money is
in exactly the same situation."

In this case by investing the money in their own names
they become, as I consider, express trustees.

In *Lord Brougham* v. *Poulett*, 19 Beav. 133-4, the same
principle is laid down, and in *Dix* v. *Burford*, *ib.* 412, to
the same effect.   These cases are noticed by Blake, V. C., in
Cameron v. *Campbell*, 27 Gr. 313, same case in appeal in
this Court, 7 A. R. 366, where the late Chief Justice Spragge,
speaking of the fund in dispute, says that it has assumed
the character of a trust fund if the executors had assented
to any one having become entitled who was named as a
legatee in the will, &c.   He reviews several authorities :
Lewin, 182, 6th ed.

In *Williams*, Executors, 130-35 (ed, 1867), it is pointed
out the danger an executor incurs as to payment of legacies
to infants without the sanction of the Court, and notices the
Imperial Act, 36 Geo. III., ch. 52, enabling him to pay it into
the Bank of England with the privity of the Accountant-Gen-
eral in Chancery, to be placed to the account of the person
entitled, who can obtain it by petition in a summary way,
&c.   I do not know of any analogous enactment here ;
but the direction and sanction of the Court could have
been obtained under our law.

The proposition now for consideration is, whether the
executors here, having clearly assumed the positions of
trustees for the infants, can, without paying the money
into Court, or acting under its directions, discharge themselves from their liability to account to the infants.   To
hand over the trust funds to the guardian to be held by
him in an analogous fiduciary character, and on a like trust

would seem to be a novel right to confer on any trustee.
We must see beyond question that the statutable rights
conferred by our Legislature on a guardian extend to enabling him to require the transfer to him of all trust funds
held by trustees for his infant wards.

Our Court of Chancery has had the question before it :
Mitchell v. *Ritchey,* 13 Gr. 445, before Mowat, V. C.; the
headnote is : "The rule is, that money belonging to an
infant is not ordered in Equity to be paid to his guardian
whether appointed by the Surrogate Court or otherwise,
but is secured for the benefit of the infant under the authority of the Court."

The Court was asked to direct the trustee, who desired
to be relieved, to pay the fund to the guardian, who
claimed as of right. The learned Vice-Chancellor said :
"No authority was cited for this demand, and I understand an opposite rule to have been the clearly settled doctrine for more than half a century, and it appears to be
supported by the soundest policy." He cites *Blake* v.
Blake, 2 Sch. & L. 26, before Lord Redesdale, where on application of the infants the testamentary guardian and executor was directed to pay the fund into Court although he
resisted it, and urged that no charge of misconduct or insolvency was made. The Vice-Chancellor cites Lord
Redesdale's language, in which he states the practice that
had prevailed of late years in Chancery, and the wisdom
and good effect of it.

Galbraith v. *Duncombe,* 28 Gr. 27, before Blake, V. C.,
is to the same effect. The executor, as here, had become a
trustee of the money left to the infants, and the Vice-
Chancellor says : "He could not, therefore, properly pay
this money to, nor could the guardian properly receive
this sum."

Flanders v. *D'Evelyn,* 4 O. R. 706, Proudfoot, V.C., adopts
the same view.

The appellant here chiefly relied upon *McCreight* v.
McCreight, 13 Ir. Eq. Rep. 314, (1849,) a decision of Brady,
L. C., of Ireland. The decision there was that the exe-
cutors were justified in transferring the personal property

which was to be paid to infants on attaining 21 to the testamentary guardians, and that the latter could give them a valid acquittance therefor. The will left his property to his 8 children on attaining 21 or marriage with consent of guardian. The property consisted of money in the funds invested in his own and partly in the joint names of himself and Andrew McCréight, and part in other names with all his other personalty. He appointed Andrew McCreight and another his executors, and one F. testamentary guardian of his children. The executor Andrew alone proved the will, and on counsel's opinion transferred certain stocks or moneys to the guardian, who could, as he was advised, give him a due acquittance therefor. The guardian died insolvent, and the bill was filed by the children against the executor.

The Lord Chancellor says, that it is singular that since the passing of the statute of Charles " to the present time no case is to be found in which this question had ever been discussed, nor is there even any judicial dictum upon the subject." He says: " Much certainty as to what has hitherto been deemed the extent of the testamentary guardian's power over personal estate under the statute cannot be attained, and there is nothing in any of the authorities to control the language of the statute * * I do not see any straightforward reading of the power to take ' the custody, tuition, and management ' of the personal estate save that which would enable the guardian to recover that personal estate from any person whomsoever. I see nothing in the section to curtail that power." The liberty to bring " such action or actions in relation thereto, as by law a guardian in socage might do, cannot, I think, be confined to real property only." His judgment is : " The guardian deriving his authority from the will of the testator was entitled by force of the power and authority given by the statute to such a guardian to give a discharge for the general personal estate of the infants, *and I think the fund in question here is not stamped with any character which distinguishes it from general personal estate, or withdraws it from the operation* of *the same principle.*"

The words which I have italicised are especially to be noted. There was no argument or suggestion in the case that the fund had been stamped with any special trust, or that (as in our case) the executor had assumed the position of a trustee in respect thereof.　The case is, therefore, to my mind, not an authority to govern as to the respective rights and duties of the trustee of a fund for infants and a statutable guardian.　Counsel cited the note of Mr. Hargrave, note 13 Co. Lit. 88 B., which strikes me as against the idea that the guardian could require a fund in a trustee's hand to be handed to him.　See on this, Vaughan, R. 186 in *Bedell* v. *Constable*.　It must also be borne in mind that this decision was on an Act placing the testamentary guardian on the same footing as guardian in socage.　The case of *Blake* v. *Blake* was not cited.

The statute, 12 Car. 2 ch. 24, sec. 9, empowers the testamentary guardian to take into his custody to the use of the child the profits of all lands, &c., and also the custody, tuition and management of the goods, chattels and personal estate of such child until 21, "and may bring such action or actions in relation thereto, as by law a guardian in common socage might do."　The preceding sec. 8 enables the guardian to maintain action against any person taking away the ward, and recover damages therefor to the use of the ward.

My learned brother Wilson in his very carefully considered judgment in *Collins* v. *Martin*, 41 U.C.R. 606, points out the less extensive powers given by our statute to the guardian, which enables him to prosecute or defend actions in the infant's name, and that he shall have the charge and management of his or her estate, real and personal, and the care of his person and education.　He adds : " I am of opinion that under such letters of guardianship the guardian has not the rights, power, and estate in the ward's property, real and personal, which the guardian in socage or testamentary guardian in England has—that he is here more in the nature of an agent, bailiff, or receiver as respects the ward's estate."　See, also, *Switzer* v. *McMillan*, 23 Gr. 538.

In *Gardner* v. *Blane*, 1 Hare 381, Wigram, V.C., appointed a receiver to the estate notwithstanding the appointment of a testamentary guardian.　He said : " The Statute enables the father to give to the testamentary guardian certain powers, but the precise extent of these powers over the property of the infant was by no means certain. The testamentary guardian had no estate, and was frequently unable to act without the assistance of this Court." See, also, *Kerr* on Receivers, p. 16.

Re Cresswell, 45 L. T. N. S. 468, the testamentary guardian applied to have funds which had been paid into Court under the Legacy Duty Act, 36 Geo. III. ch. 52, the property of infants, paid out to her as guardian. *Macreight* v. *Macreight* was cited.

Fry, L. J., held that the guardian was not the person entitled to the funds under the statute on which they had been paid into Court. He says: "I should add that by the conclusion at which I have arrived I have no intention of interfering with the decision of Brady, L. C., in *Macreight* v. *Macreight*, who had not then to deal with the statute, the terms of which compel me to refuse this application."

The counsel in argument said that the point did not seem to have been ever discussed in England, and the only authority discoverable was the Irish case, *Macreight* v. *Macreight*.

I think I am bound to hold that the decree appealed from is right : that the guardian had no right to require this fund to be paid to him; and that the trustees had no right to pay it, and are accountable for its loss.

The duties imposed by our statute on a guardian may be usefully exercised in collecting and managing his personalty, money, or chattels without giving him the right to require the trustee of any of the estate to surrender the fund or estate to him. A Court of Equity would certainly not compel the trustee to do so, and I cannot regard their usual course of directing the fund to be paid into Court as a mere compliance with a rule of equity practice. It seems to me not easy to understand that a voluntary payment by the trustees can be protected, when, if the law had been resorted to to compel such payment the guardian could not have succeeded, but the money would have been ordered into Court.

Appeal allowed, with costs.

HAGARTY, C. J. O., dissenting.

BAKER AND THE MERCHANTS' BANK v. ATKINSON ET AL.

Money paid, action to recover back—Distress.

The defendants, under assumption of a lawful distress for rent, part of
which was in arrear, and the other part of which was claimed in advance, entered and seized goods which had been assigned to the plaintiff B. in trust for the benefit of creditors. Three executions were
shortly after placed in the sheriff's hands, and the solicitor for the
plaintiffs under the first and third executions, relying upon being repaid
from the proceeds of the goods, with full knowledge of all the facts,
and to get the distress out of the way and let in the executions paid
the rent claimed to prevent the sale of the goods, though not admitting defendants' right to it. The sheriff afterwards sold for less than
the executions, and repaid the solicitor. B. did not act under the
assignment, and in no way asserted his rights against the execution
creditors.
Held, [reversing the judgment of the Queen's Bench Division, 11 O. R.
735,] that the money so paid could not be recovered back either by the
execution creditors on whose behalf it was paid, or by B. as assignee.

THIS was an appeal by the defendants from the Queen's
Bench Division, reported 11 O. R. 735, where, and in the
present judgments, the facts are fully stated, and came on to
be heard before this Court on the 4th and 5th days of
April, 1887.*

Robinson, Q. C., and *Atkinson,* Q. C., for the appellants.
Moss, Q.C., and *Rankin,* for the respondents.

June 29th, 1887.   HAGARTY, C. J. O.--The claim was first
made with Baker as sole plaintiff; afterwards the Merchants Bank was added.

The amended claim stated the demise to Brown. That
Brown assigned to plaintiff Baker in trust for creditors,
and Baker entered into possession. That defendants under
assumption of a lawful distress for alleged arrears wrongfully entered and seized the goods as a distress. That no
rent was due, nor any arrears. Defendants refused to give
up possession and threatened to sell, and to prevent this and
to get back possession, and to avoid a sale at a sacrifice,

Present.—HAGARTY, C.J.O., BURTON, PATTERSON, and OSLER, JJ.A.

the plaintiffs were obliged to pay, and did pay defendants their claim under protest.

After making the assignment executions were issued against the assignor's goods at suit of Hull & Keddie, and also at suit of the plaintiffs, the Merchants Bank, and given to the sheriff while the goods were in seizure under the distress.

That under the lease the arrear claimed by defendants did not arise, and it did not give the right to distrain, and the provisions were illegal and void as against the plaintiffs.

" 12. All parties being desirous of testing the right of the defendants to distrain for the said rent, and there being doubts as to whether as between the plaintiff William P. Baker, and the said execution creditors, which of them were entitled to priority, the moneys so paid as aforesaid were paid to the sheriff of the said County of Kent by the plaintiffs, the Merchants Bank of Canada, to be by him paid under protest, to the defendants, so as to put an end to said distress and enable the said goods to be sold so as not to sacrifice them, and the said moneys were paid on account of whomsoever should be held entitled to receive them back from the defendants in the event of their right to distrain for the whole of the rent claimed being negatived.

" 13. The plaintiffs, the Merchants Bank of Canada, are assignees of the judgment and execution of Hull & Keddie aforesaid.

" 14. The plaintiffs submit that the plaintiff, William P. Baker, is entitled to recover back the said moneys so paid by the said sheriff as aforesaid. or in the alternative that the plaintiffs, the Merchants Bank of Canada, are entitled to recover them.

" 15. If it should appear that some rent was due to the defendants for which they had the right to distrain, the plaintiffs say that the sum distrained for, and which they were compelled to pay, exceeded the sum actually due, if any, by at least $1,000.

" The plaintiffs claim,

" (1) $1,500 damages for the wrongs complained of.

" (2) Repayment to the plaintiff, Baker, or the plaintiffs, the Merchants Bank of Canada. of said sum of $1,350, with interest.

" (3) Such further, and other relief," &c.

It seems perfectly clear on the evidence, and is so found
by the trial judge, that the payment made by Mr.Craddock,
who was then solicitor for the Merchants Bank, was not
made in any way for the benefit of the assignment, or in
aid of Baker, the assignee's title.

Mr. Craddock states that he paid the money on behalf
and in the interest of the execution creditors for whom he
was acting, and that he was acting adversely to the
assignee.

He is asked if the assignee contested his right, or admitted
it. He says, there was no formal contestation, but he believes no notice was given by the assignee to the sheriff.

He paid without any instruction so to do from his clients,
out of his firm's moneys; and he adds : " We looked upon
the repayment as certain, because the goods would realise
much more than that. * * The payment was made in contemplation of getting it back out of the goods. * * It
was with the expectation of getting it back from Mr.
Atkinson we undertook to make the payment."

"Q. You thought you would get back what you had paid
out of the proceeds of the goods, or out of Mr. Atkinson ?
A. We expected to get it back out of the proceeds of the
goods. Q. And you thought if you succeeded in recovering back from Mr. Atkinson, then you would have to
appropriate it to the execution creditors. Is that it ? A.
There would certainly be so much more for the execution
creditors."

Mr. Baker, the assignee, seems to have in no way
asserted his right against the execution creditors. He does
not say that he formally abandoned his claim, but he gives
us to understand that the creditors met, but did nothing.

No creditor appears to have executed the deed. Baker
signed it, but it does not appear whether he was a creditor
or not. He says that he does not know that it was abandoned altogether; that creditors came to no agreement and
did nothing; that he attended the sheriff's sale and bought
the goods on his own account, not as assignee, and that
when he purchased he was not asserting the validity of the
assignment, nor acting as assignee, and that at the time of

purchase it was none of his business whether it had been abandoned or not.

Mr. Sheriff Mercer pressed the seizure while the goods were under defendants' distress. He swears that Baker, the assignee, told him that he withdrew—the creditors would not indemnify him and he would have nothing more to do with it, and that the sheriff might proceed. That but for this assurance from Baker he would have interpleaded. Messrs. Scane and Craddock paid the amount to defendants on their claims, and when the sheriff sold he repaid to them the amount they advanced to pay defendants' claim.

As to Baker's right to recover I am wholly unable to see what his claim can be in respect of the payment of this money. As my learned brother Cameron, who tried the case, puts it in his judgment, "The money could in no sense be held to be the money of the plaintiff, Baker, and its payment instead of giving him a right of action against the defendants, had the effect of relieving his goods if the assignment by the debtors, A. O. Brown & Co., legally transferred the goods to him, from the distress, and left him free to contract (Q. contest ?) the right of the execution creditors to take the goods as against him."

He finds that the bank was not consulted in the matter and that the solicitors " advanced the money upon the faith of being repaid out of the sale of the goods by the sheriff, and were so repaid."

I do not see any satisfactory answer to this view of my learned brother.

Baker paid nothing, and the discharge of the landlord's claim, whether just or unjust, on behalf of the execution creditors, was a most essential benefit to him as assignee.

By his own conduct and admissions he wholly failed to urge his right. The assignee gave way to the execution creditors, and then buys the property as a private purchaser at the sale.

We are not concerned here to discuss Mr. Baker's relations to the creditors. No such question is raised here.

The claim puts the demand as if there were some common interest between the assignee and the execution creditors. Mr. Craddock's evidence disposes of that. The execution creditors were acting adversely to the assignee. If the assignment prevailed their priorities would be wholly destroyed. The payment was made expressly to help the execution, and it seems to me to be the merest fiction to assert any common interest, or that any payment was made by any one in furtherance of Baker's interest as assignee. If Baker were allowed to recover either the amount paid, or the whole value of the goods, what would become of the money so recovered?

We know nothing of his position with the creditors. The interests of the latter are not represented before us. Baker, who practically abandoned his position as assignee, and chose to buy the estate for himself as an individual, cannot, in my opinion, be regarded as entitled to receive the amount. No creditor has intervened or done anything to enforce any trust. Is Baker still in a position to sue the sheriff for taking his goods in execution? His conduct deprived the sheriff of the protection an interpleader would have given him.

I am of opinion that there is nothing before us to warrant a recovery of substantial damages by Baker. as assignee for creditors, and that before making any such claim, or trying to substantiate it, we should be furnished with some evidence to shew the legal existence of an interest in creditors, or in Baker as their trustee.

The only reasonable inference of fact which I can draw from the evidence, is that of a complete abandonment of the assignment, and of all interests created thereby, both on behalf of Baker and the creditors. I see no shadow of evidence that Baker is a plaintiff here, bonâ fide acting for creditors. I infer from the evidence that his name is merely used by the execution creditors for their own purposes, and I think the allegations in paragraph 12 of the statement of claim, which is set forth in the judgment, are wholly disproved.

If Baker be allowed to recover over $1,300 here, it would be, I presume, on the ground that it should. be for

the creditors' benefit.   The whole property seized is said to
have been worth $1,600, the price paid by Baker as he
swears on his own account.

Are the creditors to be considered as having through
their assignee bought the estate for $1,600, and get back
$1,300, being thus $300 on the wrong side, or are they in
some other proceeding to charge Baker with the full value
of the estate, and thus get $1,300 over and above its value ?

I fully agree with the trial Judge in his finding that the
payment by the solicitors was made with a full knowledge
of all the facts, not in ignorance or mistake as to any
matter of fact, and was made of their own election to
get the distress out of the way so as to enforce the executions.

Mr. Craddock's evidence shews his views very plainly.
He says there was no dispute as to the rent overdue.   It
was only as to the additional year's rent—the penalty as he
calls it, mentioned in the lease.

It was paid, as I think, on a full consideration of all the
facts, and if any mistakes were made, it was wholly as to
the law governing the case ; and the payment was made
with a view to contesting the assignment, and to let in the
executions, and the law of the case was discussed between
them.

The learned Chief Justice of the Queen's Bench also considers that the payment was as held by the trial Judge.

It was not like the payment made by the execution creditors in *McMaster* v. *Garland*, 8 A. R. 1, a buying up of an
existing claim on goods held by the claimant with a view to
stand in such claimant's place.   The whole intent was to
contest the assignment, which, if it stood, was fatal to the
execution creditors ; and it was made, as I think, on full
calculation of its effect, and if any mistake was made it
was wholly one of law.

If I viewed it in a different light it might be necessary
to consider whether it could be considered as the money of
the Merchants Bank, as it was most distinctly proved that
it was paid by the solicitors on the express understanding

and faith that it was to be repaid to them out of the proceeds of the sale, and was so in fact paid by the sheriff.

Nor is it necessary, in this view, to consider the position
or right of an execution creditor, while the property or the
goods are still unchanged, to pay off a claim made thereon,
not with the purpose of obtaining the claimant's right thereto,
but for the purpose of at any time within the statute of
limitations, bringing an action to recover back the money
as having been paid on an unfounded claim. I very much
doubt the legal propriety of such a proceeding.

The rights of the parties, of the landlords, the assignee,
and the execution creditors, could all have been tried and
adjusted by interpleader. There would also have been the
ordinary remedies against a landlord distraining where no
rent was in arrear, if the argument be sound that the term
was forfeited, and all right of distress gone.

In the view I take it is not necessary to rest my decision
upon the the legal question, whether or no there was the
right to distrain for any rent whatever. I incline to the
opinion of my learned brother Cameron, that there was
still the right as to the rent actually past due.

It is insisted there was complete election to avoid the
term by the distress.

The words of the warrant are: "Distrain the goods of, &c.
&c., in the shop, &c., for the sum of $1,237.50, being the
amount of rent due to us on the same, on 31st August,
1883, six months in arrears, and one year's rent, by reason
of their having assigned for benefit of creditors."

Griffith v. *Brown*, 21 C. P. 12, as far as it goes, only decides
that the extra sum claimed in consequence of the breach
caused by assigning could not be distrained for, not that
arrears actually due could not be. Besides this the Insolvent
Law was then in force.

Young v. *Smith*, 29 C. P. 109 decided by the same Judge,
draws the distinction between the cases.

Graham v. *Laing*, 10 O. R. 248, favors my brother
Cameron's view, though Wilson, C. J., who decided it, seems
to throw doubt on it in the present case.

I do not see why, notwithstanding the distress, the landlord might not still elect to continue the relation. Must
we hold that his seizing for the amount, which would only
be coming to him by reason of the assignment, is an absolute
irrevocable election on his part to avoid the lease ? or that
his including it with other money actually due to him, and
for which he might have legally distrained, defeats his right
even as to the undoubted arrears ? By this breach of covenant on the lessees' part, he would be liable to pay the
lessor the full amount of the year's rent.

I do not see any inconsistency in holding that the lessor
might still be held not to have elected to avoid. There is
not much authority directly on the point.

In *Jones* v. *Carter*, 15 M. & W. 718, after pointing out
that it was always in the option of the landlord whether
he will elect to avoid for a forfeiture, Parke, B., says:
" The lease would be rendered invalid by some unequivocal
act indicating the intention of the landlord to avail himself of the option given him, and notified to the lessee,
after which he could no longer consider himself bound to
perform the other covenants in the lease : and if once rendered void it could not again be set up. An entry, or
ejectment in which an entry is admitted, would be necessary
in the case of a freehold lease, or of a chattel interest where
the terms of the lease provided that it should be avoided
by re-entry. Whether any other act unequivocally indicating the intention of the lessor would be sufficient to
determine this lease, which is made void at the option of
the lessor, we need not determine, because an ejectment
was brought and proceeded with to the consent rule, by
which defendants admitted an entry, and the entry would
certainly be an exercise of the option, and once determined
the lease could not be revived."

I think the appeal should be allowed, and the judgment
of the trial Judge restored.

BURTON, J. A.—If the plaintiff Baker had contested the
validity of the distress, or if the execution creditors had
tendered the rent actually in arrear, and in the event of
the defendants then proceeding to sell, had taken proceed-

ings against them for wrongfully interfering with the sheriff's execution of their writs, some interesting and probably difficult questions of law would have been presented for our decision, but upon the pleadings and the facts elicited at the trial, no such questions arise.

Mr. Craddock, with a full knowledge of all the facts, paid off the landlord's claim from his own moneys relying upon being repaid from the proceeds of the goods; and that anticipation has been realised as the sheriff, being left to the execution of the writs by the withdrawal of Baker's claim, has received the proceeds of the sale, and paid them over to him, who has thereby been reimbursed with a small sum over to apply on the first execution.

There is no ground, I think, for the contention that the money paid by Mr. Craddock was the money of the bank, but admitting, for argument sake, that the bank has adopted it as the act of their solicitor, they must adopt it as a whole, and we then find that the advance has been repaid. It was a payment made to remove the distress out of the way to enable the execution creditors to enforce their writs, and although the proceeds have not been sufficient to reach the bank's execution, they have been repaid the sum they advanced.

I can see no foundation whatever for Baker's claim. The deed of assignment does not appear to have been signed by any creditor, and the creditors seem to have refused to authorize him to act under it for them—those who had executions claiming adversely and disputing its validity. He abandoned any claim under it, and purchased the goods at the sheriff's sale—to allow him to recover would be in effect to enable him to acquire these goods for a nominal consideration.

I think the view taken of the case at the trial by the learned Chief Justice of the Common Pleas Division was the correct one, and that the appeal should be allowed, and his judgment restored.

OSLER, J. A.—I am of opinion that the appeal ought to be allowed, and the judgment of the Chief Justice of the Common Pleas Division restored on one of the grounds relied upon by him, namely, that if the moneys now sued for were advanced, or paid for or on account of the plaintiffs, or either of them, the payment was a purely voluntary payment, made with full knowledge of all the facts. The money so paid was moreover repaid to the parties who actually advanced it out of the very fund from which such repayment was expected to come, namely, the proceeds of the sale of the goods under the executions.

In this view it is unnecessary to consider or decide the other questions, some of them extremely interesting and important, raised on the appeal.

PATTERSON, J. A., concurred.

Appeal allowed, with costs.

RATTÉ V. BOOTH ET AL.

Water and Watercourses—Riparian proprietor—Navigable stream—Reservation in Crown grant—Statute of Limitations.

A water lot on the river Ottawa was granted by the Crown in 1850, to one A., the description of which covered the lot and two chains distant from the shore, reserving, however, the free use of all navigable waters found in or under or flowing through any part of the said lot. A. sold and conveyed the lot to P. with certain exceptions, including, however, the part covered by water ; and P. in 1867 conveyed to the plaintiff part of the lot down to and bounded by the water's edge.   The plaintiff had been in occupation of the premises, sold to him under a contract of purchase, for a year before the conveyance to him, and had built a dwelling house together with a floating wharf and boat house, and he carried on business there by letting out pleasure boats for hire.   In an action complaining of injuries to his business and to himself as a riparian proprietor by the deposit of saw-dust and other refuse from the mills of the defendants in the water in front of his land, hindering access from his wharf to the navigable part of the river, and fouling the waters of the stream upon or in contact with his land, it was contended the plaintiff had no title as a riparian proprietor, as P. owned that portion of the water lot outside of the plaintiff, and could bar him from access to the river, and also that the reservation in the patent was repugnant to the rest of the grant, which should be read as giving the whole lot there specified.

Held, [affirming the judgment of the Chancery Division, 11 O. R. 191, BURTON, J. A., dissenting,] that the plaintiff was entitled to recover damages for the injuries complained of.

Per HAGARTY, C. J. O., and OSLER, J. A., the plaintiff is in the position of a riparian proprietor. He owns the land on the bank and has the same right over the water as the rest of the public.   There is, however, a special injury to him, and a wrongdoer not in privity with P. cannot be heard to raise the question of P.'s rights in order to exclude plaintiff from the water. The Crown owning the bed of the river, could grant a portion thereof, reserving the public right of user which is the effect of the reservation in the patent.

Per PATTERSON, J.A.   The plaintiff is a riparian proprietor. The patent to A. granted the land without any restriction of his absolute dominion over it, and there is nothing to distinguish it from an ordinary grant of Crown lands. It was made in contemplation of the grantee occupying the land with buildings, or wharves, or otherwise at his pleasure, and so far there was, under legislative sanction, a curtailment of the *jus publicum.* The reservation of the free uses, passage and enjoyment of * * all navigable waters considered as an exception, was void as repugnant to the license.

The public right to the use of navigable waters is the right of each individual, and stands on a different footing ; it does not come by grant from the Crown, but is a paramount right to be curtailed only by Act of the Legislature. A public easement cannot be the subject of an exception in favor of the grantor. If the exception were construed as perpetuating the *jus publicum,* it would be repugnant to the grant in its operation under the statute 23 Vict. ch. 2 sec. 35, and would be void. The true reading of the patent is, that the reservation touching navigable waters is applicable only to other parts of the lot, and not to the two chains of the river bed. The whole lot vested in A. free from the asserted jus publicum, and the plaintiff as against his grantor, P. and a fortiori as against wrongdoers, had acquired a title to the river portions under the Statute of Limitations.

Per BURTON, J. A.—The plaintiff cannot be regarded as a riparian proprietor ; the person occupying that position is P., and on his filling in the lot, as he is entitled to do, to the extent of his grant the plaintiff would be entirely cut off from the stream.   The plaintiff, a trespasser, cannot complain of others trespassing on portions of the property of which he is not in possession, although it may interfere with his access to the portion of which he is in possession.   If the words of the reservation in the patent extend to the right of navigation, the reservation, is absolutely void. The statute 23 Vict. ch. 2, sec. 35, gives to the Crown the right to grant the bed of the river and the water upon it free from any rights publici juris.   The Statute of Limitations could give the plaintiff no title to any part of the land covered by water, except that actually occupied by his floating wharf and boat house.

THIS was an appeal by the defendants from the judgment of the Chancery Division reported 11 O. R. 491, where, as also in the report of the case in 10 O. R. 351, and in the present judgments, the facts giving rise to the action are fully set forth.

The appeal came on for hearing on the 9th and 10th of March, 1887*

McCarthy Q.C., and *Gormully*, for the appellants.
J. Maclennan, Q.C., for the respondent.

The cases cited and points relied on are mentioned in the reports in the Court below, and in the judgments.

June 29, 1887. HAGARTY, C.J.O.—The patent to Aumond granted the waterlot extending two chains out into the river bed, reserving the free use and enjoyment of and over the navigable waters, &c.   Then Aumond grants to Prevost the lot, with certain' exceptions previously sold by him. Prevost grants to plaintiff the lot down to and bounded by the water's edge of the river Ottawa.

At the time of the grant to the plaintiff in 1867 the latter had been on the place under a contract of purchase for a year before the conveyance. He had built his house and the floating wharf or landing stage about 60 × 16 feet.

* *Present.*—HAGARTY, C. J. O., BURTON, PATTERSON, and OSLER, JJ.A.

Some eleven years ago he increased it to the present size—forty feet out in the river and one hundred and forty feet along the shore.   This wharf or stage, according to the plans printed in appeal book, rests partly on the land inside the line designated as low water mark, and which, I assume from this plan, is conceded to be the land granted by Prevost, as Ratté's dwelling-house is also built upon it. This wharf or stage is fastened by chains at points marked also on said land ; and a stairway leads down the bank to this stage.   By far the larger part of it is afloat. ·

The evidence shews the most serious injury to the plain-tiff in the enjoyment of his property, and to his business as a hirer of boats, and the use of his boat-house, by the great accumulation of saw-dust from the defendants' mills with all sorts of rubbish, preventing access from his property to the river, engendering gas, which explodes occasionally, &c., causing foul smells, &c.

The defendants insist that the plaintiff has no title as a riparian proprietor, as Prevost owns the portion of the water lot outside of the plaintiff, and can bar him from access to the river.

It was also urged that the reservation in the patent as to free navigation is repugnant to the rest of the grant, and that we should read it as giving the whole lot there specified.

I cannot see the force of this objection.   The Crown, owning the bed of this navigable river, could grant a portion thereof, reserving the public right of user.   Prevost thus has the ownership of the river bed, but the public right remains as to the water.   He may have the minerals except gold and silver, or, I presume, could tunnel under the bottom, and use the space thus acquired if he pleased.

I cannot at present see why we must not consider Ratté the plaintiff, to be, for the purposes of this suit, in the position of a riparian proprietor, as the Chancery Division holds, him to be.   He is the grantee of land whose boundary is the water's edge of the river, and over that portion of the river outside such edge he has the same free use and enjoyment of the navigable river as the rest of the Queen's subjects. ·

His floating wharf and boat-house, if shewn to be a
nuisance or material interruption to such general right, can
be provided against by indictment.

I think he has clearly proved a damage to himself and
his property beyond the common nuisance to the general
public caused by the defendants' acts.

I cannot see how the defendants can justify the distinct
injury they cause to him by attacking his title. Prevost
owns the bed of the river outside of him, and they urge
that Prevost can block him from the water. Even if Prevost has the right so to do, how can wrongdoers in no
privity with him raise such a question ? The plaintiff has
been over twenty years in possession of his land. So far
from Prevost having in any way attempted to interfere
with the plaintiff's full enjoyment of the river as a riparian
proprietor, he conveyed to plaintiff after the latter had
been a year in actual possession, with a floating wharf or
stage, used as now for his boating business, attached to the
shore.

On the authority of such cases as *Francis* v. *Hayward,*
20 Ch. D. 773, and in appeal 22 Ch. Div. 177, the learned Chancellor considered that Prevost conveyed to him with this
as an easement used with the premises and passing as such
under the conveyance. This would be important in any
controversy with Prevost, but as between plaintiff and the
rest of the world I presume Prevost could not confer on
plaintiff any right to interfere with the general public right.

My brother Ferguson, in his judgment, held that Prevost
having granted to the plaintiff land bounded by the water
of the river, could not derogate from his grant by any act
of his to cut him off from the water or prevent his full
enjoyment of it ; and he cites the judgment of a very distinguished American Judge (Mr. Justice Cooley) in *Watson*
v. *Peters,* 26 Mich. 509, distinctly laying down this doctrine.

This also raises a question, as, I think, only requiring
consideration as between plaintiff and Prevost ; but it
strengthens much what seems to me the clear right of
plaintiff to be considered, for the purposes of this suit, a
riparian proprietor.

The special injury to plaintiff is by no means confined to that part of his wharf and boat-house which lies outside of the land conveyed to him. It affects him in many ways as to his access to the water and as to the enjoyment of his house and land.

I think the learned Chancellor has rightly distinguished the two cases of *Giles* v. *Campbell*, 19 Gr. 226, and *Eager* v. *Cockburn*, 24 Gr. 409. I have carefully examined them, and fail to see, even if they be admitted to be good in law, how they can govern the present case.

If plaintiff had carried on his business without this floating wharf and boat-house, I think his right to damages would be the same ; the existence of this appendage to his premises seems to me to be the chief ground of resistance to his claim. Apart from it there would seem to be only two arguments to be urged, first, that his right is merely that of the general public along the river bank. I have already stated that I think he has proved substantial injury to his property and the reasonable use and enjoyment thereof for his lawful purposes, which entitles him to sue for damages ; second, the existence of Prevost's ownership of the river-bed in front of plaintiff's premises. I am unable to see anything in this latter objection for the reasons already given. It is also urged that there is a good defence on the Statute of Limitations. I do not rest my judgment thereon, but I do not doubt that there is much to be urged in favor of it. It would arise more directly in a contest with Prevost.

I do not consider it necessary further to discuss this appeal. Every case involving water rights can be readily enveloped in a cloud of authorities for arguments urged on one side or the other. I think its decision rests upon a few broad-settled principles of law. I am satisfied with the result arrived at in the Divisional Court, and think its decision sound in law.

It was urged, (but not very strongly) before us as one of the reasons of appeal that the decree was wrong in directing the reference as to the damage for which the defendants are respectively liable to the plaintiff. This form of order will prevent the apparent injustice of making the defendants jointly responsible each for the other. It appears that the bill was filed and the defences put in prior to the passing of the Act of 1885, and relief was prayed by injunction against all the defendants and separate damages against each. Application was then made to the Court by each defendant objecting to the joinder with the others. The Chancellor, after hearing the parties, refused to interfere. Defendants appealed to the full Court. The case is reported in 10 Practice Reports, 649, and there is a very full judgment reviewing the authorities. The Court agreed with the Chancellor, and the case was ordered to proceed, subject to any application by any of the defendants for a separate trial. This decision has never been appealed against, nor was any application made for a separate trial.

In addition to the cases cited, I refer to *Cowan et al.* v. *Duke of Buccleuch et al.*, 2 App. Cas. 344, in the Lords. It was a case in which three several riparian proprietors applied for interdict against four or five owners of different paper mills for fouling the waters of the river Esk. The judgments of the Chancellor and the other law Lords are very instructive on the general questions of polluting a stream by the independent acts of several defendants. The case was decided on the law and practice of the Scotch Courts, but some of the remarks are of general application, and may be of use in the subsequent proceedings in this case.

Lord Cairns, C., says : "The experience of any of your Lordships who have observed trials of this kind will have shewn you that where the proceedings are directed against one individual for polluting a river, it is always a topic of defence that the pollution either comes from the works of some other person upon the river, or comes from the works of that other person in so great a degree as to render the pollution of the individual actually sued not worthy the attention of the Court. * * The tendency in this country, as has been pointed out, with reference to recent legislation, has been very much to enlarge the power of bringing parties having several interests, or interests in the alternative, before the Court."

Lord Penzance says (p. 357): "The cause of action in each case is not the mere act of pouring polluting matter into the river, for the quantity might be insufficient to do mischief by reason of dilution, or the water might purify itself as flowing water does, so that the cause of action is not complete until the result of rendering the water unfit for the pursuer's use is brought about. The result may, in some cases, be traced to the individual act of one of the defenders, but in the majority of cases the reverse is the case, and the extent of the deterioration in the water worked by the polluting acts of several other defenders would have to be inquired into * *. The cause of action against them depends upon the ultimate impurity of the water when it reaches the pursuer's land, and that impurity is the joint result of the acts of all of them."

The difficulties that may arise as to the trial in such cases against several defendants : it is pointed out that these are inevitable incidents affecting every day the most serious criminal and civil trials.

Lord O'Hagan adds (p. 361) that "It is surely for the advantage of the satisfactory administration of justice that those who complain of a common injury and those who are charged with the commission of it should all be enabled to assert themselves before the same tribunal, especially when that tribunal has ample power to prevent any individual wrong by the shaping of separate issues and the regulation of the course and conduct of the trial."

I see no ground for our interference with the judgment of the Chancery Division.

PATTERSON, J. A.—It was considered in the Divisional Court that the patent which granted to Aumond certain land described as extending two chains into the river Ottawa, left in the public the right of navigating the waters, within the limits of the grant, very much as it was before the patent, and that notwithstanding the reservation of that public right, the plaintiff was entitled to recover against the defendants damages for infringement of his rights as riparian proprietor, and also for injury to his business.

Two of the learned judges agreed in the conclusion, viz., the Chancellor and Ferguson, J., but they did not base it on exactly the same line of reasoning, though I do not understand either of them to have dissented from the views expressed by the other.

I arrive at the same conclusion upon grounds which, I think, are covered by the judgments delivered in the Court below, but I construe the patent of 1850 as granting to Aumond the land it describes without any restriction of his absolute dominion over it. It may therefore be unnecessary for me to refer with any particularity to the arguments on which, notwithstanding the assumed reservation, the plaintiff's right of action has been sustained. Nor is it necessary to do more than refer to the judgments delivered in the Court below, and the cases there cited, for a general statement of the law, particularly with reference to the paramount right of the public, even as against the Crown, to the use of all navigable highways. The cases of *Lyon* v. *The Fishmongers' Co.*, 1 App. Cas. 662, and *Williams* v. *Wilcox*, 8 A. & E. 314, contain full expositions of the doctrine and of the authorities relating to it; but for a statement at once accurate and succinct we need not go farther than the judgment of Richards, C.J., in *Attorney-General* v. *Perry*, 15 C. P. 329.

In one passage of that judgment the learned Chief Justice spoke of what had been the practice of our Provincial Government. He said : " In this country the practice has obtained in towns and cities for the Crown to grant land covered with water, and generally to the owner of the bank when adjacent to a navigable stream, and grants so made have never been cancelled for want of power in the Crown to make the grant. The right of the grantee to build wharves and warehouses for the more convenient and profitable enjoyment of the water lots so granted has never been successfully contested, that I am aware of."

That judgment was delivered in 1865.

Five years earlier the ·Act, 23 Vict., ch. 2, had been passed and had removed whatever doubts the exercise of the power had been open to. Section 35 declared that

" Whereas doubts have been entertained as to the power vested in the Crown to dispose of and grant water lots in the harbors, rivers, and other navigable waters in Upper Canada, and it is desirable to set at rest any question which might arise in reference thereto, it is declared and enacted that it has been heretofore, and that it shall be hereafter, lawful for the Governor-in-Council to authorize sales or appropriations of such water lots under such conditions as it has been or it may. be deemed requisite to impose."

There is nothing in the terms of the patent to Aumond to distinguish it from an ordinary grant of Crown lands. It conveys water lot number one in letter O in the town of Bytown, describing it by abuttals which extend to a line parallel with the shore of the river Ottawa and at the distance of two chains from the shore, and it has not been " deemed requisite to impose ' any conditions. The reservation upon which the question of construction turns is not a condition. It is the reservation usual in grants of crown lands, and appears here as part of the ordinary printed form of the Crown Lands Department, on which the patent is drawn up : " To have and to hold the said parcel or tract of land hereby granted, conveyed and assured unto the said Joseph Aumond, his heirs and assigns forever, saving, excepting and reserving nevertheless unto us, our heirs and successors all mines of gold and silver, the free uses, passage and enjoyment of, in, over and upon all navigable waters that shall or may be hereafter found on or under or be flowing through or upon any part of the said parcel or tract of land hereby granted as aforesaid."

We have in evidence a copy of part of the plan of lot letter O, on record in the department of Crown Lands. It shews water lots Nos. 1, 2, 3, and 4, each comprising a por-- tion of dry land and running two chains into the river, and two others consisting wholly of portions of the river two chains in width from the bank, which at that place is not laid out in lots but is marked " Bellevue Terrace." The lots are divided from each other by streets, the lines of the streets also being projected the two chains into the river. Upon each lot the name of the grantee is written, and there is also a note of the area, distinguishing land from water.

Thus on lot 1 the note is, " land 1.0, water 0.6=a. 1.6 ; " and, corresponding with this, we find the patent to Aumond describing the lot as containing by admeasurement one acre and six-tenths of an acre, be the same more or less.

The purpose and design evidenced by this plan are in strict accord with the historical reference by Chief Justice Richards which I have just quoted, and no doubt can be entertained that the grants made as indicated, that to Aumond being one of them, and confirmed by the statute, were made in contemplation of the grantee occupying the land with buildings or wharves or otherwise at his pleasure, and that so far there was, under legislative sanction, a curtailment of the jus publicum ; that is, a curtailment of the theoretical right, for it is not likely that the grant of any such water lot has so interfered with navigation as to cause inconvenience.

The opinion of the Legislature, coinciding with that of the Executive, has been shewn to be that such grants are for the public benefit, and there is no reason to doubt that that opinion is justified by experience. It is not there- fore probable that the patent was framed and issued with the intention that as to all that part of the lot so carefully described as extending " to a point in the Ottawa river two chains distant from the shore " it should be practically inoperative. It is our duty to give it the effect intended unless compelled by the terms of the instrument to acknowledge our inability to do so. " For," as remarked by Tindal, C.J., in *Rutter* v. *Chapman*, 8 M. & W. 1, 102, " we must never forget the rule laid down by Lord Coke, that if the King's charters will bear a double construction, one which will carry the gift into effect, the other which will make it inoperative, the former is to be adopted."

I accede to Mr. McCarthy's argument that there is nothing in this patent to compel the construction that it has so far missed its manifest intent and purpose as to preserve intact the public right of navigating the water over the granted land, though I may not follow that proposition to the con- clusion for which he contends.

I think the point is well taken that the terms of the
reservation do not point to the public right of navigating
the waters. The reservation is not of the use of navigable
waters only; it is also of all mines of silver and gold.
These are royal mines. "The King, by his prerogative,
hath all mines of gold and silver to make money, and
where in mines the gold and silver is of the greater value
they are called Royal Mines," Plowd. 336. Lord Selborne
truly remarked in giving judgment in *Attorney-General
v. Mercer,* 8 App. Cas. 767, 777, that in Crown grants
of land in British North America the practice has generally been to reserve to the Crown, not only royal mines
properly so called, but minerals generally. Here, however,
the royal mines only are reserved " unto us, our heirs, and
successors." The same words and in the same sentence,
define the reservation of the free uses, passage, and enjoyment of the waters.

We cannot, without doing violence to the language of
the deed, construe it as reserving the use of the waters in
any sense or for any purpose different from the reservation
of the mines; and the mines cannot be treated as reserved
for the public benefit except in a sense which is foreign to
the present discussion: namely, so far as they constituted
part of the territorial or other revenues surrendered in
1846 to the Province of Canada (9 Vict. ch. 114) and now
by the British North America Act assigned to Ontario.
The public right to the use of navigable waters is the
right of each individual, and stands on a different footing.
It does not come by grant from the Crown, but it is a
paramount right only to be curtailed by Act of the Legislature.

I am not concerned to inquire whether a provision framed
in the form of a reservation to the Sovereign of the use of
navigable water would not be capable, by some liberality
of interpretation, of being construed in furtherance of the
manifest intent and object of a grant, if so unlikely a situation should arise, as a declaration that the land was to
continue subject to the existing servitude in favor of the

king and all his liege subjects, or to remain the king's
highway.   The question here is, whether that construction
is so strongly compelled by the language of the reservation
as to be obligatory, although it renders nugatory the granting portion of the deed.   In my opinion the opposite is the
true construction.   The liberality called for would be to
defeat and not to carry out the purpose of the deed ; and
to attempt to read the language in one sense with regard
to the mines and in another with regard to the water would
do violence to the natural meaning of the sentence.

What force is to be attributed to the words as we have
them ?

Primarily they assume to reserve to Her Majesty the use
of the waters, just as the royal mines are reserved.   These
are not reservations in the technical meaning of that term
which strictly applies to rents and services.   " In every
good reservation three things must always concur.   1. It
must be by apt words.   2. It must be of some other thing
issuing or coming out of the thing granted, and not part of
the thing itself, nor of some thing issuing out of another
thing.   3. It must be out of such a thing whereunto the
grantor may have resort to distrain :" Shepp. Touch. 80.

They are technically " exceptions," and though the word
" reserve " is used, it is an apt word to create an exception,
as appears from examples given in the Touchstone (at p.
78) from which I again quote : " But this exception may
be in any part of the deed, and so it hath been reasoned :
Hil. 17 Car.   In every good exception these things must
always concur : 1. This exception must be by apt words.
2. It must be of part of the thing granted, and not of
some other thing.   * * 5. It must be of such a thing as
he that doth except may have and doth properly belong to
him. * * If one grant a manor excepting * * the woods
* * or excepting all the gross trees, these are good exceptions. * * If the exception be such as is repugnant to the
grant and doth utterly subvert it and take away the fruit
of it ; as if one grant a manor or land to another excepting
the profits thereof : or make a feoffment of a close of
meadow or pasture, reserving or excepting all the grass of
it, * * these are void exceptions ; * * or if the exception
be of such a thing as the grantor cannot have nor doth

belong to him by law ; as if a lessee for years assign over all his term in the land, excepting the timber trees, earth or clay ; this exception is not good." Mr. Preston adds the explanation that " In this instance the exception is void for want of interest or ownership in the thing excepted."

On these principles the mines are well reserved or excepted. They were vested in Her Majesty and would, but for the exception, have passed by the grant of the land. But not so with the public easement. It would be unaffected by the grant of the land. It is therefore not the subject of exception in favor of the grantor, and for this reason the exception, like the exception of timber-trees, earth or clay by a lessee for years, is void.

If the exception be construed as perpetuating the jus publicum, it is repugnant to the grant in its operation under the statute of 1860, " and doth utterly subvert it and take away the fruit of it," and is therefore void.

A suggestion was made at the bar, that the grant might operate by giving the grantee the exclusive right to fish in these waters. So, adopting the Touchstone's illustration of the grant of a meadow, it might be said that the grantee would have the exclusive right to extract worms from the meadow for bait to catch the fish with, and the reservation or exception of the grass ought not to be held to be void.

The purpose of the grant in each case is too obvious to leave any doubt of the repugnancy of the exception.

It would not better the argument to treat the reservation as a condition : " A condition that would take away the whole effect of a grant is void : and so it is if it be contrary to the express words of it." *Tomlin's* Law Dictionary, citing 1 Inst. 206.

There is, however, another view of the matter. It was suggested, but not much elaborated, by Mr. McCarthy, and I am inclined to think it the correct reading of the deed. It is that this reservation, touching navigable waters, is applicable only to the other parts of the lot, and not to the two chains of the river bed.

The purpose and effect of the deed, so far as it operates under the statute, are to take these two chains of the river out of the category of navigable waters.

We do not use the term " navigable water " as including
all waters on which a boat can float.   The navigable water
of the discussion is a public highway.   The use, passage,
and enjoyment reserved signify the right to navigate any
such public highway thereafter found upon the land conveyed.   This water ceased, by virtue of the statute and the
effect carried by it into the action of the Government in
granting the water lot, to be a public highway, and was
placed outside of the class of navigable waters over which
the right is reserved.

The whole lot thus, in my opinion, vested in Aumond
free from the asserted jus publicum.

Now let us see what is the nature of the plaintiff's title,
either absolutely, or as against these defendants who are
wrongdoers claiming no right or title.

In addition to the information which was before us on
the argument, the solicitors for the parties have, at my
request, procured a correct copy from the registry office at
Ottawa of a plan of the sub-division of lot 1, which supplies
some dates and other particulars, but the information is
still imperfect.

This plan appears to have been made for Aumond.   The
certificate required by the Registry Act is signed by Aumond
and the surveyor, and is dated the 10th of January, 1867.
The date of the filing of the plan in the registry office is
the 22nd of January, 1867.   The plaintiff says he bought
from Aumond a year before he got a conveyance.   Aumond
conveyed to Prevost on the 2nd of November, 1866, and
the plaintiff got his conveyance from Prevost, the deed
bearing date the 23rd of January, 1867.   The plaintiff
must have bargained with Aumond about January, 1866.

I suppose the survey shewn by the plan must have been
made for Aumond some time before the date of the certificate upon the plan, as that date is later than the conveyance to Prevost.   The deed from Aumond to Prevost gives
no description beyond this very general one : " Water lot
number one, more particularly described in the deed from
the Crown to the said Joseph Aumond, excepting certain

portions of the said last mentioned water lot number one,
sold and conveyed by several conveyances, one part to
Charles Brown and the other to Louis Joseph Benoit Lazure
and the other to Francois Xavier Guerton, which said lot
forms part of the original lot letter O of Nepean."

I shall have to found some remarks on the description
in the deed from Prevost to Ratté, wherefore we may as
well note at this place the details of that description, instead of referring to it in a general way :

" All and singular that certain parcel or tract of land
and premises, situate, lying and being in the city of Ottawa
in the county of Carleton and Province of Canada, being
composed of that part of water lot number one in lot letter
O in the city of Ottawa aforesaid (which said water lot
number one in lot letter O, was by the Crown by patent
bearing date, the 24th December, A. D. 1850, granted to
Joseph Aumond), described as follows : Commencing at a
point ninety-nine feet from the boundary stone on the
north-west side of said water lot, thence *in a southerly
direction parallel to Sussex street, a distance of ninety-nine
feet to the intersection of the line between lots numbers
three and four as laid down on the plan of the sub-division
of the said water lot number one, filed in the registry office
of the City of Ottawa, thence along the said subdivision
line produced in a westerly direction one hundred and
thirty-two feet, thence southerly parallel to Sussex street
aforesaid, ninety-nine feet to the line of Cathcart street,*
thence along the northerly line of Cathcart street in a
westerly direction to the water's edge of the river Ottawa,
thence along the said water's edge down the stream in a
northerly direction to the line of Bolton street and thence
in an easterly direction to the place of beginning."

Looking at the plan from the registry office, we see that
ten building lots are laid out, each 33 by 99 feet, and that
they occupy the whole of the original lot one, as far as the
brow of the high bank of the river, and some of them
take in part of the bank.

The line along the bank, or the western boundary of the
building lots, is not a straight line but is in three courses,
each turn being a right angle. That line forms the eastern boundary in Ratté's deed ; and it will be noticed that
its three courses, which I italicise, are the only courses of

which the distances are specified, the other three being
simply given as along Cathcart street to the water's edge,
along the water's edge to the line of Bolton street, and
along that line to the place of beginning. Notice, also,
that the area is not mentioned.

All that the deed conveys is below the brow of the bank.

There is no distinct evidence of the particulars of the
bargain between the plaintiff and Aumond. The only evidence is that of the plaintiff himself, and from some cause,
perhaps because no contest was raised about it, or because
the point was not seen to be important, that evidence is not
at all definite. If the bargain had been in writing, I should
have expected to find it refer in general terms like those
used in the deed to Prevost, to all of the lot which was not
laid out among the ten lots shewn on the plan.

The plaintiff bought for the purpose of his business of
keeping boats for hire. He had conducted that business
on the opposite side of the river, and had there a floating
wharf and boat-house 60 by 16 feet. This he moved across
the river to the locus in quo and moored it on the Aumond
water lot ; and he built a dwelling-house on the dry land,
and had lived in it several months before he got his deed.
Eight or nine years later he enlarged his wharf and boat
accommodations, making a structure 140 by 40 feet, which
floats on the water and is moored to the bank.

Neither Aumond nor Prevost ever occupied the plaintiff's part of the lot, or interfered with his possession, which,
such as it has been, has been continuous for over twenty
years.

Though it did not occur to counsel on either side at the
trial to bring out the particulars of the plaintiff's bargain
with Aumond, I should infer from what he said that he
bargained for all that Aumond had outside of the ten
building lots. That understanding is consistent with all
that we are told ; with the purpose for which the place was
acquired; the prompt and continuous occupation of the river
portion; the seeming absence of value in the land he got
except in connection with the use of that part which is in

the river, and the uselessness of the latter to any one but the owner of the shore; and the fact that neither Aumond nor Prevost ever interfered, and that they are not, nor is any one who claims under them, interfering now.

The terms in which the deed from Prevost is drawn, giving only to the water's edge, prevent its being appealed to as affirmatively supporting this theory, and make it evidence on the other side; but the deed itself supplies ground for a reasonable surmise as to how it came to be drawn as it is, and we have no explanation from any other source. We have seen that Prevost, nine months after the plaintiff had bought from Aumond, took a conveyance from Aumond in the most general terms, and that the Aumond plan was filed the day before the date of the deed from Prevost to Ratté. The description in that deed was obviously framed from the plan. We see that from the absence of any mention of the area conveyed, and of any specification of distances except those marked on the plan, and of any courses or other particulars but such as the plan supplied. The date of the patent is stated in Aumond's certificate on the plan, and was there at the draughtsman's hand. Now it happens that this plan, which was made only for the purpose of shewing the survey of the building lots, does not indicate the extension of the original lot into the river; and a person who was told to draw a deed of all the lot except the building lots, and who had only this plan to guide him, would, as a matter of course, draw just such a description as we have here. He would make the water's edge the boundary simply because he knew of no other, and the plan before him misled him.

It may, of course, be true that the deed represents Ratté's real purchase from Aumond, as it certainly contains all that Prevost, in terms, conveyed to him, and it was undoubtedly Ratté's business to see that it covered all that he had bought; but knowing the loose way in which these things are done, I do not, under all the circumstances, regard this deed as evidence of much weight against the inference that Ratté bargained with Aumond for the whole lot less

the building lots, and that that was what Aumond put him
in possession of.

I speak of the deed merely as part of the evidence touching the plaintiff's bargain with Aumond. I do not intend
to throw any doubt upon the opinion of Mr. Justice Ferguson as to the land covered by water passing under that
deed by implication ; and I have not considered that subject sufficiently to form an independent opinion upon it.

I have taken the trouble to look, in the Crown Lands
office, at the plan of which we have a tracing in evidence,
and at some other plans, including a survey of lot O in
Nepean, laying out upon it part of the town of Bytown, of
earlier date than the plan of the water lots, and I have
seen also the original plan returned by Mr. Bell, the surveyor who laid out the water lots in 1846 and 1848. The
earliest plan throws light on the design of the Government
to curtail the navigable part of the river, as the survey
into lots was not by it extended to the river, a space being
left and marked, " Reserved for wharves." This was afterwards surveyed into the water lots which extended, as we
have seen, two chains into the river. The plans of the
water lots shew that the measurements of two chains are
from the high water mark, and a line on the plans indicates that place. Upon the steep bank at the place the
distance between high water mark and low water mark
cannot be great. We are not informed what it is, but a
printed plan which forms part of the appeal book and purports to shew the lines of both high and low water seems
very far astray, apparently marking the summit of the
lofty bank as the high water mark of the river.

That Ratté was let into actual possession farther out than
the high water mark, and beyond the low water mark of
the river, is a fact which there need be no hesitation in
finding on the evidence ; and if the case were to turn on
his having possession beyond the spot he actually occupied,
I should find as a fact that he was let into possession as a
purchaser of the whole, and that his actual occupation was
therefore extended into constructive possession out to the
two chains limit.

If Prevost were now to bring ejectment against the plaintiff, it is not easy to see how, upon such evidence as we have here and without further evidence, he could hope to contend successfully against the statute of limitations, or to maintain that he has not been dispossessed, or has not discontinued the possession, of the river portion as well as of the bank for more than the statutory period.

On the subject of discontinuance, see *Doe Taylor* v *Proudfoot,* 9 U. C. R. 503; *Butler & McNeill* v. *Donaldson,* 12 U. C. R. 255 ; *Smith* v. *Lloyd,* 9 Ex. 562 ; *Ketchum* v. *Mighton,* 14 U. C. R. 99 ; *Pringle* v. *Allan,* 18 U. C. R. 575 ; *Leigh* v. *Jack.* 5 Ex. D. 264.

We are not trying title between the plaintiff and Prevost, but if the facts before us indicate that the plaintiff has title as against Prevost, they are a fortiori sufficient to prove title against wrong doers.

In my opinion the plaintiff has shewn, as against the defendants, title to all the land actually occupied by him in his business, which is enough to entitle him to recover damages for the injury done to his business, as well as for the injury from the pollution of the water ; and I further think that he shews title to the full outward limit of the Aumond lot.

I agree, therefore, that the appeal should be dismissed.

OSLER, J. A.—I agree that the appeal should be dismissed, for the reasons stated in the judgment of the Chief Justice, and in that of my brother Ferguson in the Court below.

BURTON, J. A.—Legislatures are not interpreters of the law, and although they may give a retrospective effect to their enactments and legalise acts which were previously invalid. I apprehend that notwithstanding the recital in sec. 35 of the 23rd Vict., ch. 2, "that doubts had been entertained as to the power of the Crown to grant lots in navigable waters," with the view to their being built upon and thereby interfering with navigation, no power to

make such grants did generally exist before the passing of
that statute.

Special Acts such as those we had to consider in *Hood* v.
The Harbor Commissioners, 37 U. C. R. 72 and in *Warin* v.
The London and Canadian Loan Co., 12 A. R. 327, have given
that power to the Crown.   But the right of navigation is
paramount to the right of property of the Crown and its
grantees in the bed of the river, and such property cannot
be used in any way so as to derogate from or interfere with
the public right of navigation.   *Gann* v. *The Free Fishers
of Whitstable*, 11 H. L. 192.

Any grant, therefore, of the Crown, apart from those
made under the statute, which interferes with the public
right is, with great respect to those who differ with me in
my opinion, void as to such parts as are open to such objection if acted upon so as to effect nuisance by working injury
to the public right.   *Parmeter* v. *Attorney-General*, 10
Price, 412.

The section of the statute to which I have referred I
regard as a virtual abandonment on the part of the public
of this right, so far as regards water lots laid out by the
Government in harbors and on the banks of navigable
rivers, so that as regards such lots the Crown has now the
clear right to grant them free from the public right of
navigation, with the view to their being filled in and
utilised for wharves or other similar purposes.

Before proceeding to consider the facts of this case, I
wish to refer to a matter relied on by one of the learned
Judges in the Court below, as to the water lot in question
in front of the land covered by the conveyance to the
plaintiff passing under that conveyance, by analogy to cases
of lands abutting on a non-navigable stream where the
riparian proprietor's own title would extend to the centre
of the bed of the stream.

I think the answer to that contention is to be found in the
judgment of Mr. Justice Gwynne, in *Dixon* v. *Snetzinger*,
23 C. P. 235, where the question of the rights of riparian
proprietors on the banks of our great lakes and navigable

rivers was much discussed, and the conclusion arrived at
that the bed of such river does not pass under the rule of
the Common Law of England ad medium filum aquæ
to the riparian proprietors, but is vested in the Crown for
the use, benefit, and enjoyment of the public in the waters
flowing over it.

A grant of lands on the side of non-navigable streams,
in the absence of evidence to the contrary, conveys the
soil of the bed to the middle of the stream; on the other
hand, any grant of land by the Crown on the banks of a
navigable river like the Ottawa would, primâ facie, be
bounded by the edge of the stream. It requires an
absolute grant of the bed of the stream, there being no
presumption of law, in such a case, that the ownership of
the bed of the river goes along with the ownership of the
shore.

If it requires an absolute grant from the Crown to pass
the land within the limits of the stream, can any good
reason be suggested why the same should not be required
in order to pass the land to the grantee of the patentee ?
Why should any greater effect be given to the patentee's
conveyance than would have been given in a patent to him
of land described as extending to the edge of the river ?

The plaintiff, claiming under the patentee, must be presumed to know the terms of the grant and that the description comprised two chains within the river, and he must
be presumed to know the law which entitled the patentee
to fill in in front of his lot, at least to the extent of the
land covered with water not sufficiently deep to be
navigable ; and I cannot see therefore how the plaintiff can
be regarded as a riparian proprietor; the person filling that
position is Prevost and on his filling in the lot, as I think
he is entitled to do to the limits of his grant, the plaintiff
will be entirely cut off from the stream.

The case would, I think, be free from difficulty but for
the appearance in the patent of a reservation or exception
to be found in most grants from the Crown at that date ;
"Saving, excepting, and reserving nevertheless unto us,

our heirs and successors, all mines of gold and silver, the free uses, passage, and enjoyment of, in, over, and upon all navigable waters that shall or may be hereafter found on or under, or be flowing through or upon any part of the said parcel or tract of land hereby granted as aforesaid."

Such a reservation, though probably quite unnecessary and not very happily expressed, is intelligible enough when contained in a patent of a large tract, but partially known, and where streams which may turn out to be navigable may pass through them. It would have been more to the purpose to have excluded from the grant the beds of such streams, and it was quite unnecessary to except the use and enjoyment in and over the navigable waters thereof, as that is a matter which the Crown has no power to grant, and the exception therefore is useless.

The form is a printed one, and the reservation is, I apprehend, to be found in all the patents then issued, but becomes very inapplicable to such a grant as the present. The grant itself professed to transfer a piece of land two chains in extent which the Crown had had surveyed and knew that it was covered with water which was navigable, that being presumably the most valuable part of the grant.

The defendants contend that this was not a voluntary grant by the Crown, but was sold at a large price to the purchaser ; and they urge, and the argument is entitled to great weight, that it could never have been the intention of the Crown to grant with one hand and take away with the other ; that it was sold for value and for the evident purpose of being utilised for wharves or warehouses, and was granted by metes and bounds, and that under these circumstances the ordinary rule of construction must govern, and the first part of the deed which contains the grant must prevail, and the reservation which would appear to be repugnant to it rejected.

But if the words do extend to the right of navigation over this water, it appears to me the reservation is absolutely void. That right, as I have pointed out, is paramount to the rights of the Sovereign. The Sovereign could not make a grant of it to any one and deprive the public of their rights; and if so, it follows that she could not reserve it to herself and her successors, which, if it means anything, means a transfer not to a subject, but to the Crown.

Then we come to the statute, which I regard as a virtual abandonment by the public, expressed through their duly constituted representatives, of this right, so far as it extends to lots of this kind laid out in harbors or on the banks of rivers, and at the same time vesting in the Crown the right both to grant the bed of the river and the water upon it free from any rights publici juris.

The Act of Parliament and the grant together vest in the purchaser the absolute right to use that land covered with water, unconditionally; as his own for all purposes.

If that be so, can the plaintiff maintain this action? Upon the best consideration I have been able to give the matter, and with a very strong inclination to stretch the law, if possible, in favor of the plaintiff, I have come to the conclusion that he cannot.

I can understand that a person having no title but his bare possession can maintain an action against any person invading that possession, but I do not see upon what principle he himself, a trespasser, can complain of others trespassing on other portions of the property of which he is not in possession, although it may interfere with his access to the portion of which he is in possession : it being clear that the party in whom the legal estate in the land is vested could build over the whole of that land and interfere with the access to the property.

I thought that the judgment might possibly be upheld on the ground that the owner Prevost had discontinued possession for over twenty years, and that the plaintiff might be held to have acquired a title by the Statute of Limitations, but I have been unable to bring myself to that conclusion.   .

The contract for the purchase which was about a year before the execution of the deed, is not produced, but presumably it covers the same land as is described in the deed.

The plaintiff says that when he made the purchase he brought over his boat house from the other side of the river and anchored it in front of his lot. The former owner having exercised acts of ownership over certain portions of the lot may be said to have been in actual possession of the whole of the land covered by his grant, whether covered by water or not. If we look at the conveyance alone, it tends to negative any intention to discontinue the possession of that portion of the lot which was covered with water. The mere circumstance of the owner not making use of this land by building upon it either permanent structures or such floating structures as the plaintiff is using, which probably is the only way in which he could use and enjoy it, can be no evidence of discontinuance. It is said that the occupation of it by this floating boat house and wharf, is however, a dispossession, but whatever may be the effect of that occupation I do not see upon what principle it can be extended beyond the actual limits of the structure itself. If it had been shewn that the contract itself extended to the whole of the two chains under water, although the deed had erroneously restricted the description to the dry land, there would be no difficulty in extending the plaintiff's possession to the limits of the land contracted to be sold, but in the absence of any evidence of that kind it would, I fear, be very dangerous to place such a construction upon the plaintiff's occupation, more especially as no such case is made upon the pleadings, or pointed at in the evidence, or in the reasons of appeal, and no such point was made upon the argument.

It is unnecessary to express any opinion as to what his rights may be as to the portion of the land covered by his boat house and wharf, but beyond that I cannot hold that he has acquired any title to the land not so covered or occupied.

I ought, before concluding, to refer to a portion of the Chancellor's judgment in which he treats the case as one of an easement which would pass under the conveyance from Prevost to the plaintiff, but the easement to pass under the conveyance would be an easement which the grantor had previously owned and enjoyed, not one which the grantee was then in the enjoyment of.

I fail to see any ground on which the plaintiff can be entitled to maintain this action, and think that it should be dismissed.

Appeal dismissed, with costs.

BURTON, J. A., dissenting.

[This case has been carried to the Privy Council.]

PARTLO v. TODD ET AL.

*Trade Mark—The Trade Mark and Design Act of 1879—42 Vict. ch.
    22 (D.)—Prior user—Registration, effect of—Injunction.*

The fact of proprietorship or ownership is a condition precedent of the
    right to register a trade-mark or to obtain any advantage under the
    "Trade-Mark and Design Act of 1879," and registration thereunder
    does not create or confer such status on an unqualified person, and his
    right thereto may be disallowed.
In an action to restrain the infringement of a registered trade-mark it
    was shewn that the defendants had, after the registration of such mark,
    made use of the words "Gold Leaf," which formed an important
    feature of the mark, for the purpose of branding their flour, but did not
    represent it as made by the registrant. .It was proved, however, that
    those words had been in common use, before such registration, for a
    like purpose in this and the sister provinces. On appeal the Court
    affirmed the judgment of PROUDFOOT, J. (12 O. R. 171), refusing an in-
    junction. [BURTON, J. A., dissenting.]

THIS was an appeal by the plaintiff from the judgment
of Proudfoot, J. (12 O. R. 171), and came on to be heard
before this Court on the 12th of May, 1887.[*]

W. Cassels, Q. C., and *Jackson*, for the appellant.
Moss, Q. C., and *Ball*, for the respondents.

The facts appear in the former report.

September 6th, 1887.   HAGARTY, C. J. O.—The plaintiff
made out a primâ facie case of infringement of his trade
mark—the defendant sought to prove that the term "gold
leaf" flour was a term known and used in the trade for a
considerable time before plaintiff registered his mark.

In his application for registration, 17th December, 1884,
after describing and furnishing a copy of his design, he
states the words "gold leaf" and adds, "which words
designating a particular brand of flour, are the words I
particularly request registered."

Mr. Cassels, both at the trial and before us, strenuously
argued that it was not open to defendants to contradict
plaintiff's right to the exclusive user, and that evidence

Present.—HAGARTY, C.J.O., BURTON, PATTERSON, and OSLER, JJ. A.

could not be received as offered. The learned Judge chiefly on the authority of *McCall* v. *Theal*, 28 Gr. 48, admitted the evidence, and held that "gold leaf" was a common brand for patent flour in use before the registration of plaintiff's trade mark, well known in the Lower Provinces on flour sold there by active manufacturers—in effect that plaintiff was not correct in his assertion on which he obtained registration, that the special characteristic of his mark, viz.: "gold leaf" was not in use by any other person than himself.

He dismissed plaintiff's bill.

If the defence was admissible, I think we cannot say that it was not proved as found by the trial Judge.

The evidence warrants the conclusion, according to Haine's testimony, that the words were in use before 1881.

King and Spink's evidence may also be referred to.

On the facts as found in evidence, I cannot think that the plaintiff was entitled to have this mark registered.

The learned Judge has pointed out some of the very striking differences between our statute of 1879, and the Imperial Act of 1875, and also that of 1883.

Our Act is singularly bald in its provisions. We have nothing before us to indicate that any rules or regulations referred to in sec. 2 have ever been promulgated.

A register is to be kept.

By sec. 4, registration is made a condition precedent to the right to sue for infringement.

Sec. 5, the Minister may refuse to register on certain specified grounds ; none of them, apparently, covering the grounds of defence here urged.

Sec. 7, the Minister shall give his certificate to the effect that the trade-mark has been duly registered, " and every such certificate purporting to be so signed, shall be received in all Courts of Law or of Equity in Canada as primâ facie evidence of the facts therein alleged, without proof of the signature."

This is the only statement in the statute as to the legal effect of the certificate.

Sec. 8 enacts that all marks, names, labels, &c., adopted for use in trade, &c., to distinguish any manufacture, &c., no matter how applied, &c., shall be considered and known as trade-marks, and " may be registered for the exclusive use of the party registering the same," and thereafter " he shall have the exclusive right to use the same to designate articles manufactured by him."

Sec. 10, a specific trade-mark, registered, shall endure for 25 years, subject to renewal.

Secs. 13 and 14 allow cancellation, on application of the owner and provide for assignments.

Sec. 15 enables the Minister, on application, to register a mark already registered, to cause parties interested to appear, and to decide the respective rights. In his absence his deputy may act for him, " and any error in registering trade-marks, or any oversight about conflicting registrations of trade-marks may be settled in the same manner."

I do not consider that this last cited clause, or anything in this 15th section, confers any power on the Minister to interpose in a case like that before us.

Sec. 16 makes it a misdemeanour fraudulently to mark goods with the registered mark, &c.

Sec. 17. A suit may be sustained against any person using the registered trade-mark, or any fraudulent imitations, or selling articles bearing such trade-mark, or any such imitations thereof, or contained in packages being, or purporting to be his (i. e. registered owner) contrary to the provisions of this Act.

In the sections specially applicable to trade-marks in the statute, I see no further provision bearing on this case.

In the sections from 20 to 36, which are declared applicable only to industrial designs, there is a section 29 which provides that if any person, not being the lawful proprietor of a design, be registered as proprietor, the rightful owner may bring an action, and the Court, if it appears that the design has been registered in the name of a wrong person, may direct cancellation or substitution of names on the register. But even if this section applied to trade-marks, it would apparently not give a remedy in a case like this, as the ownership is not claimed by any rival. The defence in the present action is not that some other person owns the trade-mark, but that no one is entitled to register it.

If Mr. Cassels's able argument be sound, there is apparently no redress whatever when once the certificate is granted.

We were asked to regard it as a case of Crown Patent, which could not be impeached except in the known way by sci. fa. or other proceedings, where the Crown, the grantor, is before the Court.

I do not see how the illustration holds good. Here there is no record under the Great Seal, nothing but the certificate of a Minister, who may, under the statute (sec. 3), have a seal for the sealing of trade-marks and other instruments and copies from his office. Even such a seal has not been used here, if it exists. Its use, however, would hardly help the plaintiff's argument on this : See *Sebastian* on Trade Marks, p. 13.

The Imperial Acts contain very full provisions. For five years from registration it shall be primâ facie evidence of his right to the exclusive use of the mark, and after five years it shall be conclusive evidence of his right to the exclusive use as to this section.

" Until the end of five years from registration the only effect of it is as was said in the Court of Appeal in *Nuthall* v. *Vining*, 28 W. R. 330, to qualify the registered proprietor for suing infringers, in other words, registration is 'simply a condition precedent to suing.' Per Chitty, J., in *Monson* v. *Boehm*, 28 Sol. J. 361, and the mark remains liable to removal from the register. * * After the expiration of five years from registration the title of the registered proprietor appears to be secure against individual rival claimants, but as the Act only says that after five years the person who has registered a trade-mark shall be entitled to the trade-mark, but does not say the mark as registered shall be deemed to be a trade-mark. See per Jessel, M. R., *In re Palmer*, 21 Ch.

D. 47, the trade-mark remains liable to removal for inherent defects in it, e. g., that it contains no one of the essential particulars specified in sec. 64." *Sebastian*, p 318.

Full remedies are provided in the Imperial Acts for the rectification of the register, by removing a registration improperly granted. This is done by motion in the Court of Equity.

Sebastian at p. 327 fully explains the matter. He refers to *Rose* v. *Evans*, 48 L. J. Ch. 618, in which it was said that any person aggrieved in case of a wrongful registration, was a person in the same trade with the registered proprietor. See also *In re Ralph*, 25 Ch. D. 194.

He cites *Re Hyde*, 7 Ch. D. 724.

There, on motion, the registration was cancelled on application of persons in the trade proving that it had been commonly used for years. Sir Geo. Jessel's remarks are important.

On notice of the registration, which had passed unopposed, the trade at once came forward and said in effect: "This registration is illegal—it interferes with our trade, we are as much entitled to have our sealing wax stamped " Bank of England," as the persons who have registered it. If we do not interfere speedily they will get an absolute title under the Act, and therefore we come forward to remove the mark from the register as being a wrongful registration.

See, also, *Re Leonard & Ellis*, 53 L. J. Ch. 233; *In re Palmer*, 21 Ch. D. 47 ; 24 Ch. Div. 504, when, as he says, " marks publici juris have been registered as private property."

It seems clear that the lapse of the five years is no bar to the removal from the register of a mark not authorized to be registered as a trade-mark.

Re Palmer was a registration as a mark of " Braided fixed Stars," a kind of lucifer match.

Sir Geo. Jessel refers to the opinions in Mr. Sebastian's work, and to a section from *Brice* on Trade-Marks, which states the opinion that the right may be contested after the five years on any ground going to shew that it ought never to have been registered at all.

It does not appear very clearly the extent a five years' registration will protect.

Sir Geo. Jessel's remarks *In re Hyde*, are relied on to claim that such a thing as prior user by others of the peculiar mark could not be urged after five years.

In re Wragg's Trade-mark, 29 Ch. Div. 551, Pearson, J., ordered the registration to be cancelled after eight or nine years, on the ground that at the time of registration the mark or brand was in use in the trade, and therefore ought not to have been registered. The language of Jessel, M. R., was relied on. Sub-sec. 3 of sec. 74 of the Act of 1875, says : " Any device * * which was before 13th August, 1875, publiclyused by more than three persons on the same or a similar description of goods shall, for the purposes of this section be deemed common to the trade in such goods."

Pearson, J., says : " It is said that because Mr. Wragg has registered, he has got an exclusive right (*i. e.* after five years). To my mind he could get an exclusive right only to that which he was authorized to register under this Act, and it is quite plain that no person can, with propriety, ask the comptroller to register as his exclusive property a mark which is common to all persons engaged in the same trade."

The case of *Lloyd's* Trade-mark, 27 Ch. D. 649, before Chitty, J., is to the same effect, and registration was cancelled after the five years on the same grounds. Stress is laid on the words in the section as to exclusive use after five years from registration, "subject to the provisions of this Act."

Edwards v. *Dennis,* 30 Ch. Div. 454, was decided, on appeal, some months afterwards. The precise point in the preceding cases did not arise. The register was rectified after the five years by restricting the trade-mark to certain goods manufactured in the registering party's trade. It was too large and covered goods not made by him.

Cotton, L. J., points out that the object of the Acts was not to give new rights, but to place restrictions on the bringing of actions, by requiring registration before suing

—and that they were also to facilitate evidence, by directing that for five years it was to be primâ facie evidence of
right to exclusive user, and after five years conclusive
evidence of user. He adds: " When the alleged infringement consists of using not the exact thing upon the
register, but something similar to it, the Court must, in
considering whether there has been an infringement or
not, proceed upon the old principle which prevailed both
at law and equity before the Act, that a man is not to pass
off his goods as the goods of another "   *   *   referring
to *In re Palmer*, " although it may have been on for five
years, if it ought not to have been on at all, then it can
be taken off."

As before remarked our Act omits all provisions for
rectification of the register, and names no limit for exclusive right to succeed primâ facie right.

Must we therefore agree that our Legislature intended
no matter by what fraud and misrepresentation a trade-
mark has been successfully placed on the register an exclusive right of user was thereby conferred, and that in no
way could such a right be resisted?

If, as Cotton, L. J. points out, the Act was not intended
to regulate the right to sue and to facilitate evidence—if
the substantial object be to aid the honest trader in preventing others from palming off their goods as his goods, the
intention could hardly have been to give a positive twenty-
five years exclusive right to a trade-mark to a man who
never owned or used it, but who was merely securing to
himself the property of another, or a name or term common to all men.

Sec. 1 says, that a register shall be kept in which any
proprietor of a trade-mark may have it registered by complying with the provisions of the Act.

Sec. 6 declares that the proprietor of a trade-mark may
have it registered.

Must we not consider that only such proprietors can do so?

If not, then clearly a new right is created by the statute wholly independent of ownership or even user, if only
a false declaration be made and registration thus obtained.

Thus sec. 7 says that " upon compliance with the requirements of this Act," there shall be registration.

Must we not consider that proprietorship is one of these requirements ?

Sec. 11 the proprietor of a trade-mark applying for registration must, &c., &c.

And sec. 16 as to marking of goods and exclusive rights, already cited, speaks of the trade-mark as registered under the provisions of the Act.

All which expressions point to a registration by the proprietor.

I think the object of the Act was not to create new rights but to facilitate the vindication of existing rights.

Our first step in this direction seems to have been the Act of 1860, 23 Vict. ch. 61, which says nothing of registration, but makes it a misdemeanour to mark goods " with the known and accustomed trade-mark, name, or device of any manufacturer," and also in sec. 3, providing that a suit may be maintained by any manufacturer against any person using his trade-mark., &c, or selling goods bearing such trade-mark, &c., or any imitation thereof contrary to the provisions of the Act.

All this legislation is based upon the further protection of existing rights.

Next year 24 Vict. ch. 21, was passed for the first time establishing a register.

It declares it "expedient to make provision for the better ascertaining and determining the right of manufacturers and others to enjoy the exclusive use of trade-marks claimed by them."

In *Browne* on Trade Marks, p. 253, sec. 357, the principle is discussed.

He points out the distinction between a patent and certificate of registry : " A patent is a grant—a new creation. It makes a right that did not previously exist, and one that must expire with it.

A trade mark is not granted by the government *   *
The patent is a modern invention, the trade-mark is vener-

ab.e for its antiquity, its origin being coeval with that of
property itself.   All the patent office does with the latter
is to recognize and record it   *   *   the symbol of commerce exists ex proprio vigore, by virtue of an immutable
law."

The subject is discussed in *United States* v. *Stevens*, U. S.
Reports, vol. 100, p. 82, where the Supreme Court held
the legislation by Congress as to trade-marks to be uncon-
stitutional, though they could legislate as to Patent Law
and Copyright.   See especially the judgment Miller, J.,
p. 94.

The case seems in my mind to be reduced to this : Does
our statute create a new right vesting in any person who
succeeds in registering a trade-mark, rightfully or wrongfully, the exclusive use of it for say twenty-five years ?   Is
not the fact of proprietorship or owner of such trade-mark
the necessary condition precedent of the right to register
or obtain any advantage under the Act ?

On the best consideration I can give the case, I come to
the conclusion that from the beginning our legislation has
been and is based upon the fact of proprietor and ownership, and that registration does not create or confer that
status on an unqualified person, and that his right thereto
can be challenged.

All through the Acts the provisions are that the proprietor may have his mark registered, and that when registered such person shall have certain rights.

In construing an Act so bald as ours, it would be pre-
sumptuous in me to speak without some natural hesitation,
and I have had many doubts in arriving at this conclusion.

PATTERSON and OSLER, JJ.A., concurred.

BURTON, J.A.—We are not called upon in this case to
consider what remedy, if any, would be open in the event of
a word or name which was merely descriptive of an article,
or which was indicative merely of its quality or composition, and which therefore could not properly be the subject

of a trade-mark having been placed upon the register by the Minister of Agriculture.   Here the words used were properly the subject of a trade-mark, apart altogether from the statute, but sec. 8 of the statute declares that for the purposes of the Act, all marks, names, and brands, or other business devices, which may be adopted for use by a person in his trade for the purpose of distinguishing any manufacture, product or article of any description, by him manufactured, shall be considered and known as trade-marks, and may be registered for the exclusive use of the party registering the same in the manner provided by the Act.

The Act provides that, the proprietor of such trade-mark may have it registered by forwarding a drawing and description of it in duplicate to the Minister of Agriculture, with a declaration that the same was not in use to his knowledge by any other person than himself *at the time of his adoption thereof.*

The Minister may refuse to register in four cases :

1. If it resembles a trade mark already registered.

2. If it appears that it is likely to deceive or mislead the public.

3. If it contains any immorality or scandalous figure.

4. If it does not contain the essentials necessary to constitute a trade-mark properly speaking, but in addition he may cancel a certificate already granted improvidently, from which it follows that if the same facts were known to him at the time of the application he might refuse to grant it.

After the Act came into operation no person who had not registered a trade-mark to which he had become entitled could institute any proceeding for its infringement, although he might still maintain an action against persons fraudulently marking merchandise, or forging a trade-mark contrary to the provisions of the 35 Vict. ch. 32.

What then were the rights of a person, who claiming to be the proprietor of a trade-mark, has registered in the terms of the Act ?

It is contended on the one hand that having registered
he has an indefeasible right, the words of the Act being,
that thereafter, that is to say, after registration, " he shall
have the exclusive right to use the same, and may maintain a suit against any person using his trade-mark, or any
fraudulent imitation thereof, or selling articles bearing such
trade-mark, or any such imitation thereof."

On the other hand it is contended that there being no
other provision, statutory or otherwise, in which the validity or regularity of the alleged trade-mark could be
questioned, they must necessarily have the right to do so
in this action.

The last of these contentions is not warranted in fact;
but even if true, the argument based upon it would be,
I think, more plausible than sound. If the Legislature
has neglected to provide a remedy, it by no means
follows that the Courts should take upon themselves to do
so. It would be impossible for us to say why that omission
was made, or whether it has been designedly made or not;
and then the question also arises, whether under section 15
sufficient protection is not given to the person entitled to
protection, that is to say, to a person who might, if notified
originally, have resisted the plaintiff's application, and
whether that is not all that the Legislature proposed to do.

As I understand that section any person claiming to be
entitled to the trade-mark may, notwithstanding the plaintiff's prior registration, himself apply to be registered, and
the Minister of Agriculture may call before him all parties interested, including of course the registered party, and
upon hearing them may cancel the former application and
enter the last, or make such other order as to right and
justice may appertain.

I think that section may be so read without doing any
violence to its language; but if no remedy has been provided by the Legislature, I cannot accede to the argument
that we are at liberty to supplement the Act by legislation
of our own.

When we refer to the English Act we find the language
used by them not nearly as strong as that of our own Act;

but we find also that there is ample provision for rectifying
the register at any time.

The words of the English Act are these: "The registration of a person as proprietor of a trade-mark shall be
primâ facie evidence of his right to the exclusive use of
such trade-mark, and shall, after the expiration of five
years, be conclusive evidence of his right to the exclusive
use of such trade-mark, subject to the provisions of the
Act."

Our Act is even stronger; it is not treated as a question
of evidence, but is in the form of a positive declaration that
he shall have the exclusive right to use the same.

In an action, therefore, under the English Act, the plaintiff is apparently required to set forth all the material facts
on which he relies, and particularly the user by himself or
his predecessors, and then the statute for the first five years
is primâ facie evidence of these allegations, and after five
years conclusive evidence of them. Under our Act I apprehend all that the plaintiff would be bound to allege, would
be, his registered title.

No doubt under section 15 his right to continue on the
register may be contested by any person who claims to be
himself entitled; but the question still remains whether
the defendant is entitled to any relief in this action, or
whether so long as the registry remains uncancelled, it is
not conclusive as to the plaintiff's right.

I should gather from the remarks of several of the
Judges in some of the English cases, in accordance with
what (apart from these remarks I should consider to be the
well-understood canons of construction relating to statutes),
that if the section which gives the power of rectification
had been omitted, there would be no relief there after the
expiration of the five years.

In *Lloyd's Case*, 27 Ch. D. 649, Chitty, J., says: "Without
going through other parts of the Act, it is sufficient to say
that the statute which enacts that registration shall after
the expiration of five years be conclusive, &c., by the concluding words, 'Subject to the provisions of this Act' lets
in and is controlled by sec. 90," which is the section which
enables any party aggrieved to apply to get rid of the

entry, leading rather to the inference that but for that
section the plaintiff's right was conclusively established at
the expiration of that period.

It is true that there is no express provision under our
Act as is found in the English Act, for giving notice by
advertisement of the application to be registered, and the
person to make the application is under our Act, described
as the proprietor, instead of, as in the English Act, the
person claiming to be entitled, if that can make any difference. If the party could, mero motu, register, I should
think the fact of his being proprietor would be a condition
precedent to the claim of exclusive right but it cannot be
overlooked that the person claiming cannot get a certificate
until he has satisfied the Minister of Agriculture that he
is entitled, including of course the material fact that he is
proprietor, and the Minister of Agriculture is invested
with the fullest powers to make such rules and regulations
as will best insure the proper working of the Act. Once he
has passed upon it, his decision is binding upon every one,
subject only to a cancellation as provided in the 15th sec.
which is a matter also placed entirely under his control.
This would appear to be the only mode which the Legislature deemed necessary for the protection of the true owner,
except, perhaps, in the case of fraud, which avoids everything : but in the absence of fraud, is not the object of the
Act best insured by making the registered title absolute
and conclusive, unless attacked by the party who has a
prior or better claim ? An Act of this nature would be
of comparatively little use if the person charged with infringing can put the plaintiffs to the trouble of investigating and resisting other claims which the wrong doer asserts
are preferable to those of the plaintiffs ; claims which the
parties alleged to own do not think proper to assert—such
an answer would appear to be entirely without merit where
the person infringing is undoubtedly as between himself
and the registered owner a wrong doer, and is not claiming
under the alleged rightful owner.

For my own part, I regard the decision of the Minister of Agriculture as res judicata, as binding upon us as any decision of the ultimate Court of Appeal; but even if I am wrong in that view, I have a very decided opinion that mere prior user by some one, not shewn to have been continued down to the time of the application, would be insufficient to defeat the plaintiff's right under the Act; on the contrary, it would tend to defeat the very object which the Legislature had in view when passing the enactment. The very form of the declaration which the applicant is required to make when seeking to register, seems to shew this, for it is that it is not in use to his knowledge by any other person at the time of his adoption of it.

That such prior user would not at Common Law in itsself be sufficient, was the view entertained by the Master of the Rolls in *Hall* v. *Barrows*, 32 L. J. N. S. 548, where he says:

"If the brand or mark be an old one formerly used, but since discontinued, the former proprietor of the mark, undoubtedly cannot retain such a property in it, or prevent others from using it, but provided it has been adopted by a manufacturer and continuously and still used by him to denote his own goods when brought into market and offered for sale there, I apprehend, although the mark may not have been adopted a week, and may not have acquired any reputation in the market, his neighbours cannot use that mark," and then comes a passage shewing the usefulness of an Act of this kind, for he proceeds: "Were it otherwise, and were the question to depend entirely on the time the mark had been used, or the reputation it had acquired, a very difficult, if not an insoluble inquiry would have to be opened in every case namely, whether the mark had acquired on the market a distinctive character denoting the goods of the person who first used it."

The Act contemplates that there may be other parties entitled to this trade-mark at the time, for it makes provision for such persons taking proceedings to cancel the registration, but until cancelled I apprehend it would remain good. In other words, the fact that such person had apart from the registration a preferable right to that of the person upon the register would not per se, avoid the trade mark, although it might be liable to be cancelled on a proper application.

But if the actual user by some one else at the time of the application would be a defence, there is, in my opinion, no evidence to shew that at the time the plaintiff adopted the mark, which he subsequently registered, it was in use by others so as to deprive him of the right to appropriate it to his own exclusive use.

Great efforts appear to have been made before the trial to obtain particulars.

On the 13th March the defendants furnished particulars, stating that it was in use by W. S. King prior to the registration, and by James King, and on the 18th March the defendants furnished an additional name of a person named Cawthrop.

On the 23rd March the plaintiff obtained an order for better particulars, and under that order the defendants again gave the name of W. S. King as having used it in 1881 and 1882, Paul Haines in 1876 and in each year since, and Spink Brothers.

I refer to this because I incline to think from the reference made by the learned Judge to *McCall* v. *Theal*, that he treats previous cases of user as equivalent to evidence of the mark being in common use at the time of its adoption by the plaintiff.

The parties named in the particulars were examined at the trial, with the exception of Cawthrop, and their evidence entirely fails to establish that the name was in use by any one but the plaintiff at the time he adopted it.

Wm. S. King states that he did at one time use the word " Gold Leaf " as a brand, but after using it on 1,000 sacks he discontinued it, and used it afterwards only on oatmeal flour; he was so using it on oatmeal only when the plaintiff adopted it as a trade-mark, and he distinctly disclaims any wish or intention to apply to cancel the plaintiff's trade-mark ; and the conversation related by him as having taken place with the plaintiff, though not admitted

by the latter, amounted to a waiver of any right or claim
to the mark.

R. S. King does not carry the matter any further. Spink
says he had a brand "Gold Leaf" cut in 1883, and sent to
Mr. Haines, of Cheltenham, who branded with it 2,000
barrels for Spink which were sent to Quebec and Montreal,
and that would seem to be the extent of his dealing with it.
Haines is called, and speaks of having used the words as a
trade-mark in 1881, and probably two or three years before
that, and he speaks of having shipped, in 1883 and 1884
the flour referred to in Spink's evidence, and he says
that is the last shipment that he made with that brand,
and he leaves it rather uncertain, upon cross-examination,
whether he is not mistaken about that being the brand
used : the brand itself not being produced.

This is all the evidence of user, from which I infer that
what the learned Judge means when he speaks of this
being a common brand in use before the registration of the
plaintiff's trade-mark, that he treats a prior user as des-
tructive of the plaintiff's title. If it is, I think the conclusion of the learned Judge is right, but I do not think
that sufficient to invalidate the title which the plaintiff
claims by his registration. It would be necessary at least,
in order to defeat his right, to shew not that there had at
one time been such an user, but that such user was in
actual existence at the time of the plaintiff's adoption of it.

That the defendant did, after the registration of the
plaintiff's mark, sell flour with the distinctive mark is
clearly established, and the plaintiff should, in my opinion,
be entitled to have the appeal allowed, and the injunction
originally granted made perpetual, with the costs of the
suit.

Appeal dismissed, with costs.
BURTON, J.A., dissenting.

[This case has been carried to the Supreme Court.]

WALLBRIDGE V. GAUJOT.

Landlord and tenant—Lease of mines—Exhaustion of ore—Surrender of term—Determination of lease.

The plaintiff, by deed of 30th December, 1882, created a term for ten years, which became vested in the defendants, of "all the mines of ores of iron and iron stone, as well opened as not opened, which can, shall, or may be wrought, dug, found out, or discovered within, upon, or under ten acres square of the north half of lot number 12 in the 6th concession of Madoc": Yielding and paying $1 per gross ton of the said iron stone or ore for every ton mined and raised from the land and mine, payable quarterly on the 1st days of March, June, September, and December, in each year. The lessees covenanted to dig up, &c., not less than 2,000 tons the first year and not less than 5,000 tons in every subsequent year, and "pay quarterly the sum of $1 per ton for the quantity agreed to be taken during each year :" * * And if the same should exceed the quantity actually taken, such excess to be applied towards payment of the first quarter thereafter in which more than the stipulated quantity should be taken: "Provided, that if the iron ore or iron stone shall be exhausted and not to be found or obtained there, by proper and reasonable effort, in paying quantities, then the parties of the second part shall be at liberty to determine this lease."

The defendants entered, and proceeded to work the mines until September (or December), 1884, when, having taken out about 300 tons, they ascertained that the ore could not be obtained in paying quantities, whereupon they notified the lessor thereof and of their desire to surrender their lease, which surrender the lessor refused to accept, and instituted proceedings to recover the amount of two quarters' rent (all prior rents having been regularly paid). The defendants counter-claimed for the rents already paid by reason of failure of consideration.

Held, (1) that, in the absence of any specified mode of surrendering the term having been provided for by the lease, the act of the defendants was a sufficient determination thereof ; (2) [in this reversing the judgment of FERGUSON, J.], that the consideration for the lease had not failed, so as to bring it within the class of cases where the subject matter could be treated as non-existent, and by the true construction of the lease the plaintiff was entitled to be paid quarterly for the quantity of ore agreed to be got out; that the defendants were not entitled to recover back any of the rents paid, and that the lessor was entitled to judgment for such rent as accrued due between the 1st of June and the giving of the notice of surrender.

THIS was an action instituted by Jane Alexander Wallbridge against Earnest Gaujot, Hannah Francis Stewart and Philip R. Palmer, the statement of claim in which, filed 17th February, 1885, alleged that the defendants by indenture of 30th December, 1882, agreed with the plaintiff to dig up, mine, and carry away in each year during the term of ten years, therein mentioned, a quantity of iron ore not less than 2,000 tons for the first year, and not less than 5,000 tons for each subsequent year of the said term, and to pay a rent or royalty of $1.00 per ton therefor. And they further covenanted to pay such rent or royalty upon the quantity agreed to be taken out, and if the rent or royalty so paid in any quarter should exceed the quantity actually taken out, such excess should be applied towards payment of the first quarter thereafter in which more than the said quantity should be taken ; and it further alleged that the defendants had not paid the two quarters rent due 1st September and December, 1884, and asked judgment therefor and costs.

The defendants, by their statement of defence, set out the lease verbatim, and alleged that the plaintiff. represented herself to be the owner of an iron mine on the lands in the lease mentioned, and the defendants believing the same entered into the said lease, which contained a proviso for determining the same, as set out in the judgment of the Court, *infra*. That afterwards the defendants sunk a shaft and expended a large sum of money in opening and developing the said mine, and soon exhausted the iron ore, and found the said mine to be a failure. That they obtained only 306 tons of ore, but paid much larger sums, believing that there was merchantable ore in the mine, but finding there was no more they abandoned the same, and told the plaintiff they were prepared to surrender the lease. The plaintiff refused to accept a surrender, and asked for the report of an expert, which was procured and a copy served on plaintiff, and the defendants alleged that the consideration for the lease wholly failed.

And by way of counter-claim they asked to have the lease cancelled, and the covenants therein rescinded, and the money paid in excess of the royalty upon 306 tons repaid ; and they alleged that the defendants Gaujot and Stewart had sold their interest to the defendant Palmer.

By an order made by the local Master at Belleville on the 23rd of February, 1885, under the provisions of Rule 105, O. J. A., one William Coe was added as a third party to the action on the application of the defendants, and he, by way of defence, set up that by reason of the failure of ore the lease was bad from the beginning, but if not so, it was determined before action commenced; and claimed that he was improperly added.

The plaintiff by her reply to the counter-claim denied the right of all or any of the defendants to have the lease cancelled.

The action came on for trial before Ferguson, J., at Belleville, on the 18th November, 1885, who after reserving judgment, found in favor of the defendants; dismissed the action, with costs, and ordered the plaintiff to repay to the defendants all moneys paid prior to the action in excess of $306, being the amount of royalties payable on the 306 tons of ore admitted by the defendants to have been taken from the mine.

From this judgment the plaintiff appealed, and the appeal came on to be heard before this Court on the 8th of March, 1887.*

Robinson, Q. C., and *Dickson*, Q. C., for the appellant. The plain meaning and the true construction of the language used in the instrument in question shews that the parties to it intended that the lessees should pay a minimum rent of $2,000 for the first year and, $5,000 for every other year of the term thereby created, in equal quarterly payments, and the conduct of the lessees after the execution of the lease evidences this intention. The terms of the covenant are to pay quarterly for the quantity of iron ore "agreed" to be taken out, not on the quantity actually mined and got out. The plaintiff's contention is that she is entitled to the two quarters of rent sued for whether the mine had become exhausted or not, because the lessees did not pretend or seek to determine the lease until the commencement of the last quarter for which rent is claimed; and the determination could not defeat the rent accruing for the then current quarter, but in any event the lessor must be entitled to an apportionment of rent for that quarter: and it is insisted that what is here shewn to

*PRESENT – HAGARTY, C.J.O., BURTON, PATTERSON, and OSLER, JJ.A·

have been done by the defendants was not such an unequivocal act as effected a determination of the lease, which,
being an option given or reserved to the lessees, could only
be validly exercised by writing: *Doe dem. Burr* v. *Davison*, 8 U. C. R. 185. The proviso in the lease gives to the
lessees the right to determine the lease, and, in effect, establishes that there was at the time of the execution of that
instrument a mine; the lessor, however, did not warrant
that there was or that it would continue to exist, and the
lessees therein provided against the contingency of its
becoming exhausted. The money which has been paid from
time to time by the defendants was paid as rent under the
lease, and to enable them to continue the term created by
it, and the use, possession, and enjoyment of the demised
premises, so that under no circumstances can this be
recovered back. *Bridges* v. *Potts*, 17 C. B. N. S. 314;
Clifford v. *Watts*, L. R. 5 C. P. 577; *Bute* v. *Thompson*, 13
M. & W. 487; *Bishop* v. *Goodwin*, 14 M. & W. 260; *Jefferys*
v. *Fairs*, 4 Ch. D. 448, were cited.

J Bell, Q. C., *W. Cassels*, Q. C., and *Burdette*, for the
respondents. The appellant here admits the facts as found
by the learned Judge at the trial, who found, as the facts
really are, that at the time of the execution of the lease,
there was no minable ore upon the lands and premises
embraced in the lease.

According to the true construction of this instrument,
there was in reality no dead rent or minimum rent payable,
the payment being in the nature of a royalty, payable out
of the iron stone or ore to be mined and raised from the
land and mine.

Viewed in any light the language here used must
be taken to mean that the plaintiff professed to lease
a mine, from which the lessees would be able to dig up and
mine and carry away in each and every year during the
existence of the lease a quantity of not less than 2,000 tons
of iron ore in the first year, and a quantity not less than
5,000 tons a year in every subsequent year of the term;
and the lessees were only bound to pay the sum of $1 per

gross ton for every ton mined and raised from the land and mine.

It was never contemplated or agreed by the defendants that a rent should be paid unless there was iron ore upon the premises out of which such rent or royalty could be paid, and the respondents contend that it having been ascertained as a fact that there was no minable ore upon the demised lands at the date of the lease, the royalty payable never accrued, and that the learned Judge was correct in ordering the plaintiff to refund the moneys paid to her by mistake. There was, in fact, a failure of consideration, and the respondents are entitled to have the amount repaid; they having been so paid under a mistake of fact.

Featherstone v. *Van Allen*, 12 A. R. 133; *Durrant* v. *Ecclesiastical Commissioners* 6 Q. B. D. 234; *Earl of Beauchamp* v. *Winn*, L. R. 6 H. L. 234; *Daniell* v. *Sinclair*, 6 App. Cas. 181; *Gowan* v. *Christie*, L. R. 2 Sc. App. 273; *Griffiths* v. *Rigby*, 1 H. & N. 237; *Smith* v. *Morris*, 2 Bro. C. C. 311; *Scioto Fire Brick Co.* v. *Pond*, 38 Ohio State 68; *Cooke* v. *Andrews*, 36 Ohio State 178; *Reed* v. *Beck*, 23 North Western Reporter 159, were referred to.

September 6, 1887. The judgment of the Court was delivered by

HAGARTY, C. J. O.—It was not seriously contested before us that the plaintiff could deny that the defendants had the right to determine the lease under the clause to that effect. But it was denied that it had been legally determined until the execution of a proper surrender.

If the learned Judge was right in holding that it was legally determined in September, 1884, then only one quarter, being that due on September 1st, was claimable by the plaintiff. If not determined till January by written surrender then a second quarter would be claimable, due 1st December, 1884.

I think the learned Judge was right in holding that in order to exercise this right to determine the lease it was not necessary to execute a formal instrument of surrender, but that it could be done by an unequivocal act or declaration if the lessees communicated to the lessor. A well drawn lease with such a power usually prescribes how it may be exercised, generally by a notice in writing to be given at a named time. Here the lease provides that on the happening of named events the lessees " shall be at liberty to determine this lease." No method of determining is stated, and I do not see how we can add to the clause that it must be determined by deed or notice in writing. It is not correct to apply the maxim " naturale est quidlibet dissolvi eo modo quo ligatur." *Broom*, 577. It is the exercise of a power or right created by the deed.

The lessees have the right to determine. Their election to determine to be effectual must be absolute, irrevocable and final. *Com. Dig.*, Election, c. 2 : " It shall be made by express words or by act." *Ib.* ch. 1, cited in *Clough* v. *London and North-Western R. W. Co.*, L. R. 7 Ex. 26, and in *Morrison* v. *Universal Marine Insurance Co.*, L. R. 8 Ex. 197 ; *Jones* v. *Carter*, 15 M. & W. 718.

The learned Judge says, at p. 353 : " The plaintiff in her examination said : ' I was led to suppose from their visits that they wanted to surrender the lease.' From all the evidence on this subject I am of the opinion that what was done by Palmer and Coe who were then the parties interested in the contract, Palmer being one of the parties to it, was of an unequivocal character, and sufficient as the consummation of their election to determine the agreement or lease, and that the getting of the opinion of the expert and giving it to the plaintiff was done merely for the purpose of satisfying her and probably saving further trouble. I do not think that the evidence shews that there was any suspension of the election or notice of election until the opinion of the expert should be obtained, or that the election should depend at all upon the character of the opinion when obtained. Gaujot and Stewart had assigned their interests to Palmer, and Palmer had transferred a half interest in the contract to Coe, and I think this was a good election to determine the lease. As before stated, I think there was the right to determine it, and I am of the opinion that the lease was determined at the time of this interview. The date of the interview is left in doubt, but I cannot on the evidence place it later than some time in September, 1884. The burden of proof in respect of this date was upon the defendants, and as against them I think it must be placed after the first day of September, 1884, when, according to the terms of payment mentioned in the contract, one of the quarter's rent or royalty would have accrued due, but before the first day of December, 1884, when the other quarter sued for would fall due."

I must confess that if I had to form my opinion wholly from a perusal of the evidence I would have found some difficulty in arriving at the conclusion that there was a final and absolute election then expressed to determine the lease. The accounts given of the interviews, getting the experts' report, and the vacillating course pursued afterwards as to executing a formal surrender would cause me to hesitate. But I hardly feel justified in refusing to accept the finding of the trial Judge.

Accepting this finding we have next to consider an important point in the case, viz., the true meaning of the contract. The learned Judge holds that the real meaning of the parties was, that the royalty should be paid upon ore that had an existence in the premises and could be taken by defendants, and that defendants did not covenant to pay any rent absolutely unless there was ore available to pay the same at the rate per ton specified. It has been frequently said that in all these mining bargains each party takes upon himself certain risks.

In *Mellers* v. *Duke of Devonshire*, 16 Beav. 252, the Master of the Rolls says : " That the lease was granted in ignorance of the amount of coal under the surface there can be no doubt, but such is the case in all mining leases ; it is always a speculation; both the lessor and the lessee are equally ignorant of the amount of coal which may be gotten, and they provide for these circumstances."

The learned Judge here says, p. 348 : " There is no doubt that at the time of the execution of the lease all believed that there was a valuable mine on the property in question."

The original lessees had sunk a shaft, and had the fullest opportunity of satisfying themselves before the execution of the lease.   There is no pretence whatever for supposing that as between lessor and lessee there was any misrepresentation whatever.

The demise is of "all the mines of ores of iron and iron stone as well opened as not opened which can, shall, or may be wrought, dug, found out, or discovered within ten acres," &c.   Yielding and paying &c., $1 per gross ton &c., of the said iron stone or ore for every ton mined and raised from the land and mine, payable quarterly on the 1st days of March, June, September, and December in each year.   Then the lessees covenant to dig up &c., not less than 2000 tons the first year and not less than 5000 tons in every subsequent year, and "pay quarterly the sum of $1 per ton for the quantity agreed to be taken during each year."   *   *   And the said party of the second part covenant and agree to and with the party of the first part that they will pay the said quarter's rent or royalty upon the said quantity, quarterly in each year, and if the same shall then exceed the quantity actually taken, such excess shall be applied towards payment of the first quarter thereafter in which more than the said quantity shall be taken. Provided, that if the rent or royalty hereby reserved shall be behind, in arrear, or unpaid for two quarters, then the lessor may at her election then, or at any time before actual payment, declare the lease void and the term hereby created, at an end and the term shall cease and be determined.

Provided also, that if the iron ore or iron stone shall be exhausted, and not to be found or obtained there by proper and reasonable effort in paying quantities, then the party of the second part shall be at liberty to determine this lease."

Some 306 tons have been raised, and the lessees appear to have paid rent on the quarter days down to 1st June, 1884.   The quarter due on the 1st September, is unpaid. The quarter claimed due 1st December, cannot be recovered if the lease was determined in September, 1884.

It was urged before us in argument that there was no "mine" in the land demised.   The learned Judge does not so find.   I do not see how this can be said.   It may have been a mine, although a very poor one.   All the witnesses agree that there was a "vein," or "string," or "stock" from the adjacent Wallbridge mine running into this land.   Some call it a wedge shaped mass from that mine.

Professor Chapman, after describing this "string" or
wedge shaped mass, says : "Well, of course it is a mine
because it has a shaft and three drifts in it, but at the
same time it is a mine that would not pay for working." See his description of the generally poor ore and
"nobs or bunches of clear ore mixed with a great deal of
earthy matter,"* &c.

MacSwinney on Mines &c., p. 1, *et seq.*, gives all the definitions in legal and other dictionaries of "mine," "vein,"
"seam," &c. He says : "Vein and seam appear to be
convertible expressions." If there are a particular number of veins within or under a piece of land there
are precisely the same number of mines occupying
the same areas. In this sense the primary meaning
of mine is vein. Consistently, however, with this, each
word seems to have a distinct meaning of its own.
In strictness a mine is not, it would seem, properly
so called until it is opened. It is at best but a vein
(of coals), citing Sir George Jessel, in *Lord Abinger* v.
Ashton, L. R. 17 Eq. 358 : "The word mine is clearly
used in its primary sense of vein."

MacSwinney, p. 3 : "That portion of a vein which is
confined within the ambit of a particular property is, in
common parlance, and may with propriety be called a mine.
It is so considered for rating purposes."

I am of opinion that in the case before us there was an
existing "mine."

If we had to judge of the rights of the parties as a new
case arising for the first time, I cannot but think that we
should regard it as a venture or risk undertaken by the
tenants to pay the specified quarterly rent, with the right and
privilege of fully protecting themselves by determining
the lease if they could not work the mine at a profit, or
the ore becoming exhausted.

---

* The witness further stated : "It runs in very poor, or if you can call
it so, the stuff is really indeed only fit for lining puddling furnaces or for
material ; of course there are nobs and bunches of clean ore mixed with a
great deal of earthy matter and surrounded by this lying stuff, and in
these bunches in some places perhaps there would be on an average a foot
to fifteen inches clean ore there : perhaps on an average three feet bunches
of ore and rock intermingled with earth and stuff."

The defendants insist that all these covenants are based upon the understanding that iron ore existed in the mine fully to answer the terms of the contract, and that its non-existence is a full defence.

The judgment appealed from adopts that argument as sound.

The tendency of modern decision seems clearly to indicate that when two persons contract for the doing of certain specified acts or things in respect of a subject matter assumed in good faith by both as existing, and it turns out in fact to be non-existent, that the contracts in respect of it are at an end or cannot be enforced.

It is therefore insisted here that all the contracts for payment fail as soon as the iron ore fails, or, in other words, that no more iron ore is to be paid for than can be found, by reasonable effort.

But in this bargain it is evident that both parties contemplated that the ore might be exhausted, or could not be found in paying quantities. In such event they did not provide for the ceasing of the payments or their reduction in proportion to the quantity of ore to be raised by reasonable exertions, but the sole remedy provided is to determine the tenancy. Therefore the possible failure of the subject matter was a thing not overlooked, but was a matter deliberately provided for and a protection specially inserted for the lessees.

Again, if the reddendum be strictly adhered to that the $1 per ton was only payable for every ton mined and raised why, it may be asked, are the quarterly payments fixed absolutely at that rate for the mininum quantity agreed to be raised each year, followed by the peculiar provisions that if the fixed quarterly payment shall exceed the quantity actually taken, (from the mine) the excess should be applied to payment of the next quarter in which more than the quantity should be taken?

Here seems to be a direct provision for the absolute sum payable for the quarter happening to be more than the quantity raised. This might be carried on for several

quarters, and seems to me to be inconsistent with any
construction of the bargain, except the fixed payment
of the stipulated sum per quarter.

Thus, we find the lessor may declare the lease void if the
rent or royalty be in arrear for two quarters. If the lessees
had been neglecting to raise the stipulated quantities, the
two quarters' rent in arrear would for the purposes of this
forfeiture clause be surely the full sum stipulated as quarterly payments. The lessees could hardly be allowed to
resist the avoidance of the lease because they had failed to
raise the stipulated quantity. The right of avoidance is
not given for breach of the covenant to raise the minimum
quantity, but for non-payment of two quarters' rent. The
contract is express to pay quarterly for the quantity agreed
to be raised, not to pay if raised.

I have not seen any case so near in its facts to the present as to be an authoritative guide. *Lord Clifford* v. *Watts*,
L. R. 5 C. P. 577 seems to be the nearest, but, as I think,
differing substantially in the language of the demise. The
demise is of mines, veins, &c., of clay, as well pipe as potter's
clay under certain lands. Reddendum to Lord Clifford in
respect of all pipe and potter's clays being to be dug or
obtained, &c. under said lands, the sum of 2s. 6d. per ton,
and for other clay being to be dug, &c., 6d. per ton weight.
Covenant by lessee to pay the several dues, &c., so respectively made payable as aforesaid, free and clear of taxes,
&c.   *   *   Also that lessee shall and will dig and procure
to be dug and removed from the lands, in pursuance of the
demise, an aggregate amount of not less than 1,000 tons,
nor a larger quantity than 2,000 tons of pipe or potter's
clay in each and every year of the term hereby granted :
then a clause for re-entry in default of payment of the 2s.
6d. and 6d. per ton of all merchantable clay got from the
lands.

The action was for not making trials for clay according
to covenant. 2nd. That the defendant did not dig each year
an amount not less than 1,000 tons. Defence to last
breach on equitable grounds, that there was not at demise

or at any time since, 1,000 tons within the meaning of the
covenant; that performance was impossible, but such impossibility was unknown to defendant, &c.

On demurrer the plea was held a good answer. The
authorities are reviewed by Willes, J. He minutely criticises the language of the demise. He notices that there is
no covenant to pay any dead or minimum rent, or any
rent in event of no clay being raised, or not being there to
be raised, nor any provision for putting an end to the
term in case the clay should be exhausted—a point also
urged by the counsel in argument. The learned Judge
then proceeds :

" The result to my mind is, that the covenant upon which
this breach is assigned is one of a series of subsidiary covenants introduced for the purpose of carrying out the substantial object and intention of the parties, viz.: that Watts
should have the right during the term of working out all
the clay under the land, and pay for it at the price specified
per ton, and this subsidiary covenant deals with the rate
at which the clay is to be worked out. The bare statement
of the provision of the deed leads me to the conclusion that
the tenant never intended to warrant that there was clay
upon the land, and that neither party contemplated that
he should in the event of no clay being found there at all
events pay a minimum fixed rent during the term. It is
a bare stipulation as to the rate of payment for the clay
that should be raised. It turned out that there was no
clay of the description mentioned in the deed. The covenant therefore became inapplicable and has not been broken."

It is clear that if the action in *Clifford* v. *Watts* had
been, as here, for non-payment of rent based on the minimum
quantity to be raised, it would also have failed.

The differences between *Clifford* v. *Watts* and our case
are marked. 1st. It is a claim for not raising the contracted quantity. 2nd. There is no covenant to pay
except for clay actually raised. 3rd. There is no provision
as here, for payment in a quarter of rent beyond the
quantity actually raised. 4th. There is no proviso, as here,
determining the lease if clay be exhausted or working thereof unprofitable. These are formidable differences. The dif-

ferences in the subject matter of the actions, the first being
for not raising a quantity admitted by the demurrer to be
non-existent, the present suit being for the rent on the
stipulated quantity. I consider the law views two such
claims on different principles.

A case before Page Wood, V.C., (*Ridgway* v. *Sneyd*, 1854,
Kay, 632) is very instructive on this point. He points out
the difference between the two cases, and his remarks on
the risks undertaken by lessees in mining cases are instructive. He comments largely on *Phillips* v. *Jones*, 9 Sim.
521, where the Vice-Chancellor speaks of the case where
the Court of Equity might relieve against a covenant to
continue working though the coal had been exhausted, and
that in such case the lessee could relieve himself under a
clause enabling him to determine the lease.

Gowan v. *Christie*, L.R. 2 Sc. Ap. p. 273, (1873), was chiefly
on Scotch law taken from the civil law. But there are valuable opinions expressed on the common law. It was an action
by a lessee to be released from a mining lease because
there was no mineral there capable of being worked at a
profit. It was a demise of all minerals. Lord Selborne
says: "Lord Stair, the authority on the law of Scotland
chiefly relied on, as it seems to me lays down the true
principle in the most unequivocal terms. He says that
there is peril or risk undertaken by the lessee; that he is
at the risk of the quantity and the value of the subject
matter, but he is not at the risk of the being or existence
of it." * * He notices that it is very common with parties in mining leases to contract that the tenant shall not be
obliged to go on working when he cannot work at a profit :
that there was nothing to that effect in the lease before
them but a clause that he could throw up the lease at 3,
7, or 14 years.

Lord Selborne says that such a provision was wholly
irreconcilable with the whole principle of appellants' argument, because if the lease was vitiated from the beginning
and liable to reduction, it must have been on grounds
wholly independent of the exercise of the option of throwing it up. "I had great difficulty in understanding

whether it was seriously meant to be contended that because the lessee. had made no profit he would not only have a right to throw it up, but he would also have a right to a repetition [or repayment] of the rent he had paid." He adds: "That would be utterly inconsistent with the whole intent and purpose of the express contract between the parties."

Lord Chelmsford says it is most reasonable to hold that when a special contract like this is entered into (that is, as to throwing up the lease,) it is impossible to say that the tenant can be fairly and reasonably entitled to reduce the lease, even supposing circumstances existed which without a contract would have entitled him to do so.

Lord Colonsay points out that " he had protected himself as if he had no basis of common law to rely on " by reserving this right to break the lease.

Lord Cairns points out that it is a common covenant in mining leases that the lessee may give up in certain cases. He does not think that there is any common law right applicable to the case, but that if there were he does not see why it might not co-exist with a lease providing for power to break. He says he considers "these provisions are to be regarded as proof that it never was imagined by those who entered into it that there was any such common law right, because if there were such a common law right these provisions, to a great extent at all- events, would have been unnecessary."

The " breaks " allowed in the lease were to give up absolutely, not apparently for any named reason.

In applying this case to that before us we must remember that in the Court below the lease seems to be in effect treated as subject to "reduction ab initio " and the plaintiff directed to refund the rents received, less the value of the ore actually raised and one quarter's rent which was paid, as alleged, with full knowledge of the failure of the iron ore.

I am unable to reconcile the decision on this branch of the case with the views expressed in *Gowan* v. *Christie* and other cases.

60—VOL XIV A.R.

There was no misrepresentation here, there was some ore raised and sold ; there is more ore there but it is proved neither to be workable at a profit nor to exist in sufficient quantities to meet the covenants. Therefore the lessee has the admitted right to determine the lease and he has exercised that right.

But I am wholly unable to understand the principle on which it has been held that he can recover back the moneys voluntarily paid as rent. To support this it can only be on the ground of the whole failure of the demise, on the ground of the non-existence of the subject matter.

But so far from it not being a matter contemplated by the parties, we find the express agreement providing for the contingency of exhaustion or profitless working.

I cannot agree that any of the moneys paid can be recovered back, as money paid under a mutual mistake of fact. The facts were equally known to both parties, each had the same amount of knowledge as to the existence or non-existence of iron ore, or as to its probable quantity and extent. No fact was suppressed or concealed. The parties stood on equal ground as to knowledge or means of knowledge.

If the defendants mistook their legal right and paid under their covenant each quarter based on the stipulated minimum quantity to be raised. this is not a mistake of fact but of legal obligation and construction.

The learned Judge below cites three cases as shewing that equity will relieve against a mistake in law. One is *Earl Beauchamp* v. *Winn*, L. R. 6 H. L 223 ; *Daniell* v. *Sinclair*, 6 App. Cas. 181 ; *Durrant* v. *Ecclesiastical Commissioners*, 6 Q. B. D. 234.

The last is the only one to recover back money paid, and it was paid solely on a mistake of fact, no question about mistake in law.

The case of Lord Beauchamp, was not to recover back money, but to obtain relief on a contract for exchange of property on the ground of mutual mistake as to each other's rights.

Daniell v. *Sinclair*, was a New Zealand Appeal as to how the account should be taken on a mortgage ; no money appears to have been paid, but an account had been settled between the parties on the footing of compound interest, with half-yearly rests, both parties wrongly understanding that the mortgage deed required the same. It was held such account might be re-opened. There was no express agreement shewn, nothing more than "a general acquiescence on the part of the plaintiff in the defendant's mode of stating the account between them." It was held that the plaintiff was not concluded by this.

Sir R. Collier says: "In equity the line between mistakes in law and mistakes in fact has not been so clearly and sharply drawn," citing *Beauchamp* v. *Winn*, and such cases as *Cooper* v. *Phibbs*, L. R. 2 H. L. 149. But *Rogers* v. *Ingham*, 3 Ch. Div. 351, is very clear.

James, L. J., says: "No authority whatever has been cited in support of the proposition that an action for money had and received would lie against a person who has received money from another with perfect knowledge of all the facts common to both, merely because it was said that the claim to the money was not well founded in law * * the law on the subject was exactly the same in the old Courts of Chancery as in the old Courts of Common Law. There were no more equities affecting the conscience of the persons receiving the money in the one Court than in the other Court, for the action for money had and received, proceeded upon equitable considerations * * relief has never been given in the case of a simple money demand by one person against another, there being between these two persons no fiduciary relation whatever, and no equity to supervene by reason of the conduct of either of the parties."

Mellish, L. J., is equally emphatic. The whole case is very instructive on the general question. The cases are noted in notes to *Marriot* v. *Hampton*, American ed. of Sm. L. C. of 1885, at p. 434, vol 2 part 1.

In conclusion, I am of opinion that there is no case made out for declaring the consideration for the lease to have failed so as to bring it within the class of cases where the subject matter could be treated as non-existent. It is as is laid down in *Gowan* v. *Christie*, the case of "a peril or risk undertaken by the lessee of the quantity and the value of the subject matter, but he is not at the risk of the being or existence of it." There was iron ore raised under the lease and there is ore there still, but not worth working.

In that view it is impossible, as I think, to treat it as void or not binding because there was no existing subject matter. The risk that he took upon himself as to quantity and value he fully protected himself against by the clause for avoiding it on the contingency as to exhaustion or unprofitableness.

Had he filed a bill to be relieved he would be told that the Court would not interfere as he had the remedy in his own hands. I think him bound to pay the rent on the quantity contracted to be raised. That there is no equity entitling him to a refund of any of the payments. That the appeal must be allowed and a decree made for plaintiff's recovering the quarter due on September 1st, being the last due before determination, as found by the learned Judge, and the counter-claim to be disallowed.

I refer to some of the cases on the subject: *Strelley* v. *Pearson*, 15 Ch. D. 113; *Lord Bute* v. *Thompson*, 13 M. & W. 487; *Bishop* v. *Goodwin*, 14 M. & W. 260; *Brydges* v. *Cox*, 17 C. B. N. S. 332; *Jeffreys* v. *Fairs*, 4 Ch. D. 234; *Jarvis* v. *Tomlinson*, 1 H & N. 195.

Appeal allowed, with costs.

[This case has been carried to the Supreme Court.]

MINNIE GRAHAM v. THOMAS E. O'CALLAGHAN.

AND

MARGARET CELESTINE RUSSELL v. THOMAS E. O'CALLAGHAN.

Replevin—Value of goods lost or eloigned—Retaining possession of goods—
Damages—Detinet—Detinuit.

'The practice, generally, as to damages in actions of replevin is that where
the goods are promptly returned, only sufficient will be given to cover
the expense of preparing the replevin bond, but where the party distraining acts in a manner unnecessarily harsh or oppressive, substantial
damages may be recovered.   And where the sheriff was unable to
replevy some of the articles mentioned in the writ, by reason of their
having been lost or eloigned by the defendant, the plaintiff was held
entitled to recover their value as damages; the count being in the
detinet as well as in the detinuit..

THESE were two actions of replevin brought by the
·respective plaintiffs against the defendant for unlawfully
·seizing and detaining their trunks containing their clothing and a few articles of jewellery, valued respectively at
:$62 and $48. It appeared that the plaintiffs had been
residing in the house of the defendant, the former for
about two years and a half, the latter for about 17 years,
performing, as far as they could, all the domestic duties,
and for some two or three years nursing and caring for the
invalid mother of the defendant.

The actions came on for trial before the Judge of the
County Court of Middlesex, and a jury, on the 8th of Jan-
·uary, 1887.

The facts giving rise to the litigation are thus stated in
the judgment of the County Judge when disposing of the
application to set aside the verdict of $200 in each case,
that is, $138 for the detention of the clothing and $62 for
the loss of the jewellery caused by the act of the defendant,
in the first case, and $152 and $48 in the second case.

"It appears that the plaintiff, who is twenty-five years of age, had
lived with the defendant, and his mother, as a member of their family for
seventeen years. In the month of September last some misunderstanding
had occurred between the plaintiff and defendant, owing to the unwilling-

ness of the former to acknowledge the validity of a subsequent will of the mother by which a legacy to the plaintiff was much reduced in amount.

"On the 16th September last it appears that Mr. Frank O'Callaghan, who acted on behalf of the defendant, ordered the plaintiff and Miss Graham, who also resided in the same house, to leave. Upon receiving this order the plaintiff says that she and Miss Graham packed up their things in trunks ready for removal. They, however, did not leave on that day, as it was stormy, and on the following morning they went out to procure legal advice, and on their return to the house they found the outer door locked in such a manner that their accustomed mode of entry by a latch key was impracticable. So the goods of the plaintiff, as well as those of Miss Graham, remained in the house of defendant, and for these goods this suit of replevin and that of Miss Graham were instituted.

"It is very apparent that at this time a very angry feeling existed between the plaintiff and the defendant and his brother Frank, who appears to have been an active agent of the defendant, and this feeling, no doubt, prevented any personal approach between the parties in view of an amicable arrangement. The plaintiff and Miss Graham then took refuge in the house of Mrs. Duff, who recommended them to employ Mr. Stewart, a solicitor practising at Glencoe. Mr. Stewart, being instructed, had an interview with the defendant and his brother, which resulted in his demanding the goods ineffectually. It seems that the defendant was under the impression that the plaintiff and Miss Graham had removed already or secreted articles which did not belong to them, and this impression seems to have actuated the defendant throughout. Some jewellery which belonged to the plaintiff was taken out of one of the trunks and left on a bed by Mr. Frank O'Callaghan. This jewellery has never been recovered by the plaintiff. Two or three days after the 17th September the goods were taken by the defendant or his brother Frank to Hamilton ; ultimately the articles, except the jewellery, were brought to London and replevied to the plaintiff.

"The evidence * * * is sufficient to shew that the principal question discussed was whether the goods claimed by the plaintiff really belonged to her ; upon this question the jury have found in the affirmative, and they have also found that the plaintiff did not intermix any goods of the defendant with her own. Also that the defendant took the plaintiff's jewellery, which they value at $48, and the damages for the taking and detention of the goods they have assessed at $152, making their verdict $200. * * *

"Now, had he the right to remove all these articles to Hamilton, leaving the plaintiff without her necessary wearing apparel for three weeks, with the exception of what she wore at the time ?

"On this application it is urged that goods of the defendant had been intermixed with goods of the plaintiff in the trunks, and therefore the defendant was justified in holding them. Whether he would or not it is unnecessary to consider ; for the jury found that there was no such intermixture, and I see no sufficient reason for the rejection of their finding. * * *

"Mr. Mills, for the defendant, speaks of a bailment ; but there is here no semblance of a contract on which to found a bailment.   He also urges that, primâ facie, the goods belonged to the defendant, as they were in his possession.   But his possession was wrongful, according to the finding of the jury.   *   *   *

" In this case the defendant or his agent, with his authority, took this jewellery out of the plaintiff's trunk and left it on a bed, and it has been lost to the plaintiff.   I do not see how the defendant can escape responsibility for the loss.

"There was much in this case to excite the commiseration of the jury. The plaintiff being a delicate and interesting young person and, moreover at one period of her cross-examination, being in a fainting condition, was sure to create a powerful sympathy on the part of the jury, which was heightened by the impressive address of her counsel as he dwelt upon the harsh conduct of the defendant in suddenly without notice locking her out, and, as her counsel expressed it, turning her out in the street without a stitch of clothing except that which she then wore, and putting her to the pain and obligation of having to entreat the loan of suitable articles from a neighbour.   All this, I am afraid, inflamed the minds of the jury, and thereby led them to give damages beyond what is reasonable.   *   *

" According to *Mayne* on Damages, 3rd ed. 364 : 'The manner in which the property is seized may be the source of substantial damages in addition to any which may be given in respect of the detention,' and reference is made to *Brewer* v. *Drewe*, 11 M. & W. 625 ; and at page 390 Mr. Mayne says : 'In actions of trespass where there is no special damage, the jury are not limited to the actual injury inflicted, but may take all the circumstances in consideration.'

"I think the jury allowed their feeling of sympathy to sway their minds unduly : Instead of estimating the damages, irrespective of the jewellery, at $152 ; I think $100 is nearer to what is reasonable, thus making the whole amount of damages $148 instead of $200.   If the plaintiff shall elect within a week to reduce the verdict to the sum of $148 with costs, this application will be dismissed, otherwise a new trial, without costs."

Counsel for the plaintiff elected to reduce the verdict in the manner suggested by the learned Judge, and the application was dismissed, with costs.

In the firstly mentioned case the County Judge reduced the damages to $100 also, making the amount $162, for which judgment should be entered.

From these judgments the defendant appealed, and the appeal came on for hearing on the 13th September, 1887.*

* *Present.*—HAGARTY, C. J. O., PATTERSON and OSLER, JJ.A.

Moss, Q.C., for the appellant.

R. M. Meredith for the respondents.

September 29, 1887. HAGARTY, C.J.O.—It seems clear, on the authorities, that a recovery in replevin for personal chattels is a bar to any further proceedings for damages in respect of the taking or detention, and also that substantial damages may be recovered in replevin.

The case of *Gibbs* v. *Crookshank*, L. R. 8 C. P. 454, very fully discusses and states the law. Where the goods are, as is generally the case, promptly recovered, the practice was to give as damages the supposed expense of preparing the replevin bond. But where the plaintiff is unlawfully deprived of the use of the goods for a considerable time and is damaged thereby, there seems to be no reason whatever to prevent damages being recovered, See also *Deal* v. *Potter*, 26 U. C. R. 578 ; *Lewis* v. *Teale*, 32 U. C. R. 108.

We have examined the evidence in these cases. We cannot say that there was not evidence on which reasonable men might not properly have found verdicts for the plaintiffs. The facts sworn to would naturally weigh heavily against the defendant, and it is highly improbable that another jury would find differently.

The learned Judge below has reduced the damages in each case to $100. We do not see any well founded complaint against the manner in which the cases have been dealt with by his Honor.

If the objection that the damages were excessive were open to the defendant on this appeal, we cannot see how we could give effect to it.

The defendant's proceedings, to say the least of them, were conducted in a very harsh and oppressive manner, and it is not easy to see how we could hold that $100 damages would be so excessive as to warrant interference.

OSLER, J.A.—I think the appeal in each case should be dismissed. I see no reason to interfere with the privilege of the jury on the questions submitted to them, and that disposes of the objection that the plaintiffs had taken goods of the defendant and intermixed them with their own, so that replevin would not lie 'until they had separated and distinguished them, and made a demand for the precise articles in the trunks which belonged to them.

Two points were made on the question of damages; the first that the plaintiffs have recovered the value of certain articles of jewellery which the sheriff was commanded to replevy but which he was unable to find ; and second, that special damages were awarded for the trespass and detention by the defendant of those goods which were replevied. As to the first, it is abundantly clear from authority that if the sheriff is unable to replevy the articles mentioned in the writ in consequence of their having been lost or eloigned by the defendant, the plaintiff is not obliged to proceed upon a capias in withernam, but may recover the value of the goods as damages, where, as in this case, the count in replevin is in the detinct as well as in the detinuit : *Gibbs* v. *Cruickshank*, L. R. 8 C. P. 454 ; *Deal* v. *Potter*, 26 U. C. R. 575 ; *Lewis* v. *Teale*, 32 U. C. R. 108.

From the same authority it is also to be seen that special damages are recoverable for the trespass to the goods actually replevied, and that the plaintiff is not confined to nominal damages usually given for the costs of the replevin bond.

There were certainly in these cases circumstances to warrant the jury in giving special damages, and if they erred in being too liberal their error has been corrected in the Court below. In strictness I do not think these objections were open to the defendants as they were not taken at the trial, or in the Court below, on the order nisi. The motion was on the ground that the damages were excessive, but that is not the point. The objection now urged on the argument is that the learned judge misdirected the jury as to the mode of assessing the damages, or the nature of the damages which the plaintiffs were entitled to recover. But the charge was not objected to on this ground, nor, for the reasons given, do I think it was open to objection. The judgment in each case should therefore be affirmed.

PATTERSON, J. A., concurred.

Appeal dismissed, with costs.

FORSE v. SOVEREEN.

Landlord and tenant—Purchase for value without notice—Reformation of lease—Termination of tenancy by intervention of mortgagee.

M. being possessed of certain lands subject to a mortgagee, made a lease thereof for a term of years to the plaintiff, which provided, amongst other things, that $15 should be expended in the first year of the term in procuring manure for the purposes of the farm. Afterwards he created a mortgage in favour of the defendant, and assigned to him this lease as collateral security. The defendant distrained for rent claimed to be due, and plaintiff replevied the goods seized, claiming there was no rent due ; and proved the payment of certain moneys to the first mortgagee, and claimed also credit for $15 a year in respect of manure furnished and expended in each year on the premises, which, at the trial, was proved to have been the true agreement between the landlord and tenant, though not so expressed in the lease, and the lease was ordered to be reformed accordingly.

Held, that the lease should not have been reformed as against defendant, he being a bonâ fide purchaser for value without notice of the facts on which the plaintiff's equity rested.

Held, also, that although a new contract of tenancy may be inferred from the fact of a notice by a mortgagee to pay rent to him, and acquiescence by the tenant by payment of the rent, still as the circumstances showed that it was not intended to create such a contract, but rather that the interest being paid, the possession of the mortgagor and his tenants was to remain undisturbed, it could not be said that the plaintiff's tenancy had been put an end to by the intervention of the first mortgagee.

THIS was an appeal from the judgment of the County Court of the County of Norfolk pronounced on the 3rd of June, 1887.

The action was one of replevin and came on for trial before the county Judge without a jury, who found in favour of the plaintiff and five dollars damages. From this judgment the defendants appealed, on the grounds, amongst others : (*a*) That in an action of replevin no reformation of a deed can be ordered or decreed. (*b*) That the learned Judge was wrong in admitting parol evidence to vary the terms of the written lease produced at the trial. (*c*) That the evidence shewed that the defendant Sovereen was a bonâ fide purchaser for value, without notice of the facts upon which the Court decreed a reformation of the lease, and was therefore not affected by the equities between the plaintiff and his landlord, and consequently the lease could not be reformed as against him.

The appeal came on for hearing on the 14th and 15th days of September, 1887.*

Aylesworth, for the appellants.
W. M. Douglas, for the respondent.
The other facts appear in the judgment.

September 29' 1887. OSLER, J. A.—This is an appeal by the defendants from the judgment of the Judge of the County Court of the County of Norfolk in an action tried by him without a jury.

The statement of claim contains the usual count in replevin.

The defendants avow and make cognizance, as landlord and bailiff, for a distress for rent under a lease from one Wilson Macpherson to the plaintiff, assigned to the defendant Sovereen. To this the plaintiff replies riens en arriere.

It appeared that Macpherson, being the owner of the demised premises subject to a mortgage to one Gibson, leased them to the plaintiff by indenture dated 23rd March, 1884, for a term of five years from the 1st April, 1884, at a rent of $80 per annum, payable half yearly. On the 23rd March he made a second mortgage of the same land to the defendant Sovereen, and at the same time executed a special assignment of the lease as collateral security for payment of the mortgage. On the 17th November, 1886, the defendant distrained for $85, being, as expressed in the

Present.—HAGARTY, C.J.O., PATTERSON and OSLER, JJ.A.

warrant, " the amount of. a year and six months' rent due
on the 1st October, 1886." At the trial the plaintiff's case
was, that the rent for the whole period (which would be
$120) had been paid or discharged. He proved the pay-
ment of two sums of $65.15, and $35 to the solicitor
of the first mortgagee, and of $8.85 for taxes assessed
to, and payable by the lessor. He also claimed a
deduction of. $15 for a quantity of manure expended by
him on the demised premises under an alleged agreement
with the lessor. His difficulty, however, was that an
allowance had already been made for the manure supplied
during the first year of the tenancy, while the lease had
not been so expressed as to shew what he asserted was
the true agreement—namely, that it was to be supplied,
and the price deducted from the rent during each year
of the tenancy. Evidence was admitted in support of
this contention, and the plaintiff was allowed to amend
his pleadings by alleging that the lease had been drawn
up in its present form by mistake, claiming that it should
be rectified or reformed so as to express the real agreement, and setting up the grounds on which, in equity, on
the lease so reformed, no rent was in arrear at the time of
the distress.

The learned Judge held that the payments to the first
mortgagee should be allowed to the plaintiff as having been
made under constraint; and, upon the evidence, that the
lease ought to be reformed in accordance with the plaintiff's contention, notwithstanding that the defendant Sovereen was, as he found, a bonâ fide mortgagee and assignee
of the lease for value without notice. The plaintiff therefore
had judgment, the value of the manure expended by him
being equivalent to the balance of the rent distrained for.

The defendants appeal on the ground, inter alia, that
Sovereen, being a bonâ fide purchaser for value without
notice of the facts on which the plaintiff's equity depends,
the lease ought not to have been reformed as against him.

This objection appears to me, (apart from the further
and serious difficulty that Macpherson is not a party to

the suit) to be well taken. The learned Judge's reasons for
holding that such an equity was entitled to prevail against
a person in the defendant's position are not given, but it
was argued before us that the parties being lessee and
mortgagee, respectively, of an equity of redemption, the
defence of bonâ fide purchaser for value without notice
could not be set up by the defendant, it being inapplicable, as was contended, between persons interested in or
claiming a merely equitable estate. This, however, is an
entire misconception of the nature of the plaintiff's claim
and the defence in the present action.

It is not the case of a contest for priority between two
persons who claim merely equitable estates or interests, but
a claim for relief on the ground of an equity not dependent upon or arising out of the nature of the estate or title :
and to such a claim the plea in question, if maintained, is
a perfectly valid defence.

It is only necessary to refer to the judgment of Lord
Campbell in the important case of *Phillips* v. *Phillips*, 4
DeG. F. & J. 208, where the law on the subject is summarised. "There appear," he says, "to be three cases
in which the use of this defence is most familiar: first,
where an application is made to an auxiliary jurisdiction
of the Court by the possessor of a legal title as by an heir-
-at-law, * * and the defendant pleads that he is a bonâ
fide purchaser for value without notice. In such a case the
defence is good, and the reason given is, that as against
a purchaser for valuable consideration without notice the
Court gives no assistance—that is no assistance to the legal
title. * * The second class of cases is the ordinary one
of several purchasers or incumbrancers each claiming in
equity, and one who is later and last in time succeeds in
obtaining an outstanding legal estate, &c., the possession
of which was to be a protection to himself or an embarrassment to other claimants. He will not be deprived of
this advantage by a Court of equity. * * This is the
common doctrine of the tabula in naufragio. Thirdly,
where there are circumstances that give rise to an equity
as distinguished from an equitable estate—as, for example,
an equity to set aside a deed for fraud, or to correct it for
mistake—and the purchaser under the instrument main-

tains the plea of purchase for valuable consideration without notice, the Court will not interfere."

The case before us is clearly one of the latter class, and.
therefore, as the defendants proved their defence, the
learned Judge ought not in our opinion to have reformed
the lease in favor of the plaintiff. See also *Garrard* v.
Frankel, 30 Beav. 445 ; *Story's* Eq. Jur., 13th ed., vol. 2, pp.
151, 152.

The appeal should therefore be allowed, as there was
rent due at the time of the distress, unless the plaintiff
can succeed on another ground suggested by Mr. Douglas
on the argument, viz., that his tenancy had been put an
end to by the intervention of the first mortgagee, Gibson,
and the payment of the rent, or a portion of it, to her
solicitor.

This objection was not taken at the trial, and is not raised
on the pleadings, nor do we think that the evidence, fairly
considered, supports it.   It is, moreover, quite inconsistent
with the contention mainly relied on that the lease, as
an existing instrument, ought to be reformed.   The payment to the first mortgagee, and the payment of the
lessor's taxes were set up and allowed as a discharge
pro tanto of the rent, because made under constraint,
and in discharge of claims to which the lease was subject, and not, as regards payment of the rent, as determining the old tenancy and creating a new one between
the plaintiff and the first mortgagee.   The law on this
subject is stated by Willes, J., in the note to *Moss* v.
Gallimore, 1 Smith's Leading Cases, 4th ed., 470-
479 : "A tenant of the mortgagor, whose tenancy has
commenced since the mortgage, may, in case of an
eviction by the mortgagee, either actual or constructive
(for instance, an attornment to him under threat of eviction), dispute the mortgagor's title to either the land or
the rent (which is no more than any tenant may do upon
an eviction by title paramount); and further * * he
may, although there has been no eviction, defend an action
for rent by proof of a payment under constraint in discharge of the mortgagee's claim, which right is analogous
to that of an ordinary tenant in respect of payments on

account of rent-charges and other claims issuing out of the land."

And in *Hickman* v. *Machin*, 4 H. & N. 716, Bramwell, B., says :

"I have always understood that in a case like the present (an action for use and occupation) a defendant could only get rid of the tenancy by shewing a notice by the mortgagee and payment of rent to him, which operates either as 'determining his landlord's interest, and so is equivalent to eviction; or, if notice is given and acted upon, it may be considered an answer to the claim for rent, in the same way as the payment of any other charge would be."

Johnson v. *Jones*, 9 Ad. & E. 809, was an action of replevin, and the tenant pleaded payment of the rent to the mortgagee, who had demanded payment from him, and threatened to put the law in force in case of refusal.

Littledale, J., says: "This is not a plea of nil habui nor of eviction ; nor is it a voluntary payment to one who claims under a prior title. The plaintiff does not deny that he holds as tenant to the defendant; but he shews that the lease was made subject to a prior charge which he was compelled to pay."

In this case the mortgagee had served upon the tenant and other subsequent incumbrancers the usual notice of sale in default of payment of the principal or interest, and her solicitor insisted that the interest should be paid to him out of the rent, or that the tenant should "take the consequences." The solicitor swore that his object was to avoid putting his client in the position of mortgagee in possession. All he appears to have required was, that the interest should be paid, and receipts were accordingly given as for rent paid on account of the lease in discharge of the interest. It is evident, that so long as the interest was paid the mortgagee did not desire to interfere with the lease or with the rights of others to the rents reserved by it ; and although there is no doubt that a new contract of tenancy may be inferred from a notice by the mortgagees to pay the rent to them, acquiesced in by the tenant by payment of the rent, I think the circumstances of this case shew that it was not intended to create such a contract, but rather that, the interest being paid, the possession of the mortgagor and his tenants was to remain undisturbed. This would distinguish it from the recent case of *Corbett* v. *Plowden*, 25 Ch. Div. 678, where the mortgagees having given notice to the tenant to pay " the rent due this day, and all future rent " to them, was held, payment having been made in accordance with the notice—to have done away with the existing agreement, to have withdrawn the mortgagor's authority to receive the rents under it, and to have created a new tenancy from year to year between the tenant and themselves. The present case, in short, falls within the other authorities already cited. In my opinion, the plaintiff has no answer to the residue of the rent distrained for, and the appeal should be allowed.

HAGARTY. C. J. O., and PATTERSON, J. A., concurred.

Appeal allowed, with costs.

MURRAY V. HUTCHINSON.

Sale of chattels—Deposit on sale—Breach of contract—Waiver—Recovery of deposit—Contradictory evidence—Finding of jury.

On the 9th of July, 1885, the plaintiff, a cattle dealer, bought from defendant 42 head of cattle for $2,772, and paid $200 on account, the defendant to retain the animals on his pasture until in a condition fit for the English market, for which they were to the knowledge of the defendant purchased by the plaintiff. The defendant insisting that he was bound to retain the cattle until the 20th of August only, on the 18th September, wrote to the plaintiff requiring him to "settle for the cattle and take them away before the 27th instant, or I will sell the cattle again to get my money out of them." The plaintiff not having acted upon this notice, the defendant on the 5th of October sold forty of the cattle at a loss, and refused to refund the deposit. In an action brought by the plaintiff the evidence, as to the exact terms of the contract, was contradictory, but the jury found in favor of the plaintiff's version, and gave a verdict for the full amount of deposit, which on a motion made in term, the learned Judge of the County Court refused to disturb. On appeal, this Court being of opinion that the plaintiff could waive the breach of contract and simply sue for recovery of the money paid, affirmed the judgment of the Court below, with costs.

THIS was an appeal by the defendant from the judgment of the County Court of the County of Oxford in an action in which D. G. Murray was plaintiff and Donald Hutchinson was defendant.

The appeal was against the refusal to grant a rule to set aside the verdict for the plaintiff, and to enter judgment for the defendant on the ground that the verdict was contrary to law and against evidence, &c.

The statement of claim set forth that on the 9th of July, 1885, the plaintiff purchased from the defendant 42 head of cattle at the price of $66.00 a head on the terms that the defendant should keep the same on his premises until they should be in a condition fit to ship for export to England; and paid the defendant $200 on account of such purchase; that plaintiff afterwards demanded a delivery of the cattle from the defendant, which the defendant wholly refused; and in breach of his contract sold and delivered the cattle to another person, and the plaintiff never received any part thereof.

The plaintiff, under the circumstances, claimed that he was entitled to, and was willing to accept his said deposit, and demanded the same from the defendant before suit, which was refused.

The defendant counter-claimed, alleging that it was part of his business to raise cattle for sale, and that on the 9th of July, 1885, the plaintiff purchased from him 42 head of cattle at the price and on the terms substantially as set forth in the statement of claim, but plaintiff was to pay the balance of the price and remove the cattle from defendant's premises on or before the 20th of August, 1885; that after such sale, and before the said 20th of August, the cattle market became depressed, and the price fell, and continued to fall further from time to time thereafter. The plaintiff did not (as he had agreed to do) pay the balance of the purchase money or remove said cattle on or before the said 20th of August; whereupon defendant demanded from the plaintiff payment of such balance, and requested him to remove said cattle from the defendant's premises, and the defendant was always ready and willing to accept payment of such balance, and to allow plaintiff to remove the cattle on payment of such balance; but the plaintiff refused and neglected so to do, wherefore the defendant on the 5th of October, 1885, sold 40 of the said cattle for the price or sum of $59.25 per head, being the then market value thereof, and the best price he was able to obtain for the same. Before proceeding to sell the cattle the defendant on the 18th of September, 1885, wrote to the plaintiff as follows :

"To Donald Murray :—Please call and settle for the cattle, and take them away before the 27th inst., or I will sell the cattle again to get my money out of them   *   *
                              " DONALD HUTCHINSON."

That defendant lost the difference between the price for which the plaintiff purchased the cattle and the price for which he (defendant) afterwards sold the same; and also the value of depasturing the said cattle from the 20th of August to the 5th of October, 1885, &c.

The action came on for trial before the County Court Judge and a jury on the 16th December, 1886, when evidence was taken establishing substantially the facts set up by the plaintiff and defendant respectively; in other words, each party swore to his view of the bargain; and the witnesses on either side also differed in their views of the facts.

The jury found in favor of the plaintiff for the full amount of his deposit, and on the 4th of January the defendant moved to set aside such verdict, and enter a verdict for the defendant, which application the Judge, on 8th of January, 1887, refused.

The appeal came on for hearing on the 14th of September, 1887.*

Holman, for the appellant, contended that the finding of the jury was contrary to the weight of evidence, and that they should have found that the terms of the agreement between the plaintiff and defendant were, that plaintiff was to pay the price of the cattle and remove them from off the premises of the defendant on or before the 20th of August, 1886, and having made default in so doing he had forfeited any claim to the money deposited with or paid to the defendant on account of the purchase money; his only remedy being an action for damages for not delivering the cattle. That the evidence established clearly that between the date of the agreement and the re-sale the price of cattle had greatly fallen in the market: that the cattle were re-sold for the best price that could be obtained, and that the loss attending such re-sale greatly exceeded the $200 paid on account of the price.

Aylesworth, for the respondent. On all the questions of fact the evidence, if believed by the jury, was sufficient to sustain the findings of the jury, who were the proper parties to pass upon the character of that evidence. They have distinctly found that the evidence given by the plaintiff and his witnesses was to be relied on, and therefore the Court below acted properly in refusing to disturb their finding.

Chinery v. *Viall,* 5 H. & N. 288 ; *Phippen* v. *Hyland,* 19 C. P. 416 ; *Furniss* v. *Sawers,* 3 U. C. R. 76 ; *Campbell* v. *Green,* 10 C. P. 295 ; 11 C. P. 231 ; *DeLong* v. *Oliver,* 26 U. C. R. 612 ; *Valpy* v. *Oakley,* 16 Q. B. 94 ; *Griffiths* v. *Perry,* 1 E. & E. 680 ; *Benjamin* on Sales, (4th Am. ed.), secs. 1125, 1156, 1169, 1174-1180, were referred to.

Present.—HAGARTY, C.J.O., PATTERSON and OSLER, JJ.A.

The other facts in the case are mentioned in the judgment.

September 29, 1887. HAGARTY, C. J. O.—The plaintiff
sets out a sale to him by defendant of certain cattle on 9th
July, 1885, at so much per head, on the terms that defendant should keep them until they should be in condition
to ship to England : that he paid $200 on account : that he
afterwards demanded delivery, but defendant refused, and
afterwards, in breach of his contract, sold the cattle to
others. Under these circumstances the plaintiff is entitled
to and is willing to take his deposit (of money), and
demanded same ; defendant refused, and plaintiff now
claims it.

Defendant denies the facts, and states that even if
true they disclose no legal liability to repay the $200.
And he then counter-claims for the large loss sustained by
him in consequence of plaintiff not taking the cattle and
paying the price agreed, and that plaintiff should have
removed them by 20th August : that the market fell considerably : that he required plaintiff to take and pay for
them, and was always ready to accept payment and deliver
up to the time of the sale by defendant : that plaintiff
neglected to take or pay, and defendant then sold them for
the best attainable price, but for far less than plaintiff's
contract price, and defendant has thus lost the difference,
and claims damages over and above the $200.

A letter was sent by defendant, dated September 18,
calling on plaintiff to settle for and take the cattle before
the 27th instant, or that he, defendant, would re-sell them
to get his money out of them. On the 26th September
plaintiff telegraphed to defendant to have patience and he
would take the cattle in a few days. On the 28th September defendant telegraphed back that he could not give
any more time. On the 6th October defendant sold the
cattle in Toronto.

Some days before this the parties met, and there was
contradictory evidence as to whether the cattle were fit for

-export or not, and they failed to come to any terms of
compromise.   On the 26th October plaintiff went to defendant's place and found the cattle had been sold, and he
wrote a letter to defendant:

HARRINGTON, October 26, 1885.

Mr. Hutchinson—Dear Sir : I called at your place to-day for the cattle
I got from you, but the boys told me you had shipped them some time
ago. Now you will kindly remit me the two hundred dollars that I deposited on them, and save costs. You can remit by registered letter to
Harrington P. O.   .   D. G. MURRAY.

Before the action the plaintiff swears that he tried to
get back from the defendant the money paid, and offered
to make a large reduction rather than have any trouble.
Defendant refused.   The defendant admits that before the
suit the plaintiff demanded the $200 back.

The case went to the jury without any special questions
and they found for plaintiff.

The learned Judge stated the respective versions as to
the bargain.

  " The plaintiff says, ' I purchased these cattle from the
·defendant at a certain price, the defendant undertook to
keep them till they were fit for the market.'   The defen-
·dant in answer to that says, ' true you purchased those
·cattle from me at the price you named, but I only agreed
to keep them until the 22nd August.   The plaintiff says
·that is not true, that you agreed to keep them until they
were properly fit for the market.'   Now, that is the whole
·case for you to decide, there is nothing very difficult about
it.   Has the plaintiff satisfied you that the bargain was as
put by him ?

*   *   *   *   *   *   *   *   *   *

The plaintiff says I have paid $200 to the defendant on
·account of these cattle ; I was prepared to carry out my
bargain, you were not prepared to carry out yours, and
you sold the property before you had a right to ; for that
reason you put it out of my power to carry out my part
·of the contract, and I am at all events entitled to recover
back the money I paid you.   Are you satisfied that the
defendant did anything more than a reasonable man ought
to do ?   Has the plaintiff satisfied your minds that he
had until the cattle were fit for market, and that they

remained with the defendant who sold them before that.
time ? If you are so satisfied from the evidence the plaintiff is entitled to the verdict.

*   *   *   *   *   *   *

The plaintiff undertakes to satisfy you as twelve reasonable men that the case as put by him is such a case as
entitles him to a verdict. Has the plaintiff so satisfied
you ? Is the contract as he says : That he was to pay
this price, and that the defendant was to keep the property until they were properly fit for use ? If that was
the contract, did the plaintiff come within a reasonable
time when they were fit for the market and offer to carry
out the contract ? If he did, and the defendant sold them
before he had a right to sell them, the plaintiff is entitled
to a verdict. If, on the other hand, the plaintiff did not
carry out his contract, did not come to him at the time
agreed upon, that he allowed that time to lapse after
getting a notice that they would be sold, and he did not
come there to pay the money and take the property, the
defendant is entitled to a verdict at your hands."

It appears clearly that the jury, on this charge, must
have found their verdict for plaintiff on their belief that
the plaintiff's version of the bargain was the correct one ;
that the defendant wrongfully sold the cattle before he
had a right so to do ; and that his act was a wrong to
plaintiff.

There does not seem to be any ground for interfering
with the finding of the jury on the questions of fact.

This view of the facts seems to answer most of Mr.
Holman's able argument for the defendant. The latter
has done a legal wrong to the plaintiff, and thus put it out
of his power to fulfil his contract.

We cannot see any reason why in such a case the plaintiff may not, as it were, waive the tort or breach, and
assenting to the improper disposition of the cattle, merely
require the defendant to repay to him the money paid on
account.

He offered to settle with defendant before action, by
taking back this money with a considerable reduction,
and in his claim he offers to take it back, claiming no

other relief, and his letter of Oct. 26th seems to be to the same effect.

Had the jury found the facts to be different, and adopted defendant's version of the contract, we might have to consider the legal difficulties pointed out by Mr. Holman and the cases cited by him.

The appeal must be dismissed.

OSLER, J. A.—I agree in dismissing the appeal, as I think there was evidence from which it may be inferred that the property in the goods did not pass under the contract. The plaintiff bought cattle to be fit for export. They were to be kept for the plaintiff for that purpose, and he was not bound to take them unless they were fit.

The defendant sold them before any default had been made by the plaintiff, and that, as it seems to me, would put an end to the contract, and enable the plaintiff to recover the money paid on account of the purchase money as money paid upon a consideration that had failed. In such a state of things, none of the difficulties suggested by such cases as *Chinery* v. *Viall*, 5 H. & N. 288; *Martindale* v. *Smith*, 1 Q. B. 389; *Heffernan* v. *Berry*, 6 U. C. R. 207, and other authorities relied upon by the defendant would arise, and the result is, that the defendant sold his own cattle, not the plaintiff's, and that the latter was properly entitled to recover what he paid on account of the bargain.

PATTERSON, J.A., concurred.

Appeal dismissed, with costs.

Logg v. Ellwood.

Verdict of jury—Findings of referee—Interference by Court.

In an action for wages, there was a dispute as to the nature of the agreement for hiring; there was evidence at the trial which would have supported a finding for either party. The question was wholly one of fact, and of the credibility of witnesses. The jury found in favor of the plaintiff; but the Judge set it aside, and sent the case to a referee, who found substantially as the jury had done. Upon motion the Judge made an order sending the case back to the referee with instructions to find against the plaintiff on one branch of the case.

Held, that the case was one specially proper for the decision of a jury, and that the verdict as also the finding of the referee should not have been interfered with.

THIS was an action commenced in the County Court of the county of Elgin by James Logg, a carpenter by trade, against Charles Ellwood, a building contractor.

The statement of claim filed by the plaintiff set forth that on the 2nd of April, 1883, the defendant engaged the plaintiff to work for him for one year for $150, and when that term of engagement was ended it was agreed that plaintiff should continue to work for defendant at the rate of $1.75 per day, under which arrangement plaintiff continued such work until 20th June, 1884, for which he claimed to be paid $109.37½, and had received from defendant during these periods of service $104.50 on account of wages, leaving a balance due plaintiff of $154.87½, which he claimed to be due, with interest, from June, 1884.

The defendant counter-claimed, alleging that plaintiff agreed to work for him as an apprentice for one year, and that during that time plaintiff was to receive such remuneration as defendant should consider him entitled to: that defendant supplied him with board, washing, and lodging during that year, and alleged that they were worth more than his services: that after the expiration of that year plaintiff remained in defendant's employ, without any definite agreement as to wages, only except that he was to pay such amount as plaintiff was reasonably worth; and defendant insisted that plaintiff had been paid all the wages he was entitled to for the time he worked after the first year; and also claimed that plaintiff was indebted to him $182 for board, &c., during the year from 2nd April, 1883, to 2nd April, 1884.

The action came on for trial before the County Judge, with a jury, at St. Thomas, on the 10th of June, 1886, when the plaintiff was examined and swore substantially to his demand as set forth in his statement of claim. He also proved that during the first year of his working for defendant he had been paid by him, in small sums varying from twenty-five cents to ten dollars on twenty-seven different occasions, the sum of $52.20; and during the summer of 1884 he had, on thirteen different occasions, been paid small sums, varying from $3.00 to $5.00, aggregating $52.50. In other words, he had been paid $104.70 during the two seasons.

The defendant was also examined, and denied ever having made the agreements alleged by plaintiff, and claimed that he had overpaid plaintiff to the amount of $39.08.

The learned Judge, in the course of his charge to the jury, said :

"This plaintiff admits having got altogether $104.70, and you have to decide whether he is entitled to anything more than that, all things being considered, and the whole evidence being passed through your minds. He certainly does claim more, and it is for you to say whether he is entitled to more. It is not for me to tell you how you are to decide, but you have to reconcile the evidence, and you have to attach that importance to the testimony you think it justly entitled to."

After retiring and considering their verdict as directed by the Judge, the jury brought in a verdict for the plaintiff, and $154.67 damages.

In the following term, counsel for the defendant moved to set the verdict aside, which was done; and, on the 14th of December, 1886, an order was made, under sec. 48 of the O. J. Act, referring all questions in the action to be tried by David McLaws, Esquire, clerk of the court, costs to be costs in the cause.

After having heard the evidence taken at the trial, and that of several other witnesses adduced before him, the referee, on the 11th of January, 1887, made his report, finding:

" that there was a contract made between the plaintiff and defendant, and
that the plaintiff was to have for the first year $150 and board, and for
the second year sixty-two and a half days at $1.75, making in all $259.37½,
less cash paid the plaintiff $106.33, thus leaving a balance due the plaintiff
of $153.04½ on the 20th of June, 1884, and interest from that date up to
the date of this my report, at six per cent., making $23.49, making a total
of $176.53 due the plaintiff.   All which, &c."

On the 21st of the same month a motion was made on
behalf of the defendant for an order setting aside this
report,

" Or varying the same by declaring the plaintiff to be entitled for the first
year to the amount paid him in that year by the defendant instead of the
sum of $150 and board ; and for the second year to the sum of $1.50 per
day instead of $1.75 as found by said report or to refer back the report for
further consideration on the grounds that the findings contained in said
report are contrary to evidence and the weight of evidence."

After hearing counsel for both parties the learned Judge
on the 12th of February disposed of the application as
follows :

" The case must therefore be referred back to the referee for amendment
of his report with instructions to find that the first year's services were
paid for, and directing him to find what balance (if any) is due the plaintiff
for the second year's services, after deducting the payments that were
made by the defendant on the second year's employment the plaintiff being
allowed for sixty-two and a half days at the rate of $1.75 per diem."

From this decision the plaintiff appealed, and the appeal
came on to be heard before this Court on the 13th of
September, 1887.*

J. A. Robinson, for the appellant.

The finding of the referee ought to be looked upon quite
as favorably as the verdict of a jury : here the report of
that officer was made after reading the evidence taken at
the trial ; and after hearing the oral testimony of other
witnesses called upon the reference.   There having been no
other person present on the occasion of the defendant
employing the plaintiff, the parties themselves were the
only persons who could testify as to the terms of the engagement ; and the jury as well as the referee having seen fit
to give credence to the statements of the plaintiff in prefer-

Present.—HAGARTY, C. J. O., PATTERSON and OSLER, JJ.A.

ence to those made by the defendant, it was clearly a case in which the report of the referee should not be interfered with.

The finding of the learned Judge, himself, that the terms of the second agreement of hiring had been agreed upon, shews that credence was given by him to the statements of the plaintiff in preference to those made by the defendant, who swore positively that no agreement had been entered into ; so that the account of the agreement as to the first year's contract, given by the plaintiff was entitled to prevail, even if the case was one in which the jury were not, as the learned Judge told them they were, the parties " to decide."

Doherty, for the respondent. This is clearly a question as to the credibility of witnesses, and the learned Judge who heard the witnesses at the trial was so impressed with the improbability of the plaintiff's story that in making the rule absolute to set aside the verdict of the jury he remarked : " I know it is unusual to set aside the verdict of the jury in such a case as this, but I cannot allow a verdict so unjust to stand."

This Court therefore is now asked to interfere with the discretion exercised by the County Judge who from his personal knowledge of the parties, and seeing the manner in which they gave their testimony before him, had a much better opportunity of judging of what effect should be given to it than this Court can possibly have from reading the shorthand writer's notes.

On the whole I submit the appeal should be dismissed.

September 29th, 1887. HAGARTY, C. J. O.—This was an action for wages, and was tried in the ordinary way by a jury. The jury found for plaintiff for his whole claim. There was clear evidence in favor of the finding—the defendant directly denied the plaintiff's version of the bargain, and it was for the jury to say to which of the witnesses credence was to be given.

Having carefully examined the evidence, and speaking only as to my own impressions and from my experience in such matters, I do not think, on motion against the verdict, on the weight of evidence, the Court *in banc* would have interfered whether the jury, on a fair charge, had found, on such evidence, either for plaintiff or for defendant. I think the Court would not have interfered, considering it was for them, and not for the Judge, to decide on the conflict of testimony.

We gather from the appeal book that the learned Judge in term disapproved of the finding as unreasonable and unjust, and that he could not allow a verdict so unjust to stand ; that it was never a proper case for a jury ; and that if either party applied to him he would appoint a referee to try the case.

An order was accordingly made referring the case to Mr. McLaws, the clerk of the Court. That gentleman made his award, after apparently a very careful consideration of the evidence ; and we are furnished with his reasons. He fully adopts, in substance, the finding of the jury in favor of the plaintiff.

On an appeal to the learned Judge against the award it was ordered to be referred back to the referee to amend his report by finding that the first year's work had been paid for by defendant, thus in effect declaring that plaintiff was not entitled to the $150 wages for the first year and very substantially reducing his claim, which had been allowed first by the jury, secondly by the referee.

We can hardly understand the course taken in the court below. The practical result, of course, has been that the learned Judge considered both jury and referee to have taken an erroneous view of the credibility of the witnesses on mere questions of fact and direct contradictory statements, and has given judgment according to his own view as to what ought to have been the proper finding.

We find great difficulty in accepting as right this course of proceeding.

The case seems one specially proper for the decision of a jury, so long as that mode of trial forms part of our jurisprudence. It was a matter wholly of disputed fact and credibility, unembarrassed by any legal question whatever. It went down to trial in the ordinary way.

In such a case it would, we think, require some very extraordinary reason to change the tribunal of trial.

On proper grounds, the Court could have directed another trial by another jury, although this is rarely done merely because the Court happens to differ from the jury's conclusion of fact on directly contradictory evidence.

When the Court takes the case away from the jury and refers it, and then exercises its right to direct the award to be altered to meet its views of what was the proper result of the evidence, it of course, in effect, compels adoption of its own view of the disputed facts. There is a very intelligible distinction between this action of the Court and its decision previous to the trial as to what the mode of trial should be.

We can also understand the action of the Court in altering the mode of trial, if jurors persist in disregarding the directions of the court on legal questions arising at the trial. But the course adopted in the present case is, we think, not one to be followed.

We think we are bound to allow this appeal, and to direct judgment to be entered in the Court below on the findings and report of the referee, with costs below, and of this appeal.

OSLER, J. A.—I agree in allowing the appeal. The case both at the trial and before the referee, resolved itself into a conflict of evidence between the plaintiff and defendant as to the existence of an agreement in respect of a hiring for the first and succeeding year. If the jury believed the plaintiff, their verdict in his favor was right and should not, in my opinion, have been set aside. If evidence to corroborate his story was necessary, there was evidence of that kind; and the case was peculiarly one within the

province of the jury, and a claim fitting for them to determine. There was evidence which would have supported a
finding for the defendant; but there was also evidence
on which reasonable men, believing it, might find, as they
found for the plaintiff. Their verdict, however, was set
aside, and the case sent to a referee, although, as I
insist, it was one which, from the nature of the claim—a
dispute about a tradesman's hiring, and the character of
the evidence, which of the parties was telling the truth—
was a case which ought to have been tried by a jury. The
referee, after hearing the former and further evidence, having had the parties themselves before him, and being in a
position to judge by every circumstance in the case which
of their stories ought to be accepted, has again found for
the plaintiff, that he was to be paid $150 and his board for
the first year, and $1.75 per day for the time worked in
the second year.

To my mind the referee in his written reasons for his
findings has handled the evidence very well, and if he
believed the plaintiff, as he says he did, on what ground is
his finding to be impeached? Certainly there are circumstances which corroborate the plaintiff's story, but the case
is one of that kind which depends, yea or nay, whose oath
do you accept as to the terms of the agreement? That being
so, and there being nothing in the remainder of the
evidence to indicate that the plaintiff's statement was of so
extraordinary a character that the officer ought judicially
to have disbelieved it, his finding in favor of it ought not
to have been disturbed.

PATTERSON, J. A., concurred.

Appeal allowed, with costs.

COYNE v. LEE.

Chattel mortgage—After-acquired chattels—Interpleader issue—Transfer to County Court—Jurisdiction—44 Vict. ch. 7 (O.)—Appeal in special case.

A chattel mortgage conveyed to the plaintiff the stock in trade of the mortgagor, which purported to be enumerated in a schedule (A,) and was described as being on certain named premises. The schedule after setting out the goods proceeded : "And all goods * * which at any time may be owned by the said mortgagor and kept in the said store for sale * * and whether now in stock or hereafter to be purchased and placed in stock."

Held, [affirming the judgment of the County Court of York] that after-acquired stock brought into the business in the ordinary course thereof, became subject to the chattel mortgage as against execution creditors of the mortgagor, notwithstanding that their writs were in the hands of the sheriff at the time such stock was brought into the business ; the equitable right of the mortgagee under such agreement attaching immediately on the goods reaching the premises.

In an action pending in the High Court, an interpleader issue and all subsequent proceedings were transferred under the 44 Vict. ch. 7, sec. 1 (O.) to the county court of Middlesex. By a subsequent order made on consent, the trial of such issue was withdrawn from Middlesex, and a special case was agreed on, and the venue changed from Middlesex to York, where the special case was argued.

Held, [*per* PATTERSON and OSLER, JJ.A.], that in strictness the appeal should be quashed. The transfer to the Middlesex County Court was final, and there was no jurisdiction under the statute or otherwise to transfer the issue or any part of it, or to change the venue to any other County Court. The proceedings in the County Court of York could therefore only be regarded as a summary trial by consent from which no appeal lay.

THIS was an interpleader issue in an action in the High Court originally directed to be tried before the County Court of Middlesex, but subsequently by an order made in Chambers by consent in the original cause, the trial of the issue was withdrawn from Middlesex, and a special case agreed on by the parties was ordered to be argued in the County Court of the county of York, all other questions in the issue being reserved for disposition by the former county court.

The appellants were execution creditors of one Henry Potts. The respondent claimed under a chattel mortgage executed prior to the recovery of the appellants' judgment.

The goods in question came into the possession of Potts subsequent to the execution of the chattel mortgage ; some of them prior and some subsequent to the renewal of the mortgage.

The respondent claimed that such goods were within
and covered by the terms of the mortgage.

The parties agreed on a special case which was argued
before the County Judge who, after stating the facts as
set forth above and in the present judgments, proceeded:

" Two points were argued by Dr. McMichael for the defendants, the
execution creditors : First, that under our Act no valid and effectual
mortgage can be made of after-acquired goods unaccompanied by some
actual and immediate change of possession ; and second, that if such a
mortgage could be made, that the mortgage in question was invalid in the
description of the locality of after-acquired goods, the words of the mortgage being ' All of which said goods and chattels are now lying and being
on the premises,' claiming that the description of the locality was appropriate only as applied to the existing goods at the date of the mortgage ;
and it was admitted during the argument of the case that substantially
all the goods in dispute were after-acquired goods.   *   *

" Under the case of *Perrin* v. *Wood*, 21 Gr. 492, and the judgment of
Blake, V. C., the question of the validity of a mortgage upon after-
acquired property is settled. He held in that case that there could be no
doubt on the authorities that a mortgage could effectually charge after-
acquired property, and although at law it might be necessary to have the
novus actus, yet in equity when the property came into the possession of
the mortgagor it was at once operated upon by the instrument, and effectually charged as against a subsequent assignee or a judgment creditor.

" This disposes of the Doctor's first point in favor of the mortgagee.

" As to the second point, I am of opinion that looking at the whole instrument and reading the schedule as part of the mortgage, that the after-
acquired property is sufficiently identified in locality by the expression in
the schedule, ' and general merchandise which at any time may be owned
by the said mortgagor and kept in the said store for sale by him.'   *   *
No question has been raised as to the bona fides of the parties, and the
endeavour is made to set the mortgage aside on an alleged technical defect
only.

" I think it may be reasonably gathered from within the four corners of
the instrument, including the schedules, that the locality of the after-
acquired goods was to be the store which is properly described as the
locality at which at the date of the execution of the mortgage the then
stock was situate.

" I therefore hold that the goods mentioned in the interpleader order
were, at the time of their seizure by the sheriff, the property of the said
J. W. Coyne."   *   *

From this judgment the defendants appealed, and the
appeal came on for hearing before this Court on the 13th
and 14th of September, 1887.*

Present.—HAGARTY, C. J. O., PATTERSON and OSLER, JJ. A.

McMichael, Q.C., for the appellants.

J. M. Clark, for the respondent.

October 26th, 1887.   HAGARTY, C. J. O.—The chattel mortgage conveys the stock in trade of the mortgagor, as a general hardware merchant and dealer in stoves and tin-ware, more particularly described in schedule A.; and also horses, wagons, &c., used in mortgagor's livery business, and all other horses, &c., mentioned in schedule B. thereto annexed, all which goods and chattels were situate and lying on certain specified premises of the mortgagor.

Schedule A. sets out all the property and proceeds thus :

" And all goods and chattels, stock in trade, and general merchandise which at any time may be owned by the said mortgagor and kept in the said store for sale by him as a general hardware merchant and dealer in stoves and tin-ware, and whether now in stock or hereafter to be pur-chased and placed in stock ; and notwithstanding that por-tion of said stock and goods now in said store, may be sold and replaced by other goods ; the intention being that all the goods of any of the above descriptions at any time in said store shall be covered by the said mortgage."

The question raised on the case submitted is, whether the after-acquired property brought into the business in ordi-nary course is covered by the chattel mortgage as against the defendants, execution creditors.

Whether the mortgage in terms professed directly to convey the future acquired goods to the mortgagee, or merely covenanted that they should become liable to the mortga-gee's claims as soon as received, does not seem to be of much importance

No title in either case passes at law, the claim must rest wholly on the mortgagee's equitable title.

Sir George Jessel says, in *Collyer* v. *Isaacs*, 19 Ch. D. 342, 351 :

" The assignment in fact constituted only a contract to give him the after-acquired chattels.   A man cannot in equity any more than at law assign what has no existence. A man can contract to assign property which is to come into existence in the future, and when it has come into existence equity, treating as done that which ought to be done, fastens upon that property, and the contract to assign thus becomes a complete assignment."

This seems a concise and clear statement of the equity on which the claimant here has to rely.

I do not think the objection of vagueness as to the future acquired property, applies. As soon as it may be brought upon the named premises, and into the named business, it is identified, and the equity attaches. .

This point is fully discussed by Lord Esher in *Official Receiver* v. *Tailby*, 18 Q. B. D. 25 (as to assignment of book debts.)

As between the parties, of course, this equitable interest is enforceable ; the contest is as to its being a valid right to prevail against execution creditors. The executions attached prior to any steps being taken by the mortgagee to claim or enforce his equity, and the after-acquired property was then in the posssession and disposition of the mortgagor in his business.

We may conveniently discuss the case in the first place apart from any effect attributable to our Chattel Mortgage Act.

Beyond the fact of registration of the mortgage there is no question as to notice of its existence to defendants or other creditors of the trader.

The case always cited as to this equity is *Holroyd* v. *Marshall*, 10 H. L. C. 191. The mortgagor of a hull and machinery covenanted that all new machinery to be brought into the hull should be subject to the trusts, &c., of the mortgage, and that he would do all necessary acts to vest same in the mortgagees. The deed was registered. Execution issued against the mortgagor, and the sheriff seized and sold, but only the new machinery. A bill was filed by the mortgagees against sheriff and other necessary parties praying for assessment of damages &c. After very full argument the Lords decided in favor of the mortgagees against the execution creditors. The doctrines laid down are so often referred to that I do not repeat them.

Apart from all special legislation, the principle enunciated in this case seems clear that in the absence of fraud, the title to after-acquired goods may prevail as against execution creditors.

It leaves a case of this kind unembarrassed by any consideration as to how far the title of an assignee in insolvency, or trustee in liquidation, can be placed any higher than that of the insolvent. It is a direct contest between mortgagee and execution creditor. The authority of the case seems to be always admitted. It must be borne in mind that under it the future-acquired goods must be so clearly identified or distinguished that specific performance of a contract to assign or convey them would be enforceable.

As said by Lindley, L. J., in *Official Receiver* v. *Tailby* : " Apart from the doctrines of specific performance, I do not see how there can be any passing of after-acquired property at all. The question, therefore, in such a case as this must be determined with reference to the doctrine of specific performance."

Lazarus v. *Andrade*, (1880,) 5 C. P. D. 318, was an interpleader issue between mortgagee claiming after-acquired property and execution creditor.

Lopes, L. J., decided that the mortgagee must prevail. He says, after noting *Holroyd* v. *Marshall, &c.* :

" The principle deducible from these decisions is, that property to be after-acquired, if described so as to be capable of being identified, may be, not only in equity but also at law, the subject-matter of a valid assignment for value. The contract must be one which a Court of Equity would specifically enforce."

In *Joseph* v. *Lyons*, 1884, 15 Q. B. D. 280, at p. 286 Cotton, L. J. says of *Lazarus* v. *Andrade* :

" I think that the decision in that case was right ; but I cannot agree with what I gather to have been the view of the learned judge as to the effect of the Supreme Court of Judicature Acts." * *

And in an earlier part of his judgment the same learned Judge remarks :

" I think that the clause enacting that the rules of equity

shall prevail shews that it was not intended to sweep away altogether the principles of the common law. And it was not intended that a conveyance void at common law should, after the passing of those statutes, become valid as a conveyance at common law."

In that case a mortgagor assigned his after-acquired stock in trade. Before the mortgagee took possession he had pledged a portion with defendant, who had no notice of the mortgage.

The Court held that the legal interest remained in the mortgagor, and that he transferred to pledgee a legal, not an equitable right—the mortgagee had only the equitable right, and the defendant the legal interest. Therefore the defendant prevailed, and the plaintiff could not maintain a legal remedy like conversion or detinue.

The defendant was a pawnbroker, and it was said that he was not bound to search the register for bills of sale of goods pledged to him. If he had notice of it he should have searched.

Lindley, L.J., adds :

" It seems to me that the modern doctrine as to constructive notice has been pushed too far, and I do not feel inclined to extend it."

In the same volume the next case is *Hallas* v. *Robinson,* where *Joseph* v. *Lyons* is followed.

Leatham v. *Amor,* 47 L. J. Q. B. 581, in appeal, the principles of *Holroyd* v. *Marshall,* are followed. The after-acquired property was chiefly, if not wholly, as in the Holroyd case, renewal of plant and machinery. The assignment was held good against an execution creditor.

Clements v. *Matthews,* 11 Q. B. D. 808, may be referred to on the general subject. It was not against an execution creditor.

Roberts v. *Roberts,* 13 Q. B. D. 794, relied on by Dr. McMichael cannot, I think, help his argument.

It seems to turn chiefly on the special effect of the Bills of Sale Acts, 1878, and Amendment Act of 1882, which are to be read together. The head-note points out that "the bill of sale was void as against execution creditors of the grantor in respect of after-acquired property, and also as to household furniture and effects, because they were not specifically described within the meaning of sec. 4." The bill of sale was supported as to the rest.

Under this clause the assignment is to have effect only as regards personal chattels specifically described in the schedule. Under sec. 5 it is still good against the grantor.

Macaskie's Law of Bills of Sale, p. 102, et seq., discusses these new clauses; at p. 105 he discusses the law of *Holroyd* v. *Marshall*.

It is not necessary for the decision of this case to discuss further the peculiar effect of the Imperial Acts as to bills of sale.

An anonymous case, Weekly Notes 1876, p. 64, before Archibald, J., who held on one interpleader issue that since the Judicature Act of 1873, the sheriff seized subject to all the equities which attached in after-acquired property, saying that he followed the opinion of Lush, J., at p. 202 Weekly Notes 1875, as to future acquired chattels under a marriage settlement.

The learned Judge in the Court below based his judgment against the execution debtor on the authority of Blake, V. C., in 1874, *Perrin* v. *Wood*, 21 Gr. 492.

That decision fully supports his view, and the learned Vice-Chancellor reviews the authorities resting on *Holroyd* v. *Marshall*.

We need not further notice those referred to in that judgment.

It remains to be considered whether any Ontario legislation interferes with these views. I cannot find anything in our Acts which can in any way affect the question as to this after-acquired property.

If the instrument professing to convey, or agreeing to convey such property, requires registration, then it appears that registration has been duly effected with the prescribed affidavits, &c.

If it can take effect outside the statute, we need not

consider the latter, so long as it does not directly, or by necessary intendment, forbid the creating of this equitable interest in non-existing property.

The Imperial Act 17 & 18 Vict. ch. 36, which was in force when *Holroyd* v. *Marshall* was decided, does not seem to bear upon this point.

On this statute Lord Chelmsford, at p. 227, speaking of notice of the equitable claims to the judgment creditor says:

" It appears that the deed was registered as a bill of sale under 17 & 18 Vict. ch. 36. It was argued that Act was intended to apply to bills of sale of actual existing property only, and it probably may be the case that sales of future property were not within the contemplation of the Legislature, but there is no ground for excluding them from the provisions of the Act; and upon the question of notice the register would furnish the same information of the dealing with future as with existing property, which is all that is required to answer the objection."

It was objected on the argument for the appellants before us that a covenant by a debtor for value to convey after-acquired property might, without registration or public notice of any kind, prevail against the creditors of the debtor and enable him to obtain credit by false appearances, &c.

We need express no opinion on such a case until it arises. It will be for the Legislature if necessary to provide further safeguards. But it must be borne in mind that if we decide against this claimant, we practically make it almost impossible to grant a valid mortgage on the stock of a retail dealer. It may be, say, of the value of $5000, but to supply the waste of daily sales to keep it up to anything like the value, new goods must be constantly coming in, so that in six or twelve months two-thirds of the stock may consist of " after-acquired property."

If a valid charge cannot be created on the latter, of course any security on a retail dealer's stock would be almost valueless. The more active might be his sales, the more worthless the security.

The class of case before us is a mortgage security on a stock of goods in a particular business, and whatever new goods come in to supply those sold, and to keep up the stock, become, in effect, the substantial property mortgaged, viz., a stock of goods.

It is wholly unlike the case of a man mortgaging several distinct kinds of property, and covenanting to charge all subsequently acquired chattel property of other kinds.

Our case is more like the substitution of new for worn out plant or machinery, where the subsequent matter of the business mortgaged requires such additions or substitutions to preserve its character as a going concern.

PATTERSON, J.A.—I agree on the grounds expressed by his lordship the Chief Justice, that the pledge in question is outside of the purview of the statute, and that the opinion of the learned Judge of the County Court should be sustained. But I am also satisfied, for reasons which will be given by my brother Osler, that the case is not properly before us, the reference to the County Court of the county of York not being authorized by statute, but having force only by consent of the parties, who are bound by his decision.

OSLER. J.A.—If this case is properly before us for decision, I think, as at present advised, that the judgment below may be supported, and the cases relied upon by the appellants distinguished.

If the mortgage in question, so far as it relates to after-acquired property, is within the statute, and requires registration, then it has been registered, and creditors have received all the notice it is said to have been the object of the statute to give them. If it is not within the statute it did not require registration, and the execution creditor's claim is subject to the prior equitable charge. The law is thus summarised by Kay, J., in the recent case of *Re Bell*, 54 L. T. N. S. 370 (1886), where the leading authorities are collected. The question there arose upon a

charging order, but the law is the same as to any process
by which a creditor seeks to affect his debtor's property :

 " It has been decided in many cases, of which I need only
refer to *Beavan* v. *Earl of Oxford*, 6 D. M. & G. 507 ; *Scott*
v. *Lord Hastings*, 4 K. & J. 633 ; *Haly* v. *Barry*, 18 L. T.
N. S. 491 ; L. R. 3 Ch. 452, 457, that a charging order
only effects a charge upon such interest as the debtor had
in the property at the date of the order nisi.   A judgment
creditor is not in the position of a mortgagee.   He simply
takes under his process such interest as the debtor happens to have (*Whitworth* v. *Gaugain*, 1 Ph. 728).   He is
subject to all prior charges, legal and equitable, whether he
knows of them or not, and cannot by a charging order
obtain priority over them."

 See also *Dominion Bank* v. *Davidson*, 12 A. R. 90 ;
Federal Bank v. *Canadian Bank*, 13 S. C. R. 384, 394.

 The cases-in the English Courts which were so strongly
relied upon by the appellants, are plainly distinguishable.

 In *Collyer* v. *Isaacs*, 19 Ch. D. 342, the point decided was
that the contract to assign the after-acquired property had
been discharged by the bankruptcy of the covenantor.
The claim in respect of it was one provable in bankruptcy,
and therefore that after the bankrupt had been discharged,
the covenantee could no longer enforce it by seizing the
property which would otherwise have been affected by it.

 Joseph v. *Lyons*, 15 Q. B. D. 280 ; *Hallas* v. *Robinson*,
ib. 288 ; *McAllister* v. *Forsyth*, 12 S. C. R. 1, are cases in
which the legal title to the after-acquired property having
been transferred by the covenantor to a bonâ fide mortgagee, pledgee, or purchaser, for valuable consideration
without notice of the equitable interest of the covenantee
therein, and before he had obtained possession of the goods,
he was prevented from setting up such interest by the
application of the well known rule that a purchaser for
valuable consideration without notice of a prior equitable
right, obtaining the legal estate, is entitled to priority in
equity as well as at law.

 And in *Roberts* v. *Roberts*, 13 Q. B. D. 794, the bill of
sale holder failed as to the after-acquired property, because

the Bills of Sale (1878) Amendment Act, 1882, expressly rendered such an instrument void as against an execution creditor.

The question may require further consideration in view of the case of *Ex parte National Mercantile Bank* v. *Phillips,* 16 Ch. D. 104, to which, however, *Brantom* v. *Griffits,* 2 C. P. D. 212, seems at first sight opposed.

I am, however, of opinion, that in the case before us no appeal lies. The action out of which the proceeding has arisen, was in the Common Pleas Division of the High Court, and we must assume that the facts were such as to authorize the interpleader issue and subsequent proceedings to be transferred to a County Court under 44 Vict. ch. 7, sec. 1, (O.), namely, that the amount claimed under the execution, or the value of the goods seized, did not exceed $400.

The statute enacts that when this is the case the order directing the issue to be tried may direct that it shall be drawn up and tried in the County Court in which the issue would, under sec. 22 of the Interpleader Act, be tried, that is to say, either in the County Court from which the process issued, or in that of the county in which the goods are taken in execution.

Then the section proceeds : " And in such case the issue shall be drawn up and tried in the County Court, and all subsequent proceedings therein up to and inclusive of judgment and execution, shall be had and taken in the County Court, which shall have jurisdiction in the premises, as fully as though the writ of execution or attachment had issued out of a County Court."

I am not aware of any other authority to direct the tria in, or to transfer to a County Court an interpleader issue or proceeding arising out of an action or execution in the High Court : *Barker* v. *Leeson.* 9 P. R. 107 ; *Beaty* v. *Bryce, ib.* 320; *Arkell* v. *Geiger, ib.* 523; *Christie* v. *Conway, ib.* 529 ; *Close* v. *Exchange. Bank,* 11 P. R. 186.

I think the right to make such an order hangs entirely upon the 44 Vict. ch. 7 (O.). It is optional with the Judge of the High Court to dispose of the interpleader application in that way; but if he does so, the jurisdiction over the future proceedings is declared by the Act to belong to the County Court.

The original interpleader order has not been brought before us, but it appears from the order by which the special case was sent to the county of York, to have been made on the 23rd December, 1886, and to have directed the trial of an issue between the parties in the County Court of Middlesex. The jurisdiction over the interpleader proceedings was then absolutely and finally transferred from the High Court to, and vested in, that County Court, so far as the trial and disposition of the issue was concerned.

Under what authority, then, was the order of the 1st March, 1887, made by the Master in Chambers in the original cause, withdrawing the trial of the issue from the Middlesex County Court, and directing a special case (which the parties had agreed to, and the judgment upon which is attempted to be brought under review on this appeal), to be argued before the County Court of the county of York? It is not a special case under the Common Law Procedure Act (secs. 185, 187); nor under the Judicature Act (Rule 248), for that can only be agreed upon after writ issued in an action; and even if it can be regarded as a case stated in a proceeding " incidental to an action " (Rule 253), no case under any of these clauses can be sent by the High Court to the County Court. Indeed, it would seem to be an entire reversal of the ordinary procedure for the High Court to transmit a question of law to be argued in the County Court.

The order of the 1st of March recites that the parties have consented that the issue directed by the former order shall be determined by the decision of the County Court of York, on the special case agreed on by them; and orders " that the venue for the trial of the issue be and the same is thereby changed from the county of Middlesex to the county of York," and then directs the parties to proceed to the argument of the special case before the County Court of the latter county.

I do not think there was any authority to make such order under sec. 155 of the C. L. P. Act, which provides for changing the venue in County Court actions. The jurisdiction conferred upon the particular County Court selected by the interpleader order is a special jurisdiction, and is conferred upon it once for all. It "shall have jurisdiction as fully as if the execution had issued out of a County Court."

If the execution had issued out of a County Court, proceedings must have been initiated in the County Court of the county where the goods were taken, and carried to a conclusion there, *unless* the Judge of that Court, upon the return of the interpleader summons, should deem it more convenient to order the proceedings to be taken in the County Court of the county from which the process issued. Nothing in that event, could be reserved to be disposed of in the former Court : *Nicholls* v. *Lundy,* 16 C. P. 160.

If the proceedings were retained in the Court where they were initiated, they could not subsequently be sent to the Court from which the execution issued. If they were sent to the latter court, there they would have to stay. The "venue," so to call it, of such proceedings, is selected once for all, by the first Court, and the latter Court cannot change it back again. I do not think sec. 155 applies to these proceedings, providing as it does that :

" In all *actions brought* in a County Court the Judge of the court where the proceedings are commenced, or a Judge of one of the Superior Courts in Chambers may change the venue, and that in that event the clerk of the court where the action was commenced, shall transmit all papers in the cause to the Court to which the venue is changed, in which Court all subsequent proceedings shall be entitled and carried on."

If, however, the section can by any construction be held to apply to the case of an interpleader issue, or if the High Court could otherwise interfere with the original order, the order in question is still open to the objection that it divides the disposition of the issue between the County Court of York and the County Court of Middlesex, sending the question of law to the one, and referring any remaining questions of fact to the other; whereas sec. 22 of ch. 54, and sec. 155 of the C. L. P. Act, require that the whole, whether issue or action, shall be sent to and disposed of wholly by either one or the other.

It may be contended that the High Court can send an interpleader issue to be tried in the County Court, under some power derived from the old jurisdiction of the Court of Chancery. I think there is no such power for the reasons mentioned in *Close* v. *Exchange Bank*, 11 P. R. 186; but even if there is, could the High Court do more than send an issue, that is, an issue of fact, there? Could it send a special case? And if it could do either under a jurisdiction of that kind, to what tribunal would the appeal lie? Surely to the High Court out of which the issue or special case had been sent—not to the Court of Appeal: *Cole* v. *Campbell*, 9 P. R. 498; *Barker* v. *Leeson, ib.* 107; *Wilson* v. *Wilson*, 3 A. R. 400.

The very fact that the appeal is here taken to the Court of Appeal direct from the County Court, argues that that court is supposed to have acquired jurisdiction under the 44 Vict. ch. 7, (O.) and hence that an appeal lies under sec. 23 of the Interpleader Act, with which the former Act is to be read and is to form part of. But the only Court which acquired jurisdiction under the interpleader order of the 23rd December, 1886, by force of the former Act, was the County Court of Middlesex, and it could not be deprived of that jurisdiction by any consent order, such as that of the 1st March, 1887.

The result, therefore, would seem to be either that by means of that order and the special case, the merits of the case have been summarily (and therefore finally) disposed of by consent of the parties; or that the Master in Chambers had no jurisdiction to make the order for, and the judge of the County Court of York none (except as a mere arbitrator) to dispose of the special case, and so quâcunque viâ, that no appeal lies. I think the appeal should be quashed. We may, perhaps, simply dismiss it, as the parties have not taken the objection.

Appeal dismissed, with costs.

MITCHELL V. VANDUSEN.

Costs in discretion of Court—O. J. A. Rule 428—Successful party ordered to pay costs.

> An action by the bailiff of one Division Court against the bailiff of another Division Court to recover the proceeds of goods seized and sold by the latter, such goods being at the time of such seizure and sale already under seizure by the plaintiff upon executions in his hands against the execution debtor, was tried before the Judge of a County Court, without a jury, who held that the plaintiff was entitled to recover, but, under the circumstances, deprived the plaintiff of his costs, and ordered that the defendant's costs of the action and the costs of the seizure and sale should be deducted from the amount of the judgment. On appeal from such exercise of discretion, this Court reversed the decision of the learned Judge and ordered judgment to be entered for the plaintiff with costs.
>
> HAGARTY, C. J. O., reserved his opinion as to the existence of any right in any judge to make a defendant pay the costs of a plaintiff who has failed to establish a right to recover, or to make a plaintiff who substantially proved his right to recover, pay the costs of the defendant.
>
> *Per* PATTERSON, J. A.—Rule 428 gives full discretion over the apportionment of costs, and in proper cases to deprive the successful party of costs, but does not extend to make any party, whether plaintiff or defendant who is wholly successful in his action or defence, pay his defeated opponent's costs.
>
> *Per* OSLER, J. A.—The jurisdiction in question is one which existed in the old Court of Chancery, though the circumstances in which it was exercised, were of a very special and unusual character.

THIS was an appeal from the judgment of the Junior Judge of the County Court of the county of Grey.

The trial took place before him, without a jury, at the sittings of the Court on the 15th and 16th December 1886, when judgment was reserved.

It appeared that the plaintiff was bailiff of the 4th Division Court of the county of Grey. Executions on judgments obtained in that Court at the suits of one Dyre, and of the Molson's Bank, against one William Boyd and others, were issued against the goods and chattels of those defendants, and delivered to the plaintiff to be executed, on the 16th June and 9th July, 1885, respectively.

The plaintiff swore that, under those executions, he had seized the goods and chattels of Boyd on or about 11th July, 1885, and advertised the same for sale on or about 20th October following.

On the 24th and 27th October, the defendant Vandusen, who was bailiff of the Fifth Division Court of said county, under executions in his hands at the suit of the defendant McFarland and others, issued out of the last named Court, seized the goods and chattels in question ; and before the sale thereof by Vandusen, the plaintiff notified him of his prior seizure. Vandusen, however, by direction of Mc-Farland disregarding such notice, sold the goods in question.

The other facts out of which the proceedings arose, appear in the following extract from the judgment of the learned Judge, delivered on the 8th January, 1887 :

"The plaintiff swears he seized the goods in question about 11th July, 1885 ; that at the time of seizure the grain was growing, and that he deemed it advisable not to sell until it was harvested, and that the horses, &c., would be required in the harvesting, and that he therefore informed Boyd of the seizure and placed him in charge of the goods seized with his consent and with the understanding and agreement that he should keep possession for the plaintiff and harvest the grain with the view of saving expense, and this statement Boyd confirms. The next thing that happened, according to the plaintiff's account, was, that he heard that Boyd had threshed the grain : that he went to his premises on or about the 20th October, and, after satisfying himself that the grain had been threshed, advertised the seized property for sale ; he says he placed one notice on a bin of oats on the premises, and others in Clarksburg and Thornbury ; he did not produce a copy of this notice, neither was there any endorsement of the date of seizure on the writs ; he thinks the sale was fixed for 31st October, and that he posted the notices of sale on 20th October. The defendant Vandusen, as bailiff, seized the goods in question at two different times—namely, on the 24th and 27th October, under the defendant McFarland's execution and another. At the time of the seizure by him there was nothing to indicate that the goods were under seizure ; he swears that when he seized the grain on the 24th he was not informed by any one that the goods had been seized by Mitchell ; he also says that he does not recollect being so informed when he made the seizure of the horses, &c., on the 27th, but the defendant Boyd says he did inform him at that time that Mitchell had seized ; he had, however, previous to the sale by him received a letter from the plaintiff demanding the goods, and stating that they were under seizure by him. The defendant Vandusen, however, apparently did not believe the statements contained in this letter, and judging from the evidence given at the trial, I am not surprised at this fact. There are several objections raised to the plaintiff's recovery : 1. That there was no seizure, or as I understand it, that if there was, there was an abandonment of it, and that at the time of the seizure by Vandusen the goods were not in custodia legis ; 2. That the writs were not in force, not having been renewed by instructions from the plaintiffs in the suits ; 3. Growing crops are not liable to seizure ; 4. No endorsement on writs of date of seizure, as required by sec. 174 of Division Courts Act ; 5. That the plaintiffs in the suits under which plaintiff seized, stayed or delayed proceedings. It is also objected that there is no evidence to connect defendant McFarland with the seizure."

The learned Judge overruled all these objections, stating fully his reasons for so doing, and proceeded :

"I will give judgment for the plaintiff for the sum of $162.85, being the amount realized by the sale of the goods ; but inasmuch as I believe this suit has been brought about by the carelessness of the plaintiff, and his neglect in following legal requirements as well as in adopting the ordinary precautions taken by officers in his position, I will not give the plaintiff costs, but will allow the defendants their costs as also the costs of the seizure and sale of the goods in question, to be deducted from the amount of the judgment. There will be judgment against both defendants."

The plaintiff thereupon appealed to this Court, and the appeal came on to be heard on the 12th of September, 1887.*

Creasor, Q. C., for the appellant. The appellant having wholly succeeded in his action, the learned Judge had no jurisdiction to allow the respondents their costs of action ; and much less could he order the costs of the seizure and sale to be deducted from the amount realised ; and admitting for the moment that the learned Judge had the power to give the respondents their costs, there was no good cause for his so doing on this occasion ; and there was certainly no good cause for depriving the appellant of his costs of action which ought to have been allowed to him. See *Foster* v. *Great Western R.W. Co.*, 8 Q. B. D. 25, 515 ; *Jones* v. *Curling*, 13 Q. B. D. 262 ; *Johnstone* v. *Cox*, 19 Ch. D. 17.

George Kerr, for the respondents, contended that the question of costs was one entirely in the discretion of the Judge who tried the case, and he having exercised his discretion, this Court would not interfere.

Present.—HAGARTY, C.J.O., PATTERSON and OSLER, JJ.A.,

September 29, 1887. PATTERSON, J. A.—This is an action by the bailiff of a Division Court against the bailiff of another Division Court in the same county, for seizing and selling under executions in his hands goods which the plaintiff had already seized under executions.

It was tried in the County Court without a jury, and the learned Judge, after a careful consideration of the facts, thus stated his decision: "I will give judgment for the plaintiff for the sum of $162.85, being the amount realised by the sale of the goods, but, inasmuch as I believe this suit has been brought about by the carelessness of the plaintiff and his neglect in following legal requirements as well as in adopting the ordinary precautions taken by officers in his position, I will not give the plaintiff costs, but will allow the defendants their costs, as also the costs of the seizure and sale of the goods in question, to be deducted from the amount of the judgment."

The appeal is from the adjudication of costs against the successful plaintiff, or from the direction to deduct the amount from the damages assessed.

The learned Judge speaks of the defendant's costs of defence and the costs of the seizure and sale of the goods in the same manner, but I do not think they are intended to be put on quite the same footing. I understand him to mean that what the defendant realised by the sale of the goods was the price they brought, viz., $162.85, less what it cost him to effect the sale, or his disbursements out of pocket; and that that balance, which can be easily ascertained when it is known what amount was disbursed, is to be the award of damages.

I do not see any objection to that, and therefore would not sustain the appeal so far as those disbursements are concerned.

The allowance to the defendant of his costs of the defence in which he failed against the plaintiff who wholly succeeded, raises a question of importance and of some nicety under rule 428.

The learned Judge granted leave to appeal from his decision, which removes any objection to our reviewing

the exercise of the discretion vested in the Court by
that rule over the costs of an action; but there is the
larger question whether that discretion extends so far
beyond the refusal of costs to a successful party as to
authorise an order that he pay the costs of the party
against whom he has succeeded in the action.

The question, though not yet formally decided in this
province, is yet not altogether new.

In the English Supreme Court Orders of 1875, order
55, rule 1, was identical with our rule 428, and though
somewhat changed in the orders of 1883, where it is
order 65, rule 1, it is still essentially the same so far
as applicable to the matter before us.

The effect of these orders has been discussed in cases,
several of which were cited to us.

In *Foster* v. *Great Western R. W. Co.*, 8 Q. B. D. 25,
decided in 1882, the Lords Justices pointed out that the
jurisdiction conferred by the rule upon the High Court
was the same formerly exercised in Chancery, and which
had not been considered to extend to making a successful defendant pay the costs of the plaintiff who wholly
failed in his action.

The same view had been acted on a year earlier in
Dicks v. *Yates*, 18 Ch. D. 76, and has since that time been
followed in many cases, and in one or two expressly
affirmed. See *Farrow* v. *Austin*, 18 Ch. D. 58; *Turner*
v. *Hancock*, 20 Ch. D. 303; *In re Silver Valley Mines*,
21 Ch. D. 381; *Snelling* v. *Pulling*, 29 Ch. D. 85; *Re*
McClellan, 29 Ch. D. 495; *Re Mills's Estate*, 34 Ch. D. 24;
Williams v. *Jones*, 34 Ch. D. 120; *Willmott* v. *Barber*, 17
Ch. D. 772; *Butcher* v. *Pooler*, 24 Ch. D. 273.

The subject of decision in *Foster's* case, and in most if
not all those I have cited, was the liability of the successful defendant to be ordered to pay the costs of the
plaintiff.

It was so also in *Dicks* v. *Yates*, but there the Lord
Justice James alluded to the form of the question with
which we are now more directly concerned, when the

plaintiff succeeds and it is sought to make him pay the
defendant's costs. He said (p. 85): "There is an essential difference between a plaintiff and a defendant. A plaintiff
may succeed in getting a decree and still have to pay all
the costs of the action, but the defendant is dragged into
Court and cannot be made liable to pay the whole costs
of the action, if the plaintiff had no title to bring him
there."

We cannot tell what class of cases the Lord Justice
had in his mind in thus referring to the plaintiff's
liability, when successful to the extent of obtaining a
decree, to be made pay the whole costs of the action.
He cannot have intended to assert that a plaintiff who
wholly succeeded in establishing a substantial cause of
action against a defendant who sets up a defence which he
cannot sustain was, under the old practice, liable to be
ordered to pay the defendant's costs. There would be no
essential distinction in principle between a case of that
kind and the case of a defendant sued by a plaintiff who
had no title. He must have had in his mind some peculiar and exceptional state of facts justifying a departure
from the general rule of the Court.

The general rule was differently stated by Cotton, L.J.,
in *Harris* v. *Petherick*, 4 Q. B. D. 611. In that case
plaintiff sued for two claims which seem to have had no
connection with each other. One was for £85 as commission for obtaining a partnership, and the other was for
six shillings, being the cost of an advertisement relating to
the sale of a horse. He failed as to the £85, but recovered
the six shillings, and he was ordered to pay the defendant's costs. The Court of Appeal consisting of Bramwell,
Brett, and Cotton, L.JJ., affirmed the order made at the
trial by Manisty, J., holding that the plaintiff had failed
as to the substantial cause of the action. Cotton, L.J.,
whose opinions as an experienced equity counsel and
judge are of great weight on any question of equity procedure, said : " I have had some doubt whether the plaintiff
who has obtained judgment for a small amount can be
ordered to pay the defendant's costs ; but as the other

Lords Justices are of opinion that he can be made to do so, I do not dissent from that view. Under the old practice in Chancery I do not think that a successful plaintiff was ever ordered to pay costs," &c.

The two claims in *Harris* v. *Petherick* were apparently as distinct as if each had been the subject of a separate action. The hesitation of Cotton, L. J., may therefore be a little difficult to understand, but it serves to give point to his statement of what the old practice was, and distinguishes that statement, which was his ratio dubitandi, from an obiter dictum like the remark of James, L. J., in *Dicks* v. *Yates*. I imagine that the rule against multifariousness in the Chancery procedure would have prevented a situation like that in *Harris* v. *Petherick* from arising in that jurisdiction.

There is a case of *Williams* v. *Ward*, reported in 55 L. J. Q. B. 566, as decided in the Court of Appeal on 30th June, 1886. It was an action for libel in which a plea of justification was pleaded, and the jury found for the plaintiff with one farthing damages. The report states that on application of the defendant under order 65, rule 1, the Judge deprived the plaintiff of costs and ordered him to pay the costs of the defendant. The plaintiff appealed to the Court of Appeal and the appeal was dismissed. On this bare statement the case would look very much like a precedent for the judgment now in review. But for several reasons it seems impossible to rely on that part of the report which states that the plaintiff was ordered to pay the costs. No other case is to be found, so far as I am aware, in which, under analogous circumstances, such an order was made: *Harris* v. *Petherick* is obviously not a case of the kind. If, therefore, the order was made, and was sustained by the Court of Appeal, the decision would have been too important to have escaped the attention of other reporters. Yet I have been unable to find any trace of it any where but in the Law Journal report. It does not appear even in the *London Times* reports, and in the *Weekly Notes* there is merely the memorandum : " *Williams* v. *Ward.* Appeal from order of Field, J., dismissed"—in the record of business for the day. Then, when we read the judgment of the Court which was delivered by Lord Esher, M. R., without calling on the counsel for the respondent, we find no allusion whatever to the order to pay the defendant's costs, but we find the order treated as of the same extent only as in the order in *Harnett* ·v. *Vise,* 5 Ex. D. 307, which merely deprived the plaintiff of costs, and the whole discussion turning on the question whether there was the " good cause" required by order 65, rule 1, to enable the Judge to deprive the plaintiff of costs in place of leaving them to follow the event of the verdict. In *Harnett* v. *Vise* the Court had heard an appeal on the existence of "good cause," and in *Jones* v. *Curling,* 13 Q. B. D. 262, had formally decided that it was the subject of appeal. In *Williams* v. *Ward,* Lord Esher, after a reference to the facts, concluded his judgment by saying : " This is oppression, and therefore good cause for the Judge to exercise his discretion *as to depriving the plaintiff of his costs.* We must stop here and decline to consider how far he exercised that discretion rightly."

The case is thus seen to have been merely an exercise of the appellate jurisdiction, which, in *Jones* v. *Curling,* was decided to belong to the Court, not involving any point of such novelty or interest as to seem to any of the reporters, but the one, fit for insertion in the reports.

Re Mills Estate, 34 Ch. D. 24, was decided some months later than *Williams* v. *Ward,* and while the whole subject is there pretty fully discussed, there is no hint that the sanction of the Court had been given to the proposition that a plaintiff under circumstances like those in *Williams* v. *Ward,* could be ordered to pay the defendant's costs.

I have no doubt of the propriety of holding that the jurisdiction over costs, given by rule 428, does not extend to make any party, whether plaintiff or defendant, who is wholly successful in his action or defence, pay the costs of his defeated opponent.

That interpretation is, I think, supported by the tenor of all the decisions on the subject, and is in accordance with sound policy.

It avoids the recognition of a power which would be dangerous as well as unnecessary ; while it leaves full discretion, not only over the apportionment of costs, but in proper cases to deprive the successful party of costs.

It is a power which would be apt to be exercised by way of punishing the litigant for some supposed offence, the means of judging of which would, in most cases, be insufficient.

The discretion to be exercised is, as was observed by Lord Coleridge in the course of the vigorous criticism of the decision of the Court of Appeal in *Jones* v. *Curling*, 13 Q. B. D. 262, with which he prefaced his decision upon an application respecting costs in *Huxley* v. *West London Extension R. W. Co.*, 17 Q. B. D. 373 : " A judicial discretion to be exercised on legal principles, not by chance medley, nor by caprice, nor in temper."

It is to be feared that this sound and useful canon would be in danger of being sometimes lost sight of in the exercise of the penal power we have been discussing.

We have to decide how the costs are to go.

We should, in any case, observe the salutary rule laid down in *Gilbert* v. *Huddlestone*, 28 Ch. D. 549, that even when there is an appeal by leave of the Court below from the exercise of discretion in awarding costs, regard must be had to the discretion which has been exercised, and which should not be interfered with unless there has been a violation of principle or misapprehension of facts.

We shall find a useful statement of the principle which ought to guide us in the language of Jessel, M.R., in *Cooper* v. *Whittingham*, 15 Ch. D. 501, 504, where he said : " As I understand the law as to costs, it is this, that when a plaintiff comes to enforce a legal right, and there has been no misconduct on his part, no omission or neglect which would induce the court to deprive him of his costs, the Court has no discretion, and cannot take away the plaintiff's right to costs. There may be misconduct of many sorts: for instance, there may be misconduct in commencing the proceedings, or some miscarriage in the procedure, or an oppressive and vexatious mode of conducting the proceedings, or other misconduct which will induce the Court to refuse costs; but when there is nothing of the kind the rule is plain and well settled and is as I have stated it. It is, for instance, no answer where a plaintiff asserts a legal right, for a defendant to allege his ignorance of such a right, and to say, 'If I had known of your right, I should not have infringed it.'"

These last words might fairly be put in the mouth of this defendant, and would express the whole of his ground for being relieved from the ordinary incidence of the costs of the suit which he has unsuccessfully defended.

I may also refer to *Upmann* v. *Forrester*, 24 Ch. D. 231, where Chitty, J., acting on the same principle, said (p. 257): "Although as against the defendant the case may be a hard one, he must not on that account be excused the payment of costs. As the late Master of the Rolls said in *Cooper* v. *Whittingham*, he cannot be allowed to escape by saying 'I never intended to do wrong'; and to use an observation of the same learned Judge, as there is no fund out of which successful plaintiffs can receive costs, their costs must be paid by defendants, although they may be innocent"; and to *Goodhart* v. *Hyett*, 25 Ch. D. 182, where North, J., after commenting on the conduct of the plaintiff in bringing the action, which related to an easement, without first giving notice to the defendant, the effect of which might have been to avert the litigation, said: " Under these circumstances I have felt very much disposed, if I could, to say that there ought to be no costs of the action. I do not think I can do that; but I think it is a case in which, there being a right set up by the plaintiffs and denied by the defendant, the plaintiffs must have the costs of the action so far as relates to the house in the course of erection by the defendant."

A complication is introduced into this case by the form of the judgment, which directs the defendant's costs to be paid out of a fund which does not belong to either plaintiff or defendant, being the proceeds of the sale of goods under executions.

But, apart from that circumstance, there is nothing which, consistently with principle, can take the case out of the ordinary rule.

In my opinion we should allow the appeal with costs, and direct judgment for the plaintiff for $162.85, less whatever sum the Judge shall ascertain to have been necessarily expended by the defendant in effecting the sale of the goods, and with full costs.

OSLER, J. A.—This is an appeal from the Junior Judge of the County Court of the county of Grey. The action was brought by the plaintiff, the bailiff of the 4th Division Court, against the defendant Vandusen, bailiff of the Fifth Division Court of the county, and one McFarland, to recover the proceeds of goods seized and sold by the latter bailiff under an execution against one Boyd at the suit of the defendant McFarland, which at the time of such seizure and sale, were actually under seizure, and had been advertised for sale by the plaintiff under executions which he also held against the same judgment debtor.

The case was tried by the learned Judge without a jury. He held that the plaintiff was entitled to recover, but deprived him of his costs, and ordered that the defendants' costs and the costs of the seizure and sale of the goods should be deducted from the amount of the judgment.

The plaintiff's right to recover is not in question, but he has by leave of the learned Judge appealed from the order in respect of costs, and the questions we have to decide are, 1st, whether the Judge had jurisdiction to make the order which he did make; and 2nd, if he had, whether it was wrongly exercised.

The case having been tried without a jury the jurisdiction as to costs is governed by the 1st part of rule 428, viz., that subject to the provisions of the Act the costs of and incidental to all proceedings shall be in the discretion of the Court.

Then the question is, what are the limitations upon that discretion? The rule itself points out two; the first that where certain classes of persons such as trustees, mortgagees, &c., were according to the former practice in equity entitled to costs out of a particular fund, they are not to be deprived of that right in the future ; and 2nd, that in cases tried by a jury costs are to follow the event, unless upon application and for good cause shewn, the Judge or Court otherwise orders.

A further and more general limitation has, by construction, been placed upon the rule, and in *Foster* v. *Great Western R. W. Co.*, 8 Q. B. Div. 515, which was followed and approved in *Re Mills's Estate*, 34 Ch. Div. 24, the Court of Appeal held that the intention of the Legislature in passing the corresponding English rule was to confer upon the Chancery and Common Law Divisions of the High Court the same jurisdiction as to costs which the Court of Chancery had before the Judicature Act, and that the meaning of the order was that there should be an absolute discretion over all costs within the jurisdiction of the High Court, and that the jurisdiction of the High Court should be precisely what the jurisdiction of the Court of Chancery formerly was. "The true construction of the order," says Brett, L.J., "is that it adopts the jurisdiction of the Court of Chancery as to costs, with the same limitation of jurisdiction as formerly existed in that Court." See also per Cotton, L.J., in *Re Mills's Estate*, *supra*, at p. 33.

Now the Court always had power where the justice of the case seemed to require it to excuse the defeated party from payment of his adversary's costs, in other words to deprive the successful party of costs ; (Dan. Chy. Pr. vol. 1, pp. 1243, 1244, 5th ed. ; *Cooper* v. *Whittingham*, 15 Ch. Div. 501 ; *Dicks* v. *Yates*, 18 Ch. D. 85 ; *Harnett* v. *Vise*, 6 Ex. Div. p. 307,) though where the case is tried by a jury, that can now only be done upon application, for good cause shewn ; and whether the facts exist which constitute good cause is the subject of appeal without leave : *Jones* v. *Curling*, 13 Q. B. Div. 262. But as regards the power to make a successful party pay the costs of his opponent, a distinction appears to exist between the case of a successful plaintiff and that of a successful defendant.

I think we must take it as distinctly settled for us by
the course of decision under the English rule, and notwithstanding the observations to be found in the judgment of
the Divisional Court in *Church* v. *Fuller*, 3 O. R. 317, that
where the defendant succeeds in the action he cannot be
ordered to pay the plaintiff's general costs of suit, as distinguished from the costs of particular issues, or costs
occasioned by his misconduct in the course of the litigation;
because that is a power which the Court of Chancery did
not possess.   I do not enter into a general examination of
the cases, or the text books upon this subject, as I
think it sufficient to quote the language of the late Master
of the Rolls, Sir George Jessel, in the case of *Dicks* v. *Yates*,
18 Ch. Div. 76, which was approved by the Court of
Appeal, in *Foster* v. *The Great Western R. W. Co.*, 8 Q. B.
D 515, and *Re Mills's Estate*, 34 Ch. Div. 24-35 :

" Now, if a plaintiff has no title, are the costs of the action
in the discretion of the Court so that the Court can give the
whole of them to the plaintiff ?   It seems to me that they
are not. No one ever heard of a defendant being ordered
to pay the costs of the plaintiff who has failed to make
out any title."

Witt v. *Corcoran*, 2 Ch. Div. 69, is to the same
effect.   A successful plaintiff, however, would seem,
in some very exceptional cases, to have stood in a
different position.   In *Dicks* v. *Yates, supra*, James, L. J.,
observes :   *   * "There is a difference between a plaintiff
and a defendant. A plaintiff may succeed in getting a
decree, and still have to pay all the costs of the litigation ;
but a defendant is dragged into Court and cannot be made
liable to pay the whole costs of the action if the plaintiff
had no title to bring him there."

In *Foster's Case*, (1882) Cotton, L. J., said :

"According to the practice of the Court of Chancery,
relief was sometimes granted on condition that the
plaintiff should pay all the costs of the action."

Harris v. *Petherick*, 4 Q. B. Div., (1879) was an action
tried with a jury, in which the plaintiff sued for two
sums of money, £85 for a commission on a sale effected

by him, and 6s. the cost of an advertisement. He
failed to recover the first but succeeded as to the second.
This was held to be good cause for directing him to
pay the costs as he had substantially failed in the suit,
and had harassed the defendant with a vexatious action.
Bramwell and Cotton, L. JJ., also held, and Brett, L. J.,
seems to agree that when "good cause" is shewn, the
discretion of the Judge under the proviso at the end
of the order, is as large as that under the first clause
though Cotton, L. J., said that he had had some doubt
whether a plaintiff who had obtained judgment for
a small amount could be ordered to pay the defendant's
costs, and that he did not think that under the old practice in Chancery a successful plaintiff was ever ordered to
pay costs.   The dictum which subsequently fell from the
same learned Judge in *Foster's Case*, is probably a more
accurate statement of the practice.   In *Daniell's* Chancery
Practice, 5th ed., pp. 1244-1266, the writer says that cases
of the kind (*i.e.*, of the successful party being ordered to
pay his opponent's costs), are very limited.

Two instances are given.   Where a bill for specific performance stated the agreement in one way ; the agreement
as proved by the only witness was different, while the
answer set forth an agreement different from both. Specific
performance was decreed according to the agreement stated
in the answer with costs against the plaintiff.   Again,
where at the instance of the grantee, an annuity, in
payment of which no default had been made, was
declared charged on the lands of the grantor, the plaintiff
was ordered to pay the costs. Upon the whole it seems
that the jurisdiction in question is one which does exist,
though the circumstances in which it has been exercised,
are of a very special and unusual character, as where the
plaintiff was not entitled to a decree as of right, but
ex gratiâ, and upon condition, or where, though having a
strict right, the action was unnecessary or precautionary. I
do not suppose any case can be found where a defendant
who has wrongfully resisted a just demand, has recovered
his costs from the plaintiff.

We have then only further to say, whether in our opinion the order as a whole was, under all the circumstances, one which ought to have been made.

It by no means follows that because leave has been given to appeal, the Court will readily interfere with the discretion which a Judge has exercised. They will only do so where there has been some disregard of principle or some misapprehension of the facts : *Re Gilbert*, 28 Ch. Div. 549. In the present it is manifest that there was no sufficient reason in principle, having regard to the manner in which the jurisdiction has hitherto been exercised— for refusing costs to the plaintiff, much less for casting upon him, in addition, the payment of the defendants' costs. Substantially, the action is for a mere money demand, and by the judgment the plaintiff is declared entitled to recover just what he has sued for ; the effect of the order practically is to deprive him of the greater part, if not the whole of it, though it is a fund which in point of fact belongs not to himself but to the execution plaintiffs in the division court actions. The reason assigned by the learned Judge for making the order is, that if the plaintiff had observed the statutory direction (section 174, D. C. Act) as to indorsing the date of seizure on the executions held by him it would have prevented the doubts which had been thrown on the question of his seizure. But, inasmuch as it appears from the evidence as reported in the judgment, and from the findings of the learned Judge that an effectual seizure had been in fact made, under which the debtor's goods had been advertised for sale before the issue of the warrant under which the defendant bailiff acted, and that the plaintiff had given him written notice of such seizure, which he and his co-defendant the other execution plaintiff chose to disregard, I think he should have been treated in all respects as having proceeded upon the warrant of the latter at his own risk, and that there was nothing to take the case out of the general rule that costs are to follow the event. The learned Judge's discretion was exercised on a wrong principle, and therefore the appeal should be allowed.

HAGARTY, C. J. O.—I agree in the result. But I wish
to add as to any future discussion of this question, that I
reserve my opinion as to the existence of any right in any
Judge to make a defendant pay the costs of a plaintiff who
has failed to establish a right to recover, or on the other
hand to make a plaintiff who has substantially proved his
right to recover, pay the costs of the defendant. I shall
regret if it be found that such a power exists, as I do not
think it should be entrusted to any Judge or Court. Even
if it exist, I for one would be most unwilling to exercise it.
These remarks do not apply to costs of issues or to any
order as to costs improperly or unnecessarily incurred by a
successful party.

Appeal allowed with costs.

RYAN V. THE BANK OF MONTREAL.

Bill of exchange payable to order of drawer—Forgery of drawer's name—
Acceptance, what it means—Forgery of drawing and indorsement—
Action by drawee to recover back money paid to retire forged bill—
Estoppel—Delay.

The plaintiff at the request of Y., the business manager of the Hamilton
Cotton Company, received from him a draft in the name of the company on a New York firm for $4,989.65, at three months, which
plaintiff discounted at the Toronto agency of the defendants, and in
pursuance of an arrangement to that effect, Y. drew on the plaintiff
in the name of the Cotton Company, payable to their own order for
$4,800, which plaintiff paid on presentment out of the proceeds of the
New York draft. About seven weeks afterwards plaintiff discovered
that the signatures to, and indorsements on both these drafts had
been forged by Y., and immediately communicated such information to
the defendants, and demanded from them a return of the amount paid
by him to retire the $4,800 draft which was refused. Plaintiff, how-
ever, paid the draft on New York at maturity.

In an action brought to recover the money paid to retire the $4,800 draft,
the Queen's Bench Division held that the plaintiff was entitled
recover : An appeal from this judgment was dismissed, the Judges of
this Court being equally divided.

THIS was an appeal by the defendants from a judgment
of the Queen's Bench Division, reversing the judgment of
the trial Judge, reported 12 O. R. 39, where and in the judgments on the present appeal the facts are clearly set
forth.

The appeal came on for hearing on the 28th of March,
1887.*

Bruce, Q. C., for the appellants.

J. Maclennan, Q. C., and *Haverson*, for the respondent.

September 6, 1887.   HAGARTY, C. J. O.—This case is to
be viewed in two aspects ; first, as if the plaintiff had duly
accepted the bill and was sued by the bank on the acceptance ; second, under the actual state of facts that he voluntarily paid the amount to the holders, equally innocent
with himself of any evil practice connected with the
bill, and on discovery, as he alleges, of the truth, claims
to have the money refunded as paid under a mistake.

The whole point relied on under the first branch of the
case was, that although the acceptor could not deny

Present—HAGARTY, C. J. O., BURTON, PATTERSON, and OSLER, JJ. A.

the drawing he could traverse the indorsement. I must say that the law on that point is not in a very satisfactory state. ·

In *Robarts* v. *Tucker*, 18 L. J. Q. B. 173, (1849), Sir J. Patteson says:

" No doubt if a man drew on his debtor in favor of a third person who indorses over, the acceptance does not admit the handwriting of the third person. But if a man draws payable to his own order, and then indorses, the acceptance, if made after the indorsement, admits the indorsement as well as the drawing."

··The case did not call for a decision on that point. The payees were third persons.

In *Ashpitel* v. *Bryan*, 3 B. & S. 489, (1863), fourteen years afterwards, Wightman, J., delivering judgment, says: " Primâ facie the acceptor is not admitted to deny the handwriting of the drawer, and I think the same rule applies to an indorsement by the drawer, the indorsement being on the bill when it was accepted. It may be that he would not be bound to admit the handwriting of a person who was a stranger; but here the indorsement is in the same handwriting as the drawing." Crompton and Mellor, JJ., agree in the judgment. But it turned on peculiar grounds that under the facts the acceptor was, as it were, estopped by his own act and conduct in the case. The judgment was affirmed in Error 5 B. & S. 723.

In *Cooper* v. *Meyer*, 10 B. & Cr. 471, Lord Tenterden says:

" The acceptor ought to know the handwriting of the drawer, and is therefore precluded from 'disputing it, but it is said that he may nevertheless dispute the indorsement. Where the drawer is a real person he may do so; but if there is in reality no such person, I think the fair construction of the acceptor's undertaking is, that he will pay to the signature of the same person that signed for the drawer."

It was shewn there that the handwriting and indorsement of the drawer's names was the same, and were fictitious persons.

Bayley, J., adds:

" The defendants ought not to have accepted the bills without knowing whether or not there were such persons as the supposed drawers.   If they chose to accept without making the inquiry, I think they must be considered as undertaking to pay to the signature of the person who actually drew the bills."

Allport v. *Meek*, 4 C. & P. 268, a bill drawn by Williams, and indorsed by him to the plaintiff, and accepted by the defendant.   There was as no proof of handwriting, but only an admission by defendant that he had accepted the bill.   It was urged that the jury might look at the indorsement to see whether it was the same handwriting as the drawing.

Tindal, C. J.—" I think you must call some witness to lay some evidence before the jury on which they may decide;" this the plaintiff could not do, and thus a nonsuit.   In the same volume is the case of *Jones* v. *Turnour*, (p. 204) a bill declared on as drawn by Hannah Pickersgill on the defendant, accepted by him and indorsed by the drawer to plaintiff.   A witness proved that the signature of the drawer: *Per pro* H. Pickersgill, John Pickersgill, and the indorsement in same form were in the handwriting of John Pickersgill.   Witness did not know Hannah Pickersgill—he heard from John—she was his mother;   no authority in John was proved, but the witness said he had seen other bills in the same form and handwriting as the drawing and the indorsement on this bill.   It was objected that the indorsement was not proved.

Lord Tenterden says :

" I am of opinion that as against this defendant, it must be taken to be an indorsment by Hannah Pickersgill.   If the defendant had intended to dispute the existence of any such person, or of any such authority to draw, he should not have accepted the bill in that state; but he having done so, I consider that his acceptance admits the authority to draw in that particular form, and the indorsement being in the same form and handwriting, it may be taken to have been made with the same authority."

In the following term, it was again raised, objecting also to the admission of evidence that other bills in the same form had been seen.

Bayley, J., intimated an opinion that the proof was sufficient in all repects, except that there was no evidence
of the name being " Hannah," the bill being merely " H."
A rule was granted and the Court allowed an affidavit to
be filed that the name was " Hannah," &c., and the rule
was discharged.

I think if in *Allport* v. *Meek*, a witness had proved that
the handwriting of the drawing and indorsement were the
same, it would have sufficed to satisfy Tindal, C. J. It
must be remembered that at that date proof by comparison
of handwriting was not generally allowed.

There are strong statements in the text writers to the
effect that acceptance while admitting the drawing, does
not admit the indorsement, even when the bill is to the
drawer's own order.

Robinson v. *Yarrow*, 7 Taunt. 455 (1817), is always
cited. The headnote is : The acceptance of a bill drawn
by procuration admits the drawer's handwriting, and the
procuration to draw. But though the bill is indorsed by
the same procuration, the date thereof not appearing, the
acceptor does not admit the procuration to indorse.

At the trial no evidence was given of the handwriting
of the agent. The Court upheld a verdict for defendant.

Gibbs, C. J., says :

" The defendant admits that Henry, the agent, as the
attorney of the drawers, had authority to draw the bill ;
but it does not appear at what date the indorsement was
made, and the defendant has not admitted that Henry had
a right to indorse that bill."

The Court refers to an earlier case, *Smith* v. *Chester*, 1
T. R. 654. There were several indorsements on the bill
before it was accepted, and the holder could not prove the
writing of the first indorser.

Buller, J., said :

" When a bill is presented for acceptance the acceptor
only looks at the handwriting of the drawer, which he is
afterwards precluded from disputing, and it is on that
account the acceptor is liable, even though the bill be
forged."

If in *Robinson* v. *Yarrow*, it had been proved, as in our case, that the bill was discounted by the bank on the day of date and of drawing, with the payee's indorsement on it, and that the drawing and indorsement were in the same handwriting, and presented the next day for acceptance, possibly the decision might have been different.

Then in *Cooper* v. *Meyer*, 10 B. & Cr. 468, Lord Tenterden remarks as I have already quoted.

The same very learned Chief Justice, a couple of months afterwards, in the same year, decided the case of *Jones* v. *Turnour*, already noticed, where there was no suggestion as to the non-existence of the drawer, and in which case also *Robinson* v. *Yarrow* and *Smith* v. *Chester* were cited.

In *Beeman* v. *Duck*, 11 M. & W. 255 (in 1843). it was urged that *Cooper* v. *Meyer* only decided the case of the drawer being a fictitious person. Parke, B., in directing a new trial, as the plea traversing the indorsement had not been noticed until after verdict for the plaintiff, discussing the distinction between that case and *Cooper* v. *Meyer*, says, that there is great weight in the argument that the acceptor does not admit that it was indorsed by the drawers, if the defendant accepted in ignorance of the forgery.

The latest case that has been cited is, *Garland* v. *Jacomb*, L. R. 8 Ex. 216 (in Ex. Chr.), (1873).

In that case a bill was drawn by Williamson and Blackburn, a firm of solicitors to their own order on, and accepted by defendant. The drawing and indorsing was in the handwriting of Blackburn one of the firm, for his own debt, without his partner's sanction, to pay a debt to the holder who knew all the facts. It was held that the acceptor was only estopped from denying the drawing, and not from disputing the indorsement, and that the plaintiff who took it for his private debt would not have acquired any title to the bill unless Williamson, the other partner and drawer, had either expressly authorized or ratified the indorsement.

Blackburn, J., adds :

" Of course the plaintiff's title against the defendant arising from an estoppel cannot be better than it would have been had everything which the defendant is estopped from denying been literally true."

In this view, even if both the partners had joined in drawing the bill, there was nothing to authorize one of them without the other's assent to indorse it over to a person, knowing the facts, for his private debt.

The text books hardly discuss the question. They merely state the point, and cite some of the cases.

In *Chitty* on Bills (ed. 1878) p. 383, it is said the acceptance does not admit the authority of the drawer to indorse, citing *Garland* v. *Jacomb*; or the authority of an agent who draws by procuration; nor does it admit the genuineness of the indorsement, though it was on the bill at the time it was accepted : citing *Robinson* v. *Jarrow*, *Beeman* v. *Duck*, and *Robarts* v. *Tucker*.

Byles on Bills, (ed. 1885) 269, is to the same effect, citing same cases.

See also 1 Daniel, p. 429, sec. 538, citing some American authorities ; *Story* on Bills, secs. 262-3.

I think the authorities on this subject are in a most unsatisfactory state. As to the text writers, we find, as usual, very little examination of the cases beyond the mention of their names. Some of the authorities to which I have referred are not to be found cited.

If, as I find it laid down, the acceptor cannot deny the drawing, one of the reasons assigned being that he is assumed to be acquainted with his handwriting, and the indorsement is plainly in the same writing with which he is supposed to be familiar, I cannot see why he does not acknowledge them both. It is quite different where an independent payee is introduced whose indorsement is required, and is unknown to him. In the present case he only knew of the cotton company; the drawers, through H. Young, the person who arranged all with him, and arranged for drawing on him, assuming to represent the drawers. When the bill is presented to him he sees it in the shape in which he would naturally expect it to be—a draft on him to the drawers' order.

Two or three days before he had indorsed a draft of the company on the New York firm of Billup & Co., drawn and indorsed as this bill is by the payees ; then Ryan indorses it, and obtains the proceeds of it by discounting it in Toronto. In the Billup case he admits the goodness of the indorsement by putting his own name under it, and then dealing all the time solely with Hamilton Young, the bill now in question is drawn, indorsed, and presented to him, and he pays it out of the funds then in his hands—the proceeds of a previous alleged forgery of the same man. Under such circumstances I hardly see how he can now be heard averring that the indorsement was not made.

But we have further to consider the subject matter of this action. It is not a suit by the Bank of Montreal against Ryan on the bill. It is a claim by Ryan to recover back from the bank the money paid to them as money to which ex æquo et bono he is entitled, and which it is against equity and good conscience that the defendants should be allowed to retain.

We may assume that the bank and Ryan are equally innocent persons—that neither had any reason to suspect a fraud—both were imposed on by Young.

The plaintiff says he ought to recover, as he paid the money under the belief that the bill was really drawn and indorsed by the company. He is not allowed to deny that it was drawn, but he may deny the indorsement, and therefore can recover.

The bank were equally deceived, both as to the drawing and the indorsing. They paid the proceeds of the bill to H. Young, and the following day the plaintiff Ryan, as drawee, pays it to them, both parties believing that Ryan was legally bound to pay, and the bank to receive. It is not easy to perceive any superior equity on Ryan's side.

On the facts in evidence he had a far closer knowledge of Young's dealings in this and the preceding transactions than the bank.

The case seems reduced to this :—By Young's fraud the
bank was induced to discount the draft on Ryan. By the
same person's fraud Ryan paid it. Each was equally
deceived.

The language of Lord Mansfield, in *Price* v. *Neal*, 3 Burr.
1354, as to the recovery of money between two innocent
persons, may be referred to. The language is cited with
approval, and emphasised by additional comment, by Mr.
Justice Story, when delivering the Supreme Court judgment in *U. S. Bank* v. *Bank of Georgia*, 10 Wheat. 348.

In another case, 2 Burr. 1012, Lord Mansfield, in describing the action, says :

"In one word, the gist of this kind of action is, that
the defendant, upon the circumstances of the case, is obliged
by the ties of natural justice and equity to refund the
money."

In considering this it must not be forgotten that, after
paying this money as a legal obligation, no notice of the
forgery was given to the bankers for five or six weeks
after. It may be said that Ryan did not know it till then.
That is his misfortune. Had it been notified promptly the
bank would, of course, have at once communicated with
the Cotton Company, the alleged drawers. We can gather
from the evidence that had this been done the latter,
having funds of Young in their hands, would have
recouped the bank.

In August, two or three weeks after the payment of this
bill, a bill drawn and indorsed like this was discounted by
the bank, and was refused acceptance by Ryan and protested. This bill was also a forgery; but as soon as it
came back protested it was paid by Mr. Lucas, one of the
two partners in the Cotton Company. As I understand
the evidence, it was paid out of the moneys of H. Young
in the hands of the firm.

I think it right to state that I have arrived at this opinion with very great hesitation, and great doubt as to the
correctness of my judgment.

I have seldom seen a case in which the true state of the
authorities appeared to me to be more obscurely stated

As to the text-books, their compilers seem to satisfy themselves by stating the names of the cases, at least of most of them, but there seems to be no attempt to examine or distinguish.

BURTON, J. A.—This case comes by appeal from a judgment of the Queen's Bench Division, reversing the learned Judge at the trial, and holding that the plaintiff is entitled to recover, as for money paid, from the Bank of Montreal, a sum of $4,800, paid by him as the drawee of a bill which had been discounted by the bank for a party who had forged the name of the drawers, and having made the bill payable to the drawers' own order had forged also their indorsement.

It was strongly urged by the plaintiff's counsel that a previous negotiation of a forged bill by the same party in the name of the same drawers upon Billup & Co., of New York, which this plaintiff had bought from him, and discounted with his own bankers, had no connection with this suit, and that all evidence of that transaction ought to have been rejected; but when it is shewn that the present draft was for the proceeds of the bill so negotiated and we consider the nature of this action, and that it may become a question whether there is anything unconscionable in the defendants' retaining the advantage they have at present, it is difficult to see how the evidence could be excluded, and it is desirable that all the facts out of which the transaction arose should be before the Court.

It would seem then, that the plaintiff, who had no prior dealings with the Hamilton Cotton Company, or either of the partners of that firm, was waited upon by one Hamilton Young, a clerk in their employment, in the month of July, 1883, and requested to negotiate a draft purporting to be a draft of the Hamilton Cotton Company, at three months, upon a firm in New York known as J. P. Billup & Co., for $4,989.65, the drawers' names having been forged by Mr. Hamilton Young.

The plaintiff being resident in Toronto, and not acquainted with the standing or position of the drawers, sent a clerk to Hamilton to make inquiries, and ascertained that they were men of large means and good standing, but he had no communication with the members of the firm, and the defendants' counsel urged with much force that the plaintiff's suspicions ought to have been aroused when he found a firm of their standing, instead of applying to their bankers, apparently seeking to negotiate this draft with a stranger at an unusual and exorbitant rate of discount.

Having made these inquiries he agreed to negotiate the bill, and having done so, he in turn discounted it with his bank, and if he had then and there given a cheque for the amount at which he had agreed to negotiate it to Mr. Hamilton Young, the loss, if loss eventually resulted, would have been his.

Mr. Hamilton Young had, however, in the meantime, returned to Hamilton, and on the 23rd July he draws upon the plaintiff for the proceeds of this forged bill, the draft now in question.

If he had made this draft payable direct to the Bank of Montreal, and the plaintiff had then accepted and paid it, it is difficult to understand upon what principle he could seek to recover it back. The money would have been paid into the hands of the very man with whom he dealt, and to whom he intended it should be paid.

The draft purported to be the draft of the Hamilton Cotton Company, and was payable to their order. It was drawn by Mr. Hamilton Young in that manner, and was indorsed in the same way to the bank; and it is contended that although by the acceptance or payment the plaintiff is precluded from disputing the genuineness of the drawers' signature, he can dispute the indorsement. and as that was not the genuine indorsement of the firm no title passed to the bank, and having paid it to them who had no right to receive it, he could, on discovering the fraud, recover it back. Is this contention sound?

The general rule no doubt is, in the case of a genuine drawing but a forged indorsement, in accordance with this contention.

The acceptor having, or being supposed to have funds of the drawers in his hands, does not discharge his liability to them unless he pays the money to the person the drawers have directed him to pay it to.

But how does that apply to the present case, the acceptor having no transactions whatever with the real firm ? the payment of this draft did not leave him exposed to being called upon by them again, for they had no claim against him.

The case is in its circumstances peculiar. The acceptor's liability was not to the true firm, but he had in his hands a sum of money to the amount of the draft now in question as the proceeds of the other forgery.

Mr. Hamilton Young the party who had successfully imposed upon him was the person entitled to that money, and in furtherance of the fraud he drew this draft, again forging the name of the firm, and in that name he drew payable to the drawers' own order.

Now what is the effect of that ? It certainly was not intended that the true firm should be the payees ; what was intended was, that the same persons who drew the bill should indorse it.

What then is the effect of a person accepting or paying a bill so drawn ? It operates as an admission of the drawer's capacity to draw the bill, and when it is payable to the drawer's own order, of his capacity to indorse.

In *Drayton* v. *Dale,* 2 B. & C. 297, it was held that when a party makes a note payable to the order of a particular person, it was intimation to every one that he considered that person capable of making an order sufficient to transfer the property in the note, and that it was a general principle applicable to all negotiable securities that a person shall not dispute the power of another to indorse such an instrument when he asserts by the instrument that the other has such power.

The capacity to indorse, and the genuineness of the indorsement are two very different things.

If, for instance, after Mr. Young had drawn this bill, some one had abstracted it from his possession and following the precedent he had set, had forged the indorsement, that would not have passed the title to the bill, and the payment to the holder would not have altered the relations between Mr. Young and the plaintiff.

The cases referred to in the judgment of the Divisional Court appear to me to be very clearly distinguishable; some, as for instance *Robinson* v. *Yarrow*, 7 Taunt. 455, are cases where the alleged drawing was by procuration; the acceptor, by accepting, admitted not only the drawing, but the authority of the person who signed by procuration; but as an authority to draw would not amount to an authority to indorse, the acceptor could dispute the indorsement, and, unless the authority to indorse were proved, no title would be shewn in the holder.

In the present case the forged bill does not profess to be a bill drawn by procuration, but purports to be drawn by one of the members of a commercial partnership and initialed by him. *Garland* v. *Jacomb*, L. R. 8 Ex. 216, which is referred to, was the case of a partnership of solicitors where one partner had no authority to bind the firm by drawing or indorsing bills, and although the acceptor, by his acceptance, was estopped from denying the right of the firm to draw, he was at liberty to dispute the right of the same firm to indorse upon the same principle as in *Robinson* v. *Yarrow*, inasmuch as the special authority to indorse had to be proved; but I apprehend the decision in that case would have been different if the drawers had been a commercial firm instead of a firm of solicitors.

Lord Blackburn, in the course of his judgment in that case, says:

"A doubt occurred to some of us during the argument, whether, if Williamson had really assented to the bill being drawn by his partner in the firm's name, he would not have conclusively established as against himself that the indorsing of this particular bill was necessary for the purposes of the firm, and consequently that his partner had the same authority to endorse it as he would have had if the business of the firm required the drawing and indorsing of bills."

But it became unnecessary to decide it inasmuch as even if the right to indorse had been shewn, it would not have been an authority to indorse for the private purposes of one of the firm.

But these cases appear to me to have very little applicacation to the one we are now considering, where the drawing is a forgery, but is very material to a case where the drawing is genuine, but the indorsement forged, or in cases where the drawing purports to be per proc, and no authority to indorse per proc is shewn. When the drawing itself is a forgery, it does not appear to be very material that the payees' indorsement is also forged.

Here the acceptance would admit not only the capacity to draw, but the capacity of the same person to indorse; and it was proved that the drawing and indorsing were in the same handwriting : that the draft was taken in that state to the bank by the person who had forged them both, and the payment by the plaintiff was a good payment and discharge as against the drawers.

It appears to me that under such circumstances the bank got a good title to the bill, and could, if it had been accepted, have enforced it against the acceptor. The plaintiff, however, instead of accepting, paid it on presentation.

Tucker v. *Robarts*, 16 Q. B. 560, decides nothing more than that a banker cannot debit a customer with a payment made to one who claims through a forged indorsement. The payment there did not discharge the insurance company from their liability to the claimant under the policy.

It is said that the case might have been different if the bill had been discounted by the bank after the acceptance; but under the circumstances of this case that cannot affect the question. In all such cases, either of acceptance or payment, the foundation upon which the drawee is made to suffer the loss, is the imputed negligence in accepting or paying until he has ascertained the bill to be genuine.

Here the payment reached the party that the plaintiff intended it should reach. It does not differ in substance from the payment of a cheque given to Hamilton Young, by the plaintiff for the $4,800, which was payable by the plaintiff as the proceeds of the other discounted bill. The learned counsel for the plaintiff referred to the bank shifting its responsibility for the loss upon the plaintiff, but the facts warrant the remark. The plaintiff had already been imposed upon by discounting the first bill, the proceeds of that bill he held for the party who had practised the fraud upon him, the bank was the mere conduit pipe for transferring those funds to the party whom the plaintiff intended should receive them. Is there anything against conscience in the bank retaining the money thus paid to it ? With great deference, it would seem to me much more unreasonable if the plaintiff could shift the loss he had already incurred, upon parties equally innocent with himself who have been guilty of no want of care in taking the paper as they did.

I think the appeal should be allowed, and judgment entered for the defendants.

PATTERSON, J. A.—Two gentlemen named R. A. Lucas and J. M. Young carried on business at Hamilton under the name of the Hamilton Cotton Co. Their manager, Hamilton Young, forged a bill purporting to be drawn by the Hamilton Cotton Co. by J. M. Young, upon the plaintiff for $4,800. It bore date the 23rd of July, 1883, and was payable on demand to the order of the company. Hamilton Young then forged the company's indorsement of the bill, and on the same 23rd of July, took it to the defendants' office in Hamilton where it was discounted, and the proceeds, being $4,794, credited to the company, and paid out upon cheques purporting to be the cheques of the company, though now understood by the bank manager to have been forged. This was all done on the 23rd, and the bill was sent to the Toronto office of the bank, and was on the next day, the 24th, presented to the plaintiff, who paid it by a cheque against money then at his credit in the bank.

The plaintiff supposed the bill to be genuine and the bank to be the lawful indorsee of it, and did not discover the real state of the case until about the 11th of the following September, when he promptly demanded back his money. That is the demand which he seeks by this action to enforce.

So far, we have a case of money paid under a mistake of fact which the person who paid it has primâ facie a right to recover back. *Jones* v. *Ryde,* 5 Taunt. 488 ; *Bruce* v. *Bruce,* 5 Taunt. 495 *n.* ; *Wilkinson* v. *Johnson,* 3 B. & C. 428, and numerous other cases in notes to *Marriott* v. *Hampton,* 2 Sm. L. C. 436.

Against the recognition of this right the defendants, in the first place, invoke the maxim *In æquali jure melior est conditio possidentis,* and rely on the authority of *Price* v. *Neal,* 3 Burr. 1354 ; 1 W. Bl. 390. In that case two forged bills drawn on the plaintiff were indorsed to the defendants. The plaintiff paid one of them when presented, without acceptance, and the other he accepted and afterwards paid. At the trial of the action brought to recover back the amounts as money received to his use, his counsel " gave up the accepted bill on the authority of *Jenys* v. *Fawler,* Tr. 2 Geo. II. Stra. 946, where it is held that proof of forgery shall not be admitted on behalf of the acceptor of a bill, because it would hurt the negotiation of paper credit," and " as to the first bill which was never accepted, they insisted the case was different : no credit had been given to that bill by an acceptance ; therefore the same inconvenience would not follow." The decision was against the plaintiff. The reasons given by Lord Mansfield are more condensed in W. Bl., which is the report from which I quote, than in the report in *Burrow,* but are in substance alike in both reports. The reasons are thus given :

"In the present case nobody knows the handwriting of the drawer but the plaintiff. The first bill is taken up by him ; the second is accepted by him before it comes to the defendant. The negligence in the plaintiff is greater than can possibly be imputed to the defendant. Where the loss has fallen there it must lie. One innocent man must not relieve himself by throwing it on another."

The case of *Price* v. *Neal* certainly resembles the case before us in several important particulars, but I do not regard it as an authority for deciding this case on the principle of portior est conditio possidentis, or the doctrine of equal equities.

In *Broom's* Legal Maxims the necessity is pointed out for great caution and careful consideration of the particular circumstances of the case in the application of the principle, " because it frequently happens that when money has been paid and received without fault on either side, it may, notwithstanding the above maxim, be recovered back either as paid under a mistake of fact, or on the ground of failure of consideration, or in consequence of the express or implied terms of the contract"; and amongst the cases cited for this is *Jones* v. *Ryde.*

In *Wilkinson* v. *Johnson*, 3 B. & C. 428, Lord Tenterden remarked that the decision of Lord Mansfield against the plaintiff in *Price* v. *Neal*, appears not to have been grounded on the delay, but rather upon the general principle that an acceptor is bound to know the handwriting of the drawer, and that it is rather by his fault or negligence than by mistake if he pays on a forged signature ; and he spoke of the cases of *Price* v. *Neal* and *Smith* v. *Mercer* (6 Taunt. 76), as exceptions to the clear and undisputed general rule of law that money paid under a mistake of facts may be recovered back as being paid without consideration.

It is worth noting that Dallas, J., when expressing his opinion in *Jones* v. *Ryde*, 5 Taunt. 495, that the plaintiff was entitled to recover, under that general rule of law, money paid for a forged navy bill to the defendant, who passed it to him without knowledge of the forgery, remarked that the case was one in which the parties were equally innocent, and had equal knowledge, and equal means of knowledge, rather giving that as a reason in favor of the recovery than against it.

So also in *Smith* v. *Mercer*, 6 Taunt. 76, Chambre, J., who criticises the judgment in *Price* v. *Neal*, and is rather severe on Blackstone's report of it, makes some observations on the application of the doctrine of equal innocence, which are pertinent to the facts we have to deal with. He says :

" Blackstone, J., has, in his report, rather jumbled together the observations applicable to the case on one of the bills with those applicable only to the other. Among other things the acceptance is relied on as applicable to both. All that he makes the Court say respecting the unaccepted bill is, 'The negligence in the plaintiff, who had taken up the forged bill, is greater than can be possibly imputed to the defendant.' That is a singular subject of calculation. He says, 'where the loss has fallen there it must lie : one innocent man must not relieve himself by throwing it on another.' So I should say here. The defendants have paid their money for that which is of no value ; they have thereby sustained a loss, and they ought not to be permitted to throw that loss upon another innocent man, who has done no act to mislead them."

The learned Judge referred at some length to *Jones* v. *Ryde* and *Bruce* v. *Bruce,* to shew that in those cases a great part of the doctrine of *Price* v. *Neal* seemed to be wholly repudiated by the Court.

On this point see *Bigelow* on Estoppel, 440, citing *The Canal Bank* v. *Bank of Albany,* 1 Hill 287, and other cases. The case of the Canal Bank is a clear decision against a contention very similar to that now advanced, upon grounds which seem to me consistent with the authority of the English cases.

Mr. Bruce contended, on behalf of the defendants, that the parties before us were not equally innocent, and that the plaintiff was more to blame than the defendants. His argument was occupied to some extent with occurrences of later date than the payment of the bill, which I shall have to advert to by and by in connection with the subject of laches. The plaintiff appears to have had no dealings with the cotton company except the discount transactions in which Hamilton Young professed to act for the firm, and not to have had through his hands any genuine signatures of the firm, but only forged ones like those on this bill. On the other hand the firm, though they did not keep their account at the Bank of Montreal, were occasional customers of that bank at its office in Hamilton. Cotton drafts on the firm frequently came through that bank, and the manager says that, besides the discounts in 1883, he thinks he had done business for them before 1883. There was thus no lack of opportunity to become familiar with the genuine signatures of the firm, or for testing the genuineness of any signature presented.

In *Smith* v. *Mercer*, 6 Taunt. 76, the forged acceptance had imposed on the bankers, who paid the money for their customers. Dallas, J., said in that case:

"If an acceptor is bound to know the drawer's handwriting, is it less the duty of a banker to know the handwriting of his customer? In degree it is more so, for he sees it every day."

These remarks would not apply in their full force to a case like this, where the parties are not regular customers of the bank, but, on the facts as we have them in evidence, the respective positions of the parties might, without unfairness, be contrasted in much the same way.

The defendants discounted the bill before acceptance by, or presentation to the plaintiff, and were not induced by any act or word of his to part with their money. They relied on their own knowledge of the firm, and were perhaps, by reason of misplaced confidence in Hamilton Young, less careful to use their means of testing the genuineness of the paper than they might have been; and when they presented the bill for payment, they did so in the character of holders under a valid indorsation by their customers.

If we weigh the vigilance of one party against that of the other, as of the date of the payment of the money, the balance will not be in the defendants' favor.

The plaintiff had made inquiries respecting the firm when he was applied to to discount some drafts on parties in New York, out of which the transaction in question arose, and it is urged that he might have been so much more thorough in those inquiries as to have got into personal communication with the partners.   There is, however, no practical force in the suggestion.   The negotiation was being conducted by Hamilton Young, who was the accredited manager for the firm.   There was nothing to suggest bad faith; and the object of the inquiries was to learn the financial standing of the persons to whom he was asked to give credit, or for whom he was asked to pledge his credit.

The negotiations had resulted in the plaintiff procuring, by his indorsation, from the Bank of Montreal at Toronto, the discount of a bill drawn upon a New York house.   It is said that the bill was forged by Hamilton Young; but, however that may be, it was dishonored when it matured in October, and the plaintiff had to pay it.   In July the proceeds of the bill were at the plaintiff's credit in the bank at Toronto, and it was against that account that the bill of the 23rd of July was drawn.

If that bill had reached the plaintiff as a genuine order of the firm to pay the money to the bank, the validity of the draft on New York would have been a matter of less importance, as he would have had his remedy against the firm for the money paid : *Fuller* v. *Smith*, Ry. & M. 49.

It has been urged for the defendants, and it is very important for them to maintain, that the plaintiff is not at liberty to dispute the indorsement of the bill to the defendants.

On the part of the plaintiff, Mr. Maclennan has not contended that the plaintiff can dispute the drawing of the bill, and has expressly disclaimed the intention to raise a question on that point.   I therefore assume for the purpose of this judgment that the question is not to be raised, and resist the temptation which springs from the fact that the defendants discounted the bill without reliance on its having been accredited by the plaintiff by acceptance or otherwise, to discuss the reason on which the doctrine rests that the acceptor cannot dispute the drawing, whether contract, or what in the formal order made in *Ashpitel* v. *Bryan*, 3 B. & S. 474, is called quasi estoppel in pais, or simply the ordinary rule of estoppel in all the cases from *Pickard* v. *Sears*, 6 A. & E. 69, to *Carr* v. *London and North Western R. W. Co.*, L. R. 10 C. P. 307, and which in *Sanderson* v. *Collman*, 4 M. & G. 209 was formally pleaded and held to be a good replication to the plea by the acceptor that the nominal drawer did not make the bill ; and, thus forbearing to discuss the reason, we have not to inquire how far the maxim cessante ratione cessat ipsa lex might apply to the transaction.

But it does not follow, nor does Mr. Maclennan by any means concede, that the indorsement by the drawer is also admitted by acceptance or payment. I do not think the authorities support the contention on that point, nor do I see why in principle it should be so.

Mr. Bruce relied a good deal on *Price* v. *Neal*, and urged that in that case the indorsement as well as the drawing must have been the work of the forger ; and he certainly spared no pains to verify his hypothesis, having endeavored, though without complete success, to obtain particulars of the indictment and trial on which the forger had been h anged for other forgeries.

Nothing is said in the very precise looking statement of f acts in *Price* v. *Neal*, of the indorsement being forged, nor is any such circumstance alluded to in the judgment. The report in Blackstone says, that one of the bills was i ndorsed to the defendant "in the course of trade." I take it that those indorsements were understood to be genuine The bills were not payable to the order of the supposed drawer, but to the order of another person whose name appeared as first indorser ; and Mr. Bruce's suggestion would therefore prove too much, and would go beyond the authority or any semblance of authority supplied by other cases.

Cooper v. *Meyer*, 10 B. & C. 468, was the case of drawing and indorsing in a fictitious name. Lord Tenterden there stated the general rule in these terms :

" The acceptor ought to know the handwriting of the drawer, and is therefore precluded from disputing it ; but it is said that he may nevertheless dispute the indorsement.

Where the drawer is a real person he may do so; but if there is in reality no such person, I think the fair construction of the acceptor's undertaking is, that he will pay to the signature of the same person who signed for the drawer."

In *Beeman* v. *Duck*, 11 M. & W. 251, the facts, as stated by Parke, B., were, that "the bill was drawn in the name of Bradshaw and Williams and indorsed in the same name. * * On the part of the defendants it was shewn that this firm was a real one, and proved by both members of the firm that the drawing and indorsement were forgeries."

It was contended on the one side that the case ought to be governed by *Cooper* v. *Meyer*, and on the other that it was distinguishable by the fact that the drawers were not, as in *Cooper* v. *Meyer*, fictitious persons, but that they really existed though their signature was forged, and that in such a case the acceptor, though he admits that the bill was drawn by the parties by whom it purports to be drawn, does not admit the indorsement by the same parties; a doctrine which, Parke, B., observed, is clearly established as to bills wherein the signature is not forged—citing *Robinson* v. *Yarrow*, 7 Taunt. 455. "In analogy to that case," the learned Baron continued, "the defendant, it is said, admits by his acceptance that the bill was drawn in the name of Bradshaw & Williams, by themselves or some agent authorized to draw in their name; but it does not admit that it was indorsed by themselves or some agent authorized to *indorse*, which is a different species of authority; and one cannot help thinking there is great weight in that argument, if the defendant accepted the bill in ignorance of the forgery; but if he knew of it, and intended that the bill should be put into circulation by a forged indorsement, in the name of the same firm, by the same party who drew it, the case seems to fall within the principle of *Cooper* v. *Meyer*."

There is a dictum of Wightman, J., in *Ashpitel* v. *Bryan*, 3 B. & S. 474, 489, which seems to express an opinion somewhat broader than any reported decision. "Primâ facie," he said, "the acceptor is not admitted to deny the handwriting of the drawer; and I think the same rule applies to an indorsement by the drawer, the indorsement being on the bill when it was accepted. It may be that he would not be bound to admit the handwriting of a person who was a stranger; but here the indorsement is in the same handwriting as the drawing." That was a case of a drawing and indorsement in the name of a deceased person, and so made in pursuance of an understanding among the parties to the bill. Wightman, J., said that for the purpose of the case the bill might be treated as drawn and indorsed by a fictitious person, and accepted by the defendant for a valuable consideration, with full knowledge of all the facts. His reasoning, in the course of which the dictum I have quoted was uttered, proceeded on that basis, and the decision turned mainly on the estoppel arising from the arrangement in pursuance of which the bill had been drawn and indorsed. The opinion expressed touching the admission of the indorsement was not part of the ratio decidendi further than, relating as it did to the hypothetical case of a bill taken on the faith of the signature of the acceptor who had thereby accredited the drawing and indorsing of the bill, it aided the learned Judge's argument on the subject of estoppel. The dictum is thus only remotely, if at all, applicable to the facts of this appeal, and it is not easily reconcilable with what is said in other cases, and notably in *Robinson* v. *Yarrow*, to which I am about to refer.

In *Garland* v. *Jacomb*, L. R. 8 Ex, 216, one of two solicitors, who were partners, drew and indorsed to the plaintiff, in the partnership name, a bill which the defendant accepted without consideration. The indorsement was in respect of a private matter unconnected with the business, and was not authorized by any actual or implied authority in the partner. The defendant was held not estopped from shewing that there had been no indorsement by the firm. Blackburn, J., in delivering the judgment of the Court, said:

" If the defendant had accepted the bill with the intent that Blackburn should indorse the bill and so raise money on it, it might have been a serious question whether she would not have been estopped from denying the indorsement: see *Beeman* v. *Duck;* but no such fact has been found. And in the absence of such a fact the acceptor (generally,) though he admits the authority of the person drawing the bill to draw it, does not admit the authority of the same person to indorse it."

The law was stated, a century ago, in *Smith* v. *Chester*, 1 T. R. 654, to be settled that an indorsee of a bill of exchange, in an action against the acceptor, was obliged to prove the handwriting of the first indorser. There was no question there of the first indorser being the same person as the drawer, but that was the case in *Robinson* v. *Yarrow*, 7 Taunt. 455, where *Smith* v. *Chester* is cited by Park, J., as applicable. Park, J., said:

"The mere acceptance proves the drawing, but it never proves the indorsement. It is not at all necessary that a power given to draw bills by procuration should enable the agent to indorse by procuration. The first is, power to get funds into the agent's hands: the other, to pay them out. The case of *Smith* v. *Chester* decides that, even if the indorsement be there, the acceptance does not admit the indorser's handwriting, and that the acceptor is bound to look only at the face of the bill."

The case of *Allport* v. *Meek*, 4 C. & P. 267, has been supposed to bear on this discussion, but I cannot see that anything of use to us can be extracted from it. The action was on a bill of exchange drawn by one Williams on and accepted by the defendant, and indorsed by Williams to the plaintiff. At the trial before Tindal, C. J., a witness was called to prove the drawing and indorsement, but he swore that neither of them was written by Williams. Then it being shewn that the defendant had admitted his acceptance, the plaintiff relied on proving that the indorsement was in the same handwriting as the drawing, but he had not proper evidence of that fact for the jury, and was nonsuited. What took place certainly did not imply that either Judge or counsel thought the acceptor estopped from disputing the indorsement, which, however, may, for all that appears, have been written after the acceptance. The case seems to me to have been reported as a decision on the rules of evidence in the matter of handwriting, and without any idea of its bearing on the law affecting bills of exchange. The case is not cited in Taylor on Evidence in connection with the subject of bills of exchange, but is cited as shewing what the old law was as to comparison of handwriting.

The expression, so often made use of, that the acceptance admits the handwriting of the drawer, seems to me to be calculated to mislead, and to have sometimes led to equivocal dicta. It is explained in several cases, and perhaps most distinctly in *Beeman* v. *Duck*, that what is admitted is that the writing is, that of the nominal drawer or of some one authorized to draw in his name. This understanding of the extent of the admission gives force to the distinction, pointed out in *Cooper* v. *Meyer*, between cases where the name of a real person appears as drawer and others where a fictitious name is used, and satisfies me that when it is said, as was said by Lord Tenterden in that case, that the acceptor ought to know the handwriting of the drawer, the meaning is that he vouches not for the name being written by the drawer's own hand, but for the drawing being, so far as he is concerned, valid and indisputable.

The theory on which, in *Allport* v. *Meek*, it was proposed to shew that the indorsement was in the same handwriting as the drawing, no estoppel as to the indorsement being asserted, may have been that the primâ facie inference from the admission was that the handwriting was that of the drawer himself, but that inference the acceptor would be at liberty to rebut without impugning the validity of the drawing.

Something like this was observed upon during the argument of *Robarts* v. *Tucker*, 16 Q. B. 560, 577. Counsel argued that the effect of the practice of the company accepting the bill in that case was, that, by accepting the company admitted that they had satisfied themselves of the genuineness of the indorsements. " WILLIAMS, J.—That would be evidence against them that the indorsement was genuine if that was in dispute; but does it preclude them from proving that it was forged? PARKE, B.—It would not do so unless it amounted to a prior authority to pay this particular bill without inquiry, or to a subsequent admission that the indorsement was genuine, in reliance on which the bankers were induced to alter their position."

Of the same character as the dictum of Wightman, J., in *Ashpitel* v. *Bryan* is one by Patteson, J., in *Tucker* v. *Robarts*, 18 L. J. Q. B. 169. *Tucker* v. *Robarts* was an action by or on behalf of a life insurance company to recover from their bankers the amount of a draft made by the company payable to the order of the representatives of a deceased policyholder, and delivered to the solicitor for the representatives, who forged his clients' signatures as indorsers and obtained the cash from the bank. The action was twice tried, and was finally decided against the bankers on a bill of exceptions tendered at the second trial: *Robarts* v. *Tucker*, 16 Q. B. 560.

The defence, which failed, was, that under the facts connected with the insurance company's mode of doing business, and the relations between the company and the bankers, the latter were not bound to see that the right persons indorsed the bill. The dictum of Patteson, J., is found in the report of the argument of the rule for a new trial after the first trial. He said:

"No doubt if a man draws on his debtor in favor of a third person who indorses over, the acceptance does not admit the handwriting of the third person. But if a man draw payable to his own order and then indorses, the acceptance, if made after the indorsement, admits the indorsement as well as the drawing. Suppose there had been money of the company kept in a box by the bankers, and the company's agent had stood by and saw the bankers pay Winterbottom [the solicitor] without objection, could the company afterwards have turned round and disputed the payment?"

Now, without stopping to answer this question, or to consider whether the answer would necessarily be in the negative, it is sufficient to point out what is apparent from the whole passage, and is emphasised by the illustration

558 ONTARIO APPEAL REPORTS. [VOL.

from the payment of money, whatever may be the proper
answer to the concluding question, that the learned Judge
was evidently dealing with the idea of estoppel by conduct,
and when he speaks of the acceptance being made after
the indorsement, means also, "and before the person who
relies on the acceptance pays value for the bill." This
distinguishes the case he puts from the present case, and
makes it unnecessary to compare the opinion expressed
with the other cases I have referred to.

It will be worth while to quote a passage from the
judgment of Chief Justice Taney in the case of *Hortsman*
v. *Henshaw*, 11 Howard 177; *Bigelow's* Bills and Notes,
541, which was cited to us, which covers most of the
ground of the present discussion. "The general rule,"
the Chief Justice said, "undoubtedly is, that the drawee
by accepting admits the handwriting of the drawer, but
not of the indorser, and the holder is bound to see that the
previous indorsements, including that of the payee, are in
the handwriting of the parties whose names appear upon
the bill, or were duly authorized by them; and if it should
appear that one of them is forged, he cannot recover
against the acceptor, although the forged name may be on
the bill at the time of the acceptance; and if he has
received money from the acceptor, and the forgery is afterwards discovered, he will be compelled to repay it. The
reason of the rule is obvious. A forged indorsement
cannot transfer any interest in the bill, and the holder,
therefore, has no right to demand the money. If the bill
is dishonored by the drawee, the drawer is not responsible,
and if the drawee pays it to a person not authorised to
receive the money, he cannot claim credit for it in his
account with the drawer."

The facts in *Hortsman* v. *Henshaw* were peculiar,
the drawers having put the bill in circulation with the
names of the payees indorsed on it, that indorsement being
the forgery. It was therefore held that the drawers could
not dispute the indorsement, and that the acceptor was
entitled to credit in his account with the drawer for the
money he paid, and therefore could not recover it back
from the indorsee to whom he had paid it. "We take the
rule to be this," the Chief Justice said, (p. 184) "wherever the

drawer is liable to the holder, the acceptor is entitled to a credit if he pays the money ; and he is bound to pay upon his acceptance, when the payment will entitle him to a credit in his account with the drawer."

What I have said respecting the use of the word " handwriting" in the cases, and the qualification with which it has to be understood, is supported by this judgment of Chief Justice Taney ; for, while he speaks of the acceptance admitting the handwriting of the drawer, he expressly shews in one of the passages which I have quoted, and in others which I have not quoted, that he means the handwriting of some one authorised to draw, and not necessarily that of the nominal drawer himself.

In my opinion the defendants' title to the money in question is displaced and the plaintiff's right to recover it back, as paid without consideration, is established, unless there is something in the delay or other circumstances in evidence to prevent his assertion of that right.

The plaintiff lost no time in giving notice to the defendants after he knew of the forgery, but that was nearly two months after the payment of the money. But, though the delay was thus inadvertent and unavoidable, the law seems to be that it would afford an answer to the plaintiff's demand, if it prejudiced the defendants in their relation to other parties to the bill.

I understand that to be the ground of the decision in *Smith* v. *Mercer*, although the opinions of the Judges who decided the case were not altogether in accord. Chambre, J., dissented, holding that the plaintiff was entitled to recover. Heath, J., appears to have proceeded on the opinion that the acceptor, whose signature was forged, could not have recovered back the money if he had himself paid it, and that the banker who paid it as his agent was in no better position. Dallas, J., concludes his judgment by saying: " The ground, therefore, on which I rest my opinion, and to which I wish to confine it, is the want of due caution in having paid the bill, the effect of which has been to give time to different parties, which the plaintiffs were not authorised to do." And Gibbs, C. J., while

expressing his concurrence with Heath and Dallas, JJ.,
puts his own judgment on what he calls the narrower
ground of the discharge of other parties to the bill by want
of notice.

In *Cocks* v. *Masterman*, 9 B. & C. 902, the delay of one
day was, upon the same ground, held to disentitle the
plaintiff to recover, and the case was distinguished from
Wilkinson v. *Johnson*, 3 B. & C. 428, in which the plaintiff recovered, by the circumstance that in the latter case
notice of the forgery had been given on the day the money
was paid, and in time to hold the earlier parties.

In *Mather* v. *Maidstone*, 18 C. B. 273, the remedy against
prior parties had been lost by the lapse of time before the
discovery of the forgery.

There was here no one against whom a remedy on the
bill existed ; but it was argued that, if the defendants had
known of the forgery sooner, they might have had an opportunity of averting the loss.

To support this argument the defendants shewed by
evidence that on the 8th of August, 1883, a month before
the discovery of the forgery of the bill of the 23rd of July,
another bill, said also to have been forged by Hamilton
Young, was drawn in the name of the Hamilton Cotton
Company on the plaintiff. It was for $5,110.40, and was
in other respects similar to the former one, except that
besides being indorsed in the name of the drawers, it was
also indorsed by Hamilton Young, and was apparently
discounted for him. The bank manager mentions that the
money was handed to him at once, not checked out. The
plaintiff refused to accept that draft, not from suspicion of
forgery, but because it was not drawn against any funds
in his hands. On its return to the bank at Hamilton, Mr.
Lucas paid it, the firm happening to have money of Hamilton Young's in their hands, out of which they were able
to recoup themselves.

The point made is that the July draft might have fared
in the same way if the forgery had been announced
sooner.

That is a suggestion too speculative to be the foundation of a legal right.

It is not helped by the principle of cases like *Cocks* v. *Masterman,* and no authority has been produced in aid of it. The bank has still its remedy against Hamilton Young quantum valeat.

Upon all points I concur in the judgment pronounced by Wilson, C. J., in the Divisional Court, and am therefore of opinion that the appeal should be dismissed, with costs.

OSLER, J. A., concurred in the views expressed by PATTERSON, J. A.

The Court being equally divided the appeal was

Dismissed, with costs.

[This case has been carried to the Privy Council.]

NOTE.—See Imp. Stat. 45 and 46 Vict. ch. 61, sec. 54 (2) (*b.*)

RAYMOND v. SCHOOL TRUSTEES OF THE VILLAGE OF CARDINAL.

Public school, trustees of—Dismissal of teacher—49 Vict. ch. 49, (secs. 165, 168, (O.)

The right of public school trustees to dismiss for good cause a teacher engaged by them, necessarily exists from the relation of the parties. 49 Vict. ch. 49, (O.) secs. 165, 168), provides a proceeding by which the status or qualification of the teacher may be determined; and the result of such proceeding may be in effect the same as dismissal; but such enactment does not deprive the employers of the inherent right to dismiss.

THIS was an appeal from the judgment of the Junior Judge of the County Court of the united counties of Leeds and Grenville, whereby the plaintiff's action was dismissed with costs.

The plaintiff, a public school teacher, sued the defendants for wrongful dismissal.

The defence was, in substance, that the defendants were justified in dismissing the plaintiff inasmuch as he did not conduct the school in accordance with the requirements of the School Act and his written agreement with them.

The appeal came on for hearing on the 12th of September, 1887.*

Knapp (Prescott), for the appellant.
Shepley, for the respondents.

The facts appear more fully in the judgment of the Court which was delivered—

September 29, 1887, by HAGARTY, C. J. O.—The only point raised by this appeal is, whether the school trustees had the power to dismiss the plaintiff from his office of teacher, having hired him for the year; that by the statute this power can only be exercised by the action of the inspector in suspending the certificate.

Section 161 of the Act 49 Vict. ch. 49, (O.) provides that the certificate entitles the holder to teach a public school.

Present.—HAGARTY, C.J.O., PATTERSON and OSLER, JJ. A.

Section.165. The inspector may suspend the certificate of any teacher for inefficiency, misconduct, &c., and is to notify the trustees and the teacher of the reasons of sus-pension.

Section 166. If the teacher wilfully neglect to carry out his agreement at common law with the trustees, he shall, on complaint of the trustees, be liable to suspension of his certificate by the inspector.

Section 167. If the teacher holds a certificate issued by the Chief Superintendent or Council of Public Instruction, or Education Department, or Minister of Education, the inspector shall report to the Minister of Education, and such suspension shall continue till the case is decided by the Minister.

Section 168. When a teacher holds a certificate granted by the County Board of Examiners, the inspector shall forthwith call a meeting of such board for the consideration of such suspension, of which due notice shall be given to the teacher, and the decision of such board shall be final.

The appellant contends that the power of dismissal is not with the trustees, and that the only course allowed by law is, not by actual dismissal, but by the suspension of the certificate, which would at once work a disqualification to act as teacher, and would thus be equivalent to dismissal, sec. 153 requiring the existence of the certificate during the period of his engagement.

I think there is nothing before us for decision beyond the existence or non-existence of a right in the trustees to dismiss. We are not apparently concerned with the reasons on which such power of dismissal was exercised.

Unless the Legislature have expressly, or by direct intendment, taken away the right of dismissal, we should hold it necessarily to arise from the relation of the parties as master and servant, employer and person employed.

I do not think the statute here takes away such inherent right from the employers.

It provides a proceeding by which the status or qualification of the teacher to hold such employment may be determined ; and the result of such proceeding may be in effect the same as dismissal. The process is one which would possibly involve considerable delay, and we can easily conceive cases in which prompt action would be necessary on the part of the trustees.

If a teacher were guilty of such conduct as rendered it unfit that he should be allowed to act at all as teacher, as in the case of intoxication, or visibly improper behaviour in the conduct of the school, it might be essential that the promptest action should be taken, and that he should be prevented from a day's further presence as teacher.

In addition, it may be well supposed that dismissal by the trustees would be a much lighter penalty than their calling for the intervention of the inspector.

The action of the latter would apparently be confined to suspension of certificate; a fatal blow to the *status* of the teacher, disqualifying him from filling such a position.

Dismissal by the trustees would not necessarily involve any such disability. It is quite possible, that in a case like that before us, the dismissed teacher might successfully conduct a public school in another school section.

We are unable to see that the Legislature have deprived the trustees of the right usually held to be common to all employers of labour—especially of skilled labour.

We may refer to *Wood* on Master and Servant, 210; *Smith* on Master and Servant, 134-5, and the remarks of Blackburn, J., in *Fletcher* v. *Knell*, 42 L. J. Q. B. 56.

The appeal must be dismissed.

PATTERSON and OSLER, JJ. A., concurred.

Appeal dismissed, with costs.

CAMERON ET AL. V. PERRIN ET AL.

Chattel mortgage—Fraudulent preference—Executions.

The plaintiffs sold to C. their stock in trade in a country store which he
had managed for them as their agent ; and took a chattel mortgage
thereon as security for the purchase money. The mortgage also included
sundry other chattels the property of C. At the time of the sale and
mortgage there were executions in the sheriff's hands at the suit of the
defendants by which these latter goods were bound. The Judge of the
County Court found that they had been included in the mortgage in
order to defeat or delay an expected execution against C. at the suit of
S. who was no party to the proceedings and had made no claim.
Held, affirming the judgment of the County Court [Osler, J. A., dissent-
ing], that the acceptance by the plaintiffs of a mortgage on goods which
they knew belonged to C. though already bound by the defendants'
executions, with knowledge of the judgment recovered by S. against
C., rendered the whole transaction fraudulent and void against creditors, so that the stock in trade sold by the plaintiffs to C. became subject
to the defendants' executions.
Per Osler, J. A.—The sale and mortgage back of the stock in trade being
parts of the same transaction the executions bound only the interest
of C. therein, and were subject to the mortgage for the purchase money.
The mortgage of the other goods could not affect the executions which
had all along bound them, and therefore was not fraudulent against the
defendants, the only creditors who were complaining of it.
The issue might have been found distributively, and the plaintiffs could
either recover their own goods under the mortgage title as against the
executions, or equitably, as impressed with a trust to secure the purchase
money, which was paramount to any claim under the executions.

THIS was an appeal by the plaintiffs from a judgment of
the Judge of the County Court of the County of Bruce,
in favor of the defendants (execution creditors) on an
interpleader issue tried before him.

The action was commenced in that Court by Donald E.
Cameron and Donald Campbell, against D. S. Perrin and
W. J. Ramsay & Co., and the issue was directed to try the
right to certain goods and chattels, viz., one horse, one buggy,
one set of single harness, one cutter, one waggon, some
buffalo robes, and other goods and chattels, being the stock-
in-trade in a general grocery store, seized by the sheriff
of Bruce, under two executions in his hands against one
Robert A. Clow, in favor respectively of the defendants.
Perrin's writ was tested on the 17th of December, 1883,

and received by the sheriff the next day; Ramsay's on 16th April, 1886, and received by the sheriff on 20th April, 1886.

At the trial the evidence shewed that in the Spring of 1884, under the execution of Perrin, the sheriff seized and sold Clow's goods. The claimants (Cameron and Campbell) bought them in at the sale, they being at the time creditors of Clow, holding an unrenewed chattel mortgage against the goods then sold, bearing date the 9th January, 1882, for $500. It was shewn that Clow came to Cameron and represented that he could handle the goods for the claimants to good advantage, and that if they employed him for a few years the profits would exceed the loss they would otherwise sustain; he having no means of satisfying his debt to them.

An agreement was accordingly reduced to writing; Cameron not being satisfied with it a new agreement was drawn up by Mr. Traver a solicitor, in January, 1886, which recited that the claimants were the owners of the stock, &c., and that it had been agreed that Clow should carry on the business as their salesman and agent, and should account for all sales at the end of each month, and pay over the balance after deducting expenses, including his monthly salary; Clow to have no lien on or property in the goods whatever; the claimants not to be liable for any goods purchased by Clow unless they consented thereto in writing. The plaintiff Cameron also swore that,

" Under this arrangement Clow carried on the business as our servant, agent, or clerk ; he had no interest in the goods seized ; he put in no money from the day I purchased ; the goods belonged to Cameron & Campbell ; for the goods purchased by Clow we had arrangements with the firms ; they drew on us, Cameron & Campbell, direct, or if on Clow they were guaranteed by us.   *   *   Our understanding with Clow was, that he had no authority to order goods ; if I was away he would get small quantities of biscuits or tobacco, and such like, and would report to me ; I sometimes would tell the travellers it was all right, or Clow would sign the draft by way of certifying the correctness.   *   *

" On 22nd April, 1886, we made another arrangement with Clow as set out in mortgage. I sold out the stock for $1,000, including book accounts : I was to collect the book accounts and apply them upon the mortgage.   *   *

" A writ had been served in the case of *Smith* v. *Cameron and Clow* sometime before the date of the second agreement, such action being for damages for having caused proceedings to be taken against Smith ; and before January, 1886, I understood from Mr. Barrett, who had been Smith's solicitor, that the suit was at an end, and heard no more of it."

Cameron also stated that he knew the sheriff did not make enough to satisfy Perrin's execution, and that Clow had other old debts outstanding.

It was also shewn that Clow had delivered accounts after the arrangement made with the claimants in which his name was followed by the word "agent."

Several witnesses were called who swore that they had dealt all along with Clow directly, and

" George Kerr, the owner of the shop occupied by Clow, stated that he had rented the premises to Clow in November, 1885, and never heard it was for any one but Clow until lately. There was nothing to indicate that it was any one's but Clow's business. It was understood that Cameron and Campbell had a claim against Clow ; that Clow was indebted to them."

The learned judge in the Court below after setting forth fully the facts above mentioned, proceeded

" On this evidence I think I must find that the grocery business prior to 22nd April, 1886, was really Cameron 'and Campbell's. I think there is quite enough shewn to make Cameron and Campbell liable to any creditor on any claim contracted for the business since April, 1884. People dealing with Clow and selling goods to him might, without doubt, hold Cameron and Campbell for purchase money, but that is not the question here. The claims of Perrin and Ramsay are on old executions, one issued on a judgment obtained prior to April, 1884, and in full force in the sheriff's hands ever since and their right is to realise out of Clow's not Cameron's goods. I see no impropriety in such arrangement as Mr. Cameron contends existed between his firm and Clow, and there existed a good reason for Cameron and Campbell entering into it, viz., to try and realise the amount due to them by Clow, originally covered by the lapsed mortgage, and as to which they lost their priority. *   * All the probabilities are in favor of the transaction being such as Cameron describes it to have been so far as the grocery business was concerned, namely, that Clow was no more than a servant working out an indebtedness. The part of the transaction which appears curious and unexplained is, why Cameron and Campbell should,.when they knew they owned the goods and business and could defy any execution creditor of Clow's to touch the goods, alter their position by a sale to Clow for a price payable in three days, and thereby place in jeopardy that which was theretofore secure ? The only motive I can gather from the evidence is, that Cameron knowng that Clow's ownership of the buggy, harness, robes, and perhaps horse, could not be controverted, and desiring to assist him to delay iSmith in realising on his verdict just recovered against him in the suit against Cameron and Clow, thought that by including them in the sale of the stock and taking security on the whole he might assist Clow.

" I think that my decision must rest upon the answer to the question : was this sale to Clow and mortgage back to Cameron and Campbell made with intent to delay Clow's creditors, or with the intent to give Cameron and Campbell a preference ?   *   *

" On Mr. Cameron's evidence, who has such a hazy recollection about the purchase of the horse, buggy, sleigh, and harness and robes, I must find that (not being interested in the peddling part of Clow's business) they, Cameron and Campbell, had no interest in those things pertaining thereto, That coupling them with the stock in trade in the shop and taking security on them as well as on the stock, was done in order to secure Clow in a position in which he might delay Smith, who had just recovered a verdict against him for $250, and in that view of it, as so doing amounts to a legal fraud, the whole mortgage must, I think, fall, if I read correctly the law laid down in various cases, such as *Commercial Bank* v. *Wilson,* 3 E. & A. 257, where, at page 264, Robinson, C. J., says, ' Being tainted with actual fraud, and to a great extent, it should not be upheld as to any part, but in the words of the Statute 13 Eliz. ch. 5, sec. 2, being made of fraud, collusion, and guile, with intent to delay, hinder and defraud creditors of their just and lawful action and debts, it must be deemed and taken (as against the plaintiffs, who are judgment creditors) to be clearly and utterly void, frustrate, and of non effect.' The Court does not in such cases attempt, or, as it has been said they will not condescend, to go into the consideration whether any or what part of the fraudulent judgment may not have been founded on a just and legal demand. The judgment which is made of ' fraud,' that is, with the fraudulent intent to defeat creditors, is taken to be void altogether, without considering whether there may not be a portion of the sum, for which judgment was given which was honestly due. If this was not so held, the statute would [fail greatly in its effect ; for then parties would be in a position to attempt such frauds, without risk of loss of anything real in case of detection, And besides, in many cases like this, when we find that a large portion of the alleged debt is evidently fictitious, it throws such a suspicion upon the rest as makes it the duty of the courts to entertain all presumptions against the honesty of the case where there is any room for doubt. On the whole, I have come to the conclusion I must find for the defendants, and will direct judgment for them accordingly in due course."

The other facts appear sufficiently in the judgments.

The appeal came on to be heard before this Court on the 12th September, 1887.*

*Present.—HAGARTY, C.J.O., PATTERSON and OSLER, JJ.A.

Reeve, Q. C., for the appellants.

Aylesworth, for the respondent Perrin.

Holman, for the respondents Ramsay & Co.

October 25, 1887. Patterson, J. A.—In this case, which is somewhat peculiar in one or two respects, I am of opinion that there is no reason to differ from the conclusion arrived at by the learned judge of the County Court in his careful and able judgment.

Cameron and Campbell appear to have been as the learned Judge has held, owners of the stock in trade of the business carried on by Clow. Their purchase under Perrin's fi. fa., the proceeds of which paid Perrin's debt pro tanto, does not appear from anything before us to have been open to question. It would be strange to have found Perrin, who had in his pocket the money realised by the sheriff on his execution by the sale of the stock, seizing the same goods again on the same writ and insisting on having them sold again, without some very different proof of their revesting in his debtor from the arrangement under which Clow carried on the business. The stock now in question may not have included much of what was in the shop when the sheriff sold, but that circumstance falls a long way short of proof of ownership in Clow.

The other execution plaintiff, Ramsay, had not, like Perrin, been paid by any previous sale of the stock, but the question of ownership stands with regard to him on the same footing.

Both sets of creditors had their writs in the hands of the sheriff to be executed before the transaction, which is the main subject of attack in this issue ; but I do not suppose that if that transaction had not taken place either of them would have challenged the plaintiffs' ownership of the business.

The surprise one feels is, as the learned judge has noticed, at the plaintiffs' imperilling their strong position by selling the business to Clow. Looking for a motive for what they did it is impossible not to take the view which the learned

72—VOL XIV A.R.

Judge has taken, that it was to protect the other property
of Clow from an expected execution upon the judgment
recently recovered against him by Smith.

The strength of the motive, while it seems to furnish the
reason for what was done, scarcely lessens one's surprise at
the method adopted ; but when an intentional fraud upon
the statute is so strongly indicated, it will not do to pronounce the conspirators harmless as doves, because they
may not have been wise as serpents.

What was done was to transfer to Clow all the stock in
trade at the price of $1,000, and to take back from him, as
security for that sum, a mortgage upon the same stock
together with other chattels of Clow, which seem to have
been all his chattels.

The instrument recites that Cameron and Campbell have
agreed to sell to Clow the stock at the said price, and that
Clow has agreed to secure the price by that mortgage.

I was for a while impressed a good deal by the argument
that, as Clow took his title to the stock by the same
instrument which is attacked, the effect of holding the
instrument void as against creditors must be to leave things
in statu quo as if the transaction had not taken place ; and
that the plaintiffs ought therefore to succeed as to the
stock, with the further consequence, which might be considered in awarding costs, though it would not perhaps
affect the technical determination of the issue, that the
mortgage did not interfere with the recourse of the plaintiffs against the other chattels, because they were already
bound by the executions.

Upon reflection, however, I do not think that argument
sound.

It is not the fact that the instrument conveys the goods
to Clow. It contains no words of conveyance. The
operative conveyance was no doubt by delivery, or what
was equivalent to delivery, the recognition of Clow's possession being as owner when it had been as agent.

The essence of the transaction, so far as our present
inquiry is concerned, seems to be the election by the plain-

tiffs to place their title to the stock on the basis of the
the mortgage from Clow; to treat him as the owner, or
rather to make him the owner, and to take their title
from him.

I think that is the way the position was apprehended
by the learned Judge in the Court below, though I may
perhaps be wrong in so understanding what he said.

If the form of the transaction is properly found to have
been adopted with intent to defeat or delay creditors, the
parties to the fraud cannot reasonably expect the Court to
be specially astute in order to relieve them from the consequence of their own act.

The transaction, we must treat as good between the
parties to it, though the terms of 48 Vict. ch. 26 (O.) may be
wide enough to imply avoidance altogether of a fraudulent
conveyance.

It may be, and no doubt it was, the arrangement that
the passing of the property to Clow and the re-conveyance
of it by way of mortgage should be as nearly as possible
simultaneous acts and form one transaction. If, as
between them, the mortgage failed to operate, the plaintiffs would have ground to contend that the property
ought not to be held to have passed from them because
it was not to become Clow's except on the terms that he
was to pledge it for the purchase money.

What the statute does, in favor of creditors, is to avoid
the mortgage as a conveyance. It strikes at that part of
the transaction which was entered into with the fraudulent intent. The intent, it is urged, was to protect the
other goods; but I cannot see any satisfactory answer to
the charge that the intent of the whole conveyance was to
defeat or delay creditors. The other goods may have been
what the parties principally sought to cover, but they
brought the stock into the transaction as part of their
scheme, and treated it as what in law it was, and what
between the parties it remained, the property of Clow.

The matter is certainly not free from difficulty, but I
cannot say that the learned Judge's treatment of it was
incorrect.

It would be difficult to imply a charge different from that expressly created by the deed, notwithstanding that the deed cannot prevail against the creditors, and there cannot be such a thing under the circumstances as a lien for which the plaintiffs contended, and which, indeed, they made the only specific reason of appeal of which they gave notice.

As put in *Benjamin* on Sales, in the chapter on lien,. "where goods are at the time of the contract in the possession of the buyer, as agent of the vendor, the mere completion of the contract operates as a delivery of possession," and " the vendor's lien is abandoned when he makes delivery of the goods to the buyer."

A point made by Mr. Reeve for the plaintiffs was, that the mortgage was saved by 48 Vict. ch. 26' sec. 3 (1).

The second section avoids every transfer of goods by a person in insolvent circumstances, or unable to pay his debts in full, made with intent to defeat, delay, or prejudice his creditors, or to give to any one or more of them a preference over his other creditors, or over any one or more of them, or which has such effect.

This adds materially to the stringency of the former law as it was found in R. S. O. ch. 116, sec. 2. But the third section protects from the operation of the second transfers &c., made under several specified states of facts, and inter alia when made " in consideration of any present actua bonâ fide sale or delivery of goods or other property, provided that the * * goods or other property sold or delivered bear a fair and reasonable relative value to the consideration therefor."

This mortgage, it is urged, is made in consideration of the present actual bonâ fide sale and delivery of the stock in trade, and the stock in trade bears a fair and reasonable relative value to the goods mortgaged.

There need, as I apprehend, be no difficulty in assenting to the proposition that if goods, of say $1500 in value, are mortgaged to secure payment at a future day for goods bonâ fide sold and bought for $1000, the values are not necessarily disproportionate.

The question would always be one of fact depending on the nature of the goods and many other things.

The plaintiffs' difficulty here is, the absence of findings of fact in their favor. The onus is on them to bring the transaction within the saving clause.

It will be observed that the statute does not treat an actual sale as necessarily a bonâ fide sale, and, as far as the findings touch the subject, it cannot be said that a bonâ fide sale has been found. Nor have we the means of pronouncing upon the relative values or the reasonableness of securing payment for what was sold by pledging all that was sold plus the other property.

These considerations are, I think, fatal to the success of of the argument on the statute.

In my opinion the appeal must be dismissed, with costs.

HAGARTY, C. J. O., concurred in dismissing the appeal.

OSLER, J. A.—There being on the 20th April, 1886, two executions in the sheriff's hands against the goods of the judgment debtor, Clow, one at the suit of the defendant Perrin, and the other at that of the defendant Ramsay, the plaintiffs on or about the 22nd April, agreed with the debtor to sell to him the stock of goods in the store at Lucknow, the business of which they had for some time previously carried on there by him as their clerk or manager.

The evidence bears out the learned Judge's finding that these goods were then the property of the plaintiffs, and not of the judgment debtor. It was part of the bargain that he should secure the purchase money of the goods by giving the plaintiffs a mortgage therefor, and the transaction was accordingly carried out in that way. I do not understand from the evidence that the debtor ever acquired the goods as his own, free from the just claim of the plaintiffs for their purchase money and his obligation to secure it by this mortgage, or that he was at liberty to deal with them before or until he had executed the mortgage.

. The finding of the learned Judge leaves no doubt upon that point, for, in dealing with the argument that the plaintiffs had a special interest in the goods growing out of their original ownership, paramount to the defendants' executions, he says :

" This they might have possibly retained by the fact that the sale and security were one and the same transaction, and that Clow never obtained sole control of the goods as his own until the mortgage securing the price was absolutely executed, and they passed into his possession subject to C. & C.'s claim, and not otherwise."

At this time the debtor was the owner of other chattels, consisting of a horse and buggy, and set of harness, a cutter and robes, and a waggon, which were of course bound by the defendants' executions, and these chattels were included in the mortgage of the stock of store goods as security for the purchase money of the latter.

The question then is, whether this transaction, the mortgage part of which did not in the remotest degree affect the right of the defendants to the goods already bound by their executions, and which could only transfer the debtor's interest in them subject to the executions, had the effect of transferring the other goods to the execution debtor, absolutely, so as to subject them to the executions free from the vendor's claim to the purchase money, notwithstanding the agreement under which they were sold ?

I think this question would probably have been answered in favor of the plaintiffs in the Court below, but for the view which the learned Judge took of the facts I now proceed to mention.

It appears that at the time of the sale to Clow, an action for malicious prosecution was pending at the suit of one Smith against him and the plaintiff Cameron, and that Smith had just obtained a verdict against the former for $250. The learned Judge thought it a singular thing that the plaintiffs knowing that they owned the stock of store goods should alter their position by a sale to Clow, and thereby put in jeopardy that which was already secure.

Then he says:

" The only motive I can gather from the evidence is, that Cameron, knowing that Clow's ownership of the buggy, harness, robes, and perhaps horse, could not be controverted, to assist him to delay Smith in realising on his verdict just recovered against him in the suit against Cameron and Clow, thought that by including them in the sale of the stock and taking security on the whole he might assist Clow."

Accordingly he finds:

" That coupling these goods with the stock in trade in the shop and taking security on them as well as on the stock was done in order to secure Clow in a position in which he might delay Smith who had just recovered a verdict against him, and in that view of it, as so doing amounts to a legal fraud, the whole mortgage must fall."

I fail to see any evidence that the plaintiffs sold or professed to sell to Clow these articles which I have already said undoubtedly belonged to him, and the recital of the agreement in the mortgage is opposed to it; but assume that they were included in the mortgage for the purpose of embarrassing and delaying Smith as the learned Judge finds: how does that affect the defendants ?

They at all events were not embarrassed, hindered, or delayed by the mortgage. It never was and never could be fraudulent as to them in respect of Clow's goods, which had all along been bound by their executions. Smith, for aught we can see, may never think it worth his while to impeach it, and he is no party to these proceedings. As regards the defendants there is nothing in the instrument for the statute to operate upon or to avoid, and except as to those against whom it is fraudulent, an instrument or conveyance remains in full force and effect.

If, therefore, the plaintiffs could recover upon their mortgage title alone as against the executions which are prior in date, I see no reason why the issue should not be found, as it always may be found where justice requires it, distributively, for the plaintiffs as to the store goods, and for the defendants as to residue, they being in no way affected by the alleged fraud.

If, on the other hand, the plaintiffs cannot assert title under the mortgage to the goods sold by them to the execution debtor, owing to the legal title to them having passed to him while the writs were in the sheriff's hands, there is not the same difficulty in setting up their equitable right.

The debtor only acquired the goods on the faith of an agreement to secure the purchase money by reconveying them to the plaintiffs by way of mortgage, and never possessed them for an instant free from that obligation. There was, therefore, a trust which was paramount to any claim under the executions, since these could only attach upon and bind the debtor's own interest in the property. I think the principle on which the case of *Dominion Bank* v. *Davidson*, 12 A. R. 90, was decided, governs the present case. See also the authorities there referred to, *Nevitt* v. v. *McMurray*, ante 126, 140 and *Federal Bank* v. *Canadian Bank of Commerce*, 13 S. C. R., at p. 393. For these reasons I am respectfully of opinion that the appeal should be allowed.

The ground on which I rest my decision makes it unnecessary to express any opinion as to the point raised by Mr. Reeve on the 48 Vict. ch. 26 (O).

Appeal dismissed, with costs. [OSLER, J.A., *dissenting.*]

LONDON AND CANADIAN LOAN COMPANY v. MORPHY. ET AL.

Stock Exchange—Sale of seat at, under process—Sequestration.

The plaintiffs having recovered judgment against the defendants M. & N.,. both of whom were members of the Toronto Stock Exchange, each owning a seat at the board thereof, which it was considered could not be sold under *fi. fa.*, and an application was made to the Queen's Bench Division for an order to sell the seats which had been seized under a sequestration, which was refused by Wilson, C. J., whereupon the plaintiffs appealed, and on the argument it was made to appear that M. had paid off the judgment of the plaintiffs, and was carrying on the appeal for the purpose of obtaining the seat owned by N. This Court, under the circumstances, and aside from the fact that the ultimate completion of title to a purchaser could only be effected by the contingent co-operation and assent of the Stock Exchange, as provided by its by-laws, affirmed the judgment appealed from without prejudice to any right M. might have to procure himself to be substituted for the plaintiffs.

THIS was an appeal by the plaintiffs from the judgment of Wilson, C. J., (reported 10 O. R. 86, where the facts clearly appear) and came on for hearing on the 8th November, 1887*

Arnoldi, for the appellants.
C. Ritchie, Q. C., for the Toronto Stock Exchange.
Mortimer Clark, for respondent Niven.

January 10, 1888.   HAGARTY, C. J. O.—I am of opinion that the learned Chief Justice was right in refusing to order a sale.

I have very carefully examined his elaborate and instructive judgment, and do not see how the appellant can answer either the reasoning or the conclusions. He points out with clearness how grave is the objection that a Court should not order a sale of any species of property without being able to give a title to the purchaser. How this could be done in the present case, is unintelligible to me. It is not even the case where rival claims could be heard and adjusted—the difficulty arises from the ultimate

---

* *Present*—HAGARTY, C. J. O., BURTON, PATTERSON, and OSLER, JJ. A

uncertainty of giving title after the adjustment of rival claims.

If the property could pass by manual delivery the appellants could proceed, I presume, without any order for sale. In a case like this the Court could not properly undertake the task of perfecting title to a purchaser.

Both the seats claimed to be sold at the plaintiffs' suit are shewn to have been dealt with by the owners some six months before the recovery of judgment against them.

Defendant Morphy proved that after dissolving partnership with Niven he had formed a partnership with Oliver Morphy, and his seat was agreed to become partnership property, and to belong in equal shares to the partners. Niven proves a similar arrangement as to his seat with Malcolm Niven, and that he has transferred his seat to the new firm; and each claims that the debts and liabilities of the new firm bo satisfied before the seat can be disposed of.

Under such circumstances it would appear to be out of the question that the Court should direct a sale where, even after all the existing claims had been adjusted, the ultimate completion of title to a purchaser can only be effected by the contingent co-operation and assent of the stock exchange, as shewn in the by-laws.

But since the judgment of the learned Chief Justice the case has assumed a widely different aspect.

It is admitted that the defendant Morphy has paid the plaintiffs the amount of the then judgment debt, and taken an assignment thereof, and he now seeks, under the Mercantile Amendment Act, to stand in the stead of the plaintiff, and press the enforcement of the judgment by a sale of his late co-partner's seat.

This raises another question, and one of some importance.

It was stated that when the defendants dissolved in December, 1884, neither of them owed anything to the other on partnership account, except a trifling sum. This claim of the plaintiffs was apparently not taken into account, and judgment thereon not recovered till July, 1885, but the action was commenced very shortly after the dissolution.

Both the seats had been purchased with the money of the firm, $500 for one, and $750 for the other. On dissolving they agreed that each should retain his seat, and almost immediately after each formed a new partnership, and each seat was declared an asset of such new firm.

In resisting the application for the order for sale, Oliver Morphy, the new partner of George Morphy, claimed that the seat of the latter had become partnership property, and that the liabilities of the new firm must be first paid out of the sale.

Niven takes the same defence for his new co-partner. At that time both Morphy and Niven, judgment debtors, took the same line of defence.

I entertain a very strong opinion that even if the order for sale was improperly refused on the then existing state of facts, the changed positions of the parties must prevent our interfering with the decision. The judgment creditors are paid. I think it would be wholly unfair and improper to allow Morphy to use it against his joint debtor in the way proposed.

He has his remedy over against the latter and can have the partnership accounts taken. We know nothing of the existing relations between them, as to this large judgment. Morphy can use it as proof that he paid it, and of the joint liability. But it does not follow that we can assume his absolute right to recover equal or any particular contribution from his co-partner.

In *Batchelor* v. *Lawrence*, 9 C. B. N. S. 543, the effect of the statute is fully discussed, but no reference is made to the case of co-partners. I have no doubt but that the fact of Morphy being co-defendant at the plaintiffs' suit, entitled him to take the assignment of the judgment, and he had the right to claim contribution from his co-defendant. But the statute provides that he shall only recover the just proportion as between themselves.

The latter may have good cause against being held liable to him.

The firm may be liable, but one partner may, as between themselves, shew that the whole loss should be borne by one of them in consequence of the latter's culpable negligence or default and may throw the whole consequence upon him. This principle is discussed in 1 *Lindley*, 791, 805, 3rd ed.

No question of this kind could have arisen on the application for the order of sale.   Then the judgment debtors were apparently in accord as to this common line of defence, each setting up precisely the same reason against a sale of the seats, the creation of fresh interests in their respective new partners, &c., &c.

I think the learned Chief Justice rightly refused the order, and the new facts admitted on this application render it, as I think, doubly necessary that his judgment should not be interfered with.

BURTON, J.A.—The respondent Morphy who now claims to be in the position of the Loan Company, and to conduct this appeal has, in his reasons filed against the appeal when respondent, made a very strong case against his present contention, and having succeeded in obtaining a decision in his favor from the learned Chief Justice has failed to convince me that that judgment is wrong, although I do not feel called upon to express any further opinion as to its correctness.

But, I think that the moment it was stated to us that the judgment had been satisfied by one of the defendants, it was our duty to have dismissed this appeal without prejudice to any right the defendant might have to apply to have himself substituted for the plaintiffs, on proper materials shewing that he filled the position of surety only as to the original debt, or so much of it as he is now seeking to enforce by this peculiar process.

We cannot assume that he occupied that position as to the debt or any part of it, and on this short ground I think the appeal should have been dismissed.

PATTERSON, J.A., concurred.

OSLER, J. A.—As an appeal by the plaintiffs, I think they fail to shew that the learned Chief Justice was wrong in refusing to grant a writ of sequestration.

Since the appeal was lodged the plaintiffs have been paid in full by one of the defendants, who seeks to prosecute the appeal for his own benefit against his co-defendant.

In that state of things new considerations arise (assuming that an appeal by the plaintiffs on their own behalf might have been successful) which cannot now be inquired into. The judgment was recovered against the defendants as partners, and I doubt if under the Mercantile Law Amendment Act, R. S. O. ch. 116, secs. 2, 3, 4, one partner paying a judgment against the firm is entitled as a matter of right to enforce it for his own benefit ; except it may be to the extent that anything may be proved due to him upon the taking of the accounts between them, and, (as regards a judgment for such a cause of action as this judgment was recovered for), ascertaining whether the claim was one which should as between the partners themselves be borne equally or by one of them alone.

Then again (the contest being now between the partners themselves) it appears that there was a dissolution of their partnership by consent, and the seats at the stock exchange, which had theretofore been the property of the partnership, were taken over one by each of the partners who, has now entered into a new partnership, to which the seat belongs. I should not think it right to order a writ of sequestration at the instance of one of the former partners merely upon the suggestion that proceedings may hereafter be taken in aid of it to attack the bona fides of the new partnership, and of the transfer of the defendant Niven's seat thereto.

I think the appeal should be dismissed.

Appeal dismissed, with costs to be paid to respondent Niven.

Moore v. The Citizens Fire Insurance Company.

Moore v. The Quebec Fire Insurance Company.

Moore v. The British America Assurance Copmany.

AND

Moore v. The Gore District Mutual Fire Insurance. Company.

Fire insurance—Over-value—First statutory condition—Several insurances— Change of one policy—Notice.

The plaintiff being owner of a quantity of railway ties and lumber, effected insurances thereon with three companies to the amount of $4,000,
and subsequently, with the knowledge and through the agency of H.,
the person acting on behalf of the several companies, effected an additional insurance of $1,200 on the same property in "The Fire Insurance
Association." H. acted as agent for that company also, and he made
the necessary entries thereof on the three first policies. In consequence
of "The Fire Association" having ceased to take risks on that kind of
property, H. asked the plaintiff for the interim receipt of that company
which he gave up accordingly, and H. substituted one in the Gore District Company for it, he being agent for that company also, but omitted to give any notice or make any entry as to the substitution of the
Gore insurance for that of "The Fire Association."
In an action to recover the amount of the insurances, after a destruction
of the property by fire :
Held, [affirming the judgment of the Court below] that this was not such
an omission on the part of the plaintiff as invalidated the policies, in
this following : *Parsons* v. *The Standard Ins..Co.,* 43 U. C. R. 603 ; 4
A. R. 326 ; 5 S. C. R. 233.
In effecting insurances in all to the amount of $5,200, the plaintiff rep-
resented the property as being of "the cash value" of $5,339 on two
occasions, and $5,500 on a third occasion. In an action on the policies
the jury found that the value was $4,000 when first insured, and $4,200
when the additional insurance was effected ; that the plaintiff had misrepresented the value, but not intentionally or wilfully ; that it was not
material that the true value should be made known to the compan
and that the company intended that the goods should be insured to
their full value, and rendered a verdict in favor of the plaintiff for
$3,100, which the Divisional Court subsequently refused to set aside..
Held, [in this reversing the judgment of the Court below] that under the
circumstances and in view of the nature of the goods insured, the over-
valuation was such, as under the first statutory condition in the policy,
rendered the same void.

THESE actions were brought against the respective companies under policies of insurance against fire on certain
lumber and ties owned by the plaintiff.

On the 30th of January, 1886, an order was made by

the Master in Chambers consolidating the actions for the purpose of trial, &c., which took place at the Town of Welland, on the 14th of April, 1886, before O'Connor, J., and a jury ; and subsequently a judgment was directed to be entered for the plaintiff for $3,100 on the answers of the jury to the questions submitted to them, which appear in the present judgments.

An order nisi to set aside the findings of the jury was obtained in each of said actions, and notice of motion to set aside the judgment directed to be entered thereon was given in each action on behalf of the defendants, and notice of motion to increase the verdict and judgment of the plaintiff was given on the plaintiff's behalf.

By an order of the Chief Justices of the several Divisions of the High Court of Justice, of the 29th of May, 1886, it was ordered that the actions other than that against the British America Assurance Company, which had been commenced in the Chancery Division, should be transferred to that Division ; and on the 2nd of December, 1886, judgment was given by that Court, dismissing all the said motions with costs.

From this judgment, so far as it was adverse to them, the defendants appealed ; and the appeal came on to be heard before this Court on the 21st and 22nd of November, 1887.*

Osler, Q. C., and *Wallace Nesbitt*, for the appellants.
Laidlaw, Q. C., and *Kapelle*, for the respondent.

March 6, 1888. HAGARTY, C. J. O.—The three first named companies' policies were insuring from 22nd July to the 4th October.

Citizens, (further insurance) $1,500
In British America Company.......... 1,500
In Quebec Company............... 1,000
                                          ————
    In all........................ $4,000

* *Present.*—HAGARTY, C. J. O., BURTON, PATTERSON, and OSLER, JJ.A.

In the application for each insurance, the cash value of
the property is estimated at $5,339.

On the Citizens Company's is an indorsement, 22nd
August, 1884 : "Notice received and accepted, that the
other insurance has been increased to the amount of
$3,700." This was indorsed on a notice from the plaintiff,
dated 21st August, that he had further insured in the
Fire Association for $1,200, concurrent.

On the Quebec policy, a similar indorsement on a like
notice of additional insurance is entered.

The British America, to the like effect.

It appears that he did effect an insurance in the Fire
Association on or about the 21st August as notified. But
this only appears to have existed a few days. The evidence is very confused and uncertain about this insurance,
but it was stated in argument and not contradicted, that
the Fire Association had cancelled it, as they had ceased
to take risks on that kind of property.

Mr. Hill, the agent at Welland for the Association, and
also for the Gore and the Citizens, British America and
Quebec Companies, is not asked as to the cause of cancelling.

The plaintiff says that in a few days Hill asked him to
give back the Fire Association receipt, which he did, and
the Gore District was substituted for it.

The Gore District policy is dated September 1st, and
ending October 4th, like the others, and is for $1,200,
stating, "Further concurrent assurance $4,000."

Nothing was apparently communicated to the Gore
Company as to the Fire Association insurance.

Everything connected with these insurances appears to
have been wholly arranged by Mr. Hill with the plaintiff,
and the notice as to the Fire Association insurance
appears to have been sent by him to the different companies for the plaintiff.

His powers as agent seem to have been not the same for
each company. He had larger powers for the British
America, and was allowed to take risks and issue policies
for them.

For the others he issued interim receipts, and forwarded applications as ordinary agents do.

He appears to have had the policy signed in blank at Toronto, and issued by him at Welland, and on August 21st, he enters in the body of it the further insurance in the Fire Association; but after having this cancelled, he made no further entry as to the substituted Gore District insurance.

There is not, in any of the three existing insurances, any assent in writing by the company, or duly authorized agent, to a specific insurance in the Gore District Company but only in the Fire Association.

I think the British America case stands on a different footing from the others. Hill had the right to issue, and seems to have had the control of the policy to make such entries as he thought proper. He enters the Fire Association insurance. It is cancelled through him, and he, by his own action, substitutes the Gore insurance for it. I think he stands in the position as if the company in Toronto, by their President or Managing Director, had first consented in writing to the Fire Association insurance, and then obtained its cancellation, and then applied to the Gore or procured the Gore Company to substitute their insurance.

I think they must be held to have assented to the Gore insurance; and cannot insist on the difference of name, as the change took place by their own action, and they had full notice of the extent of the new risk.

As to the Citizens and Quebec Companies, the case is not so strong against them on this point, as Hill occupied a less important position, and was merely a local agent.

But I have great reluctance in acceding to the objections as to the name of the proposed underwriter.

There is no suggestion here that there was anything wrong in the substitution of the one company for the other ; or that it made or could make any difference whatever to them whether the insurance to the named amount of $1,200 was made in the one company or the other.

I cannot distinguish the case in substance from the

decision in *Parsons* v. *Standard Ins. Co.*, 43 U. C. R. 603ᵣ
4 A. R. 326, 5 S. C. R. 233.

There, in answer to the question, what other insurance
upon the property ? the answer was four of $2,000 each;
mentioning the offices, but by mistake stating the Canada
Fire and Marine Company as one of them, instead of the
Provincial.

It was objected that there was no notice of the Provincial insurance. It also appeared that he had an insurance
for $2,000 in the Western, and having agreed with the
agent to cancel it, he arranged with him, being also agent
for the Queen Insurance Company, to effect an insurance
in the same sum with them—no notice or assent was given
of this Queen insurance. He had informed the defendants' company on effecting insurance of four policies of
$2,000 each—$8,000 in all.

In the Court of first instance, I delivered the judgment,.
I say : [p. 607.]

"I cannot bring myself to hold that in an answer to a question asking what other insurances affect the property, and
in what companies, an unintentional error in the name of
one company, when the true amount of insurance is given,
shall vitiate the whole contract. So when the contract is
based upon the statement that $8,000 of insurance is
already upon the property, and one policy of $2,000 is
allowed to drop or be cancelled, and another to a like
amount is substituted therefor in another company, that
the non-communication of the new insurance, must necessarily destroy the contract. The statutable condition
just cited, requires a subsequent insurance to be communicated. The meaning is plain, and the provision is most
reasonable, that if the insured increases the insurance, the
prior insurer must be consulted."

I prefer quoting my words in that case, to using language to the same effect here, as the judgment was affirmed
by the Supreme Court.

The judgment of the Court was delivered by Mr. Justice
Gwynne, holding that the condition, as to subsequent insurance, must be construed to point to *further* insurance beyond
the amount allowed, and not to a policy substituted for one

of like amount allowed to lapse, and that the company to support their contention, should be more precise in the language used.

If, in these policies, the Fire Association insurance had been existing when the first three were effected and mentioned by name with the others, then, if a fortnight after, the Fire Association policy had expired and the plaintiff effected in substitution that with the Gore Company, the case would be precisely as in *Parsons* v. *The Standard.*

I am unable to draw any intelligible distinction between such a case and the present, and I think we must decide against the objection as to all the three companies.

As to the Gore Company. On this branch of the case, the only objection is, that the fact of there having been a cancelled insurance in the Fire Association, was not communicated to them.

We can easily understand the force of this objection if the Fire Association had refused to insure or cancelled an insurance on any ground except that assigned, viz., that they had ceased to take risks on that kind of property, and refused to confirm or continue their agents interim contract. If they had so insured and the insurance had lapsed by effluxion of time, I do not see why it would have been necessary to communicate the fact.

The law on this subject of non-communication, is fully discussed in Sir George Jessel's judgment in the *London Assurance Co.* v. *Mansel,* 11 Ch. D. 367, and the rule is stated to apply equally to insurances on ships, houses, or lives.

On the other branch of the case as to alleged misrepresentation as to value, an important question arises. It was strongly pressed upon us in argument that the statutory form requires, as it were, a warranty by the assured, of the absolute truth of the statement of value: "If any person or persons insures his or their buildings or goods, and causes them to be described otherwise than as they really are, to the prejudice of the company, or misrepresents or omits to communicate any circumstance which is material to be made known to the company in order to enable it to judge of the risk it undertakes, such insurance shall be of no force in respect to the property in regard to which the misrepresentation or omission is made."

I am of opinion that this clause leaves the law substantially unaltered, and as it has been for the last century, and it merely puts into words the rules applicable to all insurances, fire, life or marine.

The case just cited before Sir George Jessel, refers to various authorities governing the contract of insurance.

In the present case, the three first underwriters insured $4,000 on a property of the estimated cash value of $5,339. The jury find that the actual value was only $4,000, the actual sum assured. A month later these companies agree to a further assurance of $1,200, bringing the whole insurance up to within a small amount of the first declared value. The jury find that when this last $1,200 was taken the true value was only $4,200, an increase of $200.

I adopt the view so often expressed in our courts as to over value, without fraud or bad faith. On this, see *Wood* on Insurance, 426 *et seq.*, which has a review of authorities. The text books generally are to the same effect.

We have not here the usual complication caused by the owner's over estimate (however sincere) of his farm or his residence.

The property here was a quantity of lumber and railway ties—as we may suppose very readily counted in the middle of summer on a canal bank, and the market value readily ascertained as easily as if it had been a flock of sheep. The actual over-valuation the jury find to amount to twenty per cent or one-fifth beyond the true value.

They find that there was a misrepresentation, but that the over-valuation was free from fraud or any intention to deceive or mislead, and they also held that it was not material. It may be well to give the answers.

1. Q. What was the value of goods proposed to be insured on the 22nd of July and 21st of August, 1884, respectively? A. $4,000 and $4,200.

2. Q. Did the plaintiff misrepresent the value of the property to be insured at the time of the application for insurance? A. Yes.

3. Q. If plaintiff made any misrepresntation of value, was such misrepresentation intentionally and wilfully made? A. No.

4. Q. If any misrepresentation of value was made, was it material to be made known to the companies in these cases? A. No.

5. Q. Did the defendants intend to insure full value of goods? A. Yes.

6. Q. Was the stock represented on the 21st of August, as increasing? A. Yes.

7. Q. What was the amount of loss; that is, what was the value of the property destroyed? A. $3,564.51.

8. Q. Was there fraud or false statement in the proofs of loss? A. No.

9. Q. Was the cause of fire truly stated by plaintiff in proofs of loss; but, in answering this question you must consider whether plaintiff knew more of the cause of the fire than he stated? A. Yes. (In answer to a verbal question by his Lordship, the jury say they mean that he did state the cause of the fire truly, as far as his knowledge enabled him.)

10. Q. Did the insured wilfully or fraudulently over-state amount of claim in proofs of loss? A. No.

11. Q. What is the amount of loss caused by the fire? A. Same as No. 7.

(Verdict for plaintiff, $3,100.)

The jury apparently considered that their view that the defendants intended to insure to the full value was an important reason for holding the misrepresentations not material.

In the Divisional Court the learned Chancellor places a good deal of weight on the finding as to the company's intentions. He says:

" In the present case all the materiality (within the meaning of the condition) is removed from the valuation placed upon the goods at the time of insurance, because it is found by the jury, and was hardly questioned on the argument, that the companies intended to insure to the full value of this property. That is a fair inference on what took place on the 21st August on the part of all the defendants. This being so, it is evident that the extent of the value—whether less or more in the estimate of the insured—could not have influenced the judgment of the companies in undertaking the risk, or calculating the premium."

I am not prepared to attach so much importance to this alleged intention as influencing the decision as to the non-materiality of the misrepresentation, and especially as to the Gore insurance.

It may have been, and probably was, the intention of the three companies to insure to the full value, and, as a matter of fact, they did so. But when acting on such intention they took $4,000 of risk on $4,000 of value, can we say it was not material to represent to them that there was a margin of value to $1,300 over the insurance ?

Then, even assuming that the first three insurances were fairly obtained, we have to consider the effect of the further $1,200 insurance. The jury found that the value of stock had increased so that at the last insurance it was $200 better than at the first. The plaintiff states that he told Hill, the agent, that it was so increased by $200, and that he (plaintiff) then thought $5,200 was the full value. The addition of the Gore Company's $1,200 thus brought the whole risks up to the whole estimated value stated by the plaintiff.

The evidence strongly suggests that it was in consequence of the plaintiff being pressed by the bank for more security that he effected this last insurance, rather than from a bonâ fide desire to guard himself. This is his evidence :

"Q. Now, why did you insure in the Gore for this larger amount? A. Well, Mr. Hill had told me that I had better insure for full value. That is what he has always told me ; and being pressed by the bank for further security, I thought that in case loss should happen, and I was only insured for part of the value, I thought I might be in a difficulty with the bank when I agreed to insure.

"Q. Was it under pressure from the bank that you insured for this larger amount? A. Well, it was to satisfy the bank ; I wanted to please Mr. McGlashan all I could.

"Q. Now, is this the account you gave of it before—'Why did you increase the insurance in August.' 'I generally tried to insure enough to cover my liabilities?' A. Certainly ; and the bank was one.

"Q. Had you been borrowing any money?" "The bank had been making advances all along, and I had given Mr. McGlashan to understand that I would insure" (question 370).—"But you were insured for $4,000?" "Yes; but I was getting deeper and deeper into the bank all the time."— This is true? A. I think it was ; of course I cannot speak definitely ; I have not the books here.

"Q. Is your answer true or false? A. I think it is true ; I won't speak to an exact amount of figures.

"Q. Is it true—'I was getting deeper and deeper into the bank all the time?' A. Yes.

"Q. Question—'Was the bank asking you for insurance the only reason that you put on this extra $1,200?' Answer—'If the bank had not

asked me for insurance, I would not have insured, I swear that positively?"
A. I do.

" Q. Question 377—' Why should you, for a $200 increase in value, put on $1,200 increase in insurance?'—and here is your answer: 'Mr. McGlashan told me that time he had a letter from Toronto stating that my liabilities were about $7,000, and the bank and he kept wanting security, and the only security I could very easily give him was to insure, and that is the reason I put this on.'—Is that true? A. Yes.

" Q. The bank in Toronto was writing to Mr. McGlashan about your account? A. Yes.

" Q. McGlashan was pressing you, and you had no security you could give him easy, and you went off and got another policy? A. Yes; the calculation was, in case there should be a loss Mr. McGlashan's account should be paid first.

Q. And, of course, you had no desire to be insured, as you say there, except for the purpose of giving the bank the security they were pressing for? A. There was a certain desire.

Q. I suppose your answer is true there? A. Yes.

I think this evidence has a very strong bearing on the value and the materiality.

It is evident that the Gore Company was willing to insure to the full value, as stated to them—aware of $4,000 existing risks. But it can hardly be urged that it was of no consequence to them to know that there was really nothing in the shape of value in existence for their insurances to operate on, except to give them the privilege of sharing with the other three companies their relative proportion of the actual loss, on the basis of $5,200 of risk on $4,200 of value.

It may be, for all we know, a practice among insurance companies after insuring up to the full value, to readily consent to another company taking a further risk with a view to lessen the ratable proportion of loss; and it may also be the case that a company, for the sake of the premium, knowingly coming into such an arrangement, though there was no margin of value above the existing risks. No such case is in evidence here.

If the case depended on the question of the plaintiff's alleged guilty knowledge of the cause of fire, &c., I do not think we should interfere. I at first thought that our proper course should be to send the case to another trial.

On further consideration, I adopt the views of my brother
Patterson. He, in the judgment he will deliver, has pointed
out very clearly certain points as to the matters referred
to the consideration of the court not directly involved in
the findings of the jury. The legal effect of the fourth
insurance with the Gore Company, appears to be left to
the court, and if so, we must determine it. I think we
must regard the insurance as invalid; there was no value
to insure, and no company should be bound on such a state
of facts; granted that if he had to deal only with the
three first companies, he can recover, I hardly see how
in any view the fourth is sustainable. Nor is it easy to
see how in the face of the condition as to further insur-
rance and the non-existence of any further insurable value
therefor, of property to represent the same, his whole
claim must not be defeated.

The assent of the three companies ought not to avail to
bind them in such a state of facts.

PATTERSON, J. A.—In *Moore* v. *The Citizens Fire Ins.
Co.*, the plaintiff effected a policy with the defendants
on the 22nd of July, 1884, for $1,500, "on lumber
and ties situate on the north bank of the Welland
Canal Feeder, in the township of Moulton, county of Hal-
dimand," insuring him from the date of the policy till the
4th of October, 1884. On the face of the policy it was
stated that there was "further insurance $2,500." The
policy was expressed to be subject to the statutory conditions, and also to be subject to the fulfilment of other
voluminous conditions on which nothing in connection
with this contest turns.

The insured goods were destroyed by fire on the 16th of
September, 1884, and this action was commenced on the
23rd of December, in the same year.

The defence, as pleaded, relies on the statutory conditions,
and notably on the first condition.

This condition has often been considered in cases like
this, but notwithstanding our familiarity with it, it may be
useful to have its precise terms in view when we consider
the facts to which it is now sought to apply it.

" If any person or persons insures his or their buildings or goods, and causes the same to be described otherwise than as they really are, to the prejudice of the company, or misrepresents or omits to communicate any circumstance which is material to be made known to the company in order to enable it to judge of the risk it undertakes, such insurance shall be of no force in respect to the property in regard to which the misrepresentation or omission is made."

Several misrepresentations or concealments in connection with the plaintiff's application for the insurance are pleaded by the defendants, but we have to consider only one of them, being the only charge under this condition as to which any question went to the jury. That is a charge of misrepresenting the value of the goods.

The value stated in the application is $5,339 as " present cash value." The jury find that the value was $4,000 ; that the plaintiff misrepresented the value, but not intentionally or wilfully ; that it was not material that the true value should be made known to the company ; and that the company intended that the goods should be insured to their full value.

The " present cash value " of these goods was something capable of being stated by the applicant as a fact, not as a matter of opinion merely, like the valuation of the building discussed in *Williamson* v. *Commercial Union Ins. Co.*, 26 C. P. 591. I had occasion in that case to make some remarks on the subject which are reported at p. 597. These were goods for the market. The selling price of the lumber and the ties was to a very small extent a matter of opinion, and the statement that the goods were worth $5,339, was really a statement of quantity. That it was so understood and intended by the plaintiff is proved by his statement to Mr. Hill when he wanted to increase the insurance : " By George, Frank, I have more stuff there than I thought I had."

The insurance by the defendants, plus the other insurances of $2,500, brought the total to the exact amount ($4,000) found by the jury as the value of the goods. The coincidence of the amounts is, however, purely accidental.

The materiality of a representation, under the first condition, is a question of fact, as has often been pointed out.
See *Butler* v. *Standard Fire Ins. Co.*, 4 A. R. 391, 398.

The finding that the misrepresentation in this case was
not material means, I suppose, that the company would
have issued the policy all the same, even if $4,000 had
been represented as the value. That finding cannot be
said to be entirely unsupported by evidence. The statement is not made in reply to a specific question. If it had
been so, it might have been argued with force that the
stamp of materiality had been attached to it by the parties
themselves. Where it occurs is in the description of the
goods offered for insurance, and the jury find that the
misdescription is not due to fraud or bad faith.

I should not be surprised if a jury, on another trial,
should take a different view, but looking no farther than
the date of the policy, I do not think we could properly
say that the Divisional Court ought to have disturbed the
judgment. We may find reason to think differently when
we consider the subsequent occurrences.

Another condition relied upon is the 8th, which declares
that the company is not liable for loss if any subsequent
insurance is effected in any other company, unless and
until the company assents thereto by writing, signed by a
duly authorized agent.

In August, 1884, the plaintiff effected a further insurance with the Fire Insurance Association for $1,200
through Mr. Hill, the agent authorized by that company
to give an interim receipt, but not to issue a policy. Hill
sent the plaintiff's policy in the Citizens Company to the
St. Catharine's agency of that company, where the following indorsement was made upon it :

" ST. CATHARINES, Aug. 22nd, 1884.

" Notice received and accepted that the other insurance
has been increased to the amount of $3,700.

L. C. CAMP & SON."

The Fire Insurance Association declined to issue a policy,
the reason given being that they had ceased insuring that

description of property ; and Mr. Hill, who was authorized also to take applications for the Gore District Mutual Fire Ins. Co., took from the plaintiff an application to that company for insurance to the amount of $1,200, the value of goods being stated to be $5,500; and a policy was accordingly issued, bearing date the first day of September, 1884. The policy is for $1,300, but $100 of that amount is on cordwood.

The assent indorsed on the Citizens Company policy was undoubtedly given on notice only of the insurance in the Fire Insurance Association. But it is a general assent to the increase of the insurance, just as the note in the body of the policy assented generally to $2,500 further insurance ; and the policy in the Gore District Company being merely in substitution for the insurance in the Fire Association, the case is precisely within the decision in *Parsons* v. *Standard Ins. Co.*, 5 S. C. R. 133. Mr. Osler attempted to find a distinction in the fact that the insurance in the Fire Insurance Association died an untimely and not a natural death; not expiring by effluxion of time, but being cancelled by the company. I cannot recognise the distinction.

If the Gore District Company's policy is valid, I think the consent to the increased insurance must be held to cover it. If it is invalid by reason of anything in the Fire Insurance Association transaction, then the Citizens Company has nothing to complain of.

But another consideration arises, not involved in the operation of the 8th condition alone, but carrying us back to the 1st condition.

The materiality of the representation that the value was $5,329, in place of $4,000, has to be looked at in a new light when the total insurance is to be $5,200, and not $4,000.

The findings of the jury on the question of materiality relate only to the date of the policy, or rather to the time of the application, when the whole insurance in contemplation was $4,000.

I understand the questions arising on the further insurance to have been left to the Court, the jury being asked
to find, and having found, only one fact on that branch of
the case, namely, that the value was then $4,200.   I do
not know that any further representation of the value was
made to any company but the Gore District Company,
and that was as far from the true value as the original
representation to the Citizens Company.

There can be no doubt of the fact of the representation
of value being most material when the insurance effected
far exceeds the real value of the goods.

It is material " in order to enable the company to judge
of the risk it undertakes."

Now while we adhere to the word "value" as a convenient term, we must not forget that we are really discussing
a representation of the quantity, just as if the lumber had
been described as so many thousand feet, twenty-five per
cent. above the true quantity.

The reasoning of the jury was, that so long as the insurances did not exceed the true value of the goods it was of
no consequence towards enabling the company to judge of
the proposed risk that they were put at too high a figure,
because the intention was that they should be insured to
their full value.

Whether that chain of reasoning is sound or unsound, it
is evident from the findings of the jury that it was the
reasoning they adopted.

But if the intention had been taken to be to insure for
$5,200 on the representation that the goods were worth
$5,339, the jury would not have ventured to say that it
was of no consequence to conceal the fact that the value
was only $4,000.   The absurdity would have been too
glaring.

Yet that is the position the plaintiff must take when he
asserts the assent to the further insurance of $1,200.

He cannot hold the company to that assent without adhering to, and in effect repeating, his original valuation,
and submitting to the consequence of that material misre-

presentation. The consequence is the avoidance of the policy unless saved by the absence of fraudulent intent.

To hold such intent necessary is, in my judgment, to introduce into the condition an important qualification of the language in which it is expressed.

We are not required by anything in the language of the condition, or in the policy in view of which it is framed, to introduce any such qualification. Fraud would, of course, vitiate without the expressed conditions. On the other hand the condition does not make every misrepresentation fatal.

That effect is confined to statements of circumstances material to be made known to the company in order to enable it to judge of the risk it undertakes; and extends, not to the whole contract, but only to the property misrepresented. The case of *Sly* v. *Ottawa Agricultural Ins. Co.*, 20 U. C. R. 557, was decided on that understanding of the condition, and was, I think, correctly so decided.

The policy is in my opinion void under either the first condition or the eighth, and the choice between them is little more than a matter of words.

It was argued with more particular reference to the 8th condition, the argument being that the plaintiff could not be allowed to insist on a consent obtained as this was; while I have attempted to explain why in my opinion the first condition applies.

In either way the result is the same, and should be followed by a judgment dismissing the action.

If, however, it should go again to trial I think the defence founded on the allegation that the cause of the fire was not truly disclosed in the proofs of loss, according to the best of the plaintiff's knowledge, should be open as fully as any other issue on the record.

There is a feeling, founded on certain maxims of the criminal law, that a defence which relies on a charge savoring of crime should be dealt with on somewhat different principles from a defence founded on allegations which would not support an indictment. That is a feeling easily capable of being carried into the region of false sentiment, and made the instrument of injustice. The object is to ascertain the truth, and the facilities afforded in procedure to an insurance company, defending itself in an action on a policy, should be at least as ample when personal charges of bad faith or fraud are the ground of the defence, even though they border on an imputation of crime, or perhaps overstep the border, as when only the failure, perhaps inadvertent, to comply with some condition is in question.

MOORE V. QUEBEC FIRE ASSURANCE CO.

There is only one respect in which this case differs from that against the Citizens Company, and it is in the specification in the body of the policy of the other insurances, as being "$1,500 in Citizens, $1,500 in British America, warranted concurrent," in place of noting merely the total amount, and in preserving the same form in the notice of the $1,200 new policy, thus: "Notice received of additional further insurance of $1,200 in the Fire Insurance Association, warranted concurrent."

I am against the plaintiff's right to recover in this case on the same grounds as in the other.

I am not sure that I should not in this case add the avoidance of the policy under the 8th condition by the neglect to communicate and procure assent to the insurance in the Gore District Company.

In the judgment of the Supreme Court in *Parsons* v. *Standard Ins. Co.*, as well as in the Queen's Bench, 43 U. C. R. 603, stress was laid on the circumstance that the note in the body of the policy was of the amount of the other insurance generally, and not of the specific insurances in other companies. That feature is wanting in this policy. I do not wish to express any opinion upon the effect of this difference, because the judgment does not, in my view, turn upon that question. I merely desire to leave it open.

MOORE V. BRITISH AMERICA ASSURANCE CO.

I have to repeat in this case what I have said in the case of the Quebec Assurance Company, mutatis mutandis.

I have not been able to see that the accident of Hill, having a more extensive agency for this company than for the others, makes a difference in the legal rights of the company ; but the result is not affected by the question.

MOORE V. GORE DISTRICT MUTUAL FIRE INSURANCE COMPANY.

This policy is dated the 13th of September, 1884. It is for $1,200, in addition to the insurances in other companies specified in the body of the policy at the amount of $4,000, the other companies not being named.

The goods are valued in the application at $5,500, and were worth, according to the finding of the jury, $4,200.

There is no finding as to the materiality of this misrepresentation. It is, as I have already remarked, left to the court, if I correctly understand the report of the trial. The materiality I take to be indisputable; and the effect of the misrepresentation is, under the 1st statutory condition, to avoid the policy.

A point was made at the trial, and was pressed before us, touching the cancellation of the insurance in the Fire Insurance Association.

I have not apprehended the relevance of the point to any of the insurances but this one, and as to this I feel at a loss for facts. I do not know the terms of the interim receipt by which alone the insurance was effected. It may have been cancelled or burnt, or the insurance may have, under the terms of the contract, expired. If it were cancelled, or indeed whether cancelled or not, it should apparently have been mentioned in answer to the question " In what offices has this property been insured hitherto?" I should not like to say, without more consideration, that the fact of the cancellation of the insurance, if in any case a material circumstance, became immaterial merely because the reason assigned for cancelling it was that the company had ceased to do that class of business. I could not say judicially that that was the true reason, or that the knowledge of the facts might not have suggested important inquiries.

But, in the state of our information, any opinion would be to some extent speculative, and in the view I take of the general merits, no such opinion is called for.

The appeal should be allowed, and the actions dismissed with costs.

BURTON and OSLER, JJ.A., concurred.

Appeal allowed, with costs.

[Since carried to the Supreme Court.]

BEATY V. SHAW ET AL.

Mortgage—Executor and trustee—Void discharge of mortgage—Payment for improvements—Mistake of title.

H. by his will appointed F. and W. executors and trustees of his estate. F. for the purpose of securing a debt due by him to the estate, executed a mortgage to W. W. died intestate, and F., five years subsequently having agreed to sell the mortgaged premises to M., executed a statutory discharge of the mortgage, which he expressed to do as sole surviving executor, and then conveyed the estate to M.

Held, [affirming the judgment of BOYD, C., 13 O. R. 21,] that the act of F., in executing such discharge, had not the effect of releasing the land from the mortgage.

Held, also, [in this reversing the same judgment] that M., the purchaser from F. and his assigns, were not entitled to any lien for improvements on the lands during their occupancy thereof.

THIS was an appeal by the plaintiff and a cross-appeal by the defendants from the judgment of Boyd, C., reported 13 O. R. 21, where the facts are fully stated.

The appeal came on to be heard on the 24th November, 1887.*

J, C. Hamilton and *Alan Cassels,* for the appellant.
Bain, Q. C., for the respondents.

January 30, 1888. HAGARTY, C. J. O.—I fully agree with the decision of the learned Chancellor that the extraordinary discharge executed by the borrower and mortgagor,

* *Present.*—HAGARTY, C.J.O., BURTON, PATTERSON, and OSLER, JJ.A.

and its registration, could not operate as a discharge of the plaintiff's mortgage.

I am fully satisfied with the reasons, and adopt them as governing my decision.

But a very embarrassing question is raised by the reference as to improvements.

The bill is in the ordinary form asking payment of mortgage or foreclosure.

The defence is a purchase for value from the mortgagor in ignorance of the mortgage, claiming that they had made permanent improvements for which compensation is asked; and the decree directs that the defendants are entitled to a lien and charge on the lands in priority to the plaintiff's claim under the mortgage for the value of all lasting and permanent improvements made by them prior to the commencement of the suit.

If the Master find such improvements, the effect will be curious.

The first mortgagee without the slightest knowledge default, connivance, or standing by on his part, is thus converted into a subsequent mortgagee, a position that he certainly never contemplated occupying, or would wittingly have occupied.

We have to consider the rules adopted in Courts of Equity on this subject as to compensating in cases of defective title, &c., and also on statutable provisions.

In 1873, 36 Vict. ch. 22, (O.) an Act of one clause, was as follows:

" In every case in which any person has made or may make lasting improvements on any land under the belief that the land is or was his own, he or his assigns, shall be entitled to a lien upon the same to the extent of the amount by which the value of such land is enhanced by such improvements."

To this short section was added by the R. S. O. ch. 95 sec. 4, these words, " or shall be entitled, or may be required to retain the land, if the Court is of opinion, or requires that such should be done, according as may, under all the circumstances of the case, be most just, making compensation for the land if retained, as the Court may direct."

As far back as 1818, R. S. U. C. p. 205, 59 Geo. III. ch. 14, a provision was made in cases of ejectment, to assess damages, which the defendants may sustain by improving on land not their own—in consequence of unskilful survey. This provision appears again in 1839, 2 Vict. ch. 17, R. S. U. C. p. 973, with fresh provisions, but limited to cases of defendant improving land not his own, in consequence of unskilful survey.

This provision is substantially repeated in 12 Vict. ch 35, sec. 49; C. S. U. C. ch. 93, sec. 53. The jury there are to assess both the improvements and the value of the land ; claimant has to pay for the improvements or to release the land on payment of its assessed value.

The next statute, is that cited in 1873, departing for the first time from the narrower ground of unskilful surveys.

These are what are called " Betterment Laws" in many of the States. *Fee* v. *Cowdry*, 55 Am. R. 563. They seem generally framed with more care than our statute. In Arkansas the law is, " If any person believing himself to be the owner either in law or equity under colour of title, has peaceably improved, &c., any land which, upon judicial investigation, shall be decided to belong to another, &c., the value of the improvements shall be paid before the Court shall order possession to be delivered."

In Vermont, 31 Vermont, 306, if the defendant, or those under whom he holds, have purchased a title to such land, supposing at the time of such purchase such title to be good in fee, &c.

In Ohio, if he have purchased in good faith and received a deed properly authenticated, which has been recorded, and under which he has held quiet possession, and made valuable improvements supposing himself to be the actual owner, &c. : *Hunt* v. *McMahon*, 5 Ohio 132, (*n*).

In Illinois, the relief is given to any person evicted, if he can shew a plain title in law or equity from the Records without actual notice of an adverse title, with many special provisions for valuing: *Ross* v. *Irving*, 14 Ill. 172.

I feel very great difficulty in holding that our statute applies to a case like that before us. The effect of a decision in favor of the defendants would be very far reaching in its results.

I think the Legislature must have had in view the case of improvements on land wholly belonging to another person, and to which the improving occupant turns out to have no claim or title. The direction that he shall have a lien on the land for his improvements, assists this construction, and the added proviso giving power to the Court to make him retain the land, making compensation to the owner, seems to point in the same direction.

The defendants desire to apply the Act to the case of a purchaser who, though his deed professes to grant an estate in fee, only takes the equity of redemption, there being a mortgage outstanding.

Does the owner of an estate, subject to a mortgage, come within the statute?

" The mortgagor, as in the civil law, is now held until a decree of foreclosure, to be the real owner of the land and possessed of it in his ancient and original right and estate, and the mortgage is personal assets."

" An equity of redemption then is, in equity, the ancient estate in the land, without change of ownership": 1 Coote 31, ed., 1884, citing Lord Hardwicke, 1 Atk. 602.

I cannot understand that the direction that the occupant shall have a lien on the land, is reconcilable with his position as the owner of an equitable estate of inheritance.

The land is his own, subject to a charge.

The holder of this charge has done nothing whatever, either by commission or omission, in any way to deceive or mislead the occupant. We are asked, as already suggested, to turn him from a first into a second mortgagee, postponing him to the lien or charge claimed under the statute.

If the contention prevail, it must follow that every mortgagee of land, with the title clear on the registry, is subject to a prior claim for improvements by a subsequent purchaser from his mortgagor, who is ignorant of the mortgage, either from taking the assurance of his vendor that the title is clear, or from omitting to search the registry or make any inquiry.

Registration is declared to be notice, but the words of our Act seem to make "the belief that the land is his own ;" the sole foundation for the claim for improvements.

Even if the purchaser is aware that there is a mortgage on record, if he accept the assurance of his vendor that it has been paid, or that it has been discharged, and enter and improve under belief that such is the case, he will, in this view, bring himself within this Act.

In the case before us, the defendant Moran took a statutory deed in fee, and under it, if his vendor's estate were solvent, he would have had full redress on the covenant against the vendor's own acts. He bought with this covenant for his protection. His legal rights are the same whether the vendor's estate could or could not satisfy his demand.

The case is one of much hardship, but we must hesitate before adopting a construction of the statute so far reaching in its effect on incumbrances on real estate.

I cannot bring myself to the conclusion that the Act applies.

It remains to regard the claim for improvements irrespective of the statute.

I have not been able to find any case approaching in its facts to the case before us: no case bearing on the alleged right in equity to postpone a first incumbrance on an estate by granting a lien to a subsequent purchaser from the first mortgagor. Nor have we been referred to any direct decision that such lien is to be allowed to a purchaser from a person having no title and where no interest passed.

In 2 *Story* on Equity 129, *et seq.*, the subject is very fully discussed, and numerous cases are referred to, and the writer is strongly in favor of a very liberal application of the equitable rule. But none of the cases seem to touch this, even if we take this case to be one in which no legal title passed to the purchaser.

This is not the case of the owner of the paramount title seeking to make the ousted occupant account for rents and profits, nor of an owner of the equitable title, asking the aid of equity to enforce that title against the holder of the legal estate, &c.

In our own Courts there have been several decisions, but none seems applicable to this case. None as to postponing an innocent first incumbrancer.

The only case that I have seen as to allowing compensation for improvements to one who claimed under a conveyance by which no title passed, is *Gummerson* v. *Banting*, 18 Gr. 516, a decision of Spragge, C., before the passing of the Act, 1873.

He allowed compensation to the plaintiff who had purchased from the widow and administratrix.

The heir-at-law ejected the plaintiff, and he claimed that he had, at all events, purchased her estate in dower, and he claimed a lien for his improvements. As the widow died before the hearing, the only point was, as to improvements.

The learned Chancellor appears to me to state the rule of equity too broadly, when he says: " It is established that this Court regards it as equitable that a party making a purchase under mistake as to title, should be allowed for improvements as against the true owner."

No doubt he is so allowed in many cases as in *Bevis* v. *Boulton*, 7 Gr. 39 ; *Carroll* v. *Robertson*, 15 Gr. 17 ; *Wilson Graham*, 13 O. R. 661.

There is nothing in this case resembling the case of a purchase under a power of sale in a mortgage which turns out to have been defectively exercised; or where a contract, sale, or lease has been set aside as improperly obtained, and the vendee or lessee has, in good faith, improved the estate, or where he held under a purchase from a trustee and has to yield to the claim of a cestui que trust.

This case stands on wholly different ground.

With the strongest feeling of regret for the position of the respondents, I think we are bound to allow this appeal.

BURTON, J. A.—The plaintiff appeals against so much of the judgment of the learned Chancellor as declares these defendants entitled to a lien in respect of improvements upon the mortgaged premises prior to the plaintiff's mortgage.

The formal judgment as drawn up, is manifestly erroneous and unwarranted, inasmuch as it awards to the defendants a lien or charge for the value of all lasting and permanent improvements made by them, whereas, if the case comes within the statute, all that the defendants would be entitled to, would be a charge to the extent by which the value of the land is enhanced by such improvements.

But I am of opinion that the case is not within the statute, which is intended to apply to a state of things where the person making the improvement has no title or estate in the land, but has entered and made improvements under the belief that the land was his own. In such a case where the real owner asserts his title, the person making the improvements is entitled to a lien on the land, which land belongs to the owner, but becomes subject to the lien.

Here the persons making the improvements made them upon their own lands, how can they be entitled to a lien upon lands which they own? The statute does not say as in the Mechanic's Lien Acts, that they shall be entitled to a lien, even as against and in priority to an incumbrancer who has registered his security; and I venture to think that nothing short of legislation, in clear and express terms, would warrant such an interference with securities which the parties entitled to them, have registered in compliance with the laws in that behalf. The further legislation by the amending Act, 40 Vict. ch. 7, (O.) shews, I, think, very clearly that this is the proper construction, as power is there given to the Court to compel the improver to retain the land, in which case he is to pay the owner for the land, and thereby acquire a title. If this be the correct view of the statute, is there anything, as the law stood before and independently of the statute, to warrant the judgment?

The case of *Gummerson* v. *Banting*, 18 Gr. 516, decided by the late Chief Justice of this Court when Chancellor, took the profession a good deal by surprise, and was supposed to carry the law in reference to allowance for improvements, where there was no privity between the parties, no fraud, no standing by and suffering the improvements to be made, much farther than any previous decision either here or in England; and the passage of the 36 Vict. ch. 22,(O.) very shortly afterwards, probably prevented the point being further considered in a Court of Appeal; but I do not at all understand that the ratio decidendi in that case would apart from the statute, warrant the present decree.

With very great deference for the opinion of that painstaking Judge, I do not think the authorities he refers to warrant the conclusion at which he arrived in that case.

In the cases he refers to of vendor and purchaser, where the latter has paid part of the purchase money, and without any fault on his part, the vendor has been unable to complete the sale, the purchaser has, to the extent of that purchase, become equitable owner and entitled to a lien, and if let into possession with the knowledge on the part of the vendor that he intended to build, there would seem to be no good reason why the vendor should recover that estate without payment for the improvements. The case of *Brunskill* v. *Clark*, 9 Gr. 430, was decided upon that principle; it being shewn that the vendor was made aware

of the contemplated use of the property by the purchaser :
Bunney v. *Hopkinson*, 27 Beav. 565, referred to by the
Chancellor, is a case of the same description.

But I find no case in our own Court before *Gummerson*
v. *Banting*, and no case at all in England where a stranger
who has entered upon land, even under colour of title can,
as against the true owner, claim to be paid for his improvements.

The case first referred to by the learned Chancellor is *Nee-
son* v. *Clarkson*, 4 Hare 97 ; that case is commented on and
explained in *Parkinson* v. *Hanbury*, L. R. 2 H. L. 11. In
that case a married woman had, previously to her marriage,
become entitled to the benefit of a contract for the purchase of some land. The husband supposing himself to be
entitled, paid the balance of the purchase money, and took
the conveyance in his own name. He afterwards sold it,
and the conveyance contained recitals, which the Vice
Chancellor held (although it was spoken of by Lord Westbury as unquestionably a strong decision) that these
recitals gave distinct notice to the purchaser that he had
only a limited interest which ceased upon the death of his
wife. The heir-at-law of the wife brought an action to
recover possession, and it was held that the purchaser had
no title to the possession except in respect of his lien for
the purchase money. It is true, that in taking the accounts
the expenditure for improvements was allowed, but it is
stated in a note to the report that the right of the defendant to them was conceded at the hearing.

Many cases are to be found where a Court has been
applied to to grant relief against a trustee or other person
in a fiduciary position, who, without actual fraud, has made
a purchase which is improper according to the rules laid
down in Courts of Equity, and in those cases the Courts have
frequently imposed, as a condition of the relief, that the
plaintiff shall pay for improvements of a permanent and
lasting nature, which have a tendency to bring the estate
to a better sale ; such a case was *Bevis* v. *Boulton*, 7 Gr. 39,
in our own courts : the purchaser, Armstrong, had notice

of the trusts on which the property was held before he
purchased, but it was held that he was entitled to stand in
the position of the trustee, and that to the extent to which
he had added to the present value of the estate, he was
entitled to a fair allowance.

The case of *Cooper* v. *Phibbs*, L. R. 2 H. L. 149,150, does
not establish that improvements made by a stranger under
a mistake as to title, would give to him a lien for them
against the true owner, but merely that a person who filled
the position of trustee, and who had expended his own
means for the purpose of making certain improvements
authorised by Act of Parliament, was entitled as against
the cestui que trust to a lien for the money so expended.

The case of *Gummerson* v. *Banting,* was a peculiarly
hard case, one of those cases which it is proverbially said
are apt to excite the sympathies of a Judge, and lead to
the making of doubtful law. The learned Judge based
his judgment mainly on a judgment of Mr. Justice Story,
in the case of *Boyd* v. *Bright*, 2 *Story's* R. 605.

No doubt, by the rules of the civil law, the possessor of
the property of another who has made improvements in
good faith, believing himself to be the owner, was entitled
to be paid for such improvements; and this law has been
adopted by many countries whose laws are based upon the
civil law; thus it has been acted upon in Scotland, and in
some instances, but not universally, in America; but we
do not derive our laws from that source; and I know of
no instance in which, by the law of England, the principle
has been adopted except in the action for mesne profits,.
where the party has been sometimes allowed to recoup
himself by setting off the value of the improvements, and
in cases where the legal title has been in the person
making the improvements, and the equitable title in
another, who is obliged to resort to a Court of Equity for
relief, and where the court then acts upon the principle
that the party who comes to the court to seek equity,
must, himself, be willing to do what is equitable.

The old case of *Edlin* v. *Battlay,* in Levinz, *(a)* can hardly be regarded as an authority for so broad a proposition ; the amount involved, was very small, and on the recommendation of the court, a compromise was arrived at during the argument.

As against the true owner having the legal title, the Legislature has said that the person who has made the improvements in good faith, shall to the extent to which the property has been enhanced in value, have a lien ; having that lien, he has the means of course of enforcing it in the courts of the country, but apart from the legislation, I have been unable to convince myself, that except in the case of fraud, or that the aid of a Court of Equity is required, the Courts have any power against the real owner to enforce a claim for compensation for improvements ; but, however that may be, such a claim cannot be enforced as against a mortgagee who has registered his mortgage.

As to the cross-appeal, the point is not arguable. If the mortgagor had been a debtor of the testator, his appointment as executor, would formerly have discharged the debt at law, but not in equity ; but no prudent purchaser would have completed his purchase without a reconveyance of the legal estate from the heir-at-law ; but that is not the nature of the transaction ; as between him and the mortgagee, the debt was his individual debt to the mortgagee, although the money when collected would be held for the benefit of the beneficiaries under the will, but the title to the security and the right to enforce it, passed to the personal representatives of the mortgagee.

I am of opinion that the appeal should be allowed with costs, and the cross-appeal dismissed with costs.

PATTERSON, J. A.—I agree that under the proper application of the statute, the owner of the equity of redemption in this case has no claim against the mortgagee in respect of the value added to the land by his own improvements.

I am content to put my judgment upon the reasons expressed by my brother Osler in the judgment he is about to deliver.

(a) Vol. 2, p. 152.

OSLER, J. A.—The late mortgagor being the owner in fee of the lands in question mortgaged them to William Hincks, junior, to secure the sum of $5,652, which he had borrowed from the estate of the Reverend Professor William Hincks, deceased, of whom they were both trustees and executors. William Hincks, junior, the mortgagee, died, and some time afterwards the mortgagor being minded to sell the land to the defendants, assumed to discharge, and in fact executed an instrument which purported to be a discharge of his own mortgage. The plaintiff having become sole trustee of the estate of the Rev. Professor Hincks and the holder of the mortgage, brought this action in order to foreclose it or to obtain payment of the mortgage debt, and he now appeals from the judgment on the ground that although the mortgage was held not to have been discharged the defendants were declared entitled to a lien or charge upon those parts of the land respectively purchased by them, in priority to the plaintiff's claim under the mortgage, for the value of all lasting and permanent improvements made upon the lands so purchased prior to the commencement of the action.   This point may be said to have passed without discussion in the Court below, the judgment being entirely occupied with the consideration of the main question, namely the alleged discharge of the mortgage, as to which there is a cross-appeal.

The form of decree has been objected to because it directs payment of the value of the improvements instead of the amount by which the value of the land has been enhanced thereby.   This may have been an error in drawing up the decree, but in the view I take of the case, I do not think it necessary to do more than notice it.

The defendants' right to relief must depend, and has indeed been rested upon the statute R. S. O. ch. 95, sec. 4, (R. S. O. 1877, ch. 99, sec. 28.)

Independently of the statute, the case does not fall within the principle of any authority which has been cited to us.

This statute which was first passed in the year 1873,

provides for the case of improvements made under mistake of title, and if applicable to every state of facts which might come literally within its general words, is legislation of a very advanced character, as Wilson, J., observed in *Carrick* v. *Smith*, 34 U. C. R., 389, the first occasion on which it seems to have been considered. As it now appears in the Statute Book after one or two amendments, it is as follows :

" In every case in which any person makes lasting improvements under the belief that the land is his own, he or his assigns shall be entitled to a lien upon the same to the extent of the amount by which the value of such land is enhanced by such improvements ; or shall be entitled or may be required to retain the land if the Court is of opinion or requires that such should be done, according as may under all the circumstances of the case, be most just, making compensation for the land, if retained, as the court may direct."

The governing words of the clause are, " under the belief that the land is his own ;" the implication from them being that the case intended to be provided for by the legislature is that of improvements made by a person under a mistake of title on land which turns out not to belong to him—not to be his own. Do they extend to such a case as the present, where the land is really the land of the person who has made the improvements, but is subject to a mortgage or prior charge of some kind which, from accident or neglect, he has failed to discover before he purchased it ? With submission, I think the language of the section is almost in terms opposed to that construction. In the first place, what is spoken of is not lands which *are* the lands of the person making the improvements, but lands which he *believes* to be his ; and in the next place, the relief afforded by the Act, namely, giving such person a *lien* upon the land, or entitling or requiring him to retain it, making compensation as the court may direct, is appropriate only to cases where the party claiming it, has no interest in the land except such as arises from the fact of his having made improvements upon it.

The construction demanded would confer upon the true owner a prior incumbrance to the extent of the enhanced value of his land, arising from all the improvements made by him thereon in ignorance of incumbrances existing prior to his title, or under an erroneous belief (as in this case) that they had been discharged; and that, whether the real value of the land was greater or less than the amount of the incumbrances and the enhanced value caused by the improvements. Suppose a title depending upon a will, by which legacies are charged upon the land, and the purchaser either erroneously advised that the legacies are not charged, or erroneously believes that they have been paid; I see no difference in principle between such a case as that and the one now before us. Yet, neither in equity nor under the statute, can I find reason or authority for holding that the legatee's rights would be postponed to a claim on the part of the owner for the enhanced value added to the land by improvements made by him in ignorance of the charge. Equity may interpose, or the statute may apply in cases where the person who has made the improvements must otherwise lose them with the land unconditionally to the real owner, but not in favor of the real owner against an incumbrancer. If the latter is to be postponed in such a case as this I think it must be by legislation as clear as that by which he is postponed in favor of a lien under the Mechanic's Lien Act. For these reasons I am respectfully of opinion that the plaintiff's appeal should be allowed.

The defendant's appeal must be dismissed on the grounds stated by the learned Chancellor in his judgment. I agree that the case is essentially different from the case of *Bacon* v. *Shier,* and that the mortgagor could not legally discharge his own mortgage. The instrument executed by him was a mere nullity. His was the hand to pay the money, but not the hand to receive it. He was merely a debtor to his brother's estate for the money borrowed from it, and not the surviving trustee or executor, so as to give a valid discharge of his own debt. It was so much taken by him out of the estate, for which both trustees were probably liable, but William Hincks junior, and the borrower stood towards

each other in regard to it simply in the relation of mortgagor and mortgagee, and the latter or his representatives,
could alone give a legal discharge.

Plaintiff's appeal allowed, with costs.
Defendant's appeal dismissed, with costs.

ERICKSON v. BRAND.

Action for maliciously procuring order to hold to bail—Necessity to set aside
or discharge from custody before bringing action—Reasonable and
probable cause—Duty of judge.

It is not essential to the maintenance of an action for maliciously procuring a judge's order to hold to bail, that the order for the arrest should
be set aside, or that the plaintiff should procure himself to be discharged
out of custody.—[BURTON, J. A., dissenting.]
Such an order if obtained regularly and on sufficient material cannot (save
in very rare and exceptional cases) be rescinded or set aside on the
merits.
The defendant in his application for the order to hold to bail by his affidavit made out a primâ facie case, but certain facts and circumstances
were omitted therefrom, which, it was contended, might, if stated,
have satisfied the judge granting the order, that, although the plaintiff
was about to depart from the province, it was not with *intent* to
defraud, &c.
At the trial the plaintiff was nonsuited, the Judge holding that he had
failed to shew a want of reasonable and probable cause. The Divisional
Court set aside the nonsuit and granted a new trial.
Held, upon the evidence, affirming the judgment, [PATTERSON, J. A.,
dubitante,] the facts upon which the existence of reasonable and probable cause depended being in dispute, the judge was not in a position to
decide that question until the jury had found upon the facts.
Semble—Per PATTERSON, J. A., the evidence sufficiently shewed that
there was no want of reasonable and probable cause; and that the
omitted facts were not material to have been stated in the affidavit.

THE plaintiff Frederick Erickson instituted proceedings
in the Queen's Bench Division against Ole Brand; and
the plaintiff Charles Erickson sued the said Brand in the
Common Pleas Division, each plaintiff in his statement of
claim alleging that he was a merchant and railway contractor, carrying on business along the line of the C. P. R.
in the district of Algoma; and that the defendant was a
merchant carrying on business at, &c., in the said district.

That on or about the 11th April, 1885, the defendant
falsely alleging and swearing that the plaintiff was indebted

to him in the sum of $1,618.35; and that the plaintiff was, unless forthwith apprehended, about to quit this Province with intent to defraud the defendant of his said claim, applied for and obtained an order for a writ of capias, which on the same day defendant caused to be issued, directed to the sheriff of the county of Renfrew, commanding him to arrest the plaintiff and imprison him until, &c., and placed the same in the hands of the sheriff to be executed; and that the said sheriff according as he was commanded by the said writ and by the instruction of the defendant, who was present when the arrest was made, arrested the plaintiff and took him into custody in a railway car on the regular express train of the C. P. R. going east on the 20th day of April, 1885, in the presence of a large number of persons at the Pembroke railway station; and the sheriff placed the plaintiff for safe-keeping in the common goal of the county of Renfrew, where he was for a long time detained until he was able to procure bail; and that the defendant had no probable or reasonable cause for believing that the plaintiff was about to quit Ontario with intent or design to defraud the defendant; and that in consequence of the plaintiff's arrest and imprisonment, the plaintiff suffered great annoyance and disgrace and loss of credit and reputation, and was otherwise injured, and claimed $10,000 damages.

By the statement of defence, the defendant denied all the allegations made by the plaintiff, and alleged that the plaintiff resided in the State of Minnesota, * * and had, shortly before the making of the said affidavit, and the obtaining of the said order for a writ of capias completed his contract on the said railway and was disposing of his property, which consisted of goods and chattels, at Dalton, in said district of Algoma, and was preparing to leave the Province of Ontario to go to Minnesota to reside permanently. The defendant further alleged that before that time he heard plaintiff's wife say, and he was also informed by several of the plaintiff's employés, that the plaintiff had told them that he was leaving Algoma to go to Minnesota aforesaid, on or about the 9th of April, 1885 ; that the plaintiff was then indebted to the defendant in a large sum of money for the amount of an account for goods sold and delivered, and for a number of cheques drawn by the plaintiff, the payment of which had been refused because the plaintiff had no funds at his credit wherewith to pay them, and the defendant was unable to obtain payment from the plaintiff of his indebtedness or any part thereof. The defendant further alleged that from these and other facts he had reasonable and probable cause for believing, and did believe, that the plaintiff, unless apprehended, was about to quit the Province of Ontario with intent and design to defraud him of his said claim ; and that the plaintiff did leave on or about the 9th of April, and when arrested on the said writ, was on the express train of the C. P. R. Co., at the town of Pembroke on his way to Montreal ; and that as soon as the plaintiff procured bail he left Pembroke and went to Montreal and thence to Minnesota, and the plaintiff had not since returned, and never had any intention of returning to Algoma or to this Province.

The plaintiffs joined issue in each case, and proceeded to trial at Pembroke before Thomas Deacon, Q. C., sitting at the request of. Rose, J., on the 5th November, 1885, when, after hearing the evidence of the two plaintiffs and of Robert G. Deithe, the effect of which sufficiently appears in the present judgments, the actions were dismissed and judgment ordered to be entered for the defendant.

Against that judgment the plaintiffs moved the several divisional courts, when the finding of the learned Queen's Counsel was set aside, and a new trial ordered, costs of the first trial and of such motion to be costs to the plaintiffs in any event.

Thereupon the defendant appealed to this Court, and the appeal came on for hearing on the 22nd and 23rd of November, 1887.*

*PRESENT — HAGARTY, C.J.O., BURTON, PATTERSON and OSLER, JJ.A.

McCarthy, Q. C., and *Wallace Nesbitt*, for the appellant.
Arnoldi, for the respondents.

The authorities cited appear in the judgments.

January 30th, 1888.　HAGARTY, C. J. O.—Mr. McCarthy
has urged an important legal objection as a bar to the action,
viz., that so long as the order to arrest remains unrescinded
the action does not lie.

In *Gibbons* v. *Alison*, 3 C. B. 181, it was held a misdirection to leave it to the' jury whether there was or was not
a reasonable or probable cause, as the issue.

It seems clear that in the language of Rolfe, B., in
Daniels v. *Fielding*, 16 M. & W. 206, the foundation of
the action is, "that the party obtaining the capias has
imposed on the Judge by some false statement, some suggestio falsi or suppressio veri, and has satisfied him thereby
not only of the existence of the debt to the requisite
amount, but also that there is a reasonable ground for supposing the debtor is about to quit the country ;" also that
it is essential to allege that the plaintiff should allege
falsehood or fraud in obtaining the order, and that it is an
error to rest the action on the arrest at a time when there
was no reasonable or probable cause for believing the
plaintiff was about to leave the country.　This was in
1847.

In 1869, the same principle, on the same authority, is
laid down by the Court of Common Pleas, per Gwynne,
J., in *Baker* v. *Jones*, 19 C. P. 370.

I cannot find any express decision on the point in any
of the English cases cited.

Whitworth v. *Hall*, 2 B. & Ad. 695, is frequently cited.
It was for maliciously, &c., suing out a commission of bankruptcy, and it was held that the plaintiff must both aver
and prove that the commission had been superseded.

Lord Tenterden said : " There is no sound distinction as
to the point raised in this case between a malicious prosecution by indictment, or a malicious arrest and malicious

suing out of a commission in bankruptcy," and Littledale,J.,
repeating the same words, adds : " In all of them it is necessary to shew that the original proceeding which formed the
alleged ground of the action is at an end."

There is no doubt but that wherever the alleged wrong
is for arresting where no debt is due, or for too much, that
the determination of the suit must be shewn.

Parton v. *Hill,* 12 W. R. 754 was for maliciously suing
out an attachment from the Mayor's Court, whereby certain
moneys due to the plaintiff were attached, and then swearing that plaintiff owed a debt to defendant, and to remove
the attachment plaintiff had to pay a large sum to the defendant.   The declaration was held to be bad for not shewing
the termination of the proceedings in the Mayor's Court.

Cockburn, C. J.,said : " It appears that the act complained
of was a process incident and ancilliary to a suit, therefore
the rule applies that it cannot be made matter of action
till the suit is terminated."

Blackburn, J.—" The defendant has done nothing which
he would not be perfectly justified in doing, if a real cause
of action were actually pending in the Mayor's Court.
The averment of want of reasonable cause is of no use
unless it be averred that no cause of action really existed,
and the general rule is laid down in *Gilding* v. *Eyre,* that
this can only be shewn by alleging ' a judicial determination or other final event of the suit in the regular course
of it.' "

Granger v. *Hill,* 4 Bing. N. C. 219, was referred to,
where in an action for abusing the process of the Court in
order illegally to compel a party to give up his property,
it is not necessary to prove that the action in which the
process was improperly employed, has been determined.

In *Burness* v. *Guiranovich,* 4 Ex. 520, the Court was
asked to set aside a Judge's order rescinding his former
order to hold to bail, and all proceedings thereon, additional
facts being brought before him.   The Court held his first
order must stand, and that he should not have revoked it.

Alderson, B.—The statute says nothing about setting
aside the writ, the proper course is to order the discharge ·

of the party out of custody. The order of the learned Judge cannot be revoked ; can the defendant shew any instance of such an order being revoked ? * * As long as the order exists the person who obtained it is not a trespasser. If the party has obtained the order by fraud the other party has a remedy against him by an action on the case.

Parke, B.—The defendant may still have his remedy by an action on the case.

Per Curiam, Pollock, C. B., Parke, Alderson, and Rolfe, BB.—The proper course was to apply to discharge the defendant out of custody. The rule must be made absolute to set aside the order of 15th September, so far as it relates to rescinding the order of 1st September.

I understand this case to decide that if the order to arrest was made on statements to the Judge warranting its issue, it cannot be rescinded on fresh facts being shewn.

Bullock v. *Jenkins*, 20 L. J. Q. B. 92-3, supports the same view. The rule was to rescind the order to hold to bail, and to discharge defendant from custody.

Bovill and Garth supporting the rule, said: " With regard to that part of the application that seeks to rescind the order of Platt B., it is conceded that only the affidavit used before Platt, B., can be looked to."

Patteson, J.: "The application is divided into two parts. The granting or refusing the first part must depend upon whether the affidavit on which it was founded was sufficient to justify the learned Judge in making the order. I take it to be quite clear that on a motion to set aside an order of a Judge warranting the arrest of a party, it is not competent for the party making the application to produce affidavits as to collateral facts not submitted to the notice of the Judge. * * .* I am yet quite clear that on a motion to set aside the order no affidavit can be received as to any collateral facts not submitted to the Judge, such as to shew that there was no cause of action, or that the defendant had no intention of leaving the country, though proof of these facts may well be received on a motion to discharge

the defendant from custody. * * In considering, therefore, whether the order of Platt, B., ought to be set aside,
I must confine myself to looking at the affidavit on which
the order was made. *   *   * He calls it ' an ex parte
proceeding.' "

These cases are specially commented on in the very
able and exhaustive judgment of Gwynne, J., in *Damer* v.
Busby, 5 Pr. Rep. 356, which contains a very full review
of all the cases up to its time (1871).

Mr. Justice Gwynne had not to decide the point now
before us ; but I gather from his remarks especially at
page 388, that he regards the law to be as it is laid down
in the two last cases cited, which he also notices very fully.

Archbold's Practice, p. 796, (1885,) states the law as in
Bullock v. *Jenkins*, citing that case. See also 1 *Mew
& Fisher's* Digest.

Stewart v. *Gromett*, 7 C. B. N. S. 191, was an action for
maliciously, &c., causing plaintiff to be held to bail to
keep the peace, and it was held not to be necessary to aver
that the proceedings before the magistrate terminated in
favor of the plaintiff, such a proceeding being ex parte,
and the truth of the statement made by the defendant to
the magistrate not being controvertible.

Erle, C.J., p. 200, says: "If you shew that the magistrates
here acted judicially in deciding between the parties, you
advance your argument a long way." At p. 204 he points out
that it was an ex parte proceeding not controvertible, and
although it attains the result, " it is not a judgment but is in
the nature of a writ or process * * If a party goes before
a Judge (under 1 & 2 Vict. ch. 110) with an affidavit of debt
for the purpose of procuring a capias to arrest his debtor
upon a suggestion that he is going abroad, and that is done
falsely and maliciously, &c., an action lies. *   * Can it
make any difference here that the proceeding took place
before a magistrate" ?

Williams, J., p. 206, points out the distinction between the
case and such cases as *Whitworth* v. *Hall*, and that it is impossible to say that the existence of the proceedings, and
the fact that they did not terminate in favor of the plain-

tiff is any evidence that there was reasonable and probable cause for instituting them, that the magistrate does not exercise any judicial function.

Crowder and Byles, JJ., agree. The latter says [p. 207]:

"Whether the proceeding was of a judicial nature or not depends upon whether the plaintiff had an opportunity to be heard before the magistrates in answer to the charge. * * Under the statute 1 & 2 Vict. ch. 110, the Judge does not allow a capias as a matter of course, and yet it has been held that an action lies against a party for maliciously, &c., procuring a capias to be issued against the plaintiff, although he has a right to come before the Judge to shew why the writ should not issue."

I presume the learned Judge means, although he can afterwards move to rescind or to be discharged from arrest.

It seems clear to me that the opinion of the Judges in this case, was against the argument that it was necessary to shew the annulment or rescinding of the order or a discharge from the arrest. The order was not an adjudication between the parties, but an ex parte proceeding.

In *Griffith* v. *Hall*, 26 U. C. R. 94, (1868) it was expressly held that the right of action for malicious arrest, it was no objection that the plaintiff had not moved to rescind the order or to be discharged: "If the groundwork of the action exist, the subsequent fate of the order may not affect it, and the plaintiff need not move against it." *Eakins* v. *Christopher*, 18 C. P. 532, adopts the same rule.

Richards, C. J., [p. 537] says: "The grievance here complained of has nothing to do with the result of the suit." He had previously noticed the objection that the plaintiff had not averred that he had been discharged from the arrest and the order therefor set aside, and he clearly points out the distinction between the suit for maliciously arresting on a charge of leaving the country, and for arrest for too much, or where no debt was due: *Griffith* v. *Hall*, was not cited. It appears to be the independent judgment of the Court.

Fahey v. *Kennedy*, 28 U. C. R. 301, was an action for maliciously, &c., obtaining an order for an attachment against the plaintiff, as an absconding debtor, by falsely swearing, &c., on which plaintiff's property was seized, &c. Held not necessary to aver that the attachment had been set aside; that the wrong complained of was complete whatever was the determination of the action.

The distinction between a case like the present, and the case in the Lords, *Metropolitan Bank* v. *Pooley,* 10 App.Cas. 214, is very obvious. It had long been held that an action for maliciously suing out a commission in bankruptcy would not lie so long as the adjudication remained unsuperseded. There there was a true adjudication—a judicial determination of a matter between parties. There was a creditor's petition—notice to the debtor to appear and shew cause, and he can be fully heard, and can dispute the facts alleged, give security, &c.

The proceedings are set forth in *Robson,* 146. The adjudication in the case in the Lords was under the law noticed in the text book cited. The case was a very gross one ; the bankrupt had tried to set aside the adjudication, and had been refused.

Independently of authority it would be a most dangerous proceeding after possibly a large estate had been administered in bankruptcy, and the status of the debtor completely altered.

Lord Fitzgerald specially calls attention to a case of *Muncey* v. *Black,* 7 Irish C. L. R. 475, as stating the law "scientifically."

The defendant was charged with having maliciously, &c., by false affidavits, caused an injunction to be issued from the Incumbered Estates Court, &c., and the plaint was held bad on demurrer for not averring the end or determination of the proceedings.

But the orders were obtained on affidavits of service on plaintiff, and on statements said to have been made by him in default of attorning as tenant to the defendant : the plaintiff had notice that an injunction would issue to put defendant in possession. The plaint averred that the affidavits were false, &c., and the injunction was obtained thereon, &c.

This case is no guide to us. There was an adjudication, but it was not ex parte, in the usual sense, but based upon apparent proof of service on and notice to the plaintiff; and it was held, no doubt, most correctly, that so long as these orders stood, the action could not be maintained.

Pigott, C. B., gives the judgment of the Court, and noticing the Judge's orders for arrest under 1 & 2 Vict., says :

"In no case cited, while the process remains, has any action been sustained for the malicious issuing of it by means of the deception of the Judge. * * The case is one *primæ impressionis* to make a process still remaining in force and effect the subject of a suit for maliciously putting in force the action of the Court."

None of the authorities bearing on the present question were noticed. With great deference I must suggest that this language is hardly warranted by the authorities. I have examined them to no purpose if the language cited is correct.

A recent case, of *Hope* v. *Evered*, 17 Q. B. D. 338, was for maliciously &c., issuing a search warrant under a late statute, giving (as Lord Coleridge said) "very unusual powers," enabling a magistrate to issue it if there is reasonable cause to suspect that a woman or girl is detained for immoral purposes.

It was held that the magistrate acted judicially, and if the defendant only "stated the grounds of his suspicion, and says that on those grounds he reasonably suspects the girl is improperly detained, and if the magistrate agrees with him, and thinks that it has been made to appear that a person acting bonâ fide has reasonable cause for his suspicion, then that decision of the magistrate is an answer to such an action as the present."

It was pointed out that of course the action would lie if defendant knew he had no reasonable ground for suspicion, or desired to use the act for oppression, in a false and fraudulent manner obtained the warrant. "But when bona fides was present, and the matter is stated fully and fairly to the magistrate, and he concludes there is reasonable ground for applicant's suspicion, then his conclusion is an answer to any proceeding."

This case is in accordance with the general law in such matters. It is no authority in favour of the setting aside of an order, being a condition precedent to the action. The Court finally held : "On the facts, and on the true construction of this Act of Parliament, I am of opinion there was no ground for leaving this case to the jury."

If it be urged, as now suggested, although not urged on the argument, that although the person arrested cannot set aside the Judge's order, yet that at least he should have himself discharged from arrest on the shewing of facts proving the falsity of the statements to the Judge; it may be answered that he may find it necessary for the prompt regaining of his liberty to pay the creditor's claim, and thus obtain his discharge. But it may be said he could still apply to have his arrest declared unwarrantable. I cannot believe that any such proceedings would be either necessary or allowable—and prefer believing, in the absence of authority, that the law would not require such a useless formality. I think if he asked to be so discharged he would be told that he had been discharged already, and told as in *Burness* v. *Guiranovich*, 4 Ex. 520, that he had his remedy by action if he could falsify the statement made to the Judge.

I look upon the power given to discharge from custody to be merely to restore to liberty a person who proved that he had been unjustly arrested, in fact to provide a quick remedy for a proved wrongful restraint, and not in any way intended as an essential preliminary to bring an action for the wrong done by procuring the order to arrest by false statements. His discharge from arrest or the refusal to discharge cannot in my opinion affect his right of action. As said by Rolfe, B., in *Daniels* v. *Fielding*, 16 M. & W. 206, "the discharge affords no ground of action to the party."

I come to the conclusion : 1st. That the Judge's order

here would not have been set aside by the Court on the only ground open—viz., the insufficiency of the affidavit on which it issued ; it being apparently primâ facie sufficient ; 2nd, that moving to discharge the plaintiff from the arrest was not necessary, especially as the plaintiff discharged himself by settling the defendant's claim ; 3rd, the plaintiff's cause of action here, in which he must stand or fall was, that the wrong done to him (if any) was, that the Judge's order was obtained in bad faith, either by suggestio falsi or suppressio veri, and this he is entitled to shew without proving either that the order was rescinded or that he was discharged from arrest ;. 4th, I hold that the order of the Judge was not an "adjudication" between parties, but merely an ex parte proceeding. It is so called by Sir J. Patteson, in *Bullock* v. *Jenkins*, 20 L. J. Q. B. 92, and nine years later the same view is upheld in *Stewart* v. *Gromett*, 7 C. B. N. S. 191.

I consider that the cause of action is complete where an arrest has been made on false statements to the Judge.

I can find no direct authority to the effect that either the rescission of the order or the discharge from custody is a condition precedent to the maintenance of the action.

I am wholly unable to consider the decisions as to the adjudications in bankruptcy as applicable.

For more than twenty years the decisions of two of our Courts have been the other way, and I see no reason for differing from them.

I regard *Burness* v. *Guiranovich*, and *Bullock* v. *Jenkins*, as express authorities against the rescission or setting aside the order on any grounds not laid before the Judge.

For several years after the passing of the 1 & 2 Vict., the practice seems to have been very loose and unsettled, and the Act was some years old before its scope was distinctly stated and illustrated.

It all comes back to one point. The only "adjudication" here was the Judge's ex parte decision on the materials before him. This decision was right, and cannot and ought not to be set aside by new matter, or matter not before him.

On the remaining branch of the case I think we cannot interfere with the Court below in setting aside the judgment, dismissing the action, and ordering a new trial.

The pleadings were very inartificially drawn.

An amendment was allowed as to the debt not being due.

Objections were stated to the plaintiff's statement of claim, and it is certainly open to grave objection. But I see nothing that could not have been amended then or now.

I find, after perusing thirty pages of discussion after the evidence was closed, that the point on which the dismissal took place was distinctly that it was for the Judge to decide whether there was shewn a want of reasonable or probable cause.

Mr. McCarthy, " I move for judgment because the Court has to determine that plaintiff has not proved the want of just and reasonable cause, therefore I am entitled to judgment."

And at the end the Judge says :

" Well, I think the onus was on the plaintiff to make out the absence of reasonable and probable cause, and I think he has failed," and he dismissed the action, with costs.

It is of course the province of the Judge to rule on this question, but he should see that the facts on which he rules are either proved without contradiction, or are admitted, or found by the jury.

Here there was no evidence, and I cannot but agree with the learned Chief Justice of the Queen's Bench, that the case should not have been stopped, but should have been left to the jury. The jury could have found any question submitted to them, and on their findings of any disputed matter, the Judge could have ruled.

I need not review the evidence again, as I agree in the main with the view taken of it below.

The onus was on the plaintiff to prove the gist of the action that the defendant had not given to the Judge a fair bonâ fide statement of the facts put forward to warrant the arrest.

I think the plaintiff disclosed a state of facts, uncontra-dicted on defendant's part, which raised fairly a question for the jury whether the bald statement of defendant's affidavit for arrest fairly state$_d$ the case. I do not wish in any way to suggest what view should be taken by a jury. I merely state that I agree there was a case proper for their consideration on the points suggested by the learned Chief Justice, and as to 'plaintiff's real position at the time as a contractor, to whom a very large amount of money was due by the Canadian Pacific Railway Company, returning to his own home, &c.

For myself I should certainly not have stopped the case, and I think we must dismiss the appeal.

BURTON, J.A.—The ground of objection taken in the first reason of appeal, if valid, would render it unnecessary to consider the other questions argued before us on this appeal, as it would necessarily be fatal to the plaintiff's right to recover in this action.

I thought it at first untenable, and 'that is the view which has, I believe, generally been taken of the matter since the change in the law introduced by the Act, 22 Vict. ch. 96 ; but my opinion was much shaken on finding that Bullen and Leake, and other authors of eminence, have in their precedents for declarations in actions of this nature, introduced an averment that the order has been so far varied as to order the defendant to be discharged from custody.

It becomes necessary, therefore, to consider this ques-tion, and, after a very careful examination of the author-ities, I have come to the conclusion that on principle this action is not maintainable unless it be shewn that the proceeding which was authorized by judicial authority has in some way been vacated or annulled.

Before the passing of the Act referred to, there was no check on the arrest of a debtor upon mesne process but the conscience of the creditor. The Legislature very pro-perly interfered and passed the Act so as to prevent the liberty of the subject being left at the arbitrary will of the creditor, and provided that no person should be arrested unless under the order of a Judge ; and in order to obtain such an order the Judge is to be satisfied not only of the indebtedness, but such facts and circumstances, must be shewn as to satisfy him that there is good and probable cause for believing that the debtor, unless he be forthwith apprehended, is about to quit the Province with intent to defraud his creditors generally, or the plaintiff in particular.

The Judge is bound to exercise his judgment on those affidavits, and, if satisfied, to grant the order; that order is his judicial decision on the facts submitted to him.

I must confess that I can see no distinction in principle between such a decision, and that of the full Court on any question upon which they deliver a judgment.

The order thus granted is necessarily an ex parte order, but the same Act which effected this change in the law gave to the party arrested liberty to apply to the same or any other Judge, or to the Court, to be discharged from custody. Such other Judge or the Court may be satisfied that even on the original affidavits the first Judge had come to a wrong conclusion, or, upon additional affidavits, the tribunal applied to may decide that on the facts as then appearing, there was no ground for the arrest or the detention of the party.

This question ought not to be confounded with that which was discussed in one of the actions during the trial, as to the right of the plaintiff to dispute the debt until the action for the debt had been determined in his favor. That was always an essential to the maintenance of such an action where the ground of complaint was that there was no debt, even when it was not necessary to obtain an order for the arrest.

The point here is, that there has been an adjudication resulting in an order for the plaintiff's arrest, and whether an action can be maintained where no application has been made for his discharge, and the original order and the proceedings under it remain in force.

The case is not distinguishable in principle from *Munce* v. *Black*, 7 Ir. C. L. 475 decided by the Court of Exchequer in Ireland.

That was an action for maliciously obtaining from the Commissioners of the Incumbered Estates Court an order, or injunction, for possession of certain lands by means of a false affidavit whereby the commissioners were deceived. The application was ex parte, there, as it was here, but inasmuch as it appeared upon the face of the complaint that the order still remained in force, the Court, on demurrer, held that the action was not maintainable.

Pigott, C. B., in delivering the judgment of the Court very clearly draws the distinction between those cases where the issuing of process is the act of the party and those where it is the immediate act of a Court of competent jurisdiction exercising a judicial act, and he refers by way of illustration to proceedings before and since the Act passed in England similar to our own Act, ch. 96.

It is, with great respect, a mistake to say that the application was not ex parte, but was only made after service of notice on the party affected. That is not the case ; the order was made ex parte upon affidavits filed, but part of the order was, that if the tenant did not, within ten days after service of it upon him, comply with its terms by attorning, the order should be put in force : there was no opportunity afforded to shew cause, but the order was absolute in the first instance that if the tenant did not comply with its requirements the injunction should go. It differs from the present case only in this, that there the Court was alleged to have been deceived into granting an order for possession of land ; here that it has been deceived into granting an order for the arrest of the person.

And in *Metropolitan Bank* v. *Pooley*, 10 App. Cas. 210, in the House of Lords, Lord Fitzgerald refers in terms of the strongest approval to the decision in the Irish case, stating that the law has been properly and scientifically put there upon its proper ground, without one word of disapproval of the reference to the proceeding under the Act abolishing arrest made by the Chief Baron, which he would presumably have done had he disagreed with it.

I have had great hesitation in coming to a decision in this case, inasmuch as my learned brothers have come to a different conclusion, and the length of time that a different view has been taken of this law in practice; but it is singular how sometimes a practice grows up, and is acquiesced in for years as law, which, upon investigation, turns out to be without foundation.

In the case in the House of Lords, Lord Fitzgerald remarks that the question there raised, and the applicability of *Whitworth* v. *Hall,* to the case then under adjudication, came from the Lord Chancellor, and did not come originally from the bar, and had not been raised before the Judge of first instance, the Divisional Court or the Court of Appeal. In the present case, so confirmed had become the practice that the learned counsel who took the objection before the Judge at the trial, admitted that he did not rely upon it so much as upon his other grounds of objection, but he urged it with more confidence before us, and his argument and the cases I have referred to, have satisfied me that no action will lie so long as the order for the arrest remains in force.

When I speak of the order remaining in force, I mean that what was directed by the order remains unreversed. The order remains for the protection of the sheriff, and in fact for the protection of all parties against any action for the trespass, which no doubt is the reason why the statute authorises an application for the discharge of the party arrested, and not for the setting aside of the order; but so long as the judicial direction for the arrest remains unreversed I submit that it is impossible to say that the defendant had not reasonable cause for doing the act complained of.

I am aware that there are dicta in *Griffiths* v. *Hall,* 26 U. C. R. 94, and *Eakins* v. *Christopher,* 18 C. P. 532, opposed to the view I am now expressing. I say dicta, because they were quite unnecessary to the decisions in

those cases which arose upon demurrer as to the sufficiency of the declaration ; and Richards, C. J., remarked
that the form given in the schedule to the Act had been
followed, and must be held sufficient, although the plaintiff
might perhaps be required at the trial to prove more than
alleged.   But however that may be, I look upon the
recent decision in the House of Lords as a distinct affirma-
tion of the principle, that in order to maintain an action
for malicious prosecution of proceedings, where the particular proceeding is the immediate result of the adjudication of a Court of competent jurisdiction, as such a
proceeding as the present is, it must be shewn that the
adjudication is no longer in force.

The learned Chief Justice of this Court adheres to the
opinion he expressed in *Griffiths* v. *Hall*, and I have therefore been at some pains to examine the authorities referred
to in his judgment—there are dicta—not decisions—in some
of the cases to which he refers, which apparently support
his view, but none of them are directly at variance with
the view which I am expressing.

The case of *Steward* v. *Gromett*, 7 C. B. N. S. 191, is
clearly distinguishable because the proceeding before the
magistrate, being founded upon a statement which the
party charged is not at liberty to controvert, is an ex parte
proceeding in the strictest sense, and although it attains
the result which is sought, it is not a judgment, but is in
the nature of a writ or process.

In the course of the argument Erle, C. J., remarked:
" If you shew that the magistrates have acted judicially,
deciding between the parties, you advance your argument
a long way," and Williams, J., says in the same case,
the authorities shew that the magistrates are bound to
act upon the statement made to them, and do not exercise
any judicial functions at all.

The case of *Gilding* v. *Eyre*, 10 C. B, N. S. 502, is distinguished in the case of *Huffer* v. *Allen*, reported in L. R.
2 Ex. 15.   In the former case an action was held to be
maintainable where the defendants had of their own motion

endorsed a ca sa for more than was due, and caused the plaintiffs to be arrested ; but in the latter case where a judgment had been signed by default for the whole debt, although a portion of it had been paid, which reduced the amount due to a sum for which a party could not be arrested, and the defendant nevertheless issued a ca sa, and caused the plaintiffs to be arrested, the Court held the action not maintainable, on the ground that it was not competent to any " party to an action to aver anything in contradiction of the record which, while it stands, is as between them ' an evidence of uncontrollable verity.' "

The case of *Burness* against *Guiranovich*, 4 Ex. 520, is not much in point, but is rather in favor of the view I have expressed, and supports the reasoning I have ventured to urge why the order should still stand for the protection against the act which would without it be a trespass.

In that case that portion of the order which rescinded the original order was set aside, leaving in force so much of it as discharged the defendant out of custody. It was such an order directing the discharge of the defendant that Parke and Alderson, B., were referring to when they said : " The defendant may still have his remedy by an action on the case."

But it is said if the party arrested pays the debt or remains in custody, is he to have no action ? This appears to me to be a petitio principii ; it is quite possible that that may be the result, and depends entirely upon the question of whether the arrest was made by virtue of an adjudication of a Court which is still unreversed ; such cases have frequently happened, thus in *Mellor* v. *Baddeley*, 2 C. & M. 675, an action on the case was brought for maliciously and without probable cause, causing an information to be laid for trespassing on land in pursuit of game, and causing the plaintiff to be imprisoned ; but the plaintiff was nonsuited on the ground that he should have appealed, and that a conviction unreversed was a complete answer to the action ; that instead of appealing, he had suffered the imprisonment, and having acquiesced in it, that was evidence of probable cause.

But when we come to consider the pleadings, and the evidence offered at the trial, I am by no means clear that the learned Queen's counsel at the trial was wrong in his conclusion, that the plaintiff had failed to establish the absence of reasonable and probable cause.

We have to bear in mind what is the nature of the action.

The action and the statement of claim appear to have been entirely misconceived. The plaintiff apparently founds his claim on the ground that the defendant had no probable or reasonable cause for believing that the plaintiff was about to quit Ontario with intent and design to defraud the defendant.

The whole foundation of the action is the maliciously laying before the Judge a false statement of facts, and so inducing him to act. The fact that the defendant did not himself believe that the plaintiff was about to leave the country, would seem, according to the authorities, to be perfectly immaterial if, in point of fact, he has succeeded in satisfying the Judge, upon a statement of facts fairly laid before him, that that is the plaintiff's intention. An affidavit, which merely stated that the defendant had reasonable cause for believing that the debtor was about to do so, would not satisfy the statute, and would not be likely to influence the Judge in making the order.

Now, the plaintiff here does not allege that the defendant, by means of any false statement of facts, induced the Judge to act, but merely stated that the debtor was about to leave, and bases his action not on any false statement of fact, but on the ground that the defendant had no reasonable or probable ground for believing that he was about to leave, on which immaterial fact—immaterial, as I shall presently have occasion to shew, the parties went down to trial.

In truth the defendant made no such affidavit. He stated a number of alleged facts, and upon those facts he

stated that he had good and probable cause for believing
that the plaintiff was about to leave. It was, however,
immaterial what he believed, and it is not likely that the
Judge would be much influenced by what an interested
plaintiff might believe. The question with him would be,
whether the facts so stated in the affidavit should reasonably lead a disinterested party to such a conclusion. If
they would, they would justify the order, and no action
could be maintained against a party acting on such an
order unless it could be shewn by the party bringing such
an action that the Judge had been deceived by false statements into granting it.

As I have already said, both parties appear to have misconceived the nature of the action; but assuming that the
pleadings had been amended so as to disclose a cause of
action, I think the learned Queen's Counsel was right in
holding that the plaintiff had wholly failed in shewing the
absence of reasonable and probable cause.

After a good deal of discussion, the plaintiff's counsel,
admitting all the other facts stated in the affidavit not to
have been in any way controverted, is asked to amend the
second paragraph of the statement of claim by inserting,
after the word " plaintiff," in the second line, the words,
"had sold and disposed of all his property at Dalton," which
would not have been a proper amendment, or one that would
have assisted him, inasmuch as that was not the statement
made in the defendant's affidavit, which was that the
defendants are selling and disposing, and have sold and
disposed of all their property at Dalton, which could
bear no other reasonable meaning than that they have
sold a portion of that property, and are selling and disposing of the rest, which was strictly true.

I am, therefore, of opinion that, upon the facts as they
stood, the plaintiff, even if his statement had been framed
in a manner to disclose a cause of action, failed, and that
it was the duty of the Judge to hold that he had not
established the absence of reasonable and probable cause,
which it was incumbent upon him to make out.

I think the learned Chief Justice in the Court below must have omitted to notice that the suppressio veri on which he founds his judgment was not one of the matters relied on at the trial, and could not, under any circumstances, be a question for the jury.

Suppose, for instance, those matters which are now alleged to have been fraudulently suppressed had been brought under the notice of the learned Judge who granted the order on a motion for the debtor's discharge, and he had said, as I think I should have said, instead of furnishing any reason for his discharge, they confirm me, in my view, that the order was properly made. Is the plaintiff to appeal from that decision to a jury, and secure a different result?

If the plaintiff had succeeded in obtaining his release on the presentation to the Judge of those additional facts which had been suppressed by the defendant, then a foundation would have been laid for this action; he can then shew the jury that the statements on which the arrest was made were false to the knowledge of the defendant, or were false in consequence of his wilful suppression of some fact not originally brought to the notice of the Judge. And this, I think, goes far to confirm the view which I expressed in the commencement of this judgment, that no action is maintainable until the party arrested has succeeded in shewing that he is entitled to be discharged.

But I agree that there was no question for the jury in this case, the Judge having come to the conclusion, upon the undisputed facts, that the statements in the affidavit had not been shewn to be either fraudulent or false, and that the defendant had therefore reasonable and probable cause for doing what is complained of.

There are two actions, in both of which the judgment of the learned Judge at the trial was, in my opinion, correct, and should be restored, and that of the Queen's Bench reversed.

PATTERSON, J. A.—Appeals in two separate actions have been consolidated and argued as one appeal. One of the

actions, in which Frederick Erickson is plaintiff, belongs to
the Queen's Bench Division. and the other in which Charles
Erickson, the son of Frederick, is plaintiff, belongs to the
Common Pleas Division.   The judgment of each Divisional Court set aside a judgment of the trial Judge, dismissing the action, and ordered a new trial. The questions
before the Divisional Court were identical in each action ;
but the issues on which the actions were taken down to
trial were not precisely alike, although they became so as
the trial proceeded, both actions being tried together. It
may be useful, in view of one of the questions involved,
to recall what the difference was, and how it was got
rid of.

The defendant had, on the 11th of April, 1885, made an
affidavit in an action which he began that day against the
plaintiffs jointly, in which affidavit he swore that the
plaintiffs owed him $1618.35, and then proceeded to state
facts to found an application for an order to hold the
plaintiffs to bail.   I extract this part of the affidavit.

"4. That the defendants are selling and disposing, and.
have sold and disposed of, all their property at Dalton, in
the District of Algoma, where they have had a contract
for the building of a portion of the Canadian Pacific Railway.

"5. That the property of the defendants in this Province is, as I believe, entirely composed of goods and chattels.

"6. That I was in the store of the defendants on Tuesday evening, the 7th April last, when I heard the wife of
one of the defendants ask a blacksmith, who was in the
store at the time, to fix her trunk by Wednesday, as they
were leaving for home on Thursday, which would be the
9th April.

"7. That I have been informed by two or three of the
defendants' teamsters that the defendants had told them
that they (the defendants) intended leaving for the State
of Minnesota, one of the United States of America, on
Thursday, the 9th April, instant.

"8. That I have also learned from one Louis Tyberg, a
walking-boss of the defendants, that the defendants had
told him they intended going to their home in Minnesota
aforesaid, on the said 9th April.

" 9. That I have good and probable cause for believing, and do believe, that the defendants, unless forthwith apprehended, are about and intend to quit the Province of Ontario, with intent to defraud the plaintiff of his said claim."

Upon this affidavit the defendant obtained a Judge's order, and issued a capias, upon which the plaintiffs were, on the 20th of April, arrested. They gave bail, and on the 28th April commenced these actions. It is said that the debt was afterwards paid. I understand the payment to have been made after these actions were begun, and that no further proceedings were taken by either party in the defendants' action after the arrest.

The difference between these actions as they stood when taken down to trial was that the plaintiff Charles, in his statement of claim, expressly denied the debt, while there was no such issue raised by the plaintiff Frederick. In other respects their statements of claim were identical.

'At the trial a contest arose respecting the right of Charles Erickson to dispute the debt, counsel for the defendant contending, amongst other things, that a complaint for issuing a capias when there was no debt could not be made the foundation of an action until the action for the debt had been determined.

This contest, which related only to the younger plaintiff's action, ended by the plaintiff agreeing to give no evidence on the issue respecting the debt, and thenceforward there was no difference between the two actions.

I do not care to refer at any length to the pleadings. They are, on both sides, loose and inartificial. The plaintiffs found their claim on an allegation that the affidavit contained a statement which is nowhere found in it, namely, that they were about to quit the Province, with intent, &c. They do not say they were not about to do so, but only that the defendant had no probable or reasonable cause for believing that they were ; and the defendant does not, in the defence he pleads, rely to any extent whatever on the statute under which he took the proceeding, but undertakes to shew that he had in fact reasonable and probable cause for believing, &c.

The statute is ignored by the pleaders on both sides.

I think it will be more satisfactory to pay no attention at present to the pleadings ; but to examine the facts disclosed, as we should have to do if the pleadings on both sides had been properly framed.

The plaintiffs have their home in Minnesota, upon a farm belonging to Frederick, but Frederick has for a number of years undertaken contracts for work upon railways, sometimes in the United States and sometimes in Canada. The contract that comes into the present discussion was for the construction of a portion of the Canadian Pacific Railway, on the North Shore of Lake Superior. His son Charles was associated with him, and it makes no difference, his liability for the debt being out of the question, whether he was partner or only manager. The name of F. Erickson and Son was used. Nothing turns on the respective positions of the father and son, as between themselves, in relation to the business.

The work upon the contract lasted two years. Frederick Erickson had a house at a place now called Dalton, but at first called Erickson, and lived there with his family consisting of himself, his wife, his daughter, and his son Charles, the Minnesota farm being left to the management of some one else. His book-keepers lived in his house, and he boarded some of his men.

There were some 1,300 men employed at the points where the work was being done, and to supply them a store was kept by Charles at Dalton, and another at Tunnell Hill, fourteen miles further east.

The work on the contract was finished in March, or early in April, 1885, and the plaintiffs, finding difficulty and delay in getting money to pay the men, gave cheques on Ray, Street & Co., bankers, of Port Arthur, with whom they had an arrangement for the bankers to receive the money coming from the railway company and to pay the cheques.

It appears that the delay in getting money from the company caused Ray, Street & Co. to cease paying while cheques to the amount of $77,000 were still outstanding.

The defendant became the holder of some of these cheques, amounting to a little over $1,300.

In the beginning of March, 1885, the position, as the plaintiff Frederick explains it, was that there was this large amount for which cheques had been given, and there was, besides that, upwards of $50,000 due to the men, who were clamorous for payment, while he had a very much larger amount due to him upon his contracts, which for the time he was unable to get paid. The work was done and the men idle, but unable to go away without their money.

At the beginning of March he received $30,000, and paid it out among the men. Later on in that month he received $12,000 more, and paid it out in like manner. An incident occurred at this time which strikes me as important to bear in mind on the question of reasonable and probable cause, though I take a very different view of its effect in evidence from that urged on the part of the plaintiffs. It was about the first of April, as Mr. Deithe, the bookkeeper, says; between the [5th and 10th, according to Frederick Erickson ; and a day or so before the defendant heard reports of the intention of the plaintiffs to leave, as is stated in the defendant's examination, which is put in as part of the plaintiffs' evidence.

The defendant presented, and was paid, a due bill for $330, and Frederick Erickson, being told by Deithe that the defendant held some of the cheques, says that he asked the defendant for them, saying that he wished to pay them. He further says that he would have paid them if they had been presented, though by doing so some other people would have been left without their money. But the cheques were more than 300 miles away, at Port Arthur.

" Q. What did you say to him? A. I says, " I wish you had them here, I would pay you ; I understand you got a good deal of them." Q. You told him you wished he had them here, you would pay them, you understood he had a good deal of them? A. Yes; he said he did not have them here; he said no hurry for them, 'We can fix that in the Spring when you come up to Port Arthur.' Q. That conversation you had with him you say between the 5th and 10th April? A. Yes, that was about it."

The defendant had before that asked Charles Erickson if he wished to pay the cheques at Dalton, as, if so, he would telegraph to Port Arthur for them, when Charles said they would send Ray a draft to pay all the cheques. That is the way the defendant relates the conversation. Charles gives a version which differs in some details.

" Q. Did he ever ask you for payment of these cheques? A. He did not. Q. Did he ever speak to you about that? A. He came into the store one time and he asked where those cheques would be payable. 'Well,' I says, 'if the C. P. R. pays up they will be payable at Port Arthur; if not we will pay them up here.' Q. That was at Dalton? A. Yes. Q. Do you remember when that was? A. I think that was in March sometime; I cannot tell the date. Q. The latter end or beginning of March, or when? A. I think it was the beginning of the month, somewhere around the 18th of March."

But the result of the evidence is the same whichever version we take, namely, that the cheques were not intended to be paid out of the $42,000 being disbursed all through the month of March; and that the defendant, though his inquiry was doubtless prompted by the fact that money was then being paid, was content to wait until, as put by Erickson senior, they should come up in the Spring to Port Arthur.

But when, a day or so after speaking to Mr. Erickson of meeting him at Port Arthur in the Spring, he learned, casually and not from his debtors, that they were about to leave Dalton in a couple of days and return to Minnesota, it is not a matter of surprise that he should feel some alarm.

The information he received on the point and set out in his affidavit turned out to be correct.

He further stated in the affidavit that the plaintiffs were selling and disposing of, and had sold and disposed of all their property at Dalton. The paragraph is not well worded, but is not likely to have been understood by the Judge to import that they had divested themselves of all property in the province liable to execution, The contrary is in so many words asserted in the next paragraph, which expresses the belief that the property of the defendants in the province is composed entirely of goods and chattels.

The point intended to be made, as I should understand the affidavit, is that the residence of the defendants at Dalton is being broken up, their business no longer requiring their presence here, and that whatever property they have in the province is chattel property. It is the character of the property, being portable or easily convertible into money, that is pointed at rather than its value.

What they had at Dalton was the stock-in-trade of the store, which they were avowedly desirous of selling off in order to close the business, and were in fact selling at rates reduced 25 to 60 per cent. They had a large number of horses and mules, but just at the time in question, that is between the 10th and the 14th of April as Charles gives the dates, one hundred and ten head of them were sent to Michipocoton, which is the shipping port, 55 miles from Dalton and from the railway, for shipment when navigation opened, leaving at Dalton "six poor horses, picked out." There was also the plant, described as, "horse-power, the derricks, carts, waggons, sleighs, hammers [probably a misprint for harness], and all such things as that, regular railroad plant." That was not removed at the time.

It certainly does seem to me that, in view of the object of the affidavit, the statement respecting the property at Dalton is not open to serious cavil.

The effort on the part of the plaintiffs, as is made very clear by the argument before the learned Judge at the trial, with a full report of which we have been furnished, and particularly by the wording of a proposed amendment of the statement of claim, was to have the affidavit read as if it positively stated that the plaintiffs had already sold and disposed of all their property at Dalton, and then to give a literal contradiction to that statement.

I think the statement, properly and fairly read, is substantially established.

The chattel property of the plaintiffs, other than what they had had at Dalton, seems to have been some dynamite at Port Arthur and at Michipocoton, and some rope and tools at the latter port. The dynamite is said by Charles Erickson to have been worth $2,000. He does not say how much of it was at Michipocoton. He puts the other things at $2,000 more.

All the stuff at Michipocoton, he says, was shipped the following June, which was apparently what was always intended to be done with it.

Now it is not disputed that the onus was upon the plaintiffs to shew that the affidavit was made without reasonable and probable cause.

Whether that was made out was a question for the Judge. His decision would be liable to be reviewed and overruled, as was done in *Gibbons* v. *Alison*, 3 C. B. 181, but still the question is for him. The learned Queen's Counsel who tried these actions held that the plaintiffs had failed to shew want of reasonable and probable cause, and after a careful study of the evidence, the leading features of which I have now referred to, I am unable to say that he was wrong.

In the Queen's Bench Division the learned Chief Justice, Sir Adam Wilson, discussed the pleadings and evidence at some length. Mr. Justice O'Connor, who sat with him, concurred in the order for a new trial, but said that he did not agree with some remarks in the judgment of the Chief Justice respecting the pleadings and the sufficiency of the grounds which the defendant had for making the affidavit to obtain the Judge's order. No reasons were given for the order made in the Common Pleas Division. We are thus left to form our opinions rather of the course taken at the trial than of any grounds which can be with confidence regarded as those on which the judgments in review proceeded. My impression from the evidence, as I read it, differs from that expressed by the learned Chief Justice of the Queen's Bench. I think, as I have said, that the actions were properly dismissed.

The argument upon the evidence, on the side of the plaintiffs, is not so much that the facts set out in the defendant's affidavit have been disproved, or that any material fact has been disproved, as that the defendant suppressed facts which he ought to have stated in order to bring the position, as he knew it to exist, honestly before the Judge on the application for the order to hold to bail.

The facts alleged to be suppressed are the existence of property at Dalton other than what was disposed of, or in process of being disposed of, and of the goods at Michipocoton, and of what is called the offer to pay the cheques if the defendant would present them on that day in the first week of April.

I have sufficiently shewn that the incident connected with the cheques would go far in my view of the evidence to remove any ground of complaint on the part of the plaintiffs.

The salient points are the understanding, which appears on the whole history, that the fund from which the cheques were to be paid was money to be received from the railway company ; the belief of the defendant, encouraged by the plaintiffs, that that money was to be paid into the hands of their bankers at Port Arthur, and that in the spring the plaintiffs themselves would be at Port Arthur to meet the defendant and arrange matters ; the open expression of that belief by the defendant, as sworn to by Frederick Erickson, who gave no hint that he would, long before spring, have left Ontario and returned to Minnesota ; followed closely by the discovery of the design to leave the Province. I am not saying a word against the possibility or the probability of the plaintiffs fulfilling all the hopes they held out of their receiving their money

from the company through the hands of Ray & Co., and
even being themselves at Port Arthur to meet their creditors in the spring.   I am looking only at the question of
reasonable and probable cause for the course taken by the
defendant, and I take the incident in question to afford
valuable evidence in support of the view acted on by the
learned Queen's Counsel.

I have not been able to appreciate the force of the argument concerning the existence of goods in the storehouse
at Michipocoton, awaiting the opening of navigation for
shipment out of the province.   I do not find in the affidavit, as I have already hinted, any suggestion that the
Dalton goods were all that the plaintiffs had; but why
the defendant should have been expected to mention those
other goods unless to strengthen the presumption that
before a judgment could be obtained in a defended action,
there would be nothing within reach of an execution, is by
no means apparent.

I do not assent to Mr. McCarthy's contention that under
the pleadings it was not competent to the plaintiffs to
prove a suppressio veri, and that they were confined to the
suggestio falsi.   How it would have been if the pleadings
had been more carefully framed, I don't pretend to say.
If any issue is presented by the pleadings as they are, it is
whether the defendant had reasonable and probable grounds
for asserting his belief that the plaintiffs were about to
depart with intent, &c.; and his assertion of that belief,
unnecessary though it may have been, would with sufficient reason be held to involve the assertion that he knew
of no facts calculated to qualify [the inference which he
asked the Judge to draw from the facts he stated.

Still, I take it that the absence or presence of reasonable
and probable cause is always a question for the Judge,
whether suggestio falsi, or suppressio veri is the form of
the charge.   I think the case of *Gibbons* v. *Alison*, 3
C. B. 181, to which I have referred, is an illustration of
this.

Nor do I assent to the argument which was advanced

for the defendant, though advanced without much confidence, that when the complaint is that the statements
contained in the affidavit on which an order to hold to
bail are falsely and fraudulently made, the action must
be at an end, or the order set aside before an action, such
as the present, can be maintained.

If the complaint concerns the debt sworn to, the rule
applies. This was correctly argued early in the trial, as
already noticed. There the debt is the very subject of the
action. Where, however, the complaint is respecting the
facts asserted to lead to the inference that the defendant is
about to quit the country with intent to defraud his creditors, the principle ceases to apply. I shall not occupy time
by referring to cases on the subject, beyond merely citing
Steward v. *Gromett,* 7 C. B. N. S. 191 ; *Burness* v. *Guiranovich,* 4 Ex. 520, and *Eakins* v. *Christopher,* 18 C. P. 532.

But there is a difference where the complaint is not that
the facts stated are untruly stated, but that some other
fact has been suppressed. It scarcely requires to be said
that the omission to state a fact can be of consequence
only when the fact is a material fact ; and a fact can only
be material so far as it is calculated to influence the decision, which is a judicial decision, upon the application for
the order to hold to bail. How is the materiality to be
determined ? Only, as it appears to me, by a Judge.

The question whether facts within the knowledge of the
deponent were fraudulently suppressed would of course be
for the jury, but only, as I apprehend, after the materiality of the facts had been pronounced upon and affirmed
by the Judge. The materiality could, and would necessarily, be decided upon an application founded upon those
facts, for the discharge from custody under the ca. re. If
held on such an application not to be material, it surely
could not afterwards be left to a jury, in an action for
malicious arrest, to review the Judge's opinion, and say
that the facts were material. There is something to be
said in favor of requiring an application to be made for
discharge from arrest before an action can be sustained for

alleged suppression of facts, but I am not at present able to satisfy myself that that course is obligatory. I do not see that the opinion of the Judge upon the question of materiality may not be given at the trial when the facts are proved before him ; but, whether on an application or at the trial, the question must, in my opinion, be decided by the Judge.

Suppose the case of the trial being before the same Judge who made the order to hold to bail, and who may, therefore, be supposed to be better able than any one else to say how the new facts would have affected his mind if they had been before him on the affidavits. Is he to tell the jury that it would not have made any difference to have had those facts before him but that he would have made just the order he did make, and yet to ask the jury's opinion about it ?

The question remains the question of reasonable and probable cause. The facts presented in the affidavit being true, the Judge, if he held the new facts to be immaterial, and a fortiori if he thought they would have strengthened the application, would of course rule that the plaintiffs had failed to disprove reasonable and probable cause.

It may not be quite clear from the report of the trial that the learned Queen's Counsel applied his mind to the bearing of the facts now alleged to have been suppressed ; and if we are not prepared now to pronounce upon them and to hold that upon all the evidence the ruling was correct, it will be proper to leave the order for a new trial, undisturbed.

I should be, for my own part, prepared to hold that upon the whole evidence, the ruling was correct, and to allow the appeal.

Some stress was laid, in the judgment of Sir Adam Wilson, on the circumstance that the plaintiffs were returning to their own home as inconsistent with the assertion that they were leaving the country with intent to defraud their creditors. With great respect for the opinion of that learned and eminent Judge, I think sufficient weight was

not given to the circumstances that the debt in question
had been incurred in this province in the proscution of an
enterprise here, and while the plaintiffs had here, for the
purpose of, and in connection with the work, a residence
and temporary home. These circumstances, I think, distinguish the case from one where a resident of a foreign
state comes for a merely temporary purpose into the Province, happening to owe a debt to some one who takes
advantage of his casual visit to arrest him. Even in that
case much would depend on the history of the debt, and
the existence of the foreign domicile would by no means
conclude the question. This is well shewn by the judgment of Sir Adam Wilson in *Kersterman* v. *McLellan*,
10 P. R. 122; and it is probable that in *Clements* v. *Kirby*,
7 P. R. 103, the defendant would not have been discharged
if the matter had been properly presented upon the
materials on which the motion for the discharge had to be
decided.

I do not dissent from the judgment dismissing the appeal so as to allow the action to go again to trial; though,
for the reasons I have given, I should prefer to allow the
appeal.

OSLER, J. A.—The statement of claim in this case does
not properly set forth the cause of action, though it might
possibly be held sufficient after verdict, if the real cause of
action were tried, and would then at all events be amendable. The first reason of appeal raises an objection which
strikes at the root of the case. It was not taken at the
trial, nor very confidently relied on before us. The point
is, that no action can be brought for a malicious arrest upon
a ca. re. issued under a Judge's order until the order has
been set aside.

It does not appear in the present case, either that the
order was set aside, or that the plaintiff was discharged
out of custody under section 36 of the C. L. P. Act.

It is admitted that the decisions of our own Courts are
adverse to this contention, but Mr. McCarthy argued that

they should not be followed in consequence of the dicta of Lord Fitzgerald in the recent case of *Metropolitan Bank* v. *Pooley*, 10 App. Cas. 214. That case merely affirms the law long since laid down in *Whitworth* v. *Hall*, 2 B. & Ad. 695, that an action cannot be maintained for maliciously procuring a person to be put into bankruptcy until the adjudication of bankruptcy has been set aside. His status as bankrupt having been settled after what is equivalent to a formal trial and judgment, or an opportunity of opposing it, and remaining unreversed on appeal, cannot be impeached in a collateral proceeding. These cases are only illustrations of the general rule that in actions for maliciously and without reasonable cause setting the law in motion to the damage of any one, it is essential to shew that the proceeding alleged to have been instituted maliciously and without probable cause, has terminated in favor of the plaintiff, if from its nature it be capable of such a termination. The reason seems to be that if, in the proceedings complained of, the decision was against the plaintiff, and was still unreversed, it would not be consistent with the principle on which law is administered, for another Court, not being a Court of Appeal, to hold that the decision was come to without reasonable and probable cause. Per Crompton, J., *Castrique* v. *Behrens*, 3 Ell. & Ell., at 721 ; *Basebe* v. *Mathews*, L. R. 2 C. P. 684.

To this rule an exception occurs where the proceedings are taken ex parte, and of necessity terminate unfavourably to the plaintiff, and the question is, whether the proceeding which gave rise to the present action is of that character.

The nature of the action must be borne in mind. It is not an action for maliciously arresting the plaintiff at a time when the defendant had no reasonable or probable cause for believing that he was about to leave the country. The foundation on which it rests is, as Rolfe, B., said, in *Daniels* v. *Fielding*, 16 M. & W. 200.

" That the defendant has imposed on the Judge by some false statement—some suggestio falsi or suppressio veri—

and has thereby satisfied him, not only of the existence of a debt to the requisite amount, but also that there is reasonable ground for supposing that the debtor is about to quit the country."

An order for a ca. re. appears to me to be strictly an ex parte proceeding. The Judge no doubt exercises a judicial discretion upon the facts submitted to him, but he hears one side only, without notice to the other, and the order when made, may be acted upon and the party arrested, without any opportunity of moving against or setting it aside.

It is a mere matter of procedure in the action, collateral to its object, and not directly affected by its result. If the material on which it was granted were irregular or insufficient it may be appealed from as any other order of a Judge may be appealed from, but if regularly obtained, that is, on materials technically sufficient it cannot (save in very rare and exceptional cases) be set aside on the merits, as is shewn by the cases of *Burness* v. *Guiranovich*, 4 Ex. 520, *Bullock* v. *Jenkins*, 1 L. M. & P. 645 ; and *Brown* v. *Riddell*, 13 C. P. 457, 461.

The proceeding is therefore complete in itself and terminated by the issue of the writ of ca. re. and the arrest of the party. It is not the less an ex parte proceeding because a special mode is provided by another statute by means of which the defendant may obtain his liberty, not by way of appeal from the original order, but by making, as he may do at any time after his arrest, a substantive application to the Court or a Judge either the Judge who ordered the arrest, or any other Judge, for an order to shew cause why he should not be discharged out of custody. That is an entirely independent and original proceeding, in the decision of which the tribunal is invested with a very large discretion.

" The Court or Judge may make absolute or discharge any such rule or order, and direct the costs of the application to be paid by either party, or make such other order therein as to such Court or Judge may seem fit." C. L. P. Act sec. 36.

What is affirmed by an order for the debtor's discharge ?
In most cases probably that the Judge is satisfied that he
did not intend to quit Canada, though that is perhaps not
the only ground on which it might be made. It is in effect
an original proceeding upon new material in which the
question of the debtor's intention to leave Canada is tried.
But the proceeding under which the arrest took place is
not at an end or reversed, nor can it be, nor is the falsity of
the creditor's affidavit proved by the subsequent discharge
any more than its truth is affirmed by the discharge being
refused or not applied for. If the original order was fairly
obtained, the discharge affords no ground of action, and
that is because it does not affect or touch the real cause of
action, viz., the procuring of the order by means of a fraudulently false affidavit.

Assume an order to have been made for the discharge,
still, being made upon new material and not being an
appeal from or reversal of the original order, it is as much
a decision that there was no reasonable and probable cause
for holding the party to bail, as the first order was a decision to the contrary. There are two different and independent decisions. Yet in the subsequent action for
procuring the arrest by means of a false affidavit, the
judgment may be for the plaintiff, or for the defendant,
without being inconsistent with either, because the falsity
or fraud in the original affidavit was not brought into
question in them.

Although there are no express decisions on this point in
cases arising under the Imperial Act, 1 & 2 Vict. ch. 110
such dicta as are to be found are in favor of the plaintiff's
contention.

The observation of Alderson, B., in *Burness* v. *Guiranovich*, that if the party has obtained the order by fraud the
other party has a remedy against him by an action on the
case, seems opposed to the notion that the right to maintain
such an action depends upon the granting or refusal of the
discharge. So also is much of what is said by the Court in
the case of *Stewart* v. *Gromett*, 7 C. B. N. S. 191.

In our own Courts it has been so held since 1866: *Griffith* v. *Hall*, 26 U. C. R. 94 ; *Eakins* v. *Christopher*, 18 C. P. 592 ; *Bäker* v. *Jones*, 19 C. P. 365, 374 ; *Bank of Montreal* v. *Campbell*, 2 C. L., J. N. S. 18 (*n*). The case of *Lee* v. *Patterson*, 7 Ch. D. 866, may be referred to. There the defendant had been arrested under writs of ne exeat, after the commencement of the action, the plaintiff giving an undertaking as to damages. The defendant counter-claimed for damages, alleging that the writs had been " improperly obtained." Fry, J., said the writs had been granted on affidavits which satisfied the Court of the propriety of granting them, and as the defendant had submitted to them instead of moving to discharge them, he must take it that they had been properly issued, which even on the merits he was disposed to think was the case.

The language of Willes, J., in *Gilding* v. *Eyre*, 10 C. B., N. S. 502, though no doubt used in a different case from the present, is not inapplicable to it.

" The Court on an application for a discharge from custody will, no doubt, look at affidavits of the facts for the purpose of informing its conscience in the exercise of its equitable jurisdiction, but the Court by its order either discharging or refusing to discharge a party from custody does not necessarily decide or affect to decide any disputed question of fact, so as to preclude the parties from having that fact subsequently ascertained by the verdict of the jury. No conflict of decision therefore could occur in the present case, nor could the want of probable cause be affected by an order not necessarily decisive of any question involved in it."

So here, it may be said that the granting or refusal of the discharge does not decide the question involved in the action, viz.: whether the defendant's affidavit fairly stated the facts on which he procured the Judge to make the order, or suppressed material facts which should have been brought to his notice.

The case of *Munce* v. *Black*, 7 Ir. C. L. R. 475, referred to by Lord Fitzgerald, in *Metropolitan Bank* v. *Pooley*, 10 App. Cas., 214, was one entirely analogous to the

case there in judgment, but, with deference, is not
so to the case before us. It was an action for maliciously
exhibiting a false affidavit to the Commissioners of the
Encumbered Estates Court, and thereby causing an injunction to be issued, whereby the plaintiff was turned out of
possession of certain lands. The plaint was held bad on
demurrer for not shewing that the injunction was at
an end, or had been reversed. It appears that it had
been issued upon proof of service of an order nisi upon
the plaintiff, requiring him, within ten days after service, to attorn and become tenant to the defendant,
who had purchased the land from the commissioners,
and on default of his so attorning that the injunction
should issue to put the defendant into actual possession. There was an affidavit of service of this conditional order upon the plaintiff, and of his refusal to
comply with it, upon which the injunction was granted
and issued and acted on. There was therefore a formal
judgment of the Court, based, it may be, upon a false
affidavit of service, but still a judgment in a litigious proceeding upon the whole matter in litigation, viz., whether
the plaintiff should attorn or be ejected ; not different in
its effect from a judgment by default in an ordinary action
signed upon a false affidavit of service of the writ. In
neither case is a judgment so obtained an ex parte proceeding, nor in either case could an action be maintained
for anything done under it, whether by turning the party
out of possession of the land, or by taking his property
in execution until the judgment had been set aside. That
was the point decided in *Munce* v. *Black*; and against the
dictum of Pigott, C. B., as to the necessity for setting
aside the order for arrest before bringing an action of this
kind, which, according to the English cases, cannot be
done, may be set the dicta of Erle, C. J. and Byles, J., in
Stewart v. *Gromett*, 7 C. B. N. S. 191.

For the reasons already given, namely that the order for
arrest is ex parte, not directly controvertible as a part of
the same proceeding, and that judgment for the plaintiff in

a subsequent action like this, is not necessarily inconsistent with the former decision of the Judge in granting the order ; I think it is not essential to the maintenance of such an action that the order for the arrest should be set aside, or that the plaintiff should procure himself to be discharged out of custody.

There remains the further question whether the nonsuit was right upon the evidence, assuming the statement of claim to be amended so as properly to set forth the true ground of the action.

The material facts alleged in the defendant's affidavit, were shewn to be substantially true, and were such as to justify the usual, though unnecessary statement therein, that the deponent had good and probable cause for believing that the plaintiff, unless forthwith apprehended, was about to quit Ontario, with intent and design to defraud the defendant of his claim. That such intent exists is an inference to be drawn by the Judge from all the facts laid before him.

Under our Act the question of the debtor's intent is always material, and whatever may be the proper inference to be drawn in the case of one of our own citizens (and I adhere to what I said on that subject in *Robertson* v. *Coulton,* 9 P. R. 16,) the departure, or intent to depart from Ontario, of a foreigner, to reside in the country of his domicile, cannot, ipso facto and without reference to other circumstances, be regarded as conclusive of an attempt to defraud his Canadian creditors. I refer to *Bacon* v. *Shier,* 9 C. L. J. N. S. 226 per Strong, J., and *Clement* v. *Kirby,* 7 P. R. 103, a decision which upon the facts I see no reason to quarrel with, and do not think inconsistent with that of Wilson, C. J., in *Kersterman* v. *McLellan,* 10 P. R. 122, 126.

The cases under the English Bankruptcy Act, 1869, as to the circumstances under which an intent on the part of a foreigner in departing from England is not to be regarded as an intent to defeat or delay his creditors seem to be a good deal in point on this question. *Ex parte Crispin* L. R. 8 Ch. 374, *Ex parte Gutierrez,* 11 Ch. D. 298, *Ex parte Brandon,* 25 Ch. D. 500.

It is probable that our Arrest Act was differently expressed from the English Act, and the intent to defraud made an ingredient in the debtor's liability to arrest, because it had then come to be pretty thoroughly recognised in our system of procedure that a creditor could no longer take the body of his debtor in satisfaction of his debt or retain it in custody for an indefinite period, when he had no property wherewith to answer the claim. I hope that before long the law of arrest may be further amended on the lines of the existing law of England (32-33 Vict. ch. 62), and the last shade of resemblance to that of the XII Tables obliterated.

In the case before us the affidavit laid before the Judge may be said to make out the usual primâ facie case. The difficulty arises with regard to facts and circumstances omitted, which had they been stated, might, it is argued, have satisfied the Judge that although the plaintiff was about to quit Ontario it was not with intent to defraud. How then is such a case to be dealt with at the trial?

If the omitted facts are uncontradicted, and, as Draper, C. J., says in *Riddell* v. *Brown*, 29 U. C. R. 90, are of that distinct character that there can be no question as to the correct inference to be drawn from them, the Judge may rule at once whether they amount or not to reasonable and probable cause, but if otherwise, the opinion of the jury must be taken upon them, before he is in a position to decide that question. *Gibbons* v. *Alison*, 3 C. B. N. S. 181 : *Riddell* v. *Brown*, 24 U. C. R. 90; *Jones* v. *Baker*, 19 C. P. 365, are cases of the former class.

Without intending in any way to fetter the action of the Judge who may hereafter try the case, it seems to me there were here at least two preliminary questions of fact to be decided by the jury ; 1, whether the defendant, being aware of the existence of the omitted facts, nevertheless honestly believed that the plaintiff was going away with intent to defraud ; and, secondly, whether he had reasonable grounds for so believing : *Douglass* v. *Corbett*, 3 E. & E. 571 ; *Hicks* v. *Faulkner*, 8 Q. B. D. 167, 171.

On the finding of the jury on these questions the Judge will be in a position to rule whether the facts so found amount or not to reasonable and probable cause. Should they both be answered in the affirmative, there will be little difficulty in holding that there was no want of probable cause, and therefore that the omitted facts were not fraudulently suppressed, or material to have been stated.

 If, on the contrary, the jury should think that, although the defendant honestly believed that the plaintiff was about to depart with intent to defraud, yet that the facts afforded him no reasonable ground for so believing, the Judge may hold that there was a want of probable cause, but there will then be the further question to be disposed of by the jury, viz., whether the defendant was actuated by malice in not fully disclosing the facts upon his affidavit; a question upon which the bona fides of his belief will be material, though if the jury should be of opinion that, notwithstanding such belief, he deliberately refrained from disclosing them in order to mislead the Judge, it would not be conclusive.

Upon the best consideration I have been able to give to to the evidence, I am of opinion that the facts proved are of such a nature that without the finding of the jury upon the questions I have suggested, the Judge was not in a position to decide the question of reasonable and probable cause, or to hold that such facts ought not to have been set forth, or were unnecessary to have been set forth in the affidavit in order to enable the Judge who made the order to arrive at a proper conclusion as to the intent of the plaintiff in departing from Ontario. For these reasons I think that the judgment below was right, and that the appeal should be dismissed.

Appeal dismissed, with costs.

BURTON, J.A., *dissentiente.*

WILLS v. CARMAN.

Costs—Payment of to unsuccessful party—O. J. A. rule 428—Nominal damages, power of court to give judgment for—Venire de novo.

In an action for libel the jury found that the defendant was guilty of libelling, but that the plaintiff had sustained no damage. The trial Judge dismissed the action, but ordered the defendant to pay the plaintiff's costs, and gave the latter judgment therefor. The defendant thereupon moved in the Divisional Court against the judgment for costs, which that Court varied by ordering the action to be dismissed with costs, and the plaintiff having appealed to this Court from the judgment at the trial, dismissing the action, as also from the judgment of the Divisional Court.

Held, that although rule 428, gives to the Judge or Court the power of depriving any of the parties to an action, plaintiff or defendant, of their costs, it does not confer the power of compelling a successful party to pay the costs of an unsuccessful party : *Mitchell* v. *Vandusen, ante* p. 517, considered, approved and followed.

Held, also, allowing the appeal of the plaintiff from the judgment at the trial, that a *Venire de novo* should be awarded : [PATTERSON, J. A., dissenting from such direction.]

Per HAGARTY, C. J. O., and GALT, J.—No Court has or ought to have the right *ex proprio motu* to direct judgment for nominal damages where a jury has refused to award them.

Per OSLER, J.A.—Nominal damages should not be added, unless it clearly appear that such damages are a mere matter of form, or that the omission to find them was accidental, or unintentional, or an oversight following a distinct intention to find the plaintiff's cause of action proved.

Per PATTERSON, J.A.—The jury having left no fact undetermined, the plaintiff was entitled to judgment, which might properly be entered for nominal damages with full costs.

THE action was for libel, published by the defendant, a newspaper proprietor, at the trial of which, before Cameron, C. J., the jury found the defendant guilty of publishing the alleged libel, but that plaintiff had not sustained any damages by reason thereof, whereupon the learned Chief Justice directed " that the plaintiff's action be dismissed, but that the defendant pay the plaintiff's costs, and that the plaintiff have judgment to recover the said costs."

The defendant moved the Divisional Court against so much of said judgment as ordered him to pay costs ; when on the 29th June, 1886, an order was made " that the said judgment be, and the same is hereby varied, * * and that the action do stand dismissed without costs of said action or of this motion to either party." Thereupon the plaintiff appealed to this Court from the judgment at the trial, as also from the Divisional Court; and the appeal came on for hearing on the 7th of September, 1887.*

Dickson, Q. C., for the appellant.
Moss, Q. C., and *Clute*, for the respondent.

The facts and questions raised are fully stated in the judgments.

January 10, 1888. HAGARTY, C. J. O.—It is much to be regretted that a difficulty such as we have to deal with has occurred in this case. As it comes to this Court there is a verdict or judgment in favor of defendant. This was not moved against in the Court below, but we are called on by the plaintiff to decide whether on the finding of the jury the late Chief Justice Cameron was right in entering it for defendant. The finding is reported to us thus : " The jury find the defendant guilty of libelling the plaintiff, but find the plaintiff sustained no damages."

The learned Judge construed this to be a verdict for defendant, and gave judgment dismissing the action, but that defendant should pay the plaintiff's costs, and that plaintiff have judgment to recover the said costs.

This was moved against in the Queen's Bench, and after argument the Court held that on the motion of defendant (the plaintiff not moving) they must hold the judgment for defendant must stand, and that being so the learned judge was wrong in ordering him to pay the costs.

I fully concur in holding that the order to pay plaintiff's costs cannot be supported. In a case lately decided by us of *Mitchell* v. *Vandusen*, ante 517, my learned brothers Patterson and Osler have fully reviewed the authorities on this new and curious view of the law arising since the Judicature Act, that successful parties

*Present.—HAGARTY, C. J. O., PATTERSON, OSLER, JJ.A., and GALT, J.

can be made to pay the costs of the unsuccessful parties.
The control over the costs of a suit granted by that Act,
and previously exercised for a long series of years by the
Courts of Equity, may be beneficially exercised in refusing
costs to either plaintiff or defendant, or by the refusal to
allow costs for unnecessary or immaterial steps taken by
either party. But I felt in the case just mentioned more
strongly, possibly, than my learned brethren, that to make
the successful party pay the costs of the unsuccessful was
a course so repugnant to my ideas of right and wrong
that nothing but a clear and explicit direction of the
legislature would induce me to adopt such a course. I
fail to see any such legislation. The words of the order
428 : " The costs of and incident to all proceedings in the
High Court shall be in the discretion of the Court."

As I read these words, followed in the same order by
the provisions as to trustees, mortgagees, &c., and the direction as to jury trials, I am satisfied that no such extraordinary, I might almost say astonishing, power as has
been here urged was intended to be given, and full effect
can be given to the words used by holding them to extend
the existing Chancery dealing with costs to all proceedings in the High Court ; and in jury cases costs are to follow the event except for good cause the trial judge or the
court otherwise order. The " otherwise " order would
naturally be simply to interfere with the direction as to
following the event, and for good reason depriving
the party for whom the event was found of the costs he
otherwise would have recovered.

The learned Chief Justice evidently considered that the
finding of the jury amounted to a verdict for defendant,
or in other words that the refusal to find damages was fatal
to the plaintiff. He expressed himself very strongly against
the conduct of the jury in holding it a libel, and yet refusing
damages.

We must assume that the jury's attention was clearly
called to the question of damages, and that they knowingly
and pointedly refused to find any damages.

In a case like this I do not see how it is possible for us to direct the entry of a finding of nominal damages as has been suggested.

I can understand the force of such reasoning in a case where the accidental omission to find a nominal sum for plaintiff when the actual cause of action is found to be proved. But even if this can be done to remedy such an accident, which I only assert for the argument, it seems to me that there are insuperable difficulties in so doing where the jury expressly refuse to give any damages. In entering a finding for one shilling the Court would be doing what the jury distinctly refused to do.

In such an action as libel, the only tribunal for trial (except by consent) is the jury to whom every question libel or no libel, damages or no damages is referred ; and in my judgment no tribunal but the jury can decide such questions.

I can see no more power in the Court to order a verdict for one shilling than for a hundred pounds.

It is a wholly different question whether any sufficient verdict has been given or whether there has been simply a mis-trial.

It strikes me that had I been the trial judge, after fully explaining to the jury that if the defendant was guilty of libelling the plaintiff that the law would infer at least nominal damages, and if I found the jury would give no other verdict than that here pronounced, I would have recorded the verdict as given, and afterwards decided as to its legal effect. But I should certainly not have entered it as amounting to a finding for defendant and dismissing the action thereon. As to taking such a special verdict, which it is said the Court cannot refuse if pertinent to the issue, see the old law : Co. Lit. 226 a. b.; 228 a.; 226 b.

It is held that if damages be not the only thing to be recovered, the plaintiff may supply a defect in the assessment of the damages by his release of the damages as in debt, annuity, &c.: Comyn Dig. Damages, e., 8, citing *Bentham's Case,* 11 Co. Rep. 56 a., which is in point.

Again, Com. Dig. Dam., e., 8: "But where damages only are recoverable, if the jury do not assess damages it cannot be aided by a release."

Ib. e., 1: In all cases where issue is to be tried by a jury and damages are recoverable, they ought regularly to be assessed by a jury, and if they do not where damages only are recoverable the verdict shall be void.

Bac. Ab. title verdict Z. (p. 145), is to like effect. It refers to *Cheney's Case,* 10 Co. Rep. 118 a. There it is said, as is elsewhere repeated, that an omission to assess damages may in certain cases be supplied by writ of inquiry.

The case before us for judgment is not the case of an omission but of a positive refusal by a jury to assess. See, also as to this *Anderson* v. *Matthews*, 30 C. P. 166.

Clement v. *Lewis* is a case frequently cited, 3 B. & Ald. 702, and in Error, 3 B. & Bing 297, but more fully reported 7 J. B. Moore 200.

Libel, general issue and special pleas justifying. The jury found for the plaintiff on general issue and two of the special pleas without assessing damages, and for the defendant on the other pleas. The Queen's Bench on motion for judgment *non obstante* decided that the latter pleas were bad, and awarded a writ of inquiry to assess the damages. The Exchequer Chamber reversed this judgment as to the writ of inquiry and final judgment, and remitted the record to Queen's Bench with a direction to award a venire de novo to try the general issue and the issue joined on the two pleas found for plaintiff, holding the verdict on these pleas to be void because no damages had been assessed. The case is very fully argued. The Court ordered:

"It further appears to the Court that the jury by whom the issues were tried ought to have assessed the plaintiff's damages by reason of the grievances contained in the declaration, and that by reason of their not having assessed such damages the verdict for the plaintiff on the first and last issues so far as relates to the second and sixth pleas is void in law."

It seems to me that the directing a writ of inquiry, even if lawful, would involve most inconvenient consequences in

.a suit like this, as it would be almost impossible to separate the consideration of libel or no libel from the quantum of damages.

If the jury on the inquiry viewed the matter as the last jury did, the result at best would be probably nominal damages.

As to the Court of its own right directing an award of nominal damages to be entered, it appears to me to be open to the very gravest objections.

I think, on mere technical grounds, it is never done except to supply an omission, as Lord Denman says, in the *Queen* v. *Fall,* 1 Q. B. 636:

" The entry of nominal damages in such a case as the present is quite of course and entirely a matter of form in which the jury could not exercise discretion, the omission to mention nominal damages to the jury and to enter them as part of the associate's minutes was purely accidental, and it cannot be doubted that the learned Judge intended to direct the jury to give such nominal damages,   *   *   we think the learned Judge was well warranted in making this order in furtherance of what was plainly intended, and did in substance take place at the trial."

It was the trial of a traverse to a return on mandamus: See Mayne 543.

The general subject is fully discussed in *Regina* v. *Verrier,* 12 A. & E. 336.

The present state of the law and practice is fully discussed in Mayne (4th ed.) 547.

It is thus stated : " Although amendments of the postea were allowed in order to carry out the intention of the jury by making the verdict what they meant, and had virtually found, the verdict could not be altered unless it clearly appeared that the alteration would be agreeable to the intention of the jury."

Spencer v. *Gates,* 1 H. Bl. 78. Libel—the Court said they could not alter a verdict unless it clearly appeared on the face of it that the alteration would be agreeable to the intention of the jury, the proper remedy was a new trial: In *Ernest* v. *Brown,* 4 Bing. N. C. 167, it is said :

" We are not precluded from advancing justice by correcting a mistake in entering the verdict of the jury. We certainly cannot alter the verdict against the intention of the jury; here I think we are only giving effect to that intention."

Feize v. *Thompson*, 1 Taunt. 121   When the plaintiff on a claim for average had evidently sustained some damages the jury being unable to fix on any amount found for defendants, the Court permitted the plaintiff to enter a verdict for nominal damages, Mayne, 548.

Grout v. *Glasier*, 1 Dowl. N. S. 58, was an action for injury to plaintiff's house. Pleas not guilty. 2. Denying right to support. 3. Payment into court £5, no damages ultra. Issue on two first pleas, and ultra claim on the 3rd. The jury found for plaintiff on the 1st issue without assessing any damages, and for defendants as to no damages ultra.

Parke, B., said: "The plaintiff has no right to the postea, for he is not entitled to any costs. [He notices the Statute of Gloucester.] As the postea at present stands the defendant is entitled to it. The plaintiff should apply to the judge who tried the cause to amend the postea by inserting nominal damages. If that be not done the only remedy is venire de novo. If the jury thought defendant guilty of the wrongful act complained of they should have found some damages. Not having done so, they are guilty of a default, and that is a case in which a venire de novo is awarded."

Lord Denman, the trial judge, refused to amend as asked. There the grievance was found by the jury to have been committed by finding for the plaintiff on general issue.

The celebrated case of *Rex* v. *Woodfall*, 5 Burr. 2663, seems to me very instructive on the general question. The verdict was, "Guilty of publishing only." The clear law of the Court then was that it was for them to decide libel or no libel, so that it would seem that being guilty of publishing what the Court says was a libel might suffice. Lord Mansfield, even with his emphatic view of the law, held that the word "only" must stand as part of the verdict, and adds, in ordering a venire de novo: "If a doubt arises from an ambiguous or unusual word in the verdict the Court ought to lean in favor of a venire de novo."

I cannot see how any of the modern changes in the law or practice can in any way affect our decision herein. Nor do I think any argument can be drawn from any legislation affecting the granting or withholding of costs, or on the right to costs so long rested on the Statute of Gloucester.

Posteas, records, associates, notes, &c., may have passed away to join the phantom crowd of John Doe and Richard Roe, and rejoinders and surrebutters, but the broad principles of the law governing such a case as this remain, in my judgment, unchanged.

No correction can be made to a verdict; no entry of a finding of nominal damages can be ordered unless it be to carry out the evident intention of the jury, or to supply an accidental omission. No Judicature Act has established any new principle in such matters, and that principle I understand to be that where a jury has refused to award any damages no court either has or ought to have the right, ex proprio motu, to award damages.

It is impossible to avoid the conclusion from a perusal of the evidence and judgments, and from what was conceded on argument, that the jury had no intention whatever of finding any damages, and that the law as to damages, nominal and substantial, had been fully explained to them. I think in an action of this character the question of damage or no damage rests wholly with them.

But it is suggested that finding the defendant guilty of libelling the plaintiff is sufficient in itself for a judgment in his favor.

I am unable to assent to this; although many actions for libel are brought merely to vindicate character from some injurious charge, still they all rest on the foundation of a recovery for damages.

No right is sought to be declared in such an action; nothing is or can be claimed except reparation in money for the injury set forth; and I think, on the long list of authorities that may be referred to, that damages substantial or nominal must be found.

I am not laying any stress on the old form of judgment that the plaintiff do recover, &c. But I cannot conceive how it would be proper to enter in any form or shape a judgment or declaration by the Court that the defendant had libelled the plaintiff as alleged, but that he had not sustained any damage thereby.

It may well be doubted whether a finding merely that defendant had libelled the plaintiff shews a complete cause of action. It may possibly only mean that the defendant had published libellous matter of the plaintiff.

In *Kelly* v. *Tinling,* L. R. 1 Q. B. 700, only "not guilty" was pleaded. Bramwell, B., charged the jury: "If you think all or any of these publications, defamatory and not justified by the liberty of criticism accorded to the press, then you will give your verdict for the plaintiff in respect of such part as is defamatory, but if you think none of them defamatory, or if defamatory justifiable, then you will give your verdict for the defendant."

The judgment of the Court was that "every word of the summing up of the learned Judge which has been read seems to me to have been said with the most perfect propriety."

A case may be easily conceived where an undoubted libel on plaintiff was published by defendant, but that it was provoked by or was in answer to an equally strong libel by plaintiff on defendant. A jury might properly find that the libel complained of was a libel and published by defendant, but they refused to give damages under the circumstances. In such a view they would in all probability find for defendant, but in strictness we may suppose they might simply find the fact of publication. Such difficulties seldom arise in practice, as the trial judge could by direction to and discussion with the jury fully give them to understand the only course open to them to close the litigation.

I think the Queen's Bench Division rightly held that with the judgment for defendant remaining untouched the order as to costs was wrong. But on the point brought before us by plaintiff I see no course open to us except to award a venire de novo. No costs to either party.

GALT, C. J., concurred.

PATTERSON, J. A.—I believe we all agree with the learned Judges who heard the case in the Divisional Court in holding that there is no jurisdiction to order a defendant to pay the costs of a plaintiff whose action against him has been dismissed. We have lately pronounced upon that subject in *Mitchell* v. *Vandusen, ante* p. 517.

I understand the three learned Judges in the Divisional Court to have agreed in the opinion that, under the finding of the jury, judgment might properly have been given at the trial for the plaintiff, but because the judgment dismissing the action was not moved against in that Court by a formal or substantive motion on the part of the plaintiff, two of them considered that they could not interfere with that branch of it, unless, perhaps, by ordering a new trial ; and Mr. Justice O'Connor did not, under the circumstances, dissent from the conclusion that the judgment should be merely varied by relieving the defendant from the payment of the plaintiff's costs, though he inclined to the opinion that the court might properly have entered a verdict for the plaintiff with nominal damages.

I am, myself, strongly disposed to agree with Mr. Justice O'Connor that the absence of a motion against the judgment on the part of the plaintiff would be found, if it were necessary to engage in that inquiry, not to be an insuperable objection to the court, when the judgment was complained of, making it what it ought to be, although the alteration should be different from that which the complaining party asked for.

In *Cotterill* v. *Hobby*, 4 B. & C. 465, which I shall presently cite for another purpose, the defendant obtained a rule nisi for a nonsuit, and the court reduced the verdict to nominal damages and discharged the rule.

In *Winterbottom* v. *Lord Derby*, L. R. 2 Ex. 316, on a motion, on leave reserved, for a nonsuit, the court entered a verdict for the defendant: See remarks of Channell, B., at p. 323. Several cases under the Judicature Act in England and here would have to be considered, particularly those decided on the effect of the English Order,

XL., Rule 10 of 1875, and our Rule 321, such as *Hamilton*
v. *Johnson*, 5 Q. B. D. 263 ; *Dawn* v. *Simmins*, 48 L. J.
C. P. 343 ; 40 L. T. 556 ; 41 L. T. 783 ; *Mercier* v. *Williams,*
9 Q. B. D. 337 ; *Stewart* v. *Rounds,* 7 A. R. 515 ; *Rosen-
berger* v. *Grand Trunk R. W. Co.,* 32 C. P. 349 ; *Yorkshire Banking Co.* v. *Beatson,* 5 C. P. D. 109 ; and see the
judgment of Lord Selborne in *Bowen* v. *Hall,* 6 Q. B. D.,
at p. 340, to which I shall probably make some further
reference.

But it is not necessary to discuss the power of the Court
in that particular, because the plaintiff, who was content
to submit to the original judgment which gave him his
costs while it dismissed his action, and therefore did not
move in the Divisional Court, has now availed himself of
the alternative course open to him under rule 510, and has
appealed to this court from the original judgment as well
as from the judgment pronounced in the Divisional Court.

The question for decision is what is the proper judgment
in an action for the publication of a libel upon a finding of
the jury that the defendant is guilty, but that the plaintiff
has suffered no damage.

The opinion of the learned Judges in the Divisional
Court evidently was that a judgment dismissing the action
was not the proper judgment, though they did not see
their way, under the circumstances in which the matter
came before them, to disturb it. It was mentioned by one
of them that the judgment had been apparently directed
by the learned Chief Justice of the Common Pleas, who
tried the action, on the authority of a judgment delivered
a year earlier in *Lemay* v. *Chamberlain,* 10 O. R. 638.

That was an action of libel tried before a Queen's Counsel, who held that the publication was privileged, and dismissed the action, but asked the jury to assess damages in
case the court should hold the plaintiff entitled to recover.
The jury found that no damage had been sustained. A
motion on behalf of the plaintiff was heard before a
Divisional Court of the Queen's Bench Division, composed
of the Chief Justice and Mr. Justice Armour. The ques-

tion of privilege was decided against the defendant, but
the judgment was allowed to remain, the Chief Justice
being of opinion that unless a right was involved, such as
a right of way or ferry, or the like, the plaintiff was not
strictly entitled to nominal damages, and that the finding
that there were no damages was in effect a verdict for the
defendant under our present system ; and Mr. Justice Armour holding that the learned Queen's Counsel who had
charged the jury only with reference to actual damage,
ought to have told them that they might give nominal
damages, but thinking that a new trial ought not to be
ordered merely for nominal damages, wherefore he concurred in the dismissal of the action, without costs.

The judgment in *Lemay* v. *Chamberlain* is thus incidentally brought under review, and if the effect of our
present judgment is to overrule it we have the satisfaction
of knowing, from what was said by the Chief Justice and
Mr. Justice O'Connor in the Divisional Court, that it is
overruled with the concurrence of those learned judges.

When the jury in this case said that the plaintiff had
not suffered damage by reason of the libel of which they
found the defendant guilty, they obviously spoke of actual
or special damage.

No question would have been suggested if they had
accompanied their finding with an assessment of nominal
damages, as *e. g.*, if they had said, " we find that the plaintiff has suffered no damage, and we therefore assess his
damages at one cent."

The idea that upon the findings as rendered the action
could with propriety be dismissed must, as it strikes me,
have arisen from overlooking the purpose and meaning of
nominal damages.   To sustain the judgment for the defendant would in my opinion be to declare that actual damage
is essential to a right of action for libel, while there is no
proposition of law more firmly settled than the contrary.

"Nominal damages," as remarked by Maule, J., in *Beau-
mont* v. *Greathead*, 2 C. B. 494, 499, " are a mere peg on
which to hang costs   *   *   Nominal damages, in fact mean

a sum of money that may be spoken of, but has no existence in point of quantity."

In *Gowens* v. *Moore*, 3 H. & N. 540, judgment was entered
up for £20, which was the penalty of a bond conditioned for
the payment of £12, and one shilling damages. The question was whether the plaintiff had recovered more than
£20, so as not to be liable to be deprived of costs under a
statute. Some members of the Court thought that the £12
was all that within the meaning of the statute was recovered,
but, taking the recovery to be for the £20, they all held
that that amount was not increased by the nominal damages of one shilling. See also *Joule* v. *Taylor*, 7 Ex. 58.

But though judgment cannot properly be given in favor
of the defendant whom the jury have pronounced guilty of
what was charged against him, will that finding, accompanied as it is by the further finding that no damage has
been sustained, authorise a judgment for the plaintiff, or
must something further be done or found, by Court or
jury, before any judgment can be given ?

If anything further is required, the necessity must arise
from some merely formal or technical reason.

The existence of any such obstacle would be at variance
with the spirit and aim of our present system.

I do not think any insuperable obstacle would have been
found under the old state of things even before the Common Law Procedure Act, and it would be a surprise to find
that our recent legislation had so far missed its purpose as
to create difficulties that did not before exist.

The object of a recovery of nominal damages may not
have been only in order to entitle the successful party to
costs, the plaintiff under the Statute of Gloucester, 6 Edw.
1 ch. 1, and the defendant under statutory extensions of
that Act. That was undoubtedly a main object, but the
form of the judgment in those actions at law which sounded
in damages may have required the recovery to be in that
shape.

In either case I understand the entry of nominal damages
to have been a matter of form made necessary by the

exigencies of the procedure, rather than of substance, following as of course upon the establishment of the right in respect of which the action was brought, and the invasion of that right by the defendant. The principle would be equally applicable whether the right in question was the right to enjoy one's property without molestation, or one's character without slanderous defamation.

In *Feize* v. *Thompson*, 1 Taunt. 121, the jury being unable to determine the proportion of certain damages proved, to which the plaintiff was entitled, were going to give a verdict for the defendant, whereupon the plaintiff took a non-suit, and on motion in term the Court of Common Pleas made a rule absolute to enter a verdict for the plaintiff with nominal damages.

Cotterill v. *Hobby*, 4 B. &. C. 465, was an action for injury to the plaintiff's reversion in a close by cutting branches from trees growing in the close, and there was a count in trover for the timber. There was no proof of value given. The jury returned a general verdict for the plaintiff for £5, and on motion for a non-suit the Court reduced the verdict to nominal damages, and discharged the rule.

Marzetti v. *Williams*, 1 B. & Ad. 415, was an action against a banker for dishonoring a customer's cheque. No actual damage was proved, and the contest was as to the party entitled under those circumstances to judgment. The plaintiff was held to be entitled to nominal damages. The action of slander for words actionable in themselves was referred to in argument by counsel on both sides as an instance in which the law presumes damage.

In *Regina* v. *Fall*, 1 Q. B. 636, the issues on the traverse of the return to a writ of mandamus had been tried before Lord Abinger, C. B., who directed a verdict for the Crown, which was entered, " Verdict for the Crown," nothing being said as to damages. The Master refused to tax costs, because no damages were found by the jury, whereupon a summons was taken out before Lord Abinger, who, after hearing counsel, ordered that the verdict should be entered with one shilling damages. That being moved against,

Lord Denman, C. J., delivering the judgment of the Court, said : "The entry of nominal damages in such a case as the present is quite of course, and entirely a matter of form, in which the jury could not exercise any discretion."

This remark of Lord Denman proves that his refusal to amend the postea in *Grout* v. *Glasier*, 1 Dowl. N. S. 58, in the same year (1841), in which *Regina* v. *Fall* was decided, was not owing to any doubt as to his power. In *Grout* v. *Glasier* a verdict was taken before Lord Denman, for the plaintiff, upon a count for removing support from the plaintiff's house, without any assessment of damages. Parke, B., held that inasmuch as without a judgment for damages the plaintiff was not, under the Statute of Gloucester, entitled to costs, the defendant was entitled to the postea, and said that the plaintiff should apply to the judge who tried the cause to amend the postea by inserting nominal damages, and if that was not done his remedy was by venire de novo. The reporter adds that the plaintiff thereupon applied to Lord Denman, who refused to make the amendment.

In *Dods* v. *Evans*, 15 C. B. N. S. 621, the jury, on an inquisition after judgment by default, in an action for arrears of rent of a mine and for breach of covenants to keep in repair and to work the mine properly, found a verdict for £50 in respect of rent, and expressly found that the plaintiff had sustained no damage in respect of the breach as to dilapidations, or in respect of the breach in not properly working the mine. The question was the plaintiff's right to recover the expense of witnesses called to prove damage under these breaches. Erle, C. J., said:

"The defendant suffered judgment by default; and no doubt without the plaintiff calling any witnesses upon the inquiry the jury would have been bound to give nominal damages, and if they omitted to do so the court might rectify the omission at any time," and Williams, J., said : "I think this matter is to be looked at as if that had been done which might and ought to have been done, viz., the inquisition amended by adding a finding of nominal damages upon the second and third breaches."

These cases leave, to my mind, no room to doubt that under the former system a postea shewing a finding for the plaintiff of all the issues in an action of libel, but not returning any assessment of damages, might have been amended by adding a finding of nominal damages. The jury's statement that no damage had been sustained gives their reason for not assessing substantial damages. If they said that nominal damages had not been sustained they would make a meaningless assertion. They could not negative the damages that the law presumes in case of a libel any more than the damage confessed in *Dods* v. *Evans* by suffering judgment by default.

The action would be sent again to a jury, if sent at all, by an order analogous in effect to what was called a venire de novo in the days when jury process was in use. That process was awarded when there had been a mis-trial, and it differed from a new trial by being as of right and not of discretion. To refuse it when it might have been granted, or to award it improperly, was ground of error. It would be granted for the reason, amongst others, that there had been an imperfect or defective finding, as when sufficient facts were not found on a special verdict, as in *Tancred* v. *Christy*, 12 M. & W. 316, or where in trespass or in case there was a verdict for the plaintiff and no damages, as in *Grout* v. *Glasier*, 1 Dowl. N. S. 58, to which I have already referred. The nature of the process is fully explained by Willes, C. J., in *Witham* v. *Lewis*, 1 Wils. 55, and the difference between it and a new trial pointed out. After noticing some points of difference, he said: "They likewise differ in this respect, that new trials are generally granted when a general verdict is found, a venire facias de novo upon a special verdict. But the most material difference between them is this, that a venire facias de novo must be granted upon matter appearing upon the record, but a new trial may be granted upon things out of it. If the record be never so right, if the verdict appear to be contrary to the evidence given at the trial, or if it appear that the judge has given wrong directions, a new trial will be granted; but it is otherwise as to a venire facias de novo, which can only be granted in one or other of these two cases, as 1st, If it

appear upon the face of the verdict that the verdict is so
imperfect that no judgment can be given upon it; 2nd,
When it appears that the jury ought to have found other
facts differently; and it cannot be granted in any other
case.   The best way of explaining these rules will be by
instances, and I will mention two upon the head of imperfect verdicts : *The Mayor and Corporation of Shrewsbury*
v. *Corbett Kinaston*, about six years ago [or 150 years
from the present date]. That was a mandamus, whereupon there were pleadings to issue, a special verdict was
found and error brought, and it was insisted that neither
upon the verdict nor judgment was there any damages
taken, and, therefore, that it was so imperfect that a venire
facias de novo must be awarded."

I need not read the other instances given under the first
head nor two others given to illustrate the second head.

We have what is in all substantial respects a special
verdict with the judgment of the court upon it, when the
jury return special findings of fact, and upon them the
judge directs such judgment to be entered as in his opinion
the special findings warrant.   Under section ,263 of the
C. L. P. Act, R. S. O. ch. 50, the jury must give a special
verdict if the judge so directs, except in actions of libel.
In actions of libel they are, by R. S. O. ch. 56, always at
liberty to give a general verdict; but they may, if they
please, give a special verdict.

Is the record in this case so imperfect that the court
cannot give judgment upon it ?   If it is so imperfect, can
the imperfection be removed without sending the case
again to a jury ?   If it can it ought to be done.   The
asserted imperfection is the absence of an assessment of
damages, and we have seen that a defect of that kind in a
postea was amendable, as laid down by Parke, B., in *Grout*
v. *Glasier*, if I correctly understand his judgment, and as
done in other cases which I have cited.   *Regina* v. *Fall*, in
which Lord Denman said that the entry of nominal damages was quite of course, and a matter of form in which
the jury could not exercise any discretion, was a mandamus
case like that cited by Willes, C. J., in *Witham* v. *Lewis.*
The case, *Kynaston* v. *The Mayor, Aldermen, and Assist-*

ants of Shrewsbury, is reported in 2 Strange 1051. It exactly resembled *Regina* v. *Fall* in this that " a rule was pronounced for a peremptory mandamus, and the plaintiff prepared to enter up a judgment for his damages and costs, when it was found that at the trial there was an omission of damages, and consequently there could be no judgment for costs." To supply the defect the Court was moved for a writ of inquiry, and the contest was as to the right to proceed by that process, which was negatived, and a venire de novo awarded. A similar contest, with similar results, arose in *Clement* v. *Lewis*, 10 Price 181, 7 J. B. Moore 200, 3 B. & B. 297, where on making a rule absolute for judgment for plaintiff, non obstante veredicto, the Court of King's Bench (*Lewis* v. *Clement*, 3 B. & Ald. 702) had ordered a writ of inquiry as to damages. The main ground on which the decision that the damages must be assessed by the same jury that tries the issues, and not by another jury upon a writ of enquiry, was that the defendant would lose his remedy by attaint in the event of the jury finding excessive damages, the proceeding by attaint being treated as not obsolete, notwithstanding that the practice of granting new trials had caused it to fall into disuse.

There is nothing in cases like these to militate against the power of the Court to amend a postea or complete a record by the award of nominal damages, or to shew a venire de novo to be necessary when only nominal damages are in question.

That process, or the equivalent order, is awarded in order that the jury may find some fact not found by their verdict.

The jury here have left no fact undetermined. They say that the defendant is guilty, and that the plaintiff has not suffered damage: in other words, that a wrong has been done to the plaintiff by the publication of the libel, but no actual injury has resulted from it. These are all the facts. To say that damage to the extent of one cent has been suffered would be either to state a fact or to comply with a form. If the former, it would contradict the finding already made. The verdict does not omit to find upon the fact of damages, for it declares that in fact there are none. If the latter, which it clearly would be, it would simply put in formal words what is not a fact but a fiction, for the purpose of enabling the plaintiff, by the technical recovery of nominal damages where the law presumes damage though none has been actually suffered, to satisfy an exigency of the common law action on the case.

Assuming, as for the sake of argument I am so far assuming, that a formal adjudication of damages is still essential to a recovery of judgment, I see nothing to prevent the adjudication of nominal damages by the court, even if its powers were no more extensive than when the cases I have referred to were decided.

None of those cases arose upon a special verdict. They are not less instructive as authorities on that account, and they go, I think, quite as far in illustrating the power exercised by the court as the argument requires. I see no reason to doubt that upon a special verdict in an action for libel, finding the same facts that have been found by this jury, the Courts in those days would not have considered any amendment necessary, as in the case of a postea, but would have held that the plaintiff was entitled, on the facts found, to judgment for nominal damages.

The powers of the High Court are as ample as those of the Courts whose place it has taken. In the particular in discussion they are, if not more ample, at least more distinctly and authoritatively defined.

By rule 321, upon a motion for judgment, or for a new trial, the Court may, if satisfied that it has before it all the materials necessary for finally determining the questions in dispute, or any of them, or for awarding any relief sought, give judgment accordingly.

This rule appears to me precisely to fit the present case without giving rise to any question of conflict between the functions of the Court and those of the jury.

We have before us all the materials necessary for finally determining the contest—the jury's finding of guilty, and the presumption of damages.

I have already noted several cases under the corresponding English rule. I do not refer to any of those decided
under the altered form of the rule in the English orders of
1883, such as *Millar* v. *Toulmin*, 17 Q. B. D. 603, and in
the House of Lords, 12 App. Cas. 746.

I may be allowed to quote the language of Thesiger, L.
J., from his judgment in *Yorkshire Banking Co.* v. *Beatson*,
5 C. P. D. 109, delivered in 1880, which, mutatis mutandis,
is not inapplicable to the present case. He said (p. 127):

" We have entertained some doubt whether the case ought
not to go to another jury to be decided upon the principles laid down in this judgment, but we have come to the
conclusion that the Court ought not to put the parties to
this expense. The case is one in which no additional facts
remain to be proved, and in which, upon the facts proved,
no jury would be justified in finding a verdict adverse to
the defendant Mycock. It is one, therefore, in which, to
use the words of Rule 10 of Order XL. of the General
Rules of the Supreme Court, we have before us, as the
court below had, all the materials necessary for finally
determining the question in dispute."

In *Watkins* v. *Rymill*, 10 Q. B. D. 178, the court acted
on reasoning which led to a similar conclusion, though no
allusion seems to have been made to the rule. The action
was for an alleged wrongful sale of a carriage, and the
question was whether the plaintiff was bound by conditions
printed on the receipt for the carriage given to him at the
repository kept by the defendant for the sale of horses and
carriages. The jury found that the defendant had not
given the plaintiff reasonable notice of the conditions.
Stephen, J., who delivered the judgment of the Divisional
Court, discussed the decisions on the subject of such conditions, and said towards the conclusion of his judgment :

" It is in some cases difficult to say what is a question of
law, and what is a question of fact, but in this case a test
may be applied which to us seems conclusive. Suppose
that the case were sent for a new trial and that the jury, on
the undisputed facts, were to find that the defendant had
not taken reasonable means to give notice of the conditions
to the plaintiff, would it not be our duty to set that verdict

aside as being in direct opposition to the evidence ? as
being a verdict which, upon the evidence, no intelligent
men could justly return. We think it would, and that
being so, it seems to follow that the question is one of law
and not of fact. It is in one sense a question of fact, but
it is a question of fact to which, by law, one answer only
can be given, and this is the same thing as a question of
law."

After the fullest consideration I have been able to give
the case, in the aspect of it I have been discussing, I cannot see it to be our duty to send the case again to a jury.
I think that under the older procedure it would be unnecessary, and that it would deprive the plaintiff, who in
my view has a verdict in his favor upon all that depends
on the opinion of the jury, of the benefit of the system
established by the Judicature Act.

In my opinion the plaintiff is entitled to judgment, and
it may properly be entered for nominal damages, with full
costs.

The question whether in an action of libel, or in any
other in which the cause of action is complete before actual
injury sustained, an adjudication of damages is now essential to a recovery of judgment, as it was in the old action
of trespass or case, was raised in argument before us, and
deserves consideration.

I am inclined to the opinion that it is not essential, but
is one of the old things that have passed away.

It is not, however, a matter of much consequence in the
present case, except as enforcing the conclusion that the
award of nominal damages is a mere formality.

The right to costs no longer depends on the recovery of
damages, but under rule 428 is put on a new footing,
looked at from a common law standpoint.

There had been statutory innovations upon the old doctrines before the Judicature Act. Some instances are
mentioned in chapter 15 of Lush's Practice, where the subject of costs is dealt with, one being the provision of the
C. L. P. Act, by which money recovered was allowed to be
awarded without distinction of debt or damages, and an-

other, the case of payment into Court where, under the statute, the judgment was for costs eo nomine, and not as formerly for nominal damages in order that costs might attach as an accessory.

Then, as an award of damages is not essential to entitle to costs, what purpose does an award of nominal damages now serve?

Its effect in former times was to declare that the plaintiff's rights, in respect of which he sued, had been invaded by the defendant; that a wrong had been done him, or a contract broken, but that no actual damage had resulted.

It seems to me that to make such a declaration in so many words, as the judgment of the Court, would be to act upon the spirit of our present system.

We are accustomed to look for an award of relief in some shape in a judgment pronounced in favor of a plaintiff; and there is, no doubt, some difficulty, particularly to minds practised in the procedure of Courts of Common Law, in recognising the validity of a judgment by which no relief is awarded.

Relief may be by way of damages, or by way of injunction. The power to grant injunctions in libel suits, or at all events interlocutory injunctions, was possessed by the Common Law Courts, under the C. L. P. Acts, before it was exercised in equity. See *Quartz Hill Mining Co.* v. *Beall*, 20 Ch. D. 501; *Thomas* v. *Williams*, 14 Ch. D. 864; *Saxby* v. *Easterbrook*, 3 C. P. D. 339; *Hill* v. *Hart Davies*, 21 Ch. D. 798.

Whether the remedy by injunction would always be applied when the libel affected character only without being likely to cause special damage, or only in cases of the latter class, there is no doubt of the jurisdiction to grant it, and in so doing to give judgment for the plaintiff before damage is done.

A judgment for nominal damages awards relief in form only, for nominal damages are nothing.

It may be that actions for wrongs such as libels were not in direct contemplation when it was enacted by 48 Vict. ch.

13, sec. 5, (O.) that " no action or proceeding shall be open to
objection on the ground that a merely declaratory judgment or order is sought thereby, and the Court may make
binding declarations of right whether any consequential
relief is or could be claimed or not ;" but it would be entirely within the spirit and principle of that enactment to
hold a judgment perfectly good, which, in an action for
libel, declared the facts as found by this jury, shewing the
wrong done by the defendant to the plaintiff, and thereupon, without giving consequential relief even to the extent-
of nominal damages, adjudging that the defendant pay all
the costs of the action.

These are the grounds on which my opinion inclines, as
I have said, against the necessity for any formal award of
damages in order to support a judgment for the plaintiff in
a case like the present. There may be reasons, though
they do not just now occur to me, for adhering to the
forms of the old procedure in the particular in question ;
and, if so, I have already explained why I think the court-
may award nominal damages.

I may refer to the case of *Bowen* v. *Hall,* 6 Q. B. D. 333,
as an instance in which the Court did not confine itself to
the form in which the parties had framed their proceedings,
in which respect it might have been of service to us if we
had to decide only on the appeal from the Divisional Court,
and also as an instance in which the alternative relief by
damages or injunction was in question.

It was an action against three defendants, against Hall
and Fletcher for enticing Pearson to leave the employment
of the plaintiff, and against Pearson who was supposed to
be about to transfer his skilled services to Hall and Fletcher.
An injunction was asked against all three, but damages
against Hall and Fletcher only. Pearson succeeded at the
trial and in the Divisional Court. The Court of Appeal
ordered a new trial as to him (affirming a rule for a new
trial as to Hill and Fletcher who had failed below), and
directed that in the event of a verdict for the plaintiff the
jury should find specially what damages should be awarded
against Pearson, for the purpose of enabling the Court to-

deal with his particular case as might be just : first in the event of the Court thinking his case a proper one both for an injunction and for damages ; and secondly, in the event of the court thinking it a proper case for damages only, and not also for an injunction. The judgment on this part of the case was delivered by Lord Selborne, and is found at p. 340.

It has not been contended that in any particular, material to the questions we have to decide, an action of libel is to be dealt with on different principles from those which govern the procedure in other actions, and no such contention could, as I apprehend, be successfully maintained. The effect of R. S. O. ch. 56, which applies the provisions of Fox's Act to civil actions for making or publishing any libel, requires that the question of libel or no libel shall be dealt with by the jury, and that has been done. The judge, as required by the Act, gave his "opinions and directions to the jury on the matter in issue as in other cases," and the jury found the defendant guilty. The statute was therefore satisfied.

In *Thomas* v. *Williams*, 14 Ch. D. 864, Fry. J., treated the action as on the same footing as others even as to the mode of trial. His argument on that point was founded a good deal on the circumstance that Fox's Act applied only to proceedings by way of criminal information or indictment, and that opinion would therefore be inapplicable here in view of R. S. O. ch. 56, and of section 45 of the Judicature Act read along with section 252 of the C. L. P. Act, R. S. O. ch. 50 ; but the judgment supports my proposition that except as affected by the statute there is nothing exceptional in the nature or incidents of the action of libel.

If the discretionary power of the Court were supposed to be narrower in these actions than in others, one would expect to find some allusion to it in a case like *Belt* v. *Lawes*, 12 Q. B. D. 356, where the Court of Appeal elaborately discussed and formally affirmed the right, in an action for libel, to reduce the damages with the assent of

the plaintiff, and thereupon to discharge the rule nisi for
a new trial which the defendant had obtained on the
ground, amongst others, of excessive damages; but no distinction between actions for libel and other actions seems
to have been suggested.

The formal disposition of the two appeals which I should
suggest is as follows:

The plaintiff succeeding in his appeal from the original
judgment, there would be no longer any difficulty in the
way of his retaining the award of the costs. He should,
therefore, have judgment in the action, with full costs.

I have not thought it necessary to consider exhaustively
whether, if the appeal from the Divisional Court had been
the only one before us, we might not properly have held
that that Court ought to have so modified the judgment as
to let the plaintiff retain the award of costs, which was in
itself just, and which he would retain in the result.

But, inasmuch as there can be only one final judgment
in the action, I think our proper course would be to treat
the case as a whole, and allow both appeals.

The fact of there being the two appeals cannot have
made the costs much more than if there had been only
one.

I think the appeal from the Divisional Court should be
allowed, without costs, and that each party should bear
his own costs of the motion in that court.

The other appeal, I think, should be allowed, with costs
to be taxed as if it had been the only appeal, but not to
include charges for anything which may have been peculiar to the appeal from the Divisional Court.

OSLER, J. A.—In this action the defendant has pleaded
(1) not guilty; (2) that the libel was published on a
privileged occasion; and (3) publication of a full apology
in the manner provided by sec. 4 of R. S. O. ch. 56, "An
Act respecting actions of libel and slander." No money
was paid into Court by way of amends with the last
mentioned defence, the defendant rightly relying upon

the apology alone as a bar to the action; as we have no statute
similar to the Imperial Act, 8 & 9 Vict. ch. 75, sec.
2, which makes such a plea a mere nullity unless accompanied by payment into court of a sum of money by
way of amends.

After a very full and clear charge from the learned Chief
Justice the jury returned into court with the following
finding or verdict :

"The jury find the defendant guilty of libelling the
plaintiff, but find that the plaintiff sustained no damage."

The learned Chief Justice, considering himself bound by
the recent decision of the Queen's Bench Division in *Lemay* v. *Chamberlain*, 10 O. R. 368, that such a finding
amounted to a verdict for the defendant, entered judgment
dismissing the action, but at the same time ordered the
defendant to pay the plaintiff's costs.

The defendant moved in the Divisional Court against
the latter part of this judgment. The plaintiff did not
move against the former part in that Court, and confined
himself there to shewing cause to the defendant's motion,
which was granted. He now appeals to this court direct,
(as he is at liberty to do under Rule 510,) from the
judgment at the trial dismissing the action, and also
from the judgment of the Divisional Court, so far as it
varied that part of the judgment at the trial which was
in his favor and deprived him of costs. The latter appeal
is rested entirely on the ground that the Chief Justice had
jurisdiction to order the defendant to pay the plaintiff's
costs even though the action was dismissed, and that
the Divisional Court had no power to interfere with
with the exercise of his discretion in that respect. This
appeal assumes that the judgment at the trial dismissing
the action was rightly entered on the findings of the jury.

The other, or principal appeal is on the ground that upon
these findings the plaintiff was entitled to nominal damages,
and that judgment should have been entered for him at

the trial for one shilling damages and costs, or that a new trial should be ordered.

If the appeal succeeds the judgment of the Divisional Court falls to the ground, and the appeal therefrom is allowed as a mere matter of course quite apart from its merits, and not upon any ground which has been urged against it.

It is only necessary to say that, as the case was presented to the Divisional Court, and so far as they were at liberty to deal with it, the plaintiff not complaining *there* of the judgment at the trial, I think their judgment was right for the reasons given in the case of *Mitchell* v. *Vandusen*, ante p. 517. The nature and extent of the jurisdiction over costs conferred upon the Court or Judge by the Judicature Act has been explained in decisions of the House of Lords, (I refer more particularly to *Garnett* v. *Bradley*, 3 App. Cas. 944), and the Court of Appeal in England, and it has been laid down over and over again in the most emphatic manner that there is no jurisdiction to make a defendant pay the plaintiff's general costs of the cause when the action is dismissed, that being a power which the Court of Chancery never possessed

Proceeding now to the appeal from the judgment at the trial. As the verdict of the jury stands, it would before the Judicature Act have been merely a void verdict, and would not warrant a judgment for either party. I am not prepared to say that it now stands in a different position. The only question is, how it should be dealt with, whether by amending it so that it may stand as a verdict for nominal damages, or by directing a venire de novo. I think we should not take the former course, because upon reflection I regard it as by no means clear that the jury did intend to find for the plaintiff all that was necessary to establish his cause of action, or that they have completely disposed of the issues they were to try, there being no finding as to the apology. The case was not tried as one in which nominal damages would satisfy the plaintiff, nor does it appear to have been suggested to the jury from

the Bench that if what they intended was to find a verdict
for the plaintiff without substantial damages, their verdict
should, in form at least, be for nominal damages. If that
suggestion had been made it would have been within their
right to retire and reconsider the whole case, and it is impossible to say what verdict they would have rendered.
If they intended to find for the plaintiff they would
probably have accepted the suggestion; or they might have
found for the defendant, having already approached so
nearly to that result ; or, which is very unlikely, they
might have deliberately determined simply to find for the
plaintiff upon the issues, and to refuse to assent to a verdict even for nominal damages. In the latter case the
question would be squarely presented, whether, in a case in
which damages have hitherto always been treated as the
gist of, and not collateral to the action, the plaintiff seeking no consequential relief or declaration establishing a
continuing right, an award of nominal damages is essential to a recovery. Under the old system it undoubtedly
was so. If there were no damages no judgment could be
entered : *Kynaston* v. *Shrewsbury*, 2 Strange 1050. Opinions of the Judges in the House of Lords : *Queen* v. *Fall*,
1 Q. B. 636; *Heydon's Case,* 3 Rep. 18; *Cheney's
Case*, 10 Rep. 118. But under the new procedure the
right to costs in a common law action no longer
depending upon the Statute of Gloucester, an award
of nominal damages where nothing is proved but the
invasion of a legal right and the mere legal damage which
the law infers therefrom, is if possible more essentially a
matter of form than before. Actions of libel, slander,
criminal conversation, seduction, malicious arrest and prosecution and false imprisonment, may if the parties consent,
be tried by a judge instead of by a jury. Must the Judge
award nominal damages as part of a judgment for the
plaintiff? And, if so, for what purpose ? Mr. Pollock in
his recent book on Torts, has the following observations
on this subject, p. 158 :

" The enlarged power of the Court over costs since the

Judicature Acts had made the nominal damages, which under the old procedure were described as 'a mere peg on which to hang costs,' of much less importance than it formerly was. But the possibility of recovering nominal damages is still a test to a certain extent of the nature of the right claimed."

See also *Thorley's Cattle Food Co.* v. *Massam*, 14 Ch. D. 763 ; *Fleming* v. *Newton*, 1 H. L. Cas. 363, 376 ; *Hatchard* v *Mége*, 18 Q. B. D. 771 ; *Hermann Loog* v. *Bean*, 26 Ch. D. 306 ; *Liverpool Association* v. *Smith*, 4 T. L. R. 93.

In this case I have no assurance that the finding of the jury is not a mere compromise or incomplete finding. It was most probably intentionally so ; and I fear if we convert it into an absolute verdict with or without nominal damages of with a consequent judgment for the plaintiff, we may be usurping the right of the jury, and finding what it was their peculiar privilege in an action of this kind to find " a verdict of guilty or not guilty upon the whole matter put in issue in the action." For this, if for no other reason, I think we are not in a position to exercise the powers conferred upon the court by rule 321 of the Judicature Act, not being satisfied that we have before us all the materials necessary for finally determining the question in dispute. But I am satisfied, after a careful examination of the authorities, that it has not been the practice to amend by adding nominal damages unless it has clearly appeared that such damages were a mere matter of form as in *Regina* v. *Fall*, or that the omission to find them was an accidental or unintentional omission or oversight, following a distinct intention to find the plaintiffs cause of action proved, and that there is no authority in the decided cases from *Feize* v. *Thompson*, 1 Taunt. 121, to *Lafone* v. *Smith*, 3 H. & N. 735, which warrants us in supplying in that manner an omission to assess damages contrary to the expressed intention of the jury. In the last case, as in *Dods* v. *Evans*, 15 C. B. N. S. 621, the cause of action, and therefore the existence of nominal damage was admitted on the pleadings.

I am of opinion that our proper course is to allow the appeal from the judgment at the trial, and to direct a venire de novo (to use a convenient and intelligible, even if no longer a precisely accurate, term) in the court below, as was done in *Anderson* v. *Matthews*, 30 C. P. 166. The consequence of that is, as I have already said, that the judgment of the Divisional Court is also reversed.

The principal appeal resulting in the award of a venire de novo, there should be no costs of that appeal or of the trial. And the appeal from the judgment of the Divisional Court not succeeding upon any of the grounds urged it must equally be allowed without costs.

Appeal allowed without costs.
PATTERSON, J.A., dissenting.

CARTER v. GRASETT.

Easement—Light from adjoining premises—Express or implied grant—Registration—Discharge of mortgage, effect of—Finding of jury—New trial.

The plaintiff was the owner of lot 8, and the defendant of the adjacent lot (9.) At the time the plaintiff's lot was conveyed to him it had a house upon it with windows looking over lot 9, which was then vacant, and was also the property of the plaintiff's grantors, subject to a mortgage.

The equity of redemption in lot 9 was afterwards conveyed to one through whom the defendant acquired title ; and G., the immediate predecessor in title of the defendant, satisfied the mortgage, and obtained and registered a discharge of it. Buildings were erected on lot 9 by the defendant and his predecessors, and the plaintiff complained of the interference by such erections with the access of light to his house on lot 8, contending for an express or implied grant of light over lot 9, and invoking the principle that a grantor cannot derogate from his grant :

Held, reversing the judgment of the Common Pleas Division, (11 O. R. 331) that by payment of the mortgage and registration of the discharge, G. did not acquire a new and independent estate such as would have the effect of enabling him to derogate from the grant of light, if any, made to the plaintiff by their common grantors.

Booth v. *Alcock*, L. R. 8 Ch. 663, and *Lawlor* v. *Lawlor*, 10 S. C. R. 194, distinguished.

The jury were asked : "Did the defendant's house interfere injuriously with the light of the plaintiff's house ?" They answered, "Yes, but not injuriously."

Held, that in effect a question of law had been submitted to the jury and that the finding was too uncertain to support a judgment for the defendant.

Per OSLER, J. A., dissenting, that the finding of the jury plainly was; that the defendant's house did not interfere injuriously with the light, and and had caused no substantial diminution of the light necessary for the enjoyment of the plaintiff's house. Under all the circumstances, no objection having been made on the ground of misdirection the justice of the case did not require that a new trial should be granted.

Held, also, *per* PATTERSON, J. A., and FERGUSON, J., that ;there was an express grant to the plaintiff by the conveyance to him of lot 8, which was, under the "Short Forms Act," of all light used and enjoyed with the house; but *per* PATTERSON, J. A., that upon the evidence the defendant's house intercepted no light to which the plaintiff was entitled.

Per BURTON, and OSLER, JJ.A., that the grant of light was an implied one, the conveyance of the .house carrying with it all those incidents necessary to its enjoyment, which it was in the power of the vendors to grant; and the general words in the conveyance did not enlarge or limit the grant.

Per BURTON, J. A., that under the conveyance to him the plaintiff became entitled to the enjoyment of the right to the light from the vacant land to the same extent as enjoyed by his grantors at the time of the conveyance.

Held, also, *per* PATTERSON, J. A., that the conveyance to the plaintiff was, as regards lot 9, unregistered, and in the event of the plaintiff proceeding to another trial the defendant should be allowed to set up the registry laws as a defence.

THIS was an appeal by the plaintiff from the judgment of the Common Pleas Division, reported 11 O. R. 331, where, and in the present judgments, as also in the report of the case of *Grasett* v. *Carter*, 10 S. C. R. 105, the facts giving rise to the litigation, and the points raised by counsel, are clearly and fully stated, and came on for hearing before this Court on the 14th January, 1887.*

McCarthy, Q. C., and *George Bell*, for the appellant.
Robinson, Q. C., for the respondent.

January 10, 1888. BURTON, J. A.—We are, I believe, all agreed in holding that the judgment of the Divisional Court cannot be sustained on the grounds relied upon by the late learned Chief Justice.

In equity the mortgagor was always regarded as the owner of the property, though charged with the debt, and as I understand his position, he is invested with all the incidents of ownership as regards all persons save the mortgagee and those claiming under him.

Any person claiming an interest under the mortgagor is, of course, liable to have that interest swept away by a foreclosure of the mortgage, but, subject to that contingency, his title is as complete as if no mortgage existed.

* *Present.*—BURTON, PATTERSON, OSLER, JJ.A., and FERGUSON, J.

The result of the transactions referred to in the evidence was, that the Very Rev. Dean Grasett became owner subject to the charge which he was bound to pay as part of his purchase money, and upon payment and registration of the statutory certificate, the charge was extinguished, and the legal estate vested in him, but the vesting of such estate had not the force or effect of enabling him to derogate from the grant, if any, made by his predecessors in title.

- The question is not, whether the mortgagee if she had perfected her title by foreclosure could have obstructed the plaintiff's lights, but whether the trustees of Pim, the then owners of this land, subject to that charge, could have done so immediately after the conveyance made by them to the plaintiff. If they could not have obstructed the lights, neither can the defendant.

What then was the effect of the grant by the trustees of Pim to the plaintiff by the deed of the 12th March, 1869 ?

They were then the owners of the house, and of certain vacant land adjoining. The house had windows through which the light, not as an easement, but as a matter of enjoyment, had come for some time.

It is needless to say that they could have no easement over their own property whereby during the unity of possession one portion of it was servient to the other.

As I understand the law, on the severance of the ownership of two or more tenements the law makes an absolute presumption that each tenement conveyed shall, in the absence of words to the contrary, retain all incidents essential to it that consistently with the conveyance the grantor could grant, and such incidents will be annexed to it although they shall affect as easements other tenements of the grantor. For as a man shall not be allowed to derogate from his own grant, essential incidents must be held to pass with the subject granted, though they burden other subjects of the original owner; although I am quite free to admit that what shall be considered as essential to the dominant tenement so as to create that presumption is a question of fact and degree.

It does not appear to me material in this case to consider whether the plaintiff took this right by implication merely, or by express grant, although nice questions have sometimes arisen in cases where a right existed before the unity of possession, and which was extinguished during such unity : as to these the distinction appears to be, that such as before the unity were continuous and apparent easements, and easements of necessity, would pass with the dominant tenement, though not conveyed by specific words; but those which were discontinuous or non-apparent, will not revive upon the severance, or pass with the dominant tenement, unless specifically mentioned either by express description, or positive indication. ~ I refer to *James* v. *Plant*, 4 A. & E. 749 ; *Worthington* v. *Greenson*, 2 Ell. & Ell. 618 ; *Polden* v. *Bastard*, L. R. 1 Q. B. 156 ; *Pearson* v. *Spencer*, 1 B. & S. 571, 583.

In the present discussion no such questions arise, and the case, as it seems to me, must be decided by the terms of the deed.

But as my brother Patterson is of opinion that the right granted was not as extensive as I assume it to be, and that the plaintiff consequently failed in proving what it was essential for him to establish, in order to recover, and should therefore have been nonsuited, I have thought it right to give my reasons fully for adopting a different view.

The deed contains no express grant of light over the adjoining lot. It does, however, contain general words : " All lights, easements, privileges, and appurtenances to the said land belonging, or in any wise appertaining, or with the same held, used, or enjoyed," These words were, of course, unnecessary, because the conveyance of the house carried with it all those incidents necessary to its enjoyment which it was in the power of the vendor to grant; and it makes no difference whether he grants the house simply, or the house with the windows, or the lights thereto belonging.

Looking at the deed alone no implication arises that it

was intended to convey more than the lot itself, and the light above it. It is necessary to look outside the deed, and to consider the surrounding circumstances, to see that more than this was intended. When we do so, we find that the trustees of Pim owned the adjoining vacant land; if he had, previously to that time, entered into a valid contract of sale of that land, there could be no implied grant, as the vendor had already parted with the light; if the vendor's interest in the vacant land had been for a term merely, the implied grant would be only to the extent of that term; or, if the vendor, though owning the adjoining land, held it merely as trustee for some one else, that would, of course, be sufficient to rebut any presumption of an implied grant; or as in the recent case of *Birmingham Banking Co.* v. *Ross*, Times L. R. vol. 4, p. 108, the implied grant might possibly be modified or restricted by circumstances known both to the grantor and grantee at the time of the grant, as in that case, that the adjoining land had been purchased with the view to the erection of warehouses, and a street actually laid out along the sides of which it was contemplated putting up such warehouses.

So, in a case where the grantor of a lease of a house for twenty-one years was, himself, lessee for four years of some neighbouring premises, which were so low in construction as not to prevent the light coming to the windows of the house, and he subsequently purchased the low buildings in fee, it was held that the implied grant of right to light was limited to the term the grantor had in the buildings, and that the subsequent purchase in fee of the buildings did not extend the implied grant.

If the grant is to be treated as express, and not implied, there would perhaps be greater difficulty in limiting or restricting the words used; the light used and enjoyed therewith, being the light then actually used and enjoyed; and I know of no rule of law which in such a case would permit parol evidence to restrict the generality of the words employed. Previous conversations might in some cases be referred to with a view to a reformation, but only

87—VOL XIV. A.R.

for that purpose, and such statements of intention could not control the express words of the deed. It would be a still greater infringement of the rule to allow an inference that such was his intention to be drawn from the absence of windows on the first floor, or that a certain space was left apparently for the purpose of securing light for the windows that were there.

The plaintiff is only complaining of the interference with the access of light to the windows which were there at the time of the purchase. The existence of the space of six feet will diminish the restriction pro tanto of the defendant's right to build on the vacant lot; but in my view, these matters have no other significance.

Under any circumstances, if the evidence were admissible, it would be a question for the jury. The plaintiff makes out a primâ facie case by shewing how the light was actually enjoyed at the time of the grant. If that primâ facie right can be limited or restricted, the jury have a right to pass upon it.

If the vendors desired to reserve any right to themselves at all inconsistent or at variance with the grant, or in any way in derogation of it, they might have done so; but it must be in plain and express terms, and such a reservation cannot be implied: *Bell* v. *Love,* 10 Q. B. D. 547 ; 9 App. Cas. 286 ; *Munday* v. *The Duke of Rutland,* 23 Ch. D. 89 : the only exception being the cases of easements of necessity : *Wheeldon* v. *Burrows,* 12 Ch. D. 31 ; *Russell* v. *Watts,* 25 Ch. D. 559.

The case of *Swansborough* v. *Coventry,* 9 Bing. 305, has been referred to as warranting a different rule of construction, but I do not so understand it. The description in that case referred to the adjoining land as a piece of freehold building ground, and it was contended that there was upon the face of the instrument itself notice that the right was not intended to be granted, but that the purchaser took the house subject to future erections. The court, however, whilst refusing to control the general words of the grant, and thereby to defeat the rights expressly conveyed by the deed, held, nevertheless, that as the sales of the two parcels were made simultaneously, each grantee was in the same position as if his had been the first grant, and had become entitled to the quasi easement over the other land which had been previously enjoyed; that is to say, the one to erect a building which would not interfere with the plaintiff's right to light to any greater extent than the old building had done—the plaintiff to have the enjoyment of the lights as they had previously to the demolition of that building been enjoyed.

The plaintiff's house in that case was an ancient house enjoying the right to light except to the extent to which it had been interfered with by a one story building on the defendant's land. That building had been taken down, but the evidence was admitted merely for the purpose of shewing the height of the building so removed, or in other words, the extent to which the defendant had the right to interfere with the plaintiff's light.

The same rule is laid down by Lord Justice Cotton, in giving judgment in *Russell* v. *Watts*, 25 Ch. D. 573, that where there are several grants not absolutely at the same moment, but so far at the same moment that they are to be considered as one transaction, and done at the same time, then each of the grantees gets the benefit of an implied grant of easement; each purchaser is entitled in favor of the house he buys to the benefit of the maxim that no one shall derogate from his own grant, but at the same time he has the burden of the same maxim in favor of his neighbour's house; and the result is, that all the quasi easements which existed between the two lots in the hands of the one owner, the vendor, are perpetuated by way of implied grant in the hands of the respective purchasers.

I quite agree that surrounding circumstances may also be looked at in order to enable the court to understand the meaning of the words contained in the instrument itself; but where the words used are free from ambiguity in themselves, and where external circumstances do not create any doubt or difficulty as to the proper application of the

words to the subject matter, the instrument must be construed according to the strict plain common meaning of
the words themselves, and that in such case evidence
dehors the instrument for the purpose of explaining it
according to the surmised or alleged intention of the parties is not admissible.

I think it highly probable that the grantor when executing that deed never gave the matter a thought, and that
if the matter had been brought to his notice he would
have limited the grant of the light to the limit of the lot he
was conveying ; but that is not what he has said, and call
it what we may, the effect of such a construction as would
limit the grant in that way, would be directly to contradict
the grant itself.

The case of *White* v. *Bass*, 7 H. & N. 722, furnishes a
strong illustration of the rule. There the owner of land
and of a certain house which had windows through which
the light, not as an easement but as a matter of enjoyment,
came, leased the land subject to certain covenants as
to building which, if complied with, would prevent the
new buildings interfering with the light.

That being the position of matters, it was followed by a
conveyance of the reversion to the lessees.

Here in the lease was as clear an intimation as could be
given, that only a particular class of building was to be
put up, which would not interfere with the plaintiff's
building; but the deed being silent the Court refused to
interfere, and the Chief Baron, in giving judgment, says : "I
think in construing a conveyance of land, we must collect
what the parties intended from the language they have
used."

I am therefore of opinion that by this deed the plaintiff
became entitled to the enjoyment of the right to the light
from the vacant land to the same extent as it was enjoyed
by the vendors at the time of the grant.

But I must confess that under the circumstances of this
case I feel great difficulty in arriving at a conclusion as to
the proper judgment to be entered upon the finding of the
jury.

How can we say what the jury meant by the words "not injuriously."

What is or is not an interference such as will support a claim for damages in respect to an injury to a building by the obstruction of light, is one of considerable difficulty and nicety involving matters, as expressed in one case, passing by gentle gradations from simple annoyance, which is not the subject of damages, to annoyance to the extent of rendering the habitation uncomfortable.

The nature and extent of the right is defined in another case thus: to have that amount of light which was sufficient, according to the ordinary notions of mankind, for the comfortable use and enjoyment of the house, if it were a dwelling house; or for the beneficial use and enjoyment, if it were a warehouse, shop, or other place of business; or, in other words, a right to prevent your neighbour from building upon his land so as to obstruct the access of sufficient light to such an extent as to render the house substantially less comfortable and enjoyable.

It would have been manifestly improper to have received the bald statement of witnesses that the light had been injuriously affected. How can we say that what the witness thought injuriously affected the light was an actionable obstruction within the meaning of the decided cases. Nor would it have been proper to submit the case to the jury upon such evidence, which would have been, in fact, to substitute the judgment of the witnesses for that of the jury; nor if the facts in detail upon which he formed that impression had been shewn, would it have been proper to submit the question, which was submitted in this case to the jury, without a clear direction to them of what would or would not have been such a substantial diminution of light as substantially to interfere with the enjoyment of the house, and the comfort of the residents.

I cannot agree that in leaving the case to the jury as it was done, it was left more favourably for the plaintiff in one sense than it ought to have been. The miscarriage which I cannot help feeling that there has been, arises from the

learned judge having in effect submitted what was a question of law to the decision of the jury.

If the learned Judge had pointed out that if they adopted
a certain view of the facts, that would not be an injurious
interference; but in the other alternative it would be, entitling the plaintiff to maintain the action, and in such case
to assess the damages, we could not well interfere with
their finding whether we did or did not agree with it upon
our view of the evidence: and even in the absence of such
clear direction I should be much impressed with the view
taken by my brother Osler, that we ought not to interfere
with a verdict given by a jury under such circumstances,
inasmuch as the learned counsel for the plaintiff allowed
the case to go to the jury without objection. But we
have to deal with a further difficulty, and are embarrassed
by the fact, that a judgment has to be entered upon a
finding which is in itself uncertain, taken in connection
with the charge.

I cannot, therefore, see my way to supporting the judgment upon this finding, and much as it is to be regretted,
am of opinion that if the plaintiff desires it, there should
be a new trial in order that there may be a clear finding
upon this point; and I quite agree that in that case the
defendant should be at liberty, if so advised, to set up the
Registry Act, as to the applicability of which, to a case
like the present, I offer no opinion.

I agree that there is no reason for interfering on the
other point as to the water—no right to throw water on
the plaintiff's land being pretended, and the injury not
such as to entitle the plaintiff to substantial damages.

I am of opinion, however, that the plaintiff is entitled
to succeed upon this appeal to the extent mentioned.

As the plaintiff has succeeded in part, and failed in part,
there should be no costs of the appeal, and under the circumstances the new trial should be granted without costs.

PATTERSON, J.A.—The plaintiff complains that his enjoyment of his dwelling house on lot 8, on the west side of

Simcoe street, in Toronto, has been interfered with by the obstruction of the access of light and air to six windows in the north wall of his house, by a house upon lot 9 which adjoins lot 8 on the north.

The house on lot 9 was built by Dr. Temple, who sold in 1877 to the late Very Rev. Mr. Grasett. It is charged that the injury occasioned by the house, as built by Dr. Temple, was increased by the raising of the height of a porch by Mr. Grasett, and the construction of a platform for a verandah, the injury being not only the diminution of light, but also the throwing on the plaintiff's land of some water and snow from the roof of the porch and the verandah platform.

Mr. Grasett died in 1882, devising lot 9 to his wife, who was a defendant in this action but who died before the argument of this appeal. She had in 1884 conveyed to her son and co-defendant Dr. Grasett.

The relief asked was damages for the alleged nuisances from the 20th March, 1882, until the commencement of the action against Mrs. Grasett, and an injunction to restrain the defendants from continuing the nuisances, and from making additions to the dwelling house, or other erections upon lot 9 which would further interfere with the access of light and air through the six windows.

This part of Simcoe street was, at the date I am speaking of, called William street, having received that name when dedicated, before Toronto was incorporated as a city, by the Hon. William Dummer Powell, who gave his other baptismal name to another street which also he dedicated, laying out two series of building lots, I think 60 by 120 feet, fronting on each street, and uniting on the centre line between the streets.

The names were changed by decree of the city council, William street becoming Simcoe street, Dummer street William street, and the name of Dummer sharing the fate of other family names of pioneer citizens by which the streets they laid out once were known.

I have been somewhat at a loss for particulars which

one expects to find furnished by plans in cases of this kind ;
and I am not sure that I have gathered a correct idea of
several things about which I should have liked to feel
more certain ; e. g. the way the plaintiff's house, as originally built, was divided into rooms, &c.; how the rooms
were lighted; their sizes; and the changes made by the
plaintiff. I find the dimensions of lot 9 stated in one of
the deeds, and I suppose the lots are all of the same size.

The house now owned by the plaintiff was built on lot
8 by a Mr. Pim in 1855. Pim at that time owned lot 9,
which was not built upon. He died in 1860, and in 1869
the plaintiff bought from his devisees lot 8, together with
lot 7 on Simcoe (William) street, and lots 7 and 8 on
William (Dummer) street. Lot 9 was still vacant and the
property of the devisees subject to a mortgage.

The streets run north and south, and the lots number
from the south ; lot 9 is therefore north of lot 8.

Pim did not build up to the line between the lots, but
kept his wall six feet south of that line. The distance is
a few inches short of six feet from the line as settled by
recent litigation, but it was meant to be six feet. The
plaintiff so understood it, and for our present purpose we
may call it six feet.

The house was built fronting towards Simcoe street, and
having the north wall pierced by the six windows for
which the plaintiff now asserts an easement over lot 9.

I think I understand the relative position of these windows to each other and to some other parts of the house,
but, as I have said, there are other particulars which I have
no means of knowing.

No one of the windows is near the front of the house,
but how many feet away the nearest is I do not find anywhere explained.

The front room of the ground floor at the north side of
the house is the drawing room. It is and always was
lighted from the front, and had no window in the north
side. Under it, in the basement, there is a room sometimes
spoken of as a dining room, sometimes as a breakfast room,

and described by one witness who had been servant to a tenant of the house as having been used as a servant's bedroom until finding it very damp, her mistress found accommodation for the servants up stairs. This room is also lighted from the front or east, and has no window to the north.

When we reach the rear of these rooms, whatever the distance may be, we have the first windows. One of them is a window into the basement or cellar. It is three feet high, having two feet below the level of the ground and one foot above. The room it opens into is described by the plaintiff as used for the ordinary purposes of a cellar ; one instance mentioned by him in which light was required in it was when painters who were working in the house, manipulated their paints there. The tenant's servant, whom I have referred to, did not remember either the room or the window, though she lived seven or eight years in the house. We learn from her that at the south side of the house there were other rooms in the cellar, a front one which was the basement kitchen, and one behind it with a window to the south. She is most likely mistaken in the statement, to which she strongly adhered, that at the north there was only the one basement room, being the one under the drawing-room, and that there was no cellar window at the north ; but if her evidence is honest, which I see no reason to doubt, it shews that the other room was not much used.

Over this cellar window there is a window in the ground floor, and west of it another which, as Pim built and as the plaintiff bought the house, opened into two pantries ; still further west, or towards the rear of the house, was another window into a dining-room. Of the size or shape of this room I have no information. The plaintiff speaks of it in its altered form, as thirty-two feet long; and I think from what another witness says it attained that length by the removal of a partition and taking in a room still farther to the rear, which received light from the west. In its original shape, however, it seems to have had a

window at the south end as well as the window at the
north.   Mr. Fowler, an architect, tells us that it was lighted
from the north and south ; and I infer from what he says
that it and the room in rear of it were in a wing that was
not so wide as the main building.

On the next floor, or the bed-room story, Pim made no
windows on the north side.   The plaintiff has made one,
but it does not count as one of the six, and he makes no
claim with regard to it.   Here, again, it would have
been of some use to know what rooms there were on this
floor, and how they were lighted.

It may, however, be fairly inferred from the fact that
there were at first no windows in the north wall of that
story, that an amount of light reasonably sufficient for
practical purposes was obtained from somewhere else.
The window made by the plaintiff gives, I suppose, a
useful light, and would have been useful to his predecessors if it had been there.   The inference is natural that
there was a reason for not making it when the house was
built.

The other two windows of the original six are in the
attic.   Their light and air have not been interfered with

The plaintiff asserts the same servitude over lot 9 in
respect of each of these windows.   He is as careful to shew
by his own evidence, and by that of his scientific witnesses,
that the cellar has suffered from diminution of light as the
dining room ; and he claims, in respect of all the rooms
alike, the right to the full amount of light they received
before Dr. Temple built his houses, notwithstanding that
the light they still receive may be reasonably sufficient for
the uses for which the rooms were intended when the house
was built, and to which they had been confined up to the
time of his purchase.

The claim is thus wide enough to raise more than one
important question, the first in order as well as first in
importance being whether the asserted easement ever
appertained to the house.

The question is not one of ancient lights, but of contract

—the nature and effect of the contract between the plaintiff and his grantors.

The defendant's title comes from the same grantors. He contends, and in the Court below effect was given to the contention, that he has a right to claim under the mortgagee, whose mortgage on lot 9 was older than the plaintiff's title to lot 8, but I do not see my way to adopt that view.

The mortgage was made in 1855 by Mr. Cameron, who then owned the lot in fee, to Miss Jarvis. In 1856 Cameron conveyed the lot to Pim, who covenanted to pay off and satisfy the mortgage according to the terms and tenor thereof. The mortgage was for £470, payable on the fifth of November, 1865, with interest half-yearly, at six per cent. per annum. It is not shewn to have ever been in default, though it was not paid at the time limited by the defeasance clause.

There is in evidence an agreement dated the 23rd of August, 1864, between Miss Jarvis and Pim's executors, by which the time for payment was extended to the 5th of November, 1875. Before that time arrived, viz., on the 14th of September, 1874, Dr. Temple had taken a conveyance of the lot, and had covenanted to pay the mortgage moneys on the several days and times therein stated for the payment thereof; and when he conveyed to Mr. Grasett on the 17th of November, 1877, he took a similar covenant to pay the moneys " on the days and times when they shall respectively become due and payable."

The papers before us do not shew how or when the time was extended beyond the 5th of November, 1875, but Mr. Grasett's covenant recites the amount of the mortgage debt as being $1,800, which was something less than the original amount, and that interest was payable on it at seven per cent. per annum from the 5th of November then instant; shewing a change in the rate of interest, and that the interest had been paid up; and it treats the debt as payable at a future day. The extension is therefore sufficiently proved as against both Dr. Temple and Mr. Grasett. It would seem to have been until the 5th November, 1878.

which is the date of the statutory certificate of discharge
given by Mary Caroline Jarvis to the Very Rev. H. J.
Grasett.

The argument for the defendant is that this certificate,
when registered as it was on the 8th of May, 1880, took
effect as a conveyance of the legal estate to Mr. Grasett,
under the 67th section of the Registry Act, R. S. O. ch. 111,
which declares that "such certificate so registered shall be
as valid and effectual in law as a release of such mortgage,
and as a conveyance to the mortgagor, his heirs, executors,
administrators or assigns, or any person lawfully claiming
by, through, or under him, or them, of the original estate
of the mortgagor;" and that he took that title unencum-
bered by the servitude (if any) created fourteen years after
the date of the mortgage by the conveyance from Pim's
devisees to the plaintiff.

The case of *Booth* v. *Alcock*, L. R. 8 Ch. 663, was taken
in the Court below, to sustain this contention; but that
case proceeded on a principle which does not aid the
defendant, if indeed it has not, as Mr. McCarthy submitted
that it has, a contrary tendency.

A lease was made for twenty-one years of a house
which derived some light over an adjoining tenement, of
which the lessor had a term of a few years. He afterwards bought the reversion. It was held that when the
interest which he had in the adjoining tenement at the
date of the lease expired, he had the same right as the
reversioner from whom he purchased had to build to
a height that interfered with the light of his tenant,
or as he would have had if the reversioner had raised
the height of the building and had then sold it to him.
One ground of the decision was that, in the lease, in
which the grant of lights was general, there was no contract that the plaintiff should enjoy them during the whole
twenty-one years, nor any representation that the lessor
had power to make a grant of that nature. James, L. J.,
said it was a mere grant of a legal right without any
equity; and Mellish, L. J., remarked, in a passage quoted
by the learned Chief Justice in the Court below, that,

" There may, perhaps, in this case be no great difference in result between a general grant of lights and an express grant of lights to continue during the existence of the grantor's then interest; but there is a very material difference between such grants with regard to the question whether the grantee is in equity entitled to any right after the determination of the estate which the grantor had in the other property at the date of the grant. General words in a grant must be restricted to that which the grantor had then power to grant, and will not extend to anything which he might subsequently acquire."

The decision did not turn to any extent on the distinction between legal and equitable estates, but on the circumstance that by purchasing the reversion, an entirely new estate was acquired, the expiration of the term leaving the termor in the position of a stranger to the title.

The same principle is involved in other decisions. *Davies* v. *Marshall*, 1 Dr. & S. 557; 7 Jur. 720, is an instance, but is rather the converse of *Booth* v. *Alcock*. A landlord there took a surrender of the term in the servient tenement, and was held not to have acquired a right, which his tenant might have exercised, to obstruct new lights which the dominant tenant had opened under contract with or licence from himself, and when he made a new lease of the servient tenement in consideration of the tenant pulling down and rebuilding the house, the tenant was restrained from building so high as to interfere with the lights.

In *Beddington* v. *Atlee*, 35 Ch. D. 317, where dominant and servient tenants of houses both held under the same landlord, the lease of the dominant tenement being the earlier one, the plaintiff bought the reversion of the dominant tenement, and evicted the tenant for breach of a condition in the lease. The defendant bought the reversion of the other premises over which the evicted tenant had had, by implied grant under his lease, a right of light ; and in these transactions the order of priority was reversed, the defendant's purchase being some days earlier than that of the plaintiff. The plaintiff sought to maintain his right of light against the defendant for at all events the residue of

the term for the forfeiture of which he had entered, but
his effort did not succeed. The right was held to terminate
with the term, and his title as purchaser of the reversion,
like that of the purchaser in *Booth* v. *Alcock*, was treated
as operative only from its own date.

The fallacy of the judgment under appeal in the particular now in discussion arises, I think, from placing undue
stress on the technical incident of the legal estate being in
the mortgagee.

After Cameron made the mortgage he remained the
owner of the property, though it was charged with the
mortgage debt. That was his position in equity. It is
thus neatly put by Lord Blackburn, in the recent case of
Bradford Banking Co. v. *Briggs*, 12 App. Cas., at p. 36:

"As I understand it, the principle of *Hopkinson* v. *Rolt*,
9 H. L. C. 534, 536, is explained by Lord Campbell, then
Lord Chancellor, and it is this : 'The owner of property
does not by making a pledge or mortgage of it, cease to be
the owner of it any further than is necessary to give effect
to the security which he has thus created.' "

The mortgage debt was paid in accordance with a series
of covenants from Pim and those claiming under him, and
as part of the consideration for which he bought and sold ;
and the conveyance from Miss Jarvis was from a trustee to
her cestui que trust.

The case of *Lawlor* v. *Lawlor*, 10 S. C. R. 194, was mentioned in the Court below and was cited to us as strength-
ening the defendant's argument upon the effect of the
certificate. In that case a tenant-in-tail had made a
mortgage in fee simple, which gave the mortgagee an
estate in fee simple under our disentailing Act. The
mortgagor paid off the mortgage after it was overdue and
took a statutory discharge. That was held by the Supreme
Court, Henry, J., dissenting, to vest in the mortgagor, not
his original estate tail, but the fee simple which had passed
by the force of the disentailing Act to the mortgagee, just
as that estate would have vested if the mortgagee had
executed a formal conveyance in fee simple. The main

question, if not the only one, was the effect to be given under the circumstances to the words, " the original estate of the mortgagor" in the Registry Act. In the case before us the original estate was a fee simple, and there is no dispute that Miss Jarvis's certificate vested in Mr. Grasett the fee which had been in her. So far *Lawlor* v. *Lawlor* does not affect the case. But it was cited in support of the contention that a mortgagor who takes only the statutory discharge holds thenceforth, not by his original title freed from the charge, but by title derived from the mortgagee. The decision seems to go in that direction, and the learned Chief Justice of Canada, who discusses the transaction on the basis of a re-settlement of the estate, seems so to have regarded it. The judgments of Strong and Gwynne, JJ., do not follow that line of illustration. But the decision cannot properly be treated as of wider scope than its immediate subject matter, viz., the discharge, by a statutory certificate, of a mortgage in fee simple made by a tenant-in-tail.

The substance of the matter is that Mr. Grasett was owner subject to the charge, and when he paid the mortgage money he extinguished the charge, and Miss Jarvis was simply a trustee for him.

The latest case on the general subject of the present appeal is the case I have referred to of *Beddington* v. *Atlee*, 35 Ch. D. 317, decided by Mr. Justice Chitty since the argument on which we are now pronouncing judgment. Both parties claimed there, as here, under the same person, one Whitaker, who had mortgaged both the dominant and servient tenements, a circumstance which gave occasion for some remarks which are apposite to our immediate point. Whitaker demised the house to one Hartshorn.

" At that time," the learned Judge said, " Whitaker had an equitable estate in the adjoining land, and for the convenient enjoyment of the house so demised, access of light over this adjoining land was requisite. I am satisfied that in these circumstances equity would follow the law. The law is simply this : when a man is owner of a house, and owner also of an adjoining field, and he grants the house,

he grants by implication a right of light over the adjoining
field, so far as is necessary for the proper enjoyment of the
house. Consequently, on the demise to Hartshorn, he
obtained for his term the right to light as against the
landlord who was the owner in equity of the adjoining
land. I am satisfied, as I have said, that although the title
here is altogether equitable, equity would follow the law."

This opinion was followed up by the decision of almost
the very points now made as to the effect of adding the
legal to the equitable title, occasion being given for it by
rather peculiar facts. I have already mentioned that the
plaintiff had bought the reversion in the dominant, and
the defendant that in the servient tenement, the purchase
by the plaintiff being the later of the two. The purchases
which stood in this order of time were agreements to purchase, which as laid down by Lord Cairns in *Shaw* v
Foster, L. R. 5 H. L. 321, in a passage quoted by Mr. Justice Chitty, made the purchasers beneficial owners from
the dates of the agreements—defendant first, plaintiff
second. These agreements were followed by conveyances
in which the mortgagee (who had been paid off) joined for
the purpose of conveying the legal estate ; and the plaintiff, whose agreement was second, got his conveyance before
the defendant who had the first agreement. He had thus
the legal estate in his tenement while the defendant's title
was only equitable, but their respective rights were held
to be acquired as of the dates of the equitable titles.

We have now to consider what are the plaintiff's rights

His title deed of the 12th March, 1869, is made in pursuance of the Act respecting Short Forms of Conveyances.
On its face it simply grants

" All and singular those certain parcels or tracts of land
and premises, situate, lying and being lots numbers seven
and eight on the west side of William street, and lots
numbers seven and eight on the east side of Dummer
street, being parts of the front part of park lot number
twelve, formerly in the township of York, now in the
said city of Toronto, according to a plan prepared by James
G. Chewett, and registered in the Registry Office of the
said city of Toronto, to have and to hold unto the said

party of the second part, his heirs and assigns, to and for his and their sole and only use for ever : subject, nevertheless, to the reservations, limitations, provisoes and conditions expressed in the original grant thereof from the Crown, and also to the said indenture of mortgage hereinbefore mentioned."

But by the effect of the statute it included " all houses," &c., " ways, waters, watercourses, lights, liberties, privileges, easements profits, commodities, emoluments, hereditaments and appurtenances whatsoever, to the lands therein comprised belonging or in any wise appertaining, or with the same demised, held, used, occupied, and enjoyed, or taken or known as part or parcel thereof."

Whatever right of light the plaintiff took by this deed must, I think, be held to have been granted expressly and not by implication.

The deed, as expounded by the statute, speaks of lights used and enjoyed with the land, and not with any house on the land. A right to the access of light and air to land, irrespective of buildings, cannot, it seems, be acquired by prescription or by implication of grant; *Roberts* v. *Macord*, 1 M. & Rob. 230 ; *Potts* v. *Smith*, L. R. 6 Eq. 311. But it may be the subject of an express grant ; and if a deed of land, which includes the houses upon it, grants in express terms the lights used with the land as such, it would seem to be arguable that the implication of a more extensive grant would be forbidden by the rule expressio unius, &c.

That construction of the deed might negative any grant express or implied, of lights to the houses on the land conveyed. I think it would be too narrow a construction to give the conveyance its intended effect, and that lights used and enjoyed with houses upon the land are intended, or at least included. The plaintiff therefore took by express grant, under the general words imported from the statute into the deed, all lights used and enjoyed with the house, whatever, under the circumstances, those words applied to.

Rights of light conveyed by general words in a deed and

rights granted by implication do not appear to differ in
nature or extent. The rule that a man shall not derogate
from his grant applies to both classes of rights. Nor do
they differ in extent from rights gained by prescription, as
appears from recent cases. See *Moore* v. *Hall*, 3 Q. B. D.
178; *Kelk* v. *Pearson*, L. R. 6 Ch. 809; *Allen* v. *Taylor*,
16 Ch. D. 355; *Scott* v. *Pape*, 31 Ch. D. 554.

The great question here is not the extent of such rights
when established, though that question has been argued,
but whether in the contract between the plaintiff and his
vendors there was any subject matter for the general words
imported by the statute into the conveyance to act upon.

The claim is for an easement over lot 9 ; and the use and
enjoyment of lights, to be made out as within the terms of
the grant and the contemplation of the parties to it, are a
use and enjoyment of that nature. The right over lot 8
passed, of course, by the grant of that lot.

The subject of the grant is the lot 8 on which Pim had
built the house, not building up to the line of the lot, but six
feet back from it, arranging his windows so that every room
which for comfortable occupation required any considerable amount of light, or let us say unobstructed light, obtained
it from other directions. He had a wide street in front.
Behind his house he had probably a wider tract before
reaching the rear of the Dummer street lot, on which tract
nothing would be built in the ordinary course of things,
except the outhouses of his residence, and he had a large
part of lot 8, and, as I understand, all of lot 7, on the south
of his house, at his own disposal. At all events he did
provide for such access of light as he desired and found
sufficient, without depending on light from the north for
any important room, although some of the principal rooms
in the house were on that side. There was the drawing
room with no northern window; there was the whole first
floor with a dead wall to the north, though no doubt a
window would have been useful there, as the plaintiff
shewed by making one ; and there was the basement room
under the drawing room lighted only from the front. The

dining room was presumably an important room, but it was not left to depend on its northern window alone.

The rooms receiving light only from the north were the room in the cellar, which was obscure in the other sense that the woman who served seven years in the house could not remember it and left the witness box unconvinced of its existence, and the pantries. There were, it is true, the attic windows, but so high up as not likely to suffer from any building six feet away. We have no information as to the rooms they lighted. They doubtless were and are still useful windows, but they scarcely affect the present discussion except as evidence furnished by Pim, of which we have the benefit, and which the plaintiff understood when he bought the house, that windows in the next story below would also have been useful, but were dispensed with for good reason.

It is knowledge common to every one who walks along the streets of this city that it is a very usual thing to build houses, and of a class fully as good as the plaintiff's house, with windows in every story from the cellar to the attic looking out upon an adjoining house. Sometimes one sees a space of five or six feet allowed from each of the adjacent lots, giving ten or twelve feet between the houses; but such windows looking into a space not over six feet wide are far from unfrequent. We see it in good houses built within the last year or two, and in others of date as old as the plaintiff's house and older. We have evidence in this that light and air are derivable to a useful extent from these narrow spaces. This is admissible evidence on the question of contemplation and intent, which are usually matters to be inferred rather than directly proved, and it fits in with evidence given at the trial of a proposal by the plaintiff that Dr. Temple should build far enough back to leave ten feet between the houses.

The idea that Pim, when he built his house and made the cellar window, which looks into the six foot space at the height of twelve inches from the ground, had any

intention, or that the plaintiff when he bought lot 8
understood or supposed, that lot 9 was to be in any
way servient to the cellar window, belongs to a region
which is not that of real life.

The owner of lot 9 could not put up a board fence
six feet high on his line without preventing light at an
angle of 45° from reaching the lower panes of the window, and if he built a house forty feet high he would
have to keep it away fully half the width of the lot to
avoid obstructing the light which the plaintiff insists on
his right to have for that cellar window.

The plaintiff's claim would be the same in law if the
space left on lot 8 had been twenty or thirty in place of
six feet. The difference in extent would have gone only
to the weight of evidence upon the question of intent.

I need not at present further labour the proposition that,
as a matter of fact, Pim built on the design of having from
his six foot space all the light and air which were to be
used and enjoyed as of right by means of the windows in
question, and that the plaintiff so understood the matter.
I may, incidentally, have something more to say about it.

I do not use the words " as of right." as necessarily
meaning what they mean in the Prescription Act where
they are not applied to rights of light. I mean that Pim
provided by the six foot space for all the light and air
which his design in building contemplated, or which he
intended to attach to the house. Any more that might be
temporarily enjoyed, by reason of the next lot remaining
vacant, came by accident and not as part of the design.

The action is not brought in serious assertion of any different state of facts, but is based on what is claimed to be
the effect of the conveyance, and upon the theory that
because in fact these windows received light across lot 9,
that light must be held to be used and enjoyed with the
house within the meaning of the contract.

I do not think the proposition is by any means so incontrovertible as the plaintiff assumes, and if I correctly apprehend the bargain apart from the technical effect of the

deed, it would be to be regretted if any rule of law or canon of construction compelled us to expand it so as to give the purchaser of lot 8 rights which he never purchased over lot 9. We should be trying rather severely the rule of law on which the plaintiff relies.

It is important, when referring to English decisions, to bear in mind that what was here bought and conveyed was not the house, eo nomine, but the lot—a definite sub-division of land recognised as such by the registry law, and as to which, and as to every lot on the plan referred to in the plaintiff's deed, the registrar had to keep in his books a separate index. A purchaser of lot 9 investigating the title ought to find, as pointed out by the learned Chief Justice in the Court below, this deed indexed as affecting lot 9, if it granted an easement over that lot· That had been the law for many years. When the plaintiff bought in 1869, the Act of 1868, 31 Vict. ch. 20, was in force, section 30 of which required the registrar, in addition to the former entries, to keep an " Abstract Index," in which each separate lot or part of a lot of land as originally patented by the Crown, or as defined on any plan of the sub-division of such land into smaller sections or lots, after the filing of the plan in the registry office, was to be entered under a separate and distinct head. This deed would not appear in that index because the registrar's duty was to enter in it only every deed, &c., in which the particular lot was *mentioned*.

The general clause respecting plans, continued in this Act from former statutes, is section 75. It required the registrar, after the filing of a plan, " to keep an index of the lands described and designated by any number or letter on such map or plan, by the name by which such person, corporation or company [filing the plan] designates the same in manner provided by this Act," and then enacts that " all instruments affecting the land or any part thereof, executed after such plan, shall conform thereto, otherwise the same shall not be registered." In other words, any instrument *affecting* land on a registered plan must *men-*

tion the land by the designation given to it by number or letter on the plan, otherwise it is not to be registered. Carry this into connection with section 30, and the effect is, that every instrument *affecting* a lot on a registered plan ought to appear on the abstract index of that lot as well as on the general index of it.

There is no pretence that the plaintiff asserted title to the easement over lot 9 by procuring his deed to appear in either index of that lot.

The practical result would probably be the same whether this deed should be held not to affect lot 9, or not to be a registered deed as to lot 9 ; but I do not see how it can be regarded as a registered deed. I am referring to the registration itself, not to the index.

A deed may, I apprehend, be validly registered though the registrar by error or inadvertence should omit it from the proper index. An error something of that sort led to the liability of the registrar in *Harrison* v. *Brega*, 20 U. C. R. 324.

This deed does not mention lot 9. Therefore as a deed affecting lot 9, it was, under sec. 75, incapable of registration, and the registration of it as affecting lot 8 which it does mention, is no registration as against lot 9.

The case of *Swansborough* v. *Coventry*, 9 Bing. 305, which was cited at the bar, will be found useful in relation to the effect of the deed. The statement with which the judgment of Tindal, C.J., as reported, commences, that the action was for obstructing ancient lights, is misleading, for there were no prescriptive rights in question. The plaintiff's dwelling house, and also the site on which the defendant was erecting the building of which the plaintiff complained, were both the property of the postmaster-general. There was therefore unity of ownership resembling that of Pim in lots 8 and 9. But there had stood on the defendant's lot for many years a low building which had been removed a year before the sales to the plaintiff and defendant. While it stood it kept light from the lower windows of the house which the plaintiff afterwards bought.

That house was an ancient house, and the upper windows had received light over the lower building long enough to have given a prescriptive right as against a stranger. In that sense only, as I understand, they were ancient lights. The properties were sold by auction on the same day in separate lots. The plaintiff bought the house, and it was conveyed to him " with all the lights, easements, rights, privileges, and appurtenances to the same belonging, or in any wise appertaining," and was described as " bounded on the east by a piece of ground described in the particulars of sale as a piece of freehold building ground, constituting lot 11 at the aforesaid sale, purchased by John Coventry." The plaintiff contended that the defendant had no right to erect a building on the lot purchased by him, so as to obstruct any of the windows of the dwelling house, and the defendant, on the other hand, contended that he had a right to build to any extent he thought proper, notwithstanding the obstruction of the plaintiff's lights. So far we have a counterpart of the case before us. The actual decision of the court upon the contest is of secondary interest to us. The important circumstance is the reference to matters outside of the deed in order to gather the intention of the parties to it and to give it the effect, and no more than the effect intended. Tindal, C.J., stated the general rule that when the same person possesses a house having the actual use and enjoyment of certain lights, and also possesses the adjoining land, and sells the house to another person, although the lights be new, he cannot, nor can any one who claims under him, build upon the adjoining land so as to obstruct or interrupt the enjoyment of those lights ; and that the parties to that action came within the application of the general rule of law. " It is contended, however," he continued, " on the part of the defendant, that the circumstances of this case form an exception to the general rule, inasmuch as it appears by the description of the plaintiff's own conveyance that his house was bounded by a piece of ground described in the particulars of sale as building ground, and purchased by the defendant; that such description operated as notice to the plaintiff that he bought subject to the defendant's right to build ; and that as there was no restriction or limitation as to the exercise of such right, he might build to any extent or height he thought proper, although to the obstruction of the plaintiff's lights, without any derogation of the grant of the vendor to him. But we think, with reference to the facts in this case, this conclusion cannot follow. The vendor conveyed to the plaintiff a messuage with all its rights and easements without any restriction or qualification ; and we think it would be attributing too much force to the description of boundary in this case if it was to be held to operate indirectly to the destruction of the rights expressly conveyed by the deed. The very term ' building ground,' is a loose and general expression, and may well be satisfied by the power of erecting a building which should leave the plaintiff's lights altogether undisturbed, or partially obstructed only, or altogether blocked up. The question, therefore, is, what is the meaning most consistent with the grant of the vendor to both parties ? And as we find that in point of fact, there had been a building on the ground in question, for a very long period of time, and recently demolished, which extended only to the height of the first floor of the plaintiff's house, we think that gives the limit and extent intended by the terms of the description so as at once to satisfy those terms, and at the same time to prevent the vendor from frustrating his own grant. This is in effect not a contradiction, but an explanation of the terms of the grant."

I cite this case for the sake of the principle on which the question is dealt with. The actual decision is, as I have said, of secondary interest; yet it is worth noting that the result was to limit the words "all lights" to part only of the light that had access to the house at the date of the conveyance.

The decision is referred to in several recent cases. In *Wheeldon* v. *Burrows*, 12 Ch. D. 31, and in *Allan* v. *Taylor*, 16 Ch. D. 355, it is spoken of as having been influenced by the circumstance that the conveyances were executed as the completion of sales made at the same auction, and stood therefore in the position of contemporaneous conveyances. However well founded this explanation of the decision may be, I do not think it weakens its effect for the purpose for which I cite it, as I apprehend it must be regarded as dealing with legal rights only.

It is noticed, along with *Compton* v. *Richards*, 1 Price 27, in *Beddington* v. *Atlee*, as instances in which the court proceeded to some extent on matters relating to the adjoining land which were outside of the grant itself ; and the most recent decision of all, that of Mr. Justice Kekewich, in *Birmingham, Dudley, &c., Bank* v. *Ross*, delivered a few weeks ago, and at present only accessible to us in the Times' Reports, at p. 108 of volume 4, seems to me to proceed on the principle on which I found my opinion, and on facts very much like those we have to deal with *(a)*. The same principle I take to be affirmed by *Rigby* v. *Bennett*, 21 Ch. D. 559, to which Mr. Justice Kekewich refers, although it was not there necessary to decide the point which arose for decision before him.

The easement of light does not differ, as to its acquisition by contract, from other easements. There was a difference in the kind of enjoyment which would give title under the prescription Act, particularly in the use of other easements having to be " as of right." With us, rights of light can no longer be acquired by prescription. They must now, when not acquired by twenty years user before the 5th of March, 1880, depend altogether on contract, (43 Vict. ch. 14, sec. 1). The rules and principles applicable to contracts in general must apply to them, as they do to the case in hand.

We shall not be helped towards the true construction of the contract, or its application to the facts, by a discussion of doctrines touching ancient lights, or the extent of rights gained by prescription. I therefore avoid that subject. Nor shall I enter upon the subject, which was also dwelt on in the argument, of the alterations made by the plaintiff in his house, and the addition which blocks up the end of the six foot space and must affect the windows by excluding the light from the west.

The claim is for an easement conferred by contract. The

(a) Affirmed on app. 4 *Times* L. R., 437.

lights " used with the house," as described in the general
words,of the conveyance, along with other easements and
appurtenances, are lights used and enjoyed before the conveyance with the house, not as easements in law, which
are rights in the land of another person, but so far of the
nature of easements as to be burdens on land other than
that which was conveyed.

The same general expressions in the deed apply to
ways. Suppose the very common case of a short cut diag-
onally across an adjoining vacant lot to reach the back
part of the house. If the grantee under a deed like this
made so extravagant a claim as that such a right of way
passed by the express grant of ways used with the house,
what would be the answer ?   Not that as a matter of fact
the way was not used and enjoyed with the house.   It was
literally so used and enjoyed.   The answer would be that
the use was temporary and accidental, not appurtenant to
the house, or in the nature of an easement; that access
from the street to the rear had been provided on the land
conveyed, possibly not so convenient when coming from
one direction as the short cut, but still what the vendor
intended and the purchaser understood when the bargain
was made and the price agreed upon ; and that all the
surrounding facts were evidence of this ; the nature of the
property ; the ordinary course of dealing, known to every
one, in cases of the kind ; and the facts that access had
been provided on the granted lot, while the so-called way
had not been defined or made into a road like the track
across the farm yard in *Langley* v. *Hammond*, L. R. 3 Ex.
161 ; and possibly other facts ; but all being matters of
evidence.

One of the most instructive cases on this subject, is
Kay v. *Oxley*, L. R. 10 Q. B. 360, where the question
decided was that a right of way which had been actually
used, but only by license of the owner of the soil, passed
by his grant of a messuage with all ways, &c., with the
premises " occupied or enjoyed or reputed as part or
parcel of them or any of them, or appurtenant thereto."

The whole of the judgments of Blackburn and Lush, JJ.,
are instructive, but I shall confine myself to reading one
short passage from that of the former Judge, which I
quote for its recognition of the propriety of testing the
character of such actual use as there may have been of the
privilege in question by whatever evidence may throw
light upon it. The passage is this:

"It cannot make any difference in law whether the
- right of .way was only de facto used and enjoyed, or
whether it was originally created before the unity of possession and then ceased to exist as a matter of right, so
that in the one case it would be created as a right de novo,
in the other merely revived. But it makes a great difference, as matter of evidence on the question whether the
way was used and enjoyed as appurtenant."

That is the question to be decided under the evidence.
Was the light which was de facto used and enjoyed by the
plaintiff's windows, used and enjoyed before and at the
time of his purchase as appurtenant to the house ?

In my opinion the whole evidence is to the contrary.

I have sufficiently referred to what is shewn by the construction and arrangement of the house, and the reservation of the six foot strip. I have pointed out the fact that
no assertion of right over lot 9 appears from the deed, or
was made by the plaintiff by any such act as the registration of the deed as a deed affecting that lot. I have alluded
to evidence respecting a proposal by the plaintiff to Dr.
Temple in 1875, when he was about to build, that there
should be ten feet left between the houses. The plaintiff
admits the proposal, but says he made it as a compromise,
and that he disputed Dr. Temple's right to interfere with
his lights to any extent. This evidence would, of course,
go to the jury with the facts that Dr. Temple did not keep
away ten feet; but though the body of his house was built
fifteen feet from the plaintiff's house, leaving room on his
own land for a verandah, yet at the rear, and in front of
the plaintiff's dining room window, the doctor built up to
his line; and that the plaintiff, who is not shewn to be so
averse to litigation as to be likely to submit quietly to

what he believed to be an encroachment on his rights, brought no action for the nuisance against Dr. Temple. The present action, commenced eight or ten years after Dr. Temple built, is not against him.

The only finding by the jury is, that the defendant's house interferes with the plaintiff's light, but not injuriously. I have not been able to satisfy myself as to what is meant by that. It is probably capable of expressing what is, in my opinion, the true state of the case, that while the defendant's house intercepts light it does not intercept any to which the plaintiff is entitled ; but after reading the charge to the jury I do not feel clear that is what they meant, and as far as that point is concerned, I am not averse to granting a new trial if it be desired by the plaintiff, although, on the whole, my opinion would be that upon the facts as we have them in evidence it could not be reasonably found that the rights now claimed were used or enjoyed with the house in the character of an easement or appurtenance, and that being an issue which the plaintiff had to sustain, there was not a case for the jury.

If the case goes again to trial, the important question I have alluded to under the registry law should be open. I should say, as Mr. Justice Chitty said with respect to the plaintiff's claim as purchaser for value without notice, in

Beddington v. *Atlee*: " There is no pleading to that effect on the part of the plaintiff [defendant], but I should make all proper amendments which would enable me to do justice, and I should not dispose of the case as against the plaintiff [defendant] on the ground that he has not pleaded this point, if I thought it could be maintained on the facts."

The facts I have in view are these : The plaintiff claims under a deed certain rights in lot 9 ; that deed is not indexed in the registry books as affecting lot 9, and in my present view of section 75 of the Act of 1868, which I have explained but which is of course subject to reconsideration, the deed is, with reference to lot 9, unregistered ; it is made incapable of registration, not because of anything in

the nature of the right alleged to be conveyed, but by the
act or neglect of the plaintiff in not complying with section 75.

The deed is made in 1869.

The opposing deed is from the devisees of Pim to Priestman, made the 29th of October, 1873. I am assuming it
to be registered, for the fact does not appear on the appeal
book.

The title of Priestman was conveyed to Dr. Temple in
September, 1874.

The decision in *Ross* v. *Hunter*, 7 S. C. R. 289, may perhaps bear on this question.

The other question of the throwing of water on the plaintiff's land cannot be said to be really before us, and I do not
understand that anything substantial is involved in it.
The only mention of it in the reasons of appeal is in the
13th paragraph, where the appellant submits that the finding of the jury that water was thrown on his land though
it did not affect him injuriously, is a finding that his right
of property has been infringed, and that therefore he should
have judgment. No such result is involved in the finding.
The defendant does not claim any right to throw water
on the plaintiff's lot.

OSLER, J. A.—The plaintiff sues for the interference
with the access of light to his dwelling-house through
certain windows looking over the adjoining premises of
the defendant; and also for injury caused to the dwelling-
house in consequence of water being allowed to flow upon
the plaintiff's land from the platform of the defendant's
verandah.

The plaintiff purchased his lot No. 8, with the dwelling-
house thereon, on the 12th March, 1869, from the trustees
of one Pim, who were also the owners, under a different
chain of title, of the adjacent lot No. 9, which was then
vacant, and which they subsequently on the 29th October,
1873, conveyed to one Priestman, through whom the
defendant claims.

The plaintiff's deed purports to be made in pursuance of the Act respecting Short Forms of Conveyances, C. S. U. C. ch. 91, (R. S. O. ch. 102) and therefore by force of the 3rd section, comprises a general grant, not only of all existing and acquired easements appurtenant to the land conveyed, but also of all quasi easements, with the same used, occupied, and enjoyed. It is sufficient, however, to say that as Pim's trustees were then the owners of both lots, the plaintiff's case rests upon the implied grant of light over lot 9, arising from the principle that a grantor cannot derogate from his grant. The general words in the conveyance do not, under the circumstances, enlarge or limit the implied grant.

In 1875 Dr. Temple, the then owner of lot No. 9, erected thereon a dwelling house, and in 1878 the defendant (who had in the meantime become the purchaser), added a porch with a platform verandah thereto, which, it is alleged, cause the injuries of which the plaintiff complains.

At the trial the learned Judge, at the close of the evidence, stated to counsel the questions which he proposed to leave to the jury on the principal points of the case.

No objection was made by the plaintiff's counsel, but counsel for defendant asked that the jury might be directed in accordance with the views expressed by the Lord Chancellor in *Clarke* v. *Clark*, L. R. 1. Ch. 16, viz., that there was a difference between the right to protection of a person residing in a town, and the right of a person residing in the country, who would have reason to expect a greater amount of light in his dwelling.

The learned Judge, however, refused, and, as I understand the subsequent cases, properly refused thus to direct the jury, and after stating the facts briefly, left the case to them in this way:

"The first question I submit to you is this: Did Dr. Temple's (the defendant's) house interfere injuriously with the light of the plaintiff's house?"

And again, after some further observations:

"You have heard the evidence, however, and it is for you to say if the light is injuriously interfered with."

Other questions which need not be noticed here were also left to the jury, and then on the other branch of the case the learned Judge said :

" Does the construction of the platform bring water injuriously on the plaintiff's land ? If so, what damage has the plaintiff sustained ? "

After discussing the evidence shortly, he continued :

"If the evidence satisfies you that the construction of the platform brings water injuriously on the plaintiff's land, you will say what damages the plaintiff has sustained to the present time."

The defendant's counsel objected to the charge on the ground previously taken by him, but no objection whatever was taken by the plaintiff's counsel, except as to one of the other questions, which the jury did not answer, and are here not important.

The jury answered the questions (which I repeat) thus :

Q. "Does Dr. Grasett's house interfere injuriously with the light of the plaintiff's house ? A. Yes, but not injuriously."

Q. Does the construction of the platform bring water injuriously on the plaintiff's land ? A. Yes ; but not injuriously."

And upon these findings, judgment was entered for the defendant.

Notwithstanding the awkward phraseology of the answers, which shew that the jury treated the questions as double in their form, the findings plainly are that the defendant's house does not interfere injuriously with the light; and that the platform does not bring water injuriously on the plaintiff's land.

In such an action as this, speaking for the moment of the claim for obstruction to the light, the plaintiff must prove that he has sustained some material and substantial injury, and that is the issue here raised (almost in the terms of the question put to the jury) by the statement of defence.

In *Dent* v. *The Auction Mart Co.*, L. R. 2 Eq. 238-245, Wood, V. C., considering what is sufficient to support a claim for damages in respect of an injury done to a building by the obstruction of-light, cites with approval, subject to a slight verbal correction, the language of Best, C. J., in *Back* v. *Stacey*, 2 C. & P. 410. He says :

" The Lord Chief Justice told the jury ' in order to give a right of action and sustain the issue, there must be a substantial privation of light sufficient to make the occupation of the house uncomfortable, and to prevent the plaintiff from carrying on his accustomed business (that of a grocer) on the premises as beneficially as he had formerly done.' With the single exception of reading *or* for *and*, I apprehend that the above statement correctly lays down the doctrine in the manner in which it would now be supported in an action at law."

See also *Kelk* v. *Pearson*, 6 Ch. D. 809 ; 9 Ch. D. 219 ; *Rudkin* v. *Kino*, 6 Ch. D. 160.

Now, although the charge of the learned Judge does not explain very fully to the jury the extent of the injury which would, according to the authorities, be necessary to sustain the action ; yet in leaving it as he did, to some extent at large, his charge was more favorable to the plaintiff than it ought to have been. The plaintiff had the benefit of that, and his counsel, no doubt, felt it and commented upon the evidence, and claimed the benefit of it, in the largest sense of the question which the learned judge said he would put to the jury. Their view was, notwithstanding, adverse to the plaintiff, and there is no reason to think that it would have been different had the question as to the light been presented to them in its more limited and accurate form. I consider that it is not now open to the plaintiff to complain of the charge on the ground of misdirection ; and while the finding of the jury as to the light might well have been the other way, if indeed in its present shape it is not, as I am inclined to think it is, against the weight of evidence, I am not of opinion, looking at all the circumstances, that the justice of the case requires us to interfere by granting a new trial.

As to the other cause of action the plaintiff has less

reason to complain of the charge, and the finding of the jury. Nothing is determined against him except that he has hitherto sustained no damage, a finding that is warranted by the evidence. If hereafter the defendant allows the water to flow upon the land in such a way as to be injurious to the plaintiff, he is not precluded from bringing a new action.

I wish to add a word as to the ground on which the judgment below proceeded. In the case of *Booth* v. *Alcock*, L. R. 8 Ch. 663, which was relied upon, the defendant was at the time of the grant to the plaintiff possessed of the residue of a term of years in the adjoining property. He subsequently purchased the reversion in fee expectant on the term. It was held that the general grant of lights arising upon words similar to those in the deed in the present case, anb also the implied grant, existing, as here, even in the absence of such words, were limited to the term the defendant held in such property at the date of the grant to the plaintiff, and that the subsequent purchase of the fee did not extend them to a longer term. In other words the plaintiff was not entitled to any right of light after the determination of the estate which the defendant had in the other property at the date of the grant to the plaintiff.

In the present case the vendors had the equitable fee simple in both lots, and so were in equity the real owners of the land, possessed of it in their ancient right and estate. Lot 9 was subject to the implied grant of light over it to the purchaser of lot 8. in the same way as if the vendors had possessed the legal fee. If they had discharged the mortgage on lot 9 I do not see how it can be said that they had acquired a new and different estate or title, paramount to the equitable estate, to which the implied grant would not extend. They would simply have discharged an incumbrance. Their grantee would be in the same position. No doubt, in the hands of the mortgagee the legal title was paramount to the implied grant, and pro-

bably the plaintiff as grantee of lot 8 could not have compelled the owners of lot 9, or those claiming through them,
to discharge the mortgage. But although they did pay
it off and obtained and registered a statutory discharge, I
think the case of *Lawlor* v. *Lawlor*, 10 S. C. R. 194, cannot
be treated as an authority for the proposition that they
thereby acquired a new and independent estate, as in the
instance of the acquisition of the freehold by the termor.
They simply had their old estate relieved of the incumbrance. The expressions of the Court in that case,
were, I venture to think, intended to apply simply to
the question with which they were dealing, viz., the
destruction of the estate tail by the execution of the mortgage in fee. The estate which the tenant in tail conveyed
to the mortgagee, was an estate in fee, and that was the
estate he got back by or upon the discharge of the mortgage.

For the reasons already given, I think the appeal should
be dismissed.

FERGUSON, J.—I concur in the judgment of Mr. Justice
Burton, except that I am of the opinion that there is an
express grant of the light in question.

This view, assuming it to be correct, does not, however,
oppose or militate against the opinion there stated as to
the application in this case of the general rule, that the
grantor who wishes to retain to himself any right of dero-
gating from his grant must reserve it in express terms; on
the contrary, I think it makes the more strongly in favor
of that opinion.

I think there should, if the plaintiff desire it, be a new
trial upon the terms, and for the reasons stated by that
learned judge, and that in such case the defendants should
be at liberty to amend their pleadings as suggested, if they
desire so to do.

Appeal allowed, without costs.

[OSLER, J. A., dissenting.]

ARCHER V. SEVERN.

Will—Specific bequest of mortgage to mortgagor—Right of executors to insist on payment of other claims against mortgagor—Statute of Limitations.

J. S. directed his executors to cancel and entirely release the indebtedness of his son W. S. upon a mortgage made by him to the testator, such release to operate and take effect immediately on and from the testator's death. W. S. was also indebted to the testator on a promissory note and for goods, which, together with interest, amounted to upwards of $3,740. This amount the executors claimed they were entitled to demand payment of before they could be called upon to discharge the mortgage, which contention was sustained by the Master in an action for the administration of the estate ; but, on motion, his finding was reversed by PROUDFOOT, J. (12 O. R. 615).

On appeal to this Court the judgment of the Court below was affirmed, with costs [BURTON, J. A., dissenting].

Per BURTON, J. A.—The bequest of the mortgage was not a specific bequest ; and without reference as to what the original purpose of filing the bill was, W. S. had claimed to have his mortgage released and had obtained an order for its unconditional discharge so that he stood in the same position as if he had brought an action for that purpose expressly, and had thus brought himself within the rule, that he who seeks equity must do equity : whereas the effect of the judgment appealed from by reason of the operation of the Statute of Limitations was to leave the legatee free from the debt due by him to the estate and to expose the executors to a liability to make good that loss.

THIS was an appeal from the judgment of Proudfoot, J., reported 12 O. R., 615, where, and in the present judgments, the facts and points involved are fully stated, and came on to be heard before this Court on the 31st January and 1st February, 1888.*

S. H. Blake, Q. C. and *W. Cassels,* Q. C., for the appellants, the executors of John Severn.

Moss, Q. C., and *W. Barwick,* for Elizabeth Pannell, and *Snelling,* for Mary Davison beneficiaries under the will of J. Severn.

Clement and *Sherry,* for William Severn.

March 6, 1888.   HAGARTY, C. J. O.—I agree with my brother Proudfoot's decision that the bequest in favor of William Severn is a specific legacy, or in the nature of a specific legacy.

* *Present.*—HAGARTY, C.J.O., BURTON, PATTERSON, and OSLER, JJ.A.

The testator possessed a good deal of property, real and personal. After devising certain property to several children, he leaves the residue of realty and personalty to his executors to convert into money, with large powers as to sale and re-sale on trusts.

"(K.) And as to the money to arise as aforesaid, and the stock, funds, and securities whereon the same shall be invested (hereinafter designated my Trust Fund), my said trustees or trustee shall stand possessed thereof in trust:

1. To pay to my said daughter Elizabeth Pannell the sum of $7,000 within five years after my decease, with interest after the first year of my decease.

2. To cancel and entirely release and discharge the indebtedness of my son William to me upon and by virtue of his mortgage to me for $17,000 or thereabouts, such release to operate and take effect immediately on and from my decease.

3. To pay to my son Henry the sum of $5,000 within five years after my decease, with interest after the first year of my decease.

4. To pay to my daughter Sophia Atkinson the sum of $2,000 within five years after my decease, with interest after the first year of my decease. And also to cancel and entirely release and discharge the indebtedness due by her husband or herself, or by them jointly, to me in the sum of $4,000 or thereabouts."

It will be observed that he postpones the payment of three of these bounties to several years after his decease, and in addition, in Mrs. Atkinson's case, he directs the cancellation and discharge of a large debt due by her and her husband.

As I view this provision as to William Severn, I think that this mortgage security, and the debt therein, was gone for ever on his death, nothing being left beyond what I look upon as a mere perfunctory act of the executors in executing, on reasonable request, a formal discharge to clear the title. This is, of course, based on the fact of there being no rights of creditors intervening, as is admitted to have been the case.

I do not see the importance of the discussion before us,.

and elsewhere, as to the assent or dissent of the executors. I think the evidence of testator's intention to be perfectly clear from his language. As soon as he died the specified debt and security therefor were satisfied.

If no difficulty had arisen as to the necessity of clearing the title in the registry, I think the debtor and his property were at once freed from the burden.

The will was made in 1877, the death did not occur till 1880, three years later.

Between this date of the will and his death, the testator had been advancing money to help his son William in business, taking several promissory notes from him therefor; the first $1,000 made about six months after the will, the last less than two months before his death, not due till four months after the death.

The executors insist that they are not bound to release the mortgage debt to William without his (in effect) paying the amount of these notes, and large arrears of interest as a condition.

As I understand it, they put it on two grounds; first, that equity will direct such a course as but fair and just; second, that William Severn by his course in the suit brought by them, has submitted his rights to the direction of the Court. On this latter branch also arises the question as to the Statute of Limitations.

The bill filed March, 1881, by the executors Archer and Booth, sets out the will, and that they ask the Court to construe it, as they are embarrassed by its provisions as to George Severn, the other executor, who was claiming a large sum from the estate as a charge on the land devised, arising out of dealings between him and testator; that they are advised that they cannot safely proceed to distribute the estate till George Severn's claims are disposed of, and they state the question between him and them, and pray construction of the will in respect of these matters, and to determine the rights of all parties in connection therewith; and that for that purpose all necessary inquiries be made, accounts and directions, &c.

All the testator's children, including William, are made parties.

William's answer gives his view of George Severn's claim, and then says in regard to his mortgage debt, which is not referred to in the bill beyond its appearance in the will, which is fully set out:

6. I submit that I am entitled to have my mortgage for $17,000 or thereabouts, referred to in said testator's will, released and discharged as by the said testator directed in and by the said will; and I pray that the plaintiffs the executors named in said will, and the defendant George Severn, may be ordered and decreed to release and discharge said mortgage.

7. I am willing that the said will should be construed by this honourable Court, and the rights of the parties thereunder determined; and I pray to be hence dismissed, with my costs herein.

The Court adjudicated on George Severn's claim, and ordered a reference to the master for an account of the personal estate come to the hands of the executors; an account of testator's debts, funeral expenses, testator's legacies, personal estate, outstanding account of his realty, incumbrances thereon, rents, &c., received by executors; and as to who are entitled to share in the realty and personalty.

After much protracted litigation and appeals to this Court and the Supreme Court, the reference proceeded in the master's office.

William Severn was examined at length as to his dispute with the executors, and their insisting on making him pay his debt to the estate as a condition for their releasing the mortgage.

In June, 1886, the master reported that William was not entitled to the discharge until he paid the executors his debt of over $3,700.

William Severn appealed on this ground, and also that the claim on the first and second notes given by him to the testator was barred by the Statute of Limitations.

His appeal was decided in his favor by Mr. Justice Proudfoot on both these, and the executors appeal to us.

I find very great difficulty in differing from the careful and well considered judgment of my learned brother. I think he is undoubtedly right as to this being treated as a specific legacy to William. The subject is very fully discussed in *Ashburner* v. *McGuire*, 2 White & T. L. C. 254, in the notes to Lord Thurlow's judgment. See Sir G. Jessel's definition in *Bothamley* v. *Sherson*, L. R. 20 Eq. 309 : see also Theobald's Summary of Cases, 3rd ed. p. 103.

2 *Williams* on Executors, 8th ed. p. 1163, fully discusses the distinctions : "A legacy is specific when it is a bequest of a specified part of testator's personal estate which is so distinguished ;" and it points out its advantage as such, that it is not liable to abate if there be a deficiency of assets, while, on the other hand, it is liable to be adeemed.

The main controversy is, as to the executors' right to require payment of William's debt to the estate before releasing the mortgage.

I think this claim would appear much stronger and fairer if the bequest to William had been different in this— if it involved their payment unto him of a named sum. If the testator had given to William $17,000 due by or secured by mortgage from A. B., it would still, I think, be clearly a specific legacy ; but the executors would have to collect the money from A. B., and might then with some fairness require payment from William of his debt to the estate.

But here it is wholly different. No money is payable to William, and a large sum is required from him from his own resources. I cannot think that the testator evinced any other intention than that of an immediate unconditional benefit to his son, and the liberating of that son's estate from the mortgage debt. This liberation was to take effect directly on his death.

Part of the advances made to the son were not due till months after the father's death. If the executors' argument be sound, they could apply it equally if the whole debt from William had not matured till four or five years after the death. Thus they could defeat what I consider to be the testator's intentions. It is evident that the testator contemplated changes taking place in his property between his will and his death. Provision L. in the will shews this. (a)

No case has been made out or argued to favor the idea that this specific legacy had been pro tanto adeemed. Practically on the executors, contention it would amount to an ademption, if they can deduct these advances. The case does not warrant the application of this principle.

But it is urged that as William has to seek the aid of the court to compel the release of his mortgage, he must be held to make this payment, and also that he submits in his answer to this.

It is, however, the executors who have brought him into court, and for a wholly different purpose, and for matters wholly apart from this question, and his submission to the direction of the Court seems merely to amount to what the law compels him to do ; that is, to leave it to the court to direct what is right.

The executors throughout wish to treat the case as if they had to pay William $17,000 out of the assets of the estate, and the master apparently adopted that view.

I am unable to assent to it, and I concur in the view of my brother Proudfoot.

The nearest case, and almost the only one bearing very directly on the subject, is that of *Harvey* v. *Palmer*, 4 DeG. & S., 425.

In the Court below that decision is discussed, and also the comment on it in 2 *Williams* on Executors, 8th ed. 1315, where it is said :

" His Honor see med to doubt whether in any case where a specific legatee is indebted to the testator, the legacy can be withheld till the debt is paid."

(a) Clause L. provided that in case of the sale by the testator of any lands specifically devised, the consideration money therefor should become a charge on the whole real estate, and be payable to the devisee to whom the land was specifically devised within five years from the death of the testator.

Theobald, 117 :   " It seems doubtful whether a specific legacy can be subject to the executor's right to retain for a debt due from the legatee to the estate," citing *Harvey* v. *Palmer*.

There is a class of cases as to a legatee bankrupt at the death of the testator, where there is no right to retain, "since there never was a time at which the same person was entitled to receive the legacy, and liable to pay the whole debt," following *Cherry* v. *Boultbee*, 2 Keen 319; 4 M. & Cr. 442; *Hodgson* v. *Fox*, 9 Ch. D. 673; *Bell* v. *Bell*, 17 Sim. 127.

I think the distinction is reasonably clear between a case like the present, and the ordinary case in which executors are, as it were, to pay with one hand, and to receive with the other ; there the right of retainer is usually exercised.

As is said in 2 *Williams* on Executors, p. 1311, the term " set-off" is somewhat inaccurately used in cases of this kind,   *   *   " a right of this nature [retainer] is rather a right to pay out of the fund in hand, than a right of set-off."

There is nothing here for the executors to pay. I hold the debt discharged by the testator's direction in his will. It is a mere fiction of the law to hold this to be a case of the executors paying the $17,000 to William, less his debt to the estate.   I think the case is at least as strong in favor of the specific legatee as *Harvey* v. *Palmer*.

In *Ballard* v. *Marsden*, 14 Ch. D. 374, it was held that executors who have set apart and appropriated assets to meet a legacy, cannot retain or impound any part of the appropriated assets to meet a debt from the legatee to the general estate. Fry, J., said: " That when they set apart the legacy it ought to be considered as so set apart, so as to facilitate the dealing with it by the legatee for every purpose."   The legatee had mortgaged the legacy.

It seems to me, on the general principle, that the testator's act had acquitted William's estate for all purposes from the mortgage debt, and that his vendee or mortgagee of the premises a week after testator's death, would hold free of the original mortgage debt, and no right of retainer here asserted could affect him.

As to the operation of the Statute of Limitations, I hardly see why it is necessary to deal with it in this suit, if we agree with the Court below in disallowing the right to retain.

I think the operation of the statute could best be determined in a suit to be brought by the executors against William. But if it must be determined here, I am not at present prepared to dissent from the decision of my brother Proudfoot.

I have read the cases cited and others on this point, but it is very hard to deduce any decisive principle to govern this case.

If this suit had been at all in the nature of a claim for this debt against William Severn, we can well understand that the lapse of six years before its determination could not affect the claim. But, as is clearly pointed out, it is nothing of the kind, but is brought for a wholly different purpose. As is said in the judgment: "It was only at the hearing that an administration was asked and, not being objected to, was granted."

None of the debtors to the estate lost their right to the protection of the statute. It is insisted that it is different in the case of a party. I agree to this, if he be a party to a suit to enforce the claim against him.

Did his consent to the directing an inquiry as to "what parts, if any, of the testator's estates are still outstanding," bind him to pay at any future period whatever amount might be reported as due by him?

I do not think that his being a party bound him beyond the purposes for which he was made a party, or, at all events, beyond any further express arrangement as to the ultimate settlement of the estate's claim on him.

Mr. Cassels urged that after the appointment of a receiver (March, 1885), the statute could not run as to the parties.

Kerr on Receivers, 121, was referred to. We do not

find much there to aid us; but several cases are cited, most of which refer to real estate. Lord St. Leonards' judgment in *Harrison* v. *Duignan*, 2 Dru. & W. 295; *Wrixon* v. *Vyze*, 3 Dru. & W. 123; *Grome* v. *Blake*, 6 Ir. C. L. 400; *ib.*, 8 Ir. C. L. 428.

I refer to *Whitley* v. *Lowe*, 25 Beav. 421; in appeal, 2 DeG. & J. 704, where the position and powers of a receiver to prevent the running of the statute by payment on behalf of a party to the suit is discussed. See also *Hill* v. *Stawell* (Irish, 1842), 2 Jebb & Sym. 389, as to the findings and report of the master as to the existence of a debt not being an acknowledgment under the statute to prevent its operation.

On the whole, I am not prepared to differ from the conclusion of the Court below, and think the appeal should be dismissed.

BURTON. J.A.—I think Mr. Clement's contention is correct: that the rule which prevails in the case of a legatee entitled to a pecuniary legacy to be paid in cash, who is at the same time a debtor of the estate, does not apply to a case like the present, where the legacy consists of a debt due by the legatee to the testator, and the legatee is also debtor to the estate for a further sum.

The rule itself is a perfectly fair and equitable one, viz., that the legatee having already in his hands some of the assets of the estate from which alone the debts and legacies are payable, is bound either to bring in those assets or credit them upon his legacy. That, in other words, his legacy is pro tanto discharged. Here, however, there is nothing payable by the executors, nothing against which the debt can be set-off, but simply a further debt due by the legatee to the estate.

I, therefore, agree with him that the rule is inapplicable, and if the legatee had chosen to rely upon the release created by the will itself, the executors would have been driven to enforce their claim for the debt due by him in the ordinary way; and being a co-executor the remedy before the recent changes in the law would necessarily have been in a Court of Equity.

If, however, he thinks proper to go into Court to compel the executors to assent to the legacy, and release the mortgage, he brings himself, in my opinion, within the rule that he who seeks equity must himself be willing to do equity; and certainly a fairer and more equitable rule than the general rule I have referred to it would be difficult to find.

It is immaterial to consider for what purpose the bill was originally filed ; William, the legatee, in his answer submitted his rights to the Court, and claimed to have his mortgage released, and prayed that the executors might be ordered to release and discharge the same. To such a demand the executors might well counter-claim for the debt due to the estate by their co-executor, instead of being driven to a separate suit.

Upon this he has obtained a decree or judgment, directing the executors unconditionally to discharge the mortgage without reference to the further indebtedness of the legatee to the estate, so that the matter stands precisely in the same position as if he had brought a suit expressly for that purpose.

The effect of the decree, as it stands, is to leave the legatee free from the debt due by him to the estate, and to expose the executors to a liability to make good that loss to the estate.

Upon the evidence I agree with the master that the executors never did assent to the legacy except upon the terms that the legatee should discharge his own indebtedness to the estate.

If this had been a pecuniary legacy, it is quite clear that the executors might have retained out of it so much as would be sufficient to satisfy a debt due from the legatee to the testator, even though the remedy for the recovery of such debt was, at the time of the death of the testator, barred by the Statute of Limitations. Or if, in the case of a pecuniary legacy, it had been accompanied by a direction similar to that to be found in this case, that it should be paid immediately on the death of the testator, and at that time the legatee was found to be indebted to the estate for a debt not due for some time, can there be any question that the executors would have been entitled to retain from the legacy so much as would fully represent that indebtedness, making such a discount as would make it equivalent to cash? If so, how does it differ in principle from the present case?

Assume, for the purpose of illustration, that the legatee here had granted a subsequent mortgage on the same property far exceeding its value, and was only interested in obtaining a release from the executors in consequence of his having given security to the subsequent incumbrancer to do so, and that he was also indebted to the testator in a large sum unsecured, and was insolvent. Assume further that that debt was almost the only asset for the payment of the testator's debts and legacies. It would surprise me if it should be held under such circumstances that the executors, notwithstanding the direction that the release should operate and take effect immediately, were not justified in witholding their assent; and that, on a bill filed to compel a release, the court would not refuse to grant the relief, except upon such terms as would secure so much of the fund as would be necessary for the payment of the creditors, and a ratable proportion to the legatees.

It is not shewn that the assets are not ample to pay the creditors, but at the time of the filing of the bill a very large amount was claimed against the estate by George Severn, and it is even now claimed that there will be a deficiency to meet the legacies, and in fact one of the paragraphs of the decree is made at the instance of one or more of the legatees, with the view to making the executors responsible to make good the deficiency. I think, therefore, that the equitable rule I have referred to would have been very properly invoked. It is inequitable and unjust that the legatee should recover the full amount of his legacy whilst he retains in his hands a sum to which the other legatees may be driven to resort for payment, or be driven to the still more unfair course of making the executors personally responsible.

I repeat that so long as the legatee was content to rely simply on the incomplete release given by the will itself, there would be no means of enforcing payment except by an ordinary action; but whenever he takes active steps to compel a release by the executors they have a right to say, bring in that portion of the assets which you have in your hands, and which we require properly to discharge our duties, and we will grant you the release.

Whilst placing my decision on this ground, it must not be supposed that I acquiesce in the view that this is a specific legacy, in fact some of the reasoning on which I have come to this conclusion would be inapplicable if it were. A debt forgiven is regarded with great reason in the light of a general legacy, and like other legacies not to be sanctioned by the executors in case the estate be insufficient for all the claims upon it. The mere circumstance that the debt is secured or is referred to as being secured cannot, in my opinion, alter the matter. It is very different from a bequest to A. of a debt due to the testator by B.; that is just as much a specific bequest as a bequest of "my diamond ring," but being in the nature of a general legacy, and liable to all the incidents of a general legacy, I think the executors were justified in refusing their assent so long as any debts or legacies remained unsatisfied.

I think, with great submission, that the findings of the master were right, and should not have been overruled, and this appeal should be allowed.

PATTERSON, J.A.—The principal question in this appeal is, whether the executors are entitled to refuse to release William Severn's mortgage until he pays the amount of his promissory notes.

A good deal of the argument on this question has been addressed to the character of the benefit taken by William under the trust to cancel and entirely release his indebtedness to the testator upon and by virtue of his mortgage for

$17,000, or thereabouts, such release to operate and take effect immediately on and from the decease of the testator ; the question debated being whether this is a specific legacy or a general legacy of $17,000.

The question is somewhat embarrassing. The inclination of my mind is towards treating the legacy as specific, but I do not see the necessity for settling the question.

The simple state of the facts is, that at the death of the testator his son William owed him two debts, or debts which we may for our present purpose speak of as two, namely, the mortgage debt of $17,000, and the promissory note debt of three or four thousand. The duty of the executors was to release the mortgage debt, and to collect the other debt, and that was their duty, whether the release of the mortgage debt is called a specific legacy, or a general legacy.

I do not understand that there is a deficiency of assets, or any question of abatement among the legatees. No facts suggesting any such question are to be gathered from the evidence brought before us on this appeal ; and the executors not having to pay money to William, the doctrines touching retainer have no application.

The effect of the bequest would, under the circumstances, be to extinguish the debt ; and the direction to release the debt, if it is understood to require any action by the executors, was probably superfluous. The idea may have been to direct the executors, to whom the mortgaged premises were devised, to release the mortgage or reconvey the legal estate ; but whether the release of the debt was to be effected by the direct operation of the bequest, or by some act of the executors, it was to date from the decease of the testator. At that date the debt ceased to exist and the security was satisfied.

The executors refuse to release the mortgage until the promissory note debt is paid. They took that position, as we learn from the evidence of the executors themselves as well as from that of William Severn, a long time ago, apparently within the first year after the decease of the testator. George Severn, who took the leading part in the administration of the estate, and who insisted on refusing the release when his co-executor Mr. Booth appears to have been willing to give it in connection with an arrange-ment proposed by William, but to which George did not accede, seems to have had a very proper idea of the impor-tance of bringing the dispute to an issue in some way. I gather that from what he tells us of a conversation with his solicitor; and one cannot help seeing, from the present litigation, how correctly he judged of the importance of moving in good time.

What he insisted on when [William applied for the release, and what is contended for now, is, in effect, though not put forward in that ostensible form, the right to tack to this satisfied security a simple contract debt which never was a lien on the mortgaged property. This carries the doctrine of tacking to a length which no authority has been produced to justify. See *Fisher* on Mortgages, 3rd ed., 616, citing *Challis* v. *Casborn*, Pre. Ch. 407, and other cases; 1 *Story's* Equity Jurisprudence, sec. 418, citing *Powis* v. *Corbit*, 3 Atk. 556, and other cases: and see *McLaren* v. *Fraser*, 17 Gr. 533, and *Ferguson* v. *Frontenac*, 21 Gr. 188, where Spragge, C., says: "The law is now set-tled that for subsequent advances the mortgagee has no equity to charge the land mortgaged merely because he held a mortgage for money advanced."

The other question is the right of William Severn to set up the Statute of Limitations in answer to the demand for payment of two of the promissory notes. It was held in the Court below that he had the right, for reasons in which I concur, and which I do not think have been displaced by anything urged on this appeal.

Another matter which was made a formal subject of appeal was, I think, not pressed on the argument before us. It was an order referring the accounts back to the master with liberty to the defendants, other than George and William Severn, to prosecute their surcharge against the executors in regard to the amount of the indebtedness of William Severn to the estate.

That was an order with which this Court could not interfere.

I agree that the appeal should be dismissed, and that it should be dismissed, with costs.

OSLER, J. A.—I agree with Mr. Justice Proudfoot. I think that clause K 2 of the will must be read as isolated from and independent of clause H. (*a*) It is to me impossible to suppose that the testator can have intended that the mortgage in question should be gotten in by the executors and form part of the trust fund referred to in clauses H. K. (*b*.)

I think the legacy a specific one, and that it is immaterial that it is to the debtor himself. The bequest of the thing so identified to a third party would undoubtedly be specific, and its incidents, when made to the debtor, are similar. If not to be described as a specific legacy, it probably amounts to an extinguishment or release of the debt.

I agree that the Statute of Limitations is not affected by the action as regards the notes of Wm. Severn.

It follows that the appeal should be dismissed.

Appeal dismissed, with costs.

[BURTON, J. A., dissenting.]

(*a*) By clause H. all the other real and personal estates of the testator at his decease were devised to the executors and trustees upon trust to sell and convert into money in their discretion, and until sale such estates were declared to be subject to the trusts in the said will contained, concerning the money to arise therefrom, and the real estate was to be considered as converted in equity.

(*b*) For clause K., see judgment of HAGARTY, C. J. O., ante p. 274.

SEYMOUR v. LYNCH, ET AL.

Indenture—Short forms of Leases Act—Construction—Lease or license.

By an indenture expressed to be under the " Short Forms of Leases Act,"
in which the parties were designated " Lessor " and " Lessees," and
wherein it was expressed that the lessor did "give, grant, demise, and
lease unto the said lessees, their successors or assigns, the *exclusive* right
* *   of entering at all times   * *   during the term of ten years
* *   in and upon that certain tract * * consisting of * *   reserving that portion thereof occupied or thereafter to be occupied as a
roadway,   *   *   *   and with agents to search for, dig, excavate, mine,
and carry away the iron ores in, upon or under said premises ; and of
making all necessary roads," etc.

The lessees amongst other provisions were to have the right to use any
timber found on the premises for the purpose of carrying on their operations, and on the termination of the lease they were to deliver up possession to the lessor, who covenanted for quiet enjoyment by the lessees.

The lessees covenanted that they would not allow any manufacture or
traffic in intoxicating drinks on the premises, nor carry on any business
that might be deemed a nuisance thereon.

On an interpleader to try whether the plaintiff (the lessor) had a right to
claim $2,500, being a year's rent, as against the defendants, who were
execution creditors of the parties designated lessees in the indenture,
PATTERSON, J.A., before whom the trial took place without a jury, gave
judgment in favor of the defendants, on the ground that the instrument was a license merely and not a lease ; On a motion made to
the Queen's Bench Division this judgment was reversed, and an appeal
to this Court, owing to an equal division of the Judges, was dismissed
with costs.

Per HAGARTY, C. J. O., and BURTON, J. A., the instrument was a license.
Per OSLER, J. A., and FERGUSON, J., it was a lease.

THIS was an appeal by the plaintiff from the judgment
of the Queen's Bench Division reported 7 O. R. 471, and
came on for hearing before this Court on the 12th of
of January, 1887.*

Northrup, for the appellant.

Clute, for the respondent.

The facts are fully stated in the report in the Court
below and in the present judgments.

March 1, 1887. BURTON, J. A.—I am unable to agree
with the Court below in the construction placed by them
upon the instrument under which the question in this case
arises.

The deed does not in terms purport to grant the land or
the minerals, but is on the contrary confined to granting
" the exclusive right, liberty, and privilege of entering at
all times during the term of ten years" on a certain 100 acres

Present.—HAGARTY, C. J. O., BURTON, PATTERSON, and OSLER, JJ.A.

"of land" with an exception which I shall presently refer to, "and with agents, laborers, and teams to search for, dig, excavate, move, and carry away the iron ores in, upon, or under the said premises, and of making all necessary roads for ingress and egress to, over, and across the same to any public roads or places of shipment."

Some of my learned brothers appear to be of opinion that if the words "and with servants," &c., were omitted so that the grant would read "the exclusive right of entering to search," it would be a license only, but the introduction of the word "and" indicates that the intention of the grantors was first to give the exclusive right of entry, or, in other words, the exclusive possession of the land, coupled with the additional right of mining. I admit there is a good deal of force in that contention, but, upon the best consideration I have been able to give the matter, I am of opinion that the utmost extent to which that argument can be pushed, is, that an ambiguity arises in the granting part of the deed, and that the rest of the instrument may be looked at for the purpose of ascertaining whether the enlarged meaning is to be given to it, or whether, taking the whole together, it is to be regarded as a mere exclusive privilege of entering for the purpose of mining, and not as a demise of the land itself.

The words which immediately follow, so far from extending the effect of the grant, would seem to be quite unnecessary if the soil itself were granted. They are,

"Also the right, liberty, and privilege to erect on the said premises the buildings, machinery, and dwelling houses required in the business of mining and shipping the said iron ores, and to deposit on said premises all refuse material taken out in mining said ores. The said parties of the second part to do no unnecessary damage to said premises, and at the termination of this indenture, and for three months thereafter, as well as during its continuance, the said parties of the second part, their successors and assigns are to have the right to take down and remove their erections before named and to take away ores mined, and to use such timber as may be found on the premises as may be required in carrying on mining operations, and such use of the surface as may be needed for all other purposes appertaining thereto."

I assume that the liberty granted is an exclusive one, so as to debar even the grantor from exercising the right of taking the ore during the term; but that does not necessarily give the licensee any estate or interest in the soil, or, before actual digging, in the minerals authorized to be dug.

It is true the owner or the tenant of the surface holds it subject to this easement or right of the licensee to enter at all times for the purpose of digging and searching for ore, and to having his crops interfered with by the working of the mines; but I am unable to agree with the Court below that the language used indicates an intention on the part of the grantor to divest himself of the possessson of the land, although I fully concede that any form of words, which, (when properly construed with the aid of all that is legitimately admissible to aid in the construction of a written document) indicates an intention to grant a lease will operate as a lease,

The case of *Roads* v. *The Overseers of Trumpington*, L. R. 6 Q. B. 56, does not, in my opinion, at all conflict with this view. The question there arose as to whether a party was liable to be rated to the relief of the poor as the occupier of land; and it was shewn not only that he was in occupation, but that the peculiar business in which he was engaged, rendered an exclusive occupation of the surface necessary, as the whole had to be removed in order to get the coprolites, and then to restore it to its original state.

In *Doe Hanley* v. *Wood*, 2 B. & Ald. 724, where the instrument to be construed was held to be a license it was contended that the words, " the land hereby granted," " the ground and premises hereby granted," and " the land or ground hereby granted," which occurred in many of the clauses of that instrument shewed an intent on the part of the grantor to divest himself of the possession for a time.

and to vest it in another, but the Court held that they could have no further effect than to shew that the grantor who used them supposed that the soil or minerals and not a mere liberty or privilege passed by his deed ; and if the words used in the granting part of the deed were of doubtful import and would bear the construction for which the plaintiff there contended, such doubtful words of grant, aided by the others shewing the intent, might be sufficient to pass the land or soil or minerals themselves, but were not sufficient to vary the construction that must be given to the granting part of the deed as those words were in themselves alone plain and not of doubtful import.

The exception of the land reserved for the railway does not to my mind assist the construction that this was a lease : that having been reserved for the railway, the right to dig on the portion so reserved was of necessity excluded, and was as essential in the case of a mere license as in the case of a lease.

I have already said that the express power to erect buildings and to cut timber rather militates against the view that this was intended as a lease when the power would exist without any express authority, and inasmuch as the licensee had power to erect buildings, it deprives the covenant against using them for the manufacture or sale of intoxicating liquor of any special significance.

The answer as to the insertion of a clause for re-entry is to be found in the judgment of C. J. Abbott in the case I have already referred to as not less applicable to a license than to a lease.

The covenant or warranty to secure the rights and privileges thereby granted is, I admit, consistent with either view, whilst the previous portion of this covenant for quiet possession, and that the grantor is the lawful owner of the premises, is as much required in the case of a license as a lease.

Perhaps under these circumstances, the question, not being free from doubt, it may be said this Court should not interfere with the conclusion arrived at in the divisional

Court ; and if the effect of my individual opinion were to reverse that decision, I should hesitate before delivering this judgment, notwithstanding that that principle of dealing with an intermediate judgment, has been considerably weakened by some recent decisions here.

As, however, I agree with the Judge of first instance, and the result of our decision is, to leave the judgment, which reverses him, untouched, I think it better to state my opinion, which is, that the judgment of the learned Judge at the trial was correct, and ought to be restored.

HAGARTY, C. J. O.—After very full consideration, I agree with the judgment just pronounced. The canon of construction cited from *Bacon's* Abridgement by my learned brother Armour, is of undoubted authority, but its application to this case involves, as it were, a begging of the whole question.

I do not think that there are words here shewing the intention that the " one shall divest himself of the possession and the other come into it."

Some stress seems to be laid on the form of the grant ; that there is first a demise and lease of an exclusive right. to enter at all times for the ten years on the lot, *and* with agents and labourers to search for and excavate, &c., the iron ore ; the latter being thus, as it were, in addition to the exclusive right of entry. But the construction of the whole sentence seems to me to point the other way. After the " and with agents," &c., comes the words. "*and of* making all necessary roads," &c. This is only intelligible by the former grant of the exclusive right and privilege, which has to be carried through all the things allowed— the right and privilege of exclusive entry for the purposes named, the right of searching and digging for ore, " and of" making necessary roads, &c.

The clause as to the limited use of the surface and other provisions as to making buildings and houses required for mining purposes, and to the use of timber for such purposes, all point, as I read them, to the conclusion arrived at by the trial Judge. Covenants to pay taxes, to deliver peaceable possession, and a clause for re-entry, do not affect the legal character of the instrument: *Doe Hanley* v. *Wood*, 2 B. & Ald. 740. See, also, *London and North Western R. W. Co.* v. *Buckmaster*, (in error) L. R. 10 Q. B. at p. 447, where the provision for delivering up possession afforded no inference that an actual demise was intended, as it would be as suitable to a lodger as to a tenant. In *Jones* v. *Reynolds*, 4 A. & E. 808, Lord Denman, after noticing that in *Doe Hanley* it was decided that ejectment would not lie being only a license or permission, added, " but it does not seem to follow that the permission actually demised and actually exercised would not be a hereditament enjoyed by the lessee." The Court held that an action for use and occupation would lie. In *Davis* v. *Shepherd* L. R. 1 Ch. 415, Lord Cranworth says : " In the case of a demise of unworked minerals there can hardly be said to be actual possession of any part of them except of what the intended lessee is actually working, but I think that when the lessor allows his intended lessee to take possession and the lessee does take possession and commences working accordingly, he must be considered as constructively in possession of all which the lessor had bound himself to demise."

That case arose on an agreement for a demise of minerals : *Davis* v. *Treharne*, 6 App. Cas. 460; *Smith* v. *Darby*, L. R. 7 Q. B. 722, may be referred to as shewing the nature of actual leases of minerals.

The general question is discussed in *MacSwinney's* Law of Mines, 1884, 251, 252, 253, at p. 253 it is stated that an exclusive licensee may recover possession against any person who ousts him and maintains trespass for encroachment on his workings Several cases from 2 Wilson downwards are cited to support this : *ib.*, 254, s. 5, 6, 7 ; *Collyer* on Mines, p. 11.

Doe Hanley v. *Wood*, is the most important case on the main question. It seems to be very well and fully considered by Lord Tenterden. The Court of King's Bench as then constituted was probably one of the strongest if not the very strongest of which we have any knowledge, and I need hardly say that its considered judgment is of formidable strength.

I do not find its authority on the main point of the decision has ever been questioned beyond the expression of opinion (as in *Roads* v. *Trumpington*, L. R. 6 Q. B. 56, by Blackburn, J., p. 62), the grantee might perhaps have had a right to bring ejectment for mines within the limits of his workings."

But *Doe Hanley* v. *Wood*, is hardly open to the charge of being questioned even as to this, for at p. 737, Lord Tenterden shews that a party who should have actually opened and worked, and was in actual possession of a mine might, if ousted, maintain an ejectment.

He very fully meets the argument, based on the use of various expressions in the deed which it was contended, shewed that there was an actual demise. They will be found in full at pp. 739, 40, 41.

In our case there is granted, demised, and leased the exclusive right, liberty, and privilege of entering at all times during the named term upon the land to search for, excavate, and carry away the iron ores.

The word "lease," several times used, means, in my opinion, merely a lease of certain privileges. The licensee is allowed "such use of the surface as may be needed for all other purposes appertaining thereto;" that is, to his enjoyment of the privileges granted. These words are most significant.

I do not see why, conceding the existence of an exclusive right to the iron ore, the grantor could not have made a lease the next day of the lot to any tenant, whose user of it would, of course, be subservient to the full enjoyment by the licensee of his mining privileges.

There are a great many mining cases in the books, both where only a license is given, and where there is a direct demise of the minerals.

Much stress is laid on *Roads* v. *Trumpington.* It must be borne in mind that it was a rating case, and the whole question was, whether the appellants had the exclusive occupation of the five acres for which they were rated.

A careful examination of the facts will shew that under the agreement, as explained by the process of working, the appellants had the right to enter and exclusively occupy from time to time certain portions : to do the work they had to remove the surface soil, and where the coprolites were they had to replace it properly, and yield up possession to the tenant of the whole property. During such occupation the tenant was allowed £3 rent per acre for every acre dug by the appellants. The entire acreage was 293 acres, and the tenant's assessment was reduced by five acres—the quantity held for actual working by appellants. The rate was struck for the years in which they had this actual and exclusive occupation.

The agreement was very special, secs. 2, 5, and 6, may be referred to with the statement of the facts and mode of working.

I am of opinion that as against an execution there was no right in the plaintiff respondent to be paid a rent under the statute.

OSLER, J. A.—The question in this case is, whether the instrument relied on by the plaintiff operates as a lease or merely as a license to excavate or dig and search for iron ore.

The former appears to me to be the proper legal construction and that which was contemplated by the parties. I need hardly say that I do not for a moment impugn the authority of *Doe Hanley* v. *Wood*, 2 B. & Ald. 739, which the appellants so strongly relied on, or attempt to argue against the reasoning upon which the instrument in question there was held to be a license, and not a lease. On the contrary, when the difference between it and the one with which we are now dealing is considered, I think that most of that reasoning applies quite as forcibly to shew that the latter is a lease, as it does to shew that the former was a license. It was a deed by which one Thomas Carlyon granted to Hanley, " his partners, fellow-adventurers, executors, administrators, and assigns * * free liberty and license power and authority to dig, work, mine, and search

for" tin-ore and other minerals in certain lands of the
grantor.

There it was said, as it was said here, and as must be
admitted, that in order to make a demise, or pass such
an interest in soil as would support an ejectment, formal
words were not necessary, and that words importing an
intent in the grantor to divest himself of the premises
for a time and vest it in another, would operate in law
as a lease, whatever might be their form. There were
no such words in the granting part of the deed, but it
was argued that words shewing such intent appeared in
different clauses and covenants of the deed, such as, "the
land being granted," or "the land and ground hereby
granted;" and in particular a clause of re-entry was relied
on.

Abbott, C. J., after pointing out that the instrument,
though inaccurate, was a regular formal deed, containing
all the formal or ordinary parts of a deed of conveyance,
(and *inter alia*) the premises, or granting part, one of the
proper offices of which is, as stated by Lord Coke, to
comprehend the certainty of the tenements to be conveyed, says:

"The argument rests upon the particular expressions
used in the deed, and not upon the nature or quality of
the clauses or provisions in which they are used. These
expressions may probably be attributed to want of care
or caution in the preparation of the deed; but supposing
them not to be attributable to inadvertency, still they
can have no further effect than to shew that the grantor
who used them supposed that the soil or minerals, and
not a mere liberty or privilege passed by his deed; and
if the words used in the granting part of the deed were
of doubtful import, and would bear the construction for
which the plaintiff contends, such doubtful words of grant,
aided by others, shewing the interest, might be sufficient
to pass the land and support an action of ejectment.
But, whatever doubt these expressions may cast, yet we
think they are not sufficient to vary the construction that
must be given to the words of the granting part of the
deed, as those words are in themselves alone, plain and not
of doubtful import; and as the proper office of that part of

the deed is to denote what the premises or things are that
are granted, and is the place where the intent of the
grantor and what he has actually done in that respect, is
more particularly to be looked for, recourse must be had to
the proper and efficient part of the deed to see whether
he has actually granted what it is urged that his expressions denote that he supposed he had granted, for the
question properly is, not what he supposed he had done,
but what he really has done by his grant."

Now, to-apply this passage to the present case, we have
here, as in the case from which it is taken, a formal deed
containing the formal or orderly parts of a deed of conveyance, but with this important distinction, that there are
words in the granting part larger and of more extensive
import than those found in the deed which the court
were there considering ; and which are alone sufficient
according to the canon of construction, quoted from *Bacon's*
Abridgment, *Lease* K., to create a presently vested right to
enter and take possession of the land itself from the
future period therein named as the commencement of the
term.   These words are, " doth give, grant, *demise,* and
lease unto the said parties of the second part, their successors and assigns, the *exclusive* right, liberty, and privilege of *entering* at all times during the term of ten years
from the first January, 1879, in and upon the west-half
of lot 11, containing 100 acres : reserving that portion
thereof occupied or to be occupied as a roadway by the
Belleville and North Hastings Railway."

That is the first part of the grant, and as is said by the
Court below, its language excludes any right of entry by the
lessor, and indicates his intention to divest himself of the
possession of the land.   Then the granting part proceeds :

" And   *   *   to search for, dig, excavate, mine, and
carry away the iron ores, in, upon, or under the said premises."

This, although no doubt the principal object of the
grant, is cumulative and additional to what has been
already granted by the previous words, and cannot, as I
respectfully submit, be made use of to cut down the
exclusive right of entry on the premises to a mere exclu-

sive license to enter thereon for the single purpose of
searching for ores. The rights and privileges conferred
by these words, and the subsequent provisions of the
same clause as to making roads, erecting and removing
buildings required for mining purposes, depositing refuse,
and use of the surface, while they are all consistent with
the instrument, being what the parties themselves call it,
a lease, confer, except as to erecting and removing buildings, additional rights, which, as lessees merely, the parties
of the second part would not possess.

As, therefore, we do find in the granting part of this
instrument, terms in themselves sufficient to constitute a
demise or grant of the soil, the judgment may well be supported upon the construction properly attributable to these
terms alone, looking at the way in which the parties
have chosen to frame the clause, and giving to each part
of it its full significance; and the more so because from
the general scope of the instrument, we might have expected to find some clause or provision saving the rights
of the grantor in respect of the soil, if it had been
intended to reserve any such, or to give no more than a
mere license to mine. But if it be said that inasmuch as
the technical words usually employed to denote a demise
of the soil are wanting, those which are used, though
capable of the construction contended for, are yet of
doubtful meaning, then, according to the authority already
quoted, other clauses and expressions in the deed may be
invoked in aid of that construction. The instrument is
expressed to be made in pursuance of the Act respecting
Short Forms of Leases, and the parties more than once
speak of it as a lease, and describe themselves as lessor
and lessees. The covenants of the lessees are strong to
shew the exclusive nature of the possession of the " premises" in, and upon which the exclusive right of entering at all times during the term, has been " demised."

These premises plainly are the parcel of land described as
the west-half of lot 11, and upon that parcel, that is
to say, upon the whole of it, the lessees covenant that

they *will not allow* any manufacture or traffic in any intoxicating drinks, and will not carry on any business that may be deemed a nuisance during the term of the lease. There is nothing to limit the operation of these covenants to the particular part of the 100 acres in which, at any given time, the lessees may be exploring. They apply generally and in terms to the whole, and they seem as Mr. Justice Armour says, wholly inconsistent with the idea of a mere license and of the lessor continuing in possession of the land subject to the right of search.

The clauses for delivering up of possession of, and for re-entry " upon the said premises" in case of non-performance of covenants, also aid the plaintiff's construction, (though I do lay so much stress upon them,) upon the principle already alluded to ; and the clause of warranty at the end, is not inconsistent with it, and found in company with a covenant for quiet possession of the premises, may well be regarded as having been inserted for the sake of greater caution.

I refer to 4 *Cruise*, Tit. 32, ch. 7, sec. 3 ; *Morgan* v. *Powell*, 7 M. & G. 980 ; *Jones* v. *Williams*, 4 A. & E. 805 ; *Funk* v. *Haldeman*, 53 Pa. State, 229 ; *Carr* v. *Burns*, L. R. 3 Ch. 525 ; *Chetham* v. *Williamson*, 4 East, 469.

I think the judgment should be affirmed.

FERGUSON, J.—As was stated by counsel on each side at the argument, (and as appears) the only question for determination is, as to whether the instrument dated the 12th November, 1878, and made between the plaintiff of the first part, and Pusey and Humphreys of the second part is a lease or a mere license. This document states that the party of the first part doth give, grant, demise, and lease unto the parties of the second part, the exclusive right, liberty, and privilege of entering at all times for ten years from the first day of January, 1879, upon the tract of land mentioned, the same being 100 acres more or less, (reserving the portion thereof occupied, or to be occupied, by a railway company) and with agents, labourers, and teams to search for, dig, excavate, mine, and carry away the iron

ores in, upon or under the said premises, and of making
all necessary roads for ingress and egress to, over, and
across the same to public roads or places of shipment.
Also, the right, liberty, and privilege to erect buildings,
machinery, and dwelling-houses required in the business
of mining and shipping the ores, and to deposit on the
premises the refuse material, taken out in mining the
ores; the parties of the second part to do no unnecessary
damage to the premises, and at the determination of the
indenture, and for three months thereafter, as well as during its continuance, to have the right to take down and
remove the erections and take away any ores mined, and to
use such timber as might be found on the premises as might
be required for carrying on mining operations, and to have
such use of the surface as might be needed for all other
purposes appertaining thereto.

Then follows the consideration to be paid, and the
way and manner in which the payment was or is to
take place.   Then the document provides that the parties
of the second part shall pay the taxes and perform the
statute labour assessed upon the premises; and that they
will not allow any manufacture or traffic in intoxicating
drinks on the premises, nor carry on any business that may
be deemed a nuisance thereon.

There is then a provision whereby the parties of the
second part may, on the happening of certain events, and
giving thirty days notice, and paying all arrears of
royalties, determine the lease; and that the party of the
first part shall have quiet and peaceable possession of the
premises.

There is then a provision whereby the parties of the
second part are, upon the determination of the lease, to fill
up or protect any holes they may have made in mining or
exploring for ores; and that upon default for thirty days in
respect of the obligations of the parties of the second
part, the party of the first part shall have the right of
" re-entrance" upon the premises, and that the lease shall
determine and become null and void.   Then the party of

the first part covenants for quiet possession, that he is
the lawful owner, and that he will warrant, secure, and
forever defend the parties of the second part, *"in the
rights and privileges herein granted them,"* from all and
every other person or persons whatsoever.

The parties to this document chose to call it a lease,
and it is drawn professedly in pursuance of the Act
respecting Short Forms of Leases.

In *Woodfall* on Landlord and Tenant, 12th ed., at p.
115, it is said:

" A lease for years is a contract for the exclusive possession of lands or tenements for some certain number of
years or other determinate period. An instrument is not
a demise or lease, though it contain the usual words of
demise, if its contents, shew that such was not the intention of the parties."

Apart from the words of the granting part of the deed,
there are contained in the document some provisions and
stipulations which, I think, would strongly favor the
view that what was meant by the parties to it was not a
lease of the land, but only the right or privilege of mining
upon the land upon certain terms and conditions for
and during the period of time mentioned in the instrument. Apart from the granting part, there are also
provisions, I think, favoring the view that what was meant
was a lease of the land, and some provisions that are in
this respect indifferent.

In the case of *Doe Hanley* v. *Wood*, 2 B. & Ald., [referred
to, and apparently much relied on] where the learned Chief
Justice in delivering the opinion of the Court, when speaking
of expressions appearing in the deed, apart from the words of
the granting clause, said (p. 740): " If the words used in
the granting part of the deed were of doubtful import and
would bear the construction for which the lessor of the
plaintiff contends, such doubtful words of grant, aided by
the others showing the intent, might be sufficient to pass
the land or soil, or the minerals themselves, and to support an action of ejectment. But whatever doubt these
expressions may cast, yet we think they are not sufficient

to vary the construction that must be given to the words
of the granting part of the deed, as these words are in
themselves alone plain and not of doubtful import, and as
the proper office of that part of the deed is to denote what
the premises or things are that are granted, and is the
place where the intent of the grantor and what he has
actually done in that respect are more particularly to be
looked for, recourse must be had to the proper and efficient part of the deed to see whether he has actually
granted what it is urged his expressions denote that he
supposed he had granted, for the question is not what he
supposed he had done, but what he really has done by his
grant."

In that case it was decided that the deed did not amount
to a lease, but only a license to dig and search for minerals.   The granting words were : "granted unto * *
free liberty, license, power and authority to. dig, mine and
search for tin ore, &c., and all other metals and minerals
whatsoever throughout all that part of the lands," &c
which I think differ much from the granting words in the
deed in the present case, in which the grant is a grant of
the exclusive right, liberty and privilege of entering at all
times for and during the period of ten years in and upon
the land, and with agents, laborers and teams to search
for, &c. If the words of the granting part had stopped
immediately before the words " and with agents," &c., the
grant would have been simply a grant of the exclusive
right of entry upon the land during the. term or period
mentioned. This would have been the equivalent of a
grant of the exclusive right of possession, which, according
to the authorities referred to by Chief Justice Wilson,
would be a lease of the land. A lease of the land would
not authorize the lessee to mine upon the lands unless
the mines had been opened. Saunders' Case, 3 Coke part
5, 12 a, referred to by Chief Justice Wilson, as in 5 Rep.
12 a.

I apprehend it is not doubted that a grant of the exclusive right of entry upon lands for a specified term, is the
equivalent of a grant of the exclusive right of occupation
or possession of the lands for the same term, or that such
a grant having full effect given to it would be a demise of
the land for the term.

In the present case I think there is such a grant in very plain words. Words that I think would be entirely unmistakable if the granting words stopped at the place that I have before mentioned. Then what follows ?

" And with agents, laborers, and teams, to search for, dig, excavate, mine, and carry away the iron ore in, upon, or under the said premises."

Is this additional to the grant that precedes it, or does it lessen the force or meaning of the grant, or does it create any doubt as to the meaning of it ? I think it is additional to it and according to *Saunders's Case* it was necessary in order to entitle the grantee to mine upon the lands, assuming that the mines were not open at the date of the deed, and I do not see how this addition creates any doubt as to the meaning. I think the real meaning of the granting part of the document is, that it made a lease of the lands for the term mentioned in it, and in addition thereto it granted the described right and liberty of mining upon the lands during the same term. I think this is the meaning of the granting part of the document, and that the words employed are not of doubtful import, and I think they will not bear the construction contended for, namely, a grant of a mere license. Being of this opinion, I think the other provisions contained in the deed cannot properly be employed for the purpose of shewing what was intended; for, as said by Chief Justice Abbott, in *Doe Hanley* v. *Wood,* the question is not what the grantor supposed he had done, but what he really had done by his grant.

If I could perceive that the words employed in the granting part of this deed were of a doubtful meaning, were capable of having two meanings attached to them, and would bear the construction contended for by the appellant so that other parts of the deed could properly be looked at for the purpose of ascertaining or aiding in ascertaining what the meaning really is, I should be of the opinion that these other parts of the deed contain more that to me indicate that what was intended was a mere license than that it was a lease; but I think I need not here discuss such other provisions of the deed, as my opinion is based upon what plainly appears to me, that the character of the grant, as shewn in the granting part of the deed, is unmistakable, and that its meaning is as I have stated it to be.

I am of the opinion that the document is a lease of the land with the addition of a license (such as described in the deed) to mine upon the lands, and I do not think that any of the authorities that were referred to or that I have seen shew that this deed can have any other effect.

I think the judgment should be affirmed.

The Court being equally divided, the appeal was dismissed with costs.

[The case was subsequently carried to the Supreme Court, where also there was an equal division of the members of the Court.]

A DIGEST

OF

ALL THE REPORTED CASES

DECIDED IN

THE COURT OF APPEAL,

CONTAINED IN THIS VOLUME.

APPEAL, RIGHT OF.

See PRACTICE, 1 — DISTRICT COURTS, 1, 2.

ARBITRATION.

In the conduct of arbitrations the rule is inflexible that the arbitrators must be scrupulously guarded against any possible charge of unfair dealing towards either party; therefore where one of the parties to a reference, who had been examined as a witness, after the evidence had been closed and the matter argued, sent by mail his affidavit explaining some portion of his evidence, to the arbitrator, but which was not received by him until after he had written out the view in accordance with which he subsequently made his award; the Court affirmed the judgment of the Court below setting aside the award. *Race* v. *Anderson et. al.,* 213.

ASSIGNMENT FOR BENEFIT OF CREDITORS.

See BANKRUPTCY AND INSOLVENCY.

BANKRUPTCY AND INSOLVENCY.

The mere fact that a creditor has disputed the validity of an assignment made by his debtor for the general benefit of creditors, is no ground for the assignee refusing to pay him a dividend out of the money realised from the estate; the assignment having been sustained in the action brought by the creditor to impeach it.

The law on this question under assignments for the benefit of credi-tors prior to 22 Vict. ch. 96, and the cases thereunder, considered.

Decision of the Queen's Bench Division, 10 O. R. 415, reversed. *Klœpfer* v. *Gardner,* 60.

[Affirmed by the]Supreme Court.]

BAWDY HOUSE,

CONVICTION FOR KEEPING.

See VAGRANT ACT, 2.

BILL OF EXCHANGE.

The plaintiff at the request of Y., the business manager of the Hamilton Cotton Company, received from him a draft in the name of the company on a New York firm for $4,989.65, at three months, which plaintiff discounted at the Toronto agency of the defendants, and in pursuance of an arrangement to that effect, Y. drew on the plaintiff in the name of the Cotton Company, payable to their own order for $4,800, which plaintiff paid on presentment out of the proceeds of the New York draft. About seven weeks afterwards plaintiff discovered that the signatures to, and indorsements on both these drafts had been forged by Y., and immediately communicated such information to the defendants, and demanded from them a return of the amount paid by him to retire the $4,800 draft which was refused. Plaintiff, however, paid the draft on New York at maturity.

In an action brought to recover the money paid to retire the $4,800 draft, the Queen's Bench Division held that the plaintiff was entitled to recover: An appeal from this judgment was dismissed, the Judges of

this Court being equally divided.
Ryan v. The Bank of Montreal, 533.

[After perfecting the bonds required to carry the case to the Privy Council the action was settled between the parties, the defendants paying a sum about equal to the claim, without costs.]

BONUS TO RAILWAY.

See MUNICIPAL CORPORATION, 2.

BREACH OF CONTRACT.

See SALE OF GOODS, &c.

BY-LAW.

See MUNICIPAL CORPORATION.—
RAILWAYS, 1.

CASES.

Abouloff v. *Oppenheimer*, 10 Q. B. D. 297, discussed.—See FOREIGN JUDGMENT, &c.

Booth v. *Alcock*, L. R. 8 Ch. 663, distinguished.—*See* LIGHT, 1.

Campbell v. *Davidson*, 19 U. C. R. 222, followed. — *See* COUNTY COURT, 1—PLEADING.

Cunningham v. *Dunn*, 8 C. P. D. 443, applied and followed.—*See* CONTRACT.

Canada Atlantic v. *Ottawa*, 12 A. R. 234 ; 12 S. C. R. 377, followed.—*See* MUNICIPAL CORPORATION.

Doe Hennessey v. *Meyers*, 2 O. S. 424, observed upon.—*See* ESTOPPEL BY DEED.

Doe Irvine v. *Webster*, 2 U. C. R. 234, observed upon.—*See* ESTOPPEL BY DEED.

King v. *Davenport*, 4 Q. B. D. 402 distinguished.—*See* DISTRICT COURT.

Lawlor v. *Lawlor*, 10 S. C. R. 194, distinguished.—*See* LIGHT, 1.

Lawrence v. *Faux*, 2 F. & F. 435, distinguished.—*See* LANDLORD AND TENANT.

Mead v. *Creary*, 8 P. R. 274 ; 32 C. P. 1, affirmed.—*See* DIVISION COURTS.

Mitchell v. *Vandusen*, *ante* p. 517, followed.—*See* COSTS IN DISCRETION OF COURT.

Parsons v. *Standard Ins. Co.*, 43 U. C. R. 603 ; 4 A. R. 326 ; 5 S. C. R. 233, followed.—*See* FIRE INSURANCE, 2.

Price v. *Cataraqui Bridge Co.*, 35 U. C. R. 314, considered.—*See* NEGLIGENCE.

Regina v. *Arscott*, 9 O. R. 541, not followed.—*See* VAGRANT ACT, 2.

Sherwood v. *Hamilton*, 38 U. C. R. 410, considered.—*See* NEGLIGENCE.

Toms v. *Whitby*, 37 U. C. R., 104 considered.—*See* NEGLIGENCE.

Ward v. *Pilley*, 5 Q. B. D. 427, followed.—*See* PRACTICE, 2.

Whistler v. *Hancock*, 3 Q.B.D., 83, distinguished.—*See* DISTRICT COURT.

CASTING VOTE OF CLERK.

See MUNICIPAL CORPORATION, 2.

CERTIFICATE OF ENGINEER.

See RAILWAYS, 1.

CHANGE OF TENANTS.

See LANDLORD AND TENANT.

CHATTEL MORTGAGE.

A chattel mortgage conveyed to the plaintiff the stock in trade of the mortgagor, which purported to be enumerated in a schedule (A.) and was described as being on certain named premises. The schedule after setting out the goods proceeded : "And all goods * * which at any time may be owned by the said mortgagor and kept in the said store for sale * * and whether now in stock or hereafter to be purchased and placed in stock."

Held, [affirming the judgment of the County Court of York] that after-acquired stock brought into the business in the ordinary course thereof, became subject to the chattel mortgage as against execution creditors of the mortgagor, notwithstanding that their writs were in the hands of the sheriff at the time such stock was brought into the business ; the equitable right of the mortgagee under such agreement attaching immediately on the goods reaching the premises. *Coyne* v. *Lee*, 503.

COMMISSION TO AGENT.

See PRINCIPAL AND AGENT.

COMMITMENT, WARRANT OF.

See JUSTICE OF THE PEACE, 2—VAGRANT ACT, 2.

COMPENSATION.

See MUNICIPAL CORPORATION.

——, FOR LANDS TAKEN.

See NIAGARA FALLS PARK, 2.— WILL, 1.

CONDITIONAL ACCEPTANCE.

See PRINCIPAL AND AGENT.

CONDITIONAL OFFER.

See ESTOPPEL BY DEED.

CONTEMPT OF COURT.

The decision of PROUDFOOT, J., 11 O. R. 633, finding that the solicitor for the respondent in a quo warranto proceeding had committed a contempt of Court by reason of having written a letter which he published in a newspaper commenting upon a decision of the Master in Chambers, and directing the solicitor to pay costs to the applicant, the relator in the proceeding, was affirmed.—[BURTON, J. A., dissenting.]

Per BURTON J. A.—As it appeared that the ground on which the application was based, viz., prejudice to the applicant's case had ceased to exist at the time the application was heard, the proper course would have been to dismiss it so far as the applicant was concerned. The Court might on its own motion have punished the contempt shewn to its officer, even though the quo warranto proceedings were not still pending, but that course was not adopted ; the learned Judge proceeded solely on the ground that the applicant had a locus standi, and gave him the costs of the application ; and the appeal should therefore be allowed. *Regina* v. *Howland*, 184.

CONTRACT.

Where an executory contract is entered into respecting property or goods, if the subject-matter be destroyed by the act of God or *vis major*, over which neither party has any control, and without either party's default, the parties are relieved. *Mc-Kenna* v. *McNamee*, 339.

The defendants who had a contract with the Government of British Columbia for the performance of a public work, but had forfeited it, after a part of the work had been done, agreed with the plaintiffs that the latter should do the remainder of the work under the contract and should receive ninety per cent. of the amount of every estimate issued till the completion of the work. The written instrument embodying the agreement referred to the contract as an existing one, but the fact was, as was fully shewn by all the parties, that at the time of making the agreement the contract had been forfeited, and the Government had taken possession of the works. No advantage was taken by the defendants; the plaintiffs had examined the contract with the Government, and understood as well as the defendants the exact position of affairs; but all trusted to the possession of certain influence by which they hoped to get back the contract, and resume work upon it.

Held, affirming the judgment of the Q. B. D., that the failure to obtain a restoration of the contract destroyed the whole consideration for each party's agreement or undertaking.

Cunningham v. *Dunn*, 8 C. P. D. 443, applied and followed. *Ib.*

[Affirmed by the Supreme Court.]

CONVERSION OF GOODS.

Held, [reversing the judgment of the C. P. D.] that the defendant was not liable for a conversion of the goods in question, by reason of his having joined in a bill of sale of them, and having accepted and assigned a mortgage for the balance of purchase money thereof; no other act of interference with the property on his part being shewn, they never having been in his possession or control, and he never having had the power to deliver up or retain them so as to make a demand upon and refusal by him, evidence of a conversion; he having acted in such sale of the goods as the agent, and by the authority of another only.

The plaintiff J. I. D. could not maintain an action for the conversion of the property in question; for assuming that it was the property of those under whom he claimed, which was one of the matters in controversy, it did not become vested in him until after the alleged conversion; neither could J. D. maintain the action, he never having had the actual possession of the property, but a mere right as receiver appointed by the Court to obtain the custody if it belonged to those whom he represented, which would not support the action, though it might form the ground of a special application to the court for a mandamus or attachment or other appropriate relief. *Dickey* v. *McCaul*, 166.

_____

CONVICTION.

See JUSTICE OF THE PEACE— VAGRANT ACT.

COSTS.

See JUSTICE OF THE PEACE, 2.

————

———— IN DISCRETION OF COURT.

1. An action by the bailiff of one Division Court against the bailiff of another Division Court to recover the proceeds of goods seized and sold by the latter, such goods being at the time of such seizure and sale already under seizure by the plaintiff upon executions in his hands against the execution debtor, was tried before the Judge of a County Court, without a jury, who held that the plaintiff was entitled to recover, but, under the circumstances, deprived the plaintiff of his costs, and ordered that the defendant's costs of the action and the costs of the seizure and sale should be deducted from the amount of the judgment. On appeal from such exercise of discretion, this Court reversed the decision of the learned Judge, and ordered judgment to be entered for the plaintiff with costs.

HAGARTY, C. J. O., reserved his opinion as to the existence of any right in any Judge to make a defendant pay the costs of a plaintiff who has failed to establish a right to recover, or to make a plaintiff who substantially proved his right to recover, pay the costs of the defendant.

Per PATTERSON, J. A.—Rule 428 gives full discretion over the apportionment of costs, and in proper cases to deprive the successful party of costs, but does not extend to make any party, whether plaintiff or defendant who is wholly successful in his action or defence, pay his defeated opponent's costs.

Per OSLER, J. A.—The jurisdiction in question is one which existed in the old Court of Chancery, though the circumstances in which it was exercised, were of a special and unusual character. *Mitchell* v. *Vandusen*, 517.

2. In an action for libel the jury found that the defendant was guilty of libelling, but that the plaintiff had sustained no damage. The trial Judge dismissed the action, but ordered the defendant to pay the plaintiff's costs, and gave the latter judgment therefor. The defendant thereupon moved in the Divisional Court against the judgment for costs, which that Court varied by ordering the action to be dismissed with costs, and the plaintiff having appealed to this Court from the judgment at the trial, dismissing the action, as also from the judgment of the Divisional Court.

Held, that although rule 428, gives to the Judge or Court the power of depriving any of the parties to an action, plaintiff or defendant, of their costs, it does not confer the power of compelling a successful party to pay the costs of an unsuccessful party: *Mitchell* v. *Vandusen*, *ante*, p. 517, considered, approved, and followed.

Held, also, allowing the appeal of the plaintiff from the judgment at the trial, that a venire de novo should be awarded: [PATTERSON, J. A., dissenting from such direction.]

Per HAGARTY, C. J. O., and GALT, J.—No Court has or ought to have the right ex proprio motu to direct judgment for nominal damages where a jury has refused to award them.

Per OSLER, J. A.—Nominal damages should not be added, unless it clearly appear that such damages are a mere matter of form, or that the omission to find them was ac-

-cidental, or unintentional, or an over-sight following a distinct intention to find the plaintiff's cause of action proved.

Per PATTERSON, J. A.—The jury having left no fact undetermined, the plaintiff was entitled to judgment, which might properly be -entered for nominal damages with full costs. *Wills* v. *Carman,* 656,

———

———, SECURITY FOR.

On the 5th Nov., 1885, an order was made requiring the plaintiff to give security for costs within four weeks and in default that the action should be dismissed with costs, unless the Court or Judge on special application for that purpose should otherwise order. Within the four weeks the plaintiff obtained a summons, with a stay of proceedings, for "further time to perfect security for costs," and on the 10th Dec., 1885, an order was made extending the time till the 23rd Dec. 1885, but not providing that the dismissal of the action should be the result of non-compliance with its terms. Security was not furnished within the time so extended, and it was contended that after that the action was dead, and there was no jurisdiction to make an order in it.

Held, that the action never became dismissed under either of these orders, and that a motion to dismiss was regular and necessary. *Whistler* v. *Hancock,* 3 Q. B. D. 83; *King* v. *Davenport,* 4 Q. B. D. 402, distinguished. *Bank of Minnesota* v. *Page,* 347.

———

COUNTY COURT.

1. In an action of trespass for pulling down fences and for mesne profits the plaintiff alleged his title

at the time from which he claimed to recover mesne profits; and the defendant in his statement of defence, denied that he committed any of the wrongs in the plaintiff's statement of claim mentioned, and denied that he was liable in damages or otherwise on the alleged causes of action.

Held, that on these pleadings the title to land was expressly brought in question, and the jurisdiction of the County Court ousted.

Held also, that the defendant was not estopped from raising the question of jurisdiction at the trial, because of his omission to file an affidavit under R. S. O. ch. 43, sec. 28, that his pleading was not vexatious, or for the mere purpose of excluding jurisdiction; such an omission being a mere irregularity for which the plea might have been set aside, but not operating to confer jurisdiction where the defence in fact raised the question of title. *Campbell* v. *Davidson,* 19 U. C. R. 222, followed. *Seabrook* v. *Young,* 97.

2. The statement of claim presented a cause of action within the jurisdiction, and the defendant could not have demurred; it depended upon his pleading whether the jurisdiction would be ousted, and therefore Rule 189 did not apply to prevent the raising of the question of jurisdiction at the trial. *Ib.*

———

COURT, INTERFERENCE BY.

See VERDICT OF JURY.

———

COVENANT TO BUILD FENCES.

See LEASE.

DAMAGES.

See COSTS IN DISCRETION OF COURT, 2—REPLEVIN.

DEED, CONSTRUCTION OF.

See LEASE.

DEFAMATION.

See LIBEL.

D EFENCE.

See FOREIGN JUDGMENT, &c.

DELAY.

See BILL OF EXCHANGE.

DEPOSIT ON SALE.

See SALE OF GOODS, &c.

DESTRUCTION OF SUBJECT MATTER OF CONTRACT.

See CONTRACT.

DETERMINATION OF LEASE.

See LANDLORD AND TENANT 2.

DISCHARGE OF MORTGAGE [EFFECT OF].

See LIGHT, 1.

—— VOID.

See MORTGAGE, &c.

DISMISSAL OF ACTION.

See COSTS, SECURITY FOR.

DISMISSAL OF TEACHER.

See PUBLIC SCHOOL.

DISTRICT COURTS.

1. There is an appeal to the Court of Appeal from the judgments of the District Courts of the Provisional Judicial Districts. Section 34 of R. S. O. c. 90 imports that when by the law in force with regard to County Courts an appeal lies from those Courts to the Court of Appeal, it lies also from the District Courts. *Bank of Minnesota* v. *Page*, 347.

2. 47 Vict. c. 14, s. 4 (O.), assumes the existence of the right of appeal from District Courts; and the optional right to move against the verdict in the High Court, provided by sub-sec. 5, is not the appeal referred to in the first part of the section, in the words "subject to appeal." *Ib.*

DIVISION COURTS.

The judgment of the Queen's Bench Div. (11 O. R. 138) refusing to order prohibition to a Division Court, was affirmed on appeal on the ground that the defendants were liable to repair the road in question, which was not a public road "vested as a Provincial work in Her Majesty or in any public department or board," and that the title to land was not brought in question : but

Held, (disagreeing with the Court below, and affirming *Mead* v. *Creary*, 8 P. R. 374, 32 C. P. 1), that the notice under 48 Vict. ch. 14, sec. 1, amending 43 Vict. ch. 8, sec. 14, disputing the jurisdiction, is only required when a suit otherwise of the proper competence of the Division Court has been brought in the wrong division, and the want of such notice cannot give the Division Court jurisdiction if the title to land is brought in question. HAGARTY, C. J. O., expressing no opinion on this point. *Re Knight* v. *Medora and Wood*, 112.

DRAINAGE.

See MUNICIPAL CORPORATION, 1.

DRAWBRIDGE.

See MUNICIPAL CORPORATION, 3.

DRINKING TO EXCESS.

See LIQUOR LICENCE ACT.

EASEMENT.

See LIGHT.

EJECTMENT.

It was contended that the defendant was estopped from disputing the plaintiff's title by his admissions and by reason of the plaintiff having recovered a judgment in ejectment against the defendant's tenants ; but the plaintiff's claim was for damages for pulling down fences and for mesne profits for a period of five or six months prior to the date of the ejectment, and the admission of title did not go further back than the ejectment.

Held, that the judgment against the tenants was evidence against the defendant, at the date of the writ of ejectment, but that title was really in question, and necessary to be proved in respect of the period for which mesne profits were claimed prior to the ejectment. *Seabrook* v. *Young*, 97.

EQUALITY OF VOTES.

See MUNICIPAL CORPORATION, 2.

ESTOPPEL.

See BANKRUPTCY AND INSOLVENCY —COUNTY COURT, 1—BILL OF EXCHANGE—LANDLORD AND TENANT.

———, BY DEED.

McM., in building a house, by mistake built part of it on the land of the adjoining owner B. On discovering this he applied to B. with a view of purchasing a portion of B.'s lot, and B. on 29th July, 1880, wrote : " I hereby offer to sell you twenty-five feet frontage for the sum of $250, to be paid six months from this date, otherwise this offer to be null " * *. and B. accepted such offer at the foot in the words, " I hereby accept the above offer." McM. seven days after registered a plan as No. 327, alleged to be of his own property, but which included the 25 feet as part of lot M., and the next day executed a mortgage on lot

M. with a description, which included the 25 feet, and which was assigned to the defendants the O. S. Co. B.'s offer to sell to McM. was not acted on within the six months limited, and B. afterwards, in January, 1883, sold and conveyed the 25 feet (which was called lot 40 on his [B.'s] plan No. 396, registered 26th January, 1883,) to McM. for $400, payable $100 cash and mortgage for $300, and which mortgage was at the instance of B. taken to his daughter N., the plaintiff. The O. S. Co. subsequently sold under the power of sale in their mortgage to the defendant W.

In an action by N. to realise her mortgage, it was

Held, [reversing the judgment of PROUDFOOT, J.,] that the original dealing between B. and McM. created no binding contract on the latter, it being merely an option given him; and he not having completed the purchase within six months the subsequent sale and conveyance by B. to McM. was upon a new and distinct contract. No interest in the 25 feet [lot 40] passed to the O. S. Co. under McM.'s mortgage, and the subsequent conveyance to him fed the estoppel created by his prior mortgage to the extent only of McM.'s interest which was that of owner of the equity of redemption, or owner of the 25 feet (lot 40) charged with $300, and it made no difference that the $300 mortgage was taken to the plaintiff instead of to B., the effect of the whole transaction being that W. was the owner of lot 40 subject to a first mortgage of $300 in favor of the plaintiff and to a second mortgage of the O. S. Co.

B. having by his dealing with McM. created in him the status of owner, and in the plaintiff that of

mortgagee, was not, nor was the plaintiff in a position to complain of the registration of plan 327.

Doe Irvine v. *Webster*, 2 U. C. R. 234 ; *Doe Hennessey* v. *Meyers*, 2 O. S. 424, observed upon. *Nevitt* v. *McMurray*, 126.

EVIDENCE.

See ARBITRATION—EJECTMENT—LEASE—LIBEL—LIFE INSURANCE, 1 — RAILWAYS, 2, 3. — VERDICT OF JURY.

EXECUTIONS.

See FRAUDULENT CONVEYANCE.

EXECUTORS.

Moneys bequeathed directly to infant legatees and which had been invested by the defendants, the executors of the testatrix, were demanded of and received from them by one F., a solicitor who had obtained from the Surrogate Court his appointment as guardian of the infants. F. subsequently misapplied the moneys and absconded.

Held, [reversing the judgment of FERGUSON, J., HAGARTY, C. J. O., dissenting,] that the defendants were not liable. *Huggins* v. *Law, et al.*, 383.

———, RIGHT OF, TO INSIST ON PAYMENT OF OTHER CLAIMS AGAINST MORTGAGOR TO WHOM MORTGAGE BEQUEATHED.

See WILL, 2.

EXECUTOR AND TRUSTEE.

See MORTGAGE, &c.

EXPERT EVIDENCE.

See LIBEL.

EXPRESS OR IMPLIED GRANT.

See LIGHT, 1, 2.

EXPROPRIATION.

See NIAGARA FALLS PARK.

FELLOW SERVANT,

[NEGLIGENCE OF.]

See MASTER AND SERVANT.

FENCES, COVENANT TO BUILD.

See LEASE.

FINDINGS OF JURY.

See LIGHT, 2—SALE OF GOODS, &C.—VERDICT OF JURY.

FINDINGS OF REFEREE.

See VERDICT OF JURY.

FIRE INSURANCE.

1. The plaintiff applied to the agent of the defendant company whose head office was in London, England, to insure a house which was described as a building two-stories high and built of *burds*, which was written and intended by the agent for the word "boards." On the back of the application was a diagram of the building which was marked in black, the color in which all frame buildings were required to be shewn. The house was destroyed by fire during the currency of the policy issued by the head office, which was for a brick house, the general manager swearing that he had read the application as being in respect of a brick house, the premium charged being that charged on a brick while one-half per cent. more would have been charged on a wooden building. The agent, however, swore that he considered a solid board house (that is one with the boards laid flat on each other, in this case being six inches wide) was a safer risk than a brick house, and he fixed the premium rate at one and one-half per cent., and it was admitted that he had authority to do so.

The company having refused payment of the insurance, an action was commenced to recover the amount after a lapse of more than thirty days from completion of the proofs of loss but less than sixty days thereafter which, by a variation and addition to the statutory conditions, indorsed on the policy was stipulated for.

After action the company, under the 16th statutory condition, demanded an arbitration as to the value of the premises destroyed, the result of which was an award finding the value to have been $2,500, and the loss payable to the plaintiff $1,700; while the jury at the trial of the action found that the plaintiff had truly represented the property as having been worth $3,500, and estimated his loss at that amount.

Held, [affirming the judgment of the Court below, 11 O. R. 38] that there having been no misrepresentation on the plaintiff's part, no mutual mistake, and the defendants not having proved that they granted the policy in consequence of any mistake on their part, the parties were *ad idem* and the plaintiff was entitled to judgment for the amount of the award.

Held, also, that the stipulation that no action should be brought until the expiry of sixty days after proof of loss was not a just or reasonable variation of the statutory conditions.

Per BURTON, J. A.—The words of the 17th statutory condition being that the loss should not be payable until 30 days after completion of the proofs of loss created a privilege in favor of the companies, and the statute does not contemplate any further extension, but simply that the company shall be entitled to that delay unless under their charter or by agreement that period is shortened. *Smith* v. *The City of London Ins. Co.*, 328.

[Affirmed by the Supreme Court, March, 1888.]

2. The plaintiff being owner of a quantity of railway ties and lumber, effected insurances thereon with three companies to the amount of $4,000 and subsequently, with the knowledge and through the agency of H., the person acting on behalf of the several companies, effected an additional insurance of $1,200 on the same property in "The Fire Insurance Association." H. acted as agent for that company also, and he made the necessary entries thereof on the three first policies. In consequence of "The Fire Insurance Association" having ceased to take risks on that kind of property, H. asked the plaintiff for the interim receipt of that company which he gave up accordingly, and H. substituted one in the Gore District Company for it, he being agent for that company also, but omitted to give any notice or make any entry as to the substitution of the Gore insurance for that of "The Fire Insurance Association."

In an action to recover the amount of the insurances, after a destruction of the property by fire:

Held, [affirming the judgment of the Court below] that this was not such an omission on the part of the plaintiff as invalidated the policies, in this following; *Parsons* v. *The Standard Ins. Co.*, 43 U. C. R. 603 : 4 A. R. 326 ; 5 S. C. R. 233; *Moore* v. *The Citizens Fire Insurance Company; Moore* v. *The Quebec Fire Insurance Company; Moore* v. *The British America Assurance Cmopany, and Moore* v. *The Gore District Mutual Fire Insurance Company*, 582.

3. In effecting insurances in all to the amount of $5,200, the plaintiff represented the property as being of "the cash value" of $5,339 on two occasions, and $5,500 on a third occasion. In an action on the policies the jury found that the value was $4,000 when first insured, and $4,200 when the additional insurance was effected ; that the plaintiff had misrepresented the value, but not intentionally or wilfully.; that it was not material that the true value should be made known to the company, and that the company intended that the goods should be insured to their full value and rendered a verdict in favor of the plaintiff for $3,100, which the Divisional Court subsequently refused to set aside.

Held, [in this reversing the judgment of the Court below] that under the circumstances and in view of the nature of the goods insured, the over-valuation was such, as under the first statutory condition in the policy, rendered the same void. *Ib.*

FOREIGN JUDGMENT, ACTION ON.

In an action upon a foreign judgment the defence was that the same had been recovered by reason of the plaintiff fraudulently misleading the Court at the trial by swearing to what he knew to be untrue. The matter in dispute was a claim for extra services in hauling logs for a greater distance than required by a written contract, and the contest was upon the question whether the services were or not within the terms of that contract. On this question the evidence of the plaintiff and of one of the defendants, and of other witnesses, was given at the trial in the foreign court, when the contract and certain letters were put in, and the judge's charge to the jury shewed that the whole evidence had been clearly brought to the attention of the court, and it was now sought to establish the falsehood of the plaintiff's evidence with regard to the claim for extra services.

Held, [affirming the judgment of the Common Pleas Division, BURTON, J. A., dissenting] that evidence under the defence was properly rejected at the trial; for what the defendants proposed to do was to try over again the very question which was in issue in the original action. The charge of fraud was superadded, but that charge involved the assertion that a falsehood was knowingly stated, and before the question of scienter was reached a conclusion of fact adverse to that which had been arrived at by the foreign jury would have to be adopted.

Per BURTON, J. A.—In admitting evidence under the defence the Court would not be assuming to re-try the issues disposed of in the foreign Court. The finding upon those issues being conclusive, cannot be questioned here; but it can be shown that the decision arrived at was obtained by fraud practised upon the foreign Court, and that right cannot be defeated, because, in order to establish it, it becomes necessary to go into the same evidence as was used on the former trial to sustain or defeat that issue. The issues are not the same, for if the facts now discovered could have been shewn at the former trial they would have secured a different result.

The authority of decisions of the English Court of Appeal, and the case of *Abouloff* v. *Oppenheimer*, 10 Q. B. D. 297, discussed. *Woodruff* v. *McLennan*, 242.

FORFEITURE.

See WILL 1.

FORM OF NOTICE.

See LIQUOR LICENCE ACT.

FRANCHISE, EXPROPRIATION OF.

See NIAGARA FALLS PARK, 1.

FRAUD.

See FOREIGN JUDGMENT, &c.

FRAUDULENT CONVEYANCE.

The plaintiffs sold to C. their stock in trade in a country store which he had managed for them as their agent ; and took a chattel mortgage thereon as security for the purchase money. The mortgage also included sundry other chattels the property of C. At the time of the sale and mortgage there were executions in the sheriff's hands at the suit of the defendants by which these latter goods were bound. The Judge of the County Court found that they had been included in the mortgage in order to defeat or delay an expected execution against C. at the suit of S. who was no party to the proceedings and had made no claim.

Held, affirming the judgment of the County Court [OSLER, J. A., dissenting], that the acceptance by the plaintiffs of a mortgage on goods which they knew belonged to C. though already bound by the defendants' executions, with knowledge of the judgment recovered by S. against C., rendered the whole transaction fraudulent and void against creditors, so that the stock in trade sold by the plaintiffs to C. became subject to the defendants' executions.

Per OSLER, J. A.—The sale and mortgage back of the stock in trade being parts of the same transaction the executions bound only the interest of C. therein, and were subject to the mortgage for the purchase money. The mortgage of the other goods could not affect the executions which had all along bound them, and therefore was not fraudulent against the defendants, the only creditors who were complaining of it.

The issue might have been found distributively, and the plaintiffs could either recover their own goods under the mortgage title as against the executions, or equitably, as impressed with a trust to secure the purchase money, which was paramount to any claim under the executions. *Cameron et al.* v. *Perrin et al.,* 565.

FRAUDULENT PREFERENCE.

See FRAUDULENT CONVEYANCE.

GUARDIAN, PAYMENT OF INFANTS' MONEY TO.

See EXECUTORS.

HABEAS CORPUS ACT.

See VAGRANT ACT.

IMPROVEMENTS, PAYMENT FOR.

See MORTGAGE.

INFANT'S GUARDIAN, POWERS OF.

See EXECUTORS.

INJUNCTION.

See TRADE MARK.

INJURY TO LAND.

See MUNICIPAL CORPORATION.

INTERFERENCE BY COURT.

See VERDICT OF JURY.

INTERPLEADER, TRIAL OF ISSUE BY CONSENT.

See PRACTICE, 1.

INTERVENTION OF MASTER.

See MASTER AND SERVANT.

INTOXICATING LIQUORS.

See LIQUOR LICENCE ACT.

IRREGULARITY.

See JUSTICE OF THE PEACE, 2.

JUDICATURE ACT.

[RULES 128, 146, 147, 148, 189, 240.]

See PLEADING.

JUDGE, DUTY OF.

See MALICIOUS ARREST.

——, JURISDICTION OF.

See PRACTICE, 2.

JUDGMENT.

See FOREIGN JUDGMENT.

JUDGMENT IN EJECTMENT.

[EFFECT OF AS EVIDENCE.]

See EJECTMENT.

97—VOL XIV. A.R.

JUDGMENT, ORDER FOR LEAVE TO SIGN.

1. An order for leave to sign judgment under Rule 80 is in its nature final and not merely interlocutory, and therefore such an order if made in a county Court would be appealable by virtue of 45 Vict. c. 6, s. 4 (O.), and is also appealable when made in a District Court. *Bank of Minnesota* v. *Page*, 347.

2. Leave to sign judgment under Rule 80 should not be granted save where the case is clear and free from doubt, and under the circumstances of this case an order for such leave, made by the Judge of the District Court of Thunder Bay, was reversed. *Ib.*

JURISDICTION OF JUDGE.

See PRACTICE, 2.

JURY.

See RAILWAYS, 2, 3.

JUSTICE OF THE PEACE.

1. The provisions of R. S. O., ch. 73, sec. 4, protect a magistrate from an action for anything done under a conviction so long as the conviction remains in force; not where the conviction does not justify what has been done under it. *Arscott* v. *Lilley*, 283.

2. The plaintiff being in custody on a warrant issued by the defendant L. on a conviction had before him under the Vagrant Act, applied to be discharged under the Habeas Corpus Act, the plaintiff electing to remain in custody at London

to attending before the Judge in Toronto, and on the 4th of February an order was made on that application for her discharge, which order was duly received by the gaoler on the sixth. Meanwhile a fresh warrant had been issued by L. on the 4th and delivered to the gaoler, who, by direction of the County Crown Attorney, detained her for two hours after receipt of the order for her discharge, when another warrant was prepared, and she was again arrested. In an action brought for such arrest and imprisonment for two hours, the jury found the plaintiff was entitled to a verdict, but that she had not sustained any damages which the trial judge treated as a verdict for the defendants, but refused the justice his costs (11 O. R. 285). On appeal to this Court the dismissal of the action was affirmed, but

Held, reversing the judgment of the Court below, that sec. 19 of R. S. O., ch. 73, has not been repealed by any of the provisions of the Ontario Judicature Act ; and therefore the dismissal of the action should be with costs to the magistrate, as between solicitor and client.

Held, also, that the plaintiff could not object to the appeal as irregular, on the ground that, having been begun by both defendants, it was continued by only one.

Per OSLER, J. A. If there was anything in the objection, it should have been taken by way of substantive motion to strike out the appeal for irregularity. *Ib.*

LANDS INJURIOUSLY AFFECTED.

See NIAGARA FALLS PARK, 2.

LANDLORD AND TENANT.

1. The plaintiffs by their agent, in June 1881, verbally leased to S. & W. for three years certain premises in which the latter carried on business in partnership for about a year when W. sold out his interest to one D. who in partnership with S. carried on the same business for about ten months when S. withdrew from the partnership and sold out his interest to D. who agreed with S. to pay all rent then due or to become due in respect of the premises which he continued to occupy and pay rent for. The plaintiffs without authority drew for a quarter's rent on S. & D. who refused to accept; and a fire having occurred on the premises the plaintiffs expended the insurance money in repairs with D.'s consent. Default having been made of six months' rent due on 15th December, 1883, the plaintiffs instituted proceedings against S. & W. for the recovery thereof :

Held, [reversing the judgment of the Court below] that although the plaintiffs were cognizant of the several changes in the partnership and the occupation by D. of the premises, these acts were not evidence of a surrender in law, and that they were not estopped from enforcing payment of the overdue rent against S. & W.

PATTERSON, J. A., *dubitante.* *Gault* v. *Shepard*, 203.

The doctrine of surrender by act and operation of law applies as well to a term created by deed as to one created by parol.

Lawrence v. *Faux*, 2 F. & F. 435, distinguished. *Ib.*

2. The plaintiff by deed of 30th December, 1882, created a term for ten years, which became vested in the defendants, of " all the mines of

ores of iron and iron stone, as well opened as not opened, which can, shall, or may be wrought, dug, found out, or discovered within, upon, or under ten acres square of the north half of lot number 12 in the 6th concession of Madoc " : Yielding and paying $1 per gross ton of the said iron stone or ore for every ton mined and raised from the land and mine, payable quarterly on the 1st days of March, June, September, and December, in each year. The lessees covenanted to dig up, &c., not less than 2,000 tons the first year and not less than 5,000 tons in every subsequent year, and " pay quarterly the sum of $1 per ton for the quantity agreed to be taken during each year : " * * And if the same should exceed the quantity actually taken, such excess to be applied towards payment of the first quarter thereafter in which more than the stipulated quantity should be taken: " Provided, that if the iron ore or iron stone shall be exhausted and not to be found or obtained there, by proper and reasonable effort, in paying quantities, then the parties of the second part shall be at liberty to determine this lease."

The defendants entered and proceeded to work the mines until September (or December), 1884, when, having taken out about 300 tons, they ascertained that the ore could not be obtained in paying quantities, whereupon they notified the lessor thereof and of their desire to surrender their lease, which surrender the lessor refused to accept, and instituted proceedings to recover the amount of two quarter's rent (all prior rents having been regularly paid.) The defendants counterclaimed for the rents already paid by reason of failure of consideration.

Held, (1) that in the absence of any specified mode of surrendering the term having been provided for by the lease, the act of the defendants was a sufficient determination thereof; (2) [in this reversing the judgment of FERGUSON, J.], that the consideration for the lease had not failed, so as to bring it within the class of cases where the subject matter could be treated as as non-existent, and by the true construction of the lease the plaintiff was entitled to be paid quarterly for the quantity of ore agreed to be got out ; that the defendants were not entitled to recover back any of the rents paid, and that the lessor was entitled to judgment for such rent as accrued due between the 1st of June and the giving of the notice of surrender. *Wallbridge* v. *Gaujot,* 460.

3. M. being possessed of certain lands subject to a mortgage, made a lease thereof for a term of years to the plaintiff, which provided, amongst other things, that $15 should be expended in the first year of the term in procuring manure for the purposes of the farm. Afterwards he created a mortgage in favor of the defendant, and assigned to him this lease as collateral security. The defendant distrained for rent claimed to be due, and plaintiff replevied the goods seized, claiming there was no rent due ; and proved the payment of certain moneys to the first mortgagee, and claimed also credit for $15 a year in respect of manure furnished and expended in each year on the premises, which, at the trial, was proved to have been the true agreement between the landlord and tenant, though not so expressed in the lease, and the lease was ordered to be reformed accordingly.

Held, that the lease should not have been reformed as against defendant, he being a bonâ fide purchaser for value without notice of the facts on which the plaintiff's equity rested.

Held, also, that although a new contract of tenancy may be inferred from the fact of a notice by a mortgagee to pay rent to him, and acquiescence by the tenant by payment of the rent, still as the circumstances shewed that it was not intended to create such a contract, but rather that the interest being paid, the possession of the mortgagor and his tenants was to remain undisturbed, it could not be said that the plaintiff's tenancy had been put an end to by the intervention of the first mortgagee. *Forse* v. *Sovereen*, 482.

See also MONEY PAID, ACTION TO RECOVER.

LEASE.

1. The lease from the defendant to the plaintiff contained the usual covenant by the lessee to repair fences, &c., but the lessor agreed " *to build the line fence between the premises hereby demised and the farm of D. M., should the same be required during the currency of the lease.*"

The evidence shewed that there was no line fence between the farms, but that there was a fence upon D. M.'s land about twent-four yards south of the boundary line. The plaintiff alleged that this fence was out of order; and that the defendant would not repair it, and that in consequence damage had been done to his crops by cattle, and he contended that the stipulation as to the line fence being "required during the currency of the lease," was fulfilled

by the fence on D. M.'s land being out of repair.

Held, [affirming the judgment of the Court below] that no liability could accrue under the defendant's covenant until something occurred to disturb the state of things existing at the time the lease was made, and that the covenant was designed to meet such a contingency as D. M. refusing to allow entry on his land to repair the fence, or his requiring the line fence to be built.

Per OSLER, J. A., the language of the covenant being indefinite, evidence was properly admitted to explain it. *Houston* v. *McLaren*, 104.

2. By an indenture expressed to be under the " Short Forms of Leases Act," in which the parties were designated "lessor" and "lessees," and wherein it was expressed that the lessor did " give, grant, demise, and lease unto the said lessees, their successors or assigns, the *exclusive* right * * of entering at all times * * during the term of ten years * * in and upon that certain tract * * consisting of * * reserving that portion thereof occupied or thereafter to be occupied as a roadway, * * and with agents to search for, dig, excavate, mine, and carry away the iron ores in, upon or under said premises ; and of making all necessary roads," etc.

The lessees amongst other provisions were to have the right to use any timber found on the premises for the purpose of carrying on their operations, and on the termination of the lease they were to deliver up possession to the lessor, who covenanted for quiet enjoyment by the lessees.

The lessees covenanted that they would not allow any manufacture or traffic in intoxicating drinks on the premises, nor carry on any business that might be deemed a nuisance thereon.

On an interpleader to try whether the plaintiff (the lessor) had a right to claim $2,500 being a year's rent, as against the defendants, who were execution creditors of the parties designated lessees in the indenture, PATTERSON, J. A., before whom the trial took place without a jury, gave judgment in favor of the defendants, on the ground that the instrument was a license merely and not a lease: On a motion made to the Queen's Bench Division this judgment was reversed, and an appeal to this Court, owing to an equal division of the Judges, was dismissed, with costs.

Per HAGARTY, C. J. O., and BURTON, J. A., the instrument was a licence.

Per OSLER, J. A., and FERGUSON, J. A., it was a lease. *Seymour v. Lynch*, 738.

See also LANDLORD AND TENANT.

LEASE OR LICENSE.

See LEASE, 2.

LEASE OF MINES.

See LANDLORD AND TENANT, 2.

LEASE, REFORMATION OF.

See LANDLORD AND TENANT, 3.

LIBEL.

On the trial of an action for a libel contained in an anonymous letter circulated among members of the legal profession, charging the plaintiff with unprofessional conduct, no direct evidence was given to shew that the defendant was the author of the letter, but the plaintiff relied on several circumstances pointing to that conclusion. The Judge at the trial refused to admit some of the evidence tendered.

Held, [reversing the judgment of the C. P. D., (11 O. R. 541,)] that evidence of the defendant being in the habit of using certain uncommon expressions, which occurred in the letter, was improperly rejected : but

Semble, a witness could not be asked his opinion as to the authorship of a letter ; and

Per BURTON, and OSLER, JJ.A.— Evidence of literary style on which to found a comparison, if admissible at all, is not so otherwise than as expert evidence. *Scott v. Crerar,* 152.

LICENSE.

See LEASE.

LIFE INSURANCE.

M. applied to the defendants to effect an endowment policy on his life, and received a printed form of application containing a number of questions. Subjoined to the questions was a declaration which he signed, to the effect that the foregoing answers were true to "the best of his knowledge and belief," and that he agreed that this proposal and declaration should be the basis of the contract, and that if any misstatements or suppression of facts were made in the said answers or in those to the medical examiner the policy was to be absolutely void and all moneys received as premiums forfeited. The policy recited the above declaration as the basis of the contract. The medical examiner's report did not propound any questions to be answered by the assured. Among the questions and answers in the application were : "Have either of your * * brothers * * ever had * * pulmonary * * or any other constitutional disease ?" to which the answer was in the negative. It appeared that one brother who had died at 17 was an overgrown lad, and had spat blood several times, and that medical men whom he had consulted had apparently thought lightly of the matter. There was no evidence that he had died of pulmonary disease.

Another brother had also spat blood, but on consulting physicians they seemed to have thought there was nothing seriously wrong.

The assured was also asked whether he had "had any serious illness, local disease, or personal injury, and if so of what nature ?" The answer was, "broken leg in childhood ; confined to bed three days with a cold." It appeared the applicant was rendered permanently lame from the effects of the accident. About three years previous to his application the assured was thrown from a load of hay and sustained personal injuries for which he brought an action against the township of S. Although bruised and shaken and incapacitated from work he fully recovered. All mention of this was omitted. He was also asked as to the medical men whom he had at any time consulted, and in his answer omitted the names of those attending him during the last mentioned accident.

Held, [affirming the judgment of the Q. B. D. 11 O. R. 120,] that it was not a misdirection to leave it to the jury to say whether the answers of the assured were reasonably fair and truthful to the best of his knowledge and belief. That the applicant's declaration was in all its parts governed by the qualification "to the best of my knowledge and belief;" that the answers were not warranted to be absolutely accurate, and that there were no such misstatements or suppression of facts as would vitiate the policy.

Held, also, that the discovery of new evidence which was merely corroborative of evidence given at the former trial was no ground for a new trial. *Miller* v. *Confederation Life Insurance*, 218.

[Affirmed by the Supreme Court.]

LIGHT.

1. The plaintiff was the owner of lot 8, and the defendant of the adjacent lot (9). At the time the plaintiff's lot was conveyed to him it had a house upon it with windows looking over lot 9, which was then vacant, and was also the property of the plaintiff's grantors, subject to a mortgage.

The equity of redemption in lot 9 was afterwards conveyed to one through whom the defendant acquired title ; and G., the immediate predecessor in title of the defendant, satisfied the mortgage, and obtained and registered a discharge of it. Buildings were erected on lot 9 by the defendant and his predecessors, and the plaintiff complained of the interference by such erections with the access of light to his house on lot 8, contending for an express or implied grant of light over lot 9, and invoking the principle that a grantor cannot derogate from his grant :

Held, reversing the judgment of the Common Pleas Division (11 O.R. 331) that by payment of the mortgage and registration of the discharge G. did not acquire a new and independent estate such as would have the effect of enabling him to derogate from the grant of light, if any, made to the plaintiff by their common grantors.

Booth v. *Alcock*, L. R. 8 Ch. 663, and *Lawlor* v. *Lawlor*, 10 S. C. R. 194 distinguished.

Carter v. *Grasett*, 685.

2. The jury were asked: "Did the defendant's house interfere injuriously with the light of the plaintiff's house?" They answered, "Yes, but not injuriously."

Held, that in effect a question of law had been submitted to the jury and that the finding was too uncertain to support a judgment for the defendant.

Per OSLER, J. A., dissenting, that the finding of the jury plainly was, that the defendant's house did not interfere injuriously with the light, and had caused no substantial diminution of the light necessary for the enjoyment of the plaintiff's house. Under all the circumstances, no objection having been made on the ground of misdirection, the justice of the case did not require that a new trial should be granted.

Held, also, *per* PATTERSON, J. A., and FERGUSON, J., that there was an express grant to the plaintiff by the conveyance to him of lot 8, which was, under the "Short Forms Act," of all light used and enjoyed with the house; but *per* PATTERSON, J. A., that upon the evidence the defendant's house intercepted no light to which the plaintiff was entitled.

Per BURTON and OSLER, JJ. A., that the grant of light was an implied one, the conveyance of the house carrying with it all those incidents necessary to its enjoyment, which it was in the power of the vendors to grant; and the general words in the conveyance did not enlarge or limit the grant.

Per BURTON, J. A., that under the conveyance to him the plaintiff became entitled to the enjoyment of the right to the light from the vacant land to the same extent as enjoyed by his grantors at the time of the conveyance. *Ib.*

3. *Held*, also, *per* PATTERSON, J. A., that the conveyance to the plaintiff was, as regards lot 9, unregistered, and in the event of the plaintiff proceeding to another trial the defendant should be allowed to set up the registry laws as a defence. *Ib.*

See also NIAGARA FALLS PARK, 2.

LIMITATIONS, STATUTE OF.

See WATER AND WATERCOURSES.

LIQUOR LICENSE ACT.

In an action by a married woman against an innkeeper, under R. S. O. ch. 181, sec. 60, for having supplied liquor to her husband, after a notice, as follows : " I hereby forbid you, or any one in your house, giving my husband William Northcote any liquor of any kind from this day," * * the jury found that the husband was an habitual drunkard, and that intoxicating liquor had been furnished to him after such notice by the defendant, who knew the husband well, as also the reason for giving the notice, and rendered a verdict in favor of the plaintiff for $20.

In the following term the defendant moved to set aside that verdict, and to enter a nonsuit or grant a new trial. After argument the learned Judge ordered the verdict to be set aside and a nonsuit entered, which on appeal to this Court, by reason of an equal division of the Judges, was affirmed.

Per HAGARTY, C. J. O., and OSLER, J. A., the notice was insufficient in omitting to state that the plaintiff's husband had the habit of drinking to excess.

Per BURTON and PATTERSON, JJ. A.—The notice as given was sufficient.

Per BURTON, PATTERSON, and OSLER, JJ. A.—It was not necessary to forbid the supplying of "intoxicating liquor," the words used "liquor of any kind" being sufficient. *Northcote v. Brunker*, 364.

MALICIOUS ARREST.

1. It is not essential to the maintenance of an action for maliciously procuring a Judge's order to hold to bail, that the order for the arrest should be set aside, or that the plaintiff should procure himself to be discharged out of custody.—[BURTON, J. A., dissenting.]

Such an order if obtained regularly and on sufficient material cannot (save in very rare and exceptional cases) be rescinded or set aside on the merits. *Erickson v. Brand*, 614.

2. The defendant in his application for the order to hold to bail by his affidavit made out a primâ facie case, but certain facts and circumstances were omitted therefrom, which, it was contended, might, if stated, have satisfied the Judge granting the order,

that, although the plaintiff was about to depart from the province, it was not with *intent* to defraud, &c.

At the trial the plaintiff was nonsuited, the judge holding that he had failed to shew a want of reasonable and probable cause. The divisional court set aside the nonsuit and granted a new trial,

Held, upon the evidence, affirming the judgment, [PATTERSON, J. A., dubitante,] the facts upon which the existence of reasonable and probable cause depended being in dispute, the judge was not in a position to decide that question until the jury had found upon the facts.

Semble—*Per* PATTERSON, J. A., the evidence sufficiently shewed that there was no want of reasonable and probable cause; and that the omitted facts were not material to have been stated in the affidavit. *Ib.*

MASTER AND SERVANT.

In an action for damages by the administrators of M., an employee of the defendant company, who was killed by an explosion of defendants' powder mills, caused by a portion of the machinery being out of repair, it was shewn that W., a director of the company, had sometime before the explosion, when the works were idle, given directions to C., the superintendent and head of the works, to have the defective portions of the machinery repaired before recommencing operations, but C. neglected to attend to it, and the repairs were not made. It was not shewn that W. in any way assumed to direct the practical working of the mills, or that he had any special knowledge or ability to do so, and there was no suggestion that C. was

: an incompetent or improper person to employ.

Held, reversing the judgment of the Queen's Bench Division, 12 O. R. 58, that the intervention of W. had not taken the case out of the general rule of law, that the defendants were not responsible for an accident due to the negligence of a fellow servant. *Matthews* v. *The Hamilton Powder Co.*, 261.

————

MESNE PROFITS.

See EJECTMENT.

————

MISDESCRIPTION OF PREMISES.

See FIRE INSURANCE, 1.

————

MISJOINDER OF DEFENDANTS.

See PENALTY, 3.

————

MISSTATEMENT IN APPLICATION FOR INSURANCE.

See LIFE INSURANCE.

————

MONEY PAID, ACTION TO RECOVER BACK.

The defendants, under assumption of a lawful distress for rent, part of which was in arrear, and the other part of which was claimed in advance, entered and seized goods which had been assigned to the plaintiff B. in trust for the benefit of creditors. Three executions were shortly after placed in the sheriff's hands, and the solicitor for the plaintiffs under the first and third executions, relying upon being repaid from the proceeds of the goods, with full knowledge of all the facts, and to get the distress out of the way and let in the executions paid the rent claimed, to prevent the sale of the goods, though not admitting the defendants' right to it. The sheriff afterwards sold for less than the executions and repaid the solicitor. B. did not act under the assignment, and in no way asserted his rights against the execution creditors.

Held, [reversing the judgment of the Queen's Bench Division, 11 O.R. 735,] that the money so paid could not be recovered back either by the execution creditors on whose behalf it was paid or by B. as assignee. *Baker and The Merchants Bank* v. *Atkinson et al.*, 409.

————

MORTGAGE.

H. by his will appointed F. and W. executors and trustees of his estate. F. for the purpose of securing a debt due by him to the estate, executed a mortgage to W. W. died intestate, and F., five years subsequently having agreed to sell the mortgaged premises to M., executed a statutory discharge of the mortgage, which he expressed to do as sole surviving executor, and then conveyed the estate to M.

Held, [affirming the judgment of BOYD, C., 13 O. R. 21,] that the act of F., in executing a discharge of his own mortgage had not the effect of releasing the land.

Held, also, [in this reversing the same judgment] that M., the purchaser from F. and his assigns, were not entitled to any lien for improvements on the lands during their occupancy thereof. *Beaty* v. *Shaw et al.*, 600.

See also WILL, 2—LANDLORD AND TENANT.

___

MUNICIPAL CORPORATION.

1. The defendants enlarged a drain running through the plaintiff's land ; the earth taken from which they deposited on either side and left it there. The plaintiff sued for damages to his land, &c., by reason of such depositing of the earth. It was admitted that the work was done under a by-law, passed under sec. 576 of the Municipal Act, (1883,) and it was not suggested that the by-law was defective in any way. The jury found that the defendants were not guilty of any negligence, but that the plaintiff had suffered damage in consequence of the execution of the work.

Held, [reversing the decision of ROSE, J.,] that upon these findings judgment should have been entered for the defendants ; that a cause of action could not accrue from the doing of a lawful act, unless in a negligent manner; and that the plaintiff's remedy, if any, was by arbitration to obtain compensation under the Municipal Act of 1883, sec. 91. *Preston* v. *Corporation of Camden*, 85.

2. In 1880, (before the passing of 46 Vict. ch. 18, (O.) a municipal council, with a view of granting a bonus to a railway company, caused to be submitted to the vote of the ratepayers a by-law to raise money for that purpose. At the voting thereon the votes for and against it were equal, and the clerk of the municipality, who also acted as returning officer, verbally gave a casting vote in favor of the by-law.

Held, [reversing the judgment of the C. P. D., 11 O. R. 392] that section 152 of the Municipal Act, R. S. O., ch. 174, is not applicable to the case of voting on a by-law, and therefore the casting vote of the clerk was a nullity, and the by-law did not receive the assent of the electors of the municipality within the meaning of R. S. O., ch. 174, sec. 317; as such a defect could not be cured by promulgation of the by-law.

Per BURTON, J. A, The provisions of section 258 of the Municipal Act 1876, 36 Vict. ch. 48, do not apply to by-laws for granting bonuses to railways and the judgment of the Supreme Court of Canada in *Canada Atlantic R. W. Co.* v. *Ottawa*, 12 S. C. R. 377, does not so decide. *The Canada Atlantic R. W. Co.* v. *The Corporation of the Township of Cambridge*, 299.

[Affirmed by the Supreme Court.]

3. The defendants constructed a bridge across a navigables tream having in it a draw or swing to enable vessels to ply on the river. There was not any gate or other protection to guard the approaches to the bridge when swung. A horse belonging to the plaintiff, broke away from the person in charge of him, escaped out upon the public road and ran a distance of about two miles to the bridge, reaching it while the draw was open to allow a vessel to pass, and rushing into the gap was drowned.

Held, affirming the judgment of the court below that the defendant municipality could not be made answerable for the loss of the horse.

Toms v. *Whitby*, 37 U.C.R. 104 ; *Sherwood* v. *Hamilton*, 38 U. C. R. 410 ; *Price* v. *Cataraqui Bridge Co.*,

35 U. C. R. 314 considered. *Stein-hoff* v. *Corporation of Kent*, 12.

See also RAILWAYS, 1.

NAVIGABLE STREAM.

See WATER AND WATERCOURSES.

NEGLIGENCE.

See MASTER AND SERVANT.—MUNICIPAL CORPORATION, 3.–RAILWAYS, 2, 3.

NEW TRIAL.

See LIGHT—LIFE INSURANCE.

NIAGARA FALLS PARK.

1. The statute 48 Vict. ch. 21, (O.) does not empower the commissioners appointed thereunder to expropriate the rights of a road company or to close up any part of the road for the purposes of the Niagara Falls Park. *Re Niagara Falls Park. Fuller's Case*, 65.

2. The statute 48 Vict. ch. 21, (O.,) authorized the taking of land for the purpose of a public park, and defined land, as including "any parcel of land, stream, * * and any easement in any land." There was no express provision for compensation for lands injuriously affected, the compensation, price, or value mentioned in the Act, being only for the land taken. Fourteen acres of an estate of 33 acres owned by B. were taken for the park. The 33 acres were separated by a road from another property owned by B. and leased by him for the purposes of an hotel for a term of twenty years from February, 1881. The water supply for the hotel was, and had been for thirty years derived from springs on the fourteen acres.

The Court refused to interfere with the amount of compensation awarded, and the appeal was therefore dismissed, except as to the question of the supply of water for the hotel property. As to that, it being an easement which passed to the tenant under the lease, and being "land" within the meaning of the Act, the fourteen acres might be expropriated, leaving the easement to be enjoyed by B. as appurtenant to the hotel property; or it might be extinguished, in which case it would be a proper subject for compensation, and it not appearing upon the material before the Court whether or not this had been considered, the award was referred back to the arbitrators, but under the circumstances without costs to either party.

Per PATTERSON, J. A., although the statute made no express provision for compensating the owner for the part of his land not taken, it was fair and reasonable to add proportionately to the price of the part taken for any diminution in value of the part left when dissociated from the other; and therefore the arbitrators were right in acting upon that view in determining the amount of compensation. *Re Bush and the Commissioners of the Niagara Falls Park*, 73.

See also WILL, 1.

NOMINAL DAMAGES, POWER OF COURT TO GIVE JUDGMENT FOR.

See COSTS IN DISCRETION OF COURT, &c.

NOTICE, FORM OF.

See Liquor License Act.

NOTICE OF CHANGE OF INSURANCE.

See Fire Insurance, 2.

OBJECTION TO APPEAL.

See Justice of the Peace.

OFFER TO PURCHASE.

See Principal and Agent.

OFFER TO SELL.

See Estoppel by Deed.

OFFICIAL REFEREE, REFERENCE TO.

See Practice, 1.

OVER-VALUE.

See Fire Insurance, 3.

PARTNERSHIP.

The plaintiff and defendant purchased land on joint account for the purpose of reselling, the plaintiff having an undivided one-third share, and the defendant the remaining two-thirds. A conveyance of the lands was ultimately made to defendant, he executing a declaration of trust as to plaintiff's one-third. The defendant with seven others subsequently formed a syndicate to which he turned over his two-thirds interest at a profit.

Held, [affirming the judgment of Boyd, C., 9 O. R. 139.] that this dealing of defendant with his interest in the land had not the effect of alienating or taking away any part of the partnership estate from the purposes of that partnership, and therefore the plaintiff had no right to participate in the profit made by the defendant on the sale of his individual share. *Mitchell* v. *Gormley*, 55.

PAYMENT FOR IMPROVEMENTS.

See Mortgage, &c.

PAYMENT OF INFANTS' MONEY TO GUARDIAN.

See Executors.

PENALTY.

In an action by several plaintiffs qui tam, against two defendants for penalties for not registering their partnership under R. S. O. ch. 123, sec. 11 of which gives the right of action to "any person" who may sue.

Held, reversing the judgment of the Court below: (1) That under the above section and the Interpretation Act, two persons might be joined as plaintiffs, in a qui tam actions for the same penalty: (2) That the circumstance that the plaintiffs resided out of the jurisdiction could not defeat their action: (3) That the joinder of two defendants in one action for several penalties was not a ground of demurrer ; and

Per OSLER, J. A.—There was no inconvenience or impropriety in joining these two defendants in one action. *Chaput* v. *Robert*, 354.

PENALTY OF £500 STERLING UNDER SEC. 6 OF HABEAS CORPUS ACT.

See VAGRANT ACT.

PLEADING.

Under the system of pleading in the High Court of Justice and in County Courts under the Judicature Act, Rules 128, 146, 147, 148, 240, where a material fact is alleged in a pleading, and the pleading of the opposite party is silent with respect thereto, the fact must be considered as in issue. *Waterloo Mutual Fire Ins. Co.* v. *Robinson*, 4 O. R. 295, approved of. *Seabrook* v. *Young*, 97.

POSSESSION OF GOODS.

See CONVERSION OF GOODS.

PRACTICE.

1. In an action pending in the High Court, an interpleader issue and all subsequent proceedings were transferred under the 44 Vict. ch. 7, sec. 1 (O.) to the County Court of Middlesex. By a subsequent order made on consent, the trial of such issue was withdrawn from Middlesex, and a special case was agreed on, and the venue changed from Middlesex to York, where the special case was argued.

Held, [*Per* PATTERSON and OSLER, JJ.A.], that in strictness the appeal should be quashed. The transfer to the Middlesex County Court was final, and there was no jurisdiction under the statute or otherwise to transfer the issue or any part of it, or to change the venue to any other County Court. The proceedings in the County Court of York could therefore only be regarded as a summary trial by consent from which no appeal lay. *Coyne* v. *Lee*, 503.

2. A Judge has jurisdiction under sec. 48 O. J. A. to make a compulsory order referring not only questions of account, but also all the issues of fact in any action to an official referee. *Ward* v. *Pilley*, 5 Q. B. D. 427, followed. *Shields* v. *MacDonald*, 118.

3. The plaintiff's claim was upon a verbal agreement entitling him to one half of certain commission received by the defendant ; and his case depended on his being able to prove the agreement, and to shew that he performed the services which were to form the consideration for it ; if the plaintiff succeeded in establishing the agreement and the performance, the taking of an account would necessarily follow. The defendant filed a counter-claim, as to which there was no question that it would be proper to direct a reference either to arbitration or to an official referee. Two days after the action was commenced, the defendant's solicitor wrote suggesting that all accounts between the parties should be settled by arbitration. The plaintiff subsequently made a motion to refer to an official referee under sec. 48, and the defendant moved to refer

to a named arbitrator, or to some other arbitrator to be named by the Court. The affidavit filed in support of the defendant's motion, stated the belief of the deponent that the whole matter could be settled by a reference to an arbitrator to be appointed by the Court, who would have authority to decide as to the validity of the alleged agreement : the Court being of opinion that the real contest was as to the person to whom the reference should be made, refused to in terfere with the discretion exercised by WILSON, C. J., in referring the action to the referee, though made without the consent of the defendant. *Ib.*

[*See Knight* v. *Coales,* 19 Q. B. D. 296, C.A.]

See JUSTICE OF THE PEACE— COSTS, SECURITY FOR—JUDGMENT, ORDER FOR LEAVE TO SIGN, 1, 2 ; RAILWAYS, 2.

PRINCIPAL AND AGENT.

The plaintiff had been employed by the defendants to procure offers for the purchase or exchange of three blocks of land owned by them and he accordingly procured from one R. an offer at an estimated price of $97,000 which he submitted to the defendants, and which they, on the 10th September, 1884 accepted conditionally that R. would agree to a variation of the terms of his offer. R. being then absent from the country, the plaintiff, without any instructions, agreed on behalf of R. to the proposed variation. R. returned shortly afterwards, and on the 18th September, signed a formal ratification of the plaintiff's act, but it was not shewn that this

was ever communicated to the defendants. Meanwhile the defendants being pressed for money by a mortgagee of one of the properties had arranged a sale of that property to one S., at a price $8,000 less than it was valued at in the offer of R., part of the consideration given by S. being some of the same lands offered by R. in exchange, of which it appeared that S. and not R. had the control ; and by a subsequent arrangement the defendants' other two properties were sold to R. The defendants and S. were brought together during the negotiations arising out of R.'s offer.

Held, [reversing the judgment of the C. P. D. 11 O. R. 265,] that as between R. and the defendants, the matter had never passed beyond the stage of negotiation ; R.'s offer was not one that he could carry out, and therefore the plaintiff was not entitled to commission upon the offer of R., or alleged contract of sale made with him ; neither was he entitled to anything either on the footing of his agreement or *quantum meruit* by way of commission on the sales that were actually made. *Culverwell* v. *Birney,* 266.

PRIOR USER.

See TRADE MARK.

PROHIBITION.

See DIVISION COURTS.

PROMULGATION OF BY-LAW.

See MUNICIPAL CORPORATION, 2.

PUBLIC SCHOOL.

The right of public school trustees to dismiss for good cause a teacher engaged by them, necessarily exists from the relation of the parties. 49 Vict. ch. 49, (O. secs. 165, 168), provides a proceeding by which the status or qualification of the teacher may be determined; and the result of such proceeding may be in effect the same as dismissal; but such enactment does not deprive the employers of the inherent right to dismiss. *Raymond* v. *School Trustees of the Village of Cardinal*, 562.

PURCHASE FOR VALUE WITHOUT NOTICE.

See LANDLORD AND TENANT 3.

QUI TAM ACTION AGAINST TWO DEFENDANTS

See PENALTY.

RAILWAYS.

1. A by-law of the defendant municipality provided that upon the construction and completion for running of the E. & H. Railway from Chatham to the C. S. railway crossing by a named day, and the construction and completion within two years from the date of such by-law taking effect of the whole track and road, with stations, freight sheds, sidings, &c., at such crossing, and upon the completion of a bridge across the Thames, &c., and the complete construction of the road in other respects to the satisfaction of the Commissioner of Public Works or an engineer appointed by him; and upon the company running the said road with all necessary accommodations for the public for one week the defendants should forthwith, after the completion of the road and the running thereof for one week, within two years from the day the by-law took effect (which was on the 30th December, 1882), deliver to the E. & H. R. W. Co. debentures to the amount of $30,000. By an agreement made prior to the passing of the by-law the company covenanted with the defendants, amongst other things, to run the road when completed and to construct a station at or near the corner of Colborne and William streets in the said municipality, and in consideration thereof (and other stipulations) the defendants agreed to submit the by-law.

This action was instituted by B. as the assignee of the E. & H. R. W. Co. to compel the delivery of the debentures: and the defendants counter-claimed for damages for breach of the agreement or for a specific performance thereof.

The Commissioner of Public Works on the 1st November, 1883, appointed an engineer for the purpose of certifying as required by the by-law.

On the same day the engineer granted a certificate as to the completion of the work.

The defendants claimed the right to have the continuous user and maintenance of the station " at or near the corner of Colborne and William streets" enforced by the Court, the plaintiffs insisting that having constructed the station and used it, though only for a few days, they were not bound to continue the use thereof :

Held, [affirming the judgment of CAMERON, C. J., at the trial (OSLER,

J. A., *dubitante*)] that the certificate by the engineer of the substantial completion of the works specified in the by-law established a sufficient performance to satisfy the requirements of the by-law coupled with the fact that the road had been actually run for a week ; that the covenants in the agreement were independent, and any non-compliance with the agreement would not constitute a defence to the demand for the delivery of the debentures : But, that under the agreement and by-law the station formed part of the general undertaking, just as much as the main line of road ; and that the obligation could not be limited to the construction merely as separable from the user ; the defendants were therefore entitled to the specific performance of the contract in respect of such station, and [in this reversing CAMERON, C.J.,] there should be a reference to ascertain the damages of the defendants on their counter-claim.

Held, also, that any objections to the by-law were cured by its registration under 44 Vict. ch. 24, sec. 28, no action or suit to set it aside having been made or instituted within three months, and that the statute applied although the debentures had not been issued

Per BURTON, J. A., apart from the effect of registering under the Act, the by-law was valid. *Bickford* v. *Chatham*, 32.

[Affirmed by the Supreme Court.]

2. In an action for negligence by reason of which it was alleged that fire had escaped from a locomotive of the defendants, and the plaintiff's property was destroyed ; there was evidence that the engine had passed only a short time before fire was discovered in a manure heap, and which communicated to the destroy-ed property ; that a strong wind blew across the track towards the manure heap ; that there was no other known source from which the fire was at all likely to have come ;. that the wind was not in a direction to have caused sparks from a steam saw-mill close by to reach the premises, and that cinders were found in the straw lying on the manure heap by those who went to extinguish the fire.

Held, that from these facts there was evidence for the jury that the mischief was caused by the locomotive.

The evidence further shewed that the engine had run ninety miles without the ash-pan having been emptied ; that ignited substances were found upon the manure heap, which were too large to pass through the net of the smoke stack, and it was alleged must therefore have come from the ash-pan ; that the ash-pan was perfectly good and so constructed that it was difficult for ashes to escape from it ; and that the possibility of any escape would be prevented by emptying or partly emptying the pan.

Held, [reversing the judgment of the Court below, 11 O. R. 307,] that the jury might have found as legitimate inferences of fact that the fire escaped because the pan was full, and that that result might with reasonable care have been avoided ; that there was therefore sufficient evidence of negligence to go to the jury, and that a nonsuit was improper. *McGibbon* v. *Northern R. W. Co.*, 91.

3. In an action for damages for negligence the complaint was, that owing to want of repair, negligent construction, or management, sparks or ignited matter had escaped from

an engine of the defendants and caused a fire which had spread and destroyed fences and trees on the farms of the plaintiffs.

The evidence did not directly shew the cause of the fire, but it shewed that an engine (No. 4) had passed the place of the fire about an hour and a half before it or the smoke from it was perceived, and that another engine (No, 406) had passed about an hour and a quarter later or about a quarter of an hour before the smoke was perceived. Engine No. 4 was said to be out of order and was a wood-burner, but it was not shewn that there was any defect in No. 406, which was a coal-burner, and it was assumed at the trial that it was properly constructed and in good condition. Evidence was given, in the shape of depositions taken before the trial, of two employés of the defendants, to the effect that an engine properly constructed and in good order could not throw dangerous sparks, or sparks which would not be dead before they reached the ground; and one of them said that a greater quantity of fire would escape from a wood than from a coal burner. Two witnesses who were near at the time of the passing of the engines said that they saw no smoke or fire till after both trains had passed.

It was contended that the probabilities were very much against the fire having been caused by No. 4, although the engine was shewn to be in bad order, and that, as the case depended altogether upon inferences from circumstantial evidence, there was not a case for the jury. The case was, however, submitted to the jury, and a verdict rendered for the plaintiff.

Held, [BURTON, J. A., dissenting,]

99—VOL XIV. A.R.

affirming judgments of the Queen's Bench and Common Pleas Divisions refusing orders *nisi*, that there was evidence from which the jury might infer that engine No. 4 was the cause of the fire; it was a presumption of fact depending on the circumstances of the case, and it was for the jury to fix the weight which should be given to it.

Per BURTON, J. A. It was incumbent upon the plaintiffs to furnish evidence not only of negligence but of its connection with the loss; and this was not done by shewing that the fire broke out an hour or two after engine No. 4 passed, another engine which might have caused it having passed in the meantime, and the judge ought to have withdrawn the case from the jury upon the ground that there was no evidence of the issue which the plaintiff was bound to establish, fit for them to take into consideration. *Moxley* v. *The Canada Atlantic Railway*, 309.

[Affirmed by the Supreme Court.]

RAILWAY STATION.

See RAILWAYS, 1.

REASONABLE AND PROBABLE CAUSE.

See MALICIOUS ARREST.

RECEIVER, RIGHT TO SUE IN HIS OWN NAME.

See CONVERSION OF GOODS.

REFEREE, FINDINGS OF.

See VERDICT OF JURY.

REFORMATION OF LEASE.

See Landlord and Tenant, 3.

REGISTRATION, EFFECT OF.

See Trade Mark.

—— OF DEED.

See Light, 3.

REGISTRATION OF PLAN.

See Estoppel by Deed.

REPLEVIN.

The practice, generally, as to damages in actions of replevin is that where the goods are promptly returned, only sufficient will be given to cover the expense of preparing the replevin bond, but where the party distraining acts in a manner unnecessarily harsh or oppressive, substantial damages may be recovered. And where the sheriff was unable to replevy some of the articles mentioned in the writ, by reason of their having been lost or eloigned by the defendant, the plaintiff was held entitled to recover their value as damages. *Graham v. O'Callaghan and Russell v. O'Callaghan*, 477.

RESERVATION IN CROWN GRANT.

See Water and Watercourses.

RESCISSION.

See Contract.

RESIDENCE OF PLAINTIFFS OUT OF JURISDICTION.

See Penalty.

RIGHT TO DIVIDEND.

See Bankruptcy and Insolvency.

RIPARIAN PROPRIETOR.

See Water and Watercourses.

ROAD COMPANY.

See Niagara Falls Park.

RULES OF COURT.

See Judgment, order for leave to sign, [under Rule 80] 1, 2.

SALE OF GOODS.

On the 9th of July, 1885, the plaintiff, a cattle dealer, bought from the defendant 42 head of cattle for $2,772, and paid $200 on account, the defendant to retain the animals on his pasture until in a condition fit for the English market, for which they were to the knowledge of the defendant purchased by the plaintiff. The defendant insisting that he was bound to retain the cattle until the 20th of August only, on the 18th September, wrote to the plaintiff requiring him to "settle for the cattle and take them away before the 27th instant, or I will sell the cattle again to get my money out of them." The plaintiff not having acted upon this notice, the defendant on the 5th of October sold forty of the cattle at a loss, and refused to refund the deposit. In an action brought by the plaintiff the evidence, as to the exact terms of the contract, was contradictory, but the jury found in favor of the plaintiff's version, and gave a verdict for the full amount of deposit, which on a motion made in term, the learned judge of the County Court refused to disturb. On appeal, this Court being of opinion that the plaintiff could waive the breach of contract and simply sue for recovery of the money paid, affirmed the judgment of the Court below, with costs. *Murray* v. *Hutchison*, 489.

See also CONVERSION OF GOODS.

SALE OF LANDS.

See PRINCIPAL AND AGENT.

—— OF LIQUOR AFTER NOTICE.

See LIQUOR LICENSE ACT.

SEQUESTRATION.

See STOCK EXCHANGE.

SEVERAL INSURANCES.

See FIRE INSURANCE, 2, 3.

SHORT FORMS OF LEASE ACT.

See LEASE CR LICENSE.

SOLICITOR.

See CONTEMPT OF COURT.

SPECIAL CASE, APPEAL IN.

See PRACTICE, 2.

SPECIFIC BEQUEST OF MORTGAGE TO MORTGAGOR.

See WILL 2.

STATUTE OF LIMITATIONS.

See WATER AND WATERCOURSES. —WILL 2.

STATUTES.

31 *Char.* 2, s. 2.]—*See* VAGRANT ACT.

23 *Vict.* ch. 2, s. 35 *(C.)*]—*See* WATER AND WATER COURSES.

R. S. O. ch. 43, s. 28.]—*See* COUNTY COURT, 1.

R. S. O. ch. 73, ss. 4, 19.]—*See* JUSTICE OF THE PEACE.

R. S. O. ch. 90, s. 4.]—*See* DISTRICT COURTS.

R. S. O. ch. 123, s. 11.]—*See* PENALTY.

R. S. O. ch. 174, ss. 152, 317.]—*See* MUNICIPAL CORPORATION, 2.

R. S. O. ch. 180, s. 80.]—*See* LIQUOR LICENSE ACT.

42 *Vict.* ch. 22 *(D.)*.]—*See* TRADE MARK.

44 *Vict.*ch.7,s.1 *(O.)*.]—*See* PRACTICE, 1.

44 *Vict.* ch. 24, s. 28 *(O.)*.]—*See* RAILWAYS,

45 *Vict.* ch. 6, s. 4.]—*See* JUDGMENT &c. UNDER RULE 80.

47 *Vict.* ch. 14, s. 4 *(O.)*.]—*See* DISTRICT COURTS.

48 *Vict.* ch. 14, s. 1 *(O.)*.]—*See* DIVISION COURTS.

48 *Vict.* ch. 21 *(O.)*.]—*See* NIAGARA FALLS PARK.

O. J. A. Rule 428.]—*See* COSTS IN DISCRETION OF COURT.

STATUTORY CONDITIONS, VARIATION OF.

See FIRE INSURANCE, 1.

STOCK EXCHANGE.

The plaintiffs having recovered judgment against the defendants M. & N., both of whom were members of the Toronto Stock Exchange, each owning a seat at the board thereof, which it was considered could not be sold under *fi. fa.*, and an application was made to the Queens' Bench Division for an order to sell the seats which had been seized under a sequestration, which was refused by WILSON, C. J., whereupon the plaintiffs appealed, and on the argument it was made to appear that M. had paid off the judgment of the plaintiffs, and was carrying on the appeal for the purpose of obtaining the seat owned by N. This Court under the circumstances, and aside from the fact that the ultimate completion of title to a purchaser could only be affected by the contingent co-operation and assent of the Stock Exchange, as provided by its by-laws, affirmed the judgment appealed from without prejudice to any right M. might have to procure himself to be substituted for the plaintiffs. *London and Canadian Loan Company* v. *Morphy, et. al.* 577.

SUCCESSFUL PARTY ORDERED TO PAY COSTS.

See COSTS IN DISCRETION OF COURT.

SUPPRESSION OF FACTS.

See LIFE INSURANCE.

SURRENDER IN LAW.

See LANDLORD AND TENANT.

SURRENDER OF TERM.

See LANDLORD AND TENANT, 2.

TENANTS, CHANGE OF.

See LANDLORD AND TENANT.

TERM, SURRENDER OF.

See LANDLORD AND TENANT, 2.

TERMINATION OF LEASE BY INTERVENTION OF MORTGAGEE.

See LANDLORD AND TENANT, 3.

TITLE.

See CONVERSION OF GOODS.

——TO LAND.

See COUNTY COURT, 1.

TRADE MARK.

The fact of proprietorship or ownership is a condition precedent of the right to register a trade-mark or to obtain any advantage under the "Trade-Mark and Design Act of 1879," and registration thereunder does not create or confer such status on an unqualified person, and his right thereunder may be disallowed. *Partlo* v. *Todd*, 447.

In an action to restrain the infringement of a registered trade-mark it was shewn that the defendants had, after the registration of such mark, made use of the words "Gold Leaf," which formed an important feature of the mark, for the purpose of branding their flour, but did not represent it as made by the registrant. It was proved, however, that those words had been in common use before such registration, for a like purpose in this and the sister provinces. On appeal the Court affirmed the judgment of PROUDFOOT, J. (12 O. R. 171), refusing an injunction. BURTON. J. A., dissenting. *Ib.*

[Affirmed by the Supreme Court.]

TRESPASS.

See COUNTY COURT, 1.

TROVER.

See CONVERSION OF GOODS.

TRUSTEE, EXECUTOR AND.

See MORTGAGE.

VAGRANT ACT.

1. The plaintiff had been convicted under the Vagrant Act and sentenced and committed to the common gaol for six months, but was discharged on habeas corpus, for irregularity in the warrant of commitment, whereupon a fresh warrant on the same conviction was sued out and the plaintiff was re-committed thereon.

In an action brought to recover the penalty of £500 stg. imposed under sec. 6 of the Habeas Corpus Act (31 Ch. 2 c. 2) as having been "again imprisoned for the same offence" the Queen's Bench Division held the section did not apply and dismissed the action, with costs.

On appeal that judgment was affirmed with costs. *Arscott* v. *Lilley* 297.

2. It is not necessary to allege in the conviction of a person under the Vagrant Act as the keeper of a bawdy house, that she did not give a satisfactory account of herself ; the keeping of the house is the offence so far as the keeper is concerned.

The views of WILSON, C. J., dissenting from *Regina* v. *Arscott*, 9 O. R. 541, approved and adopted. *Arscott* v. *Lilley* (2), 283.

VARIATION OF STATUTORY CONDITIONS.

See FIRE INSURANCE, 1.

VENDOR'S LIEN.

See ESTOPPEL BY DEED.

VENIRE DE NOVO.

See COSTS, &C.

VERBAL LEASE.

See LANDLORD AND TENANT.

VERDICT OF JURY.

In an action for wages, there was a dispute as to the nature of the agreement for hiring; there was evidence at the trial which would have supported a finding for either party. The question was wholly one of fact, and of the credibility of witnesses. The jury found in favor of the plaintiff; but the Judge set it aside, and sent the case to a referee, who found substantially as the jury had done. Upon motion the Judge made an order sending the case back to the referee with instructions to find against the plaintiff on one branch of the case. *Held,* that the case was one specially proper for the decision of a jury and that neither the verdict nor the finding of the referee should have been interfered with. *Logg* v. *Ellwood,* 496.

See LIGHT, 2.

VIS MAJOR.

See WILL, 1.

VOID DISCHARGE OF MORTGAGE.

See MORTGAGE, &c.

WAIVER.

See FIRE INSURANCE.—SALE OF GOODS, &c.

WATER AND WATERCOURSES.

A water lot on the river Ottawa was granted by the Crown in 1850, to one A., the description of which covered the lot and two chains distant from the shore, reserving, however, the free use of all navigable waters found in, or under, or flowing through any part of the said lot. A. sold and conveyed the lot to P. with certain exceptions, including, however, the part covered by water; and P. in 1867 conveyed to the plaintiff part of the lot down to and bounded by the water's edge. The plaintiff had been in occupation of the premises, sold to him under a contract of purchase, for a year before the conveyance to him, and had built a dwelling house together with a floating wharf and boat house, and he carried on business there by letting out pleasure boats for hire. In an action complaining of injuries to his business and to himself as a riparian proprietor by the deposit of saw-dust and other refuse from the mills of the defendants in the water in front of his land, hindering access from his wharf to the navigable part of the river, and fouling the waters of the stream upon or in contact with his land, it was contended the plaintiff had no title as a riparian proprietor, as P. owned that portion of the water lot outside of the plaintiff, and could bar him from access to the river, and also that the reservation in the patent was repugnant to the rest of the grant, which should be read as giving the whole lot there specified. *Held,* [affirming the judgment of the Chancery Division, 11 O. R. 191, BURTON, J. A., dissenting,] that the plaintiff was entitled to recover damages for the injuries complained of. *Per* HAGARTY, C.J.O., and OSLER, J. A., the plaintiff is in the position of a riparian proprietor. He owns the land on the bank and has the same right over the water as the rest of the public. There is, however, a special injury to him, and a wrongdoer not in privity with P.

cannot be heard to raise the question of P.'s rights in order to exclude plaintiff from the water. The Crown owning the bed of the river, could grant a portion thereof, reserving the public right of user which is the effect of the reservation in the patent.

Per PATTERSON, J. A. The plaintiff is a riparian proprietor. The patent to A. granted the land without any restriction of his absolute dominion over it, and there is nothing to distinguish it from an ordinary grant of Crown lands. It was made in contemplation of the grantee occupying the land with buildings, or wharves, or otherwise at his pleasure, and so far there was, under legislative sanction, a curtailment of the *jus publicum.* The reservation of the free uses, passage and enjoyment of * * all navigable waters considered as an exception, was void as repugnant to the license.

The public right to the use of navigable waters is the right of each individual, and stands on a different footing; it does not come by grant from the Crown, but is a paramount right to be curtailed only by Act of the Legislature. A public easement cannot be the subject of an exception in favor of the grantor. If the exception were construed as perpetuating the *jus publicum,* it would be repugnant to the grant in its operation under the statute 23 Vict. ch. 2 sec. 35, and would be void. The true reading of the patent is, that the reservation touching navigable waters is applicable only to other parts of the lot, and not to the two chains of the river bed. The whole lot vested in A. free from the asserted *jus publicum,* and the plaintiff as against his grantor, P. and a fortiori as against wrongdoers, had acquired a title to the river portions under the Statute of Limitations.

Per BURTON, J. A.—The plaintiff cannot be regarded as a riparian proprietor; the person occupying that position is P., and on his filling in the lot, as he is entitled to do, to the extent of his grant the plaintiff would be entirely cut off from the stream. The plaintiff, a trespasser, cannot complain of others trespassing on portions of the property of which he is not in possession, although it may interfere with his access to the portion of which he is in possession. If the words of the reservation in the patent extend to the right of navigation, the reservation is absolutely void. The statute 23 Vict. ch. 2, sec. 35, gives to the Crown the right to grant the bed of the river and the water upon it free from any rights publici juris. The Statute of Limitations could give the plaintiff no title to any part of the land covered by water, except that actually occupied by his floating wharf and boat house. *Ratté* v. *Booth,* 419.

WILL.

1. T. C. S. devised his estate of Clark Hill, with the islands, lands, and grounds appertaining, to his nephew M. M.'s grandmother by her will, directed her executors to pay him $2,000 a year so long as he should remain the owner and actual occupant of Clark Hill, "to enable him the better to keep up, decorate, and beautify the property known as Clark Hill and the islands connected therewith."

Held, that the expropriation, under an Act of the legislature, of a part of the Clark Hill estate, did not in any way affect M.'s right to this annuity; and therefore in awarding compensation to M. for the lands expropriated the arbitrators properly excluded the consideration of any contemplated loss by M. of this annuity.

A failure by M. to reside and occupy would be in the nature of a forfeiture for breach of a condition subsequent, and his right to the annuity would continue absolute until something occurred to divest the estate which must be by his own act or default; the vis major of a binding statute could not work a forfeiture.

Upon the evidence the Court refused to interfere with the amount of compensation awarded. *In re Macklem and the Commissioners of the Niagara Falls Park*, 20.

2. J. S. directed his executors to cancel and entirely release the indebtedness of his son W. S. upon a mortgage made by him to the testator, such release to operate and take effect immediately on and from the testator's death. W. S. was also indebted to the testator on a promissory note and for goods, which, together with interest amounted to upwards of $3,740. This amount the executors claimed they were entitled to demand payment of before they could be called upon to dis-

charge the mortgage, which conten- tion was sustained by the Master in an action for the administration of the estate; but on motion, his find- ing was reversed by PROUDFOOT, J. (12 O. R. 615.)

On appeal to this Court the judg- ment of the Court below was affirmed, with costs.

BURTON, J.A., dissenting.—The be- quest of the mortgage was not a specific bequest; and without reference as to what the original purpose of filing the bill was, W. S. had claimed to have his mortgage released and had obtained an order for its unconditional discharge so that he stood in the same position as if he had brought an action for that purpose ex- pressly, and had thus brought himself within the rule, that he who seeks equity must do equity; whereas the effect of the judgment appealed from by reason of the Statute of Limitations was to leave the legatee free from the debt due by him to the estate and to expose the executors to a liability to make good that loss.—*Archer* v. *Severn,* 723.

WITHDRAWING CASE FROM JURY.

See RAILWAYS 2, 3.